TACIT

THE
ANNALS

TACITUS

THE
ANNALS

Translated, with Introduction and Notes, by

A. J. WOODMAN

Hackett Publishing Company, Inc.
Indianapolis/Cambridge

10   09   08   2   3   4   5   6   7

For further information, please address:

Hackett Publishing Company, Inc.
P.O. Box 44937
Indianapolis, IN 46244-0937

www.hackettpublishing.com

Cover design by Abigail Coyle
Text design by Meera Dash
Maps by Bill Nelson
Composition by Agnew's, Inc.
Printed at The P. A. Hutchison Company

Library of Congress Cataloging-in-Publication Data

Tacitus, Cornelius.
    [Annales. English]
    The annals / Tacitus ; translated, with introduction and notes, by
A. J. Woodman.
        p.   cm.
    Includes bibliographical references and index.
    ISBN 0-87220-559-2 (cloth) — ISBN 0-87220-558-4 (paper)
    1. Rome—History—The five Julii, 30 B. C.–68 A. D.   I. Woodman,
A. J. (Anthony John), 1945–   II. Title.
    DG207.T3W66   2004
    937'.07—dc22

                                                      2004047334
ISBN-13: 978-0-87220-559-8 (cloth)
ISBN-13: 978-0-87220-558-1 (pbk.)

                                  ∞

CONTENTS

To David and John

PREFACE

"These days," wrote T. P. Wiseman recently, "we should be reading Tacitus with a livelier and more sensitive interest than ever." I hope that this new translation of the *Annals* will respond to and, if possible, promote just such an interest. From the start my principal aim, though subsequently and successively modified, was to produce as exact a rendering of Tacitus' Latin as lay within my power; at the same time I sought to incorporate some of the latest developments in Tacitean scholarship and even to introduce some innovations of my own. I would like to think that the resulting version will be equally appropriate for casual readers who want to make the acquaintance of a classic text and for those who, whether at school, college, or university, are studying the literature, history, or civilization of ancient Rome through the medium of English. The footnotes with which the translation is equipped are designed to meet the needs of both categories of reader. If readers discover mistakes or misunderstandings in either translation or notes, I hope most sincerely that they will bring them to my attention.

I had the singularly good fortune to begin my translation at the same time as I was reading the *Annals* with graduate students at Princeton University in the autumn of 1989, and to conduct the final revisions at the same time as I was again reading the *Annals* with graduate students at the University of Virginia in the autumn of 2003: I could not have wished for more enquiring or enthusiastic readers of Tacitus, and to all of them I would like to record my gratitude. In the intervening years, and particularly more recently, I have received various sorts of help from numerous scholars and friends, among them J. N. Adams, K. M. Coleman, E. Courtney, the late J. Ginsburg, M. T. Griffin, M. Helzle, J. Keegan, C. S. Kraus, D. S. Levene, E. A. Meyer, J. Nelis-Clément, M. Peachin, J. G. F. Powell, D. Sheldon, the late W. S. Watt, and T. P. Wiseman. David Braund, Ted Lendon, and John Rich provided invaluable comment on some of the appendices, and I am especially indebted to Juliette Moore for all the labor and expertise which she devoted to the geographical appendix.

Deborah Wilkes expended a great deal of time and trouble on a frustrating and difficult text. With good-humored tolerance Clemence Schultze allowed me on countless occasions to pester her with questions of English usage: her unfailing willingness to respond and in general to enter into the spirit of my enterprise was a constant source of encouragement: *ueteris stat gratia facti*. Without the award of a Sir James Knott Foundation Research Fellowship from the University of Durham in 1998–9 I would never have been able to bring my work to its conclusion.

Over the past fifteen years Ronald Martin has commented in detail on two drafts of my translation and has engaged in a substantial correspondence on the innumerable problems, great and small, which have arisen. My greatest debt of gratitude is owed to him.

A. J. Woodman
Charlottesville, March 2004

NOTE ON THE 2008 PRINTING

For corrections and suggestions I am most grateful to S. Bartera, A. R. Birley, E. Courtney, and D. C. Feeney.

INTRODUCTION

Tacitus is acknowledged to be the greatest historian of ancient Rome, the *Annals* his greatest work. Even though we do not possess in its entirety his account of the years between August A.D. 14, when the emperor Tiberius came to power, and June A.D. 68, when Nero committed suicide,[1] the surviving narrative has defined for generations of readers their picture of the early Roman empire—the empire whose literary, political, and monumental legacy has had so profound and persistent an influence on the shaping of the Western world.[2]

Some of Tacitus' episodes linger long in the mind: the discovery of the remains of legions massacred in the German forests (Book 1), the noble speech on freedom of expression put into the mouth of the historian Cremutius Cordus before he commits suicide (Book 4), Nero's attempt to murder his mother by means of a collapsible boat in the sea near Naples (Book 14), the dignity of the philosopher Thrasea Paetus as he faces the prospect of inevitable death (Book 16). Tacitus' sustained delineation of the emperor Tiberius in the first six books of the *Annals* is widely regarded as the most memorable and penetrating portrait of an individual in the whole of antiquity—a "miracle of art," in the words of Lord Macaulay. Since the Renaissance, when the early printings of the *Annals* first made his finest work available to a wider readership, Tacitus has attracted the attention of some of the most prominent names in literature and affairs. In the seventeenth century John Milton described him as "the greatest possible enemy to tyrants," Edward Gibbon in the eighteenth took him as his model in *Decline and Fall*, and Thomas Jefferson in the nineteenth considered him "the first writer in the world without a single exception," while at almost exactly the same time Napoleon was denouncing him for his "obscurity" and for having "slandered the emperors."[3]

---

1. Most of Book 5, some of Book 6, all of Books 7–10, and some of Book 11 are lost, while Book 16 breaks off midway through; whether Book 16 was the final book, or whether (as seems more likely) the work contained eighteen books in all, is disputed. See further below, n. 6.

2. See, e.g., M. Reinhold, *Classica Americana: The Greek and Roman Heritage in the United States* (Detroit 1984); R. Jenkyns (ed.), *The Legacy of Rome: A New Appraisal* (Oxford 1992); C. J. Richard, *The Founders and the Classics: Greece, Rome, and the American Enlightenment* (Cambridge, MA 1994); C. Edwards (ed.), *Roman Presences: Receptions of Rome in European Culture, 1789–1945* (Cambridge 1999), each with further bibliography.

3. See P. Gay, *Style in History* (London 1974) 21–34 (Gibbon); R. Mellor, *Tacitus* (New York 1993) 159 (Jefferson) and *Tacitus: The Classical Heritage* (New York 1995) 126 (Milton), 195 (Napoleon), 209 (Macaulay).

TACITUS AND THE *ANNALS*

When we read Tacitus' often chilling account of the early emperors, we should remember that he himself was a political insider, having enjoyed a successful political career in a later age. A seemingly chance story about a quindecimvir who was berated in A.D. 32 by Tiberius for a procedural mistake (6.12) comes to be seen in a different light when it is revealed, five books later (11.11.1), that by A.D. 88 the historian himself was holding the same priesthood.[4] In the latter passage Tacitus also says that he was praetor in that year; and we know from a letter of his friend, the younger Pliny, that he was suffect consul when, in A.D. 97, he spoke the funeral oration for the distinguished statesman Verginius Rufus (Pliny, *Letters* 2.1.6). From our knowledge of the career structures of Roman politicians we can infer from this information that Tacitus will have been quaestor in perhaps A.D. 81; and, if a fragmentary inscription (*CIL* 6.41106 [= 6.1574]) is correctly identified as the funerary record of Tacitus' career, as has recently been argued,[5] he was "quaestor of Augustus" (*quaestor Augusti*), thereby holding one of the two most prestigious quaestorships, before becoming tribune of the plebs (presumably around A.D. 85). Any "quaestor of Augustus" who subsequently turned historian will have had much to reflect upon if, like Tacitus, he came to record how in A.D. 66 it was a "quaestor of Augustus" who read out Nero's speech introducing the debate which would condemn the virtuous Thrasea Paetus to suicide (16.27.1). Another inscription informs us that in A.D. 112–113 Tacitus was proconsul of Asia, a position which represented the pinnacle of any politician's career. This tenure of office perhaps explains the apparently disproportionate number of references to Asia in the *Annals,* with which Tacitus was engaged in the years immediately following: the composition of Book 4 perhaps occurred in A.D. 115. We do not know when he died.

In his first major work, the *Histories,* on which he was engaged in A.D. 106/7 and which in its complete form covered the years A.D. 69–96,[6] Tacitus makes allusive reference to his political career (*Histories* 1.1.3):

> I cannot deny that I owe the launching of my career to Vespasian [emperor A.D. 69–79], or that I was advanced by Titus [79–81] and still further promoted by

4. For definitions and explanations of technical terms such as "quindecimvir" see Appendix A. For references to the *Annals'* text, see page xxx.

5. G. Alföldy, *Mitteilung des deutschen archaeologischen Instituts: Römische Abteilung* 102 (1995) 251–68. For discussion of Tacitus' career see now A. R. Birley, "The Life and Death of Cornelius Tacitus," *Historia* 49 (2000) 230–47.

6. Only Books 1–4 and the first part of Book 5 survive. St. Jerome said of Tacitus that "in thirty volumes he wrote down the lives of the Caesars after Augustus up to the death of Domitian" (*Comm. Zach.* 3.14): most scholars therefore assume that there were twelve books in the *Histories* and eighteen in the *Annals,* although fourteen and sixteen respectively have also been suggested (see above, n. 1). For a study of the *Histories* see R. Ash, *Ordering Anarchy: Armies and Leaders in Tacitus'* Histories (London 1999).

Domitian [81–96]; but those who lay claim to unbiased accuracy must speak of no man with either hatred or affection.

The references are integrated with the historian's traditional disclaimer of prejudice, but they act also as his personal credentials. Tacitus was not, like Livy (c. 59 B.C.–A.D. 17), a historian who lacked experience of affairs; nor was he, like Sallust (c. 86–35 B.C.), a historian whose political career had gone disastrously wrong. On the contrary, Tacitus' smooth progression from office to office—and in particular his relatively early acquisition of a major priesthood and his culminating proconsulship of Asia—bespeak someone who was more than happy to take advantage of the political opportunities which the system had to offer and whose debt to the emperors listed in the preface to the *Histories* was not inconsiderable. It is thus all the more curious that, as usually interpreted, his treatment of the early empire in the *Annals* represents a general indictment of the system from which he had derived such personal benefit.

To A.D. 98, the year after Tacitus' consulship, belong the two monographs which are known as *Agricola* and *Germania*.[7] The first is a biography of his father-in-law, Gnaeus Julius Agricola, governor of Britain c. A.D. 77–84. Praise and affection for his wife's parent are emphasized by damning criticism of the emperor Domitian, who prevented the further development of Agricola's career even as he advanced Tacitus' own. The *Germania* is a geographical and ethnographical account of the land and peoples of ancient Germany, partly idealizing these "noble savages" in order to throw into relief the evils of contemporary civilization at Rome.[8] Tacitus' third minor work, the *Dialogue on Orators,* is of uncertain date (possibly A.D. 102) but affects to describe a discussion which he heard as a young man in A.D. 75.[9] It is from this work that we infer his presence in Rome in that year: at what point he came to Rome is unknown, but it is generally assumed that his birth had taken place about nineteen years earlier, in A.D. 56 or so, in what is now southern France or northern Italy.[10]

*

In the *Agricola* (3.3) Tacitus said that in a future work he would cover the principate of Domitian (A.D. 81–96) and, presumably by way of contrast, the current period of Nerva and Trajan. But in the *Histories* he went further back, covering the period from 69 to 96 and excluding the present age. In the preface to the *Histories* he says that he has reserved the reigns of Nerva and Trajan, "more fruitful and less anxious material," for his old age, given the rare happiness of a period

7. For an annotated translation of both works see A. R. Birley, *Tacitus: Agricola and Germany* (Oxford 1999).

8. For a translation and commentary see J. B. Rives, *Tacitus: Germania* (Oxford 1999).

9. For a commentary see R. G. Mayer, *Tacitus: Dialogus de Oratoribus* (Cambridge 2001).

10. Birley (above, n. 5) suggests A.D. 58 in Trier.

"when you can feel what you want and say what you feel" (1.1.4). Yet in his final work, the *Annals,* he went further back still and treated the years 14–68. Whether this developing retrospection denotes an increasing disillusion with the principate of Trajan, under whom he principally wrote, is unclear; in the *Annals* he says that, if he lives long enough, he will go even further back in time and write about the principate of Augustus himself (3.24.3). It may simply be that he became increasingly interested in the earlier and formative years of the Roman empire.

The autocratic system of government about which Tacitus wrote, and which we call the Roman empire, began to come into existence on 2 September 31 B.C., when, at the Battle of Actium off the western coast of Greece, Mark Antony was defeated by Octavian, Julius Caesar's heir and adopted son. Previously the two men had been allies: after the assassination of Caesar by Brutus and Cassius in 44 B.C., they had joined forces, pursued the assassins, and defeated them at the Battle of Philippi in eastern Macedonia in 42 B.C. But circumstances and political rivalry then forced the erstwhile associates into a power struggle which lasted until Octavian's victory more than a decade later.

The victory at Actium, three weeks before Octavian's thirty-second birthday, brought to an end not only years of civil war but also centuries of republican government. In some respects nothing seemed to have changed: the magistrates (as the consuls and other officers of state were called) continued to be elected annually and to carry out most of their traditional responsibilities. Yet in other respects everything had changed: having eliminated all military and political opposition, a young man had returned the Roman world to peace (for which Tacitus has a variety of terms, such as *pax, otium,* and *quies*), thereby finding himself with unprecedented influence and power at his disposal and incurring the gratitude of the majority of citizens. In 27 B.C. Octavian was offered the unique and reverential name "Augustus" by the senate in recognition of the benefits he had brought to the Roman people. The *res publica* might survive in name, a survival aided by the convenient ambiguity whereby in Latin *res publica* means both "the republic" and "the state," but Rome had become in effect an autocracy. The magistrates might continue to be elected, but those who were elected had to be acceptable to Augustus.

Tacitus decided to begin the *Annals* neither with the Battle of Actium nor with any of the other significant events of Augustus' long rule but with his death in A.D. 14 (1.5) and his succession by Tiberius, his adopted son (1.6). Tacitus' decision is striking and significant: this was the moment at which it became clear that the autocratic system of government established and developed by Augustus over forty-five years was no transitory phenomenon but was destined to endure and that, for the period covered by the *Annals,* its endurance was inextricably associated with an imperial dynasty (which is usually known as that of the Julio-Claudians). A very great deal of Tacitus' narrative illustrates the almost obsessive concern of the emperors to ensure the succession of a chosen member of the imperial family and hence the continuance of the family's power; this concern frequently involves a judicious betrothal or marriage, alliances which others, often including rival members of the same family, sometimes did their utmost to thwart.

Most emperors, once they acquired power, naturally wished to retain it as long as possible, and, just as tyrants have always found that fear is a useful instrument in this respect, so Tacitus uses all the considerable resources of his vocabulary to create the impression that life in the first century A.D. was lived against a background of terror.[11] A recurring theme is that of the *delatores* or "denouncers." In a society which lacked an equivalent of the Crown Prosecution Service or district attorneys, it was left to individuals to bring charges against those suspected of crime; but, since a successful prosecution would lead to a handsome pecuniary reward for the prosecutor, there was every danger that among the unscrupulous a desire for financial advantage would take precedence over any thirst for justice. An example is provided by the consequences of the Lex Papia Poppaea, a law passed by Augustus in A.D. 9 to penalize childlessness.[12] Augustus' concern had been to increase the birthrate, but according to Tacitus the law failed to have the effect which Augustus had desired: instead, denouncers of the childless made large profits from the frequency of their denunciations and produced an atmosphere of generalized terror which Tiberius took measures to assuage (3.25.1, 3.28.3–4). Often, however, the terror caused by the denouncers had a direct bearing on the emperor himself, since their charges concerned *maiestas* or "treason."[13] Tacitus' narrative sometimes seems reduced to an unending succession of treason trials (4.36.1 "in the arraignment of defendants the year was so constant . . . ," 6.29.1 "But at Rome the slaughter was constant . . ."); and victorious denouncers, in addition to their monetary rewards, stood also to rise in the emperor's favor (see, e.g., 1.74.1–2).[14]

It is sometimes said that Tacitus' narrative is too concerned with domestic affairs such as these and that his opening words, "The City of Rome," betoken a lack of interest in the empire as a whole. In fact, some of his most compelling sections show that his concerns extended to foreign affairs. Romans in the *Annals* talk and act as if most of the world were theirs to dispose of; the kingdom of Parthia alone was acknowledged to be a power of comparable status to Rome. A conversation in A.D. 62 between a Roman general and a Parthian official on the subject of Armenia is represented by Tacitus in the following terms: the general points to everything the emperors had done "for the maintaining or bestow-

11. See further below, page xxii.

12. Childless persons (usually men) feature prominently in the literature of the early Roman empire because, having no descendants to inherit any fortune they might possess, they were preyed upon by legacy hunters, who are stock targets of criticism.

13. *Maiestas* is elliptical for an expression such as *maiestas laesa* or "impairment of [the state's] sovereignty."

14. In general see S. H. Rutledge, *Imperial Inquisitions: Prosecutors and Informants from Tiberius to Domitian* (London 2001).

ing of Armenia" (that is, to keep or to grant possession of it), while the latter contends that the Romans' power "of retaining or lavishing" that country is a mirage (15.14.2).[15] It is significant that the subject of this conversation is Armenia, which, though not formally part of the Roman empire, was nevertheless supposed by Rome to show allegiance by accepting a monarch nominated by the emperor. But Armenia, flanked as it was by the Parthian empire as well as the Roman, had divided loyalties. Tacitus at an early point in his narrative of A.D. 58 remarks of the Armenians that "in the situation of their country and the similarity of their habits they were closer to the Parthians, and, having merged with them through intermarriage and being ignorant of freedom, they inclined rather in their direction, toward servitude" (13.34.2). It is an interesting passage, in that it can be interpreted plausibly to show that Tacitus differentiated between Rome and Parthia in terms of freedom and servitude. No one disputes that freedom is one of Tacitus' abiding concerns,[16] but his differentiation here seems hard to reconcile with his apparent view elsewhere that Rome's relationship with its subject peoples mirrors the domestic tyranny which prevails in the capital. Yet such contradictions, whether seeming or real, are typical of this highly complex and elusive author.

★

Tacitus in the *Annals* says that as a young man he heard a story from older men about Cn. Calpurnius Piso, who, in the official version of events, committed suicide in A.D. 20 during Tiberius' reign (3.16.1). To what extent the *Annals* relies upon oral history (again at 11.27; cf. 15.41.1) is unknown; but it should be borne in mind that Tacitus was dealing with matters which took place between (roughly) forty-five years and a century before he came to write: despite the tenacity of oral memory, it is inevitable that he was heavily dependent on written sources. Tacitus, like other Roman historians, makes reference to anonymous "writers" (4.53.2, 4.65, 6.7.5, 16.6.1) or "authors" (1.81.1, 3.3.2, 4.10.1, 4.11.1, 14.2.2, 15.38.1), sometimes adding that they were contemporary with events (2.88.1, 5.9.2, 12.67.1, 13.17.2); elsewhere he varies this with such expressions as "it is transmitted" (e.g., 4.57.3) or "many/some transmit" (e.g., 1.29.4, 2.40.2) or "there was a report" (e.g., 11.34.1, 15.65.1). Very occasionally he refers by name to an earlier historical writer whose work has since been lost to us (the elder Pliny at 1.69.2, 13.20.2, and 15.53.3; Cluvius Rufus and Fabius Rusticus at 13.20.2 and 14.2.1–2; and the latter alone at 15.61.3): one of these passages (13.20.2) is particularly interesting in that he tells us that his intention is to fol-

---

15. "Lavishing" or "lavishment(s)" is my translation of *largiri* and *largitio(nes)*, words which occur frequently in the *Annals* to describe the generous giving of gifts, etc., sometimes for the purposes of bribery.

16. On freedom see C. Wirszubski, *Libertas as a Political Idea at Rome* (Cambridge 1950), esp. the last chapter (pp. 160–7 on Tacitus).

low the authorial consensus but will give the names of authors where their accounts differ. He refers once (4.53.2) to the memoirs of the younger Agrippina, sister of the emperor Gaius and mother of the emperor Nero, and once to those of the general Corbulo (15.16.1). Twice he refers to the speeches of Tiberius (1.81.1, 2.63.3), which had almost certainly been published; once he quotes a letter of Tiberius (6.6.1), which is quoted in almost identical terms by the biographer Suetonius (*Tiberius* 67.1), who was Tacitus' contemporary. Elsewhere he mentions, using variable phraseology, the daily gazette (3.3.2, 13.31.1, 16.22.3), remarking in the second passage that proper historiography, unlike the gazette, requires illustrious subject matter. What is meant by the expression *publica acta* ("public records"), to which he refers at 12.24.2, is uncertain.

It has been the conviction of many scholars—but most notably of Sir Ronald Syme, greatest of modern Taciteans—that Tacitus' distinctive excellence as a historian in the *Annals* is to be explained by his extensive and consistent use of the records of the Roman senate: the *acta senatus* (a form of *Hansard* or *Congressional Record*).[17] Though he alludes once to a senator charged with compiling this record during Tiberius' reign (5.4.1), there is only one certain occasion on which he refers to his own consultation of the *acta*—and that toward the very end of the extant *Annals* (15.74.3). What is one to make of this solitary reference? Does it simply confirm what Tacitus' silent practice has been for the narrative of the preceding fifteen books? Or does it imply that his consultation on this particular occasion was exceptional? The case may be argued either way, but other salient evidence needs to be taken into account.

In the last two decades of the twentieth century we were exceptionally fortunate with two dramatic archaeological discoveries in Spain. First was discovered the so-called *Tabula Siarensis,* an epigraphic record of the honors decreed by the senate to the deceased prince, Germanicus, in the last days of the year A.D. 19;[18] then came to light copies of "Senate's Decision Concerning Cn. Piso the Elder," an epigraphic record of the trial in A.D. 20 of the same Cn. Piso as mentioned above, who was popularly supposed to have poisoned Germanicus.[19] Together these two documents overlap with Tacitus' narrative in the later stages of Book 2 and earlier chapters of Book 3 and they place the modern reader in the unusually advantageous position of being able to compare an official and contemporary record with Tacitus' narrative written over ninety years later. In one sense Tacitus emerges extremely well from such a comparison. For example, there

17. R. Syme, "How Tacitus Wrote *Annals* I–III," *Roman Papers* (Oxford 1984) 3.1014–42, "Tacitus: Some Sources of His Information," *Roman Papers* (Oxford 1988) 4.199–222.

18. See now A. Sánchez-Ostiz, *Tabula Siarensis: Edición, Traducción y Commentario* (Pamplona 1999).

19. See W. Eck, A. Caballos, and F. Fernández, *Das senatus consultum de Cn. Pisone patre* (Munich 1996). See further the special issue of *American Journal of Philology* 120 (1999) vii–ix and 1–162; G. Rowe, *Princes and Political Cultures: The New Tiberian Senatorial Decrees* (Ann Arbor, MI 2002).

seems no doubt that he had seen and used a copy of the Pisonian document or something very like it. On the other hand, the epigraphic record clearly dates the conclusion of Piso's trial to 10 December A.D. 20, whereas before the inscription's discovery scholars had universally assumed from Tacitus' narrative that the trial had concluded before the end of May (see 3.19.3 and note). The consequence seems to be either that Tacitus is prepared to treat some basic facts in a quite cavalier fashion or that we have not yet learned to read his text in the way it was intended to be read.

Until the discovery of these two inscriptions the only occasion when one could subject Tacitus' text to a similar comparison related to the year A.D. 48. In that year the emperor Claudius delivered before the senate a speech which has been preserved, partially but substantially, on bronze tablets found in the sixteenth century at Lyon in France. Tacitus' version of the speech is given at 11.24, and here too we may be certain that he had in front of him a copy of Claudius' original: half a dozen main points are common both to the original and to Tacitus' version.[20] Yet Tacitus' version is otherwise nothing like Claudius' original. Are we then to praise Tacitus for reproducing the princeps's main points or to criticize him for changing so much of the rest? Scholars have answered the question both ways, but perhaps it is the question itself which is mistaken: perhaps these are not the terms in which Tacitus himself would have seen the issue.

In the modern world we are quite used to seeing the words of a historical figure or of a current politician summarized in indirect speech; and, since summary indirect speech occurs very frequently in Tacitus (as in other ancient historians), we think little of it but assume that, like its modern counterpart, it is a reasonably accurate representation of a speech which was actually delivered. However, in the case of Claudius' speech, we are dealing with direct speech: to us it appears that in Tacitus' text Claudius purports to say what we know he did not say in real life. If we encountered such a phenomenon in a modern history book, we would be scandalized: for example, when W. Stevenson in *A Man Called Intrepid* (London 1976) provides verbatim and undocumented reports of conversations which took place between various individuals during the Second World War and which common sense suggests cannot be authentic, we form the conclusion that his book is unhistorical. Yet, among all the history books which are published today, such works are the exception rather than the rule. Has the fortuitous survival of Claudius' speech presented us with a case which is similarly exceptional in the ancient world? Or was it in fact normal for an ancient historian to practice the kind of (as we see it) "misrepresentation" that is encountered in Tacitus?

Naturally, owing to the total lack of evidence, the question cannot be answered definitively; but let us consider the detailed exhortation to her troops which Tacitus puts into the mouth of Boudicca before a battle (14.35). This time he writes in indirect speech; but how could he possibly have known what was said by a British queen in a foreign language in a distant country fifty-five years previously

20. For translations of the Claudian inscription see the references at 11.24.1n.

at so ephemeral a moment? Common sense tells us that he could not have known: he made it up, attributing to Boudicca sentiments which seemed appropriate for such a speech. But was such a speech ever delivered in the first place? Were prebattle exhortations a feature of early British warfare? We do not know. All we do know is that such speeches are a convention of classical literature from the earliest times: we may infer from this that such speeches were actually delivered by Greek and Roman generals in real life (though even that inference is disputed by some scholars), but we cannot extrapolate that they were ever a convention of the Britons. Coleridge once, in a famous phrase, referred to "that willing suspension of disbelief for the moment, which constitutes poetic faith": a similar suspension is required—and was perhaps instinctively assumed by ancient historians to be required—when such speeches as Boudicca's are read.

If speeches in the works of ancient historians enjoy at best only a tangential relationship with the words spoken by their original speakers, as in the case of Claudius' speech, or if speeches are entirely invented, as in the case of Boudicca's speech, what can be said about the ancient historian's treatment of events? When Nero decided in A.D. 64 to abandon his plan of visiting Egypt, Tacitus reports that the people as a whole were delighted but that "the senate and leaders were uncertain whether he should be regarded as more frightening when at a distance or before them" (15.36.4). But how could Tacitus possibly have known? The answer is that he did not know: he borrowed from what his predecessor Sallust had written roughly a century and a half earlier about the African monarch Jugurtha: "it was regarded as uncertain whether he was more ruinous when absent or present" (*Jugurthine War* 46.8). It can be shown that individual sentences in the *Annals*, such as this, or even whole episodes have been borrowed by Tacitus from earlier writers whose subjects had nothing to do with the Julio-Claudian emperors. It is also a fair assumption that many such borrowings have so far gone unnoticed; and the loss of so much classical literature means that the evidence for other cases is lacking. Yet in a sense it does not matter if the evidence is unnoticed or unavailable: the key point is that, if such imaginative reconstruction is Tacitus' practice on a number of identifiable occasions, there is a strong likelihood that his method will be no different on numerous other occasions which we cannot now identify. Modern readers of more recent historical texts have become accustomed to the warning that there is no simple one-to-one correspondence between an "event" and its description and that the very act of describing is a distorting process. But such warnings are even more applicable in the case of ancient historical texts if there is no necessary correspondence at all between description and event.

It is easy to forget just how different the ancient world was from our own. The passion for the official recording of events did not imply a reciprocal passion for their being read by others at some indeterminate later date. Indeed some modern scholars have argued that Roman archives were extremely difficult to access, not because there was any intention of deterring consultation but simply because consultation was scarcely expected. If that is so, it is quite anachronistic to imagine Tacitus as a modern researcher, armed with a grant from the Mellon Foundation or The Leverhulme Trust while compiling material for the *Annals*. It is of course still possible that Syme and others are right in believing that the *Annals* is substantially dependent on senatorial records; but it is perhaps more likely that Tacitus followed the "authorial consensus" to which he refers at 13.20.2. Either way, he can only have responded to his material, however it was acquired, according to the mind-set of the ancient world.

The ancients themselves defined historical writing in terms of oratory and poetry. Cicero in the late republic represents his friend Atticus as saying to him that historiography "is a singularly oratorical task" (*On Laws* 1.5), while Quintilian, a contemporary of Tacitus, writes that "historiography is very close to poetry and is rather like a poem in prose" (*Institutio Oratoria* 10.1.31). Though these two definitions may seem to us to be quite different from each other, they are related by the fact that in the ancient world both oratory and poetry were seen as rhetorical pursuits: each was a type of "persuasive speech." We are to imagine (as it were) a sliding scale, with historiography—an equally rhetorical pursuit—positioned nearer oratory or poetry depending on a person's taste and inclination. Hence Aristides, a Greek writer of the second century A.D., said simply that historians fall "between orators and poets" (*Oration* 28[49].68). What these various statements signify in practice is disputed by modern scholars. Those who maintain that the nature of historiography has hardly changed at all over the past two thousand years are obliged either to restrict their applicability (e.g., by asserting that they denote a license for historians merely to use poetic language from time to time) or to disregard them altogether; others believe that these statements, coming as they do from the ancients themselves, should be taken seriously and at face value.[21]

If in reading the *Annals* our expectations are those of a modern reader of historiography, we shall be very surprised indeed that Tacitus invents speeches and constructs his narrative with materials borrowed from the texts of earlier authors which have nothing to do with Tacitus' subject. But, if we know that Romans expected historiography to be like poetry, such invention and borrowing immediately make sense: after all, this is precisely what (say) Virgil was doing when, in composing the *Aeneid,* he borrowed from (among many others) Homer, Apollonius of Rhodes, and Ennius (see also below, page xx). In other words, the actual procedures of the ancient historians strongly suggest (when there is the evidence to test them) that the ancient definitions of the genre are indeed to be taken seriously and at face value. On the other side it may be argued that Tacitus is "modern" in that he consulted primary sources such as the Pisonian decree and Claudius' speech and used them as a basis for those parts of the *Annals;* it may even be argued that, if further evidence had survived (or were to be found), Tacitus' dependence on one or other form of primary source would be seen to

21. The latter position is argued in A. J. Woodman, *Rhetoric in Classical Historiography* (London 1988), esp. 70–116.

be widespread. In the continuing absence of such evidence, however, readers might do well to approach the historicity of the *Annals* in a frame of mind which is at least mildly agnostic.

★

Tacitus' is an annalistic or year-by-year narrative, as the title suggests; yet, though he alludes to "my annals" (4.32.1) and though Pliny refers to his friend's earlier work as "your histories" (*Letters* 7.33.1), some scholars have doubted whether these were the author's own titles: in the manuscript the present work is entitled "From the passing of Divine Augustus," and the two works were not certainly known by their current titles of *Annals* and *Histories* before the Renaissance scholar Vertranius in 1569.

Each narrative year in the *Annals* is both dated and begun by a formulaic reference to the consuls of that year ("With X and Y as consuls," e.g., 1.55.1), on which there are occasional variations (2.53.1, 3.2.3, 3.31.1, 3.52.1, 6.1.1, 6.40.1, 6.45.3, 13.34.1, 15.48.1), some of them very slight (1.68.1, 5.1.1, 14.29.1, 15.23.1). Within each narrative year Tacitus "blocks" his material into domestic affairs and foreign affairs: I have used a single asterisk to separate these blocks from one another, but it should not be assumed that within any given block Tacitus invariably restricts himself to the events of the year in question. On three occasions he explicitly tells us that in a single block he has covered the foreign affairs of more than a single year (6.38.1, 12.40.5, 13.9.3), and the same phenomenon also occurs without our being explicitly informed of it; and, though it is foreign affairs which are most liable to exceed annalistic boundaries, domestic affairs are by no means immune. Hence the dates which head each page of the translation are sometimes no more than nominal, referring to the names of the consuls with which each narrative year begins.

In writing annalistic history Tacitus was following a major tradition which stretched back to the republic and which reached its climax with the 142-book history of Livy (above, page xi), who covered Roman affairs from the founding of the city to 9 B.C. But, whereas Livy's annalistic formulae and structuring reflected the realities of republican politics (the annual elections of the consuls, the military victories of each campaigning season), Tacitus evokes the tradition only to manipulate it and thereby to underline how different life was in imperial times. For example, a year such as A.D. 23, comprising exclusively domestic affairs, provides implicit but eloquent comment on the introspective nature of Tiberius' principate (4.1–16).[22]

No one disputes that Tacitus, in writing an ample and annalistic history of the years A.D. 14–96 in thirty books which we call the *Annals* and the *Histories*,[23]

---

22. The fundamental discussion of these matters is J. Ginsburg, *Tradition and Theme in the Annals of Tacitus* (New York 1981).

23. For the total of books see above, n. 6.

was seeking to rival the work of Livy; on the other hand, it is clear that in the *Annals* his style and manner were inspired chiefly by Livy's own great predecessor, Sallust (above, page xi). Tacitus begins the *Annals* with a sentence ("The City of Rome from its inception was held by kings") which combines allusions to two sentences of Sallust. The primary allusion is to the moment where, early in *Catiline's War,* Sallust begins his survey of early Roman history (6.1 "*The City of Rome. . . . was* founded and *held* at the start by Trojans"); the secondary allusion is to a phrase at the beginning of Sallust's now fragmentary *Histories* (1.8 "for *from the inception* of the City to the Macedonian War with Perseus"). These allusions together constitute what has been called a "motto," indicating to readers the chief inspiration behind an ancient author's work. In just the same way Virgil at the start of the *Aeneid* alludes to Homer, a similarity of practice which provides further evidence that ancient historiography differs from modern.

Tacitus' imitation of Sallust's style is neither casual nor perfunctory but all-pervasive, and it has implications which extend beyond the merely stylistic. Sallust had been fascinated and appalled by the distintegration of republican society through which he lived (*Catiline's War,* for example, was written within two or three years of Julius Caesar's assassination in 44 B.C.), and he used the medium of historical writing to express his own disenchantment with the direction in which the Roman world was moving. To underline that disenchantment he cultivated a style which was modeled on that of Thucydides, the disaffected Greek historian of the fifth century B.C., and which gave prominence to archaisms, asymmetrical expression, and all forms of variation. Not only was such a style the antithesis of the smooth cadences of Cicero, the supreme artist who had bestrode the literary scene for almost four decades, but it suited the social and political disjointedness which was Sallust's subject matter and it reflected the disillusion of the author himself. When Tacitus expressed his allegiance to Sallust's style, he was advertising also that his attitude was as critical of the early principate as Sallust's had been of the late republic.[24]

The term which best sums up Tacitus' stylistic technique is "variation" (*uariatio*). This device, which links Tacitus to Sallust just as it links Sallust to Thucydides, constitutes almost the defining feature of the *Annals* and is found in many different forms.[25] Tacitus refuses to call a spade a spade or to use the word "wheelbarrow" but prefers "the things with which earth is carried or turf cut out" (1.65.7), variations to which is later added that for "rubbish cart" (11.32.3 "a vehicle by which the clearings from gardens are carried off"). Such disdain for common or garden terms is in keeping with his declaration that the "founda-

---

24. For Sallust see R. Syme, *Sallust* (Berkeley/Los Angeles/London 1964, 2nd ed. by R. Mellor, 2002), esp. 240–73 and 292–6, and note T. F. Scanlon, *The Influence of Thucydides on Sallust* (Heidelberg 1980). Sallust's relationship with Thucydides was not of course exclusive (for Sallust and the elder Cato, for example, see D. S. Levene, *Classical Quarterly* 50 (2000) 170–91).

25. The standard discussion is G. Sörbom, *Variatio sermonis Tacitei* (Uppsala 1935).

tions and beams" of an amphitheater are inappropriate subjects for the kind of elevated annalistic history which he writes (13.31.1). His style as a public speaker was described by Pliny as "solemn" or "dignified" (*Letters* 2.11.17), and the same qualities are maintained consistently throughout the *Annals*. Other variations, while clearly related to these examples, seem more eccentric. Instead of the normal "civil wars," "Vestal Virgins," and "Martial Plain" (*Campus Martius*), Tacitus produces "citizens' wars" (1.3.7), "Vesta's Virgins," (1.8.1) and "Plain of Mars" (*Campus Martis:* 1.8.6, 3.4.1, 13.17.1, 13.31.1, 15.39.2). The normal expression for a resolution of the senate is *senatus consultum* ("senate's decision"), which Tacitus uses frequently; but twice (11.35.1, 16.9.1) he perpetrates *consultum senatus* ("decision of the senate"). Likewise we are offered *senatus decretum* ("senate's decree," e.g., 4.16.3), *decretum senatus* ("decree of the senate," e.g., 6.11.3), and *decretum patrum* ("decree of the fathers," e.g., 1.10.2). Though these variations inevitably seem much less marked to the modern reader of an English translation, Roman readers would have had their expectations thwarted repeatedly and unsettlingly.

A similar effect is achieved when the reader—especially the reader whose expectations have been formed by such an author as Cicero—is led to believe that a given construction will be balanced by another of the same kind. Tacitus likes to vary one type of clause by a different type (e.g., 1.44.5 "*If* the tribunes and legions voiced approval . . . ; but, *whenever* they united in hurling charges of greed or cruelty . . . ," 2.88.3 "unknown to the annals of the Greeks, *who* marvel only at their own, and not celebrated duly in the Roman, *since* we extol the distant past, indifferent to the recent"[26]) but is especially fond of pairing clauses with nouns, a form of variation which manifests itself in very many different ways (e.g., 2.79.3 "emphasizing *the greatness* of the Commander *and that* the state was being claimed by arms," 4.24.2 "*by the terror* of the Roman name *and because* the Numidians were unable . . .""). Such deliberate avoidance of balance, mirroring as it does the unbalanced nature of the world which Tacitus describes, is complemented by a regular preference for archaisms, which have the capacity to evoke a more idealized past and of which an obvious example is his preference for *reor* ("I deem") over *puto* ("I think").[27]

Though the loss of almost all first-century A.D. historiography makes certainty impossible, it is very likely that Tacitus was the first Sallustian historian of Rome for more than a hundred years: his choice of Sallust as his chief stylistic model was designed to be strange and to shock. Furthermore, each of his sentences is studded with surprises of word or construction to arrest and then test readers as they make their way through them, a tortuous progress from revelation to revelation, each often more painful than the last. No one else ever wrote Latin like Tacitus, who deserves his reputation as the most difficult of Latin authors.

---

26. Here there is further variation of genitive noun ("the annals of the Greeks," *Graecorum*) and ablative adjective ("the Roman [sc. annals]," *Romanis*).

27. On these matters see the section on "The Translation" below.

THE TRANSLATION

When Lawrence of Arabia translated Homer's *Odyssey*, a distinguished literary friend complained to him that he had translated *xanthos* ("yellow"), which occurs eight times in the poem, by seven different words.[28] Though the theory and practice of translating will vary greatly from translator to translator, it does seem a self-evident advantage to translate *patres*, which Tacitus uses as an archaizing equivalent of *senatores*, consistently as "the fathers" (which is what the word actually means) rather than as "the senators."[29] Another favored archaism is *claritudo* ("brilliancy") as opposed to *claritas* ("brilliance"); and in general, given a choice of synonyms, Tacitus often varies the linguistic norm by choosing the less common: *luxus* ("luxuriousness") for *luxuria* ("luxury"), *maestitia* ("sorrowfulness") for *maeror* ("sorrow"), *seruitium* ("servitude") for *seruitus* ("slavery"). It will be seen that in each case I have tried to find a less usual English synonym, hoping thereby to register something of the forcefulness of his language.

Much of Tacitus' linguistic power resides in his use of metaphors, which I have tried to render as literally—and hence as vividly—as possible; but no less impressive is his use of varied synonyms to express a single concept. A straightforward example occurs at 2.6.4, where Tacitus uses the usual noun for "name" (*nomen*) and follows it with his two standard variations, *cognomentum* and *uocabulum*, which in my normal fashion I have translated as "nomenclature" and "designation" respectively. Considerably more variation is shown in his expression of "fear," the emotion which seems to appear on almost every page of the *Annals* (above, page xiii). His favored terms are *metus* and the archaizing *metuere*, which I have rendered as "dread" and "to dread" respectively, but he also uses the cognate groups *formidare/formido* ("alarm"), *pauere/pauescere/pauidus/pauor* ("panic"), and *trepidare/trepidatio/trepidus* ("tremble," "trepidation"), for each of which, as will be seen, I have used one or at best two equivalents. Tacitus hardly uses *uereri*, as normal a verb as *timere*, so I have simply used "to fear" for both; *terror* and *terrere* (and its compounds) are generally rendered as "terror," "terrify," or "terrorize" as seems appropriate. Most remarkable of all is the number of Tacitus' varied terms for killing, dying, and suicide: indeed we are perhaps dealing here with between forty and fifty different words or expressions. I have attempted to retain some of this variety by using, as a general rule, "slaughter" (*caedes, caedo, occido*), "decease" (*defungor*), "passing" (*excessus*), "extermination" (*exitium*), "departure" (*exitus*), "extinguish" (*exstinguo(r)*), "kill" (*interficio*), "die" and "death" (*morior* and *mors*), "execute" (*neco*), "perish" (*pereo*), "butcher" (*trucido*). Yet these are just a fraction of the total: the capabilities of the English language, which has a vocabulary far

---

28. See R. Storrs, *Ad Pyrrham* (London 1959) 1.

29. Compare the remarks of C. Lynch, *Niccolò Machiavelli: The Art of War* (Chicago 2003) xxxix ("Note on the Translation"): "My goal in this book is to provide English-speaking readers with the closest possible approximation to Machiavelli's own presentation of his work.... My first rule has been to render each Italian word by a single English word."

in excess of that of Latin, seem as inadequate in this respect as they are in dealing with the fact that Latin has three different words for "and" (used, for example, to begin successive sentences at 11.13.2: *et . . . -que . . . ac*).

Official names and terminology are a source of particular difficulty and, often, confusion.[30] As Julius Caesar's heir (above, page xii), Octavian from 44 B.C. was entitled to call himself "Caesar," the name assumed by subsequent emperors to denote their position of superiority. This usage, to which Claudius was no exception despite his not belonging to the Julian family, is very frequent in Tacitus (e.g., 11.2.2, of Claudius), although—confusingly—other members of the imperial family are also referred to in the same way (thus at 1.56.3–4 and 3.17.2, for example, Tiberius' adopted son is called "Germanicus" and "Caesar" in almost successive lines). I have not attempted to avoid such confusion but have retained "Caesar" wherever it occurs and regardless of the personage to whom it is applied.

From the early 30s B.C. Octavian had also adopted *Imperator* as a form of first name, and *Imperator* too came to be used in due course for the ruler's title: this is the term from which our "emperor" derives, and indeed "emperor" is its usual translation; but, in order to keep alive the links with the verb *imperare* ("to command") and with the noun *imperium* ("command"), I have preferred "Commander" (using a capital letter to distinguish the ruler from military generals, who are also called by the same term). To these two names Octavian in 27 B.C. added "Augustus" (above, page xii): this name, as Tacitus emphasizes more than once (see, e.g., 2.14.1, 4.64.3, 12.26.1), is connected with the verb *augere*, which, if the connection is to be brought out in English, requires translating as "to **aug**ment" rather than, as is perhaps more usual, "to increase."[31]

Augustus' triple titulature was designed to underline his "powerfulness" (*potentia*, a word Tacitus often uses to suggest its distinction from the more constitutional *potestas*, "power");[32] but at the same time Rome's first emperor referred to himself as *princeps*, "leading man" or "chief." The term had impeccable republican credentials; but, whereas in the past it had been used for distinguished ex-consuls (*principes ciuitatis*, "leading men in the community") or for the senior senator (*princeps senatus*, "leader of the senate") and the like, now it was reserved almost exclusively for the ruler himself. This is emphasized by the fact that "principate" (*principatus*) is used for the system which the ruler oversees, a connection which is retained most easily if one transliterates rather than attempts to translate the term "princeps." Thus the essence of the new imperial regime is summed

---

30. It should be noted too that Tacitus will often transpose a person's names: e.g., Asinius Gallus, who features regularly in the Tiberian books, is sometimes "Gallus Asinius" (including his first appearance at 1.8.3).

31. The use of "to augment" in the sense of "to raise in estimation or dignity" or "to exalt," died out in the mid-seventeenth century according to the *Oxford English Dictionary*, but readers of my translation will soon become familiar with this and similar idiosyncrasies.

32. Unfortunately it has not proved possible always to translate *potentia* as "powerfulness" rather than as "power."

up in Augustus' nomenclature, evoking as it does both powerfulness and precedent; but Tacitus, while repeatedly acknowledging the former through his use of such words as *dominatio* (suggesting "ownership," "mastery," "despotism"), from the start considers the republic to have passed away entirely and the survival of its trappings to be a facade (1.3.7).

*

When the reader encounters the verb "to preside" used transitively (as 12.14.4 "Vonones . . . presiding the Medes"; cf. 3.39.1, 4.5.1, 4.72.3, 12.29.2) rather than intransitively (as 12.15.2, a few lines later, "who presided *over* the race of the Aorsi," and elsewhere), this is not some aberration of the translator but an attempt to render a Tacitean imitation of a uniquely Sallustian detail (above, page xx).[33] In the same spirit I have endeavored to preserve as much as possible of Tacitus' word order and sentence structure. Tacitus greatly favors arranging words or expressions in the order *a b b a:* though this arrangement (known as chiasmus) is often impossible to reproduce in English, and though the very frequency of its occurrence in the *Annals* defies the translator, I have nevertheless attempted it wherever possible (as 4.35.5 "disrepute for themselves and for their victims glory"). Likewise, if Tacitus writes a long and convoluted sentence, I have tried to preserve it (as in the programmatic *tour de force* at 1.2.1); if the main verb comes at the end of a sentence, as it often does, and contains the climax, I have sought means to reproduce a similar effect (e.g., 13.43.2); and, if the main verb of a sentence is followed by some form of subordinate "appendix," a characteristic Tacitean mannerism, I have tried to render that too (sometimes with the aid of a dash, as 3.32.2).

It stands to reason, however, that consistency in one's translating practice is not always possible, as the following example will show. At 14.42–5 Tacitus records how in A.D. 61 a slave killed his master and the custom was that in such circumstances all his fellow slaves should be executed. Since in this case the total "establishment" (as I translate *familia*) comprised four hundred slaves, the senate debated whether so harsh a reprisal should be exacted from so many. The issue was one of *mos* (14.42.2 "uetere ex more," 43.1 "antiqui moris," 45.2 "mos antiquus"), which ideally should be translated as "custom" throughout. But on its second appearance *mos* is part of a wordplay or assonance (14.43.1 "nimio **amor**e antiqui **mor**is") which, if "**cust**om" is retained, is impossible to reproduce except by "**lust**," a word I otherwise reserve for *libido.* My practice on such occasions is to allow localized considerations to prevail (here by changing the words altogether: "excessive **p**assion for ancient **f**ashion") and to hope that the main theme of an episode will nevertheless remain clear.[34]

33. In fact a transitive use of "to preside" is recognized by the *Oxford English Dictionary* in the sense of "to direct," "to control."

34. I particularly regret that it proved impossible to deal consistently with *moderatio,* a key theme of Tiberius' reign. But I hope that, by using a range of similar words ("modera-

Wordplay of this type is, like alliteration, so marked and universal a feature of Tacitus' style that I have done my best to reproduce equivalent effects wherever possible: e.g., 1.19.1 "his per**sist**ence irre**sist**ible" ("per**uic**acia **uic**ti"), 1.47.3 "he equi**pp**ed shi**ps**" ("ado**rn**auit **nau**es"), 1.61.1 "the hid**den den**es" ("occ**ulta** s**alt**uum"),[35] 2.38.2 "to **rise** and to press**urize**" ("cons**urgere** et ... **urgere**"), 6.35.1 "amid ... the **smite** of arms, men **smote** or were **smitten**" ("**pulsu** armorum **pellerent pellerentur**"), 12.1.2 "Claudius himself, sometimes **tend**ing in one direction and sometimes in another ... ordered them to **tender** their opinion" ("ipse huc modo, modo illuc ... **promptus** ... **promere** sententiam ... iubet"), 12.5.2 "Their un**certain**ty was not abandoned ... and he as**certain**ed of Caesar" ("nec omissa **cunctat**io ... per**cunctat**usque Caesarem"), 12.69.3 "Yet his **will** was still not read out" ("testa**ment**um tamen haud recitatum"), 13.21.3 "She was developing **aqua**ria on her Baiae estate when my counsels were preparing him for ... the other aspects of ac**quir**ing command" ("Baiarum suarum **pisc**ina excolebat cum meis consiliis ... cetera a**pisc**endo imperio praepararentur"), 13.36.3 "... to pitch **tent** outside the rampart; and in that insulting de**tent**ion ..." ("**tendere** extra uallum ... inque ea contumelia de**tent**i ..."), 14.26.1 "the **margins** of **Armenia**" ("**extrema Armen**iae").

It will be seen that several of these examples depend on etymology, whether real (as 6.35.1, 12.1.2) or false (as 1.19.1, 13.36.3); and Tacitus, like other Roman authors, was especially addicted to etymologizing or playing on proper names. Sometimes the cases are obvious, as when at 12.8.2 a connection is implied between Nero's family name "Domitius" and the "domination" which he will eventually enjoy as emperor ("**Domi**tii ... **domi**nationis"); but other cases are less obvious and are impossible to bring out in a translation. Readers of the translation should nevertheless be made aware of the sort of thing which is going on. When one Balbus is described as being "of callous eloquence" (6.48.4), his reputation belies his name (= "Stammerer"); the name of Eunones, to whom legates are sent to seek "foreign kindness" (12.15.2), itself suggests a foreign (Greek) word for "kind"; given that a defeat in Britain was suffered under the leadership of one Valens (= "hale"), it is ironical that the new governor does not find the affairs of the country to be "healthy" (12.40.1 *non ... integras*); and it seems almost too good to be true when the Frisians, who had taken over some disputed ter-

---

tion," "limit," "balance," "modestness," etc.) to translate both that term and others (e.g., *modus, modestia, temperamentum,* etc.), the general theme will emerge clearly enough.

35. "Dene" is my attempt to translate the exceptionally troublesome *saltus,* which means both "defile" (or "pass") and "woods" (the latter usually in mountainous country and containing glades or defiles). "Dene" is defined as "a (wooded) vale" in the *Shorter Oxford English Dictionary* and as a "deep wooded valley" by Webster, describing it as a "British dialect" term. The conventional translation of *saltus* is simply "woods," as if synonymous with *siluae* ("woods"); but, since *saltus* can be qualified by the adjective *siluosus* ("wooded": see, e.g., Livy 9.2.7), the matter is evidently more complicated.

ritory and were treating it as "ancestral" (13.54.2 *ut ... patrium*), were evicted by Dubius Avitus, whose names mean respectively "doubtful" and "ancestral."

The kind of historical narrative which has been outlined in this Introduction must strike the modern reader as being very different in nature from a contemporary work of history: in writing the *Annals* Tacitus was evidently engaged above all in a literary enterprise. And it is precisely because Tacitus is a writer of literature that it has seemed worthwhile to try to reproduce as many of his literary characteristics as possible. The English which results may seem strange and even difficult to those who expect a translation to make everything instantly clear in the familiarity of a modern idiom; yet a translation is grossly misleading if it lulls readers into minimizing the differences between our society and that of the early Roman empire. On the contrary, it is positively valuable to be reminded constantly that ancient Rome was an alien world.[36]

AFTERLIFE

It is remarkably easy to forget that our Latin texts of the *Annals* do not precisely represent what Tacitus wrote; but the loss of between a quarter and a third of the whole work (above, page ix) acts as a timely reminder that ancient books from two thousand years ago do not reach us in the state that they left their authors' hands. No autograph manuscript of any classical writer has come to light which may be compared with the modern texts currently available. When Tacitus finished writing his own personal copy of the *Annals,* he may have given readings of certain extracts to his friends and others. Such authorial recitations are described by Pliny in his letters (e.g., 1.13), and they constituted one form of "publication" in the Roman world; but, in the centuries before the invention of printing, any wider circulation depended upon the distribution of copies which had been made by hand. In the classical world such copies were often made by slaves; in later times the copyists were often monks. And, as we know from our own experience, any form of copying—whether by pen, typewriter, or word-processor—inevitably means the introduction of errors; and, the more times a text is copied, the more numerous the errors that are likely to be introduced.

36. "Much of the discussion of the practice of translation is reducible to one question. How far should the foreign text be domesticated? The most common practice in the sixteenth and seventeenth centuries was to make the incoming writing sound as like the best English of the present as possible. Since that philosophy and practice gave us Dryden's *Aeneid* and Pope's *Iliad,* we can hardly condemn it; only add that there is a good deal to be said for the alternative stratagem by which the host culture is unsettled through translations that carry with them the marks of where they have come from: the shock of the foreign and of the past; the estrangement of ourselves" (D. Constantine, reviewing *The Oxford Guide to Literature in English Translation* (Oxford 2000) in the *Times Literary Supplement* (1 June 2001), a forum where the problems of translation are frequently discussed). See also L. Venuti, *The Translator's Invisibility: A History of Translation* (London 1995).

Our earliest surviving copy of the *Annals'* text is a manuscript known as the "first Medicean" (and referred to as M or M1), which was copied in Germany in the mid-ninth century: we are thus already more than seven centuries—and presumably multiple copyings—distant from Tacitus' own autograph text. M1 comprises only the first six books of the *Annals,* the account of Tiberius' reign from which almost all of Book 5 and some of Book 6 are missing; Books 11–16 depend upon another manuscript known as the "second Medicean" (and likewise referred to as M or, to distinguish it from the preceding, M2), which was written two hundred years later in the mid-eleventh century.

We know that M2 was used during the fourteenth and fifteenth centuries, and it is generally thought that all the various later manuscripts of *Annals* 11–16, which belong to the fifteenth century, derive from it, either directly or indirectly. The first printed edition of *Annals* 11–16 appeared in 1472/3. M1, on the other hand, did not resurface until the early sixteenth century, evidently without having been copied during the six hundred years since it was first transcribed. It was used to produce the first printed edition of all the surviving books of the *Annals* in 1515, although, as we have already seen, it was not until 1569 that the work became known by the title which it bears today.[37]

Given that the interval between Tacitus' authorship and the first printed editions is so extended, it is to be expected that the text of the *Annals* will be variously defective: quite apart from the lost books, there are lacunae (i.e., gaps) in the text at some points; at other places the text is corrupt (i.e. makes no sense) and requires emendation; and there are other occasions where the text, though making sense, is regarded by scholars as suspect for one reason or another and hence as not being what Tacitus wrote. As a general rule, such problems are significantly more common in Books 11–16 than in Books 1–6. In the course of my translation I have not followed any one edition exclusively; variants from what may be regarded as the vulgate text are signaled by a symbol (+) and listed in Appendix E. Whereas some editions fill in lacunae by printing supplements suggested by one scholar or another, I have sometimes not done this but instead placed asterisks in the translation, hoping thereby to remind readers of the fragility of the tradition on which our knowledge of the text depends.

*

It has been calculated that one in every 6.5 persons in communist East Germany was an informer and that the Stasi, or secret police, held files on a third of the total population. At any average dinner party one could be reasonably certain that at least one of the guests would be an informer, and the files which survived the collapse of communism (many were shredded) stretch for one hundred eleven

---

37. For these matters see R. J. Tarrant in *Texts and Transmission: A Survey of the Latin Classics* (ed. L. D. Reynolds, Oxford 1983) 406–9.

miles. Those persons who were detected in trying to escape such a regime, for example by crossing the Berlin Wall, were shot as traitors by guards.[38]

Almost every detail of this nightmare, typifying as it does so much of the century to which it belongs, is reflected or anticipated in Tacitus' *Annals*—the files of information (1.74.2, 2.29.2, 3.44.2, 4.60.1, 4.67.4, 6.24.1–2) or of the interrogation sessions (6.47.3, 15.73.1), the dinner-party betrayal (6.5.1–2, 6.7.3, 15.58.3), the would-be escaper (6.14.2), and everywhere the informers or "denouncers." The scale is of course different: "counted," as Roland Barthes observed, "the murders in the *Annals* are few enough (some fifty for three principates)."[39] But such is the power of Tacitus' narrative that the effect is overwhelming. Indeed it seems almost to overwhelm the author himself, who is sometimes moved to apologetic comment on subject matter which was, after all, his own choice (4.32–3, 6.7.5, 14.64.3, 16.16.1–2).

We are too sophisticated nowadays to believe that lessons can be learned from history; on the other hand, as the ample evidence suggests, the belief that the past is important—that our roots lie in the past and that "becoming acquainted" with the past, as did Germanicus on his visit to Egypt (2.59.1), is an enhancing experience—seems increasingly recognized. Few would dispute that, as part of that experience, a special place is occupied by the *Annals* of Tacitus, "an historian who knew the worst, discovered few reasons for ease or hope or confidence, and none the less believed in human dignity and freedom of speech."[40]

38. See, e.g., T. Garton Ash, *The File* (New York 1997), J. O. Koehler, *Stasi* (Boulder 1999).
39. "Tacitus and the Funerary Baroque" in S. Sontag (ed.), *A Barthes Reader* (New York 1982) 162.
40. R. Syme, *Tacitus* (Oxford 1958) vi.

FURTHER READING

The period covered by the *Annals* is described and discussed from various points of view in Volume 10 of *The Cambridge Ancient History* (Cambridge ²1996). On individual emperors there are: B. Levick, *Tiberius the Politician* (London/New York 1976, ²1999), R. Seager, *Tiberius* (London 1972, ²Oxford 2005), A. A. Barrett, *Caligula: The Corruption of Power* (London/New Haven 1989, repr. 2000), B. Levick, *Claudius* (London 1990), E. Champlin, *Nero* (Cambridge, MA 2003), and M. T. Griffin, *Nero: The End of a Dynasty* (London/New York 1984, repr. 2000). For an introduction to various aspects of the Roman imperial world consult P. Garnsey and R. Saller, *The Roman Empire: Economy, Society and Culture* (London 1987); more specialized studies of individual topics include I. Gradel, *Emperor Worship and Roman Religion* (Oxford 2002); J. E. Lendon, *Empire of Honour: The Art of Government in the Roman World* (Oxford 1997); S. P. Mattern, *Rome and the Enemy: Imperial Strategy in the Principate* (Berkeley/Los Angeles/London 1999); F. Millar, *The Emperor in the Roman World* (London ²1992); R. P. Saller, *Personal Patronage under the Early Empire* (Cambridge 1982); R. Syme, *The Augustan Aristocracy* (Oxford 1986); R. J. A. Talbert, *The Senate of Imperial Rome* (Princeton 1984); P. Veyne, *Bread and Circuses* (London 1990).

The single most important contribution to Tacitean studies is that of R. Syme, *Tacitus* (Oxford 1958), although more accessible as introductions are R. Martin, *Tacitus* (London 1981, rev. 1994), and R. Mellor, *Tacitus* (London/New York 1993). Martin also wrote the entry on Tacitus in *The Oxford Classical Dictionary* (Oxford ³1996) 1469–71 (reprinted, but without the bibliography, in *The Oxford Companion to Classical Civilization* (Oxford 1998) 702–4). The standard discussion of the *Annals* as a work of literature is B. Walker, *The Annals of Tacitus: A Study in the Writing of History* (Manchester 1952). Access to the details of Tacitus' narrative is often provided most usefully by a commentary, but the only English commentary on the whole of the *Annals* remains that of H. Furneaux, *The Annals of Tacitus* (2nd ed., 2 vols., Oxford 1896, 1907), which is still extremely helpful. There are substantial and scholarly commentaries on the Latin text of Books 1–2 by F. R. D. Goodyear (2 vols., Cambridge 1972–81) and of Book 3 by A. J. Woodman and R. H. Martin (Cambridge 1996); on a smaller scale there is a commentary on Book 4 by R. H. Martin and A. J. Woodman (Cambridge 1989, ⁷2003). R. H. Martin's commentary on Books 5–6 accompanies his translation of those books (Warminster 2001).

Tacitus is usually discussed in the numerous books devoted to classical (or Roman) historiography (or historians), but most of these books are out of date and—misleadingly, in my view—treat their subject according to the criteria of modern historical writing. For a rather different introduction to the topic see C. S. Kraus and A. J. Woodman, *Latin Historians* (Oxford 1997).

Abbreviations and References

The following list explains the abbreviations used in the footnotes to the translation and in the appendices:

Braund — D. C. Braund, *Augustus to Nero: A Sourcebook on Roman History 31 BC–AD 68* (London and Sydney 1985)

CAH^2 — *Cambridge Ancient History*, 2nd ed. (references are invariably to Vol. 10, ed. A. K. Bowman, E. Champlin and A. Lintott, Cambridge 1996)

EJ — V. Ehrenberg and A. H. M. Jones, *Documents Illustrating the Reigns of Augustus and Tiberius* (2nd ed., repr., Oxford 1976)

OCD — *Oxford Classical Dictionary* (3rd ed., ed. S. Hornblower and A. Spawforth, Oxford 1996)

SCPP — *Senatus Consultum de Cn. Pisone Patre* ("Senate's Decision Concerning Cn. Piso the Elder": references are to the English translation by M. Griffin, *Journal of Roman Studies* 87 (1997) 250–3)

Sherk — R. K. Sherk, *The Roman Empire: Augustus to Hadrian* (Translated Documents of Greece and Rome 6, Cambridge 1988)

Tac. Rev. — A. J. Woodman, *Tacitus Reviewed* (Oxford 1998)

WM — B. H. Warmington and S. J. Miller, *Inscriptions of the Roman Empire A.D. 14–117* (LACTOR 8, repr., London 1996)

In the cases of Braund, EJ, Sherk, and WM, references are to **items** rather than to pages, unless it is stated otherwise; in the case of *SCPP,* references are to **lines.**

It is conventional to refer to the text of the *Annals* by book number, chapter number, and (where appropriate) section number (e.g., 6.12 or 11.11.1). Since I have sometimes reparagraphed or repunctuated the text, chapter numbers and section numbers do not always coincide with the beginnings of paragraphs or sentences respectively.

Footnotes are numbered consecutively throughout each book of the *Annals,* but cross-references to footnotes usually take the form "1.16.2n." or "6.32.3 and n." and should be easy to follow up.

Dates are A.D. unless indicated otherwise.

CORNELIUS TACITUS

FROM THE PASSING OF DIVINE AUGUSTUS

BOOK 1

The City of Rome from its inception was held by kings; freedom and the consulship were established by L. Brutus.[1] Dictatorships were taken up only on occasion, and neither did decemviral power remain in effect beyond two years, nor
the military tribunes' consular prerogative for long.[2] Not for Cinna nor for Sulla
was there lengthy domination, and the powerfulness of Pompeius and Crassus
passed quickly to Caesar, the armies of Lepidus and Antonius to Augustus, who
with the name of princeps took everything, exhausted as it now was by civil dis-
sensions, under his command.[3]

1

The Roman people of old, however, had their successes and adversities recalled by brilliant writers; and to tell of Augustus' times there was no dearth of
deserving talents, until they were deterred by swelling sycophancy. The affairs of
Tiberius and Gaius, as of Claudius and Nero, were falsified through dread while
the men themselves flourished, and composed with hatred fresh after their fall.
Hence my plan is the transmission of a mere few things about Augustus and of
his final period, then of Tiberius' principate and the remainder[4] without anger
and partiality, any reasons for which I keep at a distance.

2

lack

3

---

1. The traditional dates of Rome's foundation and of the first ever consulship are 753
and 509 B.C. respectively.

2. The decemvirs (3.27.1n.) traditionally operated c. 451–449 B.C.; from shortly thereafter until 367 B.C. military tribunes with consular power very often substituted for the
consuls.

3. L. Cornelius Cinna held four successive consulships in 87–84 B.C.; L. Cornelius
Sulla was appointed dictator in 82 B.C. but relinquished the office in 81 and died in 79;
in 60/59 B.C. a coalition was formed between Pompey the Great, M. Licinius Crassus,
and Julius Caesar, but Crassus was killed at the battle of Carrhae (53 B.C.) and Pompey
after the battle of Pharsalus (48 B.C.); in 43 B.C. the triumvirate of M. Aemilius Lepidus,
Mark Antony, and Octavian was established, but Lepidus was deposed in 36 B.C. and
Antony was defeated in 31 B.C. at the Battle of Actium by Octavian, who in 27 B.C. took
the name "Augustus" (Sherk 1B, p. 3). The civil wars, which had begun with Caesar's crossing of the River Rubicon in January 49 B.C., were formally declared at an end in January 29 B.C.

4. T. has here listed the contents of the *Annals* under four headings: "a mere few things
about Augustus" = 1.2.1–1.4.1; "his final period" = 1.4.2–1.5.4; "Tiberius' principate"
= 1.6.1–6.51.3; "the remainder" = Book 7 (no longer extant) to the end (also no longer

1

* * *

2 When after the slaughter of Brutus and Cassius there were no more republican armies and Pompeius had been overwhelmed off Sicily and, with Lepidus cast aside and Antonius killed, not even the Julian party had any leader left but Caesar, he, putting aside the name of triumvir, presented himself as consul and as content with his tribunician prerogative for protecting the plebs;[5] but, when he had enticed the soldiery with gifts, the people with food, and everyone with the sweetness of inactivity, he rose up gradually and drew to himself the responsibilities of senate, magistrates, and laws—without a single adversary, since the most defiant had fallen in the battle line or by proscription and the rest of the nobles, each in proportion to his readiness for servitude, were being exalted by wealth and honors and, enhanced by the revolution, preferred the protection of the pres-

2 ent to the perils of old. Nor did the provinces reject that state of affairs, the command of senate and people having become suspect owing to the contests of the powerful and the greed of magistrates (there being no effective assistance from the laws, which had been disrupted by violence, intrigue, and finally money).

3 Nevertheless, as buttresses for his domination, Augustus promoted Claudius Marcellus, his sister's son and just a juvenile, by means of a pontificate and curule aedileship, and M. Agrippa, ignoble in status but good at soldiering and his partner in victory, by means of twin consulships, and subsequently after Marcellus' decease took him as son-in-law.[6] Tiberius Nero and Claudius Drusus, his step-

2 sons, he enhanced with the name of "commander," even though his own house was still then intact: for he had brought Agrippa's progeny, Gaius and Lucius, into the family of the Caesars and, though the praetexta of boyhood was not yet put aside, despite a display of reluctance he had had a burning desire that they be

3 called Principes of the Youth and marked out as consuls. But, when Agrippa had departed from life, both L. Caesar, while traveling to the Spanish armies, and Gaius, while retiring from Armenia and weakened by a wound, were carried off by fatefully early deaths or by the guile of their stepmother Livia; and, with Drusus' life extinguished previously, Nero alone of the stepsons was left.[7] Every-

---

extant). It follows from this listing that the present sentence concludes the formal preface to the *Annals*.

5. Brutus and Cassius committed suicide at the Battle of Philippi in 42 B.C.; Sextus Pompeius (son of Pompey the Great) was defeated at the battle of Naulochus in 36 and killed in 35 B.C.; for Lepidus and Antony see above (1.1.1n.). "Caesar" is Octavian/Augustus, who was consul continuously between 31 and 23 B.C., when he took tribunician power instead (see App. A).

6. Marcellus, son of Octavia, was aedile in 23 B.C., the year of his death; Agrippa, one of Augustus' great ministers, held twin consulships in 28–27 B.C. and married Julia (1.53.1n.) in 21 B.C.

7. Agrippa died in 12 B.C. (see Sherk 12 = Braund 73), Claudius Drusus (Tiberius'

Nero got it all [handwritten]

thing inclined in his direction: he was enlisted as son, colleague in command, and sharer in the tribunician power,[8] and through all the armies he was put on exhibition—not through his mother's dark practices, as before, but openly with her encouragement. For she had so shackled the elderly Augustus that he deported his one and only grandson, Agrippa Postumus, to the island of Planasia—raw, certainly, in terms of good behavior, and in his physical strength stupidly defiant, but discovered in no outrage.[9] Yet, as Hercules is my witness, he installed Germanicus, Drusus' offspring, over the eight legions on the Rhine and ordered him to be affiliated by Tiberius through adoption, notwithstanding that there was a young son in Tiberius' house, but so that there would be more bulwarks on which to depend.[10] *Nero adopts brother's son: Germanicus* [handwritten]

As for war, none survived at that time except against the Germans, more to erase the infamy of the army lost with Quintilius Varus[11] than through any desire of extending the empire or for some worthy prize. At home things were calm, magistrates had the same designations. But the younger men had been born after the Actian victory, and the majority even of the elderly in the course of the citizens' wars: what size was the remaining proportion, who had seen the republic? As a result, along with the changed state of the community, nowhere did any aspect of old-time convention remain untouched: with equality cast aside, all looked to the orders of the princeps, with no alarm for the present, while Augustus had the strength and years to support both himself and his household and peace. *"equality cast aside"* [handwritten]

Yet, when his old age, already advanced, had started to be exhausted by physical illness too, and the end was approaching, and with it new hopes, a few people discussed pointlessly the advantages of freedom, more panicked about war (others desired it), but by far the greatest number spread various rumors of the masters looming over them: Agrippa was callous and blazing from ignominy, unequal

Agrippa — callous [handwritten]

4

5

6

7

4

2

3

---

brother, son of Livia by her marriage to Ti. Claudius Nero) in 9 B.C., Lucius Caesar in A.D. 2 (Braund 62), Gaius Caesar in A.D. 4 (see Sherk 19 = Braund 63 = WM 1). "Nero" is Tiberius.

8. The reference seems principally to be to A.D. 4, though the details are disputed.

9. Agrippa Postumus, son of Agrippa and Julia (Augustus' daughter) and brother of Gaius and Lucius Caesar, was banished in A.D. 7.

10. Germanicus was adopted by Tiberius, his uncle, in A.D. 4 and given the Rhine command c. A.D. 13. In *Annals* 1–2 he is the major figure apart from Tiberius himself; for his death in A.D. 19 see 2.72.2. The "young son" of Tiberius and his first wife (Vipsania, daughter of Agrippa) is Drusus Caesar, who was born c. 13 B.C. and will die in A.D. 23 (4.8.1–2).

11. P. Quintilius Varus had been consul in 13 B.C. along with Tiberius: both had married daughters of Agrippa named Vipsania. The loss of Varus and Legions XVII, XVIII, and XIX in A.D. 9 was one of the greatest disasters in Roman history (A. Murdoch, *Rome's Greatest Defeat: Massacre in the Teutoburg Forest* [Sutton, Gloucestershire 2006]) and is often returned to in Book 1 of the *Annals*. For a monument to one of the centurions who perished see Sherk 23 (= Braund 49).

Nero –
spoiled &
dishonest

to so great a task in both age and experience of affairs; Tiberius Nero was mature in years and proved in war, but with the old and endemic haughtiness of the Claudian family; and many indications of his savagery, despite attempts at their

4 suppression, kept breaking out. From his earliest infancy he had been brought up in the royal house; as a young man he had been heaped with consulships, triumphs; not even during his years on Rhodes,[12] when in a show of seclusion he had acted as an exile, had he contemplated anything other than anger and de-

5 ception and secret lusts. In addition, they said, there was his mother, with her womanly unruliness: his enslavement to the female would be compulsory, and to two juveniles as well, who for a while would oppress the state and at some time tear it apart.[13]

5   As men were churning over such things as these, there was a deterioration in Augustus' health, and some suspected crime on the part of his wife. A rumor had started that a few months previously, with only a select number as accessories and with Fabius Maximus as his one companion,[14] Augustus had traveled to Planasia to visit Agrippa; many had been the tears and signs of affection there on both sides, and as a result there was hope that the young man would be restored to his

2 grandfather's hearth, something which Maximus had disclosed to his wife Marcia, and she to Livia; that in turn had become known to Caesar, and, with Maximus' life extinguished not long afterward (it being in doubt whether he had sought his own death), Marcia's groans had been heard at his funeral, accusing herself of having been the cause of her husband's extermination.

3   Whether or not that was the case, Tiberius had scarcely entered Illyricum

A.D. 14 when he was summoned by a hasty letter from his mother; but it has not been satisfactorily uncovered whether at the city of Nola he discovered Augustus still

4 breathing or lifeless. For Livia had cordoned off the house and streets with fierce guards, and from time to time favorable news was published until, after provision for what the occasion demanded, a single report carried the simultaneous announcement that Augustus had passed away and that Nero was in control of affairs.[15]

Nero
assumes
power

6   The first act of the new principate was the slaughter of Postumus Agrippa, unawares and unarmed, whom a centurion, despite bracing himself in spirit, dispatched only with difficulty. Tiberius did not speak about the matter in the senate: he was pretending there were orders from his father, in which he had written in advance to the tribune assigned to the guard that the latter should not hesitate in putting Agrippa to death whenever he himself consummated his final day.

2 Now there is no doubt that Augustus had often made savage complaints about

---

12. Tiberius' retirement to Rhodes in 6 B.C.–A.D. 2 is another topic to which T. frequently returns (e.g., 3.48.1, 4.15.1, 4.57.2).

13. The "two juveniles" are his biological son, Drusus, and his adopted son, Germanicus.

14. Paullus Fabius Maximus had been consul in 11 B.C. and became proconsul of Asia in the following year.

15. Augustus died on 19 August A.D. 14.

the young man's behavior and had ensured that his exile was sanctioned by a senate's decision; but he never hardened himself to execute any of his own relatives, nor was it credible that death had been inflicted on his grandson for the sake of his stepson's security: more likely, Tiberius and Livia—the former through dread, the latter through stepmotherly hatred—had speeded the slaughter of a suspected and resented young man. But to the centurion's announcement (in the manner **3** of the military) that the action which he had commanded had been taken, Tiberius replied that he had given no command and that an account of the action would have to be rendered in the senate. When this was discovered by Sallustius Crispus, a partner in the secret (it was he who had sent the note to the tribune),[16] he dreaded that he might be supplied as a defendant (it being equally perilous whether he produced a fabricated or a true statement) and he warned Livia that the mysteries of the household, the advice of friends and the services of soldiers should not be made public and that Tiberius should not dissipate the essence of the principate by calling everything to the attention of the senate: it was a condition of commanding that the account would not balance unless it were rendered to a single individual.

But at Rome there was a rush into servitude from consuls, fathers, equestrians. The more illustrious each was, the more false and frantic, and, with their **7** looks composed to avoid delight at the passing—and too much gloom at the commencement—of a princeps, they blended tears with joy and mourning with sycophancy. Sex. Pompeius and Sex. Appuleius as consuls were the first to swear **2** allegiance to Tiberius Caesar, and in their presence Seius Strabo and C. Turranius, the former being prefect of the praetorian cohorts, the latter of the food supply;[17] next came the senate, soldiery, and people. And in fact Tiberius' entire **3** start was through the consuls, as though in the old republic;[18] and, being ambivalent about commanding, even when he posted the edict by which he summoned the fathers to the curia, he headed it only with the tribunician power received under Augustus. The words of the edict were few and of delimited purport: he **4** would consult about his parent's honors and was staying close by the body, and that was his sole appropriation of a public responsibility. Yet on Augustus' decease **5** he had issued, like a Commander, the password to the praetorian cohorts; there were lookouts, arms, and the other trappings of court: soldiery accompanied him to the forum, soldiery to the curia; he sent a letter to the armies as though the

Nero adhered to tribunal leading

16. For Sallustius see further 2.40.2, 3.30.1–3.

17. Seius Strabo was father of the notorious Sejanus (4.1.1–3); Turranius is not mentioned again until A.D. 48 (11.31.1).

18. The punctuation here is mine; others read "as though in the old republic and ambivalent about commanding" and begin a new sentence thereafter. In my view too the statement "Tiberius' entire start was through the consuls" is a forward reference to the formal motion which the consuls placed before the senate at its *second* meeting (1.13.4) and is equivalent in meaning to "Tiberius began his whole reign through the consuls." See *Tac. Rev.* 66–8.

principate were acquired—in no respect reluctant except when he spoke in the
6   senate.[19] (The principal reason was alarm lest Germanicus—who wielded so
many legions, untold allied auxiliaries, and remarkable goodwill among the
7   people—should prefer to hold rather than to wait for command. He was also
conceding to public opinion that he should be seen to have been summoned and
chosen by the state rather than to have crept in through wifely intrigue and an
elderly adoption. Afterward it was recognized that his hesitancy had been brought
on to gain an insight into the attitudes of the aristocracy too: he stored away their
language and looks, twisting them into an accusation.)

8   Nothing did he allow to be discussed on the first day of the senate except the
last rites of Augustus, whose will, brought in by Vesta's Virgins, had Tiberius and
Livia as his heirs; Livia was enlisted in the Julian family and the Augustan name.
For secondary bequests he had written down his grandsons and great-grandsons,
and in the third rank leaders of the community—most of them the objects of his
2   resentment, but for vaunting and glory among posterity. His legacies did not go
beyond the limits of an ordinary citizen, except that he gave 43,500,000 sesterces to the people and plebs, individual donations of a thousand to the soldiers of
the praetorian cohorts, and three hundred a man to the legionaries and the cohorts consisting of Roman citizens.[20]

3   Next there was a debate about his honors, of which Gallus Asinius and L.
Arruntius proposed those seen+ as particularly distinctive, respectively that the
funeral should be led through the triumphal gate and that at its head should be
carried the titles of his legislation and the designations of the races conquered by
4   him.[21] Messala Valerius added that the oath in Tiberius' name should be renewed
annually; and, when asked by Tiberius whether it was on his instruction that he
had produced such a suggestion, he responded that he had spoken spontaneously
and that in matters which pertained to the state he would resort to no one's counsel but his own, even at the risk of offense.[22] (That was the only display of syco-
5   phancy left to be tried.) The fathers shouted unanimously that the body should
be carried to the pyre on the shoulders of senators; but Caesar relieved them with

19.   The reference here is to the *first* meeting of the senate (1.8.1 below), the date of which
is unknown (4 September has been suggested). The "reluctance" in question is Tiberius'
refusal to speak, at this first meeting, about the formalization of his own position; three reasons for this reluctance are given in the following parenthesis. See *Tac. Rev.* 53–9.

20.   Nearly all auxiliary cohorts were formed of noncitizens (see App. B), but in emergencies Roman citizens (usually volunteers) could be enrolled as auxiliaries, and their
units were designated as by T. here. Cf. 1.31.4 and n.

21.   C. Asinius Gallus, consul in 8 B.C. and proconsul of Asia two years later, was son of
C. Asinius Pollio (1.12.4n.) and in the Tiberian books is mentioned more than any other
individual apart from members of the imperial family and Sejanus. L. Arruntius was consul in A.D. 6 and is also prominent in Books 1–6. See esp. 1.13.1–3 below.

22.   M. Valerius Messalla Messalinus (consul in 3 B.C.) was son of the famous orator M.
Valerius Messalla Corvinus (3.34.2).

arrogant restraint and warned the people by edict that, whereas they had once disrupted the funeral of Divine Julius by their excessive enthusiasm, they should not prefer Augustus to be cremated in the forum rather than the Plain of Mars, his appointed resting-place.[23]

On the day of the funeral soldiers stood as if forming a garrison, much to the derision of those who had seen personally or who had heard from their parents about that day of still undigested servitude and of freedom served up again unsuccessfully, when the slaughter of the dictator Caesar seemed to some the worst of acts, to others the finest. Now, they said, an elderly princeps, despite the longevity of his power, and having even provided the state with resources in the form of heirs, would evidently require protecting by military assistance to ensure that his burial was peaceful!   6

Afterward there was much conversation about Augustus himself, with the majority in empty wonder that the day of his first receiving command all that time ago was the same as the last of his life, and that he had ended his life in the same bedroom of the house at Nola as his father, Octavius. Also celebrated was the number of his consulships, in which he had equaled Valerius Corvus and C. Marius jointly;[24] the continuation of his tribunician power for thirty-seven years; the name of "commander," acquired twenty-one times;[25] and his other honors, whether multiplied or novel.   9   2

Among the perspicacious, however, his life was variously extolled or criticized. The former said that, because of devotion to his parent and the requirements of the state, in which at that time there had been no place for law, he had been driven to civil war, which could be neither prepared for nor maintained by good behavior. He had made many concessions to Antonius while avenging himself on the killers of his father, many to Lepidus; after the latter had aged from apathy, and the former had been sunk by his lusts, there had been no other remedy for his disaffected fatherland than that it be ruled by one man. Yet it was neither on kingly rule nor dictatorship but on the name of "princeps" that the state had been based. The empire was cordoned by the sea of Ocean or distant streams; legions, provinces, fleets, everything was interconnected; there was legality among citizens, restraint among allies; the City itself was magnificent in its apparel; just a few things had been handled by force to ensure peace for the rest.   3   4   5

It was said on the other side that devotion to his parent and the times in the state had been taken up as a screen; in reality it was in a desire for domination that veterans had been mustered by his lavishness, an army procured by a juvenile in his private capacity, a consul's legions bribed, and support for the Pom-   10

23. Augustus' famous mausoleum (see App. C) was in the Plain of Mars.

24. M. Valerius Corvus (4th cent. B.C.) was traditionally a six-times consul, C. Marius was consul seven times between 107 and 86 B.C.

25. Here "commander" refers to military acclamations (see App. A) and not to Augustus' title as "emperor."

2   peian party pretended.[26] Subsequently, when by a decree of the fathers he had assailed the fasces and prerogative of a praetor, after the slaughter of Hirtius and Pansa (whether they had been carried off by the enemy, or Pansa by poison poured into a wound and Hirtius by his own soldiers and by Caesar's engineering of guile) he had taken over the forces of both.[27] The consulship had been extorted from an unwilling senate, and the arms which he had been given to deal with Antonius were turned against the state. The proscription of citizens and dis-

3   tributions of land had not been praised even by those who did them. Of course the ends of Cassius and the Bruti had been a concession to paternal antagonisms (although it was proper to forgo private hatreds for the public good); but Pompeius had been deceived by a phantom peace, Lepidus by a display of friendship; and subsequently Antonius, enticed by the Tarentine and Brundisian treaties and by a wedding to his sister,[28] had paid the penalty of a guileful relationship with

4   his death. Peace there had been without doubt after that, but gory: there had been the Lollian and Varian disasters, and the killing at Rome of Varrones, Egnatii, and Iulli.[29]

5   Nor was there any abstention from family matters. Nero's wife had been abducted from him, and there was the mockery of consulting pontiffs on the question whether it was right for her to wed after conceiving but before producing a child.[30] [. . .] and Vedius Pollio's luxuriousness.[31] Finally there was Livia, her burden on the state as a mother being matched by that on the Caesars' family as

6   a stepmother.[32] Nothing was left with which to honor the gods, since he wished himself to be worshiped with temples and with the likenesses of a divinity by

7   flamines and priests. Not even Tiberius had been adopted as successor through any affection or any concern for the state, but, because he had had insight into the man's arrogance and savagery, by the basest of comparisons he had sought glory for himself. (Indeed a few years before, when Augustus was again demand-

26. The references are to 44 B.C.

27. The reference is to the battle of Mutina in 43 B.C., in which the consuls A. Hirtius and C. Vibius Pansa participated.

28. The "phantom peace" is the treaty of Misenum in 39 B.C.; the "display of friendship" is the triumvirate (above, 1.1.1n.). The treaties of Tarentum and Brundisium were in 37 and 40 B.C. respectively, Antony's marriage to Octavia being an element of the latter.

29. M. Lollius' disaster in Germany was 16 B.C.; for Varus' see 1.3.6n. Varro Murena and Egnatius Rufus were executed for conspiracy in 22 and 19 B.C.; Iullus Antonius was forced to commit suicide in 2 B.C. for adultery with Julia.

30. Ti. Claudius Nero was compelled to divorce Livia in 39 B.C. so that Octavian could marry her (see further 5.1.1–2).

31. This sentence begins with a textual corruption which may perhaps hide another proper name or may be a sign that something more extensive has been omitted by mistake. Vedius Pollio was a friend of Augustus and noted for his wealth and cruelty.

32. She had given birth to Tiberius and was allegedly responsible for the deaths of Gaius and Lucius Caesar (1.3.3) and Agrippa Postumus (cf. 1.6.3).

ing tribunician power from the fathers for Tiberius, despite an honorific speech he had tossed out some comments on his demeanor, lifestyle, and habits in order to decry what he seemed to defend.)

As for his burial, once it had been completed according to custom, a temple **8** and heavenly rituals were decreed.[33] Prayers were then redirected toward **11** Tiberius; and he for his part began to talk variously about the magnitude of command and his own limitations: only Divine Augustus had been mentally capable of such a great undertaking on his own; having himself been summoned by Augustus for partnership in his cares, he had learned by experience how steep, how exposed to fortune, was the burden of ruling everything. Accordingly, in a community supported by such numbers of illustrious men, it should not be the case that they tendered all things to a single individual: several would more easily carry out the responsibilities of state by sharing the labors. *change from dictatorship*

More in such a speech was impressive than credible; and Tiberius' words, even **2** on matters which he was not for concealing, were—whether by nature or habit—always weighed and dark; but on that occasion, when he was striving to hide his feelings deep down, their extra complication led to uncertainty and ambiguity. But the fathers, whose one dread was that they seemed to understand,[34] **3** poured out complaints, tears, and vows; they were stretching out their hands to the gods, to Augustus' likeness, to the man's own knees, when he ordered a booklet to be produced and read out. Its contents were the public resources, what **4** numbers of citizens and allies under arms, how many fleets, kingdoms and provinces, taxes and revenues, and also necessary expenses and lavishments—all of which Augustus had listed in his own hand, and had added the counsel of confining the empire within its boundaries (whether in dread or through resentment being uncertain). *Is Tiberius lying? Or is he really doubtful of power?*

With the senate meanwhile prostrating itself in the basest protestations, **12** Tiberius by chance said that, although he was unequal to the state as a whole, he would undertake the protection of whatever part was entrusted to him. Thereupon Asinius Gallus said, "My question, Caesar, is which part of the state you **2** wish to be entrusted to you." Shocked by the unforeseen question, he fell silent for a while; then, collecting himself, he replied that it was not at all consistent with his reserve to choose or avoid any element of that from which he preferred to be excused totally. Gallus in turn (he had inferred offense from his look) said **3** that the purpose of his question had not been that the princeps should divide what could not be separated but that by his own admission it should be proved that the body of the state was one and needed to be ruled by the mind of one individual. He added praise of Augustus and reminded Tiberius himself of his *Nero pretends he doesn't want power...*

33. On 17 September (Sherk 1L, p. 4), at the senate's second meeting of Tiberius' principate.

34. I.e., they thought they understood what Tiberius had said and were therefore singularly afraid (so *Tac. Rev.* 48–9); the usual interpretation is that the senators had indeed understood Tiberius but were afraid lest they should seem to him to have understood.

own victories and of the exceptional actions which he had performed in the toga

4   over so many years.[35] But Gallus did not thereby assuage the other's anger, since he had long been resented on the grounds that, having taken in marriage Vipsania (M. Agrippa's daughter, who had once been Tiberius' wife), he had intentions beyond those of an ordinary citizen and retained the defiance of Pollio Asinius, his father.[36]

13   After this L. Arruntius caused similar offense with a speech not very different from that of Gallus, although Tiberius felt no inveterate anger toward Arruntius; but, as the man was rich, always at the ready, and of exceptional qualities with a

2   matching reputation publicly, he was suspected. For Augustus in his closing conversations—when he was handling the question of those who, though likely competent, would decline to acquire the princeps's position; those who, though no match for it, would want it; and those who were both able and desirous—had said that M. Lepidus was capable but would spurn it,[37] Gallus Asinius greedy and inferior, and L. Arruntius not unworthy and, if the chance were given, likely to

3   dare it. (About the former two there is a consensus; instead of Arruntius some have transmitted Cn. Piso,[38] and indeed all of them besides Lepidus were trapped by various subsequent charges set up by Tiberius.)

4   Q. Haterius and Mamercus Scaurus also grated on his suspicious mind, Haterius when he had said "How long will you allow yourself, Caesar, not to attend as head of the state?," Scaurus because he had said that, since the princeps had not intervened against the consuls' motion by the prerogative of his tribunician power, there was hope that the senate's pleas would not be unavailing.[39] Against Haterius he inveighed at once; Scaurus, for whom his ire was more im-

5   placable, he passed over in silence. And, exhausted by the shouting of everyone and the solicitations of individuals, he gradually changed tack—not to the point of admitting that he was undertaking command, but to that of ceasing to refuse

6   and to be asked. (It is agreed that, when Haterius had entered the Palatium to beg forgiveness and was groveling at the knees of Tiberius as he walked along, he was almost killed by soldiers because Tiberius, whether by accident or being fettered by the man's hands, had lurched forward. Yet not even the danger to such a man did anything to soften him, until Haterius appealed to Augusta and was protected by her highly concerned pleas.)

---

35. The toga symbolized peace as opposed to war (cf. 11.7.3).

36. The famous and multitalented C. Asinius Pollio had been consul in 40 B.C.

37. M. Aemilius Lepidus, consul in A.D. 6, features prominently in T.'s Tiberian narrative: see esp. 4.20.2.

38. This is T.'s first reference to Cn. Calpurnius Piso (consul in 7 B.C.), the opponent of Germanicus (2.43.2–4 onward) and subject of the "Senate's Decision Concerning Cn. Piso the Elder" (above, page xv).

39. Q. Haterius had been suffect consul in 5 B.C.; Mamercus Aemilius Scaurus would become suffect consul in A.D. 21.

There was considerable sycophancy from the fathers toward Augusta too. **14**
Some proposed calling her "Mother of the Fatherland," others its "Parent," but
the majority that "Son of Julia" be an extra title to Caesar's name. But he for his **2**
part—insisting that honors for females should be limited and that he would
employ the same control with those which were bestowed on himself, but in reality tense with resentment and interpreting her womanly elevation as depreciation of himself—allowed not even a lictor to be decreed for her and forbade an
Altar of Adoption and other things of this type. Yet for Germanicus Caesar he **3**
requested proconsular command, and legates were dispatched to tender it and at
the same time to offer condolences on his sorrowfulness at the passing of Augustus. (The reason why the same was not demanded on behalf of Drusus was that
Drusus was consul designate and present.)

He nominated twelve candidates for the praetorship, the number transmitted **4**
by Augustus; and, when the senate urged him to augment it, he pledged on oath
that he would not exceed it. It was then that elections were first transferred from **15**
the Plain to the fathers.[40] (Up to that day, although the most important were at
the princeps's discretion, some were nevertheless subject to the support of the
tribes.) The people for their part did not complain at being deprived of their
prerogative, except in hollow rumor, and the senate, released as it was from lavishments and sordid appeals, gladly grasped it, while Tiberius limited himself to
recommending no more than four candidates to be designated without objection and canvassing.

Meanwhile the tribunes of the plebs sought to produce, at personal expense, **2**
games which, as additions to the fasti, would be called "Augustal" from Augustus' name. But the money was decreed from the treasury, and in the circus
triumphal clothing should be worn;[41] riding in a chariot was not permitted. **3**
Subsequently as an annual celebration they were transferred to the praetor who
was allotted jurisdiction between citizens and foreigners.

*

This was the condition of City affairs when mutiny befell the Pannonian legions, **16**
not from any novel causes except that it was a change of princeps which offered
the license for disruption and, resulting from civil war, the hope of prizes.

40. The Plain of Mars was the meeting-place for the "centuriate assembly," responsible
for the election of consuls and praetors. T.'s reference to "tribes" in the next sentence suggests an allusion to the "tribal assembly," which met in the forum and was responsible for
the election of lesser magistrates. But the precise significance of his remarks here is highly
controversial. For the technical terms see *OCD* 372–3 s.v. *comitia*.

41. I.e., by the tribunes. The term "fasti" (above) designates either (as here) a calendar
of annual festivals, from which Ovid's poem *Fasti* takes its name, or (as at 3.17.4–18.1) a
list of officeholders, especially consuls. See further *OCD* 588.

2   In a summer camp three legions were being held simultaneously,[42] presided over by Junius Blaesus, who, on hearing of the end of Augustus and the beginnings of Tiberius, had suspended their customary responsibilities for reasons of the recess[43] or of joy. With that as the start, the soldiers became reckless, disaffected, lent their ears to conversations with all the worst elements, and finally desired luxuriousness and inactivity and spurned discipline and toil.

3   There was in the camp one Percennius, formerly leader of a theatrical claque and later a troop-soldier, with a provocative tongue and taught to stir up crowds with his actorish enthusiasm. On impressionable minds, uncertain about what the precise condition of soldiering after Augustus would be, he exerted a gradual influence in nightly dialogues or when day had turned to evening, and when

17   the better men had slipped away, he trooped all the basest ones together.[44] At length, with others too now ready to serve the mutiny, his questions took on the style of a public meeting: why, in the fashion of slaves, were they obedient to a few centurions and even fewer tribunes? When would they ever dare to demand remedies, if they did not approach a new and still nervous princeps with pleas or

2   arms? Enough wrong had been done through shirking for so many years: old men, their bodies very often maimed from wounds, were tolerating thirty or forty

3   years' service; not even discharge put an end to their soldiering, but, pitched by the banner,[45] they endured the same toils under another designation; and anyone who survived so many hazards with his life would still be dragged off to different and distant countries to be given swampy marshes or uncultivated

4   mountains called "land." Indeed soldiering itself was heavy in cost and unprofitable: soul and body were reckoned at ten asses a day,[46] and out of this came their clothing, arms, and tents; out of this the savagery of centurions was bought off, and exemptions from responsibilities bought. On the other hand, as Hercules was his witness, the whippings and woundings, the hard winter, grueling summers,

5   frightful warfare, and barren peace were everlasting! There would be no other alleviation than if soldiering were entered upon under fixed conditions: they should earn a denarius a day,[47] the sixteenth year of service should bring an end

42. The legions were VIII, IX, and XV.

43. A "recess" (*iustitium*) was the official suspension of business and other activities which was decreed on the death of an emperor or other distinguished person (*OCD* 791). See further 1.50.1, 2.82.3, 3.7.1. Q. Junius Blaesus had been suffect consul in A.D. 10; he was Sejanus' uncle (3.35.2).

44. This rendering preserves the ambiguities of the Latin.

45. Any special detachment of troops might have its own banner (*uexillum*): here the troops in question have been discharged from service but evidently have been kept on as reservists and have pitched their tents under their own banner.

46. I.e., ⅝ of a denarius (below) or 2 ½ sesterces per day. The soldiers' annual wage was thus roughly equivalent to ¹⁄₄₄₀ of the sum needed to qualify as an equestrian (for which see App. A).

47. I.e., 16 asses or 4 sesterces per day.

to it, they should not be held further under the banners but their reward should be paid in cash in their own camp. Did the praetorian cohorts—who received two denarii a day, who after sixteen years were returned to their own hearths—really undertake more dangers? It was not that they themselves disparaged City lookouts; but in their own case, situated as they were among grisly peoples, the enemy was actually visible from their own billets.   **6**

The crowd bayed its approval from a variety of incentives, some remonstrating about the marks of their beatings, others their white hair, most of them their worn-out coverings and naked bodies. Finally they reached such a point of madness that they agitated to merge the three legions into one; but, deterred by rivalry (because each man sought that particular honor for his own legion), they turned elsewhere and placed all three eagles and the cohorts' standards together. At the same time they piled up turf and constructed a tribunal to make a more conspicuous site.   **18**
                                                                            2

As they hurried about, Blaesus arrived and started to berate individuals and tried to hold them back with repeated shouts: "Stain your hands by slaughtering me instead! It will be a lesser outrage to kill your legate than to secede from your Commander. Either, unharmed, I shall hold on to the loyalty of my legions or, with my throat cut, I shall speed your remorse." The turf continued to pile up nonetheless and had already reached chest height when finally, his persistence irresistible, they abandoned their project. With considerable oratorical skill Blaesus said that it was not through mutiny and disruption that soldiers' requirements should be conveyed to Caesar: the ancients had not made such novel requests of old-time commanders, nor had they themselves of Divine Augustus; it was also hardly the right occasion for an incipient princeps to have his cares aggravated. Yet, if they aimed in peacetime to attempt things which had not been demanded by the victors even in the civil wars, why, contrary to their habit of compliance, contrary to the obligations of discipline, were they contemplating violence? They should decide on legates and, in his presence, issue instructions.   **3**

                                                                            19
                                                                            2
                                                                            3

They cried out that Blaesus' son, a tribune, should perform the legation and request discharge for the soldiers after sixteen years; their other instructions would follow when the first had borne fruit. On the young man's departure there was moderate peace; but the soldiery behaved haughtily because the fact that the legate's son was the advocate of their common cause provided ample demonstration that necessity had extracted what they would not have achieved through moderation.   **4**
                                                                            5

greedy soldiers

Meanwhile the maniples who before the start of the mutiny had been sent to Nauportus for roadworks and bridges and other utilities, on hearing of the agitation in the camp, uprooted their banners and, ransacking the nearby villages and Nauportus itself (which was the size of a municipality), used ridicule, insults, and finally beatings to assail the centurions who were trying to hold them back—their principal anger being directed against Aufidienus Rufus, the camp prefect, whom, snatched from his vehicle, they loaded with packs and drove along at the head of the driving column, mockingly asking whether he gladly bore such in-   **20**

2   ordinate burdens, such long journeys. For Rufus—long a maniple regular, later
a centurion, then prefect in the camp—was for reviving an ancient and hard soldiering, being obsessed with work and toil and all the more ruthless because he
had endured them himself.

21   On the arrival of these men the mutiny started afresh, and, roving about, they
began to pillage the surrounding area. To terrify the rest, Blaesus ordered a few,
particularly those laden with plunder, to be subjected to beatings and pent up in
prison (even at that point the legate was still obeyed by the centurions and the
2   best of the maniple regulars); but they for their part struggled against those dragging them away, grasped hold of the knees of bystanders, and sometimes invoked
individuals by name, sometimes the century, cohort, or legion to which each maniple regular belonged, shouting repeatedly that the same fate was looming over
them all. Simultaneously they heaped abuse on the legate, besought heaven and
the gods, and left out nothing which would arouse resentment, pity, dread, and
3   anger. Everyone rushed in their direction, and, the prison broken open, no sooner
were their chains released than deserters and men condemned on capital charges
were already merging with the crowd.

22   Thereupon the violence burned more feverishly, and the mutiny had more
leaders. In particular one Vibulenus, a troop-soldier, raising himself up on the
shoulders of bystanders in front of Blaesus' tribunal, addressed the men, agitated
as they were and intent on what he was planning: "You at least have restored light
and breath to these guiltless and most pitiable men; but who is restoring life to
my brother, or my brother to me? Sent to you from the German army concerning your mutual benefits, last night he had his throat cut by *him*,[48] through the
agency of the personal gladiators whom he keeps and arms for the extermina-
2   tion of soldiers. Tell me, Blaesus, where you have flung away the corpse: not even
enemies resent burial. When with kisses and with tears I have had my fill of pain,
order me too to be butchered—provided that these men here bury us, killed for
no crime but because we paid heed to the interests of the legions."

23   He made these words inflammatory by weeping and beating his chest and face
with his hands. Then, knocking aside the men on whose shoulders he was supported, and leaping headlong to grovel at the feet of individuals, he provoked so
much consternation and resentment that some of the soldiers bound the gladiators who were among Blaesus' slaves, some the rest of his establishment, while
2   others poured out to look for the body. And, had it not quickly become known
both that there was no body to be discovered and that despite application of the
rack the slaves were denying the slaughter and that the man had never had a
3   brother at all, they were on the point of exterminating the legate. As it was, they
ousted the tribunes and camp prefect; the packs of the fugitives were ransacked;
and the centurion Lucilius was killed (to whom, with soldierly wit, they had attributed the designation "Another Here," because, when his vine-cane broke on
a soldier's back, he demanded another in a loud voice and then a third and so

48. I.e., Blaesus.

14

on).The rest found cover in hiding-places, with the exception of Clemens Julius,   4
who was kept back as being considered suitable for conveying the soldiers' instructions on account of his ready ingenuity. Further, the Eighth and Fifteenth   5
Legions were themselves preparing their swords against each other, as the former
demanded the death of a centurion with the nomenclature Sirpicus whom the
Fifteens were protecting, but the soldiery of the Ninth interposed pleas and, on
their being spurned, threats.

   News of these events drove Tiberius—though reclusive and especially given   **24**
to concealing all the grimmest matters—to dispatch his son Drusus along with
community leaders and two praetorian cohorts, with no particularly fixed instructions but to make decisions in the light of the situation; and the cohorts
were strengthened unconventionally by a select soldiery. In addition there was a   2
considerable portion of the praetorian cavalry and the hard core of the Germans
who at that time were on hand as the Commander's guards; also the prefect of
the praetorian, Aelius Sejanus (who had been given as colleague to his father
Strabo and enjoyed great influence with Tiberius), as a mentor for the young man
and, for the others, a living demonstration of perils and prizes.[49]

   On Drusus' approach the legions met him as though out of duty, not delighted   3
(as is conventional) nor glittering with insignia but disfigured by filth and, despite their semblance of sorrowfulness, with looks approaching truculence.
After he had entered the rampart, they strengthened the gates with pickets and   **25**
ordered groups of armed men to wait at fixed locations in the camp; the rest all
surrounded the tribunal in a mighty column. There stood Drusus, requesting   2
silence with his hand; whenever they for their part returned their eyes to the
multitude, they bayed with callous voices; conversely, looking again at Caesar,
they trembled. There would be an indistinct growl, a frightening roar and suddenly quiet; in accordance with their different emotions they were panicked and
terrifying. Finally, during a lull in the turmoil, he read out a letter from his fa-   3
ther in which it had been written down that his principal concern was for the
bravest of legions, with whom he had endured very many wars;[50] the first moment his spirit rested from its grief, he would discuss their demands before the
fathers; meanwhile he had sent his son to concede without hesitation whatever
could be granted immediately; the rest had to be kept for the senate, who should
properly be considered a party to either favor or strictness.

   The response of the meeting was that Clemens the centurion had the instruc-   **26**
tions to be conveyed. He began by speaking about discharge after sixteen years,
about the rewards at the end of service, that a denarius should be their daily wage,
and that veterans should not be kept under the banner. When Drusus in reply
pleaded the senate's and his father's adjudication as an excuse, there was a disruptive shout: why had he come, neither to increase the soldiers' wages nor allevi-   2

---

49. This is T.'s first mention of Sejanus, later Tiberius' notorious minister and evil genius (see esp. 4.1.1–3 and 4.57.1).

50. Tiberius had campaigned in Pannonia in 12–9 B.C. and A.D. 6–9.

senate consulted only for benefits, not for punishments (good point)

ate their toils, in fact without a license to do any good at all? Yet, as Hercules was their witness, everyone had permission when it came to beatings and execution! Tiberius had once been accustomed to frustrate the legions' requirements with Augustus' name; Drusus had brought back the same techniques: would they never

3   have any visitors except family sons? It was obviously a novelty that the Commander should refer only the benefits of soldiers to the senate: was the same senate therefore to be consulted each time reprisals or battles were declared? Or was it the case that prizes depended on their masters but punishments demanded no adjudicator?

27   Finally they left the tribunal and, whenever one of the praetorian soldiers or Caesar's friends was encountered, brandished their fists to cause disaffection and start hostilities, being especially ferocious toward Cn. Lentulus, because, as the others' superior in age and in glory from war, he was believed to be stiffening

2   Drusus and foremost in spurning "those outrages to soldiering."[51] And not long after, as he was departing+ to make his way back again to winter camp at the prospect of peril, they surrounded him, asking repeatedly where he was proceeding: to the Commander or to the fathers, so that there too he could oppose the legions' benefits? At the same time they swooped on him and hurled rocks; and it was only when he was already gory from the impact of a stone and certain of extermination that he was shielded by the hurried arrival of the crowd which had come with Drusus.

28   The menace of a night likely to erupt into crime was allayed by chance: for, when the sky suddenly cleared, the moon was seen to be waning. Ignorant of the reason, the soldiery interpreted it as an omen of their immediate circumstances, assimilating the eclipse of the planet to their own toils: there would be a successful outcome to their proceedings if the goddess's glitter and brilliancy were restored

2   to her. So they made a din with the sound of bronze and a chorus of trumpets and horns; in accordance with her increasing brightness or darkness, they were either delighted or sorrowful; and, after a bank of clouds had obstructed their view and it was believed that she had been buried in the shadows, they started (since minds once shocked are prone to superstition) to lament that for them eternal toil was being portended, it was their actions from which the gods were turning away.

3   Deeming that he should make use of this development and that what had been offered by accident should be turned to wise account, Caesar ordered a round of the tents to be made. The centurion Clemens was summoned, along with any

4   others whose good behavior was still welcome to the crowd. They infiltrated the watches, pickets, and sentries on the gates; they offered hope and brandished dread: "How long will we keep up our blockade of the Commander's son? Where will our conflicts end? Are we really likely to swear an oath to Percennius and Vibulenus? Will Percennius and Vibulenus lavish wages on the soldiers, land on

51. Cn. Cornelius Lentulus "the Augur": consul in 14 B.C. and a man of immense distinction (4.44.1).

Clemens advises that the soldiers apologize now for mutiny

the retired? In a word, will they, rather than the Nerones and Drusi, take on the command of the Roman people? Why not rather be prior with our penitence, just as we were the last in guilt? Collective demands are slow to be realized, but individual favor you would earn immediately and receive immediately." With their minds moved by these words, and mutually suspicious, recruit was detached from veteran, legion from legion. Then there gradually returned their love of compliance: they abandoned the gates, and the standards which had been gathered together at the start of the mutiny were replaced in their proper sites.

mutiny gives up

Drusus at daybreak called a meeting and, despite his rawness at speaking, censured with an inborn nobility their past course and approved the present. He said that he was not to be conquered by terror and threats: if he saw that they had turned toward moderation, if he heard them being suppliants, he would write to his father urging him to be appeased and to receive the legions' prayers. As they pleaded, the same Blaesus once again and L. Aponius, a Roman equestrian from Drusus' retinue, and Justus Catonius, a first-rank centurion, were dispatched to Tiberius.

A conflict of opinion then followed, since some proposed that they should wait for the legates and in the meantime manipulate the soldiery by being affable, while others that they should act with stronger remedies: there was nothing moderate about a crowd: they terrorized unless they were panicking; when they were thoroughly afraid, they could be despised with impunity: while they were still gripped by superstition, there should be an extra admixture of dread on the part of the leader by removing the instigators of the mutiny. Drusus was instinctively ready for the more drastic of these alternatives: he ordered Vibulenus and Percennius to be summoned and killed. (Many transmit that they were buried within the leader's pavilion, others that the bodies were flung away outside the rampart as a demonstration.) Next a search was made for the principals of the disturbance, and some while straying outside the camp were cut down by centurions or soldiers of the praetorian cohorts, some the maniples themselves handed over as evidence of their loyalty.

orders death of mutiny leaders

An early winter had increased the soldiers' concerns by constant deluges, so savage that they could neither leave their tents nor troop together or scarcely protect the standards, which were frequently snatched away by whirlwind and wave. Still persisting too was their alarm at the heavens' anger: it was not without reason that, in the face of their impiety, the planets grew dull and storms plunged down: there would be no other alleviation of their afflictions, they said, than if they were to leave their inauspicious and defiled camp and each man, thus released from his impiousness,[52] were restored to his own winter camp. First the Eighth, then the Fifteenth Legion went back; the Ninth had repeatedly cried out that they should stay for Tiberius' letter, but soon, deserted when the others departed, it chose of its own free will to anticipate the looming necessity. And

superstition

— all legions returned to their own camps

52. Or perhaps "each man, released by this act of expiation."

17

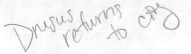

Drusus too did not wait for the legates' return but, because the immediate condition there had subsided well enough, went back to the City.

31   During the course of almost the same days, and from the same causes, the German legions were disrupted—all the more violently, given their greater numbers, and with high hopes that Germanicus Caesar would be unable to suffer the command of another and would entrust himself to the legions, who would handle[+] everything by their own force.

2   There were two armies on the bank of the Rhine. One, named "the upper," was under the legate C. Silius;[53] the lower was the concern of A. Caecina;[54] direction of the whole lay with Germanicus, who at the time was intent on conducting a census of the Galliae. Yet those whom Silius controlled did no more

3   than keep the fortune of a mutiny elsewhere under observation in an ambivalent state of mind; it was the soldiery of the lower army which fell into a frenzy, with the source arising from the Twenty-first and Fifth, and the First and Twentieth Legions swept along also (they were being held in the same summer camp in the territory of the Ubii for a period of inactivity or light responsibilities). So,

4   on hearing of the end of Augustus, it was—after a levy held recently in the City—an indigenous crowd who, inured to recklessness and intolerant of toil, filled the raw minds of the rest:[55] the time had come, they said, for veterans to demand their due discharge, young men more lavish wages, and everyone a limit on their

5   pitiable conditions and to avenge the centurions' savagery. These were not the words of one man, like Percennius among the Pannonian legions, nor were they addressed to the ears of trembling soldiers, looking behind them at other and more effective armies, but rather many faces and voices in mutiny: in their hands lay the Roman cause, they said, by their victories was the state increased, theirs

32   the nomenclature which commanders adopted.[56] Nor did the legate attempt to confront them: the derangement of the majority had deprived him of his steadfastness.

Suddenly in a brainstorm,[57] their swords drawn, they attacked the centurions (it was this group that had fueled the soldiers' hatreds longest and was the starting-point of their savagery). Knocking them down, they mauled each of them

---

53. The "upper" army comprised Legions II, XIII, XIV, and XVI (see 1.37.3). C. Silius A. Caecina Largus had been consul in A.D. 13: for his end see 4.18.1–20.1.

54. A. Caecina Severus had been suffect consul in 1 B.C.

55. The "levy held recently in the City" had been designed to make good the heavy losses suffered in the Varian disaster of A.D. 9 (above, 1.3.6n.): hence "indigenous" means "local" from the viewpoint of Rome rather than (as might have been expected) that of Germany.

56. I.e., "Germanicus," the name both of their present commander and of his father Nero Claudius Drusus, whose other descendants too were entitled to the name.

57. "Brainstorm" is here used in its primary sense of "a series of sudden, violent, cerebral disturbances" (Webster) or "a succession of sudden and severe phenomena, due to some cerebral disturbance" (*OED*).

with sixty blows, to match the centurions' number;[58] then they tipped them—mangled and mutilated and sometimes lifeless—in front of the rampart or into the stream of the Rhine. After Septimius had escaped to the tribunal and started to grovel at the feet of Caecina, they importuned for him unceasingly until he was surrendered for extermination. Cassius Chaerea, who later achieved his memorial among posterity for the slaughter of C. Caesar[59] but was at that time a juvenile of defiant spirit, opened up with his sword a passage through the armed men confronting him. No tribune, no camp prefect wielded authority any further: watches, pickets, and anything else which their immediate need indicated, were assigned by the men themselves. To anyone making a deeper diagnosis of the soldiers' spirits, a principal symptom of the extent and irremediability of their disturbance was the fact that they were neither scattered in disarray nor under the influence of a minority but flared up together and fell silent together—with such uniformity and consistency that you would have believed them to be directed.

Meanwhile Germanicus, who (as we have said) was being responsible for a census throughout the Galliae,[60] received the news that Augustus had passed away. He had the latter's granddaughter Agrippina in marriage and several children by her, being himself the offspring of Drusus (Tiberius' brother) and the grandson of Augusta, but tense from his uncle's and grandmother's concealed hatred of him, their reasons for which were all the more bitter because unjust. (The memory of Drusus among the Roman people was considerable, and it was believed that, if he had been in charge of affairs, he would have given them back their freedom. Hence goodwill toward Germanicus, and the same hope. For the young man had the instinct of an ordinary citizen and a remarkable affability quite different from Tiberius' conversation and look, arrogant and dark as they were.) In addition there were womanly affronts, with Livia's stepmotherly goadings of Agrippina, and Agrippina herself a little too volatile, except that, with her chastity and her love for her husband, she turned her (albeit untamed) spirit to good effect. Yet, the closer Germanicus now was to that highest of all hopes, the more emphatically did he strive on Tiberius' behalf: he bound both himself and his intimates and the communities of the Belgae by the latter's oath.

Subsequently, hearing of the legions' turmoil, he set off hurriedly and confronted them outside the camp, their eyes cast down toward the ground as if in remorse. After he had entered the rampart, however, discordant complaints began to make themselves heard; and some men, grasping his hand in a show of effusive kissing, inserted his fingers so that he would feel mouths devoid of teeth; others displayed limbs twisted with old age. Because the waiting meeting seemed thoroughly disorganized, he first ordered it to disperse into maniples; but "they would hear him better as they were" was their reply; next, banners must be carried in front, so that that at least would distinguish the cohorts; slowly they sub-

58. There were sixty centurions in each legion (see App. B).

59. "C. Caesar" is the future emperor Gaius Caligula, murdered early in A.D. 41.

60. See 1.31.2 above.

4   mitted. Then, after beginning with veneration of Augustus, he turned to the victories and triumphs of Tiberius, reserving his principal praise for celebrating the latter's finest actions in the Germanies with those very legions.[61] After that he extolled the consensus in Italy, the loyalty of the Galliae: nowhere was there a single element of turbulence or disaffection.

35   These words were listened to in silence or with a restrained growl; but, when he touched on the mutiny—asking where their soldierly moderation was, where the dignity of their old discipline, where the evicted tribunes were, where the centurions—they bared their bodies as one man and remonstrated about the weals from their wounds and the marks of their beatings. Then in indistinguishable utterances they censured the price of exemptions, their straitened wages, the hardness of their work and specifically the ramparting, ditches, and haulings of pasturage, fuel and wood, and anything else which was required out of necessity or

2   merely to combat inactivity in camp. A particularly frightening shout arose from the veterans, who, counting out their thirty or more years of service, begged both that he should cure their exhaustion and for an end to such grueling soldiering

3   and for a not impecunious retirement, not⁺ for death amid the selfsame toils. There were those too by whom the money bequeathed by Divine Augustus was demanded as their right, along with words of auspicious omen for Germanicus; and, if he wanted the command, they demonstrated their readiness.

4   At that, as if contaminated by their crime, he leapt headlong from the tribunal. They blocked his departure with their weapons, threatening if he did not go back; but he for his part, shouting repeatedly that he would die rather than cast aside his loyalty, snatched the sword from his side, brought it upward, and was on the verge of bringing it down into his heart, had not those nearest grasped his

5   hand, holding it fast by force. The farthest section of the meeting, clustered together as it was, and (scarcely credible to say) some individuals who came up nearer urged him to strike; and a soldier by the name of Calusidius offered his own drawn sword, adding that it was sharper. Even to the madmen that seemed savage and a sign of evil behavior, and there was an interval for Caesar to be snatched away by his friends into his pavilion.

36   There a debate took place about the remedy. For news was also coming in that legates were being organized, who would sweep off the upper army to the same cause; the town of the Ubii had been marked out for extirpation; and, once hands

2   had been dipped in plunder, they would break out to ransack the Galliae. Their dread was increased both by the enemy's awareness of the Roman mutiny and by the likelihood of his attack if the bank[62] were neglected; yet, if the auxiliaries and allies were armed against the withdrawal of the legions, civil war would be under way. Strictness was perilous, lavishness outrageous: whether nothing or

3   everything was conceded to the soldiery, the state would be on the brink. It was therefore decided, after they had turned over the calculations among themselves,

---

61. Tiberius had campaigned in Germany in 9–7 B.C., A.D. 4–6, and 10.
62. Of the Rhine.

final concession to army

that a letter should be written in the princeps's name: discharge was being granted to men of twenty years' service; those who had done sixteen were being decommissioned and retained under the banner without liability for anything except repulsing the enemy; and the bequests for which they had asked were being paid and indeed doubled.

The soldiery recognized this as a timely fabrication and importuned at once. **37** Due discharge was dispatched by the tribunes; the lavishment was deferred for each man's winter camp. But the men of the Fifth and Twenty-first did not withdraw until their money, collected from the travel-fund of his friends and of Caesar himself, was paid fully there and then in the summer camp. As for the First **2** and Twentieth Legions, the legate Caecina led them back to the community of the Ubii—a disgraceful column, since the money-chests seized from the commander were being carried along amid the standards and amid the eagles. Germanicus set off for the upper army and bound the Second, Thirteenth, and **3** Sixteenth Legions by the oath without any hesitation on their part (the men of the Fourteenth had briefly demurred); money and discharge were delivered to them even without their importuning.

Among the Chauci, however, the banner-men[63] of the disaffected legions **38** started a mutiny while manning a garrison and were briefly suppressed by instant reprisals against two soldiers. The order had been that of M'. Ennius, the camp prefect, thereby setting a good example rather than relying on any accredited authority. Subsequently, with the enlargement of the disturbance, he turned **2** fugitive but was discovered; and, when his hiding-place was found to be unsafe, his daring lent him a defense: it was not their prefect, he said, but rather their leader Germanicus, rather their Commander Tiberius whom they were violating. Simultaneously, having terrified the men who had stood in his way, he seized the banner and turned it toward the bank;[64] and, shouting repeatedly that whoever left the column would be treated as a deserter, he led them back to their winter camp, still turbulent but with nothing dared. *resolved*

Meanwhile the legates from the senate reached Germanicus, who had now re- **39** turned, at the altar of the Ubii.[65] There two legions (the First and Twentieth), as well as veterans under the banner who had recently been discharged, were wintering. Panicked, and deranged by their complicity, they were transfixed by dread, **2** thinking that the newcomers were under the fathers' orders to cancel what had been extracted by mutiny. And, customary as it is for a crowd to supply a guilty **3** party, however false the charges, they censured Munatius Plancus, a former consul and principal of the legation,[66] for instigating the senate's decision; and at bed-

discharged men feared truth of their discharge, & blamed Munatius Plancus

---

63. Regular troops on special detachment, to be distinguished from the semiretired veterans mentioned earlier (1.17.3) and again below (1.39.1).

64. The identity of this river is uncertain.

65. These are the legates dispatched at 1.14.3 above.

66. L. Munatius Plancus, son of the better known consul of 42 B.C., had been consul in A.D. 13.

[handwritten margin notes: "doubtful", "soldiers attack", "Germanicus"; left margin: "Germanicus puts soldiers at ease & explains why legates had really come"]

time they commenced to importune for the banner located in Germanicus' house, and, converging on the entrance, set to work on the doors, dragged Germanicus from his bed, and, facing him with the dread of death, compelled him to hand

4   over the banner. Then, roving through the streets, they were confronted by the legates, who, having heard the commotion, were making for Germanicus. They heaped insults on the legates and prepared for slaughter, particularly in the case of Plancus, whose rank had prevented him from flight; nor had he any other refuge in his peril except the camp of the First Legion. There, embracing the standards and eagle, he was trying to protect himself by sanctuary, and, had not the eagle-bearer Calpurnius fended off the ultimate violence, a legate of the Roman people in a Roman camp would have stained the altars of the gods with his own blood—a rarity even between enemies.

5   Finally at daylight, after the leader and the soldiery and their actions had begun to be accorded due recognition, Germanicus on entering the camp com-
6   manded Plancus to be brought to him, and received him onto the tribunal. Then, berating their frenzy as "fated" and saying that its resurgence was due not to the soldiers' anger but the gods', he revealed why the legates had come. He expressed fluent sympathy for the rights of the legation and for Plancus' own grave and undeserved plight, and also for how much disgrace the legion had incurred; and, with the meeting stunned rather than pacified, he dismissed the legates under the protection of auxiliary cavalry.

40   In a situation of such dread everyone started to criticize Germanicus for not proceeding to the upper army, where there was compliance and help against the rebels: enough wrong and more had been done by the discharge and money and
2   soft decisions; even if he regarded his own safety as cheap, why did he keep his tiny little son and pregnant spouse amid madmen and violators of every human law? Them at least he should restore to grandfather and state.

3   After much hesitation, during which his contemptuous wife attested that she was sprung from Divine Augustus and was by no means inferior in the face of dangers, finally, embracing her womb and their mutual son with much weeping,
4   he drove her to leave. There went on its way a pitiable column of women: the leader's wife a refugee, carrying her tiny little son in her lap and surrounded by friends' lamenting spouses, who were being dragged off with her. And no less
41   grim were the men who stayed behind. The scene was not that of a Caesar who was flourishing and in his own camp, but like that in a conquered city. And the groans and breast-beating turned even the soldiers' ears and faces in their direction. They emerged from their billets: what was that weeping sound? what was it that was so sad? Illustrious ladies, with neither a single centurion nor soldier for protection, no sign of her being the commander's wife or of her normal es-
2   cort! And they were proceeding to the Treviri, to people of alien loyalty! Hence arose shame and pity and the memory of her father Agrippa and of Augustus her grandfather; her father-in-law Drusus, and the woman herself, with her distinguished fertility and conspicuous modesty: already there was an infant begotten in the camp and brought up in the legions' billet, whom in soldierly designation

they called "Caligula," because he was often dressed with that covering on his   3
feet to win the affection of the crowd.[67] Yet nothing influenced them so much
as their resentment of the Treviri. They begged, they blocked the way: she must
come back, she must stay—some of them converging on Agrippina, the majority going back to Germanicus.

He for his part, fresh with pain and anger as he was, began as follows in the
presence of the men pouring around him: "Not to me are wife and son more   **42**
dear than father or state; but he at least will be protected by his own sovereignty,
the Roman empire by the other armies. My spouse and children, however,
whom for your glory I would gladly expose to extermination, I am now removing far from your madness in order that, whatever crime of yours it is which
looms, it may be expiated by my blood alone and so that slaughtering Augustus' great-grandson and killing Tiberius' daughter-in-law may not make you
more guilty.

"After all, what have you left undared and undefiled during these past days?   2
What name shall I give to this throng? Is it soldiers I am to call you, who have
invested the son of your Commander with rampart and arms? Or citizens, by
whom the senate's authority has been so flung aside? You have shattered the rights
due even to an enemy, a legation's sanctity, and the law of nations. Divine Julius   3
suppressed an army mutiny with a single word, in calling 'Quirites'[68] those who
were rejecting his oath; Divine Augustus by his look and appearance caused
terror in the Actian legions; although I am not[+] their equal, I am nevertheless
descended from them, and, if it were the soldiery of Spain or Syria that was spurning me, it would still be a remarkable thing and undeserved: as it is, are the First
and Twentieth Legions—the one in receipt of standards from Tiberius, and you
here his ally in so many battles and enhanced by so many prizes[69]—are both of
you giving to your leader the exceptional thanks he is due? Is this the news which   4
I am to carry to my father, as he listens to all the welcome tidings from other
provinces? That his own recruits, his own veterans are satisfied with neither discharge nor money? That only here are centurions killed, tribunes evicted, legates
imprisoned? That the camp and rivers are tainted with blood, and I myself drawing breath on sufferance among the hostile?

67. "Caligula" is the diminutive form of *caliga,* the Latin word for a soldier's boot. The
infant is of course the future emperor (above, 1.32.2n.).

68. The word means "citizens," but with the implication of "civilians" (as opposed to
soldiers). The reference is to an incident in 49 or 47 B.C. or both.

69. The tortuousness of the English reflects that of the Latin. Though Germanicus is
addressing both Legion I and XX ("both of you," below), he is evidently in the camp of
I (1.39.4–6): it thus seems that "you here" must be Legion I and "the one" must be XX.
His argument is as follows: it would be bad enough if he, as a member of the imperial
family, were being opposed by legions with which he had had no previous contact ("the
soldiery of Spain or Syria"); how much more deplorable it is that *the emperor himself* is being opposed by legions who are *in his debt.*

43   "Why in fact did you, on the day of the first meeting, snatch away that sword which I was preparing to drive into my heart? Oh, my misguided friends! Better and more lovingly the man who offered me his sword: at least I would have fallen without yet being an accomplice in my army's many outrages, and you would have chosen the kind of leader who, though allowing my death to go un-

2   punished, would have avenged that of Varus and his three legions. For may the gods not allow the Belgae, despite their offer, the honor and brilliancy which are yours—of having rescued the Roman name and subdued the peoples of Germany!

3   "Rather, Divine Augustus, may it be your spirit, now welcomed back to heaven, rather, my father Drusus, may it be your image and your memory which—along with these selfsame soldiers of yours, whom shame and thoughts of glory are already permeating—wash away this stain and divert the anger of civil

4   war to the extermination of the enemy. And you too, on whose now changed faces and changed hearts I am gazing, if you are restoring the legates to the senate and compliance to your Commander, if to me you are restoring my spouse and son, turn away from contagion and isolate the turbulent elements. That will be a firm foothold on the path to remorse, that will be a bond of your loyalty."

44   Supplicatory at this, and admitting the truth of his remonstrations, they begged him to punish the guilty, pardon the fallen, and lead them against the enemy; his spouse should be recalled, the legions' foster-son should return and not be handed over as a hostage to the Gauls.

The return of Agrippina he forwent, on the grounds of her looming child-birth and the winter; but his son would come; the rest they must follow through

2   themselves. Now transformed, they ran everywhere and bound all the worst mutineers, dragging them to C. Caetronius, legate of the First Legion, who enforced justice and punishment for individuals in the following manner. The legions stood, as if at a meeting,[70] with swords drawn; a defendant was presented on the dais by a tribune: if they shouted "guilty," he was pitched to them headlong and

3   butchered. The soldiery rejoiced in each slaughter, as though they were absolving themselves, and Caesar for his part did nothing to prevent it, since, without any order of his, it was the same people who were equally liable both for the sav-

4   agery of the action and for the resentment at it. (The veterans who followed their example were sent into Raetia not long afterward, in a display of defending the province on account of a looming threat from the Suebi, but in reality to wrench them away from a camp still brutalized as much by the drastic nature of the rem-

5   edy as by the memory of the crime.) Next he mustered[+] the centurionate. Summoned by the commander, each gave out his name, rank, fatherland, number of years' service, how energetic he had been in battle, and (if any) his military awards. If the tribunes and legion voiced approval of his industry and innocence, he kept his rank; but, whenever they united in hurling charges of greed or cruelty at him, the man was released from soldiering.

70. Or perhaps "stood in front of the platform."

[handwritten margin note: 1st in mutiny — 5th & 21st legions still an issue]

With the immediate situation calmed down in this way, no less an obstacle re- **45**
mained on account of the defiance of the Fifth and Twenty-first Legions, wintering at the sixtieth milestone (Vetera is the place's name). They had been the **2**
first to initiate the mutiny; the most frightful actions had all been perpetrated by
their hands; and, neither terrified by the punishment of their fellow soldiers nor
transformed by remorse, they retained their anger. Therefore Caesar prepared to
send arms, a fleet, and allies down the Rhine—proposing, if they rejected his
command, to decide the issue by war. *[handwritten: Caesar is prepared to war against rest of mutiny]*

But at Rome,[71] where it was not yet known what the outcome in Illyricum **46**
had been and news had been received of the German legions' disturbance, the
trembling community began to censure Tiberius on the grounds that, while he
toyed with the fathers and plebs—those ineffective and unarmed entities—by
fabricating reluctance, the soldiery meanwhile was in dispute and could not be
subdued by the immature authority of two still maturing juveniles. He ought to **2**
have gone in person and confronted them with his Commander's sovereignty—
and they would surely have given way, once they saw a princeps with his long
experience and supreme in strictness and munificence alike. Or was it the case **3**
that Augustus, despite the exhaustion of age, had been able to travel to the Germanies so often, whereas Tiberius, vigorous in years, sat in the senate, quibbling
at the fathers' words? Sufficient provision had been made for the City's enslavement; it was the soldiers' spirits which needed dressings applied to them, so that
they might be willing to endure peace. *[handwritten: ha]*

[handwritten margin note: Criticism of Tiberius & his reluctance to rule]

Immovable in the face of such conversation, however, was the idea, implanted **47** *[handwritten: pretense]*
in Tiberius, that he should not abandon the headquarters of affairs and entrust
himself and the state to chance. And in fact he was tense from many conflicting *[handwritten: true]*
considerations: the army throughout Germany was more effective, that in Pan-
nonia nearer; the former was supported by the resources of the Galliae, the latter
looming over Italy. Whom, therefore, should he put first? And those postponed **2**
might be inflamed by his "insult." Through his sons, on the other hand, approaches *[handwritten: sent his sons to ease his decision & responsibility]*
could be made simultaneously without impairing his sovereignty, for which there
would be greater respect from a distance. At the same time the juveniles had the
excuse of referring certain matters to their father, and any resistance to Germanicus or Drusus could be softened by himself, or broken. What other resort would
there be, if they spurned the Commander? Yet, as if always on the point of going, **3**
he selected companions, assembled baggage, equipped ships; then, pleading variously the winter or business, he subsequently deceived the perspicacious first, the
public next, and the provinces for longest of all. *[handwritten: smart]*

[handwritten: yes]

[handwritten: ?]

But as for Germanicus, despite gathering together an army and preparing **48**
vengeance against the defectors, he deemed that an interval should still be pro-

---

71. It seems to be conventional to regard chapters 46–7 as part of the narrative of foreign affairs (i.e., as integral with 16–51); but it can be argued that they constitute a domestic interlude which interrupts that narrative.

[handwritten: reasons for Tiberius' lack of involvement in military affairs]

vided to see if the men would consider their own interests in the light of the recent example, and so he sent an advance letter to Caecina that he was arriving
with a substantial unit and that, unless they exacted reprisals from the wrongdo-

2   ers in advance, he would resort to indiscriminate slaughter. Caecina read out the
letter secretly to the eagle-bearers, standard-bearers, and soundest elements in the
camp, and urged them to save everyone from disgrace and themselves from death:
in peacetime, after all, cases were looked at on their merits, but, when war was

3   closing in, innocent and guilty alike fell side by side. They for their part tested
those whom they deemed suitable and, when they saw that the greater part of
the legions was dutiful, in accordance with the legate's proposal they established
a time for an armed assault on the foulest and readiest mutineers. Then, after sig-
naling to one another, they burst into the billets and butchered the unsuspecting
occupants, with no one except the accomplices knowing how the slaughter had
begun, where it would end.

49   It was a different scene from that of all the civil wars which have ever taken
place. It was neither in battle nor from opposing camps but from the same beds
that men—whom the day had found eating together and the night resting together—split into factions and thrust in their weapons. Shouting, wounds, blood
were in evidence; only the reason for them was concealed; the rest was directed
by chance. In fact some of the loyalists were slaughtered, after the worst elements

2   too, realizing the targets of the savagery, had seized arms. And no legate or tribune was present to control: the crowd was permitted license, vengeance, and its
fill.
        On entering the camp soon after, Germanicus described the event, with very
many tears, not as a cure but a disaster, and he ordered the bodies to be cremated.

3   Into their minds, which even then were still callous, there flew the desire of
going against the enemy as an expiation of their madness: the shades of their
fellow soldiers would be appeased, they said, only if they sustained honorable

4   wounds on their impious breasts. Caesar fell in with the soldiers' fervor, and, once
a bridge had been connected, sent across[72] twelve thousand from the legions,
twenty-six allied cohorts, and eight wings of cavalry, whose self-control in that
mutiny was undefiled.

50   Delight had been the reaction of the Germans not far away, all the while that
we were detained by the recess for the loss of Augustus[73] and later by the disaffection. But the Roman with a quick column cleaved through the Caesian wood
and the causeway begun by Tiberius and pitched camp at the causeway, fortify-

2   ing himself with a rampart front and rear and with fellings on the flanks. From
there he made his way through the dark denes[74] and debated which of two routes
to follow: the short and customary or the more encumbered and untried—and

3   thus unguarded by the enemy. Once the longer way was chosen, everything else

72. Sc. the Rhine.

73. See 1.16.2n.

74. For this translation of *saltus,* which recurs quite often, see Introduction, p. xxv n. 35.

was speeded up: scouts had brought news that that very night was a festival for the Germans, and their entertainment a solemn banquet. Caecina was ordered to go ahead with the unencumbered cohorts and to dislodge the woodland obstacles; the legions followed at a moderate distance. Aided by a night illuminated 4 by stars, they arrived at the villages of the Marsi and placed pickets around the enemy, who, even then, still lay in bed or alongside their tables, with no dread and without forward watches. Indeed everything was scattered in careless disarray, and there was neither fear of war nor even peace—except the languid release existing among drunkards.

Caesar divided his hungry legions into four wedges, to enlarge their pillage; **51** fifty miles was the area he devastated with fire and sword. Neither sex nor age aroused pity; things profane and sacred alike, including the temple most celebrated by those peoples (which they called Tanfana's), were leveled to the ground. His soldiers were left without a wound, after slaying folk who were half-asleep, unarmed, or straying about.

This slaughter stirred the Bructeri, Tubantes, and Usipetes, and they installed 2 themselves in the denes through which lay the army's return. But that was known to the leader, and he advanced with journey and battle in prospect. Part of the cavalry and the auxiliary cohorts were leading, next the First Legion, and, with the baggage in the center, the Twenty-first closed off the left flank and the Fifth the right; the Twentieth Legion consolidated the rear; after them the rest of the allies. But the enemy, not moving until the column was stretched out through 3 the denes, and then making only limited dashes against the flanks and front, raided with full force against those last of all. And the light cohorts were in the process of being disrupted by the dense companies of Germans when Caesar, riding up to the Twentieth, started to shout, loudly and repeatedly, that now was the time to obliterate the mutiny: they should proceed and press on with turning guilt into honor. Their spirits blazed, and with a single attack they burst through the 4 enemy, driving him back onto open ground and slaying him. Simultaneously the first forces in the column emerged from the woods and fortified a camp. Thereafter the journey was peaceful, and the soldiers, confident from recent events and with the past in oblivion, settled in winter camp.

★

News of all this affected Tiberius with delight and concern: he rejoiced at the **52** suppression of the mutiny, but, because Germanicus had won the soldiers' goodwill by lavishing money and speeding their discharge, and also owing to his warlike glory, he was tense. Nevertheless he reported to the senate on the man's 2 achievements and commemorated his courage in a lengthy account whose verbal embellishments were aimed too much at display for it to be believed that he felt deeply. He praised Drusus and the end of the Illyrian disturbance in fewer 3 words, but more earnestly and in a convincing speech. And every indulgence of Germanicus he upheld also among the Pannonian armies.

53   In the same year Julia passed her final day,[75] who for her immorality had formerly been shut away by her father Augustus on the island of Pandateria, then subsequently in the town of the Regini who live near the Sicilian strait. She had been in a marriage to Tiberius while Gaius and Lucius Caesar flourished, and had spurned him as her inferior; and no other reason was so close to Tiberius'

2   heart for his withdrawal to Rhodes. Once he acquired command, he ensured the annihilation of the outcast by deprivation and protracted atrophy, disgraced as she was and (after the killing of Postumus Agrippa)[76] destitute of all hope, deem-

3   ing that her execution would be obscured by the length of her exile. There was a similar reason for his savagery against Sempronius Gracchus, who, from a noble family, skillful in intellect and prevaricatingly fluent, had defiled the same Julia during her marriage to Marcus Agrippa. Nor was that the limit of the man's lust: when she was passed to Tiberius, the persistent adulterer inflamed her with a truculent hatred for her husband; and the letter which Julia wrote to her father Augustus, with its assault on Tiberius, was believed to have been composed by

4   Gracchus. He was therefore removed to Cercina, an island in the African sea,

5   and for fourteen years endured exile. Then soldiers were dispatched for his slaughter, and they found him on a spur of the shore, no welcome prospect left. On their arrival he asked for a brief moment to give his wife Alliaria his last instructions by letter, and offered his neck to his assailants, being in the steadfastness of his death not unworthy of the Sempronian name. It was in life that he

6   had degenerated. (Some have transmitted that the soldiers were sent not from Rome but by L. Asprenas, proconsul of Africa, at the instigation of Tiberius, who had hoped in vain that the report of the slaughter could be turned against Asprenas.)[77]

54   The same year admitted a new ceremonial office with the addition of the priesthood of the Augustal Fellows (just as once T. Tatius had instituted the Titian Fellows to preserve the rituals of the Sabines): from leaders of the community twenty-one were chosen by lot; Tiberius and Drusus and also Claudius and

2   Germanicus were affiliated. The Augustal Games, starting then for the first time, were disrupted by disorder arising from the actors' competitiveness.[78] Augustus had been indulgent toward their entertainment during his acquiescence in Mae-

---

75. Julia was Augustus' only child (the offspring of his marriage to Scribonia and born in 39 B.C.). She was married (1) in 25 B.C. to her cousin M. Claudius Marcellus, (2) in 21 B.C. to Agrippa (1.3.1), by whom she had three sons (Gaius and Lucius Caesar and Agrippa Postumus) and two daughters (Julia and Agrippina, Germanicus' wife), (3) in 11 B.C. to Tiberius. She was exiled in 2 B.C.

76. For which see 1.6.1.

77. L. Nonius Asprenas, suffect consul in A.D. 6 and a nephew of Quintilius Varus (1.3.6n.).

78. Actors and the theater in general were a continual source of social disturbance (e.g., 1.16.3, 1.77.1–4, 4.14.3, 6.13.1, 11.13.1, 13.24.1, 13.25.4, 13.28.1; cf. 14.21.4): see N. Horsfall, *The Culture of the Roman Plebs* (London 2003) 39–42.

cenas' outpourings of love for Bathyllus;[79] and in fact he personally did not shrink from such enthusiasms and deemed it citizenlike to blend in with the pleasures of the public. Tiberius' way of behaving was otherwise; but, with the people having been handled softly for so many years, he did not yet dare to turn them in a harder direction.

too soft for Tiberius

* * *

With Drusus Caesar and C. Norbanus as consuls, a triumph was decreed to Germanicus—with the war still remaining. Although he had been preparing for it with the utmost effort, aiming at the summer season, he seized it early at the beginning of spring with a sudden sally against the Chatti. For hope had arisen that the enemy was split between Arminius and Segestes, each conspicuous for his disloyalty or loyalty toward us.

55

war a.f. Germans begins

2

Arminius was the disrupter of Germany; Segestes on various frequent occasions, and especially at the last party before hostilities were entered upon, revealed that preparations were being made for rebellion and he urged Varus to place Arminius and himself and the other aristocrats in bonds: the plebs would dare nothing with their principes removed, he said, and Varus would have time to distinguish between the accusations and the guiltless. But Varus fell to fate and Arminius' violence; Segestes, though drawn into war by the consensus of his race, remained disaffected, his hatred augmented privately because his daughter, though betrothed to another, had been snatched by Arminius, a son-in-law resented by a rancorous father-in-law; and what between mutually affectionate parties are bonds of dearness were incitements to anger between antagonists.

3

So it was that Germanicus handed over to Caecina four legions, five thousand auxiliaries and irregular companies of the Germans living on this side of the Rhine. He led the same number of legions himself, and double the number of allies; and, having sited a stronghold on the traces of his father's garrison on Mount Taunus, he swept an unencumbered army against the Chatti, with L. Apronius left for fortifying roads and rivers.[80] (With the drought—a rarity in that climate—and streams only moderate, his journey had been speedy and unobstructed, and there was a dread of deluges and swollen rivers on his return.) As it was, so unforeseen was his arrival amongst the Chatti that those weak for reasons of their age or their sex were immediately captured or butchered. The young

56

2

3

---

79. Bathyllus, who was evidently part-responsible for introducing Rome to the art form known as "pantomime," was a freedman of Maecenas, one of Augustus' great ministers (3.30.2–4), and the two of them conducted a notorious affair. See *OCD* 907 and 1107 s.vv. Maecenas and pantomime.

80. Apronius, suffect consul in A.D. 8, recurs fairly frequently in the Tiberian books (see esp. 3.21, 4.73). His son (3.21.4) became consul in 39.

Segestes fears arminius & his soldiers would rebel

men had crossed the River Adrana by swimming and began to prevent the Romans' attempts at starting a bridge; but then, beaten back by launchers and arrows, after a vain trial for peace terms some fled across to Germanicus, while the rest,

4 abandoning their districts and villages, scattered into the woods. Caesar, having burned down Mattium (that is the headquarters of the race) and pillaged the open terrain, turned towards the Rhine, with the enemy not daring to harry the rear of the departing forces (which is his custom whenever stratagem rather than alarm

5 has caused his withdrawal). The Cherusci had had a mind to help the Chatti, but Caecina deterred them by moving his armor here and there; and, when the Marsi dared to engage, he checked them in a successful battle.

57   Not long afterward legates from Segestes came begging for aid against the violence of the compatriots by whom he was being invested—Arminius being the more authoritative among them because he urged war: in the case of barbarians, the readier a man is to be daring, the more trustworthy is he regarded and, when

2 things are in turmoil, more influential. (Segestes had added to the legates a son by the name of Segimundus, but the young man had hesitated through conscience: for, though he had been made a priest at the altar of the Ubii, in the year of the Germanies' defection[81] he had torn off his wreaths and fled to the rebels. Nevertheless, induced to hope for Roman mercy, he conveyed his father's instructions and, after a kindly reception, was sent under guard to the Gallic

3 bank.[82]) It was worth Germanicus' while to turn his column around, and a fight took place against the blockaders, and Segestes was snatched away, together with

4 a large force of his kinsmen and clients: included were noble ladies, among whom was Arminius' wife, Segestes' daughter, with her husband's rather than her parent's spirit, neither overcome to the point of tears nor supplicatory in voice, but,

5 with her hands clasped together in her lap, gazing on her pregnant womb. Also brought were spoils of the Varian disaster, which had been given as plunder to many of those who now were coming in surrender. At the same time there was Segestes himself, mighty to behold and, mindful of his faithful alliance, intrepid.

58   His words were in this manner: "This is not my first day of loyalty and steadfastness toward the Roman people. From the time when I was presented with citizenship by Divine Augustus, I have selected my friends and enemies in accordance with your interests—and not through hatred of my fatherland (traitors are resented also by the side which they prefer) but because my verdict was that one

2 thing was advantageous to Romans and Germans alike, namely peace rather than war. It was for that reason that I brought the snatcher of my daughter and the violator of your treaty, Arminius, as a defendant before Varus, who presided over the army at that time. Put off by that leader's sluggishness, however, and because there was too little protection in the laws, I importuned him to bind myself and Arminius and his accomplices. That night is my witness. (And would that it had

3 rather been my last! What followed can only be deplored rather than defended.

81. A.D. 9.

82. Of the Rhine.

The facts are that I both threw chains on Arminius and endured those thrown by his faction on me.) And, at the first opportunity of addressing you, here I am putting the old before the new, peace before disruption—and not for reward but to absolve myself from disloyalty, being at the same time an appropriate conciliator for the race of the Germans, if remorse rather than ruin should be its preference. For my son's youth and error I beg pardon; that my daughter has been   4
brought here under compulsion I acknowledge. It will be yours to decide which is the more effective: that she has conceived by Arminius or that she was begotten by me."

Caesar's merciful response was to guarantee security for his children and kinsmen, and an abode in the old province[83] for the man himself. He led back his   5
army and received the name of "commander" at Tiberius' instigation. Arminius'   6
wife produced stock of the male sex: brought up at Ravenna as a boy, the mockery with which he had to contend thereafter I shall recall in due course.[84]

The report of Segestes' surrender and kindly reception having become pub   **59**
lic, it was received with hope or pain depending on whether war was regarded with reluctance or desire. Arminius, in addition to his innate violence, was driven deranged by the seizure of his wife and the subjection to servitude of his wife's womb, and he flew through the Cherusci demanding arms against Segestes, arms against Caesar. Nor was his abuse in any way restrained: it was an exceptional fa   2
ther, a great commander, a brave army, whose numerous hands had carried off one poor woman! *He* had been responsible for the prostration of three legions   3
and the same number of legates: it was not *his* habit to conduct war by betrayal or against pregnant females, but openly against armed men. Still visible in the groves of the Germans were the Roman standards which he had hung to his native gods. Let Segestes live on a conquered bank, let him restore to his son a priest   4
hood for men.[85] Germans would never sufficiently excuse the fact that between Albis and Rhine they had seen the rods and axes and toga.[86] To other races,   5
ignorant of Roman command, its reprisals were unfamiliar, its taxes unknown; but, since they themselves had cast off these things, and since Augustus, that figure consecrated among the divinities, and Tiberius, that chosen one, had withdrawn thwarted, there should be no panic at an inexperienced juvenile or mutinous army! If their fatherland, parents, and antiquity were preferable to masters and   6
new colonies, they should rather follow Arminius' lead to glory and freedom than Segestes' to outrageous slavery!

83. Presumably that part of Germany to the west of the Rhine.

84. Thumelicus' subsequent history does not appear in the *Annals* as extant (but note 11.16.3), nor do we know how he was treated by the Romans.

85. The priesthood which Segimundus had abandoned in A.D. 9 (1.57.2 above) evidently involved a local cult of Augustus, who at that time was still alive and undeified.

86. The "rods" are the fasces, symbol of Roman magistrates (see App. A) and, when combined with the axe, of the power of execution (cf. 12.34); the toga is here a symbol of Romans in general.

60   Stirred by these words were not only the Cherusci but the bordering races,
        and drawn to their faction was Inguiomerus, Arminius' uncle, whose influence
2   with the Romans was long-standing. Hence greater dread on Caesar's part; and,
        to prevent war from closing in in a single mass, he sent Caecina with forty Ro-
        man cohorts across the Bructeri to the River Amisia to disperse the enemy, while
        the prefect Pedo led cavalry through the territory of the Frisians.[87] Caesar him-
        self embarked four legions on ships and transported them across the lakes; and
        the infantry, cavalry, and fleet came together simultaneously at the prearranged
        stream. Since the Chauci were guaranteeing auxiliaries, they were enrolled as fel-
3   low soldiers; the Bructeri, who were burning their own property, were routed by
        L. Stertinius along with an unencumbered unit on dispatch from Germanicus;
        and in the midst of the slaughter and plunder he discovered the Nineteenth Le-
        gion's eagle, lost with Varus. From there the column was led to the furthermost
        of the Bructeri, and the whole area between the streams Amisia and Lupia was
        devastated—not far from the Teutoburgian dene, in which the remains of Varus
        and his legions were said to lie unburied.

61   Therefore Caesar was assailed by the desire of paying his last respects to the
        soldiers and their leader, with the whole army there present moved to pity for
        kinsmen, friends, and, ultimately, for the fortunes of war and the lot of men. With
        Caecina sent ahead to investigate the hidden denes and to install bridges and em-
        bankments on the wet marshes and treacherous plains, they entered the sorrow-
2   ful site, grotesque to behold and for its memories. First[+] there was Varus' camp,
        with its wide perimeter and headquarters measured out, demonstrating the
        handiwork of the three legions; then, in the half-destroyed rampart, in a shal-
        low ditch, their remnants, now cut to pieces, had evidently huddled together.
        In the middle of the plain there were whitening bones, scattered or piled up,
3   exactly as men had fled or resisted. Nearby lay fragments of weapons and horses'
        limbs, and also, on the trunks of trees, skulls were impaled. In the neighboring
        groves were barbarian altars, at which they had sacrificed tribunes and first-rank
4   centurions. And survivors of the disaster, who had slipped away from the fight
        or their bonds, reported that here the legates had fallen, there the eagles been
        seized; where Varus' first wound had been driven home, where he had met
        his death by a blow from his own luckless right hand; from which tribunal
        Arminius had harangued; how many gibbets there had been for the captives,
        and which were the pits; and how in his haughtiness he had mocked the stan-
        dards and eagles.

62   So the Roman army there present six years after the disaster, with none know-
        ing whether it was someone else's or his own family's remains that he was cov-
        ering with earth, but all of them sorrowing and ferocious as their anger at the
        enemy mounted, started to bury the bones of the three legions as if they were
        kith and kin. The first turf for building the mound was placed by Caesar, in a
        most welcome duty toward the deceased and sharing in the pain of those pres-

---

87. Commonly assumed to be the poet Albinovanus Pedo (see further 2.23.1n.).

ent. (But Tiberius did not approve, whether interpreting everything of German- 2
icus' for the worse or else he believed that the sight of the slaughtered and un-
buried had slowed the army for battle and increased its alarm at the enemy, while
a commander endowed with an augurate and the most olden of ceremonial offices ought not to have handled anything funereal.)

As Germanicus followed Arminius' withdrawal into trackless territory, at the **63**
first opportunity he ordered the cavalry to ride out and seize the plain where the
enemy was installed. Arminius on the other hand, having warned his men to
gather and to approach the woods, suddenly turned them around; next he gave
the signal for breaking out to those whom he had hidden in the denes. At that 2
the cavalry was disrupted by the new line; and the dispatch of supporting cohorts, which collided with the column of fugitives, had only augmented the confusion; and they were in the process of being propelled into a marsh that was
known to the victors but treacherous for the unwary, had not Caesar led out his
legions and drawn them up. Hence terror among the enemy, confidence among
the soldiery; and on equal terms they disengaged.

Subsequently, having led back his army to the Amisia, he conveyed the legions 3
back by fleet, just as he had brought them up; part of the cavalry was ordered to
make for the Rhine along the shore of the Ocean; Caecina, who was leading his
own soldiery, was warned that, although his return lay along familiar routes, he
should gain the long bridges as quickly as possible. (This was a narrow crossway 4
through the desolate marshes which had once been embanked by L. Domitius;[88]
the rest was boggy, clinging with heavy slime or unstable with watercourses; all
around were woods, sloping gradually upward, which Arminius now filled, since
by shortcuts and a fast column he had forestalled the soldiery, burdened as it was
with packs and arms.)   *Romans retreat*

As Caecina debated how to replace the bridges, which had broken with age, 5
and at the same time to repulse the enemy, he decided to lay out his camp on
the spot so that they might start the work and others the battle. For their part **64**
the barbarians, struggling to break through the pickets and throw themselves on
the fortifiers, harried, encircled, converged. The shouting of workers and warriors blended, and everything was uniformly adverse for the Romans: the place, 2
with its deep swamp, was both unreliable for footholds and slippery for those advancing; their bodies were heavy with breastplates; nor could they balance their
javelins amid the waves. On the other hand, battles in marshes were normal for
the Cherusci, who had lanky limbs and mighty spears for inflicting wounds even
at a distance. *Swamp battle*

Night finally rescued the now sagging legions from their adverse fight. But the 3
Germans, tireless from success, took no rest even then, diverting onto the low-
lying areas all the water which rises in the soaring ridges around about; and, with
the ground submerged and the completed part of their work overwhelmed, the

88. L. Domitius Ahenobarbus was grandfather of the emperor Nero and consul in 16
B.C.; his exploits in Germany c. 2 B.C. were famous (4.44.2).

4   toil of the soldiery was doubled. Yet Caecina, who was having his fortieth year's
    service as orderly or orderer, was familiar with success and uncertainty and there-
    fore unafraid. So, as he turned over the possibilities, his only solution was to con-
    fine the enemy in the woods until the wounded and more heavily armed parts
    of the column went ahead. For in between the mountains and marshes there
5   stretched enough flat ground to take a slender line. The Fifth Legion was selected
    for the right flank, the Twenty-first on the left, the First to lead the column, the
    Twentieth against their likely pursuers.

65   The night was restless for different reasons, since the barbarians at their festive
    banquet filled the low-lying valleys and echoing denes with delighted singing or
    callous sound, while on the Romans' side were ineffectual fires and fitful voices,
    and everywhere the men themselves lay against the rampart or wandered around
2   the tents, sleepless rather than watchful. As for their leader, an ominous slumber
    terrified him: he imagined that he witnessed Quintilius Varus smeared in blood
    and emerging from the marshes and heard him apparently calling, but that he did
    not follow and pushed away the hand extended to him.
3   With the start of daylight the legions sent to the flanks deserted their position
    (through dread or truculence), quickly capturing the plain beyond the wetlands.
4   Nevertheless Arminius, despite the freedom to raid, did not burst forth immedi-
    ately; but—as the baggage stuck in the slime and ditches; the soldiers were dis-
    rupted on all sides; the line of standards became indistinct and (as happens at such
    a moment) each man was quick for himself but his ears slow in response to com-
    mands—then he ordered the Germans to burst on them, shouting repeatedly
    "Here's Varus, and legions again bound by the same fate!" At the same time he
    and his picked men cleft the column and inflicted wounds on the horses espe-
5   cially; the latter, slithering in their own blood and the slipperiness of the marshes,
    threw their riders, scattered everyone in their path, and trampled people as they
    lay. Most of the toil was around the eagles, which could be neither carried in the
6   face of the hail of weapons nor planted in the boggy ground. While Caecina was
    trying to maintain the line, he tumbled from his horse, which had been pierced
    beneath him, and was in the process of being surrounded, had not the First Le-
    gion placed itself in the way. The greed of the enemy helped, as they neglected
    slaughter in their pursuit of plunder; and, as the day turned to evening, the le-
    gions struggled out onto open and solid ground.
7   Yet that was not the end of their pitiful plight: there was a rampart to be set
    up and an embankment to be fetched, despite their having lost most of the things
    with which earth is carried[+] or turf cut out. There were no tents for the mani-
    ples, no dressings for the wounded; dividing food tainted with slime or gore, they
    lamented the funereal darkness and that for men in their so many thousands one
66 day only was now remaining. By chance a horse, roving about with its bonds
    snapped and terrified by the shouting, crashed against some of those converging
    on it. Thereupon such was the consternation of those who believed the Germans
    had burst in that everyone rushed to the gates, of which the rear was the partic-

ular target, as facing away from the enemy and safer for escape. Caecina, discov- 2
ering that it was a false alarm, but nevertheless unable to block or restrain the soldiery either by his authority or pleas or even by force, flung himself down at the
threshold of the gate, finally closing off their route by appealing to their pity, since
they would have been obliged to go over the body of their legate. At the same
time the tribunes and centurions explained that their panic had been mistaken.
Then, after they had gathered into the headquarters and been ordered to receive 67
his words in silence, he warned them about the requirements of the moment: their
one salvation lay in their weapons, but this had to be tempered by counsel and
they must stay within the rampart until the enemy, in his hope of storming, came
up closer; then they had to break out on all fronts: with that breakout they would
reach the Rhine! But, if they fled, there would remain more woods, deeper 2
marshes, the savagery of the enemy; whereas the victors would enjoy prestige and
glory. He recalled what they held dear at home, what honorable in camp; about
adversity he kept silent. Then, beginning with his own, he transferred the legates' 3
and tribunes' horses without favoritism to all the bravest warriors, in order that
they should precede the infantry in their assault on the enemy.

Equally restless was the German behavior, from hope, desire, and the oppos- 68
ing opinions of their leaders—Arminius urging that their adversaries be allowed
to emerge and, once emerged, be surrounded again amid the wetlands and obstacles, Inguiomerus' message more frightening (and welcome to the barbarians),
that they should encircle the rampart with arms: storming would be ready-made,
captives more numerous, plunder undamaged.

Therefore, as dawn rose, they collapsed the ditches, flung on hurdles, and grasped 2
the heights of the rampart—the soldiery up there being scarce and apparently
rooted to the spot through dread. After they became stuck on the fortifications, 3
however, the signal was given to the cohorts and the horns and trumpets sang
out in chorus. Thereupon, shouting as they attacked, they poured around the rear
of the Germans, remonstrating that here were no woods or marshes but fair
ground and fair gods. Over the enemy, who had been contemplating easy extir- 4
pation and only a few half-armed men, there poured the sound of trumpets and
glitter of arms, magnified for being unexpected; and they fell, as incautious in adverse conditions as they had been greedy in favorable. Arminius abandoned the 5
fight unscathed, Inguiomerus after a severe wound; their crowd was butchered
as long as anger and daylight remained. Finally, at night, the legions returned and,
though exhausted by more wounds and the same lack of food, found strength,
health, resources, everything, in victory.

Meanwhile there had spread a report of the army's being surrounded and that 69
the Galliae were the target of a ferocious column of Germans; and, had not Agrippina prevented the dismantling of a bridge installed over the Rhine, there were
those who because of their alarm would have dared that outrage. As it was, a female of mighty spirit assumed during those days the responsibilities of a leader
and distributed clothing and dressings to the soldiers according to each man's

2   need or injuries. C. Plinius, the writer of the Germanic wars,[89] transmits that she
     stood at the head of the bridge, extending praise and gratitude to the returning
3   legions. That made an unusually deep penetration into Tiberius' mind: it was not
     the case that her concerns were straightforward, he reflected, nor was it with the
4   aim of opposing foreigners that she was seeking the soldiers' affections[+]; noth-
     ing was left for commanders when a female visited the maniples, inspected the
     standards, experimented with lavishness—as though she did too little canvassing
     when she carried around the leader's son in a trooper's dress and wanted him
     called Caesar Caligula! Already Agrippina was more influential with the armies
     than legates, than leaders: the woman had suppressed a mutiny which the prin-
5   ceps's name had been unable to stop. These thoughts were kept burning and piled
     high by Sejanus, who, with his experience of Tiberius' behavior, sowed hatreds
     for the distant future, to be stored away and brought out when grown.

70   As for Germanicus, of the legions which he had brought by ship, he trans-
     ferred the Second and Fourteenth to P. Vitellius for leading on an overland jour-
     ney, so that the fleet would be lighter when floating on the shallows or running
2   aground at the ebb.[90] At first Vitellius had a peaceful journey, the ground being
     dry or the incoming tide only moderate; but later under the onslaught of the
     north wind, coinciding as it did with the constellation of the equinox (when the
     Ocean's swell is greatest),[91] his driving column was caught and driven about. In
     fact the land was covered over: strait, shore, and plains all had the same appear-
3   ance, nor could unstable parts be differentiated from firm, shoal from deep. They
     were knocked over by billows, swallowed up by maelstroms; baggage-animals,
     packs, lifeless bodies flowed past or bumped into them. The maniples became
     thoroughly mixed up among themselves, sometimes protruding as far as the
     chest, sometimes only the face, and on occasion, with the ground swept from un-
     der them, scattered or overwhelmed. No voice or mutual encouragements gave
     help in the onrushing waves; nothing distinguished the energetic from the
     shirker, the wise from the incautious, calculation from chance: everything was
     engulfed in equal violence.
4   Eventually Vitellius, struggling out to higher ground, led his column up to the
     same place. They passed the night without comestibles, without fire, many with
     their bodies naked or mauled, no less pitiable than men invested by an enemy:
     for then one still has the resort of an honorable death, whereas theirs was an in-
5   glorious extermination. Daylight restored the land, and they penetrated as far as

---

89. The elder Pliny was a prolific author (see further 13.20.2n.) and uncle of T.'s friend,
the younger Pliny. According to the latter (*Letters* 3.5.4) the exact title of his uncle's work
was *Bella Germaniae* or "Wars in Germany," which T. typically avoids.

90. Vitellius was uncle of the future emperor and a member of Germanicus' entourage
(see 2.6.1); he will feature prominently in the trial of Cn. Piso (see 2.74.2, 3.10.1, 13.2,
19.1). For his death see 5.8.1–2.

91. Some associated the autumn equinox with a particular constellation responsible for
storms.

the stream for which Caesar had been making with his fleet. Thereupon the legions were embarked, with the report spreading that they had been drowned; nor was there any belief in their safety until it was seen that Caesar and his army had returned.

Already Stertinius, sent ahead to receive Segestes' brother Segimerus in surren- **71** der, had led the man and his son to the community of the Ubii. Pardon was given to each, easily to Segimerus, more hesitatingly to the son, because he was said to have made sport of the body of Quintilius Varus. As for replenishing the army's **2** losses, the Galliae, the Spains, and Italy competed in offering what each of them had ready: arms, horses, gold. Praising their enthusiasm, Germanicus took for the war only arms and horses, using his own money to help the soldiers. And in or- **3** der to assuage the memory of the disaster by affability also, he went around the injured and extolled the actions of individuals; examining their wounds, he used hope with one, glory with another, and dialogue and concern with everybody to stiffen them both for his own sake and for battle.

— pardon to Segestes' family

Decreed in that year were triumphal insignia to A. Caecina, L. Apronius, and C. **72** Silius for their achievements alongside Germanicus. Tiberius rejected the name "Father of the Fatherland," which had been thrust upon him quite often by the people; nor, despite its proposal by the senate, did he allow the swearing of obedience to his enactments,[92] insisting that all the affairs of mortals were uncertain and that, the more he acquired, the more slippery his ground. Yet he did not **2** thereby engender belief that he was citizenlike in spirit: he had brought back the law of treason. *? Wouldn't even swear obedience to his position*

This had the same name in the time of the ancients, but different matters came to court, such as the impairment of an army by betrayal or of the plebs by sedition or, in fine, of the sovereignty of the Roman people by maladministration of the government. Actions were prosecuted, talk had impunity. Augustus was the **3** first to handle a trial of defamatory documents under the category of that law, being roused by the passion with which Cassius Severus had defamed illustrious men and ladies in provocative writings;[93] subsequently Tiberius, consulted by the praetor Pompeius Macer on the question whether legal proceedings would be allowed in cases of treason, replied that the laws should be enforced. He too had **4** been stung by the publication of poems, of uncertain authorship, against his savagery and haughtiness and his disaffected relations with his mother.

It will not be irksome to record the charges brought in the test cases of Faia- **73** nius and Rubrius, modest Roman equestrians, in order to become acquainted

92. The oath to uphold the enactments of a princeps (and of his predecessors) became a regular ritual on 1 January each year: see further 4.42.3, 13.11.1, and 16.22.3.

93. Cassius Severus, one of the principal orators of the Augustan principate, had been exiled for treason in A.D. 8 or 12: see further 4.21.3.

with the initial phases from which, given the degree of Tiberius' skill, a form of extermination of the utmost severity crept in, was then suppressed, and finally

2 flared up and gripped everything. Faianius' accuser hurled at him the charges that, among the worshipers of Augustus (who were maintained in every house in the manner of colleges),[94] he had affiliated one Cassius, a mime disgraced for his use of his body,[95] and that, when selling his garden, he had disposed of a statue of Augustus at the same time. Rubrius' charge was that he had violated the divin-

3 ity of Augustus by perjury. When these matters became known to Tiberius, he wrote to the consuls that the reason for decreeing a place in heaven to his father had not been that the honor should be turned into the ruin of citizens: the actor Cassius, among others of the same profession, had been accustomed to attend the games which his own mother had consecrated to Augustus' memory; nor was it contrary to religion that likenesses of the latter should be included in the sales of gardens and houses in the same way as were the representations of

4 other divinities. As for the oath, it should be valued exactly as if the man had sworn falsely by Jupiter: the gods' injuries were the gods' concern.

74 Not long afterward Granius Marcellus, praetor[96] of Bithynia, was arraigned for treason by his own quaestor, Caepio Crispinus, with the supporting signature of Romanius Hispo. (He[97] entered upon a form of life which afterward was made notoriously common by the wretchedness of the times and the boldnesses of

2 men: needy, nameless, and restless as he wormed his way, using his secret documents, into the princeps's savagery, he subsequently made defendants of all the most brilliant people and, having achieved power in his dealings with one man and hatred in his dealings with everyone, set an example which was followed by those who, transformed into the rich and dreaded from being poor and con-

3 temptible, contrived ruin for others and, ultimately, themselves.) He incriminated Marcellus for having held malicious conversations about Tiberius—an inescapable charge, since the accuser selected the foulest of the princeps's habits and blamed their dissemination on the defendant (and in fact, because they were true, they were believed actually to have been spoken). Hispo added that Marcellus' statue had been sited higher than those of the Caesars and that on another

4 statue Augustus' head had been sliced off and Tiberius' likeness imposed. At this Tiberius flared up to such an extent that, shattering his taciturnity, he announced that he too would express an opinion in the case, openly and on oath, so that the

---

94. In domestic houses there were evidently unofficial groups, as if modeled on the official colleges (for which see App. A), devoted to the cult of Rome's first emperor. We must remember that many such houses would have a substantial establishment.

95. Here "mime" means an actor in mimes, evidently a different form of entertainment from the pantomime (above, 1.54.2n.): see *OCD* 982. T.'s description of Cassius indicates a pathic homosexual.

96. An archaism for "proconsul": see further App. A.

97. Whether Hispo or Crispinus is meant is debated. But "He" at 1.74.3 below is Crispinus.

same constraint[98] should apply to the others. Even then there remained traces of   5
dying freedom: so Cn. Piso said, "In what place will you vote, Caesar? If first, I
shall have something to follow; if after everyone else, I am afraid lest I dissent im-
providently." Shaken by these words, and passive from penitence at having boiled   6
over too incautiously, he allowed the defendant to be released from the charges
of treason; the question of extortion went to the recoverers.[99]   *Tiberius shaken?*

    Not sated with the trials held by the fathers, he sat in on the courts (at the   **75**
edge of the tribunal, to avoid evicting the praetor from his curule chair), and in
his presence many decisions were made in the face of bribery and the prayers of
the powerful. But the contribution to truth was the corruption of freedom.

    Meanwhile Pius Aurelius, a senator, complaining of subsidence to his house   2
from a massive public road and an aqueduct, called upon the fathers' aid. On the
resistance of the treasury praetors, Caesar came to his rescue and granted Aurelius the value of his house, desirous as he was of expending money honorably—   *←lol*
a virtue which he retained long after he started to cast aside the rest. On Prop-   3
ertius Celer, a praetorian seeking exemption from his rank because of poverty,
he lavished a million sesterces, once it had been sufficiently discovered that his
straitened circumstances were hereditary. When others made similar attempts, he   4
ordered them to prove their cases to the senate—his desire for strictness making
him sour even in those matters where he acted with propriety. The rest therefore
preferred silence and poverty to confession and generosity.

    In the same year the Tiber, swollen by constant deluges, had flooded flat areas   **76**
of the City; its recession was followed by the wreckage of buildings and people.
Asinius Gallus therefore proposed appealing to the Sibylline books. Tiberius re-   *no divine*
fused, his protective screen as much around divine affairs as human; but the rem-   *help*
edy for confining the river was entrusted to Ateius Capito and L. Arruntius.[100]   *sought*
As for Achaea and Macedonia, begging to be excused their burdens,[101] it was de-   2
cided that for the present they should be relieved of proconsular command and
transferred to Caesar.

    Drusus presided at a gladiatorial production which he had put on in the names   3
of his brother Germanicus and himself—rejoicing excessively in albeit worthless
blood, something which alarmed the public and which his father too was said to
have criticized. As to why Tiberius himself kept away from the spectacle, there   4
were various interpretations, some saying it was because of his aversion to gatherings, some his grimness of temperament and dread of comparison, because Augustus had attended affably. (I am not inclined to believe that his son was allowed

---

98. Viz. of taking an oath; the result would have been a collective judgment such as that
mentioned at 4.21.3.

99. A board of assessors but still called by an old name which reflected their original
function.

100. For Capito see 3.75.1n.; for Arruntius see 1.8.3n.

101. I.e., taxation.

the means to exhibit his savagery and to incite the people's disgust, although that too was said.)

77   As for license in the theater, which had begun in the immediately preceding year,[102] it erupted more seriously now, with the slaughter not only of some of the plebs but also of soldiers and a centurion and the wounding of a tribune of the praetorian cohort while they were trying to prevent abuse against magistrates

2   and public dissension. There was discussion of the mutinousness before the fathers, and proposals were expressed that praetors should have the prerogative of

3   flogging in the case of actors. Haterius Agrippa, tribune of the plebs,[103] intervened and was berated in a speech by Asinius Gallus—with silence from Tiberius, who would present the senate with such representations of freedom. The intervention was nevertheless effective, because Divine Augustus had once said in a reply that actors were immune from beatings, and Tiberius did not allow himself to infringe his words. On the limit of their subsidy and against the reckless-

4   ness of their supporters, however, numerous decrees were passed, of which the most distinctive were that a senator should not enter the homes of pantomimes, that Roman equestrians should not surround them when they went out in public, nor should they[104] put on a spectacle anywhere other than in the theater, and that praetors should be empowered to penalize by exile the unrestraint of spectators.

78   Permission was given to the Spaniards on their request that a temple to Augustus be set up in the Tarraconensian colony, and a precedent was set for every

2   province. When the people begged to be excused the one-percent tax on sales instituted after the civil wars, Tiberius said in an edict that the military treasury depended upon it for support; and also that the state would be unequal to its burden unless veterans were discharged in their twentieth year of soldiering. Thus the ill-advised decisions of the very recent mutiny, whereby they had extracted a limit of sixteen years' service, were abolished for the future.

79   Next in the senate there was a discussion, led by Arruntius and Ateius, whether control of the Tiber's inundations required diverting the rivers and lakes which cause its expansion. And legations from the municipalities and colonies were heard, with the Florentines begging that the Clanis should not be removed from its customary bed and transferred to the stream of the Arnus, which would bring

2   ruin to themselves. Corresponding to this was the Interamnates' speech: the most fertile plains of Italy would go under if the stream of the Nar were split into various watercourses (for such was the plan) and flooded over. Nor were the Rea-

3   tini silent, with objections to the damming of Lake Velinus where it pours into the Nar: it would burst over the adjacent land; nature had made the best provision for mortals' affairs by giving rivers their own mouths and their own chan-

---

102. See 1.54.2.

103. D. Haterius Agrippa, son of Q. Haterius (1.13.4n.), will become consul in 22 (3.52.1). For a tribune's "intervention" see App. A.

104. The pantomime actors.

nels, their boundaries as well as their sources; they must also look at the religious scruples of the allies, who had dedicated sacred rituals and groves and altars to their native streams: in fact Tiber himself would not at all wish to flow with lesser glory, bereft of his neighboring currents. Either the prayers of the colonies or the difficulty of the work or superstition had an effect, with the result that there was agreement with the opinion of Piso, who had proposed that nothing be changed.

    Poppaeus Sabinus' tenure of the province of Moesia was extended, with Achaea and Macedonia added.[105] This too was a habit of Tiberius, to prolong commands and often keep men in the same armies or jurisdictions to the end of their life. Various reasons are transmitted, some saying that through an aversion to any new concern he preserved onetime decisions as permanent, others that it was through resentment, to limit the numbers of beneficiaries; there are those who reckon that the astuteness of his intellect was matched by the tenseness of his judgment: he did not pursue towering excellence and, conversely, hated vice: from the best men he dreaded danger for himself, from the worst a public disgrace. Such hesitation finally carried him to the point where he entrusted provinces to certain men whose departure from the City he had no intention of permitting.

    Concerning the consular elections which occurred then for the first time in his principate and thereafter, I would dare to vouch for scarcely anything: such is the diversity discovered not only among authors but in the man's own speeches. Sometimes, having removed candidates' names, he described each man's origin, life, and military service, so that it might be understood what sort of men they were.[106] At other times, having removed even that form of suggestion, he urged candidates not to disrupt the elections by canvassing and guaranteed that he would give the matter his personal attention. Generally he announced that only those had registered with him whose names he had given to the consuls; others too could register, if they felt confidence in their favor or merits—yet this was mere verbal display, empty of substance (or deceptive)[107] and, the more impressive its covering in the image of freedom, poised to erupt in an all the more ferocious servitude.

105. C. Poppaeus Sabinus, consul in A.D. 9, was grandfather of Poppaea, Nero's second wife (13.45.1). See esp. 4.46–51.

106. The usual interpretation is "so that their identities might become known," but the procedure thus described seems absurd. The whole of this paragraph is extremely obscure and has generated an enormous amount of scholarly discussion.

107. It was "empty of substance" in the sense that Tiberius' offer was assumed to be insincere and hence not taken up; "deceptive" because, if the offer was taken at face value and acted upon, the candidates would fail to be elected.

BOOK 2

1 With Sisenna Statilius Taurus and L. Libo as consuls,[1] there were tremors in the kingdoms and Roman provinces of the East, the starting-point having originated among the Parthians when, despite his being of the family of the Arsacidae, they

2 spurned as a foreigner the king they had sought and received from Rome. This was Vonones, who had been given to Augustus as a hostage by Phraates. For Phraates, although he had repelled Roman armies and leaders, had directed toward Augustus all the duties of veneration and had sent part of his progeny to reinforce the friendship, not so much from any dread of us as distrusting the loyalty of his compatriots.[2]

2 After the end of Phraates and the following kings through internal slaughters, there came to the City legates from the Parthian chiefs to fetch Vonones, the oldest of the man's children. Caesar believed this a magnificent reflection on himself, and he enhanced him with wealth; and the barbarians received him delight-

2 edly, as often happens with new commands. But this was soon succeeded by shame that the Parthians had degenerated: a king had been sought from another world and was tainted with the practices of their enemy; now the throne of the Arsacidae was being held and given as merely one among the Roman provinces! Where was that glory of the butchers of Crassus, of the evictors of Antonius,[3] if a menial of Caesar, having endured slavery for so many years, took

3 command of Parthians? Their indignation was also inflamed by the man's very difference from the conventions of his ancestors, with his infrequent hunting and sluggish concern for horses; whenever he passed through cities, it was by the conveyance of a litter and with disdain for native banquets. Also derided were his Greek companions and his locking up of the cheapest comestibles with a seal

4 ring. Yet he was readily accessible and had a forthcoming affability, virtues unknown to the Parthians but novel as vices. And, because his forms of crookedness and honesty were alien to their own behavior, there was equal hatred for

3 both. Therefore Artabanus, who was of the blood of the Arsacidae but had grown

---

1. T. Statilius Sisenna Taurus was brother of the consul of A.D. 11 (and hence uncle of the consul of 44: 12.59.1); both were grandsons of the great Statilius Taurus (3.72.1n.). L. Scribonius Libo was probably brother of the Libo convicted later this year (2.29.2).

2. The Arsacidae, to whom T. makes frequent reference in the *Annals,* constituted the royal dynasty of Parthia, taking their name from Parthia's first king, Arsaces I (c. 247–217 B.C.): see *OCD* 177. Phraates IV, who ruled Parthia c. 38–3/2 B.C., transferred his children to Augustus in 10 B.C.; among them was the future Vonones I, whose brief rule seems to have lasted no more than a year (A.D. 8/9). Throughout the Julio-Claudian period the details of Parthian and (below) Armenian affairs, for which T. provides a background here at 2.1–4, are desperately confused and confusing.

3. The Parthians had defeated Crassus in 53 B.C. at Carrhae (a disaster which ranked with that of Varus in terms of Roman ignominy) and Mark Antony in 36 B.C.

up among the Dahae, was summoned, and, though routed in a first engagement, he reconstituted his forces and took control of the kingdom.[4]

Refuge for the vanquished Vonones was Armenia, then vacant and an object of mistrust between the Parthians' dominion and the Roman owing to the crime of Antonius, who had enticed Artavasdes, the king of the Armenians, in a display of friendship, then weighing him down with chains and finally killing him.[5] This man's son, Artaxias, ferocious toward us on account of the memory of his father, protected both himself and his kingdom by the might of the Arsacidae. On Artaxias' being slaughtered through the guile of his kinsmen, Tigranes was given to the Armenians by Caesar and escorted into his kingdom by Tiberius Nero.[6] But neither Tigranes' nor his children's command was long-lasting, despite alliances (in the foreign custom) of matrimony and kingship. Next, on Augustus' order, Artavasdes was installed, and, not without disaster to ourselves, dislodged. Then C. Caesar was selected to settle Armenia.[7] He imposed Ariobarzanes, a Mede by origin, on the Armenians, willing as they were on account of his distinguished good looks and spirited brilliance. But, with Ariobarzanes taken off by an accidental death, they did not tolerate his stock; and, after trying the command of a female (whose name was Erato) and quickly expelling her, and being now indecisive and adrift, lacking a master rather than experiencing freedom, they received the refugee Vonones into the kingship. But, when Artabanus started menacing and too little support for Vonones was coming from the Armenians (the alternative, if he was to be defended by our might, was taking up war against the Parthians), the governor of Syria, Creticus Silanus,[8] summoned him and surrounded him with guards, though his luxuriousness and royal name remained. (How Vonones attempted to escape this mockery, we shall render in its proper place.)[9]

As for Tiberius, the disruption of affairs in the East was a not unwelcome development, since with that pretext he could drag Germanicus away from his familiar legions and install him in new provinces, exposing him to guile and hazard. But the latter, the keener his soldiers' enthusiasm toward him, and his uncle's

4. Artabanus II ruled Parthia from A.D. 10/11 to 38.

5. Artavasdes II, who had ruled Armenia from c. 54 B.C., was tricked by Mark Antony in 34 B.C. and subsequently killed at Alexandria on the orders of Cleopatra.

6. Artaxias (Artaxes), son of Artavasdes II, ruled Armenia from 34 B.C. but was killed in 20 B.C., whereupon Tigranes III, another son of Artavasdes, assumed the kingship until 6 B.C.

7. Gaius Caesar, Augustus' grandson, was sent to the East in 1 B.C. to sort things out (Sherk 18) but died in A.D. 4 on his way back to Rome (1.3.3). Before Gaius' arrival in Armenia, the kingdom was evidently ruled by Tigranes IV and his sister–wife Erato as successors of Tigranes III; after the almost immediate death of Gaius' nominee, Ariobarzanes, the kingdom seems then to have been ruled by Artavasdes III until c. A.D. 12. How this relates to T.'s assertions that an Artavasdes ruled before Gaius' arrival and Erato after it, rather than the other way around, is unclear.

8. Q. Caecilius Metellus Creticus Silanus had been consul in A.D. 7.

9. At 2.68 below.

will opposed, was all the more intent on accelerating his victory, and his mind touched on the courses of battles and the savage or favorable events which had
3   befallen him, now in his third year of warfare: the Germans, he reflected, were being routed in the line and in fair positions but helped by woods, marshes, the shorter summer season, and the early winter; his own soldiery was affected not so much by wounds as by the distances of the journeys and loss of weapons; the Galliae were tired of supplying horses; a long column of baggage was suscepti-
4   ble to ambush, unfair on defenders; on the other hand, if they embarked on the sea, they could take possession readily and unknown to the enemy; at the same time the war could begin more quickly, and legions and supplies be conveyed together; by the mouths and channels of rivers his cavalry and horses would arrive intact in the middle of Germany!

6   This, therefore, was his intention. With the dispatch of P. Vitellius and C. Antius to the census of the Galliae,[10] Silius and Anteius[11] and Caecina were placed
2   in charge of manufacturing a fleet. A thousand ships seemed sufficient and were hurried along. Some were short, with a narrow poop and prow and broad belly, to withstand the billows more easily; others were flat at the keel, so they could run aground without harm; a number had tillers at each end, so that, with a sudden switch of oarage, they could land one way or the other; many were layered with bridging, on which launchers could be conveyed, and at the same time were suitable for carrying horses or supplies. Adaptable to sail, fast under oar, they were developed by the eagerness of the soldiers into objects of display and terror.
3   The island of the Batavi was prearranged as their point of assembly owing to its easy landings and being favorable for the reception of forces and to transport
4   the war. For the Rhine, a stream in one continuous channel or encircling only modest islands, at the start of Batavian territory divides into two (as it were): where it skirts Germany, it keeps its name and the violence of its course until it merges with the Ocean; but, flowing more broadly and placidly by the Gallic bank with an alteration of nomenclature (the locals say "Vahalis"), it soon changes that designation too for the River Mosa, and from the immense mouth of the latter it pours out likewise into the Ocean.

7   As for Caesar, while the ships were gathering he ordered his legate Silius with an unencumbered unit to make an irruption against the Chatti; he himself, on hearing that a stronghold adjacent to the River Lupia was being blockaded, led
2   six legions there. But Silius, owing to sudden deluges, failed to accomplish anything other than the seizure of modest plunder and of the spouse and daughter of Arpus, a princeps of the Chatti; while the blockaders failed to give Caesar the opportunity of a fight, slipping away at the report of his arrival. Nevertheless they

    10. The census had evidently been in progress since at least A.D. 14 (1.31.2). For Vitellius see 1.70.1n.

    11. It is possible that "and Anteius" should be deleted as a mistaken repetition of "and C. Antius" earlier (so Urlichs).

had demolished the mound put up recently for the Varian legions[12] and the old
altar situated by Drusus. He restored the altar and, in honor of his father, himself   3
led the legions in a march-past; to remake the mound did not seem a good idea.
And everything between the Aliso stronghold and Rhine was fortified by new
causeways and embankments.

The fleet had already arrived when, having sent the supplies ahead and dis-   **8**
tributed the ships between legions and allies, he entered the conduit which has
the name "Drusian";[13] and he prayed to his father Drusus that, by the example
and memory of his plans and achievements, he should gladly and propitiously
help one who was now engaged in the same bold enterprise. From there he traveled across lakes and Ocean on a favorable voyage as far as the River Amisia.
The fleet was quitted on the left-hand side of the Amisia stream, and it was an   2
error that he did not take it upriver: he transferred the soldiery who were destined to go into the country on the right, so several days were taken up with
constructing bridges.[14] For their part the cavalry and legions crossed the first es-   3
tuaries intrepidly, as the tide was not yet rising; but the final column of auxil
iaries, and the Batavi in the same section, got into trouble when they leapt into[15]
the water and showed off their skill at swimming, and some were swallowed up.
While Caesar was laying out his camp, the defection of the Angrivarii was an-   4
nounced from the rear: Stertinius was dispatched at once with cavalry and light
armor, and by fire and slaughter he avenged their disloyalty.

The River Visurgis flowed between the Romans and Cherusci. On its bank   **9**
with the other chiefs stood Arminius, and, having asked whether Caesar had arrived, and received the reply that he was present, he begged that he be allowed
a dialogue with his brother. The latter was in the army, with the nomenclature
Flavus, and was distinguished for his loyalty and having lost an eye to a wound a
few years before under the leadership of Tiberius. At that moment he came for-   2
ward with permission and was hailed by Arminius, who, dismissing his attendants,
asked that the archers deployed along our bank should move back; and, after they
had withdrawn, he questioned his brother on the origin of his facial disfigure-
ment. As the other repeated the occasion and battle, he inquired what reward he   3
had received. Flavus recalled his increased wages, his torque and crown, and other
military gifts, to Arminius' derision of the cheap price of servitude. Thereupon   **10**
they embarked on very different speeches: on the one side were mentioned Roman greatness and the resources of Caesar, the heavy penalties for the conquered
but the clemency waiting for him who surrendered—nor were the man's spouse
and son held as enemies;[16] on the other side, the duty to the fatherland, ances-

12. See 1.62.1.   *brother sided against arminius!*
13. The canal linked the Rhine with what is now the Ijsselmeer.
14. Both text and interpretation of the whole of section 2 are extremely controversial.
15. Or perhaps "they scoffed at."
16. See 1.57.3–4 and 58.5–6 above.

45

tral freedom, the household gods of Germany—and their mother, a partner in his prayer that his brother should not prefer to be the deserter and betrayer of kinsmen and relatives, indeed of his own nation, rather than their commander.

2   Thereafter they slipped gradually into wrangling, and not even the interposing river would have prevented them from joining a fight, had not Stertinius run up and restrained Flavus, brimful of anger and begging for his arms and horse.

3   Arminius could be seen opposite, menacing and declaring battle (for he interposed a great deal in the Latin language, as one who had served in Roman camps as leader of his compatriots).

11   On the next day the Germans' line stood on the far side of the Visurgis. Caesar, deeming it not good commandership to expose legions to a critical situation without the superimposition of bridges and of garrisons thereon, dispatched the cavalry across the shallows: in charge were Stertinius and, from the first-rankers, Aemilius, whose assaults came from separate directions to split the enemy. Where

2   the stream was fastest, Chariovalda, the leader of the Batavi, burst out. The Cherusci, pretending flight, drew him to flat ground ringed by denes; then, rising up together and pouring out on all sides, they repelled those in their path, hounded those who gave way, and, as for those who had gathered in a circle, they thrust

3   them aside, some by coming in close, others from a distance. Chariovalda, having withstood the enemy's savagery for a long time, urged his men to group and break through the companies swooping upon them, and, himself bursting into the densest throng, he tumbled under a hail of weapons, with his horse pierced beneath him and many of his nobles all around; the rest were removed from danger by their own strength or by the cavalry which came with Stertinius and Aemilius to the rescue.

12   Caesar, crossing the Visurgis, on the information of a runaway found out the place selected by Arminius for the fight: other nations too, he was told, had assembled in a wood sacred to Hercules, and all would dare a night attack on the camp. Belief was accorded the informer, and fires could be seen, and scouts who had moved in closer brought news of horses' neighing and the hubbub of an im-

2   mense and unorganized column. Therefore, given that the crisis of the whole affair was approaching, and deeming that there should be an investigation of the soldiers' morale, he debated with himself in what way such a thing might be un-

3   prejudiced: tribunes and centurions more often brought welcome than confirmed news, freedmen's instincts were servile, in friends there was the presence of sycophancy; if a meeting were called, there too the rest would growl assent to the lead taken by a few: he needed to gain an intimate knowledge of their minds at a time when they were by themselves and unguarded, disclosing their hope or dread over their soldiers' food.

13   At the start of night, leaving his augural tent[17] by secret ways unknown to the watches, with a single companion and his shoulders covered in a wild-animal pelt, he approached the roads of the camp, stopped at the pavilions, and had the

---

17. I.e., his headquarters (again at 15.30.1).

pleasure of hearing reports about himself, as one man extolled the leader's nobility, another his demeanor, many his tolerance, affability, and equal attentiveness in gravity and jest; and they declared that they must express their gratitude
in the line of battle, likewise that the disloyal breakers of the peace[18] should be
sacrificed to vengeance and glory.

In the midst of all this, one of the enemy, knowledgeable in the Latin tongue,   2
rode his horse up to the rampart and in a loud voice guaranteed, in Arminius'
name, spouses and land and wages of one hundred sesterces a day for the length
of the war, if anyone should desert. The insult intensified the legions' anger: let   3
daylight come! let the fight begin! the soldiery would take the Germans' land,
drag off their spouses! they welcomed the omen, and intended the enemies' wives
and money as their plunder! At about the third watch a dash was made against   4
the camp—but without a weapon being thrown, after they perceived the cohorts
closely stationed along the fortifications and that there had been no relaxation.

The same night brought a welcome slumber to Germanicus: he saw himself   **14**
performing ritual sacrifice and, his praetexta having become spattered with sacred blood, receiving another one, more beautiful, from the hands of his grandmother, Augusta. Augmented[19] by the omen, and with the auspices' approval, he
called a meeting and spoke of what his wise precautions had been, and other
words suited to the looming fight: the Roman soldier would find it was not only   2
plains that were good for battle but, if calculation were applied, woods and denes:
amid the trunks of trees and brushwood springing from the ground, the barbarians' immense shields and outsize spears could not be handled in the same way
as javelins and swords and coverings clinging to the body: they must pack their   3
strikes and aim for the face with their tips. The German had neither breastplate
nor helmet nor even shields reinforced with iron or ribbing, but plaited wicker-
work or thin and color-dyed boards; his first line was somehow equipped with
spears, but the rest had only scorched[20] or short weapons; as for his body, though
brutal to behold and effective for a short attack, it had no toleration of wounds:
without shame at the outrage, without concern for their leaders, they would depart or flee, panicking in adversity and, amid success, mindful of neither divine
nor human law. If in their weariness of journeys and the sea his men desired an   4
end, this battle was the preparation for it: the Albis was now closer than the
Rhine, nor would there be a war beyond, if only they should set him as victor
in the same country where he was now treading in the footsteps of his father and
uncle. — The soldiers fell in fervently with their leader's speech, and the signal   **15**
for the fight was given.

18. The reference is to the German uprising against Varus: see 1.58.2.

19. T. is playing on the etymological connection between Augusta's name and the verb
augere, which normally means "to increase"; here, however, the meaning must be "encouraged" or "strengthened." See also above, Introduction, page xxiii.

20. I.e., fire-hardened.

Nor had Arminius or any of the other German aristocrats been neglecting to call upon their own men to witness that these Romans were the fastest runaways of the Varian army, who, to avoid facing war, had invested in mutiny: in some cases it was backs burdened with wounds that they were pitting a second time against a ferocious enemy and adverse gods, in others it was limbs broken by bil-

2   lows and storms, and neither had hope of success. They had had recourse to a fleet and the trackless Ocean, to prevent anyone from obstructing their arrival or from following up their flight; but, when they fought hand to hand, vain would

3   be the help from winds or oars for the vanquished. They themselves had only to remember the enemy's greed, cruelty, and haughtiness; did they have anything else left except to hold on to their freedom or to die before servitude?

16   Fired in this way, and begging for battle, the men were led down to the plain whose name is Idisiovisa.[+] In the middle between the Visurgis and the hills, it has an irregular circumference, according as the banks of the river retreat or the spurs of the mountains stand firm. At the rear there soared a wood, its branches

2   lifting on high and with clear ground between the trunks of the trees. The plain and the edges of the woods were held by the barbarian line; only the Cherusci

3   were installed on the ridges, to raid against the battling Romans from above. Our army advanced thus: the auxiliary Gauls and Germans in front, behind whom were the infantry archers; then four legions and, with two praetorian cohorts and the select cavalry, Caesar; thereafter the same number of other legions and light armor with the cavalry archers and the other cohorts of the allies. The soldiery was alert and prepared for forming the order of the column into the line of battle.

17   Seeing the companies of Cherusci, which in their defiance had burst forth, Caesar ordered his most effective cavalry to raid the flank, and Stertinius with the remaining squadrons to go around and assail the rear, while he himself was

2   aiming to assist at the right time. Meanwhile the finest of auguries—the sight of eight eagles making for and entering the woods—attracted the commander's attention. He shouted that they should "go and follow the Roman birds, the le-

3   gions' very own divinities." At the same time the infantry line advanced, and the cavalry which had been sent ahead attacked the back and flanks. And (wonderful to tell) two columns of the enemy rushed to flee in opposite directions—those who had held the wood, onto open ground, those who had formed up on

4   the plains, into the wood! In the middle between them the Cherusci were dislodged from the hills, among whom Arminius was distinctive as, with his brawn, voice, and wound, he rallied the fight. He had borne down upon the archers, aiming to burst through there, had not the Gallic cohorts and those of the Raeti

5   and Vindelici thrown their standards against him. Nevertheless by physical effort and the momentum of his horse he made a passage, smearing his face with his own gore to prevent his identity from being known. (Some have transmitted that he was indeed acknowledged by the Chauci who were serving among the Roman auxiliaries, and sent on his way.) The same courage—or treachery—pro-

6   vided Inguiomerus with his escape. The rest were butchered everywhere. Many,

in trying to swim across the Visurgis, were overwhelmed by the discharge of weapons or by the force of the river or finally by the onrushing masses and the collapse of the banks; some, in a disgraceful flight, struggled to the tops of trees and, trying to hide themselves in the branches, were mockingly transfixed by archers who were moved up, while others were crushed when the trees were felled.

That was a great victory and not gory for us. From the fifth hour of the day **18** until night the enemy were slaughtered, and their corpses and arms covered ten thousand paces—with the discovery, among their spoils, of chains which they had been carrying for the Romans, as if the outcome were not in doubt. The 2 soldiery on the field of battle hailed Tiberius as "commander" and set up an embankment and on it placed arms after the fashion of trophies, subscribing the names of the vanquished nations.

That scene affected the Germans with greater pain and anger than did wounds, **19** grief, and extirpation. Those who only recently had been preparing to leave their abodes and withdraw across the Albis were now wanting a fight and seizing their arms: plebs and chiefs, young and old suddenly raided and disrupted the Roman column. Finally they selected a place shut in by river and woods, its center a con- 2 fined and wet area of flat ground; the woods too were encircled by deep marsh, except that the Angrivarii had raised up one side with a broad embankment to divide themselves from the Cherusci. It was here that the infantry formed up; the cavalry they sheltered in nearby groves, so it should be in the rear of the legions as they entered the wood.

None of this was unknown to Caesar: he knew their plans and locations, the **20** obvious and the hidden, and he intended to turn the enemies' stratagems into their own ruin. To the legate Seius Tubero he entrusted the cavalry and plain;[21] the line of infantry he drew up in such a way that some should have a level approach to the wood when they advanced, some should struggle up the opposing embankment; the steep tasks he gave to himself, the others to the legates.

Those allotted the flat ground burst easily upon the enemy; but those who had 2 to assault the embankment were belabored by heavy strikes from above, as if they were scaling a wall. The leader realized the inequality of the fight at close quarters and, moving the legions a little farther back, ordered the slingers and throwers to release their weapons and thrust the enemy aside. Spears were dispatched from the launchers, and, the more conspicuous the defenders, the more numerous the wounds by which they were toppled. On the capture of the rampart, 3 Caesar with the praetorian cohorts was the first to mount an attack on the woods; and there the ground was contested step by step.

The enemy was shut in at the rear by the marsh, the Romans by the river or mountains. For both of them there was constraint in their location, hope in valor, salvation from victory; nor were the Germans any the less spirited, but they were **21** overcome by the type of both fight and weapons, since the mighty crowd in the

21. L. Seius Tubero, a relative of Sejanus, became suffect consul in A.D. 18.

confined location could neither extend nor retract their overlong spears nor take advantage of dashes and their natural swiftness, compelled as they were into a standing battle; on the other hand, the soldiery, whose shields were pressed to their chests and hands resting on their hilts, pierced the barbarians' ample limbs and bare faces and opened up a way through the wreckage of the enemy—Arminius being now unavailable owing to the constant danger, or else his recently received wound had slowed him down. Inguiomerus too, though flying

2 along the whole line, was deserted by fortune rather than by valor. Germanicus, to make himself more recognizable, had pulled the covering from his head and was begging his men to press home the slaughter: they had no need of captives, he said; only the annihilation of the race would bring an end to the war. And, it being now late in the day, he withdrew a legion from the line to make camp; the others sated themselves on the enemy's gore until night. The cavalry contest was ambiguous.

22 Having praised the victors at a meeting, Caesar set up a pile of weapons with a haughty inscription: having defeated the nations between Rhine and Albis, the army of Tiberius Caesar had consecrated that monument to Mars, Jupiter, and Augustus. Of himself he added nothing, either dreading resentment or deeming

2 that consciousness of the deed was enough. Next he was for handing to Stertinius the war against the Angrivarii, had they not hastened their surrender; and as suppliants, by refusing nothing, they received pardon for everything.

23 But with the season now mature, while some of the legions were sent back to winter quarters on an overland journey, Caesar embarked the majority on the

2 fleet and ferried them by the River Amisia to the Ocean.[22] At first the sea's calm surface sounded and churned only with the oars of a thousand ships;[+] but soon hail, pouring down from a dark gathering of clouds, removed all visibility, while at the same time the billows, unpredictable in the squalls from every different direction, prevented steering; and the soldiery, panicking and ignorant of the hazards of the sea, disrupted the sailors or offered untimely help, thereby hampering

3 the jobs of the skilled. Next, the entire heavens and the sea in its entirety passed into the control of the South Wind, which—already powerful from the bulging[23] lands of Germany, its deep streams and immense expanse of cloud, and now grislier from the grip of the neighboring North—seized hold of the ships and scattered them on the open Ocean or on islands ferocious for their precipitous rocks

4 or with concealed shallows. The latter they avoided for a while and with difficulty but, after the tide had begun to change in the same direction as the wind,

---

22. In his *Suasoriae* (1.15) the elder Seneca has preserved a fragment from Albinovanus Pedo's poem on Germanicus' sailing the Ocean. Scholars usually assume that the poet and the Pedo of 1.60.2 (above) are one and the same, that the poet's Germanicus is the present Germanicus, and that there is some relationship between his poem and T.'s narrative here at 2.23–4 (perhaps esp. 24.4).

23. If the text (*tumidis*) is correct, the reference seems to be either to mountains or to a terrain swollen with moisture; others accept the emendation (*h*)*umidis* ("wet").

they were unable either to cling to their anchors or to bale out the inrushing waves: horses, baggage-animals, packs, even weapons were toppled overboard to lighten the hulls, awash through their sides and with the billows crashing down.

Just as the Ocean is more violent than the sea in general, and Germany excels **24** in the callousness of its climate, so was that disaster the ultimate in novelty and magnitude, with either enemy shores all around or the deep so desolate⁺ that it is believed to be the ultimate, landless sea. Some of the ships were swallowed up, 2 more were thrown up on islands situated farther away; and in the absence of human habitation there, the soldiery were taken off by starvation, except for those sustained by the bodies of horses, cast up on the same place. Only Germanicus' trireme managed to moor at the land of the Chauci—and along the cliffs and coastal spurs he cried repeatedly through all those days and nights that the responsibility for such extermination was his; while his friends could scarcely restrain him from meeting his end in that very same sea.

At last, with the tide receding and wind turning favorable, ships limped back 3 under scanty oarage or with clothing hoisted,²⁴ and some were pulled by the more sturdy. These, rapidly repaired, he sent to investigate the islands. Quite a few men were gathered in as the result of his concern; the Angrivarii, recently received into our trust, ransomed many from inland peoples and restored them to us; some had been swept to Britain and were sent back by its princes. Whenever 4 someone returned from a distant place, he had wonders to tell: the violence of whirlwinds, unheard of birds, marine monsters, shapes ambiguous between men and beasts—all were seen, or believed from dread.

Yet, while the report of the fleet's loss roused the Germans to hope for war, it **25** roused Caesar to pen them in. He commanded C. Silius with thirty thousand infantry and three thousand cavalry to go against the Chatti; he himself with greater forces burst upon the Marsi, whose leader, Mallovendus, recently received in surrender, informed him that the eagle of a Varian legion was interred in a neighboring grove and guarded by only a modest garrison. A unit was dispatched immediately to entice the enemy from the front, and others to go around the back 2 and open up the ground; and each was attended by good fortune. All the readier on that account, Caesar proceeded inward, pillaging and extirpating an enemy who did not dare to engage or, whenever he did stand his ground, was immediately beaten and never (as was known from captives) more panicked. They 3 pronounced the Romans unconquerable and not to be overcome by any hazards: their fleet destroyed, their arms lost, after the shores had been strewn with the bodies of their horses and men, they had burst upon them with the same courage, equal defiance and seemingly augmented in numbers.

From there the soldiery was led back to winter camp, delighted in heart that **26** they had compensated for their reverses at sea with a successful expedition on foot. As an extra contribution there was munificence from Caesar, redeeming whatever loss anyone declared. Nor was there held to be any doubt that their en-

24. I.e., to act as sails.

emies were tottering and adopting plans for seeking peace, and, if the next season were added, the war could be concluded.

2   But in frequent letters Tiberius was advising him to return for the triumph
decreed to him:[25] there had now been enough results, enough hazards; he had
had successful and great battles; but he should remember too the losses inflicted
by winds and billows, which, though not the fault of the leader, were neverthe-

3   less heavy and savage. He himself, sent nine times by Divine Augustus to Germany, had achieved more by planning than by force: thus had the Sugambri been
received in surrender, thus the Suebi and their king, Maroboduus, bound by
peace; the Cherusci too, and the other nations of rebels, could be left to their internal disaffections, since the interests of Roman vengeance had been served.

4   When Germanicus begged for only a year to complete his project, he made a
sharper attack on his sense of discipline and restraint, by offering a second consulship, whose responsibilities he should meet in person; at the same time he wove
in the further point that, if there must still be war, he should leave some raw material for the glory of his brother Drusus, who, there being now no other enemy,
could not, except in the Germanies, acquire the name of "commander" and carry

5   off the laurel.[26] Germanicus hesitated no longer, although his understanding was
that those were fabrications and that through resentment he was being dragged
away from the honor already won.

★

27   Around the same time one of the family of the Scribonii, Libo Drusus, was
denounced as planning revolution. The beginning, course, and end of the proceedings I shall discuss with particular care, because then were first discovered
the elements which during so many years gnawed away at the state.

2   Firmius Catus, a senator, from Libo's closest circle of friends, impelled the
young man—misguided as he was, and susceptible to illusions—to resort to the
promises of the Chaldaeans,[27] the rites of magicians, and even the interpreters of
dreams, while at the same time he kept pointing to his great-grandfather Pompeius, his great-aunt Scribonia (who had once been Augustus' spouse), his cousins
the Caesars, and his house full of images;[28] and he encouraged him into luxuriousness and debt, acting as the partner of his lusts and obligations in order to en-

25. Germanicus had been decreed a triumph in A.D. 15 (1.55.1).

26. For "commander" see App. A; the laurel symbolizes a triumph.

27. This term, used of certain peoples of Babylonia, is found frequently in T.'s narrative
(3.22.1, 6.20.2, 12.22.1, 12.52.1, 12.68.3, 14.9.3, 16.14.1) and is equivalent to "astrologers," since Babylonia was particularly associated with astrology. See T. S. Barton, *Ancient Astrology* (London 1994), esp. 41–9, and *Power and Knowledge* (Ann Arbor, MI 1994);
also M. W. Dickie, *Magic and Magicians in the Greco-Roman World* (London 2001) 198–201.

28. These "images," another term found frequently in T.'s narrative, are those of ancestors and might take a variety of different forms: wax face masks which were kept in cup-

trap him by additional evidence. When he had discovered enough witnesses, and **28**
slaves who would acknowledge the same things, he demanded access to the princeps, the charge and defendant having been described by Flaccus Vescularius, a
Roman equestrian, whose familiarity with Tiberius was closer.[29]

Caesar, while not spurning the evidence, declined a meeting: their conversa-   2
tion could go back and forth with the same Flaccus as intermediary. And meanwhile he decorated Libo with a praetorship, invited him to parties, and was
neither estranged from him in looks nor more volatile in language (he had so buried
his anger); and, though he could have stopped all the man's words and deeds, his
preference for knowing them was maintained until the moment when a certain
Junius, having been approached to entice infernal shades by spells,[30] denounced
this evidence to Fulcinius Trio.[31] Celebrated among accusers was the talent of   3
Trio, and greedy for an evil reputation. At once he seized the defendant, went to
the consuls, and demanded a trial in the senate. The fathers were summoned, with
the additional warning that they must debate an important and frightening affair.

Libo meanwhile, having changed his clothing,[32] made a round of the houses   **29**
with leading ladies, besought his in-laws and demanded a voice to protect him
against danger—only to be met with universal refusal and, despite the different
pretexts, identical alarm. On the day of the senate, exhausted by dread and illness   2
(or, as some have transmitted, with a pretended disease), he was carried to the
doors of the curia in a litter and, leaning on his brother and extending to Tiberius
his hands and words of supplication, he was greeted by the latter's motionless expression. Then Caesar recited the documents and authorities,[33] with such control as to avoid the appearance of softening or sharpening the charges.

---

boards in the atrium of a house and brought out for funerals, when they would be worn
by persons impersonating the ancestors; painted portraits illustrating a family tree; busts
of various kinds. See H. I. Flower, *Aristocratic Masks and Aristocratic Power in Roman Culture*
(Oxford 1996). The family relationships of M. Scribonius Libo Drusus are complicated
and disputed.

29. See 6.10.2.

30. Junius was approached by Libo Drusus to raise the spirits of the dead, presumably
so that they could be questioned about what the future held for him. See in general D.
Ogden, *Greek and Roman Necromancy* (Princeton 2001).

31. Fulcinius Trio became suffect consul in 31 (5.11.1) and committed suicide four years
later (6.38.2).

32. Dark or soiled clothing would be worn (a) by defendants in court or by other persons in a position of supplication in order to win sympathy for their plight, (b) by mourn-
ers as a mark of sorrow and distress.

33. The "documents" are presumably those containing the charges and thus to be distinguished from Libo's own "documents" mentioned at 2.30.1 below (the same Latin
word, *libelli,* is used in each case). The "authorities" are those individuals who had endorsed the prosecution.

30   Besides Trio and Catus, Fonteius Agrippa and C.Vibius[34] had become accessories in the accusation, and they started competing for the prerogative of de-
claiming against the defendant, until finally Vibius, on the grounds that they
would not yield to one another and that Libo had entered without an advocate,
pronounced that he would lay down the charges individually;[35] and he produced documents of such derangement as to indicate that Libo had consulted
whether he would have the wealth to cover over the Appian Way right to Brun-
2   disium with money. The other contents too were of this type—empty, stupid,
and, if you interpreted more leniently, pitiable; nevertheless in one document
the accuser charged that in Libo's hand frightening or secret marks had been
3   added against the names of the Caesars or senators. On the defendant's denial,
it was agreed that the slaves who acknowledged it[36] should be questioned under torture; and, because by an old senate's decision any investigation bearing
on the life of a master was prohibited, Tiberius, astute to devise a new legality,
ordered that individuals should be sold to the public agent[37]—just so that an
investigation against Libo could be conducted through his slaves, with the sen-
4   ate's decision preserved intact. For this reason the defendant sought an adjournment until the next day and, departing for home, handed to P. Quirinius,[38] his
31   relative, his final pleas to the princeps. The answer was that he should ask the
senate.

Meanwhile his house was being encircled by soldiery, and they were making
a din even in the forecourt, so that they could be audible and visible, when finally Libo, racked by the very banquet which he had laid on as his last pleasure
of all, called for an assailant, grasped the right hands of his slaves and tried to place
2   his sword in them. And, as they in their trembling retreat overturned the light
placed nearby on the table, in darkness now fatal to himself he directed two blows
into his vital organs. At the falling man's groan his freedmen ran up; and the sol-
3   diery, seeing the slaughter, stood back. The accusation was nevertheless carried
through before the fathers with the same assertiveness, and Tiberius swore that
he would have asked for the man's life, despite his guilt, if he had not hastened
his voluntary death.

32   His goods were divided between his accusers, and extraordinary praetorships
given to those who were of the senatorial order. Then Cotta Messalinus voted
that no image of Libo should accompany the exequies of his descendants, Cn.

34. The elder Vibius Serenus, later proconsul of Farther Spain (4.13.2). The manuscript
here abbreviates his first name as *C.* (= Gaius), but the heading to the Piso inscription
(above, p. xv) gives his name as *N.* (= Numerius). On him see further 4.28.1–30.1.

35. So that Libo himself could answer each in turn.

36. I.e., Libo's handwriting. On the general subject of documents and the law see E. A.
Meyer, *Legitimacy and Law in the Roman World: Tabulae in Roman Practice and Belief* (Cambridge 2004).

37. An official whose exact responsibilities seem unknown.

38. For P. Sulpicius Quirinius, consul in 12 B.C., see further 3.22.1, 48.1.

Lentulus that no Scribonius should adopt the nomenclature "Drusus."[39] Days of   2
supplication were established on the proposal of Pomponius Flaccus; and L. P★★★
and Gallus Asinius and Papius Mutilus and L. Apronius decreed gifts to Jupiter,
Mars and Concordia,[40] and that the Ides of September—the day on which Libo
had killed himself—should be a festival day.[41] (I recorded those men's sycophantic suggestions so that the chronic nature of that disease in the state should be
known.) Senate's decisions were made also about expelling astrologers and ma-   3
gicians from Italy; and one of their number, L. Pituanius, was cast down from the
Rock, while against P. Marcius the consuls, after they had ordered the trumpet
to sound, took measures outside the Esquiline Gate according to the old-time
convention.[42]

On the next day of the senate much was said against the luxuriousness of the   **33**
community by the consular, Q. Haterius,[43] and a former practor, Octavius
Fronto; and it was decreed that vessels of solid gold should not be made for serving food and that silken clothing should not defile men. Fronto went further and
demanded a limit on silver, furniture, and establishment (it was still regular for
senators, when their turn came to speak, to express whatever they believed to be
in the state's interest). Gallus Asinius spoke against: with the expansion of the em-   2
pire private wealth too had grown, and that was no novelty but in accordance
with the most olden traditions: money was one thing in the time of the Fabricii,
another in that of the Scipios; and everything was relative to the state: when it
was poor, citizens' households had been confined, but, after it reached its present
magnificence, individuals swelled in importance. Nor, in the cases of establish-   3
ment and silver and everything acquired for use, was anything excessive or modest except by the standard of the owner's fortune. The qualifications for senate
and equestrians were kept distinct, not because they were different in nature but,
just as they both took precedence in place, order, and rank,[44] so too in those
things which were acquired for mental relaxation or physical healthiness—un-

39. M. Aurelius Cotta Maximus Messalinus, consul in 20 (3.2.2), was son of the famous
Corvinus (1.8.3n.): see further 5.3.2, 6.5.1–7.1. For Lentulus see 1.27.1n.

40. L. Pomponius Flaccus became consul in 17 (2.41.2); M. Papius Mutilus had been
suffect consul in A.D. 9; for Gallus and Apronius see 1.8.3n. and 1.56.1n. respectively. The
name missing from the manuscript has been thought to be L. Piso (of whom there were
two: 2.34.1n. and 6.10.3n.) or L. Plancus (1.39.3).

41. The date (13 September) is recorded on a surviving inscription (Sherk 28A, pp.
53–4).

42. He was scourged to death: see also 4.30.1, 14.48.2, and 16.11.3. (The "Rock," above,
is the Tarpeian Rock.)

43. See 1.13.4n.

44. The first of these near-synonyms seems to refer to the places which were reserved
for senators and equestrians in the theater and to which great significance was attached
(see, e.g., 2.83.4), the second to the two "orders" (in the technical sense: App. A) which
senators and equestrians constituted, and the third to their eligibility for (or prestige ac-

less perchance all the most brilliant men were required to undertake more numerous concerns and greater dangers but to do without the assuagements of
4   those concerns and dangers. Easy assent to Gallus was provided by his listeners'
confessing to similar vices under honorable names. Tiberius too had added that
that was not the time for a review, but, if there was any slip in behavior, an instigator of reform would not be lacking and would not fail in his duty.

34   It was during this that L. Piso, berating bribery in the forum, the corrupt courts
and the savagery of advocates forever threatening accusations, started to testify
that he was retiring and withdrawing from the City to live in some remote and
distant countryside.[45] At the same time he started to abandon the curia. Tiberius
was agitated and, although he had caressed Piso with soft words, he compelled
the man's relatives too to stop his retirement by their influence or prayers.

2   No less an indication of Piso's outspoken indignation was likewise provided
subsequently when he summoned to trial Urgulania, whom friendship with Augusta had elevated above the laws. Nor did either Urgulania comply, spurning
Piso by moving to the house of Caesar, or he withdraw, although Augusta com-
3   plained of being violated and diminished. Tiberius, deeming it citizenlike to in-
dulge his mother as far as saying that he would go to the praetor's tribunal to
support Urgulania, proceeded from the Palatium, with soldiers ordered to follow
at a distance. As the people converged on him, he was observed to be calm in
appearance and spending his time on the journey in a variety of conversations,
until, with relatives restraining Piso in vain, Augusta ordered the money which
4   was being sought to be handed over. And that was the end of an affair from
which Piso emerged not ingloriously and Caesar with a greater reputation. But
Urgulania's powerfulness weighed so excessively upon the community that she
disdained to appear as testifier in a case which was being handled before the senate: a praetor was sent to question her at home, although there was an old custom that Vestal Virgins should be heard in court in the forum whenever they gave
testimony.

35   I would not record the postponement of affairs[46] in that year if it were not
worth knowing the different opinions of Cn. Piso and Asinius Gallus on the matter. Piso, although Caesar had said that he would be absent, voted that that was
rather a reason for discussions to take place, so that the senate's and equestrians'
ability to uphold their responsibilities in the princeps's absence should be a credit

---

cruing from) political office. The property qualification for an equestrian was four hundred thousand sesterces and for a senator (see 1.75.3) one million; but the speaker's point
is not that these two groups were thereby distinguished from each other but that both
were distinguished from the rest of society (as 13.27.2).

45. L. Calpurnius Piso ("the augur"), brother of Cn. Piso (1.13.2n.), had been consul in
1 B.C.

46. *Res prolatae,* which I have translated as "the postponement of affairs," is the standard
expression for the adjournment of senatorial business; but scholars have debated whether
T. is referring to a spring or autumn adjournment.

to the state. Gallus, because Piso had seized the initiative with[47] a display of free   2
speech, said that nothing was sufficiently illustrious or met the dignity of the Roman people unless it were before and under the eyes of Caesar, and therefore any
gathering from Italy and influx from the provinces should be kept for his presence. With Tiberius listening to these issues in silence, they were discussed with
great contention on both sides; but there was a deferment of affairs.

Another conflict for Gallus arose between him and Caesar. He voted for hold-   **36**
ing the elections of magistrates for a quinquennium, and that legates of legions
who were performing their military service before the praetorship should already
be marked out as praetors now, and the princeps should nominate twelve candidates for each year. There was no doubt that that proposal made a deeper penetration and that the mysteries of command were being tested.[48] Nevertheless   2
Tiberius, as if his power were being augmented, said that it weighed heavily upon
his restraint to select so many and defer so many: scarcely was offense avoided
from year to year, although the proximity of hope comforted rejection; how
much hatred would come from those who were cast aside in suspense beyond a
quinquennium! On what basis could one foresee what each man's intention,   3
family, or fortune would be over so long a period of time? Men were haughty
even with the yearly designation; what if they flaunted their office for a quinquennium? Indeed there would be a quinquiplication of magistrates and an
undermining of the laws which established the proper periods for candidates'
exercising their industriousness and for seeking or holding office.

The speech being apparently aimed at winning goodwill, he retained the   4
essence of his command. He also helped the qualifications of certain senators: **37**
hence it was the more surprising that he gave a more haughty reception to the
prayers of Marcius Hortalus,[49] a young noble, despite his obvious poverty.
(Grandson of the orator Hortensius, he had been enticed by the generosity of a
million sesterces from Divine Augustus to marry a wife and raise children to prevent the extinction of a most brilliant family.) With four sons in attendance at   2
the threshold of the curia, and (since the senate was being held in the Palatium)
gazing now at the image of Hortensius, situated among the orators, now at that
of Augustus,[50] he began in this fashion when his turn came to speak: "Conscript
fathers, I reared these children, whose number and mere boyhood you see, not

---

47. Or perhaps "had proposed."

48. The precise significance of this famous sentence is not very clear. T. seems to mean
that Gallus' proposal had implications which went beyond its apparent intention and
which affected the emperor's authority. If five years' worth of magistrates were elected,
the princeps's ability to influence elections would be reduced and elected magistrates were
more likely than electoral candidates to demonstrate some independence.

49. Until the early 1990s the transmitted *Marci* was assumed to be the genitive of the
praenomen "Marcus" and not, as epigraphic evidence has now shown to be the case, of
the family name "Marcius" (see *Journal of Roman Studies* 87 (1997) 216 and n. 119).

50. The portico of the temple of Palatine Apollo, where the senate was (as often) meet-

on my own account but because the princeps advised me; at the same time my
3   ancestors had earned the right to have descendants. For I personally—who in
the changing circumstances of the times had been able to inherit or acquire neither money nor people's enthusiasm nor even eloquence, the family advantage
of our house—considered it enough if my slender means were neither a source
of shame to myself nor a burden to anyone else. It was on the orders of my Commander that I took a wife. Look! The stock and progeny of so many consuls, so
4   many dictators![51] (And I do not make those references to invite resentment but
for the winning of pity.) As long as you flourish, Caesar, they will achieve the
honors which you will give; meanwhile defend from deprivation the great-
grandsons of Q. Hortensius, the foster-children of Divine Augustus!"

38   The inclination of the senate was an incentive to Tiberius to oppose him more
readily, using roughly these words: "If all the poor elements start to come here
and beg money for their children, individuals will never be satisfied and the state
will fail. Nor, surely, was it allowed by our ancestors occasionally to deviate from
a motion and, when it was one's turn to speak, to propose something conducive
to the common good simply in order that here we should discuss private affairs
and increase our own family fortunes, bringing resentment on the senate and
2   principes whether they concede such lavishness or decline it. For that is no plea
of yours but importunity—untimely too and unforeseen, since the fathers have
convened for other matters—to rise and to pressurize the decency of the senate
with the number and age of one's children, to transfer the same undue influence
to me and (as it were) to break open the treasury, which, if we exhaust it by
3   favoritism, must be replenished by crime. Divine Augustus gave you money,
Hortalus, but without being entreated and without any condition that it should
always be given. Besides, industriousness will languish and listlessness will intensify, if no dread or hope comes from within oneself and all, without any concern,
expect support from someone else, shirkers on their own account and weighing
heavily upon us."

4   Although these and similar remarks were heard with assent by those whose
custom it is to praise a princeps's every act, honorable and dishonorable alike, the
majority received them in silence or with concealed murmuring. Tiberius sensed
it and, when he had been quiet for a short while, said that he had replied to Hortalus, but, if it seemed good to the fathers, he would give two hundred thousand
5   sesterces to each of the man's children who were of the male sex. Some people
expressed their gratitude; Hortalus kept silent—in panic, or else retentive of his

---

ing, also enclosed a famous library, where the likenesses of distinguished orators were displayed (see further 2.83.3 below). It is an additional piquancy that Augustus' own house
was part of the same complex of buildings and that the house had previously belonged to
the very same Q. Hortensius Hortalus who was the present speaker's grandfather (above).

51. The Marcii had produced one dictator (Q. Marcius Rutilus, 356 B.C.) and numerous consuls; the Hortensii likewise one dictator (Q. Hortensius, c. 287 B.C.) but only two
consuls.

inherited nobility even amid his straitened fortunes. Nor did Tiberius take pity thereafter, although the house of Hortalus slipped into shameful deprivation.

In the same year the daring of a single menial, had not help come quickly, **39** would have struck down the state with discord and civil war. A slave of Postumus Agrippa, Clemens by name, on discovering Augustus' end, conceived the quite unservile intention of proceeding to the island of Planasia and, seizing Agrippa by trick or force, transporting him to the German armies. His act of 2 daring was hampered by the slowness of his merchant-ship; and, the slaughter[52] having been accomplished in the meantime, he turned to greater and more headlong schemes: he stole the ashes[53] and, traveling to Cosa, a promontory in Etruria, hid himself in undisclosed locations until he grew his hair and beard (in age and build he was not unlike his master). Then, through suitable persons party to the 3 secret, the news that Agrippa was alive was spread—at first in surreptitious conversations (as is customary with forbidden topics), then by unattributed rumor in the ready ears of the impressionable or, conversely, among turbulent elements desirous of revolution. As for the man himself, he would approach municipali- 4 ties when it was dark, nor was he observed in the open or for too long in the same places but—because veracity is validated by vision and delay, deceptions by dispatch and uncertainties—he was always abandoning the reports of himself or anticipating them.

It was publicized meanwhile across Italy that Agrippa had been preserved by **40** the gift of the gods, and it was believed at Rome; and his arrival at Ostia was already being celebrated by mighty numbers of people, and in the City by clandestine crowds, when Tiberius was torn by the double-edged concern of whether he should detain his own slave by a force of soldiers or allow empty credulity to vanish in its own good time. Wavering between shame and dread, he reflected sometimes that nothing should be spurned, sometimes that not everything should be dreaded. Finally he gave the business to Sallustius Crispus. He selected 2 two of his clients (some transmit that they were soldiers) and urged them to make an approach with pretended complicity, to offer him money, and to guarantee their loyalty and risk-taking. They followed through what had been ordered. Then, looking out for an unguarded night, and taking an appropriate unit, they dragged him, bound and gagged, to the Palatium. To Tiberius' inquiry about the 3 way in which he had become Agrippa he is said to have replied "The way in which you became Caesar." He could not be compelled to reveal his accomplices. Nor did Tiberius dare his punishment publicly but ordered him to be killed in a remote part of the Palatium and his body carried out secretly. And, although many from the princeps's household, as well as equestrians and senators, were said to have supported him with resources and helped him with advice, there was no investigation.

52. Of Agrippa Postumus in A.D. 14 (1.6.1).
53. Of Agrippa Postumus.

41   At the end of the year there were dedicated an arch near the temple of Saturn
for the recovery, under the leadership of Germanicus and the auspices of Tiberius,
of the standards lost with Varus;[54] a temple of Fors Fortuna by the Tiber, in the
gardens which the dictator Caesar had bequeathed to the Roman people; and a
sanctuary to the Julian family and a likeness to Divine Augustus at Bovillae.

★   ★   ★

A.D. 17

2   With C. Caelius and L. Pomponius as consuls,[55] on the seventh day before the
Kalends of June,[56] Germanicus Caesar triumphed over the Cherusci, Chatti, Angrivarii, and the other nations who live as far as the Albis. Carried in the procession were spoils, captives, and representations of mountains, rivers, and battles;
and the war, because he had been prevented from concluding it,[57] was accepted
3   as concluded. The sight of the onlookers was intensified by the exceptional scene
of the man himself and by his chariot's burden of five children; but there was an
undercurrent of hidden alarm, as they reflected that the goodwill of the public
had been disadvantageous in the case of Drusus, his father, that his uncle Marcellus had been snatched away in mid-youth from the burning devotion of the
42   plebs, and that brief and unpropitious were the loves of the Roman people.[58] As
for Tiberius, in Germanicus' name he gave to the plebs three hundred sesterces
a man and marked himself out as colleague in his consulship. Yet he did not
thereby gain credibility for the soundness of his affection and, determined to dislodge the young man by a display of honor, he manufactured reasons or seized
on those offered by chance.

2   King Archelaus had been in control of Cappadocia for fifty years—resented
by Tiberius because he had not paid dutiful court to him during his time on
Rhodes.[59] Archelaus' neglect had not been caused by haughtiness but by a warning from Augustus' intimates, since, with C. Caesar flourishing and dispatched to
3   affairs in the East, friendship with Tiberius was believed unsafe. But when, ow-

54. See 1.60.3 and 2.25.1–2; the third standard was not recovered until the reign of
Claudius.

55. C. Caelius Rufus is scarcely otherwise known; for L. Pomponius Flaccus (2.32.2)
see further 2.66.2; he died in 33 (6.27.3).

56. 26 May (see Sherk 28B, p. 54).

57. Germanicus had been ordered back to Rome by Tiberius: see 2.26.2–4 above.

58. The elder Drusus had died in 9 B.C. aged thirty (1.3.3), Marcellus in 23 B.C. aged
nineteen (1.3.1).

59. Archelaus had been appointed king by Mark Antony in 36 B.C., "fifty years" from
which brings us only to A.D. 14 (unless T. is giving a round number). During his retirement on Rhodes (1.4.4n.) Tiberius had had all the more reason to feel resentment because he had once defended Archelaus successfully in court.

ing to the eradication of the budding Caesars,[60] Tiberius acquired command, he enticed Archelaus by a letter from his mother, who, without dissimulating her son's continuing offense, offered clemency if the man came begging. He for his part, unaware of any guile or (should it be believed that he understood) dreading violence, hurried to the City. Welcomed by a ruthless princeps and subsequently accused in the senate, it was not on account of the charges (which were fabricated) but through tension—and at the same time exhausted by old age and because kings find equality (and, even more, abasement) abnormal—that he consummated, whether of his own accord or naturally, the end of his life. His kingdom was converted into a province, and Caesar, announcing that the income from it could alleviate the one-percent revenue,[61] established one half-percent for the future. At around the same time, on the decease of Antiochus and Philopator (the kings respectively of the Commageni and Cilicians), there was disruption in their nations, the majority desiring Roman, others royal, command. And the provinces of Syria and Judaea, exhausted by their burdens, begged a diminution of taxation.

So in front of the fathers he discussed these things and those concerning Armenia which I recalled above:[62] the tremors in the East could not be settled except by the wisdom of Germanicus, he said, for his own life was declining and that of Drusus had not yet sufficiently matured. Then by a decree of the fathers Germanicus was entrusted with the provinces that are separated by the sea, and, wherever he went, with a greater command than that entrusted to those who held them by lot or on dispatch from the princeps.[63]

But Tiberius had removed from Syria Creticus Silanus, who was connected with Germanicus by marriage (Silanus' daughter had been betrothed to Nero, the eldest of his children), and had placed in charge Cn. Piso, temperamentally violent and a stranger to compliance, his defiance implanted in him by his father Piso (who in the civil war helped the resurgence of the party in Africa with the keenest of service against Caesar and then, after following Brutus and Cassius, was allowed to return but refrained from seeking office until he was spontaneously solicited to accept a consulship tendered by Augustus).[64] But besides his father's

60. *Caesarum* is a defining or appositional genitive: the reference is to the two Caesars, Gaius (just mentioned above) and Lucius, grandsons of Augustus, for whose deaths see 1.3.3 and n.

61. See 1.78.2 above.

62. See 2.3.1, 2.4.3–5.1 above.

63. The sea in question is the Adriatic; the phrases "by lot" and "on dispatch from the princeps" refer respectively to "public" and "imperial" provinces (for which see App. A). With T.'s wording compare that of *SCPP* 34–5 "in whatever province he [Germanicus] entered he would have greater *imperium* [command] than the person who was governing the province as proconsul."

64. Cn. Calpurnius Piso, homonymous father of the present Piso, became suffect consul in 23 B.C.

spirit he was fired by the nobility and wealth of his wife too, Plancina: he scarcely yielded to Tiberius and looked down on the man's children as greatly beneath
4   him. Nor did he have any doubt that he had been selected for installation in Syria to curb Germanicus' hopes. (Certain people believed that secret instructions had been given to him[+] by Tiberius; and without doubt Augusta warned Plancina in
5   womanly rivalry to assail Agrippina.)[65] For the court was divided and disaffected by silent devotion to either Drusus or Germanicus. Tiberius fostered Drusus as being special and of his own blood; love for Germanicus among the rest had been increased by his uncle's estrangement from him—and because he took precedence by the brilliancy of his maternal line, his credentials being his grandfather
6   M. Antonius and his great-uncle Augustus. By contrast, the fact that Drusus' great-grandfather was the Roman equestrian Pomponius Atticus seemed to embarrass the images of the Claudii;[66] and Germanicus' spouse, Agrippina, outstripped Livia, the wife of Drusus, in fertility and fame.[67] Yet the brothers were exceptionally affectionate, and unshaken by the conflicts of their kin.

*

44   And not long afterward Drusus was sent to Illyricum to become accustomed to soldiering and to procure the affection of the army; at the same time Tiberius deemed that a young man living a reckless life of urban luxuriousness would be better in camp, and that he himself would be safer with each son holding legions.
2   But his pretext was a plea from the Suebi for help against the Cherusci: for, on the withdrawal of the Romans, they were released from their dread of the foreigner and had turned their arms against each other in the habit of their race and also in their rivalry for glory. The power of their nations and the prowess of their leaders were on a level; but the name of king made Maroboduus resented among
45   his compatriots, while Arminius enjoyed goodwill as a warrior for freedom. So it was not only the Cherusci and their allies—the old soldiery of Arminius— who took up the war, but even the Suebian races from Maroboduus' kingdom— the Semnones and Langobardi—defected to him. With their addition he was on his way to preeminent power, had not Inguiomerus with a band of his clients fled to Maroboduus, for no other reason than that the elderly uncle disdained to obey the young son of his brother.

65. The Latin here is obscure, and it is not clear whose the rivalry is.

66. Drusus' mother was Tiberius' first wife, Vipsania, daughter of Agrippa and his first wife, Pomponia, who in turn was the daughter of Cicero's great friend and correspondent, T. Pomponius Atticus. For "images" see above, 2.27.2n.

67. Drusus' wife is called "Livia" by T. and on inscriptions but "Livilla" by Suetonius and Dio. She was the daughter of Tiberius' brother, Nero Claudius Drusus, and granddaughter of Mark Antony.

The lines were drawn up, with hope equal on each side and no roving raids   2
or scattered companies (as once among the Germans):⁶⁸ by long soldiering
against us they had become accustomed to follow standards, to be consolidated
by reinforcements, and to listen to their commanders' words. And in fact at that   3
moment Arminius, surveying everything from his horse, was pointing out, as he
rode up to each lot of men, that freedom had been recovered, legions butchered,
and that spoils and weapons snatched from the Romans were even now in the
hands of many—by contrast calling Maroboduus a fugitive and inexperienced in
battle: he had been protected by the hiding-places of Hercynia and then he had
sought a treaty by gifts and legations, the betrayer of his fatherland, the satellite
of Caesar, to be evicted with no less ferocity than they had killed Varus Quintilius. They had only to remember the number of battles whose result—and the re-   4
moval at last of the Romans—had fully proved which side had the answer in war!

Nor did Maroboduus refrain from self-vaunting or from insults against the en-   **46**
emy, but, clasping Inguiomerus, claimed that it was in the latter's person that all
the prestige of the Cherusci resided, by his plans that they had accomplished
whatever had turned out successfully: Arminius, deranged and ignorant of affairs,
was assigning to himself the glory of another, since by treachery he had deceived
three roving⁶⁹ legions and a leader unaware of any trick—the consequences being a great disaster for Germany and ignominy for himself, since his spouse and
son alike were even now enduring servitude.⁷⁰ He personally, on the other hand,   2
had been the target of twelve legions under Tiberius' leadership and had preserved the glory of the Germans unmarred: soon afterward there had been a
withdrawal on equal terms;⁷¹ nor did he regret that it was in their own hands
whether they preferred a fresh war against the Romans or an unbloodied peace.

Roused by these utterances, the armies were goaded also by personal motives,   3
since the struggle of the Cherusci and Langobardi was on behalf of ancient prestige or recent freedom, and on the other side for an extension of mastery. At no   4
other time was there a convergence of greater concentration or more ambiguous result, with the right edges on each side routed; and a fight was expected
again, had not Maroboduus transferred his camp to the hills. That was the sign   5
of a beaten man; and, gradually denuded by desertions, he withdrew to the Marcomanni and dispatched legates to Tiberius to beg for help. The reply was that he
had no right to appeal for Roman arms against the Cherusci, since he had made
no effort to assist the Romans in their fight with the same enemy. Drusus was
nevertheless dispatched, as we have recorded,⁷² to be the consolidator of peace.

68. The precise meaning of the latter part of this sentence is very obscure in the Latin.

69. The Latin word of which this is a translation (*uagas*) has been questioned.

70. See 1.57.3–4, 1.58.5–6, and 2.10.1.

71. An optimistic gloss on the year A.D. 6, when Tiberius' preparations for a massive attack on Maroboduus had been thwarted by the revolt of Pannonia and Dalmatia.

72. At 2.44.1–2.

*

47   In the same year twelve celebrated cities in Asia collapsed in an earthquake at
nighttime, whereby the destruction was more unexpected and severe. Nor was
there any aid from the usual recourse in such a catastrophe, that of rushing into
the open, because they were being swallowed up by the cracks in the ground.
People recall that immense mountains sank down, what had been flat was seen
2   on high, and fires gleamed out among the ruins. The harshest affliction, that of
the Sardians, drew the greatest degree of sympathy: Caesar guaranteed ten million sesterces and remitted for a quinquennium what they owed to the treasury
3   or fiscus. The Magnesians-by-Sipylus were held to be next in loss and redress. As
for the Temnians, Philadelpheni, Aegeatae, Apollonidenses, and those who are
called Mosteni or Hyrcanian Macedonians, and Hierocaesaria, Myrina, Cyme,
and Tmolus, it was agreed that they be relieved of taxes for the same period and
that someone should be sent from the senate to inspect their immediate neigh-
4   borhoods and regenerate them. M. Ateius[73] from the praetorians was selected,
lest, with a consular holding Asia, rivalry between equals—and hence obstruc-
tion—should arise.

48   Caesar increased his magnificent public lavishness with a no less welcome generosity, in that the goods of the wealthy but intestate Aemilia Musa, which were
sought for the fiscus, he handed to Aemilius Lepidus,[74] from whose family she
seemed to have been; and the inheritance of the rich Roman equestrian Pan-
tuleius, although he was himself chosen as part-heir, to M. Servilius (whom he
had discovered mentioned in earlier and unsuspected tablets),[75] with the prefa-
2   tory remark that the nobility of each man required aiding by money. Nor did he
make a move for anyone's inheritance unless as a friend he had earned it;
strangers, or those nominating the princeps through their hostility toward oth-
3   ers, he fended off at a distance. Nevertheless, just as he alleviated the honorable
poverty of the guiltless, so he removed from the senate the prodigal or those
whose need arose from their outrages—Vibidius Virro, Marius Nepos, Appius
Appianus, Cornelius Sulla, Q. Vitellius[76]—or allowed them to withdraw of their
own accord.

49   During the same period he dedicated shrines of the gods which, destroyed by
age or fire, had been projects of Augustus': that to Liber, Libera, and Ceres near
the Circus Maximus, which A. Postumius as dictator had vowed,[77] and in the
same place the shrine of Flora established by Lucius and Marcus Publicius when

73. The name is uncertain and others have been proposed.

74. Probably M. Lepidus (1.13.2n.).

75. I.e., the writing tablets which comprised his will. M. Servilius was consul in A.D. 3
and probably father of the consul of 35 (6.31.1).

76. Brother of P. Vitellius (1.70.1n.) and L.Vitellius (6.28.1n.).

77. In 499 or 496 B.C.

aediles,[78] and the temple to Janus which had been set up in the Forum Holitorium by C. Duilius, who was the first to pursue the Roman cause successfully at
sea and win a naval triumph over the Poeni.[79] A shrine to Hope was consecrated   2
by Germanicus; A. Atilius had vowed it in the same war.[80]

Coming to maturity, meanwhile, was the law of treason: for example, because   **50**
Appuleia Varilla, granddaughter of Augustus' sister,[81] had mocked Divine Augustus and Tiberius and his mother in abusive conversations, and because a connection of Caesar's was liable for adultery,[82] a denouncer summoned her for treason.
Concerning her adultery there seemed to be adequate provision under the   2
Julian law;[83] as for the charge of treason, Caesar demanded that it be kept separate and that she be condemned for any irreligious talk about Augustus; the aspersions against himself he did not want called to trial. Asked by the consul what
he thought of the things which she was accused of having said amiss about his
mother, he kept quiet; then, on the next day of the senate, in her name too he
begged that words directed against her in whatever manner should not constitute a charge against anyone. And he freed Appuleia from the law of treason; beg-   3
ging off a heavier punishment for the adultery, he urged that on their ancestors'
example she be removed by her relatives beyond the two-hundredth milestone.
Her adulterer, Manlius, was forbidden access to Italy and Africa.

Concerning the election of a substitute praetor in place of Vipstanus Gallus,   **51**
whom death had carried off, a conflict took place. Germanicus and Drusus (they
were still then in Rome) fostered the cause of Haterius Agrippa, a relative of Germanicus;[84] on the other side very many strove to ensure that the number of children should be decisive in the case of candidates, as the law ordered.[85] Tiberius   2
was delighted that the senate was arbitrating between his sons and the laws. The
law without doubt was vanquished, but not immediately and by only a few
votes—the same way as laws were vanquished even when they were valid.

★

In the same year war began in Africa, the enemy leader being Tacfarinas. This   **52**
man from the Numidian nation—having done military service as an auxiliary in

78. In 241 or 238 B.C.

79. In 260 B.C.

80. In 258 or 257 B.C.

81. Actually of his half-sister, Octavia the elder. Appuleia was also sister of the consul of
A.D. 14 (1.7.2).

82. The "connection of Caesar's" is of course Appuleia herself. Either her father, Sex.
Appuleius (consul in 29 B.C.), or her grandfather is depicted on the Ara Pacis.

83. The "Julian law concerning adultery" (Lex Iulia de adulteriis) of 18 or 17 B.C.

84. See 1.77.3n. Haterius' father (1.13.4n.) had married a daughter of Agrippa, one of
whose other daughters (Agrippina) was Germanicus' wife.

85. The Lex Papia Poppaea of A.D. 9 (see 3.25.1, 28.3–4).

the Roman camp, but later a deserter—at first formed a troop of rovers, accustomed to banditry, for plunder and seizure; then he arranged them by detachments and squadrons in military fashion; finally he was recognized as being leader

2   not of an unorganized crowd but of the Musulamii. This effective people—close to the solitudes of Africa and even then having no form of urban lifestyle—took up arms and drew the neighboring Mauri into the war. They too had a leader, Mazippa; and the army was divided so that Tacfarinas should detain selected men, armed in the Roman way, in camp and accustom them to discipline and commands, while Mazippa with a light force should spread burning, slaughter, and

3   terror. And they had driven the Cinithii (a nation not to be spurned) to the same activities, when Furius Camillus as proconsul of Africa conducted toward the enemy the single battalion which he had produced by combining his legion with the allied elements that were under the standards—only a modest unit, if you looked at the multitude of Numidians and Mauri, but his primary concern was that they should not evade war through dread:[86] by hoping for victory they were induced to be vanquished.

4   So it was that the legion was placed in the middle, the light cohorts and two wings on the edges. And Tacfarinas did not in fact decline the fight. The Numidians were routed, and after many years military prestige was procured for the

5   name Furius. (After that famous recoverer of the City and his son Camillus, [87] praise for commanders had gone to other families, and the man whom we are recalling was regarded as inexperienced in war.) All the more readily did Tiberius celebrate his achievements before the senate; and the fathers decreed triumphal insignia, something which Camillus, owing to the modesty of his life, enjoyed with impunity.

★   ★   ★

53   The following year had as its consuls Tiberius for a third time and Germanicus for a second. But Germanicus entered upon his office at Nicopolis, a city in Achaea, to which he had journeyed down the Illyrian coast after visiting his brother Drusus, resident in Dalmatia, and having endured a troublesome voyage

2   of the Adriatic and then of the Ionian Sea. He therefore spent a few days repairing his fleet; at the same time he went to the bays renowned for their Actian victory and, enshrined by Augustus, the trophies, and the encampment of Antonius,

---

86. I.e., Camillus was concerned that the enemy, if confronted by a large Roman force, might take fright and decline battle. M. Furius Camillus had been consul in A.D. 8.

87. The famous M. Furius Camillus defeated the Gauls in 390 B.C.; his son was L. Furius Camillus (consul in 349 B.C.), but T. is thought to have confused him with the homonymous grandson of the famous Camillus (consul in 338, 325 B.C.).

everywhere accompanied by the recollection of his own ancestors.[88] For, as I have recalled,[89] Augustus had been his great-uncle and Antonius his grandfather; and vivid was the vision there of sadness and delight. From here the journey was to Athens, and his concession to our treaty with this allied and olden city was that he used only one lictor. The Greeks welcomed him with the choicest offices, parading the old deeds and words of their people so that their sycophancy might have more dignity.   3

Making next for Euboea, he crossed to Lesbos, where Agrippina in her latest **54** childbirth produced Julia. Then it was the edge of Asia, and Perinthus and Byzantium, Thracian cities; soon he entered the narrows of the Propontis and the Pontic mouth, in his desire to become acquainted with old places celebrated by fame; but at the same time he regenerated provinces exhausted by internal conflicts or magistrates' injustices. Striving to visit the rituals of the Samothracians[90] on his return, he was driven off course by an encounter with northerly winds. Therefore, after going to Ilium and the venerable places there which have experienced such variation in fortune and from which our own origins derive,[91] he again skirted Asia and moored at Colophon to avail himself of the oracle of Clarian Apollo. It is not a female there (as at Delphi) but a priest, summoned from certain families (and usually from Miletus), who hears but the number and names of the consultants; then, descending into a cave, he swallows water from a mysterious spring and, despite a general ignorance of literature and poetry, produces replies in accomplished verse on the matters which individuals have conceived of only in their mind. And it was said that he prophesied for Germanicus—in ambiguities, as is the custom with oracles—a timely departure.[92]   4

As for Cn. Piso, to hasten the start of his designs he berated the community of **55** the Athenians—already terrified by his turbulent entrance—in a savage speech, delivering a glancing blow at Germanicus on the grounds that, contrary to the dignity of the Roman name, he had, with excessive affability, paid court not to Athenians, who after so many disasters were extinct, but to that famous cesspit

---

88. For a map of the Battle of Actium (31 B.C.), showing Mark Antony's camp(s), see *CAH*² 10.60. Nicopolis (above: lit. "Victory City") was established by Augustus to commemorate his famous victory; for his extraordinary display of trophies see W. M. Murray and P. M. Petsas, *Octavian's Campsite Memorial for the Actian War* (Philadelphia 1989).

89. At 2.43.5.

90. A reference to the mystery religion of the Cabiri (e.g., Herodotus 2.51.3): see *OCD* 267 and 1352 s.vv. Cabiri and Samothrace.

91. Ilium was built on the site of Troy, a standard example of the reversal of fortune and the place from where Aeneas, legendary founder of Rome, set off on his journey to Italy.

92. The ambiguities are impossible to reproduce in English. The adjective *maturum* can mean both "occurring *at* the proper time" and "occurring *before* the proper time"; and, though the manuscript here has *exitium* ("extermination"), some scholars prefer to read *exitum*, which means "departure" or "death" (whether natural or otherwise) and is the word used by Germanicus himself in his last speech at 2.71.1 below.

of nations:[93] these were the allies of Mithridates against Sulla, he said, of Anto-
2   nius against Divine Augustus![94] He also hurled old imputations (their inauspicious actions against the Macedonians, their violence against themselves),[95]
being offended at the city on account of personal anger too, because despite his
pleas they would not give up a certain Theophilus, condemned for forgery by
the Arean court.[96]
3   Thereafter, by a fast voyage through the Cyclades and shortcuts across the sea,
Piso caught up with Germanicus at the island of Rhodes; the latter was not unaware of the assaults of which he had been the target, but he acted with such forbearance that, when a storm arose, sweeping his antagonist against cliffs, and his
demise could have been attributed to hazard, he dispatched triremes to help res-
4   cue him from his plight. And yet Piso was not softened: scarcely enduring a day's
5   delay, he took his leave of Germanicus and forestalled him. And, after he reached
Syria and its legions, by lavishness and favoritism and by helping the lowest of
the maniple regulars (since he removed the old centurions and strict tribunes and
assigned their places to his own clients or to the basest elements, allowing inertia in the camp, license in the cities, and the soldiery to rove recklessly across the
countryside) he actually reached such a degree of corruption that in common
6   conversation he was held to be "the legions' parent."[97] Nor did Plancina keep
herself within female proprieties but participated in cavalry exercises and the
marches-past of cohorts, and hurled insults at Agrippina and Germanicus—some
even of the good soldiers being ready for wicked compliance with her, because
there had spread a concealed rumor that such developments were not contrary
to the Commander's will.
        All this was known to Germanicus, but turning his attention to the Armeni-
56 ans was a more immediate concern. They have been an ambiguous race from ancient times, both in the instincts of the people and in their country's situation,
since, extending a broad frontier along our provinces, they stretch deep into the

93. Until Augustus put an end to the practice, Athens had been notorious for allowing
persons to buy its citizenship.

94. The references are respectively to the First Mithridatic War (87/86 B.C.) and Actium (2.53.2n., above).

95. Piso refers to Athens' relations with Philip II during the greater part of his reign
(359–336 B.C.) and perhaps to the oligarchic regimes of the Four Hundred in 411 B.C.
and of the Thirty in 404–403 B.C., though the latter references are by no means clear.

96. I.e., the famous Areopagus (*OCD* 151–2), which T. characteristically avoids nam-
ing.

97. Compare *SCPP* 52–7 "he [Piso] had destroyed the military discipline established by
the divine Augustus and maintained by Ti. Caesar Aug., not only by allowing soldiers not
to obey in the traditional manner those in command of them, but also by giving dona-
tives in his own name from the *fiscus* of our Princeps, a deed which, he was pleased to see,
led to some soldiers being called 'Pisonians,' others 'Caesarians,' and by going on to con-
fer distinctions on those who, after usurping such a name, had shown him obedience."

Medes: they are interposed between, and more often disaffected toward, these greatest of empires, with hatred for the Romans and resentment of the Parthian. They did not have a king at this period, Vonones having been removed;[98] but the   2 nation's goodwill inclined towards Zeno (son of the Pontic king, Polemon), because from his earliest infancy he had emulated the customs and style of the Armenians and, by hunting and banquets and the other celebrations which barbarians have, he had bound aristocrats and plebs alike to himself. So Germani-   3 cus in the city of Artaxata, to the approval of the nobles and with the multitude streaming around, placed the royal insignia on his head; everyone else in veneration hailed him as King Artaxias, nomenclature which they had bestowed on him from the name of the city. (As for the Cappadocians, converted to the sta-   4 tus of a province, they received Q. Veranius as legate;[99] and there was a diminution in certain elements of the royal taxation, so that the Roman empire might be expected to be more indulgent. Q. Servaeus was placed over the Commageni, that being the first time they were transferred to the jurisdiction of a praetor.)

The favorable settlement of everything relating to the allies did not find Ger-   **57** manicus thereby delighted—on account of the haughtiness of Piso, who, ordered to lead (either personally or by means of his son) part of the legions to Armenia, had disregarded each alternative. Finally at Cyrrus, at the winter camp of the   2 Tenth Legion, they met—with fixed expressions, Piso's against betraying any dread, Germanicus' lest he be considered threatening. And in fact (as I have recorded) he was inclined to clemency, but his friends, astute at inflaming his sense of offense, let fly with the truth, heaped up falsehoods, and in various ways incriminated Piso, Plancina, and their sons. At last, in the presence of a few of   3 their establishments, Caesar began a conversation such as is born of dissembling and anger, while Piso replied with truculent pleas. They parted in open hatred.

After this, Piso was rarely on Caesar's tribunal and, on the few occasions when he sat by him, was glowering and openly dissenting. And during a party at the   4 residence of the Nabataeans' king, when golden crowns of considerable weight were offered to Caesar and Agrippina, and lighter ones to Piso and the rest, his voice was heard saying that the banquet was being given for the son of the Roman princeps, not that of the Parthian king; and at the same time he flung away his crown and added a tirade against luxuriousness—all of which, despite its bitterness, Germanicus tolerated nevertheless.

During these events legates came from the king of the Parthians, Artabanus.   **58** He had sent them to recall the treaty of friendship,[100] and he desired the pledges to be renewed, he said, and as a concession to Germanicus' honor he would advance to the bank of the Euphrates; meanwhile he was asking that Vonones

98. See 2.4.3 above. The achievement of Germanicus which T. describes in this chapter was commemorated later on the coinage (see Braund 625 = WM 6).

99. Veranius was a friend and supporter of Germanicus (2.74.2, 3.10.1–19.1); his son became consul in 49 (12.5.1) and governor of Britain (14.29.1 and n.).

100. I.e., that established by Augustus and Phraates: see 2.1.2 above.

should not be kept in Syria[101] nor use messengers from nearby to draw the aris-
2   tocrats of the various races into discord. To this Germanicus replied handsomely
concerning the alliance of Romans and Parthians, and with decorum and modesty concerning the arrival of the king and his courting of himself. Vonones was
removed to Pompeiopolis, a maritime city in Cilicia: this was not only a concession to the plea of Artabanus but an insult for Piso, by whom he was extremely
favored on account of the very many duties and gifts with which he had bound
Plancina to himself.[102]

★ ★ ★

59   With M. Silanus and L. Norbanus as consuls,[103] Germanicus departed for Egypt
to become acquainted with antiquity. But his pretext was concern for the
province, and he alleviated the prices of crops by opening storehouses and he
adopted many habits welcome to the public—walking around without soldiery,
his feet uncovered, and in an attire identical with that of the Greeks, in emula-
tion of P. Scipio, who we have heard used to do the same things on Sicily, al-
2   though the war with the Poeni was still blazing.[104] Tiberius, after a mildly
scathing reference to his style and clothing, berated him very sharply because,
contrary to the established usage of Augustus, he had gone into Alexandria with-
3   out the princeps's consent. (Augustus, among other mysteries of his despotism,
forbade senators or illustrious Roman equestrians to enter except with permission, thereby isolating Egypt in order that no pressure should be exerted on Italy
by starvation, whoever it might be who occupied the province and the gateways
60   to it by land and sea with a garrison, however light, against mighty armies.) But
Germanicus, having not yet discovered that his departure was being censured,
traveled up the Nile, starting from the town of Canopus.[105] (It was founded by
the Spartans on account of the burial there of Canopus, ship's helmsman at the
time when Menelaus, making his way back to Greece,[106] was thrown off course
2   onto a different sea and the land of Libya.) Thence to the stream's next mouth,

101. See 2.4.3 above.

102. For Piso and Vonones compare *SCPP* 38–45.

103. M. Junius Silanus Torquatus, not mentioned again by T., married Aemilia Lepida (a
great-granddaughter of Augustus) and produced five children, all of them featuring in the
Annals: M. Junius Silanus (consul in 46: 13.1.1), D. Junius Silanus Torquatus (consul in 53:
12.58.1), L. Junius Silanus (12.3.2), Junia Lepida (16.8.2), and Junia Calvina (12.4.1–2).
L. Norbanus Balbus was brother of the consul of 15 (1.55.1).

104. P. Cornelius Scipio Africanus in 204 B.C. (Livy 29.19.11–13).

105. Part of a speech which Germanicus delivered at Alexandria, adjacent to Canopus,
has survived (Sherk 34A, p. 60 = Braund 557).

106. From the Trojan War.

dedicated to Hercules, who the natives maintain was born among them and is the most ancient one, whereas those who afterward matched his valor were merely assimilated into his nomenclature.[107] Then he visited the vast vestiges of old Thebes. And on the massive structures there remained Egyptian letters, sum- 3
marizing its former wealthiness: one of the priests' elders, ordered to interpret his native language, reported that seven hundred thousand men of military age had once lived there and that with that army King Rhamses—having gained control of Libya, Ethiopia, and the Medes and Persians, the Bactrian and Scythian, and the lands which the Syrians, Armenians, and adjacent Cappadocians inhabit— had held under his command the area from the Bithynian sea on the one side to the Lycian on the other.[108] Also read out were the taxes imposed on various 4
peoples, the weight of silver and gold, the number of weapons and horses, and gifts of ivory and perfumes to the temples, and the amounts of grain and of all the co- mestibles which each nation paid—contributions no less magnificent than those that are now at the bidding of the Parthians' might or Roman powerfulness.

Yet Germanicus directed his attention to other marvels too, the principal of **61**
which were the stone likeness of Memnon, rendering, when struck by the rays of the sun, a voice's sound;[109] and, amid the drifting and almost impassable sands, the pyramids raised up like mountains by the rivalry of wealthy kings; and the lake dug out of the ground as receptacle for the overflow of the Nile;[110] and else- where its narrows and profound depths, their penetrability beyond the range of all explorers.[111] Thereafter the journey was to Elephantine and Syene, once the 2
gateways of the Roman empire, which now extends to the Red Sea.[112]

While that season was spent by Germanicus across several provinces,[113] it was **62**
no trivial prestige which Drusus acquired by enticing the Germans into discord

107. See Herodotus 2.43–5.

108. The ruler is evidently Ramesses II (1304–1237 B.C.). The two seas are presumably the Black Sea and the northeastern Mediterranean and are a way of referring to the whole of Asia Minor.

109. Memnon was the Greek identification of the huge statue at Medinet Habu which was in fact of Amenophis III (c. 1417–1379 B.C.).

110. Lake Moeris (Herodotus 2.149–50).

111. The "profound depths" are usually explained by reference to the story of Psam- metichus, who tried to plumb the Nile with a rope (Herodotus 2.28.4–5); but that would require the text to be emended, since *spatiis* (which I have translated as "range") cannot mean "lengths of rope."

112. This is a much disputed sentence. Since "red sea" in Latin can mean either our Red Sea or the Persian Gulf, scholars have debated both the precise extent of the Roman em- pire at the time that T. was writing ("now") and the interrelated question of when that time was. In my view T. means our Red Sea and was writing this passage no later than A.D. 114.

113. Under the present season only Egypt has been mentioned, not "several provinces." For this and other reasons J. Steup in 1869 proposed to move chapters 62–7 and insert

and, with Maroboduus now broken, to press on for his actual extermination.

2   There was among the Gotones a young noble by the name of Catualda, once a refugee from the might of Maroboduus and now, with the latter's affairs in doubt, daring his revenge. With a substantial unit he entered the territory of the Marcomanni and, corrupting their chiefs into an alliance, made an irruption into

3   the palace and the stronghold situated nearby. There they discovered old plunder of the Suebi and, from our provinces, camp followers and businessmen, each of whom had been transplanted from his own abode to enemy soil by the right of trade, then by the desire of increasing his money, and finally by forgetfulness of his fatherland.

63   Maroboduus, deserted on all sides, had no other recourse than Caesar's pity. Crossing the Danube where it flows past the province of Noricum, he wrote to Tiberius—not as a refugee or suppliant but in mindfulness of his previous fortune: with many nations inviting the once brilliant king to go to them, he said,

2   it was Roman friendship which he had preferred. The reply from Caesar was that there would be a safe and honorable abode for him in Italy if he were to remain there; but, if something else suited his affairs, he could depart with the same trust

3   as he had come. Yet before the senate he said that Philip had not been a source of such dread to the Athenians, nor Pyrrhus or Antiochus to the Roman people.[114] There survives a speech in which he emphasized the greatness of the man, the violence of the races subject to him, how close to Italy he had been as

4   an enemy, and his own plans in his destruction. Maroboduus for his part was held at Ravenna and, in case the Suebi ever became overbearing, the prospect of his likely return to his kingdom was held out; but in fact he did not leave Italy in eighteen years and grew old with his brilliance much diminished by his exces-

5   sive desire for living. Catualda had the same fate and no different a refuge: beaten not much later by the might of the Hermunduri under the leadership of Vibilius, he was welcomed and sent to Forum Julium, a colony of Narbonese Gaul.

6   Lest the barbarians accompanying each man should infiltrate the provinces and disrupt their tranquillity, they were situated beyond the Danube between the rivers Marus and Cusus and were given Vannius as king, of the race of the Quadi.

64   On the announcement at the same time that King Artaxias had been given to the Armenians by Germanicus,[115] the fathers decreed that Germanicus and Drusus should enter the City to an ovation. Arches too were put up around the sides of the temple of Mars the Avenger, together with a likeness of the Caesars, Tiberius being more delighted that he had consolidated peace by wisdom than

---

them between chapters 58 and 59, the effect of which is to transpose events in Germany and Thrace to the preceding year, A.D. 18.

114. For Philip see above, 2.55.2n.; for the campaigns of Pyrrhus, king of Epirus, in 280 B.C. and the following years see *OCD* 1283; for those of Antiochus III in 190/189 B.C. (again at 3.61.2, 4.56.1, and 12.62) see *OCD* 108 and 912, s.vv. Antiochus (3) and Magnesia (battle of).

115. See 2.56.3 above.

if he had concluded war through battles. Therefore he adopted a strategic ap-   2
proach to Rhescuporis too, the king of Thrace.

That nation in its entirety had been held by Rhoemetalces. On his decease,
Augustus granted some of the Thracians to Rhescuporis, his brother, and some
to his son, Cotys:[116] in that division, the plow land, cities, and areas bordering on
the Greeks fell to Cotys; the uncultivated part, defiant and adjoining their enemies, to Rhescuporis. And as for the temperaments of the kings themselves, the
former's was mild and attractive, the latter's grisly, greedy, and intolerant of partnership. Yet at first they acted with beguiling harmony; then Rhescuporis ex-   3
ceeded his boundaries, turned over to himself what had been given to Cotys,
and, on the latter's resistance, offered force—but only hesitantly under Augustus,
since he dreaded that the architect of each kingdom would, if spurned, turn
avenger. However, on hearing of the change of princeps, he sent in groups of
bandits and extirpated strongholds—reasons for war.

Nothing made Tiberius tense so much as the possible disruption of a settle-   65
ment. He picked a centurion to announce to the kings that their differences
should not involve armed conflict. And at once Cotys dismissed the auxiliaries
he had procured; but Rhescuporis, only fabricating deference, demanded they   2
should meet at a given place: their disagreement, he said, could be managed by
dialogue. There was no long uncertainty over the time, place, and conditions,
since all the mutual concessions and acceptances were made with complaisance
by the one and with cunning by the other. Rhescuporis added a dinner party   3
to sanction (as he insisted) their treaty; and, with its delights protracted into the
late night, Cotys was quite unsuspecting because of the banqueting and wine-
bibbing; it was only after he realized the trick that—despite appealing to the sanctity of kingship, to the gods of their single family, and to his own place as a guest
at table—he was weighed down with chains.

Having taken control of Thrace in its entirety, Rhescuporis wrote to Tiberius   4
that an ambush had been laid for him and his ambusher forestalled. (At the
same time, putting forward as pretext a war against the Bastarnae and Scythians,
he consolidated himself with new forces of infantry and cavalry.) It was gently   5
replied that, if there had been no deception, he could depend on his innocence; but neither the princeps himself nor the senate would decide the justice
or injustice of the case without having investigated it: accordingly, having
delivered up Cotys, he should come and devolve the resentment of the charge.[117]
That letter was sent to Thrace by Latinius Pandusa, propraetor of Moesia, along   66

116. Rhoemetalces had died c. A.D. 12, having ruled Thrace for over twenty years. Cotys is the addressee of Ovid, *Epist. ex Ponto* 2.9.

117. The meaning of this last sentence is not at all clear. It may perhaps be inferred from
Tiberius' reference to "deception" (above) that the "charge" is of Rhescuporis' having deceived and captured an innocent Cotys (as was in fact the case). Rhescuporis has incurred
"resentment" (so Tiberius implies) because the charge was thought to be true; but, by
coming to Rome, Rhescuporis can prove the charge untrue and thus transfer the resent-

with the soldiers to whom Cotys should be delivered; but Rhescuporis, hesitating between dread and anger, preferred to be guilty of an act accomplished rather than one merely begun: he ordered Cotys to be slaughtered, and lied that his

2 death had been chosen voluntarily. Yet Caesar nevertheless did not change practices once they found favor with him: on the decease of Pandusa, whom Rhescuporis had been criticizing for hostility toward himself, Pomponius Flaccus, a veteran of campaigns and (given his close friendship with the king) all the more appropriate to deceive him, was placed—mainly for that reason—in charge of Moesia.

67   Flaccus, crossing into Thrace, by means of huge promises prevailed upon Rhescuporis, who was nevertheless of two minds and reflecting on his crimes, to go inside the Roman garrison. The king on entering[+] was surrounded by a substantial unit in a display of honor; and tribunes and centurions—by warnings, persuasion, and a form of custody the more obvious the farther away they went—

2 dragged to the City a man who was now finally aware of the inevitable. Accused in the senate by Cotys' wife, he was condemned to be held far from his kingdom. Thrace was divided between his son Rhoemetalces, who was agreed to have opposed his father's plans, and the children of Cotys;[118] and, since they were not yet mature, Trebellenus Rufus (a former praetor) was provided to handle the kingdom in the meantime, on the example of M. Lepidus, whom our ancestors

3 had sent to Egypt as guardian to Ptolemy's children.[119] Rhescuporis was conveyed to Alexandria and there, attempting flight or on a fabricated charge, was killed.

68   During the same period Vonones, whose removal to Cilicia I have recalled,[120] after bribing his guards tried to flee to the Armenians and thence to the Albani, the Heniochi, and his kinsman, the king of the Scythians. In a pretense of hunting he neglected maritime areas, making for trackless denes; then, taking advantage of the speed of his horse, he hastened to the Pyramus stream, whose bridges the locals had destroyed on hearing of the king's flight; nor were there shallows

2 where it could be forded. So it was on the bank of the river that he was bound by Vibius Fronto, prefect of the cavalry; then Remmius, a senior soldier who had been assigned to the king's guard previously, transfixed him with a sword as if in anger. Hence greater credit for the belief that it was through complicity in his crime and dread of the evidence that death had been inflicted on Vonones.[121]

---

ment to Cotys (for having tried to ambush Rhescuporis). But such an interpretation is admittedly not the only one possible.

118. Their names were Rhoemetalces, Polemon, and Cotys.

119. The references are to M. Aemilius Lepidus (consul in 187 and 175 B.C.) and Ptolemy V Epiphanes, but whether there is any truth in the story is debated.

120. At 2.58.2 above.

121. The belief in question was that Remmius had been instrumental in helping Vonones to escape and, afraid of being found out, had killed him.

As for Germanicus, on retiring from Egypt he realized that everything which   **69**
he had ordered in the cases of the legions and cities had been annulled or changed
to the opposite. Hence weighty insults for Piso, and no less bitterness aimed⁺ by
the latter against Caesar. Next Piso decided to leave Syria. But subsequently he   2
was detained by Germanicus' adverse health; then, when he heard of his recovery and vows were being paid for his preservation, he used lictors to thrust aside
the waiting victims,[122] the sacrificial accoutrements, the festive plebs of the Antiochians. Then he departed for Seleucia, waiting upon the illness which again
had befallen Germanicus. The savage violence of the disease was increased by his   3
conviction that he had been given poison by Piso; and in fact there were discovered, unearthed from the ground and walls, remains of human bodies, spells and
curses and the name "Germanicus" etched on lead tablets,[123] half-burned ashes
smeared with putrid matter, and other malefic devices by which it is believed
that souls are consecrated to the infernal divinities. At the same time envoys from
Piso were censured for probing the adverse state of his health.

All this was heard by Germanicus with as much anger as dread: if his thresh-   **70**
old were blockaded, if his breath had to drain away under the eyes of his antagonist, what then would be the outcome for his pitiable wife, for his infant
children? Poisoning seemed slow to act: Piso was wasting no time and was pressing for sole possession of the province, of the legions. But Germanicus had not
weakened as much as that, nor would the prizes for his slaughter remain with his
killer! He composed a letter in which he renounced their friendship (many people   2
add that he was ordered to withdraw from the province);[124] Piso, without delaying any further, cast off his ships—and moderated his course to reduce the distance
of his return journey, should the death of Germanicus leave Syria open.

Caesar was roused briefly to hope, but then, with his body exhausted, and   **71**
when the end was approaching, he addressed in this way his friends standing by:
"If I were succumbing to fate, my indignation even at the gods would be justified, for snatching me—in my youth, by a premature departure—from parents,
children, and fatherland. As it is, I have been cut off by Piso's and Plancina's crime,
leaving these as my last prayers in your hearts: relay to my father and brother the
embitterments with which I have been tormented, the snares by which I have
been surrounded, as I end my most pitiable life by the worst of deaths. Anyone   2
who was moved by my hopes, by kindred blood, even by resentment toward me
during my lifetime—they will shed tears that a once flourishing survivor of so
many wars has fallen to womanly foul play. But it is you who will have the chance
of complaining before the senate, of invoking the laws. It is not the principal re-   3

122. Sacrificial animals standing by the altars.

123. So-called "curse tablets," a prominent feature of ancient life (*OCD* 414–5).

124. The allegation that Piso was ordered by Germanicus to leave Syria conflicts both
with T.'s own statement above (2.69.1 "Piso decided to leave Syria") and with *SCPP* 47–9
"the province of Syria which he had abandoned while Germanicus was still alive—a deed
wicked both in its intent and in the example it provided."

sponsibility of friends to serve the deceased by means of idle complaints but to remember his wishes and to observe his instructions. Germanicus will be wept for even by strangers; but it is you who will avenge him, if it was me rather than

4   my fortune that you befriended. Show to the Roman people the granddaughter of Divine Augustus, who is likewise my spouse; count out our six children. Pity will be on the side of the accusers; and those fabricating criminal instructions

5   will either not be believed by men or not forgiven." His friends, touching the right hand of the dying man, swore that they would sooner give up breath than revenge.

72   Then, turning to his wife, he begged her, by her memory of him, by their mutual children, to cast aside her defiance, to submit her spirit to the savagery of fortune, and not, on her return to the City, to goad her superiors in power by rivaling them for it. These words openly; others were in secret, by which he was

2   believed to have shown dread of Tiberius. And not long afterward his life was extinguished,[125] to the mighty grief of the province and its surrounding peoples. Foreign nations and kings felt the pain, such had been his affability to allies, forbearance to enemies. Venerated equally by those who beheld and heard him, he maintained the greatness and solemnity of the highest fortune, while escaping its resentment and arrogance.

73   The funeral, though without images and procession,[126] was well attended by the praise and remembrance of his virtues. And there were those by whom his good looks, age, and manner of death were matched—on account of the prox-

2   imity too of the place of his demise—with the lot of Alexander the Great: each, of graceful physique and illustrious family, and not long after exceeding his thirtieth year, had fallen to the snares of his own people among foreign nations. But *this* man, they said, had been gentle toward his friends, moderate in his pleasures, with only one marriage and his children certain. Nor was he any less a combatant, even if he lacked temerity and had been prevented from pressing the Ger-

3   manies, though pounded by so many victories, into servitude. If he had been the sole arbiter of affairs, they said, with royal prerogative and name, he would have achieved military glory more readily, just as he excelled in clemency, restraint, and the other good qualities.

4   (Before his body was cremated, it was stripped in the forum of the Antiochians, the place which was marked out for burial; but there was no general agreement whether it presented signs of poisoning: interpretations differed according to whether one was more inclined toward Germanicus through pity and the presumption of suspicion, or toward Piso through goodwill.)

74   There was next a debate between the legates and other senators who were present as to who should be placed in charge of Syria. And, after only modest exertions from the others, for a long time the issue was between Vibius Marsus and Cn. Sentius. Then Marsus yielded to the seniority and keener contention of Sen-

125. The date was 10 October (Sherk 28C, p. 54).
126. For the procession of images see above, 2.27.2n.

tius;[127] and he for his part dispatched to the City a woman infamous for poison-   2
ings in the province and particularly dear to Plancina, by name Martina, in response to demands from Vitellius and Veranius and the rest, who were drawing up
charges and accusation as if against persons already cited as defendants.

As for Agrippina, although exhausted by grief and physically ill, but neverthe-   **75**
less intolerant of anything which might delay her revenge, she boarded a fleet accompanied by the ashes of Germanicus and by her children—to universal pity
that a lady preeminently noble, with but recently the finest marriage, and accustomed to the gaze and veneration of well-wishers, was now bearing in her lap
the remains of a burial, uncertain of revenge, tense for her own sake and exposed
so many times to fate because of her unfortunate fertility.

Piso meanwhile was overtaken at the island of Cos by the news that German-   2
icus had passed away. Hearing it unrestrainedly, he slaughtered victims,[128] visited
temples; and, while he did not moderate his own joy, Plancina was all the more
overbearing and now for the first time exchanged grief at the loss of a sister for
clothing of delight.[129] Centurions streamed up to him and advised that he had   **76**
the ready support of the legions: he should reclaim the province which had been
taken away improperly and was vacant. As he therefore debated what should be   2
done, his son M. Piso proposed that he should hurry to the City: no unpardon-
able act had yet been committed, he said, nor were weak suspicions or the inani-
ties of report much to be feared; his disaffection toward Germanicus perhaps
earned him rejection, but not punishment; and, by his being deprived of his
province, satisfaction had been rendered to his antagonists. But, if he returned   3
and Sentius stood his ground, there was the beginning of civil war; nor would
the centurions and soldiers last long on his side, since in their case the fresh memory of their commander and a deeply entrenched love for the Caesars were highly
influential.

Conversely Domitius Celer, from among his most intimate friends, said that   **77**
he should exploit the outcome: Piso, not Sentius, had been placed in charge of
Syria: to him the fasces and praetor's prerogative had been given, to him the legions! If an enemy attacked, who would more properly place his arms in the way
than the one who had received a legate's authority and personal instructions?
Also, time should be left for rumors to grow old (the innocent were generally   2
unequal to fresh resentment).[130] On the other hand, if he retained his army and

127. Epigraphic evidence shows that the appointment of Cn. Sentius Saturninus (suffect
consul in A.D. 4) was confirmed by Tiberius (Braund 795). C. Vibius Marsus had been
suffect consul in A.D. 17 and was later proconsul of Africa A.D. 27–30: on him see further
6.47.2–48.1, 11.10.1.

128. Sacrificial animals.

129. "Grief" is metonymy for Plancina's mourning clothes (above, 2.29.1n.).

130. Celer warns Piso that, if he returns to Rome now, as an innocent man he will not
be able to cope with the wave of popular resentment brought on by Germanicus' very
recent death; he should wait in Syria till things have cooled down.

increased his forces, many things which could not be foreseen would turn out
3   for the better fortuitously. "Are we really hastening to moor our ships at the same
time as the ashes of Germanicus, so that the breast-beating of Agrippina and an
impressionable public can snatch you off, unheard and undefended, at the first
rumor? You have the complicity of Augusta and the goodwill of Caesar, but in
secret; and none more vaunt their sorrow that Germanicus has perished than
those whose delight is greatest."

78   It was without great difficulty that Piso, always ready for defiance, was drawn
to this suggestion, and in a letter sent to Tiberius he censured Germanicus for
luxuriousness and haughtiness; he himself, driven out to leave the place clear for
revolution, had reclaimed his care of the army with the same loyalty as he had
2   held it. At the same time he embarked Domitius on a trireme and ordered him
to avoid coasting along the shore and to proceed past the islands on the high⁺
sea to Syria. He constituted in maniples the deserters who were converging on
him, he armed the camp followers, and, crossing his ships to the mainland, intercepted a detachment of recruits going to Syria, and wrote to the princes of
the Cilicians to help him with auxiliaries—the young Piso in no way shirking
the tasks of war, although he had disagreed with the war's undertaking.

79   So, skirting the coast of Lycia and Pamphylia, and encountering the ships
which were carrying Agrippina, both sides in their hostility at first prepared arms;
then in mutual alarm the issue advanced no further than wrangling, and Marsus
Vibius announced to Piso that he should come to Rome to plead his case. The
latter replied evasively that he would be there when the praetor who investigated
poisonings had prescribed a day for defendant and accusers.[131]
2   Meanwhile Domitius moored at Laodicea, a city in Syria, and, while he was
making for the winter camp of the Sixth Legion (because he deemed it particularly suitable for his revolutionary plans), he was forestalled by Pacuvius, the
legate. Sentius revealed this to Piso by letter and warned him neither to make an
3   attempt on the camp by bribers nor on the province by war. And he assembled
those whom he knew to revere Germanicus' memory (or at least were opposed
to his antagonists), repeatedly emphasizing the greatness of the Commander and
that the state was being claimed by arms. And he took the lead of a substantial
unit, prepared for battle.

80   Yet Piso, although his project was turning out amiss, did not neglect the safest
measures in the circumstances but occupied a stronghold in Cilicia, well fortified, the name of which was Celenderis. (By drafting in the deserters and recently
intercepted recruits and his own and Plancina's slaves, he had formed the Cili-
2   cians' auxiliaries, which the princes had sent, into a numerical legion.)[132] And he
testified that he, Caesar's legate, was being kept out of the province which Caesar had given him—and not by the legions (it was at their summons that he

131. "To prescribe a/the day (for)" is a legal expression = "to serve a summons (on)" (a
slightly different form at 4.19.2 below).
132. I.e., he had the right numbers for a legion.

came), but by Sentius, covering his private hatred by means of false charges. They
could stand in the line of battle, but the soldiers would not fight when they saw
the Piso whom they had once called "parent"[133]—better qualified, if the issue
were one of prerogative, and not ineffective, if one of arms. Then, in front of the   3
fortifications of the stronghold, he deployed his maniples on a steep and sheer
hill (the rest is encircled by sea); opposite were the veterans, drawn up in ranks
and supporting units: on the latter side was the ruggedness of the soldiers, on the
former that of the locality—but no spirit, no hope, not even weapons, except
rustic ones or those hurried into emergency use. When they came to grips, doubt   4
lasted no longer than the time it took for the Roman cohorts to struggle up to
level ground; the Cilicians turned their backs and shut themselves in the stronghold.

Meanwhile Piso tried in vain to assail the fleet waiting not far off; on his re-   **81**
turn he went along the walls and, at one moment striking himself,[134] at another
summoning individuals by name or beckoning them with rewards, he endeavored to start a mutiny, and had set things in motion to the extent that a standard-
bearer of the Sixth Legion transferred his standard to him. Then Sentius ordered   2
the horns and trumpets to sound, the embankment to be their target,[135] ladders
to be erected, and all the readiest men to move up, others to rain down spears,
rocks, and torches from launchers. At length, his tenacity defeated, Piso begged   3
that, after handing over his arms, he should remain in the stronghold until Caesar was consulted on whom he was entrusting to Syria. The conditions were not
accepted, nor was there any other concession except ships and a safe passage to
the City.

*

But at Rome, after the health of Germanicus had become current knowledge   **82**
and each successive item of news was (naturally, given the distance it had traveled) exaggerated for the worse, there was pain and anger. And complaints burst
out: that, of course, was the reason for his relegation to the farthest lands, that the
reason for Piso's being entrusted with the province! This was what Augusta's secret conversations with Plancina had done! Their elders had spoken altogether   2
truly about Drusus:[136] rulers were prone to be displeased with citizenlike instincts in their sons, and they[137] had been cut off only because they had aspired

133. See 2.55.5 and n.

134. I.e., beating his breast.

135. Or perhaps "an embankment to be fetched" (as 1.65.7); the Latin can mean either.

136. The elder Drusus, brother of Tiberius and stepson of Augustus (1.3.1); for his alleged republican sympathies see 1.33.1–2.

137. Viz., the elder Drusus and his son Germanicus, the latter being the adopted son of
Tiberius. There was a story (not in T.) that the former had been poisoned by Augustus
(Suetonius, *Claudius* 1.4).

to incorporate the Roman people under equal rights, with freedom restored.
3   These conversations of the public were so inflamed by the news of his death that, before an edict from the magistrates, before the senate's decision, a recess[138] was adopted and the forums deserted, houses shut. Everywhere was silence and groaning, nothing was contrived for show; and, although they did not abstain from the insignia of the grieving,[139] they sorrowed more deeply in their hearts.
4   By chance some businessmen, having left Syria while Germanicus was still alive, brought more welcome news about his health. It was immediately believed, immediately publicized: as individuals met, each passed to others what he had heard (however uncritically), and they in their turn to more people, with a further joyful accretion. They ran through the City, set to work on the doors of the
5   temples; nighttime aided belief, and assurance was readier in the darkness. Nor did Tiberius block the falsehoods, until they vanished with the passage of time. And the people's pain was the keener, as if he had been snatched away again.

83   Honors, corresponding to the strength of each man's love for Germanicus or of his ingenuity, were devised and decreed:[140] that his name should be sung in the Saliarian song;[141] curule seats set up in the places of the Augustal priests, and, above them, oaken crowns; an ivory likeness of him should precede at the circus games; no flamen or augur should be created in Germanicus' place unless from
2   the Julian family. Arches were added, at Rome and on the bank of the Rhine and on the Amanus, a mountain in Syria, with an inscription of his achievements and to the effect that he had met his death for the state; there was to be a sepulchre at Antioch, where he had been cremated, and a tribunal at Epidaphna, the place in which he had ended his life. Of the statues and places in which he was to be
3   worshiped, no one could easily arrive at the number. When they proposed that a shield, distinctive for its gold and size, be placed among the authors of eloquence, Tiberius asserted that he would dedicate a normal one, identical to the rest: eloquence was not differentiated on the ground of fortune, he said, and it was illustrious enough if he were recognized as being among the writers of
4   old.[142] The equestrian order gave the name "Germanicus' Block" to that which

138. See 1.16.2n.

139. See above, 2.29.1n.

140. Extensive but partial copies of the original decree have survived (see Sherk 36A–B).

141. The Salii were a fellowship of priests (*OCD* 1348) whose ritual song or hymn was unintelligible even in antiquity (*OCD* 292–3). See Sherk 36B, lines 5–6 (= Braund 115, end of first paragraph).

142. See esp. Sherk 36B, lines 1–4 "And [sc. it has pleased the senate] that on the Palatine in the portico by the temple of Apollo, in which the senate is accustomed to meet, amid the images of men of illustrious character shall be placed those of Germanicus Caesar and Drusus Germanicus, his natural father and brother of Tiberius Caesar Augustus, who [i.e., Drusus] was himself of creative ability" (= Braund 115, start of first paragraph; also above, 2.37.2n). When T. says (above) that the senators had originally proposed "a

had been called "The Juniors',"[143] and established that on the Ides of July the
squadrons should follow his image.[144] Many of these things remain; some were
abandoned immediately or obliterated by age.

Yet, while the general sorrowfulness was still fresh, Germanicus' sister Livia,   **84**
who was wedded to Drusus, gave birth simultaneously to two children of the
male sex[145]—a rarity which, welcome even to modest hearths, affected the princeps with such joy that he did not restrain himself from boasting in front of the
fathers that, of the Romans before, no man of the same eminence had been favored with the production of twin stock (everything, even the fortuitous, he
turned to glory). But to the people at such a time even that brought pain, as   2
though Drusus' increase in children were further pressure on the house of Germanicus.

In the same year weighty senate's decrees ensured that the lust of females was   **85**
curbed and measures taken that no one should make a profit from her body
whose grandfather or father or husband was a Roman equestrian.[146] Vistilia, off-   2
spring of a praetorian family,[147] had published with the aediles her availability
for illicit sex—adopting a custom among the ancients, who believed that sufficient punishment against immoral women lay in the actual confession of their
outrage. It was demanded also of Titidius Labeo, Vistilia's husband, why he had   3
neglected the vengeance of the law in the case of a wife clearly culpable of a
felony. Since he for his part was putting forward as his explanation that the sixty
days given for deliberation had not yet passed, it seemed sufficient to determine
only about Vistilia; and she was removed to the island of Seriphos.

There was discussion also about banishing Egyptian and Jewish rites, and there   4
was passed a fathers' decision that four thousand of the freedman class, who had
been tainted by such superstition and whose age was suitable, should be transported to the island of Sardinia to curb banditry there, and, if they died owing to
the oppressiveness of the climate, it was a cheap loss; the rest should withdraw from
Italy, unless before a certain day they had discarded their profane ceremonies.

---

shield" for Germanicus, he means a particular type of portrait or "image" (above, 2.27.2n.)
which was painted on a shield and thought esp. suitable for military men.

143. The Roscian law of 67 B.C. famously reserved the first fourteen rows at the theater
for the equestrians (see 6.3.1, 15.32); it seems that subsequently these rows had been divided into blocks for "juniors" and "seniors."

144. At the annual parade or march-past of equestrians on 15 July, a ceremony which
Augustus had revived (*OCD* 552), the men were divided into "squadrons."

145. Tiberius Gemellus ("Twin"), killed by Caligula in 37/38, and Germanicus, who dies
in 23 (4.15.1).

146. Compare Sherk 35, lines 5–6 and n. 1 (= Braund 724).

147. For her father see 6.9.2; he had a sister, also called Vistilia (5.8.1n., 11.18.1n.), who
was thus this woman's aunt.

86   After this Caesar moved that a Virgin should be appointed in place of Occia, who for fifty-seven years had presided with the utmost sanctity over the Vestal rites; and he expressed gratitude to Fonteius Agrippa and Comicius Pollio because, by offering their daughters, they were competing in their obligations to-

2   ward the state. Pollio's daughter was preferred, for no other reason than that her mother remained in the same marriage (Agrippa by divorce had diminished his family). And Caesar consoled the other for being passed over by a dowry of a million sesterces.

87   With the plebs censuring the savagery of the supply rates, he established the price for grain which the buyer should pay, and, for the businessmen, he himself would add two sesterces for each individual measure.[148] Yet he did not on that account adopt the designation "Parent of the Fatherland," which had been tendered before too,[149] and he bitterly berated those who had called his occupations "divine" and himself "Master." Hence speech was confined and slippery under a princeps who dreaded liberty but hated sycophancy.

88   I discover among writers[+] of those same times that a letter of Adgandestrius, princeps of the Chatti, was read out in the senate, in which he promised Arminius' death if poison for accomplishing the execution were sent to him; and the reply was that the Roman people took vengeance on their enemies not by foul play or concealment but openly and armed. (By this glorification Tiberius was matching himself with the old-time commanders who had prohibited the

2   use of poison against King Pyrrhus and betrayed it.)[150] Nevertheless Arminius, who on the Romans' withdrawal and Maroboduus' banishment was aspiring to kingship, had opposition from his compatriots' love of liberty and became the target of their arms, and, while his struggle with them was meeting with variable fortune, he fell to the cunning of his kinsmen. The liberator of Germany without doubt, and one who challenged not the formative stages of the Roman people, like other kings and leaders, but the empire at its most flourishing, equivocal in

3   battles but not defeated in war, he consummated thirty-seven years of life, twelve of power,[151] and is still sung among barbarian races, though unknown to the annals of the Greeks, who marvel only at their own, and not celebrated duly in the Roman, since we extol the distant past, indifferent to the recent.

---

148. The measure in question was specific and is usually translated by the (now outdated) English word "peck" (= roughly nine liters).

149. See 1.72.1.

150. This story is told of C. Fabricius (consul in 282 and 278 B.C.) in the extant summary of the lost Book 13 of Livy; for Pyrrhus see above, 2.63.3n.

151. If Arminius' power did not antedate the Varian disaster in A.D. 9, as seems likely, "twelve" years would place his death in 21 and not here in 19, as T. has it.

BOOK 3

Without having interrupted her voyage on the wintry sea, Agrippina reached the **1**
island of Corcyra, situated opposite the shores of Calabria.[1] There she spent a few
days composing her mind, violent in her grief as she was and unfamiliar with enduring. Meanwhile on the news of her arrival all her most intimate friends and **2**
numerous military men who had each done service under Germanicus, and many
unknowns too from neighboring municipalities (some deeming it their duty to
the princeps, the majority following them), rushed to the town of Brundisium,
which for a voyager was the quickest and trustiest for mooring. And, the first mo- **3**
ment the fleet was seen out at sea, not only the harbor and inshore waters but the
walls and roofs and wherever afforded the farthest view filled up with a crowd of
the sorrowful, asking one another repeatedly whether to receive her disembarka-
tion in silence or with some utterance or other. And there was still no sufficient
agreement as to what suited the occasion, when the fleet gradually neared—not
with eager rowing, as is customary, but with everything composed for sadness.
When, on disembarking from the ship with her two children[2] and holding the fu- **4**
neral urn, she cast her eyes downward, there was the same groan from everyone
and you could not distinguish relatives from others, the breast-beating of men or
women, except that Agrippina's company, exhausted by its long sorrow, was outstripped by those meeting her and fresh to the pain.

Caesar had sent two praetorian cohorts, adding that the Calabrian magistrates, **2**
and those of Apulia and Campania, should perform the last responsibilities to the
memory of his son. His ashes were therefore carried on the shoulders of tribunes **2**
and centurions; there preceded unadorned standards, reversed fasces; and, in every
colony through which they passed, the blackened plebs and purpled equestrians
cremated clothing, perfumes, and other funeral offerings in proportion to the
wealth of each place.[3] Even those from far-flung towns still came to meet them,
and, allocating victims and altars to the Shades of the Dead,[4] testified to their
pain with tears and acclamations.

Drusus proceeded to Tarracina with Germanicus' brother, Claudius, and those **3**
of his children who had been in the City.[5] The consuls M. Valerius and M.

---

1. It is not clear whether the opening of the new book coincides with the opening of
a new year: the consuls for A.D. 20 are not mentioned until 3.2.3 below.

2. Presumably Gaius (now aged seven) and Julia Livilla (2.54.1).

3. "Blackened" refers to normal funeral dress (2.29.1n.), which was also to be worn by
certain priests on anniversaries of Germanicus' death (Sherk 36A, Fragment IIa, line 3);
"purpled" refers to a distinctive garment (the *trabea*) which equestrians wore on formal
occasions, as here (Sherk 36B, lines 57–8). The cremation of clothing, etc., was standard
Roman funerary ritual.

4. For the *manes* ("spirits of the dead") see *OCD* 916–7.

5. Presumably Nero Caesar, Drusus Caesar, the younger Agrippina, and Julia Drusilla.

A.D. 20   Aurelius (they had already commenced their magistracy)[6] and the senate and a
large section of the people filled the route, scattered in disarray and weeping as
each one pleased: sycophancy was absent, everyone aware that the delight of
Tiberius at Germanicus' death was being badly dissembled.

3   Tiberius and Augusta refrained from public appearance, deeming it would be-
little their sovereignty to lament openly—or lest, with everyone's eyes examin-
2   ing their demeanor, their falsity be understood. As for his mother Antonia,
neither in the authors of affairs nor in the daily account of events[7] do I discover
that she performed any illustrious duty (although in addition to Agrippina and
Drusus and Claudius his other kinsfolk too are listed by name), whether because
she was prevented by health or because her mind, defeated by grief, could not
3   bear to endure beholding the dimension of the disaster. (I am inclined more
easily to believe that Tiberius and Augusta, who made no attempt to come out
of the house, restrained her, so it should appear that their sorrow was matching
and that it was by the mother's example that grandmother and uncle too were
held back.)[8]

4   The day on which the remains were carried into the tomb of Augustus[9] was
sometimes desolate in its silence, sometimes restless with sobbing. The streets of
the City were full, torches shining out across the Plain of Mars. There soldiers
with arms, magistrates without insignia, and the people in their tribes kept shouting that the state had collapsed and no vestige of hope remained—doing so too
readily and too obviously for you to believe that they were mindful of those in
2   command of them. Yet nothing penetrated Tiberius more than men's burning
enthusiasm for Agrippina, whom they called the glory of her fatherland, the sole
blood of Augustus, the one and only manifestation of ancient times, and, turning to heaven and the gods, they prayed that her progeny would be untouched
and would outlive those prejudiced against her.

5   There were those who missed the procession of a public funeral and compared
the honorific and magnificent things which Augustus had done for Drusus, the
father of Germanicus:[10] personally, in the roughest of winters, he had proceeded
as far as Ticinum and, staying close by the body, had entered the City along with
it; spread around the couch[11] had been images of the Claudii and Julii; he had

6. M. Valerius Messalla was son of M. Valerius Messalla Messalinus, consul in 3 B.C.
(1.8.4n.); the other consul is M. Aurelius Cotta Maximus Messalinus (2.32.1n.), the uncle of his colleague.

7. It is not known to which "authors" (= historians) T. is referring. The "daily account
[lit. writing] of events," evidently identical with "the daily record of the City" (13.31.1)
and "the journal of the Roman people" (16.22.3), seems to have been some form of gazette.

8. According to the official record, Antonia was involved in the selection of honors
for Germanicus (Sherk 36A, Fragment I, lines 6–8).

9. I.e., the mausoleum (1.8.5n.).

10. Drusus had died in 9 B.C. (1.3.3).

11. I.e., the funeral couch.

been lamented in the forum, praised before the rostra; everything devised by their ancestors, or which posterity had invented, had been heaped up. But to Germanicus had fallen not even the customary honors or those due to any noble. Of course his body, owing to the length of the various journeys, had been cremated in foreign lands in whatever manner; but it would have been only fair to grant him an even greater number of becoming tributes subsequently, given that chance had denied him his first ones. He had been met neither by his brother, except for a single day's journey, nor by his uncle even as far as the gate. Where were those established usages of the ancients? The likeness propped in front of the bier, the poems performed for the memory of virtue, and the praises and the tears—or at least the imitations of pain?

All this was known to Tiberius; and, to suppress the conversations of the public, he warned in an edict that many illustrious Romans had died for the state, but none had been celebrated with such a blazing sense of loss. And they would be doing both himself and everyone an exceptional favor if a limit were applied: what was becoming for limited households or communities was not the same as that for principes and a commanding people. Grief and the comforts of sorrow had been appropriate when their pain was fresh; but now their spirits should be restored to strength, just as formerly Divine Julius on the loss of his one and only daughter, and Divine Augustus on the seizure of his grandsons, had thrust aside their sadness.[12] There was no need of examples from more olden times, such as when the Roman people had borne steadfastly the disasters of armies, the demise of leaders, and noble families utterly lost. Principes were mortal, the state eternal. Accordingly they should revert to their usual formalities and, because the spectacle of the Megalesian Games was approaching,[13] resume even their pleasures.

Then, the recess cast aside,[14] people returned to their responsibilities, and Drusus set off for the Illyrian armies—the mind of everyone being alerted for the exacting of vengeance on Piso but[+] with frequent complaints that, as he roved meanwhile among the attractions of Asia and Achaea in an arrogant and guileful delay, he was undermining the proofs of his crimes. For it had been publicized that the life of the famed poisoner Martina, who was sent (as I said) by Cn. Sentius,[15] had been extinguished by sudden death at Brundisium, and poison had been concealed in a knot of her hair, and on her body no signs had been discovered of a self-inflicted extermination.

As for Piso, having sent his son ahead to the City and given him instructions how to soften the princeps, he proceeded to Drusus, who he hoped would be, not callous on the demise of a brother, so much as more sympathetic to himself

12. Julius Caesar's daughter Julia had died in 54 B.C., Augustus' grandsons in A.D. 2 and 4 (1.3.3 and n.).

13. Celebrated on 4–10 April in honor of the goddess Cybele.

14. The "recess," or period of mourning for Germanicus, had started at 2.82.3; see also 1.16.2n.

15. See 2.74.2.

on the removal of a rival. Tiberius, to show unprejudiced judgment, received the young man affably, enhancing him by means of the generosity customary for the
2   sons of noble families. Drusus replied to Piso that, if what was being bandied about was true, the principal one to be pained would be himself; but he would prefer it to be false and hollow, and Germanicus' death fatal to no one. These things openly, all privacy avoided; but there was no doubt that the words had been prescribed for him by Tiberius, since, being inastute otherwise and with the complaisance of youth, it was the practices of the elderly which he was then deploying.

9   Piso, having crossed the Dalmatian sea and left his ships at Ancona, traveled through Picenum and subsequently by the Flaminian Way, overtaking the legion which was being led from Pannonia to the City and thence as a garrison for Africa;[16] and the subject often discussed in rumor was how he had frequently
2   shown himself off to the soldiers on his journey with the column. From Narnia—to avoid suspicion, or because the plans of those who panic are never certain—he sailed down the Nar and subsequently the Tiber, increasing the public's anger because he had moored his ship at the tomb of the Caesars[17]—and in daylight too, the bank crowded, and himself with a great column of clients and Plancina with a company of women; and it was with eagerness on their faces that
3   they strode on their way. Among the incitements to resentment were his house looming over the forum and its festive decoration, his party and banquet; and, given the crowdedness of the place, nothing was concealed.

10   On the next day Fulcinius Trio arraigned Piso before the consuls. Yet Vitellius and Veranius and the other of Germanicus' companions maintained that there was no role for Trio; nor were they accusers themselves, they said, but as informants and witnesses of events they would deliver Germanicus' instructions. Trio for his part, having disclaimed the denouncement of that aspect of the case, secured the accusation of the man's earlier life;[18] and the princeps was begged to
2   tackle the inquiry, something which not even the defendant rejected, dreading as he was the prejudices of the people and fathers; on the other hand, he thought, Tiberius would be effective at spurning rumor and was entangled in the complicity of his mother: the distinction between truth and pejorative beliefs would be made more easily by a single judge, whereas hatred and resentment were the
3   effective factors in a larger group. Yet Tiberius had no illusions about the storm the inquiry would cause and about the reports by which he himself would be torn apart. Therefore, in the presence of a few of his establishment, he listened to the accusers' threats and the pleas from the other side, and referred the case in-
11   tact to the senate. (Meanwhile Drusus was returning from Illyricum, and, although the fathers had voted that he should enter to an ovation on account of

16. Legion IX.

17. A varied reference to Augustus' mausoleum (above, 3.4.1n.).

18. It was standard practice for the prosecution to blacken a defendant's character by directing accusations against his earlier career. See 3.13.1 below.

the reception of Maroboduus and the achievements of the previous summer,[19] it was only after deferring the honor that he went into the City.)

After this, when the defendant begged L. Arruntius, P. Vinicius, Asinius Gallus, **2** Aeserninus Marcellus, and Sex. Pompeius to be his advocates, and they gave different excuses, M. Lepidus and L. Piso and Livineius Regulus stood by him[20]— with the whole community alert to hear how great was the loyalty of Germanicus' friends, what confidence the defendant had, and whether Tiberius would manage to contain and suppress his own feelings. At no other time did a more attentive people give itself greater permission for concealed utterances against the princeps or for suspicious silence.

On the day of the senate Caesar delivered a speech with considered balance:[21] **12** Piso had been his father's legate and friend and had been given by himself, on the senate's authority, to Germanicus as his helper in the administration of affairs in the East. Whether he had there stung the young man by his truculence and tussles and had been merely delighted at his departing, or whether he had extinguished his life by some crime, must be judged with an open mind. "If the legate **2** cast aside the boundaries of his office and his compliance toward his commander and was delighted at his death (and at my grief too), I shall reject him and bar him from my house and thus it will not be as princeps+ that I shall avenge a private antagonism; but, if a deed is uncovered which in the case of the killing of any mortal whatsoever would require vengeance, you for your part must visit both the children of Germanicus and us his parents with the consolation we deserve. And **3** at the same time reflect on this: whether Piso handled his armies disruptively and mutinously, whether the soldiers' affections were acquired by corrupt methods, whether the reclamation of the province was by arms, or whether these are falsehoods, publicized with exaggeration by his accusers.

"It is the excessive enthusiasms of the latter to which I rightly take exception. **4** What was the point of stripping his body and permitting its handling by the eyes of the public or of spreading abroad, even among foreigners, that his life had been cut short by poison, if those matters are still uncertain and require examination? Of course I lament my son and shall always lament him; but I am not prevent- **5** ing the defendant from producing everything by which his innocence can be bolstered or any irregularity of Germanicus' confirmed. And I pray that you should not regard the connection between the case and my pain as a reason to receive the proffered charges as proved. Those who have become his advocates **6** because of kindred blood or individual loyalty, help the imperiled man as effec-

19. See 2.64.1 for the senators' vote, and 2.63.1–4 for Maroboduus' surrender.

20. P. Vinicius was consul in A.D. 2; M. Claudius Marcellus Aeserninus, a grandson of Asinius Pollio (1.12.4n.), was praetor in 19; Sex. Pompeius was consul in 14 (1.7.2); and Livineius Regulus was suffect consul in 18. For Arruntius and Asinius Gallus see 1.8.3n.; for M. Lepidus see 1.13.2n.; and for L. Piso, brother of the defendant, see 2.34.1n.

21. T.'s account of Piso's trial (3.12–19.1) may be compared with the senate's decision published after the trial (*SCPP*).

tively as each of you can with your eloquence and concern. I urge the same task, the same steadfastness, upon his accusers. In only one respect shall we have placed Germanicus above the laws, namely that the investigation into his death is being held in the curia rather than in the forum, before the senate rather than before the judges;[22] let everything else be handled with equal restraint. No one should have regard for the tears of Drusus, no one for my sorrowfulness, nor for any hostile fabrications against us." Thereupon a two-day period was established for casting the charges, and after an interval of six days the accused would be defended for a three-day period.

13

Then Fulcinius embarked on past irrelevancies, namely the fact that Piso's tenure of Spain had been marked by corruption and greed[23]—an allegation whose proof would not harm the defendant, if he cleared himself of the recent ones, and whose rebuttal would not acquit him, if he were found guilty of greater outrages.

2 After this,+ Servaeus and Veranius and Vitellius with like enthusiasm (and with much eloquence on Vitellius' part) cast the charge that in his hatred for Germanicus and his enthusiasm for revolution Piso, by licensing maltreatment of the allies, had corrupted the common soldiers to such a degree that the basest of them called him "parent of the legions."[24] Conversely, they said, he had been savage to all the best men, especially to the companions and friends of Germanicus. Finally he had annihilated the man himself by curses and poison: hence the rituals and abominable offerings by himself and Plancina,[25] his claiming the state by arms, and—to ensure his appearance as the accused—his defeat in the line of battle.[26]

14

The defense in general felt shaken: it could deny neither his military corruption nor the fact that he had left the province susceptible to the worst elements, nor even his insults against his commander. Only the charge of poisoning did they seem to have wiped out, which not even his accusers adequately proved with their argument that at a party of Germanicus', when Piso was reclining

2 above him,[27] his food had been tainted at the man's hands. It seemed not to ring true that among someone else's slaves and in the sight of so many attendants, in the presence of Germanicus himself, he had dared such a deed; and the defendant offered his own establishment for torture and importuned for the other's servants likewise.

3 But the judges were variously implacable, Caesar on account of the war inflicted on the province, the senate never really believing that Germanicus' demise had been without foul play *** demanding what they had written, something which

---

22. The "judges" are those of the court which would normally have dealt with cases of alleged poisoning (see *OCD* 1286–7 s.v. quaestiones).

23. Piso had been appointed legate of Hispania Tarraconensis in A.D. 9/10.

24. See 2.55.5 (and n.) and 2.80.2. For Q. Servaeus see further 2.56.4 and 6.7.2–4.

25. See 2.75.2 and compare *SCPP* 63 "wicked sacrifices were offered by him."

26. See 2.80–1.

27. I.e., to the left of his host, in the seat of honor.

[handwritten: people argued w/ Piso & intend to leave him]

Tiberius no less than Piso refused.[28] At the same time the cries of the people in   4
front of the curia were heard: they would not stay their hands if he evaded sen-
tencing by the fathers. And they had dragged Piso's likenesses to the Gemonians
and would have smashed them, had they not been protected and replaced by order of the princeps. So he was put into a litter and escorted by a tribune of a   5
praetorian cohort—a follower variously rumored to be a guard for his safety or
the agent of his death.

Plancina experienced the same resentment but had greater influence; and for   **15**
that reason it was held to be doubtful how much opposition to her Caesar would
be allowed.[29] She herself, while Piso's hopes remained poised, promised that she
would be his partner in whatever fortune and, if it should come to this, his com-   *[handwritten: Placina,]*
panion in extermination; but, when by Augusta's secret pleas she obtained par-   *[handwritten: Piso's wife]*
don, she began gradually to separate herself from her husband and to detach her
defense. When the accused realized that this meant his extermination, and he hes-   2
itated whether he should still face trial, with the encouragement of his sons he
hardened his spirit and again entered the senate. And, though he suffered to the
full the renewed accusations, the ferocious cries from the fathers and every hostility and savagery, nothing terrified him more than the sight of Tiberius—
without pity, without anger, blocked and closed against being breached by any
emotional appeal. Having been carried back home, as if considering his defense   3
for the next day, he wrote a few words, sealed them, and handed them to a freedman. Then he carried out the usual routines for bodily care. Later, after much of
the night had passed, his wife having left the bedroom, he ordered the doors to
be shut and covered; and at the start of daylight he was discovered with his throat
stabbed through, a sword lying on the ground. *[handwritten: Piso commits suicide]*

(I remember hearing from my elders that a document was often seen in Piso's   **16**
hands, which he himself did not publicize; but his friends had insisted that it contained a letter[30] from Tiberius and instructions against Germanicus, and the in-   *[handwritten: & him]*
tention had been to produce it before the fathers and to accuse the princeps, had
he not been outwitted by Sejanus with empty promises; also that his life had not
been extinguished of his own accord but after an assailant had been sent in.
Neither of these would I be inclined to assert; nevertheless I had no right to conceal what was told by those whose lives lasted into my own youth.)

Caesar, changing his expression to sorrowfulness, complained before the sen-   2
ate that the aim of such a death was resentment at himself *** and with repeated
questions asked how Piso had passed his final day and night.[31] And, after the other

[handwritten: Caesar feigns sorrow for Piso's death]

28. The gap in the manuscript makes the precise meaning of this sentence, and in particular who was demanding what and from whom, unclear.

29. Sc. by his mother, who was popularly believed to dominate Tiberius (1.4.5, 4.57.3)
and who was the friend of Plancina. See further 3.17 below.

30. Or "letters" (the Latin can mean either).

31. The gap in the manuscript must have contained references to Tiberius' having
"complained," which I have supplied, and to whichever of the defendant's two sons is

had replied (generally wisely, but sometimes injudiciously), he read out the notes
3   which had been composed in roughly this fashion by Piso: "Overwhelmed by
the conspiracy of my antagonists and by the resentment of a false charge, and insofar as there is no place anywhere for truth (and for my innocence), I call the
immortal gods to witness that I have lived, Caesar, with loyalty toward you and
with no different a devotion to your mother; and I beg both of you to look after the interests of my children, of whom Cn. Piso was not involved in my fortunes of whatever kind, since he has spent all this time in the City, and M. Piso
discouraged me from reclaiming Syria (and would that I had rather yielded to
4   my young son than he to his elderly father!). Therefore I pray the more emphatically that the penalty for my perversity should not be paid by the guiltless. By
the five and forty years of my compliance, by my collegiality in the consulship,[32]
having won the approval of Divine Augustus, your parent, and as a friend of yours
who shall not ask for anything after this, I ask for the safety of my unfortunate
son." About Plancina he added nothing.

17   After this Tiberius cleared the juvenile of the charge of civil war: there had been
orders from his father, he said, and a son could not have refused. At the same time
he expressed pity for the family's nobility and for the weighty misfortune of the
man himself, however deserved. On Plancina's behalf he talked shamefully and
outrageously, putting forward the pleas of his mother, against whom the secret
2   complaints of the best people flared all the more: so it was right for a grandmother
to behold the murderess of her grandson, to address her, to snatch her from the
senate! Though the laws obtained for the benefit of all citizens, it was Germanicus alone to whom they had not applied; Caesar[33] had been merely deplored by
the voices of Vitellius and Veranius, Plancina defended by the Commander and
Augusta: let her therefore turn upon Agrippina and her children the poisons
and practices so triumphantly tested, let her glut an exceptional grandmother and
3   uncle with the gore of a most pitiable family! A two-day period was taken up with
this phantom trial, Tiberius pressing Piso's children to protect their mother; and,
since despite competing declamations from accusers and witnesses neither of them
replied, pity rather than resentment increased.
4   Asked first for his opinion, Aurelius Cotta the consul—for, with Tiberius
putting the motion, the magistrates were performing that responsibility too[34]—

---

mentioned in the next sentence ("the other"). It has been generally assumed (from "juvenile" at 3.17.1 below) that it was the younger son, M. Piso, whom Tiberius interrogated
here; but more recently it has been argued that Cn. Piso, the elder son and formerly one
of Tiberius' personal quaestors, would have been the more natural informant.

32. Tiberius and Piso had been colleagues in the consulship in 7 B.C.

33. I.e., Germanicus.

34. Normally one or other consul would act as presiding magistrate and in that capacity would put motions before the senate; one of the consuls designate would have the
right to speak first on issues (see 3.22.4 below). Here the procedure is different because
Tiberius himself presides.

proposed that Piso's name should be erased from the fasti,[35] part of his property confiscated, and part should be granted to Cn. Piso the son, who should change his forename;[36] M. Piso, shedding his rank[37] and in receipt of five million sesterces, should be relegated for ten years, with immunity granted to Plancina on account of the pleas of Augusta. Many aspects of that opinion were softened by the **18** princeps: Piso's name should not be removed from the fasti, since those of M. Antonius, who had made war on his fatherland, and of Iullus Antonius, who had violated Augustus' family, still remained.[38] And he exempted M. Piso from degradation and granted him his father's property, being quite firmly set against money (as I have often recalled)[39] and on that occasion the more amenable because of his shame at Plancina's acquittal. Likewise, when Valerius Messalinus[40] proposed 2 that a golden statue should be set up in the temple of Mars the Avenger, and Caecina Severus an altar to Vengeance, he demurred, insisting that such conse-*Tiberius* crations were for foreign victories; domestic afflictions should be shrouded in sadness. Messalinus had added that gratitude should be expressed to Tiberius, 3 Augusta, Antonia, Agrippina, and Drusus for the avenging of Germanicus, and yet he had neglected mention of Claudius. Messalinus for his part was questioned by T. Asprenas in front of the senate about whether the omission had been deliberate (and it was only at that point that Claudius' name was finally appended); 4 but as for me, the more I reconsider recent or past events, the more I am confronted with the mockeries made of mortal affairs in every activity: for in terms of reputation, hope, and veneration, everyone was marked out for command rather than the future princeps whom fortune was keeping in hiding.[41]

A few days after, Caesar initiated the senate's granting of priesthoods to Vitel- **19** lius and Veranius and Servaeus; Fulcinius he warned, while guaranteeing him recommendation for honors, not to debase his fluency by violence.

That was the end to the avenging,+ though Germanicus' death was bandied 2 about in various rumors not only among those men who lived then but also in following times. So is it the case that all the greatest matters are ambiguous, inasmuch as some people hold any form of hearsay as confirmed, others turn truth into its converse, and each swells among posterity.

---

35. See 1.15.2n. for fasti and WM 9 for an example of the erasure.

36. See *SCPP* 98–100; he became "Lucius" (see 4.62.1).

37. Though M. Piso was not yet a senator, as the son of a senator he had the right to wear the broad-striped toga, to which "rank" here refers.

38. The references are to Mark Antony's part in the civil wars and to his son's adultery with Julia, Augustus' daughter (1.10.4n. and below, 3.24.2 and n.).

39. See 1.75.2 and 2.48.1–2.

40. Either the consul of 3 B.C. (1.8.4) or the consul of the present year (3.2.3).

41. The "future princeps" is Claudius, who on the death of Gaius Caligula (A.D. 41) hid behind a curtain and, discovered by a soldier, was acclaimed emperor almost by mistake. For Asprenas see 1.53.6n.

3   As for Drusus, having left the City to resume the auspices, he later entered to
an ovation.[42] And after a few days Vipsania, his mother, passed away, the only one
of Agrippa's children to have a gentle death: the lives of the others were extinguished, as is clear, by the sword or, as was believed, by poison or starvation.[43]

*

20   In the same year Tacfarinas, whose beating by Camillus in a previous season I
have recalled,[44] renewed the war in Africa, at first by roving pillage which went
unavenged because of its rapidity; then he extirpated villages and carried off a
great load of plunder; finally, not far from the River Pagyda, he invested a Ro-
2   man cohort. In charge of the stronghold was Decrius, enterprising in action,
trained in soldiering, and deeming the blockade an outrage. After exhorting[45] his
soldiers, he drew up the line in front of the camp to provide the opportunity of
a fight in the open. With the cohort beaten by the first attack, he appeared readily amid the weapons, converging on fugitives and berating the standard-bearers
because Roman soldiery was turning its back on the undisciplined or deserters.
At the same time he received wounds, and, despite a pierced eye, he directed his
face full toward the enemy and did not abandon the battle until, deserted by his
men, he fell.

21   After this was discovered by L. Apronius (he had succeeded Camillus),[46] who
was tense more from the dishonor to his own men than from the glory of the
enemy, in a deed rare for that time and of ancient memory he chose by lot every
2   tenth man of the disgraced cohort, executing them by cudgel. And so much was
achieved by his severity that the same forces of Tacfarinas, having attacked a garrison (whose name was Thala), were routed by a detachment of veterans, no more
3   than five hundred in number. (It was from that battle that Rufus Helvius, a troop-
soldier, brought back the honor of saving a citizen and was presented by Apronius with torques and a spear. Caesar added the civic crown, complaining rather
than offended that Apronius had not bestowed that too by his prerogative of be-

42. Earlier Drusus had laid down his command (for which "auspices" here is a synonym)
in order to enter the City after postponing his ovation (3.11.1 above). The ovation is officially dated to 28 May (Sherk 28D, p. 54), whereas the senate's decision which resulted
from Piso's trial is dated 10 December (*SCPP* 1–2, 174–5): the relative chronology of these
two dates is difficult to square with T.'s narrative.

43. Vipsania, Tiberius' first wife, was Agrippa's daughter by his first wife, Pomponia
(2.43.6n.); the other offspring alluded to here seem to be those of Agrippa's marriage
to Julia, daughter of Augustus, viz. Lucius and Gaius Caesar (1.3.3), Agrippa Postumus
(1.6.1), the younger Julia (4.71.4), and the elder Agrippina (6.25.1).

44. At 2.52 above.

45. The Latin word (*cohortatus*) plays on the proximity of the word "cohort" above and
below (*cohortem . . . cohorte*).

46. For Apronius see 1.56.1n.

ing proconsul.)[47] Yet Tacfarinas, with the Numidians now shocked and spurning   4
blockades, spread the war—yielding wherever there was pressure and contrariwise reverting to his opponents' rear. And, as long as that remained the barbarian's method, he mocked with impunity the thwarted and exhausted Roman;
but, after he had diverted to maritime areas, he became bound up with his plunder and clung to his stationary camp. Apronius Caesianus, on dispatch from his
father with cavalry and auxiliary cohorts (to which he had added the swiftest
men of the legions), had a successful fight with the Numidians and beat them
into the desert.

★

But at Rome Lepida, who besides the prestige of the Aemilii had L. Sulla and   **22**
Cn. Pompeius as her great-grandfathers, was denounced for having simulated a
birth by the rich and childless P. Quirinius. Also thrown in were charges of adul-
teries, poisonings, and that questions had been asked of the Chaldaeans concerning the family of Caesar,[48] with the accused being defended by Manius Lepidus,
her brother. Quirinius, by remaining hostile after his notification of their divorce,
had added to the pity for the albeit infamous and guilty woman.[49]

One could not have discerned easily the mind of the princeps in that inquiry,   2
to such an extent did he overturn and exchange the signs of anger and clemency.
Having at first begged the senate that the charges of treason should not be handled, he later enticed M. Servilius (one of the consulars)[50] and other witnesses to
produce what he had seemed to want kept quiet.+ Likewise Lepida's slaves, when   3
they were being held in military custody, he transferred to the consuls and at the
same time did not allow them to be questioned under torture about those things
which pertained to his own household. He also removed Drusus as consul des-   4
ignate from declaring his opinion in first place—an action which some deemed
citizenlike, to save the rest from the necessity of agreement, but which others attributed to savagery, on the grounds that he would not have withdrawn except
from the responsibility of condemning.[51]

47. The civic crown (*corona ciuica*) was awarded for saving the life of a fellow citizen
(15.12.3, 16.15.1): see *OCD* 411.

48. See 2.27.2n. for Chaldaeans.

49. Aemilia Lepida's brother, Manius Lepidus, had been consul in A.D. 11; he had the
same great-grandfather (viz. M. Aemilius Lepidus, consul in 78 B.C.: 3.27.2 and n.) as the
more prominent Marcus Aemilius Lepidus (1.13.2n.). For P. Sulpicius Quirinius, consul
as long ago as 12 B.C., see 2.30.4 and below, 3.48.1. Since no husband is mentioned as
defending her, Lepida is assumed to be now unmarried, although Mamercus Aemilius
Scaurus (1.13.4n.) had married her after her divorce by Quirinius (see 3.23.2 below).

50. See 2.48.1n.

51. If Drusus had spoken first, which as consul designate he was entitled to do (see
3.17.4n.), others might have felt obliged to agree with what he said (see 1.74.4–5); but,

23   During the days of the games, which had intervened the inquiry,[52] Lepida entered the theater with some distinguished female company and in a weeping lamentation invoked her ancestors and Pompeius himself, whose monument that was and whose attendant images were visible,[53] generating so much pity that everyone, with tears pouring, repeatedly shouted savage execrations at Quirinius, to whose old age, childlessness, and family obscurity the woman once marked out as wife of L. Caesar and Divine Augustus' daughter-in-law was being surrendered.

2   Then by the torturing of her slaves her outrages were revealed, and the vote went in favor of the proposal of Rubellius Blandus, who was for banning her from water and fire.[54] With this Drusus agreed, although the opinions of others had been milder. Later it was conceded to Scaurus, who had begotten a daughter by her, that her property should not be confiscated. Then at last Tiberius disclosed that he had discovered also from the slaves of P. Quirinius that the latter had been the target of Lepida's poison.

24   The adversities of illustrious houses (within a short space of time the Calpurnii had lost Piso, and the Aemilii Lepida) were visited with the consolation of D. Silanus' restoration to the Junian family.[55] I shall retrace briefly what befell

2   him. Though the fortunes of Divine Augustus prospered in matters of state, at home they were unfavorable owing to the immorality of the daughter and granddaughter whom he drove from the City, and punished their adulterers with death or banishment.[56] (For in calling their fault—widespread though it is between men and women—by the weighty name of "infringed obligations and violated

---

since he had withdrawn from speaking first, some people inferred that he would have spoken in favor of convicting, their grounds being that a speech for mercy would have reflected well on Tiberius and so would not have been prevented. Drusus' withdrawal thus testified to the emperor's "savagery."

52. These unspecified games are usually assumed to be the Great (or Roman) Games, which took place 4–19 September. The use of "intervened" as a transitive verb imitates a similarly strange usage in T.

53. Lepida was in the theater which Pompey the Great, her great-grandfather (3.22.1), had built in 55 B.C. See also 3.72.2.

54. C. Rubellius Blandus (again at 3.51.1 below) had been suffect consul in A.D. 18; in 33 (see 6.27.1) he married Julia, daughter of Drusus (Tiberius' son, who is about to be mentioned in the next sentence). See also 3.29.3n. below.

55. Brother of: C. Junius Silanus (3.66–8), consul in A.D. 10, M. Junius Silanus (below, 3.24.3n.), and Junia Torquata (3.69.6). A different branch of the family from that noted at 2.59.1n.; both branches were descended ultimately from M. Junius Silanus, praetor in 77 B.C.

56. The elder Julia was banished in 2 B.C. (1.53.1n.), the younger in A.D. 8 (4.71.4). Iullus Antonius (3.18.1 above) was forced to commit suicide (1.10.4); for the banishment of Sempronius Gracchus see 1.53.3–4; details of the fates of the elder Julia's other lovers are unknown. The only known lover of the younger Julia is the present D. Silanus.

sovereignty" he thereby exceeded the clemency of our ancestors and his own laws.)[57] The outcomes of the other men, as well as the remaining events of that   3 age, I shall recall if, after completing what I have intended, I prolong my life for further works;[58] but as for D. Silanus, adulterer in the case of Augustus' granddaughter, although he suffered no extra savagery beyond prohibition from Caesar's friendship, he understood that exile was being indicated to him, and it was not until Tiberius took command that he dared to appeal to the senate and princeps through the powerfulness of M. Silanus, his brother, whose distinguished nobility and eloquence made him an outstanding figure.[59] But, as Silanus was ex-   4 pressing gratitude before the senate, Tiberius replied that he too was delighted that his brother had returned from his distant peregrination, and in terms of legality it was quite permissible because he had been driven out neither by any senate's decision nor by any law; nevertheless, as far as he himself was concerned, his parent's indignation at the man remained unaffected, nor did Silanus' return annul what Augustus had willed. Thereafter the man was present in the City but acquired no honors.

There was next a motion about limiting the Papia Poppaea law, which the eld-   **25** erly Augustus after the Julian rogations had sanctioned to encourage punishment of the unmarried and to augment the treasury.[60] Yet espousals and rearings of children had not thereby increased, given the effectiveness of being childless;[61] but the number of the imperiled had kept swelling, since every house was undermined by the interpretations of denouncers, and, just as society had previously suffered from outrages, so it did now from laws.

That circumstance suggests that I should talk in more depth about the begin-   2 nings of legislature and by what means one arrived at this infinite number and

---

57. A rhetorical plural for the Julian law on adultery of 18 or 17 B.C. (2.50.2 above). I have translated and punctuated this sentence to try to make its meaning clear, viz., that Augustus regarded the behavior of his daughter and granddaughter ("their fault") in unusually serious terms and that it was in this respect that he "exceeded . . . his own laws." According to the usual interpretation, the reference to Augustus' exceeding his own laws explains the punishments that were meted out to the two Julias and their lovers ("whom . . . banishment" above).

58. In two of his earlier works (*Agricola* 3.3, *Histories* 1.1.4) T. had said that in the future he would turn to writing contemporary history; here he says that he intends to go further *back* in time and that, if he lives to produce any future works, he will deal with the period before Tiberius' accession.

59. M. Junius Silanus was suffect consul in A.D. 15; his daughter Claudia (= Junia Claudilla) will marry Caligula (6.20.1).

60. The Lex Papia Poppaea of A.D. 9, itself designed to modify an earlier Julian law on marriage of 18 B.C. (hence T.'s "Julian rogations" here), was intended to reward the production of children (see 2.51.1) and to punish childlessness.

61. Childlessness brought power, since one would be regarded as having money to dispose of in one's will. See, e.g., 3.48.2, 13.52.2.

26   variety of laws. The most olden of mortals, with as yet no evil lust, lived without scandal and crime and thus without punishment or constraints. Nor was there need of rewards, since honesty was sought entirely for its own sake, and, as they

2   desired nothing contrary to custom, they were forbidden nothing by dread. But, after equality was cast aside and ambition and force became implanted instead of reserve and shame, despotisms sprang up and, in the case of many peoples, re-

3   mained permanently; but some, either at once or after they had tired of kings, preferred laws. And at first,[+] given the rawness of men's minds, they were simple enough; and fame has celebrated particularly those of the Cretans and Spartans, which were drawn up by Minos and Lycurgus respectively, and those (already more elaborate and numerous) for the Athenians by Solon.[62]

4   As for our own case, the command of Romulus had depended merely on whim.[63] Then Numa bound the people by religious injunctions and divine leg-islation, and some developments were introduced by Tullus and Ancus; but Servius Tullius was the principal sanctioner of laws, to which even the kings

27   should have submitted.[64] But after Tarquinius' banishment the people made many arrangements against the fathers' intrigues in order to protect freedom and to consolidate harmony: decemvirs were created, and, with some exceptional features fetched from wherever they could be found, the Twelve Tables were com-posed, the culmination of fair legislation.[65] For subsequent laws, though some-times directed against malefactors in accordance with their felony, were more often carried by force amid the dissension of the orders[66] and to acquire illegal

2   honors or to banish famous men and for other crooked reasons. For example, the Gracchi and Saturnini were disrupters of the plebs; and no less its lavish bene-factor, though in the name of the senate, was Drusus:[67] the allies were bribed by

---

62. Solon was archon at Athens in 594/3 B.C.; Minos and Lycurgus are legendary fig-ures.

63. Whether the whim is Romulus' or his subjects' is unclear.

64. The traditional dates of these (almost entirely mythical) kings of Rome are: Romu-lus 753–715 B.C.; Numa 715–673; Tullus Hostilius 672–641; Ancus Marcius 640–617; Servius Tullius 578–535. The last king was Tarquinius Superbus (534–510), with whose expulsion from Rome the next sentence begins.

65. T. is referring to the struggles between the patricians and the plebs (here called "fa-thers" and "people" respectively) in the years 467–446 B.C. as described in the third book of Livy. It was as part of this process that a board of ten men (decemvirs) was created in 451 B.C. and was succeeded by a second board in 450 (see 1.1.1), the purpose of each be-ing to establish a code of laws. The result was the famous code known as the Twelve Ta-bles. See *OCD* 435 and 1565–6.

66. It seems from the next sentence ("For example") that T. means the opposition be-tween the nobility and the rest which erupted in the later part of the second century B.C.

67. Tiberius Gracchus was tribune of the plebs in 133 B.C., his brother Gaius in 123 B.C., L. Appuleius Saturninus in 103 B.C., and M. Livius Drusus in 91 B.C.

allies bribed – no honesty or humility

hope or inveigled through intervention,[68] and not even in the Italian (soon the civil) war did men neglect to pass many different resolutions, until L. Sulla as dictator, abolishing or overturning what preceded (although he had added more himself), provided some respite therefrom—albeit briefly, given the immediacy of Lepidus' disruptive rogations and not long afterward the restoration of the tribunes' license to drive the people in whatever direction they themselves wished.[69] *corrupt tribunes* And now legal proceedings were instituted not only in general but against individual men,[70] and, with the infection in the state at its peak, the number of laws was at its greatest. Then Cn. Pompeius, consul for the third time and selected to **(28)** cure morality but more severe in his remedies than were the felonies, both an author and an underminer of his own laws, lost by arms what he had been protecting by arms.[71] Thereafter there was continuous disharmony for twenty years, *too severe* no morality, no legality: all acts of the basest nature passed with impunity, and many of honesty led to extermination.[72] Finally, in his sixth consulship, Caesar 2 Augustus, secure in power, abolished the orders which he had issued during the triumvirate, and provided legislation whereby we could avail ourselves of peace *peace legislation* and a princeps.[73]

Sharper were the bonds after that. Guards were imposed on us and under the 3 Papia Poppaea law were given the inducements of rewards, in order that, if there was any slackening in the privileges of parenthood, the people, as though the parent of everyone, should take possession of the unclaimed inheritance. But they began to penetrate more deeply and had gripped the City and Italy and citizens everywhere, and many had their estates removed.[74] In fact everyone would have 4 been faced with terror, had not Tiberius established a remedy by choosing by lot five of the consulars, five from the praetorians and the same number from the rest of the senate, under whom the loosening of the law's many entanglements provided a limited and temporary alleviation.

Augustus became too powerful, & Tiberius slackened the laws

68. T. may here be referring to the veto of Livius Drusus' homonymous father, tribune of the plebs in 122 B.C.

69. The Italian or "Social" War (91–88 B.C.) evolved into a civil war which lasted until Sulla's dictatorship in 82 (1.1.1n.); M. Aemilius Lepidus was consul in 78 B.C.; the powers of the tribunes ("they themselves") were restored in 70 B.C.

70. In 58 B.C. Cicero was exiled by legislation of P. Clodius.

71. Pompey the Great, consul for the third time in 52 B.C., was defeated by Julius Caesar at the battle of Pharsalus in 48 B.C.

72. T. refers to the civil wars of 49–29 B.C. (1.1.1n.).

73. Octavian's sixth consulship was in 28 B.C.; for the triumvirate see 1.1.1n.

74. By "estates" are meant assets; the Latin term for "removed" (*excisi*, lit. "cut out") suggests removal by surgery: the guards (i.e., the denouncers mentioned at 3.25.1) are seen as a disease which "grips" and "penetrates" the body of society, whose members can free themselves only by undergoing surgery.

29   During the same period he recommended to the fathers one of Germanicus'
children, Nero, who had now embarked on his young manhood;[75] and, not without derision from his listeners, he demanded that he should be released from the
responsibility of undertaking the vigintivirate[76] and should seek the quaestorship
five years earlier than according to the laws. (He maintained that the same had
2   been decreed to himself and his brother at Augustus' request. But I would not
doubt that even then there were those who secretly mocked such pleas; and yet
those times were only the beginning of the Caesars' exaltedness, the old dispen-
sation was more visible, and the relationship of stepsons with stepfather is slighter
3   than a grandfather's to his grandson.)[77] A pontificate was added, and, on the day
he first entered the forum, a gratuity for the plebs, quite delighted as they were
to be observing the stock of Germanicus already maturing.[78] Subsequently their
4   joy was augmented by the wedding of Nero and Julia, Drusus' daughter.[79] But
the favorable talk with which they greeted these developments was matched by
their hostility at Sejanus' being marked out as father-in-law to Claudius' son.[80]
He[81] seemed to have polluted his family's nobility and to have raised Sejanus beyond the excessive hopes of which the latter was already suspected.

30   At the end of the year there passed from life the distinguished men L. Volusius
and Sallustius Crispus. Volusius' was an old family, which nevertheless had not
advanced past the praetorship; he it was who introduced the consulship,[82] also
discharging censorial power in choosing the decuriae of equestrians,[83] and the
first accumulator of the wealth responsible for the immense vigor of their house.
2   Crispus, born to an equestrian position, was affiliated into his name by C. Sal-

---

75. The date on which Nero Julius Caesar received his toga of manhood and a gratuity was given to the plebs (below) was 7 June (EJ, p. 41); he had been born in A.D. 6 and
was now thirteen or fourteen years old (the latter being the normal age for the toga:
13.15.1). In due course he will be undermined by Sejanus (4.59.3–60.3) and attacked by
Tiberius (5.3.1–2); he is killed in 31.

76. The collective name for various minor magistracies prior to the quaestorship (*OCD*
1598–9).

77. T. seems to be saying that senators under Tiberius had less reason to mock than did
those under Augustus. Augustus' stepsons are Tiberius and his brother, Nero Claudius
Drusus (1.3.1), who became quaestor in 24 and 19 B.C. respectively.

78. A gratuity (*congiarium*) was a gift to the plebs of, e.g., oil or wine or a monetary
equivalent on some special occasion (*OCD* 376).

79. This is the same Julia who will eventually marry Rubellius Blandus after Nero Caesar's death (see 3.23.2n., 6.27.1n.).

80. Viz. Drusus, one of Claudius' two children by his first wife, Plautia Urgulanilla. The
name of Sejanus' daughter is not known for certain.

81. Tiberius.

82. L. Volusius Saturninus became suffect consul in 12 B.C.

83. T. seems to be using the term "decuriae," which properly refers to panels of jury-
men (as 14.20.5), as a synonym for, e.g., the equestrians' "squadrons" (2.83.4).

lustius, the brightest flower among the authors of Roman affairs,[84] to whose sis- *Crispus*
ter he was grandson; and he for his part, though with ready access to undertaking honors, emulated Maecenas:[85] without senatorial rank he outstripped in
powerfulness many of the triumph-holders and consulars, being far removed
from the ancients' established usage in terms of style and elegance, and, in his resources and affluence, more nearly approaching luxuriousness. There was never-   3
theless an underlying mental vigor, equal to mighty tasks and all the sharper in
proportion as he displayed somnolence and inertia. Therefore during Maecenas'
lifetime he was the next, and later the principal, upon whom Commanders could
rely with their secrets, and, an accomplice to the killing of Postumus Agrippa,[86]
in advanced age he maintained an appearance rather than influence in the matter of the princeps's friendship. (That had befallen Maecenas too, since power-   4
fulness is fated to be rarely everlasting; or else satiety afflicts either one party, when
they have bestowed everything they can, or the other, when there no longer remains anything they desire.)

loss of power (Rome had taken all they could)

*   *   *

There followed Tiberius' fourth and Drusus' second consulship, distinctive for   **31**
the collegiality of father and son. (Three years+ earlier, Germanicus' same honor
with Tiberius had been neither welcome to his uncle nor so connected in respect of birth.) It was at the beginning of that year that Tiberius withdrew to   2
Campania, as if to consolidate his health but in fact giving gradual consideration
to a long and continuous absence, or so that Drusus, with his father removed,
might fulfill the responsibilities of the consulship on his own.

And by chance a small affair which developed into a great contest presented
the young man with the means of acquiring goodwill. Domitius Corbulo, a for-   3
mer praetor, complained before the senate about L. Sulla, a young noble, on the
grounds that during a spectacle of gladiators he had not given way to him.[87] On
Corbulo's side were age, hereditary custom, the support of the elders; on the other
were the efforts of Mamercus Scaurus and L. Arruntius and other kinsmen of
Sulla. And they kept up their contest of speeches, and examples were recalled of   4
ancestors who in weighty decrees had branded the disrespect of youth, until
Drusus spoke words suited to moderating their spirits; and satisfaction was rendered to Corbulo by Mamercus, who was uncle as well as stepfather of Sulla, and

84. This is the historian Sallust (above, p. xx).

85. Maecenas, who died in 8 B.C., was one of Augustus' great ministers (1.54.2 and n.,
6.11.2, 14.53.3, 14.55.2).

86. See 1.6.3; also 2.40.2–3 for the murder of the false Agrippa Postumus.

87. Cn. Domitius Corbulo was the father of Nero's famous general (11.18.1n.); the
other man is probably L. Sulla Felix, the consul of 33 (6.15.1).

Corbulo

5   the most fertile of the orators at that time. (It was the same Corbulo who, exclaiming repeatedly that very many routes across Italy were interrupted and impassable owing to the fraudulence of contractors and the indifference of magistrates, willingly undertook the administration of the task, something which was considered to be not so much publicly useful as ruinous to the many against whose money and reputation, by means of convictions and the spear, he directed his savagery.)[88]

32   And not long after, Tiberius sent a letter to the senate informing them that Africa had again been shaken by a raid of Tacfarinas' and that the fathers should use their judgment to select as proconsul one who was knowledgeable in sol-

2   diering, physically effective, and capable of the war. Sex. Pompeius, seizing on this to initiate a campaign of hatred against Manius Lepidus,[89] censured him for being insensible, impoverished, and a dishonor to his ancestors, and for that reason to be removed from the allotment of Asia too—all to opposition from the senate, however, which believed that Lepidus was gentle rather than a shirker, that his straitened circumstances were hereditary, and that a noble's life lived without scandal should be held an honor, not a disgrace. He was therefore sent to Asia, and concerning Africa it was decreed that Caesar should choose to whom it was to be entrusted.

33   It was in the midst of all this that Severus Caecina proposed that no magistrate to whose lot a province had fallen should be accompanied there by his wife (he had previously retraced at some length his own spouse's harmony with himself and her six childbirths and the fact that what he was establishing for the public good he had already observed at home, having restricted her to within Italy

2   although he himself had fulfilled forty years' service across several provinces). For it was not unreasonable, he said, that at one time it had been accepted that females should not be dragged among the allies or foreign peoples: in a company of women there were elements who prolonged peace by their luxuriousness, deferred war because of their alarm,[90] and transformed a Roman column into

(margin note: Lepidus sent to Asia)

---

88. Evidently many of the Italian roads were in a poor state because building contractors were failing to do their jobs properly and because the magistrates overseeing the roads (the *curatores viarum*) were failing to supervise. Corbulo intervened, but his intervention was memorable not for any improvement to the road system but for the convictions he succeeded in getting and for the financial penalties imposed on contractors and/or curators. The penalties were so severe that the convicted were forced to auction their property: the "spear," like our "hammer," is the symbol of the auctioneer (again at 13.28.3).

89. Sex. Pompeius is the consul of 14 (1.7.2); for Manius Aemilius Lepidus see above, 3.22.1n.

90. The point is not that women by themselves would have these effects but that they would lure their men into soft living or would infect them with their own fear of war: as a result, the men would be less enthusiastic about their military responsibilities. "Luxuriousness" hints obliquely at the sex drive by which women were often said to be characterized: so too again at 3.34.5 below (the speech in reply).

something resembling a barbarian procession. The sex was not only weak and   3
unequal to toil but—if the license were allowed them—savage, self-aggrandizing
and greedy for power: they strode among the soldiers, had centurions to hand;
only recently a female had presided at the exercise of cohorts and march-past of
legions![91] Members themselves should reflect that, whenever men were accused   4
of extortion, wives were charged with more: it was to them that the basest provincial elements immediately clung, by them that business was undertaken and
transacted. Double were the departures that were courted,[92] double were the headquarters, and more persistent and unruly were the orders from women, who,
formerly constrained by the Oppian and other laws,[93] were currently released
from their bonds and were regulating houses, forums,[94] and now armies too!

Only a few agreed with what they had heard; the majority were disruptive,   **34**
saying that there had been no motion on the issue, nor was Caccina a worthy
censor in so great a matter.[95] Soon Valerius Messalinus, whose parent was Mes-   2
sala and in whom there was an echo of paternal eloquence,[96] replied that in many
respects the harshness of the ancients had undergone a welcome change for the
better. For, he said, it was not the case, as at one time, that the City was being
blockaded in war or that the provinces were hostile; and a few concessions to females' needs were being made which were not a burden even on their spouses'
households, still less on the allies. But everything else was shared indiscriminately
with the husband, and peace presented no obstacles in that respect: of course it
was the properly girded who should go to war; but for those returning from toil
what was more honorable than wifely solace? "But some women had lapsed into   3
self-aggrandizement or greed." So? Were not many magistrates themselves susceptible to a variety of lusts? Yet no one on that account was not sent to a
province. "Husbands were often corrupted by the crookedness of their wives";
but surely not all the unmarried were therefore unsullied? Formerly the Oppian   4
laws had been acceptable, since the circumstances of the state demanded as much;

91. See 2.55.6 (Plancina).

92. A great man's departure from, or arrival at, a city or residence was the occasion for
an elaborate and ritualistic paying of respects. See further 16.10.4 (and note 11.12.3).

93. The Oppian law of 215 B.C. forbade certain luxuries to women. The law was re-
pealed in 195 B.C. after a debate in which the elder Cato attacked the repeal and the tribune L. Valerius supported it. Livy's famous version of the debate, together with the
speeches of the two parties (34.2–7), is imitated by T. throughout chapters 33–4: see further 3.34.1n.

94. The forum here stands for the law courts.

95. "Censor" alludes to Cato the Censor, whose hard line on women Caecina has been
following; likewise Caecina's opponent here shares the same name (Valerius) as Cato's opponent in Livy (3.33.4n.).

96. The speaker is M. Valerius Messalla Messalinus, the consul of 3 B.C. (1.8.4n.); his father is the great M. Valerius Messalla Corvinus (consul in 31 B.C.), who had been one of
the most famous orators of his day (11.6.2, 13.34.1).

but later there had been some relaxation and softening, because it was expedient. It was unreasonable that our own masculine failures should be expressed in
5   other terms, for it was the man's fault if a female exceeded her limit. Moreover it was wrong that, on account of the weak will of one or two, husbands should be deprived of partnership in their prosperity and adversity, while at the same time a sex which was ineffectual by nature was abandoned and exposed to its own luxuriousness and to the desires of others. Even with a constant guard, espousals remained undamaged only with difficulty; what would happen if over the course of several years they were obliterated, in the manner of divorce? Members should only confront malpractices elsewhere if they remembered the outrages in the City.[97]

6   Drusus added a few words about his own marriage: principes were often required to visit distant parts of the empire: how many times had Divine Augustus made expeditions to West and East with Livia as companion! He himself too had set off for Illyricum and, if it proved advantageous, would go to other nations, but always with a heavy heart if he were wrenched from his dearest wife, the parent of their numerous mutual children.

35   In this way Caecina's proposal was outwitted, and on the day of the next senate Tiberius in a letter, after sidelong castigation of the fathers for referring every matter of concern to the princeps, named M. Lepidus and Junius Blaesus as those
2   from whom the proconsul of Africa should be chosen.[98] Then the words of both of them were heard, with Lepidus the more intent on excusing himself, since he put forward his physical ineffectiveness, his children's ages, and his marriageable daughter; and there was understood also something which he kept quiet: Blaesus was Sejanus' uncle and for that reason highly effective in terms of power.
3   Blaesus replied with a display of reluctance, but not with the same assertiveness, and was won over without difficulty[+] by the unanimity of the sycophants.

36   Next there came into the open a matter which, given the secrecy of their complaints, many had been covering up. All the basest individuals had been overcome by a form of license whereby their stirring up abuse and resentment against good people was accomplished with impunity, since at the same time they were grasping an image of Caesar; and even freedmen and slaves were dreaded sponta-
2   neously when they raised their voices and hands against patron or master. Therefore C. Cestius, a senator,[99] said that, though principes were of course like gods, the gods did not listen unless the pleas of their suppliants were just, and no one escaped to the Capitol or the City's other temples to use them as a refuge
3   for outrageous purposes; the laws were inoperative or turned upside down when in the forum, at the threshold of the curia, abuse and threats were leveled at him.

97. Messalinus means that Rome is a den of vice and dangerous for wives who are left there; this consideration should be borne in mind when speakers make reference to the sometimes dubious activities of wives abroad.

98. For Marcus Aemilius Lepidus see 1.13.2n.; for Junius Blaesus see 1.16.2n.

99. C. Cestius Gallus became consul in 35 (6.31.1).

by Annia Rufilla, whom he had convicted of fraud before a judge, and he for his part dared not risk a trial because of her brandishing against him the Commander's likeness. Drusus was enveloped by similar cries from others (and by ones of a more frightful nature from some), and they kept pleading that he should set an example of retribution, until finally he ordered that, once summoned and convicted, she should be held in public custody. *for fraud*

And because Considius Aequus and Caelius Cursor, Roman equestrians, had **37** made the praetor Magius Caecilianus the target of fabricated charges of treason, they were punished on the princeps's initiative and by decree of the senate. Yet **2** each of these two factors was interpreted to the credit of Drusus: it was by his appearances at men's gatherings and conversations in the City, they said, that the effects of his father's seclusion were being mitigated. Nor was the young man's luxuriousness so unacceptable: better to concentrate on that, devoting his days to buildings and his nights to parties, than be alone and undistracted by pleasures, spending a sorrowful vigil on evil concerns. For neither Tiberius nor the **38** accusers were growing tired: Ancharius Priscus had arraigned Caesius Cordus, the proconsul of Crete, for extortion, adding a charge of treason (which was now the complement of every accusation); and Caesar, berating the judges, dragged **2** back Antistius Vetus, one of the chiefs of Macedonia and acquitted of adultery, to stand trial for treason, on the grounds that he had been disruptive and implicated in the plans of Rhescuporis at the time when the latter, after killing Cotys, his brother's son,+ had been contemplating war against us.[100] Fire and water were therefore forbidden to the defendant, with the additional clause that he be held on an island convenient for neither Macedonia nor Thrace. *extortion / fraud*

*

For Thrace, its empire divided between Rhoemetalces and Cotys' children (who **3** owing to their infancy had Trebellienus Rufus as their guardian), was experiencing internal disaffection through its unfamiliarity with us.[101] Censuring+ Rhoemetalces no less than Trebellienus for allowing the injuries of their compatriots to go unavenged, the Coelaletae and Odrusae and Dii—effective nations **4** all—took up arms under separate leaders, comparable only in their ignobility. That was the reason why they failed to coalesce for a frightening war: some disrupted their immediate neighborhood, others crossed Mount Haemus to muster the isolated peoples there, the majority (and the most organized) invested the king and the city of Philippopolis, situated there by Macedonian Philip. When **39** these matters became known to P. Vellaeus (he presided the nearest army), he

100. See 2.64–7 above.

101. T. here resumes the Thracian narrative from 2.67.2–3, where the guardian's name was given as "Trebellenus." By Thrace's "unfamiliarity with us" T. probably means that the Thracians failed to appreciate the severity with which Rome would respond to revolt. (Note that I have changed the vulgate text and punctuation of section 3.)

P. Vellaeus (of Thrace)

sent cavalry wings and light cohorts against those who were roving about either for plunder or to enlist auxiliaries; he himself led the hard core of the infantry

2 to raise the blockade. And on all fronts the action was simultaneous and successful, with the pillagers slaughtered, dissension arising among the blockaders, a timely breakout by the king, and the legion's arrival. Nor would it be appropriate to call that a fight or battle in which half-armed strays were butchered without bloodshed on our side.

40 In the same year, on account of the magnitude of their debt, the communities of the Galliae started a rebellion, whose keenest instigator among the Treveri was Julius Florus, among the Aedui Julius Sacrovir. Both had the advantages of nobility and their ancestors' good deeds, and for that reason Roman citizenship had been given in the past, although at the time it was a rarity and exclusively a reward for valor. In secret exchanges, having enlisted all the most defiant men (or those whose compulsion to wrongdoing was greatest owing to destitution and to the dread which arose from guilt at their outrages), Florus agreed to muster the Belgae, Sacrovir the nearer Gauls. Therefore at meeting-places and gatherings they talked mutinously about the continual taxes, the weight of interest, the savagery and haughtiness of their overseers. The soldiery, they said, was disaffected on hearing of the extermination of Germanicus; it was an exceptional moment to regain their freedom, if, while flourishing themselves, they only reflected how barren Italy was, how unwarlike the urban plebs,[102] and that no effective element thrived in the armies except what was foreign.

41 Almost no community was unreceptive to the seeds for that movement's growth. But the first to burst forth were the Andecavi and Turoni, of whom the Andecavi were suppressed by the legate Acilius Aviola after he had called out the

2 cohort which was performing garrison duty at Lugdunum,[103] while the Turoni were stifled by legionary soldiery (which Visellius Varro, the legate of Lower Germany,[104] had sent) under the leadership of the same Aviola and some chiefs of the Galliae, who brought help in order to disguise their defection and bring it

3 forth at a better time. Sacrovir too was seen urging the fight on the Roman side, and with his head uncovered—to display his valor (as he maintained); but captives claimed that he had presented himself to be recognized, so he would not be assailed by weapons. When consulted on this matter, Tiberius spurned the evidence and by his scepticism fostered the war.

42 Meanwhile Florus pressed ahead with his designs and offered enticements to a wing of cavalry—which, conscripted from the Treveri, was being held under our military discipline—in order that it should initiate war by slaughtering some Roman businessmen; and, although a few of the cavalry were corrupted, the ma-

102. A reference to the levy mentioned at 1.31.4.

103. The legate is perhaps identical with C. Calpurnius Aviola, suffect consul in 24 and proconsul of Africa in (probably) 37–8.

104. C. Visellius Varro had been suffect consul in 12 and was father of L. Visellius Varro, consul in 24 (4.17.1).

rebellion

jority remained dutiful: it was the general crowd of debtors and clients which 2
took up arms. And they were making for the denes whose name is Arduenna,
when they were stopped by the legions which Visellius and C. Silius from their
respective armies had flung against them along opposing routes.[105] Sent ahead 3
with a select unit had been Julius Indus, who was from the same community and,
being disaffected with Florus, was on that account hungrier to exert himself, and
he scattered still further the unorganized multitude. Florus, foiling the victors with
his changes of hiding-place, finally, on seeing the soldiers who had beset his escape-
routes, fell by his own hand. And that was the end of Treverican turbulence.

Among the Aedui a greater storm arose, to the extent that their community **43**
was wealthier and the garrison for its suppression far away. With armed cohorts
Sacrovir had taken possession of Augustodunum (the nation's capital) and of the
noblest progeny in the Galliae (who were working there on liberal studies), so
that with them as surety he might enlist their parents and kinsmen; at the same time
he distributed among the youth arms which he had manufactured secretly. There 2
were forty thousand of them, a fifth in legionary armor, the rest with hunting-
spears and knives and other weapons which hunting people have. Added from the
slave population were those marked out for gladiatorship, who (in the native custom) had a complete covering of iron: they call them "cruppellarii," impractical
for inflicting blows, impenetrable when receiving them. These forces kept being 3
augmented, not yet with the open agreement of the neighboring communities,
but with a ready enthusiasm individually, as well as owing to the rivalry of the
Roman leaders, between whom there was a dispute, each of the two demanding
the war for himself. (Subsequently it was Varro who, ineffectual on account of his
elderly age, yielded to the vigorous Silius.)

But at Rome it was believed that not only the Treveri and Aedui but the sixty- **44**
four communities of the Galliae had defected, that the Germans had been enlisted into an alliance, and that the Spains were wavering—and every belief (as is
the custom with report) was exaggerated. All the best people sorrowed in their 2
concern for the state; many, in their hatred of the present and desire for change,
were delighted even at dangers to themselves and they berated Tiberius because,
during such a great commotion of affairs, he was devoting his energy to the documents of the accusers: would Sacrovir too be a defendant on a charge of treason in the forum? At last real men had appeared, who would suppress his gory
letters with their weapons![106] Even war was a good exchange for a wretched
peace. Yet, composing himself into an even more emphatic attitude of uncon- 4
cern, Tiberius went through those days without changing either location or demeanor but as normal—through loftiness of spirit, or else he had discovered that
the affair was limited and less serious than publicized.

105. For Silius see 1.31.2n.

106. The speakers are imagined as saying that letters from Tiberius, who was absent in
Campania (3.31.2), frequently denounced individuals for treason. In fact T. has mentioned
only one letter in such a category (3.38.2).

Silius against rebellion (handwritten annotation)

45   Meanwhile Silius, advancing with two legions and having sent ahead an auxiliary unit, devastated those districts of the Sequani which, being at the extremity of their territory and bordering on (and allied to) the Aedui, were under arms.
Soon he made for Augustodunum with a quick column, the standard-bearers
competing with one another and even the troop soldiery roaring not to delay
for their customary rest, not for the periods of nightfall: let them only see their
2   opponents and be observed! *That* would suffice for victory! At the twelfth milestone Sacrovir and his forces appeared on open ground. In front he had placed
the ironclads, on the edges the cohorts, and at the rear the half-armed. The man
himself on a distinctive horse made a tour of inspection within the front
ranks and recalled the old glories of the Gauls and the reverses which they had
inflicted on the Romans: how prestigious was freedom for the victors, how much
46   more intolerable was slavery for those twice vanquished! This speech was neither long nor welcomed: for the line of legions was closing in, and the unorganized townsmen, ignorant of soldiering, were inadequate to the sight and sound
of it.
       On the other side Silius, even though the presumption of hope had removed
the reasons for encouragement, nevertheless shouted repeatedly that they should
be ashamed that, as conquerors of the Germanies, they were being led against the
2   Gauls as if toward an enemy. "Recently the rebel Turonus was crushed by a single cohort, the Treverus by a single wing, the Sequani by a few squadrons of this
very army! To the extent that the Aedui are rich in money and enjoy a wealth of
pleasures, convince+ them how much more unwarlike *they* are—and spare a
3   thought for the runaways!" There was a mighty shout at these words; and the
cavalry poured around, the infantry assaulted the front, and there was no reluctance
on the flanks. The ironclads caused a little delay, their metal resistant against
javelins and swords; but the soldiery seized hatchets and pick-axes and, as if
breaching a wall, sliced coverings and bodies alike; some knocked over each un-
wieldy hulk with poles or forks, and, lying there, losing the struggle to get up
4   again, they were left as if lifeless. Sacrovir with the most loyal of his men proceeded first to Augustodunum, then, in his dread of surrender, to a nearby villa.
There he fell by his own hand, the rest by mutual blows; the villa, burning on
top of them, cremated everyone.
47   It was then that Tiberius finally wrote to the senate that the war had started
and been concluded. He neither detracted from nor added to the truth: the
2   legates had been superior in reliability and courage, himself in planning. At the
same time he added reasons why neither he nor Drusus had set off for the war,
emphasizing the size of the empire; nor was it proper for principes, if only one
or two communities were disruptive, to abandon the City,+ whence came direction for the whole; but now, since dread was not a factor to influence him, he
would go to examine the immediate situation and settle things down.
3   The fathers decreed prayers for his return and supplications and other proprieties; only Dolabella Cornelius, inasmuch as he had intentions of outstripping
the rest, proceeded to ridiculous sycophancy, proposing that he should enter

the City to an ovation from Campania.[107] So there followed a letter from 4
Caesar in which he proclaimed that, after taming the most defiant nations and
accepting or rejecting so many triumphs in his youth, he was not now, as an elderly man, so devoid of glory that he requested an empty reward for a suburban
peregrination.

★

About the same time he requested of the senate that the death of Sulpicius **48**
Quirinius be attended by public exequies, Quirinius had no connection with the
old patrician family of the Sulpicii, having been born in the municipality of
Lanuvium, but, enterprising in soldiering and with keen service to his credit, he
acquired the consulship under Divine Augustus and subsequently, after storming
the strongholds of the Homonadenses across Cilicia, the insignia of a triumph;[108]
and, having been given as mentor to C. Caesar during his tenure of Armenia,[109]
he had paid court to Tiberius too during his time on Rhodes. This the latter now 2
revealed in the senate, praising his duties toward himself and censuring M. Lollius, whom he criticized as having been responsible for C. Caesar's prevarication
and disaffection.[110] But to the others any recall of Quirinius was unwelcome owing to the danger with which he had faced Lepida (as I have recalled)[111] and to
his miserly and overpowerful old age.

At the end of the year Clutorius Priscus, a Roman equestrian who had been **49**
given money by Caesar after a celebrated poem in which he had lamented the final moments of Germanicus, was seized by a denouncer, casting at him the charge
that during an illness of Drusus he had composed something which, if the man's
life were extinguished, would be published for an even greater reward. Clutorius
as a foolish boast had read[+] it at the house of P. Petronius in the presence of
Vitellia, the latter's mother-in-law, and of many illustrious females.[112] When the 2
denouncer appeared, the others were terrified into giving testimony; only Vitellia
asserted that she had heard nothing. But more belief was accorded to those whose
criticisms were aimed at his ruin, and on the proposal of Haterius Agrippa, the
consul designate, the defendant was sentenced to the ultimate reprisal. —

On the other side M. Lepidus embarked in this fashion: "If, conscript fathers, **50**
we look exclusively at how wicked the voice of Clutorius Priscus was when he

107. P. Cornelius Dolabella (on whom see further 3.69.1, 4.66.2) had been consul in 10
and would later be proconsul of Africa (4.23.2–26.1).

108. For Quirinius, consul in 12 B.C., see above, 3.22.1.

109. For Gaius Caesar in Armenia see 2.4.1 and n.

110. For Lollius, consul in 21 B.C., see also 1.10.4n.

111. See 3.22–3 above.

112. P. Petronius (again at 6.45.2) was suffect consul in 19, proconsul of Asia 29–35, and
father-in-law of the emperor Vitellius.

polluted his own mind and people's ears, neither jail nor the noose nor even
2   servile rackings would be adequate for him. But, if outrages and offenses have no
limit, while at the same time the princeps's restraint and your ancestors' and your
own precedents limit reprisals and remedies; and if there is a difference between
foolishness and crime, between words and wrongdoing—then there is a place for
a proposal whereby this man's felony should not pass with impunity and we for
our part should have no cause to repent the combination of clemency and severity. I have often heard our princeps complaining whenever someone, by choos-
3   ing death, had forestalled his pity. Clutorius' life is intact, and neither will his
preservation constitute a danger to the state nor his killing a deterrent. His literary studies, full of derangement as they are, are illusory and fleeting; nor would
you dread anything weighty or serious from a man who, in betraying his own
outrages, infiltrates the minds not of men but of unfortunate women. Let him
nevertheless withdraw from the City, and, losing his property, be banned from
water and fire—something which I propose exactly as if he were liable under the
law of treason."

51   Only Rubellius Blandus, of the consulars, agreed with Lepidus; the others followed Agrippa's proposal, and Priscus was led to jail and immediately killed. That
was censured by Tiberius before the senate with his customary ambiguities, since
he extolled the devotion of those keenly avenging the injuries (however limited)
to a princeps, deprecated such precipitate punishment of mere words, lauded Lep-
2   idus and did not admonish Agrippa. There was therefore passed a senate's decision that no decrees of the fathers should be deposited in the treasury before the
tenth day and that that was the period of life which should be allowed to the condemned by way of delay. But the senate would enjoy no freedom for repentance,
nor would Tiberius be softened by the intermission of time.

★ ★ ★

A.D. 22

52   C. Sulpicius and D. Haterius were the following consuls[113]—a year not undis-
turbed+ in foreign affairs and at home by the suspicion of strictness against luxuriousness, whose inordinate surge had reached everything on which money is
squandered. Yet general expenditure, though actually heavier, was concealed by
the frequent disguising of prices; it was the publicity given in regular conversations to the accoutrements for belly and eating-house which had caused concern that a princeps of old-fashioned frugality might take harsher measures.[114]
2   For, beginning with C. Bibulus, the other aediles too had said that the expendi-

113. C. Sulpicius Galba, who commits suicide in 36 (6.40.2), was older brother of the
emperor Galba (for whom see 3.55.1, 6.15.1): their father was C. Sulpicius Galba, suffect
consul in 5 B.C. For Haterius see 1.77.3n.

114. I.e., harsher than those already taken in A.D. 16 (2.33.1).

ture law was being spurned and that forbidden prices for comestibles were increasing daily and could not be staunched by the ordinary remedies. And the fathers, when consulted, had deferred the business intact to the princeps.

But Tiberius—having often pondered to himself whether such surging desires   3
could be confined, whether their confinement would inflict a greater loss on the state, and how undignified it would be to handle something which he could not attain or which, if sustained, would entail ignominy and infamy for illustrious men—finally composed a letter to the senate, in which his proposal was in this manner: "In perhaps all other matters, conscript fathers, it would be more expe-   **53** dient if I were present to be questioned and to say what I recommend in the interests of the state; but on this motion it is better that my eyes be withdrawn, lest, as you mark the dread on the faces of those individuals who deserve criticism for their shameful luxuriousness, I myself should see them too and (as it were) apprehend them. Yet, if those energetic men, the aediles, had had a consultation   2 with me beforehand, I would probably have urged them to ignore rampant and mature vices rather than pursue a course which revealed the outrages for which we were no match. But they at least have performed their duty, as I would wish   3 the other magistrates too to fulfill their responsibilities; in my case, however, it is neither honorable to keep silent nor expeditious to speak out, because I do not undertake the role of aedile or praetor or consul. Something greater and loftier is demanded from a princeps; and, although each person arrogates to himself the credit for his correct actions, malpractice by all results in one man's being resented.

"For what should I first attempt to prohibit and prune back to its old-time   4
condition? The boundless expanses of villas? The number and nationalities of establishments? The weight of silver and gold? The wonders of bronze and of pictures? The indiscriminate clothing of males and females, and those items individual to females for which[+] *our* money is transferred to foreign or enemy peoples?[115] I am not unaware that during dinner parties and discussions those   **54** things are censured and a limit is sought; but, if anyone were to sanction a law and impose a penalty, those same people will cry repeatedly that the community is being overthrown, that extermination is intended for all the brightest, and that no one is exempt from a charge. And yet not even in the case of the body could you inhibit chronic and far-advanced diseases except by harsh and rough treatment; corrupted and corruptive alike, sick and inflamed, the mind is not to be cooled down by remedies lighter than the lusts with which it burns. The many   2 laws devised by our ancestors, the many which Divine Augustus carried, are inoperative, the former through oblivion, the latter (which is more outrageous) through contempt, making luxuriousness a matter of less concern. For, should you want what is not yet forbidden, there is always the fear that it may be forbidden; but, if you pass across prohibited areas with impunity, no dread lies beyond nor shame.

115. The "items" are jewels.

3   "Why, then, was frugality once a force? Because each man restrained himself, because we were citizens of a single City; there were not even the same incitements when we were masters only within Italy: it is by foreign victories that we have learned to use others' products, by civil-war victories to use up our own also.

4   How trivial is that issue of yours, about which the aediles warn! How lightly, if you consider everything else, it is to be regarded! As Hercules is my witness, no one brings a motion to the effect that Italy needs foreign supplies, that the livelihood of the Roman people pitches daily through the uncertainties of sea and storms! And, if the provinces' resources do not come to the aid of masters and slaves and fields, it is evidently our copses and our villas that will protect us!

5   "This, conscript fathers, is the concern which a princeps undertakes; this, if neglected, will drag the state down to the ground. For other things the remedy must be within the mind: let ourselves be changed for the better by shame, the poor by necessity, the rich by satiety. Alternatively, if any of the magistrates guarantees such industriousness and strictness that he is able to confront the issue, I

6   both praise him and acknowledge that he is disburdening part of my labors. If, on the other hand, they want merely to accuse vices and later, when they have acquired the glory for that, they create feuds which they leave to me, then believe me, conscript fathers, I too am not greedy for affronts to be leveled at me. Although I accept the risk of them, despite their severity and frequent unfairness, for the good of the state, I rightly decline those which are unavailing and unprofitable, likely to be of no use to myself or you."

55   When Caesar's letter had been heard, the aediles were relieved of their concern for such matters; and luxuriousness of the table—which, from the end of the Actian war to the hostilities which brought Servius Galba to the acquisition of power, was practiced for a hundred years[116] with surging expenditure—gradually abated.

2   The reasons for that change are pleasant to consider. Formerly rich families—either of nobles or those distinguished by their brilliancy—had been collapsing through their enthusiasm for magnificence. (Even then it was legitimate to court, and to be courted by, plebs, allies, kingdoms: as each man displayed himself by means of his house, wealth, and accoutrements, so his greater illustriousness in

3   respect of his name and clientships was maintained.) After the savage slaughters had taken place and the greatness of one's reputation began to mean extermination,[117] the rest converted to wiser courses. At the same time new men, frequently enlisted into the senate from the municipalities and colonies and even the provinces,[118] introduced a domestic frugality, and, although by good fortune or

116. I.e., 31 B.C.–A.D. 68/69.

117. In my view the two parts of this clause refer respectively to the civil wars of A.D. 68/69 and the reign of Domitian (A.D. 81–96).

118. Elsewhere T. describes Lucilius Longus as a "new man" (4.15.1–2), the first of his family to reach the consulship (in A.D. 7); here one of the broader definitions of the term seems intended (see *OCD* 1051–2 s.v. novus homo).

industriousness many reached a moneyed old age, their former mind-set still remained. But the principal instigator of disciplined behavior was Vespasian, 4 himself a man of an old-fashioned style of living:[119] thenceforward there was compliance with the princeps, and a love of rivalry more effective than either punishment by laws or dread—unless by chance there is in all matters a certain 5 circularity (as it were), with the result that, just as the changes of season come around again, so do those of behavior. (Nor was everything better in the time of our forbears, but our age too has produced many an instance of excellence in the arts which deserves to be imitated by posterity. Whether or not this happens, however, may these be the contests of ours with our ancestors which will enjoy an honorable survival.[120])

Tiberius, having won a reputation for restraint because he had checked the **56** swooping accusers, sent a letter to the senate in which he sought the tribunician power for Drusus. (That designation for the highest exaltedness was devised by 2 Augustus in order that he should not take on the name of king or dictator and yet by some entitlement should tower over the other commands. Subsequently he chose Marcus Agrippa as his partner in that power and, on his decease, Tiberius Nero, so that his successor should not be in doubt.[121] He deemed that in this way the perverse hopes of others would be checked; at the same time he trusted the modestness of Nero and his own greatness. It was with this example that 3 Tiberius now moved Drusus close to the supremacy, although during Germanicus' lifetime he had suspended judgment impartially between the two.) After veneration of the gods at the start of his letter, praying that they should prosper his policies for the state, his motion about the juvenile's behavior was restrained and not exaggerated into falsehood: Drusus had a spouse and three children and 4 was the same age at which he himself had once been called by Divine Augustus to take on this responsibility; nor was it now hastily but after undergoing trial for eight years, suppressing mutinies and settling wars, that the triumph-holder and two-times consul was being enlisted as participant in the familiar toil.[122]

The fathers in their minds had anticipated his speech: whence their syco- **57** phancy was the more studied. Yet nothing was devised except to propose like-

119. Vespasian was emperor A.D. 69–79.

120. With the phrases "many an instance of excellence in the arts" and "these . . . contests of ours" T. seems to be alluding diplomatically to his present work, the *Annals,* suggesting its place in the later ("posterity") and earlier ("ancestors") literary tradition and hoping that it will survive to be read by future generations.

121. Augustus granted tribunician power to Agrippa in 18 and 13 B.C. and to Tiberius in 6 B.C. and A.D. 4 and 13.

122. The relevant dates of Drusus' career are: mutinies A.D. 14 (1.16–30); wars A.D. 17–19 (2.44.1, 2.46.5, 2.62.1); triumph 28 May A.D. 20 (3.19.3); consulships A.D. 15 and 21 (1.55.1, 3.31.1). Drusus will have celebrated his 35th or 36th birthday on 7 October of the present year: it seems strange that T. should refer to him (above) as a "juvenile" (*adulescentis*), but the term *iuuenis* ("young man") could be used of any adult male up to the age of forty-five.

nesses of the principes, altars of the gods, temples, and arches, and other conventional items—except that M. Silanus, in an insult to the consulship, sought an honor for the principes and gave it as his opinion that, for the commemoration of time on public or private monuments, their headings should comprise the
2   names not of the consuls but of those who wielded tribunician power. As for Q. Haterius, when he proposed that the senate's decisions on that day should be fixed in golden letters in the curia, he became an object of derision—an old man destined to enjoy only the infamy of his foulest sycophancy.[123]

58   It was in the midst of all this that, Junius Blaesus' tenure of the province of Africa having been extended, Servius Maluginensis, the flamen Dialis, asked to have Asia as his allocation, insisting that the common belief that it was not legitimate for Diales to leave Italy was mistaken and that his prerogative was no different from those of the Martial and Quirinal flamines.[124] Further, if *they* drew provinces,[125] why was it forbidden to Diales? No resolutions by the people were
2   discovered on the issue, he said, nothing in the books of ritual prohibitions. Pontiffs had often performed the Dialian rites if the flamen were hindered by health or by some public responsibility: in the seventy-two years after the slaughter of Cornelius Merula[126] no one had replaced him, yet the religious observances had not ceased; and, if for so many years it was possible for someone not to be appointed with no loss to the rites, how much easier would be his own absence for
3   a single year's proconsular command! Formerly it had been private feuds which ensured that the high pontiff prevented them from going to provinces; but now, by the gift of the gods, the supreme pontiff was also the supreme man, suscepti-
59   ble to neither rivalry nor hatred or private emotions. —Since in reply Lentulus the augur and others spoke in various different ways, recourse was had to awaiting the high pontiff's opinion.

2   But Tiberius, deferring inquiry into the flamen's prerogative, modified the ceremonial decreed on account of Drusus' tribunician power, criticizing by name the unconventional and overbearing nature of the proposal,[127] and golden letters were contrary to the fathers' custom. A letter from Drusus too was read out, which, though steered toward restraint, was construed as being extremely
3   haughty: everything had fallen so low, they said, that not even a young man in receipt of such an honor approached the City's gods, entered the senate, or so much as took the auspices on his native ground! It was a war, naturally! Or he was divorced from them by some distant land, traversing Campania's littoral and
4   lakes at that very moment! Such was the plunge being taken by the helmsman

---

123. For M. Silanus see 3.24.3n.; for Haterius see 1.13.4n.

124. Servius Cornelius Lentulus Maluginensis had been suffect consul in 10 (his death is noted at 4.16.1); for Blaesus see 1.16.2n., 3.35.1–3.

125. By lot (see, e.g., 2.43.1 and n.).

126. He had committed suicide in 87 B.C.

127. Sc. of M. Silanus (3.57.1 above).

of the human race! That was the first lesson from his father's policies! Of course an elderly Commander might be oppressed by the sight of his citizens and might plead as his excuses the exhaustion of age and the completion of toils; but in Drusus' case what except arrogance was the obstacle?

Yet Tiberius, while reaffirming for himself the essence of the principate, pre-   **60** sented to the senate an old-fashioned image in sending demands from the provinces for investigation by the fathers.[128] (There had been spreading through Greek cities a license and impunity in the setting up of asylums: temples were filling up with the worst slaves and were likewise a place of refuge for receiving those indebted to creditors and suspects on capital charges; nor had any command been sufficiently effective for curbing the mutinousness of a people who were as protective of the outrages of men as of the ceremonies of the gods. It was   2 therefore decided that communities should send legates concerning their prerogatives; and, while some spontaneously abandoned what they had falsely appropriated, many put their trust in olden superstitions or their services to the Roman people.) And great was the scene on that day when the senate had an   3 insight into the benefactions of its ancestors, the pacts with the allies, the decrees too of kings who had ruled before the period of Roman might, and the injunctions of the divinities themselves—with freedom, as formerly, regarding what to reaffirm or change.

First of all the Ephesians approached, recalling that Diana and Apollo had not,   **61** as the public believed, been born at Delos: on their own home territory they had the Cenchrian stream and grove of Ortygia, where Latona, heavy with her progeny and leaning against an olive tree (which at that time still survived), had produced those divinities; and on the gods' advice the copse had been consecrated, and there Apollo himself after killing the Cyclopes had avoided Jupiter's anger. Subsequently Father Liber,[129] victorious in war, had pardoned the suppliant Amazons who had installed themselves at the altar; thereafter the temple's ceremonial had been augmented by a concession from Hercules when he had charge of Lydia, nor had its prerogative been diminished under the jurisdiction of the Persians; and afterward the Macedonians and then we had preserved it.

Next were the Magnesians, relying on decisions of L. Scipio and L. Sulla—of   **62** whom the former after the expulsion of Antiochus, and the latter after that of Mithridates, paid tribute to the Magnesians' loyalty and valor—that the refuge of Diana Leucophryena should be inviolable.[130] After this the Aphrodisians and   2

---

128. The subject of chapters 60–3 (as of 4.14.1–2) is asylum, i.e., the territorial inviolability which was enjoyed especially by certain temples or shrines and was a source of local pride in the Greek world and often constituted the basis for rivalry between neighboring communities, some of whom were able to demonstrate that their privilege had been properly granted or confirmed in the distant past (e.g., by some Roman general): see K. J. Rigsby, *Asylia: Territorial Inviolability in the Hellenistic World* (Berkeley, CA 1996).

129. I.e., Bacchus.

130. The references are to L. Cornelius Scipio Asiagenes and Antiochus III in 190/189

Stratonicensians adduced a decree of Caesar as dictator for their longstanding services to the party and a recent one of Divine Augustus wherein they were praised because they had endured the irruption of the Parthians with no change in their steadfastness toward the Roman people. (The only difference was that the Aphrodisians' community guarded the religious cult of Venus, the Stratoni-
3 censians' that of Jupiter and Trivia.) In more depth the Hierocaesarians explained that on their home territory there was a Persian Diana, a shrine dedicated in the kingship of Cyrus; and they recalled the names of Perpenna, Isauricus, and many other commanders, who had bestowed the same sanctity not only on the tem-
4 ple but for two miles around it.[131] Thereafter the Cyprians explained about their three shrines, of which the most olden had been established to Paphian Venus by its founder Aërias, the next by his son Amathus to Venus Amathusia, and one to Jupiter Salaminius by Teucer, a refugee from the anger of his father Telamon.

63   Legations from other communities too were heard. The fathers—exhausted by their number and loquacity, and because the contest was conducted with enthusiasm—entrusted everything to the consuls, on the understanding that, after the investigation of each prerogative and especially if any irregularity was in-
2 volved, they would refer the matter impartially back to the senate. The consuls, in addition to those communities which I have recalled, recorded that at Pergamum the asylum of Aesculapius had been proved, but the others were relying on
3 beginnings which were dark because of age: the Smyrnaeans, they said, referred to an oracle of Apollo, at whose command they had dedicated a temple to Venus Stratonicis, and the Teneans to a prophecy of his, by which they had been ordered to consecrate a likeness and temple of Neptune. The Sardians' references had been more recent: theirs was a gift of victorious Alexander; and the Milesians were basing themselves no less on King Darius (the difference was that in each case the divinities' cults consisted of venerating Diana and Apollo respectively). The Cretans too were making a request on behalf of their representation
4 of Divine Augustus. —And there were passed senate's decisions whereby, albeit with much honor, a limit was nevertheless prescribed, and the various parties were ordered to fix bronzes in the actual temples for enshrining the commemoration of the record and to prevent lapses into self-aggrandizement under the guise of religious injunctions.

64   About the same time the frightening state of Julia Augusta's health necessitated the princeps's speedy return to the City, the harmony between mother and son
2 being still sound—or their hatreds hidden. (Not long before, when Julia was ded-

---

B.C. (2.63.3 and n.) and to Sulla and Mithridates in 87/86 B.C. (2.55.1 and n.). Note that the petitioners here are from Magnesia-on-Meander and not (as at 2.47.3) Magnesia-by-Sipylus.

131. M. Perpenna defeated Aristonicus in 130 B.C.; P. Servilius Isauricus was proconsul of Asia 46–44 B.C.

icating a likeness to Divine Augustus not far from the theater of Marcellus, she had written Tiberius' name after her own, an action which, as belittling the sovereignty of the princeps, he was believed to have buried away, disguising the weightiness of his affront.)[132] But afterward the senate decreed supplications to   3
the gods, and Great Games which were to be produced by the pontiffs and augurs and quindecimvirs along with the septemvirs[133] and the Augustal Fellows. L. Apronius had proposed that the fetials[134] too should preside at these games;   4
but Caesar spoke against, distinguishing the prerogatives of the priesthoods and tracing back examples: never had the fetials enjoyed that degree of sovereignty, he said; the precise reason for the addition of the Augustals was that their priesthood was peculiar to the very family for which the vows were being paid.

Recounting proposals has not been my established practice, except those distinguished by honorableness or of noteworthy discredit, which I deem to be a   **65**
principal responsibility of annals, to prevent virtues from being silenced and so that crooked words and deeds should be attended by the dread of posterity and infamy.[135] Yet those times were so tainted and contaminated by sycophancy that   2
not only community leaders (whose own brilliancy had to be protected by compliance) but all the consulars, a majority of former praetors, and many pedestrian senators[136] too competed with one another in rising and delivering their foul and excessive suggestions. It is transmitted to memory that, whenever Tiberius   3
went out of the curia, he became accustomed to call out in Greek words in this fashion: "Ah! Men primed for slavery!" Evidently even he, who disliked public freedom, was averse to such prompt and prostrate passivity from the servile.

But gradually thereafter they crossed from the discreditable to the destructive.   **66**
C. Silanus, the proconsul of Asia, arraigned by the allies for extortion, was seized

132. Both the date (23 April) and Livia's "affront" to Tiberius have survived in the official record (EJ, p. 48).

133. Septemvirs were the most recently instituted of the four major priestly colleges (see App. A). Their principal function was to organize a great feast at the games (*OCD* 1389).

134. Twenty fetials formed one of the less important priestly colleges; traditionally they had advised on matters of peace and war but this function was now largely obsolete (*OCD* 594).

135. In this sentence T. says that it is not his habit to record routine proposals made formally in the senate but that he is selective (selectivity being "a principal responsibility" of the historian): he records only those which stand out as being particularly honorable or particularly discreditable, and his purpose in so doing is twofold—to immortalize good deeds and to remind his readers that, should they be tempted into discreditable behavior in their turn, there will always be some future Tacitus to record their behavior for posterity and thus ensure their infamy. However, most other interpreters of this famous sentence understand T. to be saying "... because I deem the greatest function of history to be that virtues should not be silenced and that crooked words and deeds should be attended by dread from posterity and infamy"; but see *Tac. Rev.* 86–103.

136. A strange term for junior senators below the rank of praetorians.

simultaneously by Mamercus Scaurus, one of the consulars,[137] Junius Otho a praetor, and Bruttedius Niger an aedile, and they cast at him the charge that he had violated Augustus' divinity and spurned Tiberius' sovereignty, with Mamercus tossing down ancient examples: L. Cotta accused by Scipio Africanus, Servius

2   Galba by Cato the Censor, and P. Rutilius by M. Scaurus.[138] (Assuredly it was the same kinds of thing for which retribution was sought by Scipio and Cato or by the famous Scaurus, his great-grandfather, whom Mamercus, a reproach to his

3   ancestors, was dishonoring with his infamous efforts! And Junius Otho's long-standing skill was to operate an elementary school; later a senator owing to the powerfulness of Sejanus, he polluted his dark beginnings still further by un-

4   abashed acts of daring. As for Bruttedius, abounding in honorable attainments and—if he had proceeded along a straight path—destined to reach every brilliance, speed spurred him on, inasmuch as he had intentions of outstripping his equals, then those ahead of him, and finally his very own hopes—something which has sent to the bottom many good men too, who, spurning rewards which are late but trouble-free, hasten those which are premature but actually termi-

67   nal.) The number of accusers was increased by Gellius Publicola and M. Paconius, the former the quaestor of Silanus, the latter his legate.

There was held to be no doubt that he was liable on charges of savagery and

2   of taking money; but many factors, dangerous even to the blameless, were piling up against him, since, in addition to so many senatorial opponents, he was replying to men who were the most fluent in all Asia and chosen to accuse for that very reason; whereas he was on his own and ignorant of advocacy, and in a state of dread (which cripples even practiced eloquence) peculiar to himself, since Tiberius did not refrain from pressurizing him by language, look, and very frequent personal questioning; nor was it permitted to rebut or evade, and often even confession too was required, lest the latter should have asked in vain.

3   Silanus' slaves had also been received by the public agent in formal conveyance, so they could be questioned under torture;[139] and, to prevent the endangered man from being helped by any persons obliged to him, the charges of treason

4   were supplied—a binding obligation for silence. Therefore, having sought a few days' intermission, he deserted his own defense, after sending[+] a note to Caesar in which he had combined resentment with his pleas.

68   Tiberius, in order that his intentions for Silanus might be received more justifiably with the help of an example, ordered the documents of Divine Augustus concerning Volesus Messalla (likewise a proconsul of Asia) and the senate's

2   decision passed against him to be read out.[140] Then he asked L. Piso his opin-

---

137. C. Junius Silanus, consul in 10, had been proconsul of Asia in 20–21; for his brothers and sister see 3.24.1 and n. For Mamercus Scaurus see 1.13.4n.

138. The respective dates were 138, 149, and 116 B.C.

139. See also 2.30.3 for this maneuver.

140. M. Valerius Messala Volesus (consul in A.D. 5) had been proconsul of Asia in A.D. 11 or 12.

ion.[141] He, after a lengthy preamble on the princeps's clemency, proposed that water and fire be forbidden to Silanus and the man himself relegated to the island of Gyarus. Similarly the others, except that Cn. Lentulus said that Silanus' maternal property should be kept separate (for he was born of quite a different sort of[+] parent) and restored to his son—this to endorsement from Tiberius.

But Cornelius Dolabella, inasmuch as he was pursuing his sycophancy further,[142] after berating Silanus' behavior added that no one should draw lots for a province if he were scandalous in life and covered in infamy, and that the princeps should adjudicate the matter: felonies were indeed punished by law, he said, but how much gentler it would be for the men themselves, and better for the allies, to make advance provision that no malpractice should take place! In response Caesar said that it was not of course unknown to him what was publicized about Silanus, but it was not in the light of rumor that decisions should be made: many in the provinces had acted contrary to what one's hope or dread about them had been: some were sharpened for the better by the greatness of affairs, others grew dull; a princeps could not embrace everything in his own knowledge, and it was not expedient for him to be swayed by an ambition which was alien to him.[143] The precise reason why laws were constituted for past deeds was that future ones were in doubt: it had been their ancestors' established usage that, if felonies preceded, punishment followed; they should not invert what was wisely devised and always accepted. Principes had enough burdens, enough powerfulness too: rights were diminished whenever power swelled, nor should one resort to commanding when it was possible to conduct matters by law.

To the extent that it was relatively rare for Tiberius to court popularity, the feelings with which these words were received were all the more delighted. And he for his part—prudent at moderating his course if he was not driven by personal anger—added that the island of Gyarus was a ruthless place, without human habitation: they should concede to the Junian family, and to a man formerly of the same rank as themselves, that he retire rather to Cythnus: that was the request of Silanus' sister too, Torquata, a Virgin of old-time sanctity.[144] On this proposal the division took place.

Afterward the Cyrenaeans were heard and, on the accusation of Ancharius Priscus, Caesius Cordus was condemned for extortion.[145] As for L. Ennius, a Roman equestrian arraigned for treason on the grounds that he had converted a likeness of the princeps to put its silver to indiscriminate use, Caesar forbade him

69

2

3

4

5

6

70

141. Perhaps the consul of 15 B.C. (6.10.3n.) rather than that of 1 B.C. (2.34.1n.), but the matter is uncertain.

142. See 3.47.3 above.

143. Tiberius is not only underlining his own aloofness but also criticizing Dolabella, whose proposal, being sycophantic, was also self-seeking.

144. An inscription attests her as having been a Vestal Virgin for sixty-four years.

145. T. has here resumed the case from 3.38.1 above.

to be cited among the defendants—something openly spurned by Ateius Capito
2   with apparent freedom of speech:[146] the power of deciding ought not to be
snatched from the fathers, he said, nor should such great wrongdoing be treated
with impunity; by all means let him be slow to respond in the case of his own
3   pain, but he should not condone injuries to the state. Tiberius understood this
for what it was, rather than for what was said, and he persevered with his intervention. Capito became more identified with infamy, because, knowledgeable of
human and divine law as he was, he had dishonored his exceptional public
record[+] and fine domestic attainments.

71   There next occurred a question of religion: in which precise temple should
be sited the gift which the Roman equestrians had vowed to Equestrian Fortune
for Augusta's health.[147] (Though there were many shrines of that goddess in the
City, there was nevertheless none with such a designation.) It was discovered that
there was a sanctuary at Antium which was so denominated and that all the ceremonies, temples, and divinities' likenesses in Italian towns were under Roman
2   jurisdiction and command. So the gift was placed at Antium. And, because religious questions were being handled, Caesar produced his recently deferred reply with regard to Servius Maluginensis, the flamen Dialis,[148] and he read out a
decree of the pontiffs that, whenever adverse health befell the flamen Dialis, he
could be absent more than two nights at the high pontiff's discretion, provided
it was not on days of public sacrifice nor more often than twice in the same year.
The fact that these decisions were made in Augustus' principate, he said, was
enough to show that a year's absence and the administration of provinces were
3   not granted to Diales. And also recalled was the example of the high pontiff
L. Metellus, who had kept back the flamen Aulus Postumius.[149] So the allotment
of Asia was conferred on the man who was next of the consulars to Maluginensis.

72   In the course of the same days Lepidus[150] asked the senate that he might use
his own money to consolidate and decorate the basilica of Paulus, an Aemilian
monument. (There was even then a custom of public munificence, nor had Augustus banned Taurus, Philippus, and Balbus from contributing enemy trophies
or their own torrential wealth to the decoration of the City and their descendants' glory.[151] It was with this example that Lepidus now, though limited for
2   money, revived his ancestral honor.) As for Pompeius's theater, however, consumed by a chance fire, its building was guaranteed by Caesar on the precise
grounds that no one from the family was adequate for its restoration, though the

146. For Capito see 3.75.1n. below.
147. For her health see 3.64 above.
148. See 3.58–59.2 above.
149. In 242 B.C. (Livy 37.51.1–2).
150. This is Marcus Aemilius Lepidus (1.13.2n.).
151. T. Statilius Taurus (consul in 37 and 26 B.C.) had built an amphitheater, L. Marcius
Philippus (consul in 38 B.C.) a temple to Hercules and the Muses, and L. Cornelius Balbus (consul in 40 B.C.) a theater.

name of Pompeius would survive. At the same time he extolled Sejanus with re-   3
peated praise, to the effect that through his toil and vigilance such great violence
had stopped at this single loss. And the fathers proposed a likeness for Sejanus,
to be sited at the theater of Pompeius. And not long afterward, when Caesar   4
was exalting Junius Blaesus, the proconsul of Africa, with the insignia of a triumph, he said that his granting of it was an honor for Sejanus (whose uncle the
former was).

★

And yet Blaesus' achievements were worthy of such adornment.[152] For Tacfari-   **73**
nas, though often beaten back, had reconstituted his reserves across the African
interior, reaching such a pitch of arrogance that he sent legates to Tiberius and
spontaneously demanded an abode for himself and his army or he threatened an
ever-unfolding war. They maintain that at no other time did Caesar feel greater   2
pain at an insult to himself and the Roman people than he felt that a deserter
and looter was acting in the manner of an enemy: not even to Spartacus—at the
time when he was scorching an Italy still unavenged after so many disasters to
consular armies, and although the state was tottering under great wars with Sertorius and Mithridates[153]—had it been granted that he be received into our trust
under a pact; still less, with the Roman people having reached its finest pinnacle, would the bandit Tacfarinas be bought off with peace and a concession of
land. He gave the business to Blaesus: the others should be enticed to the prospect   3
of laying down their arms without harm, he said, but the leader himself should
be seized by whatever means.

Very many were received in surrender by that pardon; subsequently war was
waged against the techniques of Tacfarinas by means not dissimilar to his own.
For, being no match in the hard core of his army but better at stealth, he kept   **74**
raiding and eluding with several groups and at the same time attempted ambushes. So three lines of advance and the same number of columns were prepared. Of these, Cornelius Scipio the legate was in charge in the area where there   2
was plundering against the Lepcitani and refuge among the Garamantes.[154] On
another flank, to prevent the districts of the Cirtenses from being annexed with
impunity, Blaesus' son led a unit of his own. In the middle with the picked men,
installing strongholds and fortifications at suitable points, the leader himself had
made everything confined and hostile for the enemy, because, whichever way

152. T. here resumes African affairs from 3.20–1 above; for Blaesus' appointment to Africa
see 3.32.1 and 3.35.

153. Spartacus, the famous leader of a slave revolt, had defeated several consular armies
in 72 B.C.; Q. Sertorius' revolt in Spain was 80–73 B.C.; the Second and Third Mithridatic Wars were c. 83–81 and 74–63 B.C.

154. P. Cornelius Lentulus Scipio, suffect consul in 24 and later married to the elder Poppaea (11.2.2), was father of the consul of 56 (13.25.1).

they turned, some part of the Roman soldiery was in front, on the flank and (as often) in the rear; and by those means many were slaughtered or surrounded.

3   Then he divided his tripartite army into several units and placed centurions of tested courage in charge. Nor, as had been the custom, did he withdraw his forces at the finish of the summer season or settle them in winter quarters in the old province;[155] but, deploying strongholds as if at the threshold to the war, by means of unencumbered men who were knowledgeable of the wastes he kept disrupting Tacfarinas' changes of mapalia,[156] until finally, on the capture of the man's brother, Blaesus turned back—too hastily, however, for the allies' benefit, since remnants were left who would resurrect the war.

4   But Tiberius, interpreting the war as concluded, also granted to Blaesus that he be hailed as "commander" by his legions—an old-time honor for leaders who, having served the state well, were acclaimed on the joyful impulse of their victorious army; and there used to be several "commanders" simultaneously, nor any one above the equality of the rest. To some men Augustus too gave that designation, as did Tiberius then, to Blaesus, for the last time.

★

75   There died in that year the illustrious men Asinius Saloninus, distinctive for having as grandfathers Marcus Agrippa and Pollio Asinius, Drusus as brother, and marked out to be Caesar's grandson-in-law;[157] and Capito Ateius, about whom I have already recalled[158] and who achieved a principal place in the community for his civil studies, but with a Sullan centurion for a grandfather, and a praetorian for a father. His consulship had been accelerated by Augustus so that in the rank and esteem of that magistracy he should anticipate Labeo Antistius, who

2   out-stepped him in the same arts.[159] For that was an age which simultaneously produced two adornments of peace; but Labeo was a man of incorruptible freedom and on that account the more celebrated in reputation, whereas Capito's compliance was more approved by his masters. In the former's case, because he

155.   An anachronism: there had been no province of "Old Africa" since the period 46–42 B.C.

156.   Seemingly a Punic word for the huts of African nomads (again at 4.25.1).

157.   Asinius Saloninus was son of Vipsania (daughter of Agrippa and first wife of Tiberius) and Asinius Gallus (1.8.3n.), brother of the consuls of 25 (4.34.1) and 38, half-brother (on his father's side) of the consul of 23 (4.1.1) and (on his mother's side) of Drusus Caesar, Tiberius' son. The children of Germanicus and Agrippina were his cousins, one of whom he was evidently engaged to marry (as T. here notes).

158.   Most recently at 3.70 above, but also at 1.76.1 and 1.79.1.

159.   Or perhaps "who was outstanding in the same arts." C. Ateius Capito had been suffect consul in A.D. 5; M. Antistius Labeo never became consul, though there was a story (contradicting what T. says here) that he was offered the consulship by Augustus but refused it.

stopped at the praetorship, commendation of him sprang from his rebuff; in the latter's, because he acquired the consulship, hatred of him from men's resentment.

And Junia too, in the sixty-fourth year after the battle lines of Philippi,[160] con-   **76** summated her final day, begotten with Cato as her uncle, the wife of C. Cassius, sister of M. Brutus.[161] Her will was the subject of considerable rumor among the public because with all her great wealth, though she had named almost all aristocrats with honor, she neglected Caesar. That was accepted in a citizenlike man-   2 ner, and he did not prevent her funeral from being honored with praise in front of the rostra and with every other solemnity. Twenty images from the most brilliant families were carried in front, the Manlii, Quinctii, and other names of similar nobility;[162] but outshining all were Cassius and Brutus, for the very reason that likenesses of them were not on view.

160. In 42 B.C. (1.2.1n.).

161. Junia Tertia was the daughter of Servilia (half-sister of the younger Cato) by her marriage to D. Junius Silanus (consul in 62 B.C.); a previous marriage to M. Junius Brutus had produced the tyrannicide M. Brutus, who was therefore Junia's half-sister. See *OCD* 1394 s.v. Servilia.

162. For the images see 2.27.2n.

BOOK 4

1 With C. Asinius and C. Antistius as consuls,[1] Tiberius was experiencing his ninth year with the state calm and his household flourishing (Germanicus' death he reckoned among the successes), when suddenly fortune started to turn disruptive and the man himself savage—or to present control to savages. The beginning and reason lay with Aelius Sejanus, prefect of the praetorian cohorts, about whose powerfulness I recalled above;[2] now I shall expound his origin, behavior, and the act by which he moved to seize mastery.

2 Begotten at Vulsinii, his father being Seius Strabo (a Roman equestrian),[3] in his early youth he was a regular follower of C. Caesar (grandson of Divine Augustus) and rumored to have offered the sale of illicit sex to the rich and prodigal Apicius; later, by various means, he shackled Tiberius to such an extent that the latter, dark as he was toward others, was rendered uniquely unguarded and unprotected in respect of Sejanus himself—this not so much by artfulness (indeed it was by the same means that he was vanquished) as by the anger of the gods against the Roman cause, for whose extermination he alike thrived and

3 fell.[4] His body was enduring of toil, his mind daring. Always self-concealing, he was an accuser of others. Sycophancy coexisted with haughtiness. Outwardly he had a calm reserve, internally a lust for acquiring supremacy, and for that reason there was sometimes lavishing and luxuriousness, but more often industry and vigilance—no less harmful when they are molded toward the procurement of kingship.

2 He increased the influence (previously limited) of the prefecture[5] by gathering into a single camp the cohorts scattered across the City, so that they would receive commands simultaneously and, given both the number of the resulting hard core and their sight of one another, there would be a rise in their own confidence and in the dread of everyone else. He pretended that a dispersed soldiery acted recklessly; if some emergency occurred, he said, a concerted rescue would offer better help; and they would behave more strictly if the rampart were set up at some

2 distance from the allurements of the City. But, when the camp was completed, he gradually wormed his way into the soldiers' hearts by approaching and addressing

---

1. C. Asinius Pollio was son of Asinius Gallus (1.8.3n.), grandson of Asinius Pollio (1.12.4n.), brother of the consul of 25 (4.34.1) and half-brother of Asinius Saloninus, just mentioned (3.75.1). C. Antistius Vetus was son of the homonymous consul of 6 B.C.; his brother was suffect consul in 28.

2. At 3.66.3; see also 1.24.2, 3.29.4, and 3.72.3.

3. See 1.7.2, 1.24.2 for Seius Strabo. He had been appointed prefect of Egypt in A.D. 15.

4. The eventual "vanquishing" and "fall" of Sejanus in A.D. 31, to which T. refers here, were recorded in a portion of Book 5 of the *Annals* which has not survived.

5. Of the Praetorian Guard.

them by name; at the same time he selected centurions and tribunes personally. Nor did he refrain from senatorial canvassing, endowing his own clients with hon-   3 ors or provinces—with Tiberius complaisant and so well inclined that he cele-brated him as his "partner in toil" not only in conversation but before the fathers and people and allowed likenesses of him to be worshiped throughout theaters and forums and within the headquarters of legions.

Yet the house of the Caesars was full: a young son and grandsons grown up   **3** brought delay to his desires;[6] and, because the simultaneous seizure of so many by violence was unsafe, guile would demand intervals between the crimes. What   2 found favor, however, was the even more concealed method involved in his be-ginning with Drusus, against whom he was borne on a wave of fresh anger. (Drusus, intolerant of his rival and temperamentally rather volatile, had bran-dished his fists at Sejanus in a chance wrangle and had beaten him in the face when he brandished back.) As Sejanus tested every possibility, he decided that   3 the readiest recourse was to the man's wife, Livia,[7] Germanicus' sister, whose looks at the beginning of her life were unbecoming but who later excelled in beauty. As if burning with love, he enticed her into adultery and, after he had achieved this first outrage (and, with her modesty lost, a female was unlikely to reject other things), drove her to hope of espousal, partnership in a kingdom, and her husband's execution. And she for her part—who had Augustus as great-   4 uncle, Tiberius as father-in-law and children by Drusus—defiled both herself and her ancestors and descendants with a municipal adulterer, so that instead of her honorable and present circumstances she could look forward to outrage and uncertainty. Enlisted in complicity was Eudemus, Livia's friend and doctor and, under the show of his skill, accessible to her secrets. Sejanus drove from home his   5 wife, Apicata, by whom he had begotten three children, to prevent his concu-bine from suspecting him. But the magnitude of his act brought dread, postpone-ments, and sometimes conflicting plans.

Meanwhile at the year's inception the Drusus who was one of Germanicus'   **4** children assumed the toga of manhood, and what the senate had decreed for his brother Nero[8] was repeated. Caesar added a speech, with much praise of his own son for the paternal benevolence with which he was treating his brother's chil-dren. For, although it is precarious for powerfulness and harmony to exist in the same place, Drusus was regarded as being level with the juveniles, or at least not adverse to them.

Next the long-standing and often simulated plan of setting off for the   2 provinces was revived.[9] The multitude of veterans was one of the Commander's

6. The obstacles to Sejanus' desires are Tiberius' son, Drusus, and the elder sons of Ger-manicus (Nero Caesar and Drusus Caesar: see 4.4.1 below) in particular.

7. See 2.43.6 and n.

8. See 3.29.1.

9. For earlier references to the possibility of Tiberius' departing Rome see 1.47.3, 3.47.2.

pretexts, and the armies needed to be supplemented by levies: volunteer soldiery was lacking, he said, and, if a supply existed, they did not behave with the same courage and restraint, because for the most part it was only the impoverished and

3 vagrants who took up soldiering spontaneously. And he listed cursorily the number of legions and which provinces they safeguarded—something which I deem should be recounted by me too: namely, what Roman forces were then under arms, who the allied kings were, and how much more confined the empire was.[10]

5 Italy was presided by two fleets, one in each sea (at Misenum and Ravenna), and the nearby shore of Gaul by beaked ships which Augustus had seized in the Actian victory and sent with sturdy oarsmen to the Forojulian town.[11] But the principal hard core was eight legions along the Rhine, as a common defense against Germans and Gauls; the Spains, just recently tamed, were held by three.

2 The Mauri had been received by King Juba as a gift from the Roman people;[12] the rest of Africa was controlled by two legions, and Egypt by a similar number, and the whole area thereafter, which is encompassed within the mighty arc of land from the start of Syria right up to the River Euphrates, by only four legions, its neighbors being the Iberian, Albanian, and other kings who are protected by

3 our greatness against foreign empires. Thrace was held by Rhoemetalces and the children of Cotys, and the bank of the Danube by two legions in Pannonia and two in Moesia—with the same number located in Dalmatia, which, given the region's position, could be summoned from the rear by those provinces and, if Italy demanded sudden help, from not far away (although the City was occupied by its own soldiery, three urban and nine praetorian cohorts, chosen mostly from

4 Etruria and Umbria or from old Latium and the ancient Roman colonies). And at suitable points in the provinces there were allied triremes and wings and auxiliary cohorts, and not much difference in their strengths;[13] but it would be unreliable to go through them, since depending on the need of the moment they moved hither and thither and sometimes swelled in number and decreased.

6 I am inclined to believe it appropriate to review the other areas of the state too, and the ways in which they were handled up to that day, because for Tiberius that year brought the start of his principate's change for the worse.

2 From the very beginning public business, and the most important of private individuals', was dealt with before the fathers, and it was permitted for their leaders to speak, and those who slipped into sycophancy he checked himself. He handed out honors by paying regard to the nobility of ancestors, brilliancy of soldiering, and illustrious qualities at home, so there should be sufficient agreement that no others had had more powerful claims. Consuls and praetors each enjoyed

10. I.e., in comparison with T.'s own day. See also 2.61.2 above.

11. "Beaked" ships are warships. For the transitive use of the verb "preside" (again in Book 4 at 72.3) see Introduction, p. xxiv.

12. In 25 B.C.; for King Juba II see *OCD* 799.

13. I.e., their strengths were not much different from those of the legionary forces mentioned above.

their own special display; the power of the lesser magistrates too was exercised; and the laws, if the question of treason be subtracted, were in good use. As for 3 grain-dues and monetary revenues and the other sources of public income, they were managed by companies of Roman equestrians; his own affairs Caesar handed to those in his highest regard and to some unknowns on the basis of their reputation; and, once enlisted, they were held continuously without limit, since many grew old in the same activities. The plebs kept being exhausted by an ad- 4 mittedly acute food supply, but there was no blame for that on the princeps's part: in fact he confronted the problems of infertile lands and rough seas as much as he could by his expenditure and assiduousness; and he made provision that the provinces were not disrupted by new burdens and tolerated their old ones with- out greed or cruelty from magistrates: corporal beatings and deprivations of property were absent. Caesar's estates across Italy were scarce, his slaves restrained, his household limited to a few freedmen. And, if ever he was in dispute with pri- vate individuals, there was the forum and justice.

All of these things—not of course in an affable way but grisly and generally 7 alarming as he was—he nevertheless maintained until they were overturned with the death of Drusus. While he survived, everything continued because Sejanus, whose powerfulness was still only beginning, wanted to become known for good advice and dreaded an avenger[14] who did not conceal his hatred but complained frequently that, with a son alive and well, someone else was being called "assis- tant in command"; and how short the remaining stage until he was spoken of as 2 "colleague"! The first hopes of becoming master were a steep climb, he said; but, once you embarked, support and servants presented themselves: already on the prefect's initiative a camp had been constructed, soldiers placed in his hands; his likeness was visible among the monuments of Cn. Pompeius, and he would have grandsons in common with the family of the Drusi.[15] After all that, could some modestness be begged, whereby he would be content? —And it was not rarely 3 or to only a few people that he tossed out such remarks; and even his secrets kept on being betrayed through his corrupted wife. Therefore Sejanus, deeming that 8 haste was required, selected a poison which, by worming its way gradually, would resemble a chance disease. It was given to Drusus by the eunuch Lygdus, as be- came known eight years later.

As for Tiberius, throughout the days of the man's ill health he behaved with 2 no dread, or to display his firmness of purpose;[16] even in the interval between decease and burial he entered the curia and reminded the consuls (who were sit- ting in ordinary seating in a show of sorrowfulness) of their place of honor; and he rallied the senate, whose tears were pouring, by conquering his own groan- ing as well as by an unbroken speech. It was not of course unknown to him, he 3

14. Viz. Drusus himself.

15. For the statue in Pompey's theater see 3.72.3; the grandsons are the expected off- spring of the projected marriage between Sejanus' daughter and Claudius' son (3.29.4).

16. I have repunctuated section 2 of this chapter.

said, that he could be criticized because, with his pain so fresh, he had subjected himself to the eyes of the senate. The majority of grievers could scarcely endure encouraging words from relatives, could scarcely behold daylight, nor were they to be condemned for feebleness; but he had sought stronger comforts from the embrace of the state. And, having expressed pity at Augusta's extreme elderliness, the still raw age of his grandsons and his own declining years, he sought that Germanicus' children, the one and only alleviation of their present ills, should be escorted

4   in. After going out and fortifying the youngsters with encouraging words, the consuls escorted them down to Caesar and stood them before him. Grasping them, he said: "Conscript fathers, when these two were bereft of their parent, I passed them to their uncle and pleaded, although he had his own progeny, that he should foster, edify, strengthen them no differently from his own blood, both for his own

5   sake and for posterity. Now that Drusus has been snatched away, I transfer my pleas to you and before gods and fatherland I implore: undertake, direct the great-grandsons of Augustus, begotten with the most brilliant ancestry; fulfill your own function and mine. These men will be for you, Nero and Drusus, in the place of your parents: your birth is such that your good and ill affects the state."

9   These words were heard with great weeping and then with propitious prayers; and, if only he had put a limit on his speech, he would have filled his hearers' hearts with pity for himself and with thoughts of glory. As it was, recoiling onto empty and frequently derided topics (about rendering up the state and that the consuls or someone else should undertake its direction), he withdrew credibility even from what was genuine and honorable.

2   To Drusus' memory were decreed the same as for Germanicus, with numerous additions (as later sycophancy usually loves to do). His funeral was particularly illustrious for its procession of images,[17] since Aeneas, origin of the Julian family, and all the Albans' kings and Romulus, founder of the City, and after them the Sabine nobility, Attus Clausus and likenesses of the other Claudii were to be observed in a long line.

10   (In transmitting Drusus' death I have recorded what has been recalled by most authors and those of the greatest credibility; but I am not inclined to neglect from

2   those same times a rumor so effective that it has not yet abated. It was said that, after corrupting Livia into crime, Sejanus by means of illicit sex had constrained the heart of the eunuch Lygdus too, since, because of his age and good looks, he was dear to his master and among his leading servants. Then, when the place and time of the poisoning had been agreed between the accomplices, Sejanus had advanced to such a pitch of daring that he changed things and by means of anonymous information ensured that Drusus was accused of aiming to poison his father and that Tiberius was warned to avoid the first drink to be offered to him

3   when banqueting at the house of his son. Taken in by the deception, the old man on entering the party had handed to Drusus the cup he received; and he for his part had unknowingly drained it (as a young man would), increasing the suspi-

17. The date was 14 September (Sherk 28E, p. 54). For "images" see 2.27.2n.

cion that through dread and shame he was inflicting upon himself the death he
had set up for his father.

This was bandied about in public, but, beyond the fact that it is affirmed in no **11**
reliable author, you can readily refute it. What man of average prudence—still
less Tiberius, practiced as he was in great affairs—would have offered extermination to a son unheard, and that too with his own hand and no recourse for repentance? Would he not rather have racked the server of the poison, searched out
its initiator, and finally, given the innate hesitancy and delay with which he
treated even outsiders, treated his one and only, who had been discovered in no
outrage, with the same? Yet, because Sejanus was considered the deviser of every **2**
act, it was owing to Caesar's excessive affection for him and to everyone else's
hatred of them both that even the most monstrous fantasies were believed—
report being always more frightful in relation to one's departed masters. Besides,
the stages of the crime were betrayed by Sejanus' Apicata and disclosed by the
torturing of Eudemus and Lygdus; nor did any writer at all prove so hostile that
he cast this imputation at Tiberius, though they raked up and aimed everything **3**
else. In my case the reason for transmitting and criticizing the rumor was that on
the basis of a resounding example I might dispel false hearsay and ask of those
into whose hands my work comes that they should not be hungry to accept well
publicized incredibilities nor prefer them to what is genuine and uncorrupted
by the miraculous.)

As Tiberius praised his son before the rostra, the senate and people assumed— **12**
in pretence rather than gladly—the guise and voices of pain, and secretly they
delighted that the house of Germanicus was recuperating; but with this goodwill as the beginning, and given the fact that Agrippina as mother was scarcely
veiling her hopes, its ruin was merely accelerated. For, when he saw that Drusus' **2**
death went unavenged for his killers and without public sorrow, Sejanus—pro-
lific+ of crimes as he was, and because the first of them had burgeoned—turned
over privately in what way he could overthrow Germanicus' children, of whose
succession there was no doubt. Poison could not be dispensed against the three
of them, given the exceptional loyalty of their guards and Agrippina's unbreach-
able morality. He therefore made an assault upon her truculence and activated **3**
both Augusta's long-standing hatred and Livia's recent complicity so that in
Caesar's presence they should criticize her for being haughty in her fertility,
supported by popular affection, and gaping for mastery. —And all this by **4**
means of astute accusers, among whom he had selected Julius Postumus, who
through his adultery with Mutilia Prisca was among the grandmother's intimates
and highly suitable for his plans, because Prisca had influence over Augusta's mind
and made the old woman (who by her very nature was tense about her
own powerfulness) incompatible with her granddaughter-in-law.[18] Even those
nearest to Agrippina were enticed to goad her puffed up spirits by prevaricating
conversations.

18. Mutilia Prisca was the wife of C. Fufius Geminus, consul in 29 (5.1.1).

13   As for Tiberius, without interrupting his concern for affairs but welcoming business in place of comfort, he handled the legal cases of citizens and the pleas of allies; and on his initiative there were passed senate's decisions that to the Cibyratic community in Asia, and to the Aegian in Achaea, which had both suffered subsidence through earthquakes, help should be given by the remis-
2   sion of tax for a three-year period. And Vibius Serenus, the proconsul of Farther Spain who had been condemned for public violence, was deported to the island of Amorgus on account of the frightfulness of his behavior.[19] Carsidius Sacerdos,[20] a defendant on the grounds that he had helped the enemy Tacfarinas with grain, was acquitted, as was C. Gracchus of the same charge.
3   (This man while just an infant had been taken by his father Sempronius to the island of Cercina as his companion in exile. Growing up there among outcasts and those unaware of the liberal arts, he later supported himself by exchanging sordid merchandise around Africa and Sicily. Nevertheless he failed to escape the dangers of high fortune; and, had the blameless man not been protected by Aelius Lamia and L. Apronius, who had both held Africa, he would have been carried off owing to the brilliancy of his unpropitious family and to paternal adversities.)[21]
14   That year too brought legations from Greek communities, with the Samians and Coans seeking that the ancient prerogative of asylum be reaffirmed for their shrines of Juno and Aesculapius respectively.[22] The Samians were relying on a decree of the Amphictyonies,[23] which had the principal jurisdiction in all affairs at the time when the Greeks, after founding cities throughout Asia, had posses-
2   sion of the sea coast. Nor was there dissimilar antiquity on the Coans' side, and their place had an additional merit: they had escorted Roman citizens into the temple of Aesculapius when, on the order of King Mithridates, they were being butchered across all the islands and cities of Asia.[24]
3   Next, after various (and very often unavailing) complaints from the praetors, Caesar at length brought a motion concerning the unrestraint of actors: their assaults in public were many and mutinous, he said, while those in houses were simply foul; the onetime Oscan entertainment, the lightest form of enjoyment

---

19. For him see 2.30.1n. and below, 4.28–30.1.

20. Praetor in 27, deported in 37 (6.48.4).

21. C. Gracchus is perhaps identical with the accuser at 6.38.4. L. Aelius Lamia, consul in A.D. 3, had been proconsul of Africa in 15/16 or 16/17: see further 6.27.2. For L. Apronius, proconsul of Africa 18–21, see 1.56.1n. The "unpropitious family" is a reference to Ti. and C. Gracchus (3.27.2), killed in 133 and 121 B.C. respectively, while "paternal adversities" refers to his own father's killing in A.D. 14 (1.53.3–6).

22. For asylum see 3.60.1 and n.

23. Greek religious associations connected with sanctuaries and their cults (*OCD* 75).

24. In 88 B.C.

among the public,[25] had reached such a pitch of outrage and violence that it must be checked by the fathers' authority. Actors were then driven from Italy.

The same year afflicted Tiberius with other grief too, by extinguishing the life **15** of one of Drusus' twin children[26] and, not less, by the death of a friend. That was Lucilius Longus, a sharer in all his sadnesses and delights and from among the senators the only companion of his Rhodian withdrawal. So, despite his being a **2** new man, a censorial funeral[27] and a likeness in Augustus' forum were decreed for him from public money by the fathers, before whom even then everything was handled, to such an extent that the procurator of Asia, Lucilius Capito, pleaded his case in their presence when his province accused him[28]—with the princeps asserting strongly that he had given him no prerogative except over his household slaves and money; and, if the man had appropriated the praetor's power and used the muscle of soldiers, his own personal instructions had been spurned in that regard: they should listen to the allies. So, after investigation of the busi- **3** ness, the defendant was condemned. In return for this vengeance, and because in the previous year there had been retribution against C. Silanus,[29] the cities of Asia decreed a temple to Tiberius and his mother and the senate. And permission was given to build; and it was Nero[30] who expressed gratitude on that account to the fathers and his grandfather, amid the delighted emotions of his hearers, who, with the memory of Germanicus fresh, deemed that it was he whom they were beholding, he whom they were hearing. Additionally the young man had modestness and good looks worthy of a princeps—qualities which, given Sejanus' known hatred for him, were all the more welcome in the light of his danger.

Around the same time Caesar spoke about choosing a flamen Dialis in place **16** of the deceased Servius Maluginensis, as well as about approving a new law: it **2** was the olden custom, he said, that three patricians begotten by confarreate parents[31] were nominated simultaneously, from whom one was to be chosen; but such a supply was not available in the same way as formerly, since the habit of

25. The reference is to Atellan farce, which was originally performed in the Oscan language (*OCD* 200 s.v. Atellana). For the disruptiveness of actors in general see 1.54.2n.

26. Germanicus (see 2.84.1 and n.).

27. Thought to be equivalent to a public funeral (3.48.1, 6.11.3). For "new man" see 3.55.3n.; Longus had been suffect consul in A.D. 7.

28. The point is that he pleaded his case in the senate and that, though Asia was a public or "senatorial" province and governed by a consular proconsul (described by the archaizing term "praetor" below), Capito was an equestrian procurator of Tiberius whose job it was to oversee the emperor's "household slaves and money" (as is stated just below): his case thus lay strictly outside the senate's jurisdiction.

29. See 3.66–9.

30. Nero Caesar, son of Germanicus.

31. I.e., parents who had had a confarreate marriage, the most ancient and solemn form of marriage, involving a sacramental meal of *far* (spelt).

confarreate marriage had been abandoned or was retained among only a few families (and he adduced several reasons for that, the chief being the indifference of men and women); in addition there were the difficulties of the ceremonial office itself, which were being deliberately avoided, and the fact that he who acquired the flamonium, and she who took the hand of the flamen,[32] left the

3   jurisdiction of their fathers.[33] So a remedy must be found by a senate's decree or a law, just as Augustus had made certain adaptations to the well-known rigidity of antiquity in order to suit present conditions. —Having therefore handled the religious issues, they decided that in the established practice of the flamines nothing should be changed; but a law was carried whereby the flaminica Dialis should be in her husband's power for the purposes of the rituals but should come under the general legal standing of women otherwise; and the son of Maluginen-

4   sis replaced his father. And, in order that esteem for the priests should swell and they themselves have a readier inclination to undertake the ceremonial offices, a decree was passed of two million sesterces to Cornelia, the Virgin who was appointed in place of Scantia, and that, whenever Augusta entered the theater, she should sit among the seats of the Vestals.

★ ★ ★

17   With Cornelius Cethegus and Visellius Varro as consuls,[34] when the pontiffs and on their example the other priests were offering vows for the princeps's preservation, they commended also Nero and Drusus to the same gods—not so much from affection for the young men as from sycophancy, which, after behavior has

2   become corrupted, is as perilous if it is absent as when it is excessive. For, though Tiberius was never gentle toward the house of Germanicus, on that occasion he felt intolerably pained that the juveniles were being placed on the same level as his elderly self, and, summoning the pontiffs, he inquired whether that had been their concession to the pleas—or the threats—of Agrippina. And they at least, despite their denials, suffered only a moderate lashing (the majority were either relatives of his or leaders of the community); but in a speech in the senate he issued a warning for the future, that no one should encourage the juveniles' im-

3   pressionable minds to haughtiness by means of premature honors. For he was being hounded by Sejanus, who repeatedly censured the fact that the community was split as in a civil war: there were, he said, people calling themselves members of "Agrippina's faction," and, unless resistance was built up, there would be more

32. Sc. in marriage.

33. As head of his household a father enjoyed wide-ranging legal powers over members of his family (see *OCD* 1122–3 s.v. *patria potestas*).

34. C. Visellius Varro was the son of the suffect consul of 12 (3.41.2, 3.43.3, 4.19.1). Cethegus is scarcely otherwise known.

of them; and the only remedy for the swelling disaffection was if one or two of the readiest were undermined.

It was for this reason that he attacked C. Silius and Titius Sabinus. Ruinous to **18** each of them was their friendship with Germanicus, but to Silius was also the fact that, as controller of a mighty army for seven years and, after winning the triumphal insignia in Germany, as victor in the Sacrovirian war,[35] he was likely to fall with a heavier crash, thereby spreading proportionately more alarm among others. Many people believed that his offense had been magnified by his own in- **2** temperance, boasting uncontrollably that it was *his* soldiery which had remained solidly compliant when others were sliding toward mutiny, and that Tiberius' command would not have survived if his legions too had had the desire for rev- olution. Tiberius deemed that his own position was being thereby destroyed and **3** that he personally was no match for such meritorious service. Benefits are wel- come while they seem able to be repaid; but, when they become excessive, ha- tred rather than gratitude is the return.

Silius' wife was Sosia Galla, resented by the princeps on account of her affec- **19** tion for Agrippina. The decision was made to seize them both, deferring Sabinus for a time;[36] and the consul Varro was sent in, who, using his father's antagonism as cover,[37] gratified Sejanus' hatred at the cost of disgracing himself. **2** With the defendant requesting a brief delay until his accuser had left the consul- ship, Tiberius objected on the grounds that it was customary for magistrates to specify the day for private individuals:[38] one should not infringe the prerogative of a consul, on whose vigilance he relied to see "that the republic suffered no damage." (It was typical of Tiberius to cloak with old-time words crimes only recently devised.)[39] So with much assertiveness—as though Silius' trial were by **3** law or Varro were a consul or that situation the Republic—the fathers fell into line, the accused keeping silent or else, whenever he attempted a defense, not concealing by whose anger he was being crushed. The accusations were the **4** lengthy disguising of Sacrovir through complicity in his war, and a victory de- filed by greed and his wife an accessory. Doubtless the extortion charges against them would have stuck, but everything was conducted on the basis of the treason question, and Silius preempted his looming conviction by a voluntary end. His **20** property was nevertheless savaged—not that any money was returned to those

---

35. For Silius and his German command see 1.31.2n.; for his insignia and victory see 1.72.1 and 3.46 respectively.

36. Until A.D. 28 (4.68–70 below).

37. The command against Sacrovir had gone to Silius in preference to Varro's father (3.43.3).

38. "To specify a/the day (for)" is a legal expression = "to serve a summons (on)" (a slightly different form at 2.79.1 above).

39. The words quoted are those of the senate's "ultimate decision," passed in times of extreme crisis and last invoked in 40 B.C. (*OCD* 1388 s.v. *senatus consultum ultimum*).

liable for dues,[40] none of whom was demanding restitution, but Augustus' generosity to him was wrested away from his estate, with an itemized calculation of what was demanded for the fiscus. That was the first time Tiberius paid attention to someone else's money.

2   Sosia was driven into exile on the motion of Asinius Gallus, who had proposed that part of her property be confiscated and part left to her children; but M. Lepidus ensured the granting of a quarter to her accusers, as the law required, and the remainder to her children. (I am discovering for myself that this Lepidus was a weighty and wise man during that period. He frequently steered issues away from the savage sycophancies of others in a better direction, but at the same time he did not lack balance, since he thrived as much by his continuing influence with
3   Tiberius as by the latter's favor toward him. Hence I feel compelled to question whether it is by fate and the chance of birth that, as is the case with all other things, principes incline toward some men and are affronted at others; or whether there is something in our own policies which permits us to proceed between sheer truc-
4   ulence and grotesque compliance along a path cleared of ambition and peril.) On the other hand Messalinus Cotta,[41] of no less brilliant ancestry but different in temperament, proposed taking measures by senate's decision that magistrates, even if blameless and ignorant of another's wrong, should nevertheless be chastised for their wives' provincial crimes as if they were their own.

21   Next was the case of Calpurnius Piso, a noble and defiant man. For it was he who, as I recorded,[42] had cried out in the senate that he would withdraw from the City owing to the accusers' factiousness and, spurning the powerfulness of Augusta, had dared to drag Urgulania to trial and to summon her from the princeps's house. All of this Tiberius regarded in a citizenlike fashion at the time; but in a mind where anger kept circulating, even if the impact of an affront lost its
2   intensity, its memory remained effective. Q. Veranius censured Piso for having conducted a private conversation against Tiberius' sovereignty, and added that he kept poison at home and entered the curia girded with a sword. This last charge was passed over as more frightful than realistic; on the many others which were piling up, however, he was cited as a defendant but not prosecuted owing to his timely death.
3   There was also a motion concerning the exiled Cassius Severus, who despite sordid origins and a life of wrongdoing was an effective speaker and through his unrestrained antagonisms had ensured that he was banished to Crete by a sworn verdict of the senate. Once there, he continued to act in the same way, bringing upon himself fresh hatreds as well as old; and, stripped of his property, and with fire and water forbidden him, he grew old on the rock of Seriphos.

22   During the same period Plautius Silvanus, a praetor, threw his spouse Apronia headlong from a height for reasons which were unclear; and, dragged in front of

40. I.e., tax-paying provincials.
41. The consul of 20 (2.32.1n., 3.2.3).
42. See 2.34 above.

Caesar by his father-in-law, L. Apronius,[43] he replied in a disturbed state of mind to the effect that he had been heavily asleep and therefore unaware and that his wife had chosen death of her own accord. Without hesitation Tiberius proceeded 2 to the house, visited the bedroom (where the traces of her struggle and ejection were to be seen), and referred the matter to the senate. With judges appointed, Urgulania, Silvanus' grandmother, sent her grandson a dagger, an action which was believed to have been taken as if on the Commander's advice, owing to Augusta's friendship with Urgulania. Having tried the steel to no purpose, the de- 3 fendant offered his veins to be severed.[44] Subsequently Numantina, his former wife, accused of having induced derangement in the husband by spells and potions, was adjudged blameless.[45]

*

That year finally released the Roman people from their long war against the Nu- **23** midian Tacfarinas.

Whenever previous leaders believed that their achievements warranted a successful request for the triumphal insignia, they had neglected consideration of the enemy; and now there were three laurel-wreathed statues in the City, and Tacfarinas was still ravaging Africa—augmented by auxiliaries from the Mauri, who, given the youthful indifference of Ptolemy (Juba's son), had substituted warfare for the servile commands of the royal freedmen. The receiver of Tacfarinas' plun- 2 der and his ally in pillaging was the king of the Garamantes—not that the latter marched out with an army but he dispatched light forces, news of whom was exaggerated from a distance; and from the province itself all the elements who were destitute of fortune and disruptive in behavior had been rushing to him the more readily because in the light of Blaesus' achievements, as though there were no longer an enemy at all in Africa, Caesar had ordered the Ninth Legion to be conveyed back;[46] nor had the proconsul of that year, P. Dolabella, dared to retain it, dreading the orders of the princeps more than the uncertainties of war.[47]

So Tacfarinas—spreading a rumor that Roman interests were being mauled by **24** other nations too, that there was a gradual retreat from Africa, and that the remaining men could be surrounded if they were set upon by all to whom freedom was more important than servitude—increased his forces and, after pitching camp, invested the town of Thubuscum. But Dolabella gathered together what 2

43. For Apronius see 1.56.1n.; M. Plautius Silvanus was son of the homonymous consul of 2 B.C.

44. Sc. by one of his slaves.

45. Fabia Numantina was sister of Paullus Fabius Persicus, consul in 34 (6.28.1), and had previously been married to Sex. Appuleius, consul in A.D. 14 (1.7.2).

46. See 3.9.1 for the legion's journey to Africa. For Blaesus' African command see 3.35, 3.58.1.

47. For Dolabella see 3.47.3n.

soldiers there were, and, by the terror of the Roman name and because the Numidians were unable to withstand the line of infantry, raised the blockade with his own very first attack and fortified some advantageous positions. At the same time he struck dead with an axe leaders of the Musulamii who were on the point

3 of defecting.[48] Then, because from repeated campaigns against Tacfarinas it was recognized that a roving enemy could not be hunted down in a single heavy raid, he summoned King Ptolemy along with his compatriots, preparing four columns which he gave to legates or tribunes. Plundering units were led by picked Mauri, and the general himself was on hand as adviser to everyone.

25   Not long after, news arrived that the Numidians had pitched their mapalia,[49] taking up position at a half-destroyed stronghold (formerly fired by themselves) whose name is Auzea, trusting the place because it was enclosed by desolate denes all round. Then the unencumbered cohorts and the wings were swept off in a

2 fast column without being told of their destination. No sooner had daylight started than they were upon the half-asleep barbarians with a chorus of trumpets and callous shouting, while the Numidians' horses were still encumbered by tethers or else wandering across far-flung pastures. The Romans concentrated their infantry, deployed their squadrons, made every provision for battle. The enemy, on the other hand, completely unawares, had no arms, no order, no plan,

3 but, like livestock, they were dragged off, slaughtered, captured. Each and every soldier, ferocious from the memory of his toils and of the fight so often desired against his elusive opponents, had his fill of vengeance and bloodshed. Word was spread through the maniples that they should all hunt down Tacfarinas, a familiar figure after so many battles: there would be no rest from war without the leader's being killed. But he for his part—with his attendants struck down around him, his son already bound, and the Romans pouring out everywhere—rushed directly into the weapons, thereby escaping captivity by a death which was not unavenged. That put an end to hostilities.

26   Dolabella's request for the triumphal insignia was refused by Tiberius out of deference to Sejanus, lest the praise for Blaesus, his uncle, might be tarnished.[50] Yet Blaesus did not become more illustrious on that account, while the honor denied to the former intensified his glory: for with a smaller army he had brought back distinguished captives and the fame resulting from the leader's slaughter and

2 from the completion of the war. There followed too legates from the Garamantes, rarely seen in the City, whom their nation, shocked by Tacfarinas' slaughter and conscious of its own guilt,+ had sent to make reparation to the Roman people. Subsequently, when Ptolemy's support during the war was realized, an honor was revived from olden custom, and one of the senate was dispatched to give him an ivory scepter and embroidered toga, ancient gifts of the fathers, and to entitle him king, ally, and friend.

48. Dolabella was resorting to a recognized form of military punishment.

49. For which see 3.74.3n.

50. See 3.72.4.

★

In that same season chance stifled the seeds of a slave war which were stirring   **27** across Italy. The instigator of the turbulence, T. Curtisius (formerly a soldier in a praetorian cohort), was engaged in calling the defiant rustic slave population on the extensive ranges to freedom, first by means of clandestine meetings in Brundisium and outlying towns, then by openly posting up documents, when suddenly, as if by a gift from the gods, three biremes moored to meet the requirements of those traveling across the sea there. And in the same district was Cutius   2 Lupus, the quaestor whose allotted province was, according to the old custom, "the leas":[51] deploying a force of marines, he broke up the conspiracy just as it was beginning. And Staius, a tribune dispatched quickly by Caesar with a substantial unit, dragged the leader and his most daring associates to the City, where there was already trepidation owing to the number of establishments, which was swelling immeasurably, while the freeborn plebs was diminishing daily.

With the same men as consuls, in a frightful example of pitifulness and savagery,   **28** a father and son (each called Vibius Serenus) were led into the senate as defendant and accuser respectively.[52] Dragged back from exile, spattered with filth and grime, and now bound with a chain, the father prepared himself for his son's declamation. The juvenile—in elegant attire and with an eager expression—as simul-   2 taneously informant and witness said that a trap had been laid for the princeps and that inciters of war had been dispatched to Gaul, and he wove in the further charge that Caecilius Cornutus, a praetorian, had supplied money. The latter, in weariness of his cares and because indictment was considered equivalent to extermination, hastened his own death. On the other hand the defendant, rounding   3 on his son with unbroken spirit, shook his bonds and called on the avenging gods that they should restore his exile, where he could live far removed from such conduct, but reprisals should one day catch up with his son. He asserted that Cornutus was innocent and had been wrongly terrorized, something which could be appreciated easily if others were produced: he had not contemplated the slaughter of the princeps and revolution with only one partner!

At that the accuser named Cn. Lentulus and Seius Tubero, to the considerable   **29** embarrassment of Caesar, since it was leaders of the community, his own intimate friends—Lentulus a man of extreme old age, Tubero with his physical weakness—who were being summoned for hostile disorder and disrupting the state.[53] But they at least were immediately reprieved; the father was investigated through his slaves, and the investigation went against the accuser. The latter, de-   2 ranged by his crime and at the same time terrified by a rumor among the public that they were threatening him with prison and the Rock or the penalties for

51. "Leas" is my attempt to find a suitably old-fashioned word for *calles* (plur.), public pastureland in Italy allotted yearly to a magistrate as his responsibility or "province."

52. For the elder Serenus see 2.30.1n.; the son reappears at 4.36.3 below.

53. For Lentulus see 1.27.1n.; for Tubero see 2.20.1n.

parricides,[54] withdrew from the City. Dragged back from Ravenna, he was compelled to follow through his accusation, with Tiberius not concealing his own long
3   standing hatred of the exile Serenus. (After Libo's conviction, in a letter sent to Caesar he had remonstrated that his was the only zeal to have gone without profit;[55] and he had made some additional remarks more truculently than was safe in the haughty ears of one inclined to be affronted. All this was now recalled eight years later by Caesar, who made various charges against the intervening period, even though the torturing of the slaves had proved negative owing to their persistence.)

30   After it was next proposed that Serenus should be punished according to ancestral custom,[56] he intervened to soften the general resentment. And, when Gallus Asinius moved that he be confined on Gyarus or Donusa, he rejected that too, referring to the fact that each island was lacking in water and that the necessities of life should be provided for one to whom life was being granted. So Serenus
2   was conveyed back to Amorgus. And, because Cornutus had fallen by his own hand, there was a debate about abolishing the rewards for accusers in cases where someone arraigned for treason took his own life before judgment was passed. And the vote would have gone in favor of the proposal, had not Caesar—more harshly and, contrary to his custom, openly on the accusers' behalf—complained that the laws would be thwarted and the state on the brink: they might as well
3   overthrow the legislation, he said, as remove its guardians. So it was that denouncers, a breed of men invented for exterminating the people and never properly checked even by punishments, were lured on by rewards.

31   Amid these events, so constant and so sorrowful, there was a limited but welcome interval in which C. Cominius, a Roman equestrian convicted for an abusive poem against Caesar, was yielded up by the latter to the pleas of his brother,
2   who was a senator. It was therefore considered all the more amazing that a man aware of the better course, and of the reputation which followed upon clemency, should nevertheless prefer the grimmer. It was not that he did wrong through insensibility, and there is no concealing when Commanders' deeds are celebrated genuinely and when with a merely spurious delight. Moreover the man himself, who at other times was composed and seemed to heave his words, held forth
3   more expansively and readily whenever he came to someone's rescue. Yet, when the senate was in the process of banning from Italy P. Suillius, a former quaestor of Germanicus convicted of accepting money for judging a case, he voted for his removal to an island—doing so with such purposeful contention that he pledged on oath that it was in the interest of the state. The rough reception of this action at the time subsequently changed to praise on Suillius' return, since a following age saw him as powerful and venal, a man whose enjoyment of Claudius' friend-

54. Parricides were traditionally scourged, sewn into a sack (along with a cock, a dog, a viper, and an ape) and thrown into the sea (*OCD* 1116 s.v. parricidium).

55. For Libo's case see 2.27–32 (A.D. 16).

56. See 2.32.3n.

ship was for long successful but never moral.[57] The same punishment was de-   4
cided for the senator Catus Firmius, on the grounds that he had falsely made his
sister the target of treason charges. Catus, as I have recorded,[58] had enticed Libo
into a trap and then struck him down with the evidence. It was because Tiberius
recalled this service that, though pretending otherwise, he protested against his
exile; but he did not stand in the way of his expulsion from the senate.

(That much of what I have recorded, and of what I shall record, seems per-   **32**
haps insignificant and trivial to recall I am not unaware; but no one should
compare my annals with the writing of those who compiled the affairs of the
Roman people of old. Mighty wars, stormings of cities, routed and captured
kings, or—whenever they turned their attention to internal matters—discord between consuls and tribunes, agrarian and grain laws, and contests of plebs and
optimates[59]—it was these which they recalled and had the freedom to explore.   2
My work, on the other hand, is confined and inglorious: peace was immovable
or only modestly challenged, affairs in the City were sorrowful, and the princeps
indifferent to extending the empire.

It will nevertheless not be without benefit to have gained an insight into what
at first sight are trivialities, from which the movements of great affairs often
spring. All nations and cities are ruled either by the people or by leading men or   **33**
by an individual. (A form of government which is chosen from a combination
of these can more easily be praised than happen, or, if it does happen, cannot be
long-lasting.) It therefore follows that, just as formerly—that is, during the period   2
of the plebs' influence or when the fathers were a force—it was necessary to
know the nature of the public and in what ways their restraint might be maintained, and those who had acquainted themselves thoroughly with the instincts
of senate and optimates were believed astute and wise for their times—so, now
that the situation has changed and there is no salvation for affairs[+] other than if
one man is in command, it will be apposite for these matters to have been assembled and transmitted, because few men have the proficiency to distinguish
the honorable from the baser, or the useful from the harmful, whereas the majority are taught by what happens to others.

Yet, though likely to be advantageous, these matters afford very little enjoy-   3
ment. It is the localities of peoples, the fluctuations of battles, and the fates of
brilliant leaders which rivet and reinvigorate readers' minds; but in my case it is
savage orders, constant accusations, deceitful friendships, the ruin of innocents
and always the same reasons for their extermination that I link together, confronted as I am by a satiety of similar material.

Then there is the fact that ancient writers attract only an occasional dispar-   4

57. See 11.1–6 and 13.42–3 below.

58. See 2.27.2 above.

59. "Optimates" is a term for the conservative aristocracy which became current in the
first century B.C. (*OCD* 1070–1).

ager, nor does it make a difference to anyone whether you delight more in exalting the Punic or Roman lines; but many who during Tiberius' rule suffered
punishment or infamy have descendants remaining, and, even if the actual families have now been extinguished, you will discover persons who, owing to a
similarity of behavior, think that the misdeeds of others are being imputed to
themselves. Even glory and courage receive a ferocious response, as being critical of their opposites from too close at hand. But I return to my undertaking.)

★ ★ ★

34   With Cornelius Cossus and Asinius Agrippa as consuls,[60] Cremutius Cordus was
arraigned on a charge which was new and heard only then for the first time—
that, having published annals and praised M. Brutus, he had spoken of C. Cassius
as the last of the Romans. The prosecutors were Satrius Secundus and Pinarius
2   Natta, clients of Sejanus. That was ruinous for the accused, as was the callous look
with which Caesar received his defense, on which Cremutius, fixed upon leaving life, embarked in this fashion:

   "It is my words, conscript fathers, that are criticized, so completely am I innocent of deeds; but not even *they* were directed at the princeps or the princeps's
parent, whom the law of treason embraces. I am said to have praised Brutus and
Cassius, whose achievements, though many have compiled them, no one has recalled without honor.

3   "Titus Livius, quite brilliant as he is for eloquence and credibility,[61] first of all
elevated Cn. Pompeius with such praises that Augustus called him 'a Pompeian';
and that was no obstacle to their friendship. Scipio, Afranius, this very Cassius
himself, this very Brutus—nowhere did he name them as 'bandits' and 'parricides' (the designations which are now imposed) but often as distinguished men.
4   Asinius Pollio's writings transmit an exceptional memorial of the same individuals; Messalla Corvinus used to proclaim Cassius his 'commander'; and each continued to thrive in wealth and honors. To the book of Marcus Cicero in which
Cato was exalted to the sky, how else did the dictator Caesar reply than with a
responding speech as if before a jury?
5   "Antonius' letters, Brutus' public addresses contain abuse against Augustus
which is admittedly false but of much acerbity; the poems of Bibaculus and Cat-
ullus, packed with insults of the Caesars, can still be read; but Divine Julius himself, Divine Augustus himself bore and ignored them all—whether with more
restraint or wisdom, I could not easily say: what is spurned tends to abate; but, if

---

60. The father of Cossus Cornelius Lentulus was consul in 1 B.C., his brother in A.D.
26 (4.46.1); M. Asinius Agrippa was grandson of Asinius Pollio (1.12.4n.) and brother of
the consul of 23 (4.1.1n.).

61. The reference is to the historian Livy (for whom see pp. xix–xx).

you become angry, you appear to have made an admission. (I do not touch on **35** the Greeks, among whom not just liberty but license too went unpunished; or, if anyone took notice, he avenged words with words.)

"What was particularly exempt, and had no one to disparage it, was to publish about those whom death had removed from hatred or favor. For surely it is **2** not the case that, by my having Cassius and Brutus armed and holding the plains of Philippi,[62] I am inflaming the people in public addresses with civil war as my motive? Is it not rather the case that, slain as they were seventy years ago, they for their part not only come to be known by their images—which not even the victor abolished—but retain some part of their memory among writers in exactly the same way? Posterity pays to every man his due repute; and, if condem- **3** nation is closing in on me, there will be no lack of those who remember not merely Cassius and Brutus but also myself." Then, leaving the senate, he ended **4** his life by fasting.

The cremation of his books by the aediles was proposed by the fathers, but they survived, having been concealed and published. Wherefore it is pleasant to **5** deride all the more the insensibility of those who, by virtue of their present powerfulness, believe that the memory even of a subsequent age too can be extinguished. On the contrary, the influence of punished talents swells, nor have foreign kings, or those who have resorted to the same savagery, accomplished anything except disrepute for themselves and for their victims glory.

Yet in the arraignment of defendants the year was so constant that, on the days **36** of the Latin Festival, Drusus as prefect of the City,[63] having mounted the tribunal for taking the auspices, was approached by Calpurnius Salvianus with a charge against Sextus Marius. That was openly berated by Caesar and was the reason for Salvianus' exile. Against the Cyziceni was publicly cast the imputation of an in- **2** difference to the ceremonial offices of Divine Augustus, with additional charges of violence toward Roman citizens; and they lost the freedom which they had earned in the war with Mithridates, when, despite their being invested, the king was beaten off as much by their own steadfastness as by the garrison of Lucullus.[64] Fonteius Capito, however, whose concern as proconsul had been Asia,[65] **3** was acquitted, it being discovered that the charges against him had been fabricated by Vibius Serenus. Yet that did no harm to Serenus, whom public hatred made increasingly more secure. Each accuser, the more exposed he was, was as if

62. Cordus means "by the simple fact that I have written a history which describes Cassius and Brutus and the Battle of Philippi." For the battle see 1.2.1n.

63. Not the permanent prefecture of the City, whose history is given below at 6.11 (q.v.), but a temporary appointment held by an upper-class young man (like Germanicus' son here) while the regular magistrates were attending the Latin Festival on the Alban Mount outside Rome (*OCD* 1239 s.v. *praefectus urbi*). The Latin Festival was a movable festival held on several consecutive days in the second quarter of each year.

64. The Third Mithridatic War, c. 74–72 B.C.

65. C. Fonteius Capito, consul in A.D. 12, was proconsul of Asia in (probably) 23/24.

sacrosanct; it was the lightweight, the ignoble who had punishments inflicted on them.

37   During the same period Farther Spain sent legates to the senate pleading that on the example of Asia it might set up a shrine to Tiberius and his mother.[66] On this occasion Caesar, who was generally firm in spurning honors and deemed that he should reply to the rumors in which he was criticized for deviating to-

2   ward self-aggrandizement, began a speech of this kind: "I know, conscript fathers, that consistency has been demanded of me by many people, because I did not oppose the communities of Asia when recently they sought the very same thing which is under discussion. Therefore I shall expound simultaneously both a defense of my previous silence and what I have decided for the future.

3   "Since Divine Augustus had not prevented a temple to himself and to the City of Rome from being placed at Pergamum, and given that I observe all his actions and words as if law, I followed an already agreeable example more readily because the cult of myself was being joined by veneration of the senate. Yet, though a single acceptance may prove pardonable, to be consecrated throughout all the provinces by the likeness of divinities would be aggrandizing, haughty; and honor for Augustus will vanish if it is vulgarized by indiscriminate sycophancies.

38   "That I am mortal, conscript fathers, and perform the duties of men, and consider it satisfying if I fill the place of princeps—these things I both call on you to witness and wish posterity to remember. The latter will make a satisfying contribution and more to my memory, should they believe me worthy of my ancestors, provident of your affairs, in dangers steadfast, and not panicked by affronts

2   for the public good. These are my temples in your hearts, these the likenesses which are finest and destined to survive: those which are set up in stone are

3   spurned like sepulchres if the judgment of posterity turns to hatred. Accordingly I pray to allies, citizens, and to the gods and goddesses themselves—to the latter that till the end of my life they may bestow on me a mind which is peaceful and understanding of human and divine law, to the former that, whenever I depart, they may attend my actions and the reputation of my name with praise and benign recollections."

4   And he persevered thereafter even in his private conversations in spurning such cult of himself. Some interpreted this as modestness, many that he was dif-

5   fident, others as the sign of a degenerate spirit: it was the best of mortals, they said, who had the highest desires: thus it was Hercules and Liber among the Greeks, and Quirinus among ourselves, who had been added to the number of the gods; better was the reaction of Augustus, who had hoped. Principes enjoyed immediate access to everything else; they should prepare insatiably for one thing alone—a favorable memory of themselves. Contempt for fame meant contempt for virtues.

39   As for Sejanus, insensible from his excessive good fortune and inflamed besides by a woman's desire (since Livia was importuning him for the promised marriage), he composed a note to Caesar. (It was then the custom to approach

66. For the example of Asia see 4.15.3 above.

him, though present, in writing.) Its outline was as follows: through the benev- 2
olence of his father Augustus, and later through the very many tokens of Tiberius'
esteem, he had become accustomed to take his hopes and prayers not primarily
to the gods but to the ears of principes. And he had never pleaded for the glitter of honors: he preferred lookouts and toils, like one of the soldiers, for his
Commander's preservation. And yet he had nevertheless acquired the finest thing
of all, that he was believed worthy of a connection with Caesar.[67] Hence the be- 3
ginning of his hope; and, because he had heard that in the matter of engaging his
daughter Augustus had not declined to deliberate even about Roman equestrians, so, if a husband was being sought for Livia, Tiberius should bear in mind that
his friend would enjoy only the glory of the relationship. For he was not casting 4
off the responsibilities imposed upon him: he would be satisfied to think that the
family was being strengthened against the unfair affronts of Agrippina—and that
too for the children's sake.[68] In his own case any portion of his life would be full
and more, if he spent it in the company of such a princeps

In reply Tiberius, praising Sejanus' devotion and giving a modest review of his **40**
own kindnesses toward him, sought time as though for a proper and unprejudiced deliberation, adding that the counsels of all other mortals depended on
what they thought advantageous to themselves; but the lot of principes was different, since they had to regulate paramount affairs with regard to their own reputation. For that reason he was not having recourse to the ready response that 2
Livia herself could decide whether to wed in the light of Drusus' death or to endure at the selfsame hearth, and that she had a mother and grandmother, more
intimate counsels.[69] He would act more directly, in the first place concerning the 3
antagonisms of Agrippina, which would blaze far more fiercely if Livia's wedding
rent the family of the Caesars into factions, so to speak. Even as things were, rivalry between the ladies was bursting forth, and his own grandsons were being
wrenched apart by their discord:[70] what if the contest were intensified by such
an espousal?

"For you are mistaken, Sejanus, if you think that you will remain in the same 4
rank and that Livia—who was wedded to C. Caesar[71] and later to Drusus—will
be of a mind to grow old in the company of a Roman equestrian. Even if I were
to allow it, do you believe that it would be suffered by those who have seen her
brother, her father, and our ancestors in the highest commands? You, of course, 5
wish to stay within that position of yours; but those magistrates and leaders who

67. Viz. through the betrothal of his daughter to Claudius' son (3.29.4).

68. The children are Tiberius Gemellus and Julia, whom Sejanus himself had made fa-
therless by his killing of Drusus.

69. The mother is the younger Antonia, widow of Nero Claudius Drusus (and younger
daughter of Mark Antony and Octavia, sister of Augustus); the grandmother is Livia Augusta.

70. This statement seems to be an anticipation of what will happen at 4.60.2–3 below.

71. Augustus' grandson, who had died in A.D. 4 (1.3.2–3).

burst in on you against your will and consult you about every affair make no secret of maintaining that you have passed long ago the pinnacle of an equestrian
and have far outstripped my father's friendships; and in their resentment of you
they censure me too.

6   "You say 'Augustus considered handing his daughter to a Roman equestrian.'
As Hercules is my witness, is it any wonder that, when he was being rent by every
concern and foresaw the immeasurable exaltation of whichever person he raised
above others by such a connection, his conversations included C. Proculeius and
those distinguished by the same tranquillity of life, involved in no businesses of
state? Yet, if we are influenced by Augustus' hesitation, how much more effective
is the fact that it was to Marcus Agrippa and later to myself that he engaged her?

7   "These matters, in virtue of our friendship, I have not concealed; but I shall
not oppose either your designs or Livia's. What I personally have been turning
over within my mind, by what further relationships I am preparing to make you
and me inseparable, I shall omit to mention at present; this only will I disclose,
that there is nothing so lofty as not to be deserved by those virtues of yours and
by your intentions toward me, and, given the right time, either in the senate or
at a public meeting, I shall not keep silent."

41   In response Sejanus no longer talked about marriage but, with a deeper dread,
protested against the silent suspicions, the public rumors, the encroaching resentment. And, in order that he should neither break his power by banning the regular gatherings at his house nor provide his accusers with an opportunity by
continuing them, he turned to pushing Tiberius to spend his life in attractive places

2   far from Rome. He foresaw many advantages: access would be in his own hands,
and for the most part he would be the judge of correspondence, since it traveled
by soldiers; soon Caesar, his old age already declining, would be softened by the
seclusion of the place and would more easily hand over the responsibilities of
command; and for himself there would be a lessening in resentment with the
crowd of well-wishers withdrawn; and, with the inessentials removed, his real

3   powerfulness would increase. Therefore he took to berating the busy City, the
people rushing up, the multitude streaming up, while extolling the praises of quiet
and solitude, where aversions and affronts were absent, and paramount affairs in
particular could be conducted.

42   And by chance an inquiry held during those days concerning Votienus Montanus, a man of celebrated talent, drove the already hesitating Tiberius to believe
that he should avoid the gatherings of the fathers and the generally true and se-

2   rious utterances which were thrust at him when he was present. For at Votienus'
arraignment for insults spoken against Caesar, in his enthusiasm for proof the witness Aemilius (one of the military men) mentioned everything and, albeit amid
loud objections, struggled on with great assertiveness: Tiberius therefore heard
the abuse with which he was being mauled in secret and was so shocked that he
exclaimed he would clear himself either at once or during the inquiry; and it was
only after pleas from intimates and sycophancy from all that he composed him-

self with difficulty. Votienus for his part had the punishment for treason inflicted   3
on him; as for Caesar, embracing all the more persistently the mercilessness toward defendants which was imputed to him, he punished Aquilia—who had
been denounced for adultery with Varius Ligus—with exile, although Lentulus
Gaetulicus the consul designate had condemned her under the Julian law,[72] and
he erased Apidius Merula from the senatorial whiteboard,[73] because he had not
sworn obedience to the enactments of Divine Augustus.[74]

Next were heard legations of the Lacedaemonians and Messenians concern-   **43**
ing the jurisdiction of the temple of Diana Limnas, whose dedication by their
own ancestors and on their own land the Lacedaemonians supported both by its
commemoration in annals and by the poems of bards; but, they said, it had been
taken away from them by the armed force of Macedonian Philip, with whom
they had warred,[75] and afterward restored by a judgment of C. Caesar and M.
Antonius. On the other hand the Messenians adduced the old division of the   2
Peloponnese between the descendants of Hercules, and the fact that it was to
their king that the Denthaliate territory, in which that shrine was, had passed;
and the monuments to that effect, sculpted in stone and in old-time bronze, still
survived. But, if it was on the basis of testimony from bards and from annals that   3
they were being challenged, they said, theirs were more numerous and substantial. Nor had Philip's decision been due to his powerfulness but in accordance
with reality; the same had been the verdict of King Antigonus, the same that of
the commander Mummius;[76] thus had the Milesians decreed, when arbitration
was officially granted them, and lastly Atidius Geminus, the praetor of Achaea.
—So it went in favor of the Messenians.

And the Segestans demanded that the sanctuary of Venus on Mount Erycus,   4
which had collapsed through age, be restored, recalling the known facts about its
origin, which were delightful to Tiberius; and as a blood relative he undertook
the concern gladly.[77] Then the pleas of the Massilians were discussed and the ex-   5
ample of P. Rutilius approved, for, when he had been banished by law,[78] the
Smyrnaeans had made him a fellow citizen of theirs: it was by this authority that

72. Cn. Cornelius Lentulus Gaetulicus was brother of Cornelius Cossus, the consul of
the present year (4.34.1n.), and became legate of Upper Germany 29–39 (see 6.30.2–4).

73. This was a published list of members of the senate, arranged in order of seniority
and updated each year.

74. See 1.72.1n.

75. Philip II of Macedon had invaded Laconia after the battle of Chaeronea in 338 B.C.

76. Antigonus III of Macedon invaded Laconia in 222 B.C.; L. Mummius was active in
the Peloponnese c. 146 B.C.

77. Tiberius had been adopted by Augustus in A.D. 4 (1.3.3): he thereupon became a
member of the Julian family, which claimed descent from Venus via her son Aeneas, who
allegedly founded her temple on the mount (Virgil, *Aeneid* 5.759).

78. In 93/92 B.C. after a notoriously unjust condemnation for extortion.

the exile Vulcacius Moschus[79] had been received by the Massilians, leaving his property to their state as to a fatherland.

44   There died in that year the noble men Cn. Lentulus and L. Domitius. To Lentulus' glory, besides his consulship and triumphing over the Getae,[80] had been his well-endured poverty and, later, his great wealth innocently won and mod-

2   estly handled. Domitius was done credit by his father, powerful at sea in the civil war until he joined the faction of Antonius and later of Caesar; his grandfather had fallen in the Pharsalian line for the optimates.[81] The man himself, chosen to be given the younger Antonia (daughter of Octavia) in marriage, afterward crossed the River Albis with his army, penetrating Germany farther than any of his predecessors, and for those achievements he acquired the insignia of a tri-

3   umph.[82] There died too L. Antonius, whose family brilliancy was considerable but unpropitious: with his father, Iullus Antonius, punished by death for adultery with Julia, Augustus isolated his sister's grandson, while just a young juvenile,[83] in the Massilian community, where the name of "exile" could be cloaked by a show of "study." Honor was nevertheless paid at his last rites, and his bones borne into the tomb of the Octavii[84] through a decree of the senate.

★

45   With the same men as consuls, a frightful act was performed in Nearer Spain by a certain rustic of the Termestine nation. While the praetor of the province, L. Piso,[85] was making a journey and had become inattentive in the peacetime conditions, the man made an unexpected attack on him and with a single blow smote him to death; and, escaping because of the speed of his horse, he reached an area of denes, after which, dismissing the horse, he foiled his pursuers across trackless

2   precipices. Yet he did not deceive them for long: the horse was caught and led through the nearest districts, and its owner was identified. And when, once discovered, he was being driven by torture to produce his accomplices, he repeat-

79. An orator from Pergamum who had been exiled to Marseille after being condemned on a charge of poisoning.

80. Respectively 14 B.C. and c. 9 B.C. For Lentulus the Augur see 1.27.1n.

81. For this term see 4.32.1n. For L. Domitius Ahenobarbus see 1.63.4n.: his father was Cn. Domitius Ahenobarbus (consul in 32 B.C.), and his grandfather was L. Domitius Ahenobarbus (consul in 54 B.C.); the battle of Pharsalus was 48 B.C.

82. Domitius had in fact been married to the elder, not the younger, Antonia; his triumphal insignia were presumably awarded c. 1 B.C.

83. Presumably in 2 B.C., the year in which his father was obliged to commit suicide (3.24.2n.). L. Antonius' mother, the elder Marcella, was the daughter of Augustus' sister, Octavia (by her first marriage, to C. Claudius Marcellus, consul in 50 B.C.).

84. Probably not Augustus' mausoleum (3.9.2n.) but the tomb of Antonius' grandmother's family, the Octavii.

85. Probably a son of L. Calpurnius Piso (2.34.1n.).

edly shouted in a loud voice in his native speech that he was being interrogated in vain: his partners could stand by and look on; no force of pain would be so great as to elicit the truth. And similarly, when on the next day he was being dragged back for questioning, he broke away from his guards and dashed his head on a rock with such effort that he expired immediately. But Piso is considered   3
to have been slaughtered by the guile of the Termestines: his attempts at collecting money intercepted from the public treasury had been too keen for the barbarians to endure.

★ ★ ★

With Lentulus Gaetulicus and C. Calvisius as consuls,[86] the insignia of a triumph   **46**
were decreed to Poppaeus Sabinus[87] for grinding down the races of the Thracians, who on mountain uplands lived uncivilized and thus all the more defiantly. The reason for the turbulence, apart from the people's temperament, was that they scorned to endure levies and to give all their most effective men to our service, being accustomed to obey not even their kings except at whim or, if they sent auxiliaries, to appoint their own leaders and not to wage war except against their neighbors. And then a rumor had spread that, dispersed and merged with   2
other nations, they would be dragged off to different and distant countries. But, before they resorted to arms, they sent legates to recall their friendship and compliance—which, they said, would survive, if they were not tried by any new burden; but, if servitude were imposed on them as if on a vanquished people, then they had swords and youth and a spirit ready for freedom or to the death. At the   3
same time they pointed to their strongholds perched on crags and to their parents and spouses gathered there, and they threatened an obstructive, steep, and gory war.

But Sabinus, though giving mild replies until he could assemble his armies into   **47**
a single battalion, nevertheless, after Pomponius Labeo had come from Moesia with a legion, and King Rhoemetalces with those of his compatriots' auxiliaries who had not changed their loyalties,[88] added to them his existing force and proceeded toward the enemy, now arranged in the narrow denes. (Some, more daringly, showed themselves on open hillsides, but the Roman leader, moving up in line, drove them off without difficulty, the barbarians' bloodshed being only moderate owing to their nearby refuges.) Having next fortified his camp on the spot,   2
Sabinus with a substantial unit took possession of a mountain with a narrow and

86. For Gaetulicus see 4.42.3n. above; C. Calvisius Sabinus, son of the consul of 4 B.C., was later accused of treason (6.9.3).

87. For him see 1.80.1n.

88. For the king see 2.67.2 (A.D. 19) and 3.38–9 (A.D. 21). Pomponius Labeo, governor of Moesia for eight years, commits suicide in 34 (6.29.1).

level ridge stretching as far as the nearest stronghold, which was guarded by a large force, partly armed and partly unorganized. At the same time he sent selected archers against the most defiant, who were prancing about in front of their

3   rampart, singing and three-stepping in the fashion of their race. As long as their advance was at a distance, they caused frequent wounds which went unavenged; but, approaching nearer, they were disrupted by a sudden breakout and rescued by the aid of a Sugambrian cohort which the Roman had drawn up not far away, ready for danger and in its clash of songs and weapons no less callous than the enemy.

48 Next he transferred the camp close to the enemy, leaving behind at the previous fortification the Thracians whose support for us I have recalled;[89] and the latter had permission to lay waste, to burn, and to carry off plunder, provided that their pillaging stayed within daylight and they passed a safe and watchful night in camp. At first this was observed; but soon, turning to the ways of luxuriousness and enriched by their seizures, they neglected their pickets for reckless ban-

2   queting or lay prostrate from sleep and wine. Therefore the enemy, discovering their carelessness, prepared two columns, by one of which the pillagers would be assailed, while others would besiege the Roman camp—not in the expectation of capturing it but so that amid the shouts and weapons each man, intent on his own danger, would not catch the sound of the other battle. In addition, darkness

3   was selected to increase the alarm. Those who made the attempt on the legions' rampart were easily driven off; but the Thracian auxiliaries were terrified by the unexpected incursion, since some were lying against the fortifications and more of them were straying about outside, and they were slaughtered all the more ferociously to the extent that they were being censured as turncoats and traitors, bearing arms for the servitude of themselves and their fatherland.

49 On the next day Sabinus showed his army on level ground to see if the barbarians, eager from their night's success, would dare battle. And, after they made no move to come down from their stronghold or its connecting mounds, he began a blockade by means of the blockhouses which he had already been fortifying at favorably situated points. Next, interweaving a ditch and breastwork, he

2   incorporated four miles in its perimeter; then gradually, to cut off water and pasturage, he contracted the cordon and surrounded a confined area; and an embankment was set up, from which rocks, spears, and fire could be thrown on the

3   now nearby enemy. But nothing exhausted them as much as thirst, since a mighty number of combatants and noncombatants was using the one remaining spring; and at the same time+ the herds, shut in alongside (as is the custom with barbarians), expired from the dearth of pasturage; lying beside them were the bodies of men whom wounds or thirst had annihilated; everything was polluted by discharge, stench, and contagion.

50 To the disruption of affairs was added—the ultimate misfortune—discord, some preparing themselves for surrender, some for death and mutual blows

89. See 4.47.1 just above.

among themselves; and there were some who urged not unavenged extermination but a breakout. Nor was it the commoners, however divergent in their opinions, but one of the leaders, Dinis, advanced in age and through long experience well taught in Roman might and clemency, who said that they should lay down their arms: that was the one remedy for their affliction. And he was the first to entrust himself, with his spouse and children, to the victor. There followed those weak by reason of their age or their sex, and those whose desire was greater for life than for glory. But the young men were torn between Tarsa and Turesis: each designed to fall in freedom, but Tarsa, shouting repeatedly for a speedy end and for their hopes and dread to be severed simultaneously, provided an example by plunging his sword into his chest; nor was there any lack of those who met their death in the same way. Turesis with his own unit waited for night, our leader being not unaware of the fact: so the pickets were consolidated with denser groups of men.

    Night closed in with frightful rain; and the enemy with his turbulent shouting, but sometimes across a desolate and awful silence, had induced uncertainty in the blockaders, whereupon Sabinus went around and urged them not to respond to ambiguous sounds or to the pretense of stillness by providing any chance for ambushers, but each man should keep to his task unmoved and without throwing his weapons at phantoms. Meanwhile the barbarians, running down in companies, at one moment threw manageable rocks, scorched stakes,[90] and lopped off boughs against the rampart, at another they filled the ditches with brushwood, hurdles, and lifeless bodies. Some brought bridges and ladders (previously manufactured) up to the defenses, which they then grasped and tried to drag down, struggling hand to hand with the resisters; the soldiery on the other side repelled them with weapons and beat them off with shield-bosses, wielded wall-javelins, and rolled down boulders which they had collected. What added spirit to the latter was their hope of an easy+ victory and, if they yielded, a scandal even more notable; for the former it was the fact that now was their last chance of salvation, and also the presence, in many cases, of mothers and spouses and their lamentations. The night proved convenient for the daring of some and the alarm of others; blows were uncertain, wounds unforeseen; unawareness of their own men and of the enemy, and voices reverberating from the curvature of the mountain as though from the rear, had caused such general confusion that the Romans abandoned some fortifications, assuming they had been pierced. And yet no passage was made by the enemy, except just a few; the rest, with all their readiest fighters dislodged or injured, at the approach of daylight were propelled to the heights of the stronghold, where surrender was finally enforced. Neighboring areas were received in submission on the initiative of their inhabitants; as for the remainder, Mount Haemus' early and savage winter saved them from being reduced by violence or blockade.

90. For which see 2.14.3n.

*

52 But at Rome the princeps' house was shaken,[91] and, to ensure that the process leading to the future extermination of Agrippina might begin, Claudia Pulchra, her cousin, was arraigned on the accusation of Domitius Afer.[92] Fresh from the praetorship, modest in rank, and quick to shine no matter what the deed, he flung at her a charge of immorality, involving Furnius as her adulterer, and poisoning

2 and curses aimed at the princeps. Agrippina—always frightening, but now inflamed by the danger to her relative too—proceeded to Tiberius and by chance discovered him sacrificing to his father. With this incentive to her indignation, she said that the same man should not be both slaying ritual victims to Divine Augustus and pursuing his descendants: his divine spirit had not been transfused into mute likenesses: *she* was his real image, the offspring of his heavenly blood. She understood the crisis, she said, and was adopting tatters.[93] It was to no purpose that the charge sheet was headed by Pulchra,[94] the only reason for whose extermination was that she had quite foolishly chosen Agrippina as the object of her courting, forgetful of the fact that Sosia had been crushed for the same.[95]

3 Hearing this elicited a rare utterance from that secretive breast, and, taking her hand,+ he warned her by means of a Greek verse that she was not being damaged merely because she did not rule. Pulchra and Furnius were condemned;

4 Afer was added to the chief advocates after the publicity given to his talent and following an assertion of Caesar's in which he called him a skillful speaker in his own right. (Subsequently, in undertaking accusations or protecting defendants, he enjoyed a more favorable reputation for his eloquence than for his morals, except that extreme age deprived him of much of his eloquence too, inasmuch as, despite his mental exhaustion, he retained an impatience of silence.)

53 As for Agrippina, persisting with her anger and caught in the toils of a physical disease, when visited by Caesar she poured forth tears for a long time in silence and then embarked on an indignant prayer: he should succor her solitude, give her a husband; she was still suitably young, nor was there any other solace for the virtuous except matrimony; there were in the community men ★★★

2 would deign to welcome the spouse of Germanicus and her children.[96] But Cae-

---

91. By the events described in 4.39–41 above, it seems.

92. Claudia Pulchra was daughter of the younger Marcella (Augustus' niece) and M. Valerius Messalla Appianus (consul in 12 B.C.), and hence second cousin of Agrippina (who was Augustus' granddaughter). She was also the widow of Quintilius Varus (1.3.6n.). Cn. Domitius Afer, an outstanding orator, became suffect consul in 39; he died in 59 (14.19).

93. See 2.29.1n. for tatters.

94. Or perhaps "that Pulchra was the pretext" (the Latin can mean either).

95. See 4.19.1 above.

96. The insertion of *qui* ("who") would restore sense, but the gap in the manuscript suggests that several words are missing.

sar was not unaware of the demands made by the state;[97] nevertheless, to avoid betraying obvious evidence of affront or dread, he left her without a reply despite her insistence. (That incident, not transmitted by the writers of annals, I discovered in the records of Agrippina's daughter, who, as mother of the princeps Nero, recalled for posterity her own life and the fates of her family.)

But Sejanus struck more deeply at the sorrowing and misguided woman, sending in people to warn her, in a display of friendship, that poison had been prepared for her and she should shun a banquet of her father-in-law's. She for her part was innocent of all pretense and, when she reclined at his side, changing neither her look nor conversation, touched none of the food, until Tiberius noticed—by chance or because he had been told. To test the matter more minutely, he praised some fruit as it lay on the table, presenting it to his daughter-in-law with his own hand. Agrippina's suspicion was thereby increased, and she passed it over, untouched by her lips, to the slaves. Still no utterance came from Tiberius in her presence but, turning to his mother, he said it was no wonder if he had decided to be more strict with one by whom he was being incriminated for poisoning. Hence a rumor that her extermination was being prepared: the Commander did not dare it openly but was seeking seclusion for its accomplishment.

But Caesar, to deflect the report, attended the senate regularly and over several days listened to legates from Asia arguing in which community the temple was to be established.[98] Eleven cities were competing, with equal self-aggrandizement but divergent in their strengths. There was not much difference between their recollections concerning their oldness of lineage or their enthusiasm for the Roman people during the wars with Perseus, Aristonicus, and other kings;[99] but the Hypaepeni and Tralliani, along with the Laodiceni and Magnesians, were passed over as having an insufficiently strong case; not even the Ilians, although they referred to Troy as parent of the City of Rome, were a force, except in their glorious antiquity. There was brief hesitation over the Halicarnassians' assertion that in one thousand and two hundred years their site had not swayed in a single earthquake and that the temple's foundations would be on living rock. It was believed that the Pergamenes, with a shrine to Augustus situated there (the very fact on which they relied), already had an adequate acquisition; the Ephesians and Milesians seemed to have taken over their entire communities with the ceremonial of Apollo and Diana respectively. So the debate was between the Sardians and the Smyrnaeans.

The Sardians read out a decree of Etruria in their capacity as kinsmen, on the grounds that Tyrrhenus and Lydus, the offspring of King Atys, had divided their race on account of its numbers: Lydus had stayed to settle in his father's lands, and

97. Or perhaps "of the demands being made of the state [by Agrippina]." The Latin phrase is very difficult.

98. For the temple see 4.15.3.

99. The war with Perseus, king of Macedon, was 171–168 B.C.; that with Aristonicus, claimant to the throne of Pergamum, was 131–129 B.C.

it was given to Tyrrhenus to found a new settlement; and it was from the names of the leaders that designations had been applied to the former across Asia and to the latter in Italy;[100] and the Lydians' wealthiness had been further increased with the dispatch of peoples to the part of Greece which subsequently took its name

4   from Pelops. At the same time they recalled letters from commanders and treaties struck with us in the war with the Macedonians,[101] the abundance of their rivers, the temperateness of their climate, and the rich lands around.

56   As for the Smyrnaeans, having traced back their antiquity (whether they had been founded by Tantalus, born of Jupiter, or by Theseus, himself of divine stock, or by one of the Amazons), they moved on to the items in which they placed most confidence, their services to the Roman people in dispatching a naval force not only to foreign wars but to those which were endured in Italy;[102] and they had been the first to establish a temple to the City of Rome in M. Porcius' consulship,[103] when the fortunes of the Roman people were of course already considerable but not yet elevated to supremacy, with the Punic city still standing and

2   kings in power across Asia. At the same time they adduced L. Sulla as a witness that, in the severest crisis of his army owing to the roughness of the winter and a scarcity of clothing, on the announcement of those facts to a public meeting in Smyrna all who were present had pulled the coverings from their bodies and

3   sent them to our legions.[104] So the fathers, when asked their opinion, preferred the Smyrnaeans, and Vibius Marsus proposed that M. Lepidus (to whose lot the province had fallen) should be given a supernumerary legate to undertake care of the temple; and, because Lepidus himself declined through modestness to make the selection, Valerius Naso from the praetorians was sent by lot.[105]

57   Meanwhile, having long considered and quite frequently postponed his plan, Caesar at last withdrew into Campania, in a show of dedicating temples to Jupiter at Capua and to Augustus at Nola, but fixed upon living far from the City.

As to the reason for his retirement, although I have followed the majority of authors and ascribed it to the practices of Sejanus, nevertheless, because he spent six continuous years in similar seclusion after bringing about the latter's slaughter, I am often moved to ask whether it is more realistically ascribed to the man himself, concealing his savagery and lust by his location, though he exhibited

2   them in his deeds. —There were those who believed that in old age his physical appearance too had been a source of shame (he had a spindly and stooping loftiness, a summit denuded of hair, and an ulcerous face, generally patched with cos-

100. Respectively Lydians and Tyrrhenians (the latter a synonym for Etruscans, the early inhabitants of Etruria).

101. See 4.55.1n. above.

102. Respectively the war against Antiochus III in 190/189 B.C. (2.63.3n.) and the Social War of 91–88 B.C. (3.27.2n.).

103. M. Porcius Cato the Elder was consul in 195 B.C.

104. The reference is to 85 B.C. during the First Mithridatic War.

105. For C. Vibius Marsus see 2.74.1n. For M. Lepidus see 1.13.2n., 4.20.2, etc.

metic medications); and yet in the seclusion of Rhodes he had been accustomed to avoid gatherings and to bury away his pleasures.[106] It is also transmitted that he was ousted by the unruliness of his mother, whom he spurned as his partner in despotism but could not dislodge, since he had received that very despotism as her gift. For Augustus had wondered about appointing Germanicus, his sister's grandson and praised by all, to control Roman interests; and it was only when overcome by the pleas of his wife that he associated Germanicus with Tiberius and Tiberius with himself.[107] And that was the basis of Augusta's constant reproaches and demands for compensation. — **3**

His departure was made with only a restricted company: one senator who was a former consul, Cocceius Nerva, with his expertise in the law;[108] a Roman equestrian (apart from Sejanus) from their illustrious ranks, Curtius Atticus;[109] the rest were endowed in liberal studies, mostly Greeks, in whose conversations he might find alleviation. Experts in heavenly matters said that Tiberius had left Rome under such movements of the planets as denied him a return. This was the reason for the extermination of many who inferred and publicized a speedy end to his life: they did not foresee so incredible a circumstance that for eleven years he would willingly be deprived of his fatherland. But subsequently there was disclosed the narrow boundary between skill and falsehood, and by what darkness the reality was veiled.[110] That he would not go back into the City was no chance saying; but, as to the rest, they acted in ignorance, since he passed his extreme old age nearby in the countryside or on the shore, and often encamping at the walls of the City. And by chance during those days Caesar was confronted with a double-edged danger which only increased the empty rumors—and presented the man himself with grounds why he should place more trust in the friendship and steadfastness of Sejanus. They were dining at a villa whose designation is Spelunca, between the Amynclan sea and Fundanian mountains, in a natural cave.[111] In an unexpected rock slide its mouth buried some servants. Hence dread among everyone and flight by those who were celebrating the party; but Sejanus, suspended over Caesar on his two knees+ and hands, placed himself in the way of the fall, and in such a posture was discovered by the soldiers who had come to the rescue. He was more influential after that, and, though his urgings had fatal consequences, he was listened to with trust as not being anxious for himself.

58

2

3

59

2

106. For Tiberius' retirement to Rhodes in 6 B.C.–A.D. 2 see 1.4.4.

107. In A.D. 4 Augustus adopted Tiberius and obliged the latter simultaneously to adopt Germanicus (1.3.3 and 5).

108. M. Cocceius Nerva had been suffect consul in 21 or 22 and was grandfather of the emperor Nerva; for his suicide in 33 see 6.26.1–2.

109. Later to be eliminated by Sejanus (6.10.2).

110. On this topic see further 6.20–2 below.

111. For discussion of the site of Spelunca (mod. Sperlonga) see A. F. Stewart, *Journal of Roman Studies* 67 (1977) 76–90.

3   And indeed he feigned the part of champion⁺ against the progeny of Germanicus, supplying men who would take on the role of accuser and in particular would
assail Nero, closest as he was to the succession and, though with the modesty of
youth, nevertheless often forgetful of what was appropriate in the present circumstances, inasmuch as his freedmen and clients, in their haste at acquiring power,
spurred him to appear alert and confident in spirit: that was what the Roman
people wanted and the armies desired, they said, nor would opposition dare to
come from Sejanus, who was now scoffing at an old man's passivity and a young

60   man's sluggishness alike. As he listened to things such as these, no trace of a crooked
thought was his; but sometimes utterances would issue, truculent and injudicious,
which were noted down by the guards assigned to him; and, since they then reported them in an exaggerated fashion and Nero was given no chance of rebut-

2   tal, different and additional manifestations of disquiet began to emerge. One man
would avoid his approach, some after exchanging greetings would immediately
turn away, and many would break off a conversation once begun—while opposite, motioning and mocking, were the bystanders who supported Sejanus.

        Moreover, Tiberius' face was brutal or beaming falsely: whether the young man
spoke or kept quiet, silence and utterance alike drew a charge. Not even his nighttime was carefree, since his waking, his sleep, and his sighs were disclosed by his
wife to her mother, Livia, and by her in turn to Sejanus, who drew Nero's brother
too, Drusus, to his side, throwing before him the prospect of the princeps's

3   position if he removed his elder and already undermined sibling. (Drusus' frightening temperament, besides his desire for power and the hatred customary to
brothers, was inflamed by resentment that their mother Agrippina was more
readily inclined toward Nero.) And yet Sejanus did not foster Drusus without
deliberating upon the seeds of future extermination in his case too, aware as he
was of the latter's defiance and of his extra susceptibility to traps.

61   At the end of the year there passed away the distinguished men Asinius
Agrippa, of brilliant rather than olden ancestors and in his own life not their inferior, and Q. Haterius, from a senatorial family and, while he lived, of celebrated
eloquence; but the monuments of his talent have not lasted correspondingly.[112]
Evidently he thrived by impulse rather than by taking care; and, whereas the la-
borious deliberation of others continues to be effective in the future, that reso-
nant flow of Haterius was extinguished along with himself.

★   ★   ★

62   With M. Licinius and L. Calpurnius as consuls,[113] an unforeseen calamity equaled
a disaster in a mighty war. It was over as soon as it began. One Atilius, of freedman descent, having started an amphitheater near Fidenae to celebrate spectacles

112. For Asinius Agrippa see 4.34.1n.; for Haterius see 1.13.4n.
113. M. Licinius Crassus Frugi was son of the consul of 14 B.C.; "L. Calpurnius" is the

of gladiators, neither sank the foundations down into solid ground nor built up the wooden construction with reliable clasps, being one who had won the business not because of an abundance of money or for courting the municipality but for a sordid profit. Hungry for such entertainment, people streamed in, having 2 been kept far from their pleasures during the command of Tiberius—in gender both men and women, every age, spilling out in greater numbers owing to the nearness of the site. Hence the destruction was more severe, given the concentration when the massive building collapsed, inasmuch as it crashed inward or spilled down over the areas outside and an untold army of mortals—intent on the spectacle or who were standing around—was swept headlong and buried. Those who were dashed to death in the initial wreckage at least escaped man- 3 gling (as far as is allowed by such a lot); more to be pitied were those whom, despite the severing of some part of their body, life had not yet deserted: during the day they recognized their spouses or children by sight, during the night by their wailing and groans. Soon everyone else, alerted by the report, lamented a brother in one case, a relative in another, or parents in yet another. Even those whose friends or connections were absent for a quite different reason nevertheless panicked; and, since it had not yet been discovered whom the violence had struck, dread was more widespread owing to the uncertainty. As the debris began to be **63** moved away, there was a rapid convergence on the lifeless to embrace and to kiss them; and often there was a dispute in cases where a face smashed beyond recognition, but the right stature or age, had led to errors of identification.

Fifty thousand people were crippled or crushed in that catastrophe; and measures for the future were taken by a senate's decision that no one should produce a gladiatorial show if his capital was less than four hundred thousand sesterces and that no amphitheater should be installed on ground which was not of proved reliability; Atilius was driven into exile. But as an immediate response to the dis- 2 aster the houses of the aristocracy were thrown open and dressings and doctors made widely available, and the City throughout those days, though of sorrowful appearance, resembled the established customs of the ancients, who after great battles gave support to the injured with lavishness and care.

That disaster had not yet abated when a violent fire afflicted the City more **64** than usual, with the Caelian Hill burned down. People were maintaining that it was a fatal year and that the princeps's counsel of absence had been undertaken with unfavorable omens (which is a habit of the public, interpreting chance events in terms of blame); but Caesar confronted the issue by distributing money in proportion to the losses. And gratitude was expressed to him in the senate by 2 illustrious members and he enjoyed a reputation among the people because, without canvassing or pleas from relatives, even unknowns who had been summoned spontaneously were helped by his munificence. Proposals were added that 3

---

former Cn. Calpurnius Piso, who was obliged to change his first name after the disgrace and death of his father (3.17.4 and n.).

the Caelian Hill should in the future be called the Augustan, since, with everything ablaze all around, only a likeness of Tiberius, located in the house of the
senator Junius, had survived the violence intact: the same thing had once happened to Claudia Quinta, they said, and her statue, having twice escaped the fury
of fires, had been consecrated by their ancestors in the shrine of the Mother of
the Gods;[114] the Claudii were sacred and acceptable to the divinities, and there
was an obligation to augment the holiness of a place in which the gods had displayed such honor to the princeps.

65   (It would not be inappropriate to transmit that in ancient times the nomenclature of that hill was "Querquetulanus," because it was prolific and productive of
that wood,[115] and that only later was it intituled "Caelian" from Caeles Vibenna,
the leader of the Etruscan race, who, after bringing help, had received it as an abode
from Tarquinius Priscus or another of the kings (writers disagree on the point);[116]
but there is no ambiguousness in other respects, namely that large numbers of his
people also inhabited the level areas in the locality of the forum, whence "Tuscan
Street" is so called from the designation of the immigrants.)

66   But, just as the enthusiasm of the aristocracy and the lavishness of the princeps had brought comfort to counteract the misfortunes, so the accusers' violence, daily ever greater and more ferocious, was raging without alleviation; and
Varus Quintilius, a rich relative of Caesar's, had been seized by Domitius Afer,
the condemner of the man's mother, Claudia Pulchra[117]—with no one in wonder that, having been needy for a long time and having misused his recently won
2   reward, he was girding himself for further outrages. What was a source of won-
derment, however, was that it was Publius Dolabella who presented himself as
the man's ally in the denunciation, because, with his brilliant ancestry and being connected to Varus, it was his own nobility and his own blood on whose destruction he was embarking.[118] The senate nevertheless resisted and voted to wait
for the Commander, the one temporary refuge from the pressing evils.

67   But Caesar had now dedicated the temples in Campania,[119] and, although he
had warned by edict that no one should interrupt his peace, and converging

114. In 191 B.C. (Livy 29.14.2); the Mother of the Gods is Cybele.

115. The "wood" in question is oak (in Latin *quercus*), and "Querquetulanus" is used of
places and deities associated with oak woods.

116. Another version of this story is given by the emperor Claudius in A.D. 48 in the
speech which has been preserved on bronze at Lyon and which T. "re-writes" at 11.24
below (see above, p. xvi). "Intituled," a very rare synonym for "named" or "designated," is
my translation for the very rare verb *appellitatum*, which occurs in Claudius' speech as well
as in T. here. The traditional dates of Tarquinius Priscus are 616–579 B.C.

117. P. Quintilius Varus was son of the infamous general Varus (1.3.6n.); his relationship
with the imperial family was through his mother, for whom and her case see above, 4.52.1
and n.

118. P. Cornelius Dolabella (3.47.3n.) was Varus' cousin.

119. See 4.57.1 above.

townsfolk were kept away by the deployment of soldiery, he nevertheless detested the municipalities and colonies and everything situated on the mainland, so he hid himself away on the island of Capri, detached as it is from the tip of the Surrentine promontory by a three-mile strait. I am inclined to believe that it was its 2 solitude which most appealed to him, because the sea around about is harborless and there are scarcely refuges even for modest craft; nor could anyone have moored there without the knowledge of the guard. The climatic conditions in winter are mild owing to a mountain barrier which fends off any savage winds; its summer faces Westerlies and, with the open main all round, is exceptionally attractive; and it used to have the prospect of a very fine bay, until the fires of Mount Vesuvius altered the area's appearance.[120] It is transmitted by report that Greeks had been its tenants and that Capri had been inhabited by the Teleboae; but now it was Tiberius who had settled there in twelve attractive[+] and massive 3 villas, his former attentiveness to public concerns contrasting with his more concealed relaxing into luxuriousness and evil inactivity. For there still remained his rashness in suspicion and credulity, which Sejanus, accustomed to aggravate it even in the City, was stirring more keenly with his traps against Agrippina and Nero, which were no longer concealed. The soldiery assigned to them recorded, 4 as though in annals,[121] their messages, visits, disclosures, and secrets; and in addition persons were set up to warn them to flee to the armies in Germany or to embrace the likeness of Divine Augustus in the throng of the forum and to call upon people and senate for aid. And all of this they spurned, yet it was cast against them as though it were their intention.

★   ★   ★

With Junius Silanus and with Silius Nerva as consuls,[122] a foul beginning to the **68** year was made with the dragging to prison of the illustrious Roman equestrian Titius Sabinus owing to his friendship with Germanicus.[123] He had not omitted to be courteous to the man's spouse and children, acting as their attendant at home and companion in public—the only one remaining from so many previous clients, and for that reason praised among good men and a reproach for the prejudiced. This was the man whom Latinius Latiaris, Porcius Cato, Petilius Ru- 2

---

120. Primarily a reference to the famous eruption of A.D. 79.

121. The reference to "annals" is unclear but perhaps implies the detailed recording of trivia as though they were important (see 13.31.1).

122. C. Appius Junius Silanus, son of the consul of A.D. 10 (3.66.1n.), was accused of treason in 32 (6.9.3); there is a passing reference at 11.29.1 to his subsequent murder. P. Silius Nerva is scarcely otherwise known.

123. Sabinus' case had been deferred in A.D. 24 (4.19.1 above).

fus, and M. Opsius, former praetors,[124] attacked in their desire for the consulship, to which there was no access except through Sejanus—and Sejanus' blessing was not to be won except by crime.

It had been agreed among them that Latiaris, who was in touch with Sabinus on a modest basis, should set up the snare; the others should be present as witnesses; and then they should embark on the accusation. Latiaris therefore threw
3   off what at first were chance conversations, but soon started to praise the man's steadfastness because, as a friend of the household when it flourished, he had not, like everyone else, deserted it now that it was blighted. At the same time, expressing pity for Agrippina, he spoke in honorable terms of Germanicus. And, after Sabinus (since mortals' hearts are pliant in misfortune) had poured forth tears and followed them with complaints, the other, more boldly now, loaded accusations upon Sejanus and his savagery, haughtiness, and hopes; he did not refrain even
4   from disparagement of Tiberius. And those conversations, on the grounds that the two had exchanged forbidden topics, produced a show of close friendship: it was now Sabinus who spontaneously sought out Latiaris, frequented his house, and brought his troubles to him as if to the most loyal of men.

69   The individuals whom I have recalled discussed how those topics could be heard by a wider audience: the place in which they would meet had to preserve an appearance of solitude; and, if they took up a position behind the doors, there was the dread of being seen, of making a sound, or of suspicion arising by chance. Between roof and ceiling, in a lair as disgusting as their treachery was execrable,
2   the three senators lurked and applied an ear to apertures and cracks. Meanwhile Latiaris, discovering Sabinus out in public, brought him home to his bedroom on the pretext of telling him some fresh information, and then he piled up past items and current (of which there was an ample supply) and new terrors as well. The other said the same at even greater length, to the extent that sorrows are the more difficult to silence when once they erupt.
3   Thereupon the accusation was speeded up, and in a letter sent to Caesar they told of the stages of the plot and of their own disgrace. At no other time was the community more tense and panicked, behaving most cautiously of all[+] toward those closest to them: encounters, dialogues, familiar and unfamiliar ears were avoided; even dumb and inanimate objects such as a roof and walls were treated with circumspection.

70   As for Caesar, having offered solemn prayers for the starting year by letter on the Kalends of January,[125] he rounded on Sabinus, charging that certain of his freedmen had been bribed and that he himself was the target; and there was no obscurity about his demand for vengeance. Nor was there delay in its decree; and the condemned man was dragged away, shouting repeatedly (insofar as he was able, with his clothing drawn up over his head and his throat restricted) that such was

124. M. Porcius Cato was suffect consul in 36. Little is known of the others: Latiaris is mentioned again at 6.4.1, where he is called Lucanius Latiaris.

125. I.e., 1 January.

the year's inauguration, these were Sejanus' victims that were being felled in sacrifice! But, wherever he directed his gaze, wherever his words fell, there was flight   2
and desolation: the streets and forums were deserted. Some people came back and
showed themselves once more, panicking at the very fact that they had been afraid.
For what day could be free from punishment, when amid rituals and prayers, at   3
the very time that it was customary to refrain even from profane words, chains
and noose were being introduced? It was not through inadvertence, they said, that
Tiberius had incurred such great resentment: it had been studied and deliberate,
to discourage any belief that new magistrates could be prevented from unveiling
the prison in the same way as they did shrines and altars.

There followed a further letter expressing gratitude that they had punished a   4
man hostile to the state, adding that his own life was one of trepidation and that
he suspected traps from his antagonists, but inculpating no one by name; and yet
there was no doubt that the attack was aimed at Nero and Agrippina. (If it had   **71**
not been my design to refer events each to their proper year, by inclination I
would be anxious to anticipate and immediately to recall the outcomes which
Latinius and Opsius and the other devisers of that outrage had, not only after C.
Caesar took control of affairs but during the lifetime of Tiberius, who, while dis-
liking his servers of crime to be overthrown by others, nevertheless generally
dashed them down for being old and bloated once he himself was satiated and
was offered fresh men for the same special task. But the punishments of these and
other blameworthy men I shall transmit at the appropriate time.)[126] Then Asinius   2
Gallus, whose children had Agrippina as their maternal aunt, proposed that the
princeps should be asked to declare his dreads to the senate and to allow them
to be removed. But none of his virtues (as he deemed them) did Tiberius cher-   3
ish as much as his dissimulation: he was therefore all the more upset to learn of
the attempt to unveil what he was for suppressing. Nevertheless Sejanus mellowed him, not through any love for Gallus but to wait upon the princeps's hes-
itations, knowing that he was slow in deliberation but that, when he erupted, he
followed his bitter words with frightening action.

During the same period Julia met her death, the granddaughter whom, when   4
convicted of adultery, Augustus had condemned and deported to the island of
Trimerus, not far from the Apulian shores.[127] There for twenty years she had
endured exile, supported by the help of Augusta, who, though she had secretly
undermined her stepchildren while they flourished,[128] openly displayed pity
toward them when they were blighted.

★

126. Latiaris was killed in 32 (6.4.1 below); the fates of the other three must have been
given in a part of the *Annals* now lost. "C. Caesar" is Gaius Caligula, who succeeded
Tiberius in 37.

127. See 3.24.2–3 above.

128. See 1.3.3 (Gaius and Lucius Caesar), 1.6.3 (Agrippa Postumus).

72   In the same year the Frisians, a transrhenane people, cast peace aside, more because of our greed than intolerant of compliance. The tax ordered for them by
Drusus had been modest in proportion to their straitened circumstances, namely
that they should contribute ox-hides for military use—but without anyone's paying attention to questions of toughness or dimension until Olennius, one of the
first-rankers and installed as ruler of the Frisians, chose aurochs' skins as a model

2   for what was acceptable. That would have been steep even for other nations but
was endured with greater difficulty among Germans, whose denes are prolific of
mighty beasts but whose domestic herds are only modest. First they handed over
the actual oxen, then their fields, and finally their spouses and children bodily

3   into servitude. Hence angry complaints and, when no relief was forthcoming, a
remedy in war. The soldiers attending to the tax were seized and affixed to gibbets, but Olennius forestalled their ferocity by flight, being received at a stronghold whose name is Flevum, where a by no means contemptible unit of citizens
and allies presided the Ocean's shores.

73   When all this became known to L. Apronius, the propraetor of Lower Germany,[129] he summoned detachments of the legions from the upper province and
chosen men of the auxiliary infantry and cavalry, and, sailing each army down
the Rhine, brought them simultaneously against the Frisians—the blockade of
the stronghold having already been raised and the rebels withdrawn to protect
their own property. He therefore consolidated the nearest estuaries with embank-

2   ments and bridges for the transportation of a heavier column; and, having discovered a ford in the meantime, he ordered a Canninefate wing and the German
infantry that was serving alongside our men to surround the rear of the enemy,
who, now arranged in line, were beating back the allied squadrons and legionary
cavalry sent as reinforcements. Next three light cohorts and then a further two
and subsequently, after an interval of time, a cavalry wing were sent in—effective enough, if they had set upon the opposition simultaneously; but, because
they kept arriving in stages, they had not imparted steadfastness to the disrupted
men and kept being carried backward in the panic of the fugitives.

3   To Cethecius Labeo, legate of the Fifth Legion, Apronius handed what remained of the auxiliaries; and he for his part, drawn to the brink owing to the
uncertain situation of his own men, sent a message imploring a legionary force.
It was the Fifth which burst forth before any others and, with the enemy beaten
in a fierce fight, rescued the cohorts and wings, exhausted as they were by their
wounds. Yet the Roman leader did not embark on revenge, nor did he inter the
bodies, although many of the tribunes and prefects, as well as distinguished cen-

4   turions, had been laid low. Later it was discovered from deserters that at the grove
which they call Baduhenna's nine hundred Romans had been dispatched in a
fight which had dragged on into the next day; and that another unit of four hundred, after occupying the villa of Cruptorix (a former mercenary) and dreading
betrayal, had fallen to mutual blows.

129. See 1.56.1n.

★

Brilliant thereafter was the Frisian name among Germans, with Tiberius disguis- **74**
ing the damage in order to avoid entrusting anyone with the war. Nor was the
senate concerned whether the extremities of the empire were being dishonored:
domestic panic had preoccupied their minds, for which the remedy was sought
in sycophancy. So, although they were consulted on various different matters, 2
what they voted for was an Altar of Clemency and an Altar of Friendship and
likenesses of Caesar and Sejanus around about; and with frequent prayers they
importuned the two of them to provide an opportunity for being seen. But they 3
for their part did not leave for the City or the neighborhood of the City: it
seemed sufficient merely to abandon the island and be observed in the nearest
part of Campania. There came fathers, equestrians, and a considerable portion of
the plebs, all of them tense as regards Sejanus, with whom meetings were harder
and procured only through canvassing and by allying oneself with his plans. It 4
was generally agreed that his haughtiness had increased as he surveyed "that
servile filth in the forecourt." At Rome bustle is normal and, given the size of
the City, the business on which any individual is proceeding is uncertain; but lying there prostrate on the plain or shore, irrespective of whether it was night or
day, they endured his doorkeepers' favor or disdain alike, until even that too was
forbidden. The return to the City was made in trepidation by those whom he 5
had not considered worthy of either conversation or glance, but in misguided eagerness by those over whom there loomed the weighty outcome of their unpropitious friendship.

As for Tiberius, once he had personally handed his granddaughter Agrippina **75**
(the offspring of Germanicus) to Cn. Domitius, he ordered their wedding to be
celebrated in the City.[130] In Domitius he had chosen, in addition to the oldness
of his line, a blood relative of the Caesars: the man could parade Octavia as his
grandmother and, through her, Augustus as great-uncle.

130. Cn. Domitius Ahenobarbus, son of the consul of 16 B.C. (1.63.4n.), was consul in
32 (6.1.1) and escaped various charges in 37 (6.47.2). He and the younger Agrippina were
the parents of the future emperor Nero.

BOOK 5

1   With Rubellius and with Fufius as consuls, each of whom had the nomenclature Geminus,[1] Julia Augusta met her death in extreme old age, a woman of the most brilliant nobility through her Claudian family and by adoption into the Livii and Julii.[2]

    Her first marriage and children were with Tiberius Nero, who, a refugee in the Perusine War, returned to the City on the pledging of peace between Sex.

2   Pompeius and the triumvirs.[3] Thereupon Caesar, in his desire for her good looks, removed her from her husband (her unwillingness being uncertain)—and so swiftly that he allowed not even an interval for childbirth, installing her at his own hearth while she was still heavily pregnant.[4] She produced no progeny thereafter, but, being connected to the blood of Augustus through the union of Agrippina and Germanicus, had great-grandchildren in common with him.[5]

3   In the purity of her house she conformed to old-time convention but was affable beyond what females of antiquity approved; an unruly mother, a complaisant wife, and a good match for the qualities of her husband and the hypocrisy of her son.

4   Her funeral was modest, her will for long unratified. She was praised before the

2   rostra by her great-grandson, C. Caesar, who later took control of affairs.[6] But Tiberius, because he had missed the final duties to his mother, pleaded by letter the magnitude of business (though without changing his attractive life), and as if through modestness reduced the honors decreed lavishly to her memory by the senate, retaining just a few and adding that no heavenly cult be decreed for her:

2   such had been her own preference. Furthermore in part of the same missive he berated her womanly friendships, a glancing blow at the consul Fufius. (The latter had flourished by Augusta's favor, adept as he was at attracting female sympa-

---

1. Nothing is otherwise known of L. Rubellius Geminus; C. Fufius Geminus was son of the homonymous suffect consul of 2 B.C.; his death is referred to at 6.10.1. "Geminus" means "twin": T.'s choice of expression draws attention to the fact that the two men are twinned in both magistracy and name.

2. Livia (= Julia Augusta) had been born on 30 January 58 B.C. It was her father who had been adopted into the family of the Livii, becoming M. Livius Drusus Claudianus; Livia herself was adopted into the Julian family on Augustus' death (1.8.1).

3. The Perusine War between Octavian and L. Antonius, Mark Antony's brother, was 41/40 B.C.; the Peace of Misenum was 39 B.C.

4. At the time of her "abduction" by the then Octavian, Livia was pregnant with the elder Drusus, who was born in 38 B.C. See 1.10.5 and n.

5. Since Germanicus was her own grandson, and since his wife, the elder Agrippina, was granddaughter of Augustus, their numerous children were the great-grandchildren of Livia and Augustus alike.

6. Gaius Caligula became emperor on Tiberius' death in A.D. 37.

thy, while being at the same time glib and accustomed to deride Tiberius in acer-
bic witticisms, for which the powerful have a long memory.)

Thenceforward it was sheer, oppressive despotism. With Augusta safe and **3**
sound, there had still been a refuge, because Tiberius' compliance toward his
mother was deep-rooted and Sejanus would not dare to overrun her parental authority; but now, as if released from harness, they charged ahead, and a letter was
sent against Agrippina and Nero which the public believed had been delivered
previously and withheld by Augusta (it was not long after her death that it was
read out). It contained words of studied sharpness, yet the princeps cast against   **2**
his grandson imputations of neither armed force nor enthusiasm for revolution
but of love affairs with young men and immorality. Against his daughter-in-law
he dared not fabricate even that, censuring her arrogance of tongue and her truculent spirit—with the senate in considerable panic and silence, until a few who
had nothing to hope for from honorableness (and public misfortunes are interpreted by individuals as an opportunity for seeking favor) demanded that a motion be put, Cotta Messalinus being the readiest with a frightening proposal.[7]
But from other leaders, and especially from the magistrates, there was only trep-   **3**
idation. Tiberius, despite the ferocity of his invective, had left everything else ambiguous.

Now there was in the senate Junius Rusticus, chosen by Caesar to compile the   **4**
fathers' deeds[8] and thus credited with insight into his deliberations. By some fateful stroke (he had given no previous evidence of steadfastness) or by a warped
artfulness (inasmuch as he was panicked by the uncertainty but forgot the inevitable) he aligned himself with the hesitant and warned the consuls not to
instigate a motion. He argued that the highest matters turned on only the slightest movement: possibly in future the old man would regret Germanicus' fate.[+]
Simultaneously the people, bearing likenesses of Agrippina and Nero, stood   **2**
around the curia and, with propitious[+] prophecies for Caesar, kept shouting that
the letter was forged and that the princeps did not wish extermination to be
aimed at his family.

So no grim deed was done that day. Even fabricated proposals against Sejanus   **3**
under the names of consulars were being circulated, as many people—anony-
mously and thus all the more provocatively—gave practical effect to an instinc-
tive lust.[9] Hence his more violent anger, and material for his allegations that the   **4**
princeps's pain had been spurned by the senate and that the people had defected:
strange new public meetings already had audiences, strange new fathers' decisions had readers:[10] what remained but that they should take up the sword and

---

7. The consul of A.D. 20 (2.32.1n., 3.2.3).

8. The "fathers' deeds" are the senatorial records (again at 15.74.3): see above, p. xv.

9. I.e., they had the chance to fulfill their long-standing natural desire of criticizing
Sejanus.

10. "Strange new" here has the sense of "revolutionary" (see 5.8.1 below).

choose as their leaders and commanders those whose images they had been following in place of standards?

5   Therefore Caesar, repeating the abuse against his grandson and daughter-in-law and berating the plebs by edict, complained to the fathers that by the foul play of a single senator his Commander's sovereignty had been publicly outwitted; he nevertheless demanded everything to be left undecided for himself. There was no further debate—not that they decreed the extreme penalty (that was forbidden), but they testified that, though prepared for vengeance, they were being hampered by the authority of the princeps. ★★★[11]

11. The next sentence in the manuscript follows normally but relates to A.D. 31: evidently T.'s narrative of the rest of A.D. 29, of the whole of 30, and of most of 31 (including the downfall of Sejanus) has been lost at an earlier stage in the text's transmission.

Book 6[1]

★★★Four and forty speeches on the affair were delivered, of which a few on account of dread, and more by habit ★★★[2]

5.6

"★★★ I judged would bring shame upon myself or resentment upon Sejanus. But fortune has turned; and, whereas the one who had affiliated him as colleague and son-in-law pardons himself,[3] the rest in their criminality assail the man whom they supported with such disgrace. Whether it is more pitiable to be accused for friendship or to accuse a friend, I can hardly decide; yet I have no intention of putting anyone's cruelty or clemency to the test, but freely and with self-respect I shall forestall my danger. I implore you to retain a memory of me not in sorrow but delightedly, adding me too to those who by an exceptional end have escaped public calamities."

2

3

Then he took up part of the day detaining or dismissing individuals, depending on whether each had a mind to withdraw+ or to speak to him; and, while there was still a considerable throng, all of them watching his intrepid expression and believing that time still remained for some last words, he fell on the sword which he had hidden in a fold.[4] And Caesar did not assail the deceased with any charges or abuse, although against Blaesus his censure had contained many foul items.[5]

5.7

2

There was next a motion concerning P. Vitellius and Pomponius Secundus.[6] Informants argued that the former had offered the keys of the treasury (of which

5.8

1. There is nothing in the manuscript to indicate a new book (see previous n.), but since the mid-nineteenth century it has been conventional to signal that the narrative which follows belongs to Book 6, the beginning of which, on this hypothesis, has been lost (see next n.). In the sixteenth century, however, it was assumed that the beginning of Book 6 coincides with the beginning of the year A.D. 32 and that the following six chapters belong to the end of Book 5; it is usual to retain this old numbering of the chapters in question (5.6 to 5.11) despite the modern belief that Book 6 has already begun.

2. After the loss of almost three years' narrative (see 5.5n.) the text continues with a sentence which itself is incomplete: the lacuna at the end of it also deprives us of part of the following speech, which begins in midsentence.

The "affair" to which reference is made in this first sentence of Book 6 is thought to be the aftermath of Livia's (i.e., Livilla's) involvement in the poisoning of her husband, Drusus, in A.D. 23 (see 4.3.3). The identity of the subsequent speaker, who after his speech commits suicide (5.7.1), is unknown.

3. Sejanus had been Tiberius' colleague in the consulship for A.D. 31: see also 6.8.3 below, where he is again called "son-in-law" (an expression which is now generally taken to mean that at some point Sejanus had married Livia).

4. Sc. of his garment.

5. Blaesus had evidently been an earlier victim of the downfall of Sejanus, his nephew (1.16.2n., 3.35.2).

6. In the extant narrative Vitellius had last been prominent as a prosecutor of Piso in

he was prefect) and military money for revolutionary purposes;[7] against the latter there was cast by Considius, a former praetor, an imputation of friendship with Aelius Gallus, who after the punishment of Sejanus had fled to Pomponius'

2   gardens as if to the trustiest of refuges. The only help the imperiled pair received was from the steadfastness of their brothers, who stood bail. Later, after frequent postponements, burdened by hope and dread alike, Vitellius requested a sharpener[8] under the pretext of studying, and, inflicting a light blow on his veins, ended his life in sickness of spirit. As for Pomponius, with his considerable elegance of behavior and illustrious talent, he withstood his adverse fortune equably and was a survivor of Tiberius.

5.9   It was decided after this that measures should be taken against the remaining children of Sejanus (though the anger of the plebs was vanishing and many had been assuaged by the earlier reprisals). So there were transported to prison his son, intuiting the inevitable, and a girl so unaware that she asked frequently for what felony and to what place she was being dragged off: she would not do it

2   again, she said, and could be admonished by a child's beating. Authors of the time transmit that, because it was held to be unheard of for a virgin to have the triumviral reprisal inflicted on her,[9] she was violated by the executioner alongside the noose; then, their throats crushed, the bodies despite their tender ages were thrown onto the Gemonians.

*

5.10   During the same period Asia and Achaea were terrified by a rumor, shrill rather than persistent, that Drusus, Germanicus' son, had been seen around the Cyclades islands, then on the mainland.[10] And there was in fact a young man of not dissimilar age, who had allegedly been recognized by some freedmen of Caesar's; and, with the latter as his companions in the deception, various unwitting persons were lured by the fame of his name and by the temperamental readiness of

2   Greeks for novelties and wonders. For they fabricated and simultaneously be-

---

A.D. 20 (e.g., 3.13.2, 3.19.1); P. Pomponius Secundus was a well-known poet, friend of the elder Pliny, and suffect consul in 44: see further 11.13.1, 12.27.2–28.2. For Pomponius' brother see 6.18.1n.: their much married mother, Vistilia, was also the mother of P. Suillius Rufus (11.1.1n.) and the famous general Corbulo (11.18.1n.).

7. The military treasury is meant: see App. A.

8. Used for reed pens. Vitellius was evidently pretending to be about to take notes as part of his studying.

9. I.e., capital punishment, which came under the jurisdiction of a board of "triumvirs" (see App. A). With T.'s story compare the following: "Islamic judges have decreed that virgins can still go to paradise despite being executed. [. . .] A former Revolutionary Guard intelligence officer and interrogator at Shiraz [in Iran] is quoted as saying: 'Virgin women prisoners must as a rule be raped before execution'" (*The Times* (London), 31 March 1995).

10. The real Drusus was in prison (6.23.2): hence "custody" below.

lieved that, having slipped away from custody, he was proceeding to his father's armies for an invasion of Egypt or Syria. Already attended by a youthful throng and by the enthusiasm of the public, he was taking delight in the present and entertaining hopes of the impossible when Poppaeus Sabinus heard of the matter. (Though concentrating at the time on Macedonia, he was concerned with Achaea too.)[11] Therefore, to forestall events whether true or false, Sabinus bypassed   3 quickly the Toronaean and Thermaean gulfs, next negotiating Euboea, an island in the Aegean Sea, and Piraeus on the Attic coast, then the Corinthian shore and the narrows of the Isthmus; and, arriving by the Actian+ sea at the Roman colony of Nicopolis,[12] there he at last found out that the man, when asked more artfully who he was, had identified himself as the offspring of M. Silanus and that, with many of his followers having dispersed, he had boarded a ship with the apparent aim of making for Italy. And Sabinus wrote as much to Tiberius, but about the origin or end of the affair I have discovered nothing further.

⋆

At the outgoing of the year a far-advanced disaffection between the consuls   **5.11** erupted.[13] Trio, who undertook antagonisms easily and was practiced in the forum, had struck a glancing blow at Regulus for being sluggish at stifling the ministers of Sejanus; he for his part, who retained his self-control except when harried, not only blunted his colleague's attack but was for dragging him to trial as being guilty of conspiracy. And, despite many of the fathers begging them to lay aside hatreds likely to end ruinously, they remained hostile and menacing until they retired from the magistracy.

⋆   ⋆   ⋆

Cn. Domitius and Camillus Scribonianus[14] had embarked on the consulship   **6.1** when Caesar, having crossed the strait which washes between Capri and Surrentum, was skirting Campania, in two minds whether to go into the City—or, because he had already decided otherwise, simulating a scene of impending arrival. And, having landed often in the neighborhood and approached the gardens by the Tiber, he retreated again to his rocks and the solitude of the sea, in shame at the crimes and unbridled lusts with which he was so inflamed that, in the man-

11. For Poppaeus Sabinus see 1.80.1n.

12. For which see 2.53.1–2.

13. Viz. L. Fulcinius Trio (2.28.2n.) and P. Memmius Regulus (see 14.47.1).

14. For Cn. Domitius Ahenobarbus see 4.75n.; L. Arruntius Camillus Scribonianus was the biological son of M. Furius Camillus (2.52.3n.) and the adopted son of L. Arruntius (1.8.3n.): see further 12.52.1–2.

2   ner of a king, he polluted freeborn youngsters in illicit sex. Nor was it only good
    looks and becoming bodies but in some cases boyish modesty and in others the
    images of their ancestors which acted as the incitement of his desire.[15] And that
    was the first time that the previously unknown designations of "sellarii" and
    "spintriae" were devised, respectively from the foulness of their place and their
    multifarious passivity.[16] And the slaves who were charged with the searching and
    bringing resorted to gifts for the ready, threats against the reluctant and, if a rel-
    ative or parent held them back, violent seizure and personal gratification, as
    though their victims were captives.

2   But at Rome at the start of the year, as if Livia's outrages were only recently
    known and not previously punished either, frightening proposals were voiced
    also against her likenesses and memory; and Sejanus' property was to be carried
2   from the treasury for collection by the fiscus (as if it made a difference). It was
    Scipios and Silani and Cassii who, in almost identical or little changed words,
    were making these suggestions with much assertiveness when suddenly Togonius
    Gallus, aligning his anonymity with these great names, was listened to with gen-
3   eral derision. He begged the princeps to select some senators, from whom twenty,
    drawn by lot and each girded with a blade, should defend his safety whenever he
    entered the curia. (He had evidently believed the missive demanding one of the
    consuls as his bodyguard so that he might travel securely from Capri to the City.)
4   Nevertheless Tiberius, wont to mix mockery with seriousness, expressed grati-
    tude for the fathers' kind thought. But who could be left out? Who selected? Al-
    ways the same members or others in turn? Former officeholders or young men?
    Private individuals or from the magistrates? Next, what a scene there would be
    of those at the threshold of the curia taking up their—swords! Life did not mean
    so much to him if it had to be protected by arms.

5   Such was his reply to Togonius, moderating his language lest his urging should
3   extend beyond cancellation of the proposal; but Junius Gallio, who had suggested
    that praetorians on completion of service should acquire the prerogative of sit-
    ting in the Fourteen Rows,[17] he berated violently, asking him, as if to his face,
    what *his* business was with soldiers who should properly receive neither words
2   nor rewards except from their Commander. He had certainly devised something
    for which Divine Augustus made no provision! Or was it rather the case that a
    satellite of Sejanus had sought discord and mutiny in order to propel raw minds,
3   under the pretext of an honor, to corrupt the conventions of soldiery? —The
    prize carried off by Gallio for his considered sycophancy was to be driven at once
    from the curia, then from Italy; and, because he drew censure for being likely to

    15. For ancestral images see 2.27.2n.

    16. The former term is derived from *sellarium* = "privy" (see Suetonius, *Tiberius* 43.1
    "in his Capri retreat he even devised *sellaria* as the place for his arcane lusts"); the latter
    term is connected with the Greek word for catamite.

    17. For the Fourteen Rows see 2.83.4n.; by "praetorians" in this sentence are meant
    members of the Praetorian Guard.

endure exile easily on his chosen Lesbos, a noted and attractive island, he was dragged back to the City and guarded in magistrates' houses.

In the same letter Caesar struck at Sextius Paconianus, a praetorian,[18] to the fathers' great joy (he was a bold malefactor, probing everyone's secrets, and chosen by Sejanus as the man to help his guileful preparations against C. Caesar);[19] and, when this became clear,[20] hatreds previously conceived burst forth and the ultimate reprisal was in the process of being decreed—except that he offered information. But, when it was Lucanius Latiaris against whom he moved, accuser and defendant alike—both equally resented—provided a most gratifying spectacle: Latiaris, as I have recorded,[21] was formerly the principal in ensnaring Titius Sabinus, and now he took priority in paying the penalty.

Meanwhile Haterius Agrippa attacked the consuls of the previous year: why, after aiming accusations at each other,[22] were they now quiet? No doubt dread and the consciousness of guilt acted as a pact, but the fathers could not keep silent what they had heard. Regulus replied that there remained time for vengeance, and he would follow it through in the presence of the princeps; Trio, that rivalry between colleagues and the aspersions of the disaffected were better obliterated. Despite Agrippa's pressure, Sanquinius Maximus from the consulars[23] begged the senate not to increase the Commander's concerns by raking up additional embitterments: the man himself was equal to determining remedies. Thus Regulus' salvation and the deferment of Trio's extermination were assured; but Haterius became more resented because—drooping from somnolence or lustful vigils as he was, and on account of his sluggishness not dreading the princeps, however cruel—he deliberated upon the ruin of illustrious men amid his gluttony and illicit sex.

Thereupon Cotta Messalinus, author of every most savage proposal and thus the object of deep-rooted resentment, was accused on numerous counts when the chance was first presented: namely, he had said that C. Caesar was of uncertain virility, and, when dining among the priests on the birthday of Augusta, that

---

18. I.e., an ex-praetor (and not, as in the preceding paragraph, a member of the Praetorian Guard). The manuscript gives the first of the man's names as "extium," always emended to "Sextium" (the form transmitted at 6.39.1 below); but epigraphic evidence has now indicated that his name was Sextilius. I have nevertheless kept the transmitted form in both places on the grounds that any mistake is more likely to be T.'s than a scribe's. See also 6.48.4n.

19. Sejanus' designs against Gaius Caligula must have been described in the lost portion of the *Annals* above.

20. The implication of this remark seems to be that Tiberius' attack on Paconianus was expressed with his customary obscurity and required some interpretation. See, for example, the beginning of the letter quoted at 6.6.1 below.

21. See 4.68.2 and 4.71.1, where Latiaris' first name is given as "Latinius."

22. See 5.11 above. For D. Haterius Agrippa see 1.77.3n.

23. The date of his consulship is unknown; he reappears at 11.18.1.

that was a ninth-day meal;[24] and, complaining about the powerfulness of M. Lepidus and L. Arruntius, with whom he disagreed over a monetary matter, he

2   had added "They will be protected by the senate, but I by my pet Tiberius." On all these matters he was shown by community leaders to be guilty, and, as they kept hounding him, he appealed to the Commander. And not long afterward a letter was delivered in which, in the manner of a defense, he rehearsed the beginning of the friendship between himself and Cotta and recollected the latter's frequent services, demanding that perversely twisted words and the frankness of

6   dinner-party stories should not be scaled to the level of a crime. (The start of that letter of Caesar's was regarded as distinctive, for he opened with these words: "If I know what to write to you, conscript fathers, or how to write or what not to write at all at this time, may the gods and goddesses destroy me worse than the daily death I feel."[25] So was it the case that his deeds and depravities had

2   turned into reprisals for himself as well: not without reason did the most outstanding man of wisdom customarily affirm that, if the minds of tyrants could be opened up, mutilations and blows would be visible, since, just as bodies were mauled by lashings, so was the spirit by savagery, lust, and evil decisions.[26] In Tiberius' case neither his fortune nor his solitude protected him from admitting the tortures of his soul and his own punishments.)

7   Next, with the fathers given the power of deciding upon the senator Caesilianus, who had produced most of the case against Cotta, it was agreed that the same punishment be invoked as against Aruseius and Sangunnius, the accusers of L. Arruntius. Nothing more honorific than this befell Cotta, who—admittedly noble, but impoverished by his luxuriousness and infamous for his outrages— was placed on the same level as the scrupulous behavior of Arruntius by the standard of his retribution.[27]

2   After this, Q. Servaeus and Minucius Thermus were brought in: Servaeus a former praetor and once a companion of Germanicus,[28] Minucius of equestrian

---

24. A modest and symbolic meal placed on a tomb nine days after burial. Cotta's alleged remark seems aimed at the nature and fare of the priestly banquet but perhaps also implies that Tiberius' mother remained "dead and buried" and had not been deified (see 5.2.1).

25. Exactly the same quotation (with only a couple of small differences) appears in Suetonius, *Tiberius* 67.1.

26. The "most outstanding man of wisdom" is Socrates (T. often uses "wisdom" as a synonym for "philosophy"); the allusion is to Plato's *Gorgias* 524e.

27. T.'s sentence is convoluted and his meaning obscure. He seems to be saying that the disgraceful Cotta resembled the blameless Arruntius on two counts: both of them escaped punishment, and in both cases their accusers were punished instead. But interpretation is not helped by the fact that T.'s account of Arruntius' case and of the fate of his accusers has been lost.

28. Servaeus, governor of Commagene in 18 (2.56.4), took a prominent part in the case against Cn. Piso (3.13.2, 19.1).

rank, they had handled Sejanus' friendship with restraint. Hence greater pity for them. But Tiberius, berating them as principals in crime, advised the elder C. Cestius to tell the senate what he had written to him;[29] and Cestius undertook the accusation. (This was a particularly baleful phenomenon generated by those 3 times, when leaders of the senate were performing even the lowest denounce-ments, some quite openly, many in secret; and you could not distinguish relatives from others, unknowns from friends, what was recent or what obscured by age: whatever the subject of their talk, whether in the forum or at a dinner party, men were censured because each individual was frantic to forestall someone else in marking out a defendant, some as a protection for themselves, the majority tainted as if by a contagious illness.) As for Minucius and Servaeus, after condem- 4 nation they attached themselves to the informants; and drawn into the same predicament were Julius Africanus from the Santoni, a Gallic community, and Seius Quadratus. His origin I have not discovered, nor am I unaware that the per- 5 ils and punishments of many men have been neglected by numerous writers, who tire of their plentifulness or are afraid that what was excessive and sorrowful to themselves might affect their readers with an equal aversion; but I have come across numerous matters worthy of recognition, though uncelebrated by others.

For example, at the time when everyone else had fraudulently discarded the 8 friendship of Sejanus, the Roman equestrian M. Terentius, a defendant on that account, dared to embrace it, embarking in this fashion before the senate: "Of course it may perchance be less helpful to my chances to admit the charge than to abjure it; but, however the affair turns out, I will acknowledge both that I was a friend of Sejanus and that I sought earnestly to be, and that, after achieving it, I was delighted. I had seen him as his father's colleague in directing the praeto- 2 rian cohorts,[30] then meeting the responsibilities of City and soldiery simultane-ously. His relatives and connections were being enhanced with honors: intimacy with Sejanus meant an effective claim on Caesar's friendship; but those to whom he was hostile were constantly belabored by the dread of tatters.[31] I enlist no in- 3 dividual as an example; all of us who were not participants in his final plan I shall defend at the cost of danger to myself alone.

"It was not Sejanus the Vulsinian whom we courted, but part of the Claudian and Julian house, which he had taken over by his connection with it; it was your son-in-law, Caesar, the partner of your consulship, performing your duties in public life.[32] It is not ours to assess whom you exalt above the rest and for what 4 reasons: to you the gods have given the supreme judgment of affairs; to us is left the glory of compliance. Further, we look only at what is held in front of us, to whom you dispense wealth and honors, who is possessed of the greatest power

29. I.e., what Cestius had written to Tiberius. C. Cestius Gallus (3.36.2) became con-sul in 35 (6.31.1).

30. For Sejanus' collegiality with his father see 1.24.2.

31. I.e., the dread of ending up as defendants in court (see 2.29.1n. for "tatters").

32. See 3.29.4 and 5.6.2 (and n.); also, e.g., 4.2.3 and 4.7.1.

for aiding or harming (which no one is likely to deny that Sejanus had); but to search out the hidden feelings of the princeps, and his still more concealed intentions, is unlawful, perilous. Nor would you necessarily grasp them.

5   "Do not, conscript fathers, think of Sejanus' last day but of his sixteen years.[33] We actually used to venerate Satrius and Pomponius;[34] becoming known even
6 to his freedmen and doorkeepers was interpreted as magnificent. Well, then: is this defense to be offered comprehensively and indiscriminately? Rather let it divide along proper lines: plots against the state, schemes of slaughter against the Commander should be punished; but, concerning friendship and its services, let the same boundary absolve both you, Caesar, and us."

9   The steadfastness of this speech, and the fact that a man had been discovered to express what everyone was churning over in his mind, had so powerful an effect that his accusers, when their previous felonies had been added, were penalized by exile or death.

2   There next followed a letter from Tiberius against Sex. Vistilius, a praetorian whom, as very dear to his brother Drusus, he had transferred to his own retinue.[35] Whether Vistilius had composed certain things against C. Caesar, alleging immorality, or whether credence was given to a fabrication, he had caused offense. And, precluded from the princeps's society on that account, with elderly hand he tried the blade but then bound up his veins; and, his pleas in note form having been met with a ruthless rescript, he unloosened the fastenings+ once more.

3   In a batch after him Annius Pollio and Appius Silanus along with Scaurus Mamercus and Sabinus Calvisius were arraigned for treason, and Vinicianus was added to his father Pollio—all of them brilliant in lineage and likewise recipients of the highest honors.[36] And the fathers had started to tremble (for how few were there who lacked connection or friendship with so many illustrious men?), but Celsus, tribune of an urban cohort and at that time among the informers, saved
4 Appius and Calvisius from their plight. Caesar deferred the cases of Pollio and Vinicianus and Scaurus for his personal investigation along with the senate,
10 though giving some ominous signals against Scaurus. Not even females were exempt from danger, who, because+ they could not be charged with taking over the state, were indicted for their tears: the aged Vitia, mother of Fufius Geminus, was executed on the grounds that she had wept at the execution of her son.

33. Evidently A.D. 15–30 inclusive. Cf. Velleius 126.1 "The achievements of these sixteen years" (written shortly before Sejanus' fall: see 6.15.1n. below).

34. For Satrius Secundus see 4.34.1; this Pomponius is otherwise unknown.

35. Vistilius is father of the woman mentioned at 2.85.2 and brother of the much married and fertile elder Vistilia (5.8.1n.).

36. C. Annius Pollio was suffect consul in 21 or 22; his son, L. Annius Vinicianus, was father of Annius Pollio, the conspirator against Nero in 65 (15.56.4), and of Annius Vinicianus (15.28.3n.), a conspirator against Nero in 66. Appius Silanus was consul in 28 (4.68.1n.); for Mamercus Scaurus see 1.13.4n.; Calvisius Sabinus was consul in 26 (4.46.1n.).

So much for events before the senate; no differently before the princeps were   2
Vescularius Atticus and Julius Marinus driven to death, both among the most
olden of his friends, having followed him to Rhodes and inseparable on Capri.
Vescularius had been his messenger in the plot against Libo;[37] it was with the
participation of Marinus that Sejanus had stifled Curtius Atticus.[38] Hence all
the more delight at the news that their own example had rebounded upon its
counselors.

During the same period L. Piso the pontiff met a natural death (a rarity in the   3
case of such brilliancy), having spontaneously initiated no servile proposal and,
whenever necessity encroached, a wisely restraining influence. That his father had
been censorial I have recalled;[39] his age reached its eightieth year; he had won
triumphal prestige in Thrace; but his principal glory came from the fact that as
prefect of the City he was wonderful at regulating a power whose continuity was
only recent and which was made more burdensome by the unfamiliarity of obedience to it. (Previously, when the kings and subsequently magistrates set out   **11**
from home, someone was chosen temporarily to dispense justice and attend to
emergencies, lest the City should be without command; and they say that
Denter Romulius was appointed by Romulus, and afterward Numa Marcius by
Tullus Hostilius and Spurius Lucretius by Tarquinius Superbus. Next it was the
consuls who deputed; and a reflection of that endures whenever someone, owing to the Latin holiday, is made prefect in order to take over consular responsibility.[40] But it was Augustus during the civil wars who placed Cilnius Maecenas,   2
of the equestrian order, over everything in Rome and Italy.[41] Later, once he had
taken control of affairs, it was owing to the size of the population and the slow
effects of the laws that he enlisted one of the consulars to coerce the slaves and
that element of the citizens whose daring leads to disruption unless it dreads
force. Messala Corvinus was the first to undertake that power and, within a few   3
days, its termination, on the ground that he was ignorant of how to exercise it.[42]
Next Taurus Statilius, despite his advanced age, bore it exceptionally well;[43] then

37. The go-between in the plot against Libo Drusus was Vescularius *Flaccus* (see
2.28.1–2). Some scholars therefore substitute "Flaccus" for the manuscript's "Atticus" in
the previous sentence, noting that a Curtius Atticus is mentioned just below; others assume that the error is not a scribe's but T.'s.

38. The case of Curtius Atticus (for whom see 4.58.1) must have been narrated in that
part of the text which is now lost.

39. In a passage now lost. L. Calpurnius Piso ("the pontiff"), whose father was L.
Calpurnius Piso Caesoninus (consul in 58 B.C. and censor in 50 B.C.), had been consul in
15 B.C.

40. See 4.36.1.

41. For Maecenas see 3.30.2–4.

42. For Corvinus see 3.34.2n. His brief tenure fell in 26 B.C.

43. For Taurus see 3.72.1n. His tenure fell in 16 B.C.

it was Piso, who was consistently commended for twenty[44] years, and he was celebrated with a public funeral by decree of the senate.)

12   A motion was then put to the fathers by Quintilianus, tribune of the plebs,[45] about a book of the Sibyl; Caninius Gallus, one of the quindecimvirs,[46] had demanded both that it be accepted among the other books of that same seer and a senate's decision on the matter. With this passed by division, Caesar sent a letter, berating the tribune only moderately for being ignorant of ancient custom owing

2   to his youth. But Gallus he reproached on the grounds that, despite his longstanding knowledge of ceremonial, he had spoken in front of an ill-attended senate on the basis of an uncertain authority before his college had given an opinion and not (as was usual) after the poem had been read by the masters[47] and assessed. At the same time he issued a reminder that, because many spurious examples had been achieving publicity under the celebrated name,[48] Augustus had sanctioned a day within which they should be delivered to the urban praetor and that it

3   should not be lawful to hold them privately. This had been decreed by our ancestors too after the burning of the Capitol in the Social War,[49] when poems of the Sibyl—whether there was one of her or more—were sought from Samos, Ilium, Erythrae, and across Africa too and Sicily and the Italian colonies, and the priests given the business of distinguishing, as far as humanly possible, the genuine. So it was that then too that book was submitted for investigation by the quindecimvirs.

13   With the same men as consuls, there was nearly a mutiny because of a crisis in the food supply, and over several days there was much importuning in the theater, with more license against the Commander than was customary. Disturbed by this, he censured the magistrates and fathers on the grounds that they had not coerced the people by means of their official authority, and he added from what provinces he was importing the supply of grain and how much greater it was

2   than Augustus'. So, to castigate the plebs, a senate's decision was composed with old-time severity, and the consuls were no more sluggish with an edict. His own silence was interpreted not (as he had believed) as citizenlike but in terms of haughtiness.

44. If the numeral is correct, Piso will have been appointed by Augustus; but some sources (e.g., Suetonius, *Tiberius* 42.1) assign the appointment to Tiberius. Some scholars have emended *XX* (20) to *XV* (15); others assume that T. has made a mistake.

45. He became suffect consul in 38.

46. L. Caninius Gallus had been suffect consul in 2 B.C.

47. The chief officers of a priestly college were known as "masters" (*magistri*).

48. The "celebrated name" is that of the Sibyl, which had long since become a generic term for certain prophetesses and was attached to various collections of oracles (the "many . . . examples" to which Tiberius here refers): see *OCD* 1400–1.

49. The date was 83 B.C. and therefore during the *civil* war (see 3.27.2n.), as T. had correctly stated at *Histories* 3.72.1. Some scholars have emended "social" to "civil"; others assume a mistake on T.'s part.

At the end of the year Geminius, Celsus, and Pompeius, Roman equestrians, **14** fell to a charge of conspiracy; of these, Geminius for the prodigality of his wealth and the softness of his life had been a friend of Sejanus, though to no serious purpose. And Julius Celsus, a tribune, while still in bonds, stretched in different directions the chain which he had loosened and wound around himself, breaking his own neck.[50] As for Rubrius Fabatus, guards were assigned to him on **2** the grounds that in the desperate state of Roman affairs he had been fleeing to the Parthians for their pity. To be sure, when discovered in the strait of Sicily and dragged back by a centurion, he offered no likely reasons for a distant peregrination; nevertheless he survived safe and sound, in oblivion rather than by clemency.

★ ★ ★

With Ser. Galba and L. Sulla as consuls,[51] after a long search for men whom he **15** could mark out as husbands for his granddaughters, Caesar, now that the maidens' age was becoming pressing, selected L. Cassius and M. Vinicius. Vinicius had a township lineage: begotten at Cales, his father and grandfather both consulars, he was otherwise of an equestrian family, mild in disposition and with a neat fluency.[52] Cassius was of a plebeian but ancient and honored lineage at Rome, and, brought up in the strict discipline of his father, was commended more often for his complaisance than for his industry.[53] To the latter Tiberius joined Drusilla, to Vinicius Julia, both Germanicus' progeny, and he wrote to the senate on the matter along with some slight honoring of the young men. Then, having provided **2** just vague reasons for his absence, he steered toward weightier items and to affronts incurred on behalf of the state, and he asked that the prefect Macro[54] and a few of the tribunes and centurions should go in with him whenever he entered the curia. And, after a senate's decision had been passed lavishly and with- **3**

50. This Celsus, already referred to as a tribune at 6.9.3 above, is here also named Julius to distinguish him from the Celsus mentioned above.

51. Ser. Sulpicius Galba is the future emperor (3.55.1, 6.20.2); for L. Cornelius Sulla Felix see (probably) 3.31.3–4.

52. M. Vinicius (who marries Julia Livilla) had been consul in 30, the year in which Velleius Paterculus dedicated his history to him; his father, P. Vinicius, mentioned at 3.11.2, had been consul in A.D. 2; his grandfather had been suffect consul in 19 B.C.

53. L. Cassius Longinus (who marries Julia Drusilla) had also been consul in 30 but was later succeeded by his brother (12.11.3n.) as suffect consul. Their father, L. Cassius Longinus, had been suffect consul in A.D. 11.

54. In the surviving text this is the first appearance of Q. Naevius Cordus Sutorius Macro, who had carried out Sejanus' arrest and succeeded him as prefect of the Praetorian Guard.

out any prescription of their rank or number, he never once approached even the roofs[55] of the City, still less the public council,[56] on frequent detours encircling and dodging his fatherland.

16   Meanwhile a great army of accusers burst upon those who kept increasing their money by usury, contrary to a law of the dictator Caesar by which measures are taken concerning the limit of credit and of possessions within Italy—a law long since neglected, because the public good is subordinated to private advantage. (Usury was a chronic blight on the City and very regularly a reason for mutiny and discord, and it was therefore checked even in ancient times when

2   behavior was less corrupt. It was enshrined first in the Twelve Tables that no one should lend at interest of more than one-twelfth, whereas the previous procedure had been at the whim of the wealthy; then by a tribunician rogation there was a reduction to half of one-twelfth; finally borrowing at interest was banned.[57] And many resolutions by the people were required to confront the frauds which, though very often suppressed, by means of some amazing practices sprang up

3   again.) On this occasion Gracchus, the praetor to whom the question had fallen, overwhelmed by the numbers of those endangered, referred it to the senate; and the trembling fathers—for no one was devoid of guilt in such a matter—sought pardon from the princeps; and with his concession a period of a year and six months ahead was granted, within which each should settle his personal accounts according to the orders of the law.

17   Hence a dearth of currency, with everyone's debt called in simultaneously and because, with so many convicted and their property sold by lot, silver coin was held by the fiscus or treasury. In response the senate had prescribed that each man

2   was to invest two-thirds of his capital in land across Italy *** but creditors dunned for the full amount,[58] nor was it becoming for those dunned to impair their credit-worthiness. So at first there was scurrying about and pleas, then the praetor's tribunal resounded; and what had been sought as a remedy—selling and buying—had the opposite effect, because the usurers had sunk all their money

3   in purchasing land. With the flood of selling followed by depreciation, the more anyone was indebted, the greater his difficulty in disposal, and many were toppled from their fortunes. The destruction of men's personal resources cast rank

55. Or perhaps "buildings"; but "roofs" suggests the City as seen from a distance.

56. I.e., the senate.

57. T. may be unique in mentioning the Twelve Tables in this connection; Livy associates the first rate of interest with a tribunician proposal a century later in 357 B.C. (7.16.1). For the halving of the initial rate see Livy 7.27.3 (347 B.C.), and for the ban see Livy 7.42.1 (342 B.C.). These matters, like almost everything else which T. says in this section, are uncertain and controversial.

58. It seems likely from "but creditors ..." that some words have dropped out of the text just beforehand. For a fuller statement of the matter see Suetonius, *Tiberius* 48.1. The financial crisis of Tiberius' reign is discussed in C. Rodewald, *Money in the Age of Tiberius* (Totowa, NJ 1976).

and fame headlong, until Caesar brought help by distributing one hundred million sesterces among the banks and by providing the opportunity of borrowing
without interest for three years, if the debtor gave security to the people for twice
as much in the form of landed estates. Thus credit was restored, and gradually   4
private creditors too were discovered. Nor was the buying of land conducted according to the terms of the senate's decision—keenness at the inception (as often in such circumstances) but indifference at the end.

There next returned their former dreads, with the arraignment for treason of   **18**
Considius Proculus,[59] who was celebrating his birthday without panic when he
was snatched off to the curia and no sooner condemned than killed. And to his
sister Sancia water and fire were forbidden on the accusation of Q. Pomponius.
(A restless personality, he pretended that he kept doing these and other similar
things in order that, having gained influence with the princeps, he might relieve
the dangers to Pomponius Secundus, his brother.)[60] Exile was decreed against   2
Pompeia Macrina also, whose husband Argolicus and father-in-law Laco, two of
the leaders of the Achaeans, Caesar had dashed down; her father too, an illustrious Roman equestrian, and her brother, a praetorian, killed themselves as conviction impended.[61] The charge had been that Cn. Magnus had had Theophanes
the Mytilenaean, their great-grandfather,[62] among his intimates and that Greek
sycophancy had bestowed heavenly honors upon Theophanes after his decease.
After them, Sex. Marius, the richest man in the Spains, was denounced for in-   **19**
cest with his daughter and cast down from the Tarpeian Rock;[63] and, so there
should be no doubt that it was the magnitude of his money which had rebounded
on him so calamitously, his gold- and silver-mines (though they were publicly
confiscated) were set aside by Tiberius for himself.

Spurred by these reprisals, he ordered all who were being held in prison ac-   2
cused of association with Sejanus to be executed. The wreckage stretched indef-
initely—every sex, every age, illustrious, ignoble, scattered, or heaped. Nor were   3
relatives or friends allowed to stand by, to shed tears or even to gaze for too long,
but the guards posted round, intent on each person's sorrow, escorted the putre-
fying bodies until they were dragged into the Tiber, where, floating about or
beached on the banks, no one dared either cremation or contact. The dealings
which are the human lot had fallen to the power of dread, and, as savagery
swelled, pity was banished.

59. Possibly identical with the Considius of 5.8.1 above.

60. See 5.8.1–2 above. Q. Pomponius Secundus would be suffect consul in 41; see also
13.43.2.

61. Her father was Cn. Pompeius Macer, equestrian procurator of Asia and a friend of
Tiberius; her brother has been thought to be Pompeius Macer (1.72.3).

62. Theophanes was friend and historian of Pompey the Great ("Cn. Magnus" here);
whether he was grandfather or (as T. says) great-grandfather of Macrina and her brother
is disputed.

63. A previous attempt to topple Marius in 25 had failed (4.36.1).

20   About the same time C. Caesar, a companion of his grandfather's withdrawal
to Capri, received Claudia, M. Silanus' daughter, in espousal, cloaking his monstrous temper by a cunning modestness, with no vocal outburst at the conviction of his mother or the extermination of his brothers.[64] Whatever kind of day
Tiberius gave signs of having,[65] he would adopt a similar style, his words differing scarcely at all. Hence a knowing remark of the orator Passienus soon became
current: never had there been a better slave or a baser master.[66]

2   (I should not omit a prophecy of Tiberius concerning Servius Galba, then
consul. Having summoned him and tested him in a series of varied conversations,
he finally addressed him in Greek words to this effect: "You too, Galba, will one
day taste command"—alluding to the man's late and brief power[67] through a
knowledge of the Chaldaeans' skill,[68] to acquire which he had leisure on Rhodes
and Thrasyllus as his master, on whose expertise he had experimented in the fol-

21   lowing way. Whenever he was consulting on a subject of such importance,[+] he
used an elevated part of his house and the complicity of a single freedman. The
latter, illiterate but with a strong physique, went along the trackless precipices (the
house loomed over rocks) ahead of the man on whose skill Tiberius had decided
to experiment, and, on returning, if any suspicion of charlatanry or fraud had
arisen, would pitch him headlong into the sea lying below, so he could not pres-

2   ent himself as an informant on the mysteries. Thus it was that Thrasyllus was led
over the same crags, and, after he had impressed his questioner by a skillful dis-
closure of the man's command and future circumstances,[69] was asked whether
he had also discovered his own natal hour: what year and what kind of day was
he currently experiencing? Having measured the positions and distances of the
planets, he hesitated at first, then began to panic, and, trembling more and more
in amazement and dread as his insight increased, he finally exclaimed that an am-

3   biguous and almost final crisis was descending upon him. Then with an embrace
Tiberius congratulated him on the grounds that he was prescient of his perils
and would be safe and sound. And, taking what he had said as an oracle, he kept
him among the most intimate of his friends.

22   Personally, when I hear things such as these, my judgment is uncertain whether
it is by fate and immutable necessity that the affairs of mortals evolve or by

---

64. The preliminary moves against Agrippina were mentioned at 5.3.1; she was exiled
(see 14.63.2) later in 29. Gaius Caligula's eldest brother, Nero Caesar, was killed in 31; the
other brother, Drusus Caesar, is about to die at 6.23.2 below. Claudia was the daughter of
the M. Junius Silanus mentioned at 3.24.3.

65. The verb in this clause is uncertain.

66. C. Sallustius Passienus Crispus was suffect consul in 27 and regular consul in 44.

67. Galba, born in 3 B.C., was briefly emperor between June A.D. 68 and the following
January.

68. For the Chaldaeans see 2.27.2n.

69. I.e., he foretold that Tiberius would one day be emperor.

chance.[70] For you will discover that the wisest of the ancients, and those who emulate their systems,⁺ are divided and that many have an innate belief that neither our beginnings nor end nor men themselves are the concern of the gods, and that hence it happens very frequently that the good are visited by sadness and the base with delight. Contrariwise others think that fate does indeed correspond to affairs, though not as the result of roving stars but depending on first principles and the links of natural causes; they nevertheless leave us a choice in life, but, when you have chosen it, there is a fixed order of inevitable events. And they say that evil or good are not what the public thinks but that many who appear to be belabored by adversity are blessed, whereas considerable numbers, albeit in the midst of great wealth, are quite wretched, if the former endure their grave fortune steadfastly and the latter use their prosperity injudiciously. 2

However, the majority of mortals cannot be parted from the thought that things to come are marked out from the first origin of each individual but that some of them fall out differently from what has been stated, owing to the deceptions of those making their statements in ignorance: thus is corrupted the credit of a skill of which resounding evidence has been produced both by antiquity and by our own age. For the prediction of Nero's command by the son of this same Thrasyllus will be recalled at the appropriate time,[71] in case I have now departed too far from my undertaking.) 3

With the same men as consuls, the death of Asinius Gallus became public knowledge: that he had perished from a lack of food was not in doubt, but whether voluntarily or by compulsion was regarded as uncertain. And Caesar, consulted whether he would allow him to be buried, did not blush to give permission and moreover to censure the circumstances which had removed the defendant before he could be convicted in his presence. (Evidently in the intervening three-year period there had been no time for an elderly consular and parent of so many consulars to undergo the judicial process!)[72] 23

Drusus' life was extinguished next, although he had sustained himself up to the ninth day by pitiable nourishment, by chewing the stuffing from his bed.[73] Some have transmitted that it had been enjoined on Macro, if Sejanus attempted armed force, to extract the young man from custody (he was held in the Palatium) and to install him as the people's leader. But later Caesar, because a rumor was spreading that he was going to be reconciled with his daughter-in-law and 2

70. The two positions outlined in this sentence are broadly Stoic and Epicurean respectively and they are expanded in reverse order in the remainder of the paragraph.

71. Possibly at 14.9.2 (but no reference there to Thrasyllus' son).

72. Gallus had been kept under house arrest for the past three years, something which T. no doubt described in the portion of the *Annals* now missing.

73. This is the Drusus Caesar, brother of Gaius, whose death was alluded to at 6.20.1 above. (Orelli reasonably argued that the latter phrase, "by chewing ... his bed," was an explanatory gloss on the former, "by pitiable nourishment," and imported from Suetonius, *Tiberius* 54.2. More often T. eschews specific and vulgar detail.)

24 grandson, preferred savagery to repentance. Furthermore, inveighing against the deceased, he hurled allegations of bodily abuse[74] and intentions fatal for his relatives and hostile to the state; and he ordered the day-by-day descriptions of his actions and words to be read out. Nothing else seemed more frightful than this. That there had stood by, through so many years, persons to catch his looks, groans, even his secret murmurs, and that his grandfather could have heard, read, and publicly produced them—these things were scarcely credible, except that the letters of the centurion Attius and of the freedman Didymus paraded the name of

2 each slave who had beaten and terrorized Drusus as he left his bedroom.[75] The centurion had even added (as an exceptional feat) words of his own, full of savagery, and the failing man's utterances, in which at first, pretending mental alienation, as if in dementia he invoked fatalities upon Tiberius and then, when he had given up hope of living, deliberate and measured curses to the effect that, in the same way as he had killed his daughter-in-law and brother's son and grandsons and filled his whole house with slaughter,[76] so he should pay the penalty to

3 the name and lineage of his ancestors and to posterity. The fathers became disruptive, in a show of forfending;[77] but in reality they were penetrated by panic and amazement that a man once astute and dark at cloaking his crimes had reached such a degree of confidence that, as if with the walls moved aside, he displayed his grandson under the centurion's lash, amid the blows from his slaves, begging in vain for the final nourishments of life.

25 Their pain at this had not yet abated when they heard about Agrippina, who I deem lived on after the killing of Sejanus because she was nurtured by hope, and, when there was no remission of the savagery, extinguished her life voluntarily—unless by the denial of nourishment her end was made to resemble one

2 which seemed to have been chosen spontaneously. Certainly Tiberius flared up with the foulest charges, accusing her of immorality and Asinius Gallus as her adulterer and that his death had driven her to an aversion for life. (But in fact Agrippina, impatient of equality and greedy for mastery, had cast off female flaws

3 in a preference for men's concerns.) Caesar added that her decease had taken place on the same day as Sejanus had paid the penalty two years previously and that the fact should be handed down to memory, and he boasted that she had not been strangled by the noose nor thrown onto the Gemonians. Gratitude was expressed on that account, and it was decreed that on the fifteenth day before

74. Similar charges had been made against the other brother, Nero Caesar: see 5.3.2 above.

75. Drusus had evidently been subjected to the same kind of treatment as his brother Nero Caesar (4.67.4).

76. The references are to Agrippina, Germanicus, Nero Caesar (6.20.1n. above), and Drusus himself.

77. The Latin *detestandi* is here used in the sense of "warding off": we are to imagine that the senators interrupt the recitation of Drusus' curses by exclamations equivalent to "Heaven forfend!"

the Kalends of November,[78] the day of each execution, a gift should be consecrated to Jupiter in all future years.

Not long afterward Cocceius Nerva, a constant companion of the princeps,   **26**
knowledgeable in divine and human law, his estate[79] untouched, his body undamaged, made the decision to die. When this became known to Tiberius, he sat
beside him, asked his reasons, added pleas, and finally confessed that it would be
serious for his own conscience, serious for his own reputation, if the closest of
his friends, with no grounds for dying, fled life. But Nerva, deflecting all conver-   **2**
sation, continued the fasting from food. Those aware of his thoughts maintained
that, in anger and dread the more he saw the calamities of the state closing in, he
had wanted an honorable end while he was still untouched and still unassailed.

As for the ruin of Agrippina, it dragged down Plancina (which was scarcely   **3**
credible). Formerly wedded to Cn. Piso and openly delighted at the death of
Germanicus, when Piso fell she had been defended by the pleas of Augusta and
no less by the antagonism of Agrippina.[80] But, as hatred and influence ceased,
justice came into effect; and, now the target of accusations by no means unfamiliar, with her own hand she exacted a late rather than an undeserved reprisal.

The community was funereal at so many griefs, part of their sorrow being the   **27**
fact that Julia, Drusus' daughter and once Nero's wife, married into the house of
Rubellius Blandus, whose Tiburtine grandfather many remembered as being a
Roman equestrian.[81]

At the extreme end of the year a censorial funeral was the means of celebrat-   **2**
ing the death of Aelius Lamia, who, released at length from his phantom
administration of Syria, had been in charge of the City.[82] His lineage had been
becoming, his old age vigorous, and his disallowed province had added prestige.   **3**
Next, with the decease of Flaccus Pomponius, propraetor of Syria,[83] a letter of
Caesar was read out in which his censure was that all the exceptional men who
were suited to directing armies were refusing their responsibility and, given that
constraint, he was being reduced to pleas, in the hope that some of the consulars
would be driven to undertake provinces—quite forgetting that Arruntius was
now being kept back for a tenth year to prevent his proceeding to Spain.

78. 18 October (and see Sherk 28F, p. 54).

79. I.e., assets, property. For Cocceius Nerva see 4.58.1 and n.

80. See esp. 3.15.1 and 3.17.1–2. Augusta's pleas and Agrippina's antagonism are referred
to chiastically by "hatred" and "influence" respectively at the start of the next sentence.

81. For Julia and Nero Caesar see 3.29.3; she was now marrying beneath her (for Rubellius Blandus see 3.23.2 and n.; Braund 391 = WM 17).

82. Lamia (4.13.3n.), who had been governor of Syria for ten years from 21/22 but not
permitted to leave Rome, thus illustrates the point made at 1.80.3; so too Arruntius (mentioned just below). As prefect of the City, Lamia had succeeded L. Piso, who had died in
32 (6.10.3). For censorial funerals see 4.15.2n.

83. Flaccus (2.32.2n., 2.66.2) had succeeded Lamia (last n.) as governor of Syria in 32.

4   There met his death in the same year M. Lepidus too, concerning whose moderation and wisdom I allocated sufficient space in earlier books.[84] Nor need his
nobility receive a lengthier demonstration: the Aemilian lineage was prolific of
good citizens, and those from the same family whose behavior was corrupt
nevertheless enjoyed illustrious fortune.

★ ★ ★

28   With Paulus Fabius and L. Vitellius as consuls,[85] at the conclusion of a centuries-
long cycle the phoenix bird came to Egypt and provided the most learned of
both natives and Greeks with material for considerable discussion of the wonder. The points on which they agree, and the more numerous matters which are
disputed but nevertheless not inappropriate to acknowledge, make a pleasing
subject for presentation.

2   The creature is sacred to the Sun, and those who have depicted its shape con-
cur that in its beak and the distinctiveness of its wings it is different from every

3   other bird. But various alternatives are transmitted on the number of years:[86] the
most common is a period of five hundred, but there are those who assert that
the interval is one thousand four hundred sixty-one and that it was first during
Sesosis' rule, and afterward during Amasis' and then Ptolemy's (the third of the
Macedonians to reign),[87] that earlier fowl flew into the community whose name
is Heliopolis, with a considerable escort of the other birds wondering at the new

4   face. Now antiquity is of course a dark age; but between Ptolemy and Tiberius
there were less than two hundred fifty years. Hence some have believed this present phoenix to be false and not from the land of the Arabs and that it performed

5   none of the feats which ancient memory has affirmed: namely that, with the
number of its years completed, and when death is approaching, it builds a nest
in its own land and pours on it a generative force, from which its issue springs;
and the first concern of the latter as an adult is burying its father—not randomly
but, after lifting up a weight of myrrh and testing it on a long journey, then,
when it is equal to the burden and equal to the expedition, it takes up its father's
body and carries it all the way to the altar of the Sun and sacrifices it in flames.

84. See 1.13.2n. and esp. 4.20.2.

85. Paullus Fabius Persicus was son of Paullus Fabius Maximus (consul in 11 B.C.); L.
Vitellius, father of the emperor Vitellius and mentioned here for the first time, will feature prominently in the *Annals* from now on (see esp. 6.32.4 below); he was consul again
in 43 and 47 (14.56.1).

86. The "number of years" is the interval which separates the appearance of one phoenix
from another (as becomes clear later in the sentence).

87. Sesosis was a mythical king; the dates of Amasis' rule were c. 570–526 B.C., those of
Ptolemy III Euergetes 246–221 B.C.

—These matters are uncertain and exaggerated by fantasy; but that that partic- 6
ular bird is sometimes observed in Egypt is not disputed.

But at Rome the slaughter was constant, with Pomponius Labeo, whom I **29**
recorded as having been in charge of Moesia,[88] pouring out his blood through
ruptured veins; and he was emulated by his spouse, Paxaea. (Dread of the executioner was producing ready deaths of that type, and, because the condemned
had their property confiscated and were prevented from burial, whereas those
who decided for themselves had their bodies interred and their wills survived,
there was a reward for hurrying.) But Caesar in a letter sent to the senate said 2
that, whenever their ancestors broke off friendships, it had been their custom
to debar a person from the house and in that way to put an end to their cor-
diality: that had been his own resort in Labeo's case, he said; and Labeo, because
he was being accused⁺ of maladministration of his province and other charges,
had veiled his guilt by an act designed to cause resentment,[89] with needless ter-
rorization of his wife, who, though culpable, had nevertheless not shared in his
peril.

Next Mamercus Scaurus was arraigned again,[90] distinguished for his nobility 3
and at pleading cases but in his life a scandal. He was undermined not by Sejanus'
friendship but by the hatred (no less effective as regards extermination) of Macro,
who operated the same practices more secretly and had denounced the plot of
a tragedy written by Scaurus with additional verses which could be twisted
against Tiberius.[91] But the imputations cast at him by the accusers Servilius and 4
Cornelius were of adultery with Livia and of magicians' rites. Scaurus, as was
worthy of the old Aemilii, forestalled condemnation at the urging of his wife,
Sextia, whose incitement was as partner in his death.

And yet accusers themselves,⁺ if the opportunity arose, had punishments in- **30**
flicted on them: Servilius and Cornelius, notorious for their destruction of Scaurus, were removed to islands and forbidden fire and water because they had taken
money from Varius Ligus to abandon a denouncement. And Abudius Ruso, a for- 2
mer aedile, while contriving to imperil Lentulus Gaetulicus (under whom he
had been in charge of a legion) for having marked out Sejanus' son as his son-
in-law, was himself condemned and driven from the city.[92]

Gaetulicus at that time was concerned with the legions of Upper Germany
and had won from them a wonderful affection, being a man of effusive clemency,
moderate in severity and, through L. Apronius' being his father-in-law, not un-

88. See 4.47.1.

89. Tiberius means that Labeo had intended his suicide to bring odium upon the princeps (who had made the same accusation against Cn. Piso: see 3.16.2).

90. See 6.9.3–4 above.

91. The tragedy was said to concern the story of Atreus.

92. Lentulus Gaetulicus (4.42.3n.) had been consul in 26 (4.46.1). Nothing is known
about the betrothal of his daughter to a son of Sejanus.

3   popular with the nearest army too.[93] Hence the persistent report that he had
     dared to send Caesar a letter to the effect that his relationship with Sejanus had
     not been begun spontaneously but on Tiberius' advice: he had been as capable
     as Tiberius of being deceived, and their identical mistake should not be held as
     meaning no risk for *him* but extermination for others. His own loyalty, he said,
     was unaffected and, unless he were the target of some plot, would remain so: he
     would receive a successor only as an indication of his death. They should (as it
     were) affirm a treaty, by which the princeps would be in control of all other af-
4   fairs and he himself would hold on to his province. —These matters, a source of
     wonder though they were, drew credibility from the fact that, alone of all Se-
     janus' relations, he remained unharmed and in considerable favor—Tiberius re-
     flecting on his own hatred by the public, his extreme age, and that it was more
     on report than reality that his circumstances depended.

                                    ★   ★   ★

31   With C. Cestius and M. Servilius as consuls,[94] Parthian nobles came to the City
     without the knowledge of King Artabanus.[95] (His dread of Germanicus meant
     that he had been loyal to the Romans and fair toward his own; but later he
     adopted haughtiness toward us and savagery toward his compatriots, relying on
     the successful wars which he had waged against surrounding nations, despising
     Tiberius' old age as defenseless, and being greedy for Armenia, where on the de-
     cease of King Artaxias he installed Arsaces, the eldest of his own children; and as
     an additional insult sending men to demand back the treasure left by Vonones in
     Syria and Cilicia.[96] At the same time he resorted to foolish boasting and to
     threats, bragging of the old boundaries of the Persians and Macedonians and that
2   he would invade the lands once possessed by Cyrus and later by Alexander.) The
     most effective instigator among the Parthians for the sending of the secret mes-
     sengers was Sinnaces, of distinguished family and wealth alike, and, next to him,
     it was Abdus, who had been deprived of his manhood (among barbarians that is
     not despised but actually confers power).[97] They had affiliated other chiefs too,
     and it was because they had been unable to install one of the family of the Ar-
     sacidae in the supremacy, most of them having been killed by Artabanus or not

93. The "nearest army" means the four legions of Lower Germany; for L. Apronius there
in 28 see 4.73.1.

94. For Cestius Gallus see 6.7.2 and n. M. Servilius Nonianus was also a historian; his
death in 59 is recorded at 14.19.

95. For the king see 2.3.1 and n.

96. For King Artaxias see 2.56.3, 2.64.1; the story of the treasure is assumed to have
been told in the lost part of Book 5.

97. He was a eunuch.

yet grown up, that they demanded Phraates, the son of King Phraates, from Rome:[98] only a name and an authorization were required, they said, if it were Caesar's will that the lineage of Arsaces should be seen on the bank of the Euphrates. That in fact was Tiberius' desire. He decorated Phraates and girded him **32** for his ancestral pinnacle, thereby maintaining his aims of managing external affairs by plan and stratagem and of keeping arms at a distance.

Meanwhile, on learning of the subterfuge, Artabanus was inhibited by dread but sometimes he kindled with the desire for revenge; and to barbarians hesitation seems servile, immediate action regal. Practicality nevertheless prevailed, with **2** the result that Abdus (whom he had invited to a banquet in a show of friendship) was ensnared by a slow-acting poison, and Sinnaces for his part was delayed by dissembling and gifts as well as on business. As for Phraates, having abandoned the Roman lifestyle to which he had become accustomed over so many years, he was adopting the habits of the Parthians when, unequal to his native dispensations, he was taken off by disease in Syria.

But Tiberius did not abandon his undertaking: he chose Tiridates, who was of **3** the same blood, as rival to Artabanus and, for the recovery of Armenia, Iberian Mithridates, and he reconciled the latter to his brother Pharasmanes, who held command of their people; and over all his preparations in the East he placed L. Vitellius in charge.[99] (Concerning this man I am not unaware of his unfortunate **4** reputation in the City and that many foul things are recalled; but in ruling provinces he acted with old-time excellence. It was on his return from there that, through alarm at C. Caesar and association with Claudius, he changed to shameful servitude, being regarded among posterity as an example of sycophantic disgrace: the commencement of his career surrendered to its conclusion, and his moral youth was obliterated by outrages in old age.)

Of the princes, Mithridates first drove Pharasmanes to aid his efforts by guile **33** and violence: bribers were discovered, who with a sum of gold compelled agents of Arsaces to crime;[100] at the same time the Iberians burst into Armenia with large forces and took possession of the city of Artaxata. After Artabanus learned **2** of this, he prepared his son Orodes to act as avenger, gave him the Parthians' forces, and sent men to hire auxiliaries. On the other side Pharasmanes federated the Albani and sent for the Sarmatians, whose sceptuchs[101] accepted gifts from each side and, in the national fashion, assumed opposing allegiances. But the **3**

98. By "King Phraates" is meant Phraates IV (2.1.2n.). For the imminent death of his son and namesake see 6.32.2, just below.

99. Tiridates, grandson of Phraates IV (6.37.4), lasts for a year and then disappears from the story (6.44). Pharasmanes I, king of Iberia, and his younger brother Mithridates I share a complicated and bloodthirsty history, which recurs principally at 11.8–9 (A.D. 47) and 12.44–8 (A.D. 51). L. Vitellius (6.28.1n.) was governor of Syria. See in general D. Braund, *Georgia in Antiquity* (Oxford/New York 1994) 219–24.

100. By "crime" is meant the murder of Arsaces.

101. Lit. "wand-bearers"; they were important officials.

Iberians, in territorial control, hastily poured out their Sarmatians against the Armenians by the Caspian route; those who were arriving to support the Parthians, however, were easily warded off, since other approaches had been closed by the enemy, while the one remaining—between the sea and the outermost mountains of the Albani—was obstructed owing to the summer season, because the shallows become filled by the blasts of the Etesians.[102] (It is the wintry South-western which rolls back the billows, and, with the water driven in on itself, narrow shores are left bare.)

34   Meanwhile, as Orodes was bereft of allies, Pharasmanes, augmented by the auxiliary, challenged him to fight and attacked him when he declined: he rode up to his camp and struck at his pasture; and often, in the manner of a blockade, he would encircle him with pickets, until finally the Parthians, unaccustomed to such insults, surrounded their king and demanded battle. Their only strength was

2   in cavalry; but Pharasmanes was effective in infantry too: the Iberians and Albani, inhabiting as they did an area of denes, were more accustomed to hardship and endurance. (They maintain also that they are sprung from the Thessalians, at the time when Jason, after Medea had sailed off with the children whom he had begotten by her, later returned to the vacant palace of Aeetes and empty Colchis. And they celebrate many things associated with his name, including the oracle of Phrixus; nor would any of them sacrifice with a ram, given their belief that Phrixus had been carried by one, whether it was in fact an animal or the figurehead of his ship.)[103]

3   With the line formed on each side, the Parthian[104] discoursed on the empire of the East, the brilliancy of the Arsacidae, and conversely the ignoble Iberian with his hired soldiery. Pharasmanes said that his men were untouched by Parthian despotism: the grander their aims, the more prestige they would carry off as victors, or, if they turned their backs, the more outrage and danger. At the same time he gestured to their own bristling line and to the Medes' columns

35   painted with gold: men on the one side, plunder on the other! Among the Sarmatians, however, there was no single leader's voice: they each goaded one another not to allow a fight with arrows: they should anticipate with an attack and hand to hand.

Hence the warriors presented different appearances, since the Parthian, accustomed to pursue or flee with equal skill, dispersed his squadrons and sought the range for his strikes, while the Sarmatians, neglecting the bow (in which they are effective over a shorter distance), rushed with pikes and swords. Sometimes, in

102. The Etesians were northwesterly winds which blew for a month in midsummer.

103. Phrixus was the mythological figure who had fled to Colchis on the back of a golden ram, whose fleece Jason was later sent to recover (see Apollodorus 1.9.1). The suggestion that the ram was actually a ship's figurehead illustrates the way in which the ancients commonly rationalized their myths. For a similar passage in a historical narrative cf., e.g., Xenophon, *Anabasis* 6.2.1–2.

104. I.e., Orodes.

the manner of a cavalry battle, it was the turn of front and rear;[105] at others, the
line was joined, with the result that,+ amid bodies and the smite of arms, men
smote or were smitten. And now the Albani and Iberians too grappled, dislodged,   2
and presented the enemy with a twofold fight, since the cavalry was harassing
them from above and the infantry with wounds closer in. In the midst of all this,
while Pharasmanes and Orodes were supporting the energetic or helping the
hesitant, each recognized the other by his conspicuousness: with shouting,
weapons, and horses they converged—Pharasmanes the more vehemently, for he
inflicted a wound through the helmet. And yet he could not effect a repetition,
having been carried past by his horse and with the bravest of the other's satellites protecting their casualty. Nevertheless a report of his death was wrongly believed and terrified the Parthians, who conceded the victory.

Soon Artabanus embarked on revenge with the whole might of his kingdom.   **36**
With their experience of the region the Iberians fought better; but he was not
for that reason on the point of withdrawing, except that Vitellius, gathering his
legions and planting a rumor to the effect that he would invade Mesopotamia,
created the dread of a Roman war. Then Armenia was abandoned and Artabanus'   2
fortunes overturned, with Vitellius enticing people to desert a king who was savage in peacetime and ruinous by his failures in battle. Therefore Sinnaces, whose
previous hostility I have recalled,[106] drew his father, Abdagaeses, into defecting,
as well as others privy to the plan (and now the readier because of the constant
calamities), with the gradual influx of those who, as subjects more through dread
than goodwill, had plucked up their courage on the discovery of men with
initiative.

Nothing else was now left to Artabanus except his bodyguard of foreigners,   3
each an outcast from his own abode, men in whom there is neither an understanding of good nor a concern for evil but who are supported by hire to be
helpers in crime. Taking these with him, he speeded his flight into distant   4
areas bordering on Scythia in the hope of aid, because he was connected to the
Hyrcani and Carmanii by a marriage relationship; and in the meantime the
Parthians—fair-minded toward the absent but fickle to those present—might
change to remorse.

But, with Artabanus a fugitive and the minds of his compatriots turning to-   **37**
ward a new king, Vitellius urged Tiridates to capitalize on his preparations and
led the hard core of his legions and allies to the bank of the Euphrates. During   2
their sacrifices—since the one was offering the suovetaurilia[107] in the Roman
manner, the other had decorated a horse for placating the stream—
locals announced that without any violent rain the Euphrates was rising of its
own accord to an inordinate level and at the same time was coiling circles of
white spray in the shape of a diadem—an augury of a favorable crossing. (Some,

105. The meaning is obscure.
106. See 6.31.2.
107. This sacrifice comprised a boar, a ram, and a bull.

more astutely, interpreted that the initial stages of the attempt would be successful but not long-lasting, on the grounds that what was portended by earth or sky
was more reliably credible, whereas the unstable nature of rivers no sooner revealed omens than swept them away.)

3   When a bridge had been made of ships and the army sent across, the first to
arrive in the camp with many thousands of cavalry was Ornospades, at one time
an exile and a not inglorious adjuvant of Tiberius when he was finishing off the
Dalmatian war,[108] and for that reason presented with Roman citizenship; but
later, having resumed his friendship with his king, at whose hands he was much
honored, he was placed in charge of the plains which, encircled as they are by
the renowned streams of the Euphrates and Tigris, have received the name of
Mesopotamia.[109] And not long afterward their forces were augmented by Sinnaces, while Abdagaeses—the keystone of his side—added kingly treasure and ac-
4   coutrements. Vitellius, deeming that a show of Roman arms had been adequate,
warned Tiridates and his chiefs: the former should remember Phraates his grandfather and his foster-father Caesar and the fine qualities in each of them; the latter should observe compliance toward their king, respect toward ourselves, and
each his own honor and loyalty. Thereupon he retired with his legions to Syria.[110]

38   These achievements of two seasons I linked together to provide some mental
respite from domestic afflictions.

★

For Tiberius, despite its being three years since the slaughter of Sejanus, was mellowed by none of the things which customarily soften others—time, pleas,
satiety—but he punished vague or bygone matters as though they were of ex-
2   treme seriousness and recent. It was in dread of this that Fulcinius Trio refused
to suffer the encroaching accusers and in his final tablets[111] compiled many
frightful things against Macro and the principal freedmen of Caesar, to whom he
imputed a mind enfeebled by old age and, given his continued withdrawal, vir-
3   tual exile. These charges, though concealed by the heirs, Tiberius ordered to be
read out, showing off his toleration of another's free speech and contemptuous
of his own infamy—or else, having been ignorant of Sejanus' crimes for so long,
he later preferred publicity to be given to remarks of whatever kind and to become
aware, if only through abuse, of the truth which is obstructed by sycophancy.
4   During those same days Granius Marcianus, a senator arraigned by C. Gracchus for treason, ended his own life violently; and Tarius Gratianus, a former prae-
39   tor, was condemned by the same law to the ultimate reprisal. No different were

108. The reference is to Tiberius' role in crushing the rebellion of A.D. 6–9.
109. The name means "land between rivers."
110. The narrative is resumed at 6.41 below.
111. I.e., the writing tablets which comprised his will. For Trio see 2.28.2n.

the outcomes of Trebellienus Rufus and Sextius Paconianus:[112] Trebellienus fell by his own hand, Paconianus was strangled in prison for poems devised there against the princeps. These matters Tiberius learned, not cut off by the sea (as formerly) nor through long-distance messengers, but close to the City, so that on the very same day or after only a night's intermission he could write back to the consuls' letters, while almost observing the gushing blood in the houses or the handiwork of the executioners.   2

At the end of the year Poppaeus Sabinus departed from life, a man modest in origin, who by his friendship with principes acquired the consulship and triumphal prestige and for twenty-four years was installed over the greatest provinces—not for any exceptional skill but because he was equal to his business and no more.[113]   3

★   ★   ★

Quintus Plautius and Sex. Papinius were the following consuls. In that year neither the fact that L. Aruseius *** they had had death inflicted on them attracted notice as anything frightful, given the normality of evil;[114] but what did cause terror was the fact that Vibullius Agrippa, a Roman equestrian, producing poison from a fold[115] when his accusers had finished their declamations, swallowed it in the curia itself and, having collapsed on the point of death, was swept off to prison by the hurried hands of the lictors and, already lifeless, his throat was gripped in the noose. Not even Tigranes, once in possession of Armenia and now a defendant, escaped the reprisals of an ordinary citizen on account of his royal name.[116] But C. Galba, a consular, and the two Blaesi fell to voluntary deaths. Galba had been prohibited by a grim letter of Caesar's from drawing lots for a province;[117] as for the priesthoods marked out for the Blaesi when their family was unscathed, Tiberius had deferred them when it was overwhelmed,[118] and then he conferred them, as though uncommitted, on others—a signal for death   **40**

  2

112. Rufus' first name here and at 3.38.3 differs from that given on his first appearance at 2.67.2. For Paconianus and the problem of his first name see above, 6.3.4 and n.

113. For Sabinus see 1.80.1n.

114. It is thought that Aruseius is the same man as mentioned at 6.7.1 above, but the loss of some words from the text makes the passage obscure.

115. Sc. of his garment (as 5.7.1).

116. Evidently Tigranes IV (2.4.1n.), but his circumstances are by no means clear.

117. Galba was consul in 22 (3.52.1n.).

118. The overwhelming of the family of the Blaesi is a reference to its fortunes after the fall of Sejanus, whose uncle, Q. Junius Blaesus (1.16.2n., 5.7.2), was father of the two Blaesi (suffect consuls in 26 and probably 28 respectively) mentioned here. A Blaesus *fils* has appeared in the *Annals* at 1.19.4, 1.29.2, and 3.74.2.

3   which they understood and followed through. As for Aemilia Lepida, whose wedding to the young Drusus I have recorded,[119] having assailed her husband with frequent charges, she continued to live with impunity—despite her infamy—while her father, Lepidus, survived;[120] after, she was seized by denouncers for adultery with a slave, and no doubt was entertained about her outrage: therefore, abandoning any defense, she put an end to her own life.

*

41   During the same period the nation of the Cietae, which was subject to Cappadocian Archelaus,[121] withdrew to the ridges of Mount Taurus because it was being driven—in our fashion—to submit returns and to endure taxes. And, given the nature of the locality, they protected themselves against the king's unwarlike forces until the legate M. Trebellius,[122] sent by Vitellius (the governor of Syria) with four thousand legionaries and selected auxiliaries, placed earthworks around the two hills which the barbarians had occupied (Cadra is the name of the smaller, Davara of the other): those daring to break out he reduced by the sword, the rest by thirst to surrender.

2   As for Tiridates,[123] with the Parthians' blessing he took possession of Nicephorium and Anthemusias and the other cities which, being Macedonian sites, have Greek designations; and also Halus and Artemita, Parthian towns, to the competing joys of people who, having cursed Artabanus for his savagery (reared as he had been among the Scythians), were now hoping for affability from

42   Tiridates because of his Roman attainments. The greatest sycophancy was assumed by the Seleucians, a powerful community, encircled by walls and not corrupted into barbarism but with a retentive memory of their founder Seleucus. (Three hundred men are selected as a senate on account of their wealth or

2   wisdom; the people have their own influence. And, as often as the two act in harmony, the Parthian is spurned; but, whenever they disagree, each calls for support against its rivals and he,[124] summoned to take one side, becomes effective against them all. That had happened recently in the reign of Artabanus, who handed the plebs over to the chiefs for his own advantage: for, whereas command by the people borders on freedom, domination by a few approximates to the

3   fancy of kings.) On the present occasion they exalted Tiridates' arrival by means

119. In a lost part of Book 5; T. recorded the death of Drusus Caesar at 6.23.2 above (A.D. 33).
120. For M. Lepidus' death in 33 see 6.27.4 above.
121. He must be the son of the king who died in A.D. 17 (2.42.3).
122. See further 14.46.2 and n.
123. His story now continues from 6.37 above.
124. I.e., the Parthian (king).

of the honors paid to the old kings and the more lavish inventions of a recent age; at the same time they poured abuse on Artabanus, an Arsacid on his mother's side but otherwise lowborn.

Tiridates entrusted Seleucian affairs to the people; but later, as he was debating on what day he should solemnize his assumption of the kingdom, he received letters from Phraates and Hiero, who held the most substantial prefectures,[125] pleading for a short delay. He decided to await such powerful individuals, and meanwhile made for Ctesiphon as the seat of command. But, when they kept stretching one day into another, the Surena,[126] to the approval of the many who were present, wreathed Tiridates with the royal insignia according to ancestral custom. And, if he had made for the other nations in the interior at once, the hesitation of the doubters would have been suppressed and everyone would have passed to the control of him alone; but, by blockading a stronghold into which Artabanus had conveyed his money and mistresses, he allowed an interval for pacts to be cast aside. Phraates and Hiero, as well as others who had not concelebrated the day selected for his receiving the diadem, turned to Artabanus (some through dread, some through resentment at Abdagaeses, who was then in charge of the court and the new king); and he was discovered among the Hyrcani, spattered with filth and providing himself with nourishment by means of his bow.

At first he was terrified, as though some trap were being prepared; but, when their pledge was given that they had come to restore his mastery, his spirits rose and he asked what had suddenly changed. Then Hiero berated Tiridates' mere boyhood: command did not rest with an Arsacid, he said, but an empty name was being held by one whose foreign softness made him unwarlike, while power rested in the house of Abdagaeses. The veteran ruler realized that, if false in affection, they were not fabricating their hatred; and, delaying no further except to raise auxiliaries from the Scythians, he proceeded apace, forestalling any stratagems of his foes and any regret from his friends. And, to attract the sympathy of the public, he had not cast off his squalor: no trick, no plea, nothing was neglected that would entice the waverers and consolidate the ready. And with a sizable squad he was already approaching the neighborhood of Seleucia when Tiridates, shocked by the report and by Artabanus' presence alike, began to be torn between plans: should he march against him or drag out the war by delaying? Those who favored battle and a speedy outcome argued that their opponents, in disarray and exhausted by the length of their journey, had not achieved, even in their hearts, the degree of unity necessary for compliance with anyone, having only recently been deserters and enemies of the man whom once again they were supporting. But Abdagaeses proposed going back to Mesopotamia in order that, with the stream as a barrier and with the Armenians and Elymaei and the oth-

4

43

2

3

44

2

3

4

125. This word is used to denote administrative districts in Armenia and Parthia (11.8.3, 11.10.1, 13.37.3, 13.39.1, 15.28.1).

126. Commander-in-chief of the army, a hereditary position.

ers roused meanwhile in the rear,[127] they might try their fortune when augmented by allied forces and those which the Roman leader would send. The latter suggestion prevailed, because most authority rested with Abdagaeses and Tiri-
5   dates shirked in the face of danger. Yet the withdrawal had every appearance of
flight; and, a start having been made by the race of the Arabs, the others left for
their homes or for the camp of Artabanus, until Tiridates' own return to Syria
with a few men provided a general redemption from the disgrace of desertion.[128]

★

45 The same year afflicted the City with a serious fire, part of the circus adjoining
the Aventine being burned down, as well as the Aventine itself—a loss which
Caesar turned into glory by redeeming the prices of the houses and tenements.
(One hundred million sesterces were invested in that munificence, all the more
acceptably in the eyes of the public to the extent that, being restrained in his
private building, he limited even his public structures to two: the temple to
Augustus and the stage of the Pompeian theater.[129] And on their completion,
2   in contempt of popularity or else from old age, he failed to dedicate them.) To
estimate the damage suffered by each person, four grandsons-in-law of Caesar—
Cn. Domitius, Cassius Longinus, M. Vinicius, and Rubellius Blandus—were
selected, and on the consuls' nomination P. Petronius was added.[130] And honors
were chosen and decreed for the princeps in accordance with the ingenuity of
each person; but which ones he neglected or accepted was uncertain, owing to
his life's approaching end.

★ ★ ★

A.D. 37

3   For not long afterward Tiberius' final consuls, Cn. Acerronius and C. Pontius,
commenced their magistracy, with power already being exercised excessively by
Macro, who from day to day was fostering ever more keenly the goodwill—
which in fact he had never neglected—of C. Caesar. After the death of Claudia,
whose wedding to the latter I recorded,[131] Macro had driven his own wife, En-

127. The "stream" in question is the Tigris; the Elymaei lived at the head of the Persian
Gulf: scholars assume that "in the rear" is therefore an error by T. or his source.
128. "By retreating himself to Syria Tiridates gave the rest of his allies a legitimate excuse for following his example" (R. H. Martin ad loc.).
129. The temple had been decreed on Augustus' death (1.10.8); Pompey's theater had
been destroyed by fire in A.D. 22, whereupon Tiberius had promised to restore it (3.72.2).
130. See 4.75 for the marriage of Cn. Domitius Ahenobarbus; 6.15.1 for those of Cassius Longinus and Vinicius; and 6.27.1 for that of Blandus. For Petronius see 3.49.1n.
131. For the wedding of Claudia and C. Caesar (Caligula) see 6.20.1.

nia, to entice the young man into a feigned love affair and then, by a matrimonial agreement, to bind him fast, since he would not refuse anything provided he could achieve mastery: for, though he was temperamentally volatile, the falseness of hypocrisy had nevertheless been a lesson well learned in his grandfather's lap.

This was known to the princeps, and therefore handing over the state caused **46** him to hesitate, first between his grandchildren. Drusus' offspring was closer in blood and affection but had not yet entered puberty;[132] Germanicus' son[133] had the vigor of youth and the public's enthusiasm—and with his grandfather that was a reason for hatred. Even Claudius he considered, because he was of settled years[134] and desirous of good qualities; but the man's mental impairment stood in the way. If, on the other hand, a successor were sought outside the household, **2** he dreaded that the memory of Augustus and the name of the Caesars might be turned into objects of mockery and insult: his concern was not so much contemporaries' goodwill as popularity among posterity. Subsequently, uncertain in **3** his mind and physically exhausted, he entrusted to fate a decision to which he was unequal—while scattering remarks by which he could be understood to have foresight into the future. In an uncomplicated conundrum he remonstrated **4** with Macro for deserting the setting, and watching the rising, sun;[135] and, when C. Caesar in a chance conversation was deriding L. Sulla, he predicted to him that he would have all of Sulla's vices and none of his virtues. At the same time amid incessant tears he embraced the younger of his grandsons and said to the other, who had a callous look, "He will be killed by you, and you by another."[136] (But despite his declining health he abandoned none of his lusts, pretending **5** strength in his hardship and having become accustomed to flout doctors' skills and those who, after the age of thirty, required someone else's advice to distinguish what helped or harmed their own bodies.)[137]

Meanwhile at Rome the seeds of future slaughters even after Tiberius were **47** being scattered. Laelius Balbus had arraigned Acutia, once the wife of P. Vitellius, for treason.[138] When on her conviction a reward for the accuser was being decreed, Junius Otho, a tribune of the plebs, intervened: whence hatred between them and the subsequent extermination of Otho. Then Albucilla, who was no- **2**

---

132. Tiberius Gemellus, born in 19 (2.84.1), had clearly "entered puberty" in the literal sense; T. means that he had not yet formally adopted the toga of manhood, which he did only after Caligula had come to power (Suetonius, *Gaius Caligula* 15.2).

133. Gaius Caligula, born A.D. 12: the "C. Caesar" of the previous paragraph.

134. Claudius had been born on 1 August 10 B.C.

135. I.e., Macro was abandoning the elderly Tiberius and was looking toward the new generation.

136. Tiberius Gemellus was killed in 37/38 by Gaius Caligula, who himself would be killed by Cassius Chaerea (1.32.2) in 41.

137. "From the age of thirty he took care of it [his health] according to his own judgment without the aid or advice of doctors" (Suetonius, *Tiberius* 68.4).

138. For P. Vitellius see 5.8.1–2 above.

torious for her many love affairs and had been married to Satrius Secundus (the informant on the conspiracy),[139] was denounced for impiety toward the princeps; Cn. Domitius, Vibius Marsus, and L. Arruntius were implicated as her accomplices and adulterers. (About the brilliancy of Domitius I spoke above;[140]

3 Marsus too was a man of olden honors and illustrious in his studies.) The record sent to the senate maintained that it was Macro who had presided over the witnesses' interrogation and the torture of the slaves; and the fact that there was no letter against the defendants from the Commander raised the suspicion that, in his illness and perhaps ignorance, there had been considerable fabrication because

48 of Macro's known antagonism toward Arruntius. Therefore Domitius and Marsus extended their lives, the former considering his defense, the latter as though he had determined on starvation. But Arruntius, though friends urged hesitation and delays, replied that the same things were not becoming for everyone: he had lived long enough and had nothing to regret except the fact that he had endured a tense old age amid mockery and danger, resented for a long time by Sejanus, now by Macro, always by one of the powerful—and not through any fault but

2 because he was intolerant of outrages. Of course avoidance was possible during the few days to the princeps's final moments; but how would he escape the youth of the one who loomed over them? When Tiberius after so much experience of affairs had become unhinged and changed under the influence of being master, would C. Caesar—who, with his boyhood scarcely ended, was wholly ignorant or else reared on evil—embark on a better course under the leadership of Macro, who, chosen for his superior depravity to suppress Sejanus, had belabored the state with more numerous crimes? Already the prospect was of a keener servi-

3 tude, and he was therefore fleeing things past and impending alike. —Insisting thus in the manner of a prophet, he opened his veins.

4   The sequel will provide proof that Arruntius did well to die. Albucilla, having wounded herself with an abortive blow, was taken to prison by order of the senate. As for the abettors of her illicit sex, it was decreed that the praetorian Carsidius Sacerdos should be deported to an island, Pontius Fregellanus should lose his senatorial rank,[141] and the same punishments for Laelius Balbus—and that at least brought delight to members, since Balbus was held to be a man of callous eloquence, ready to take on the guiltless.

49   During the same days Sex. Papinius, of a consular family, chose a sudden and disfiguring departure by throwing himself headlong from a height. The reason was traced back to his mother, who, having been rejected long since,[142] had coaxed

139. I.e., Sejanus' conspiracy (see 6.8.3). Satrius Secundus had been an adherent of Sejanus (4.34.1, 6.8.5).

140. Esp. at 4.75, but also 6.1.1, 6.45.2. For Vibius Marsus see 2.74.1n.; for Arruntius, 1.8.3n.

141. Sacerdos was mentioned earlier at 4.13.2. Epigraphic evidence suggests that Fregellanus' first name was Pontilius (see also 6.3.4n.).

142. It is not clear whether T. means that she had been divorced by a husband or (more

the young man into the ways of luxuriousness, driving him to the sorts of thing   2
from which he could find no escape except by death. She was therefore accused
in the senate, and, although she groveled at the fathers' knees and for a long time
maintained that grief was an emotion common to them all, that females' courage
when such things befell was weaker, and other sorrowful appeals for sympathy
along the same painful lines, she was nevertheless barred from the City for ten
years, until her younger son would have departed the slippery period of his youth.

It was now that Tiberius' body and strength were letting him down; but not   **50**
yet his dissembling. There was the same inflexibility of spirit: attentive in conversation and look, sometimes he tried to cover up his failing condition (however
evident) by a studied affability; and, after numerous changes of location, he settled at length on the promontory of Misenum in a villa of which L. Lucullus had
once been owner. There it was discovered in the following way that he was ap-   2
proaching his final moments.

There was a doctor distinguished for his skill by the name of Charicles, who was
accustomed not, to be sure, to take charge of the princeps's bouts of ill health but
to afford the opportunity of advice. Leaving as if on personal business, and grasping his hand in a show of respect, he felt the pulse in the man's veins but did not
deceive him. Tiberius—possibly affronted and suppressing his anger all the more—   3
ordered the banquet to be resumed and he reclined beyond his accustomed time
as if paying honor to his departing friend. Charicles nevertheless assured Macro
that his respiration was faltering and would not last beyond two days. Thereupon   4
everything was hastily arranged by means of dialogues between those present and
by messages for the legates and armies. On the seventeenth day before the Kalends
of April,[143] with his breathing stifled, it was believed that he had consummated his
mortal span; and amid a great throng of well-wishers C. Caesar was just emerging
to take up his incipient command when the news was suddenly brought that
Tiberius' voice and vision were returning and people were being summoned to
bring food to restore his failing condition. Hence general panic, and the others dis-   5
persed in all directions, each representing himself as sorrowful or ignorant; Caesar
alone was transfixed in silence, expecting the uttermost after his highest hopes.
But the intrepid Macro ordered the old man to be smothered by a pile of clothes
thrown over him, and everyone to leave the threshold.

Thus did Tiberius end, in the seventy-eighth year of his life. His father was   **51**
Nero and on each side his origin was that of the Claudian family, although his
mother by adoptions crossed into the Livian and subsequently the Julian clan.[144]
His fortunes from early infancy were equivocal. Having followed his proscribed
father into exile, on entering Augustus' household as his stepson he contended

---

probably) that her advances had been rejected by her son. Papinius' father was presumably the consul of 36 (6.40.1).

143. 16 March (see Sherk 28G, p. 54).

144. See 5.1.1 and n.

with numerous rivals while Marcellus and Agrippa, then subsequently Gaius and
Lucius Caesar, thrived; also, his brother, Drusus, was held more favorably in the

2   affection of the citizens. But his life was especially slippery after his taking of
Julia in matrimony, enduring as he did his wife's immorality or evading it.[145]
Then, on his return from Rhodes, he remained in possession of the princeps's
now vacant hearth for twelve years and subsequently of jurisdiction over Roman interests for almost three and twenty.

3   In his behavior too there were differing phases:[146] one exceptional in life and
reputation as long as he was a private individual or in commands under Augustus; one secretive and guileful in its fabrication of virtues while Germanicus and
Drusus survived; he was simultaneously a blend of good and evil during his
mother's lifetime; infamous for his savagery, but with his lusts cloaked, inasmuch
as he felt love or fear respectively for Sejanus; lastly he erupted into crimes and
degradations alike when at last, with his shame and dread removed, he had only
himself to rely on.[147]

145. The evasion relates to his retirement on Rhodes in 6 B.C.–A.D. 2, mentioned in the
next sentence.

146. The five phases which follow are: to A.D. 14; to A.D. 23; to A.D. 29; to A.D. 31; to
A.D. 37.

147. See *Tac. Rev.* 157–61 for the interpretation on which the translation of the last seven
words is based; everyone else translates "he simply indulged his own inclinations" or the
like.

Thereafter Suillius was constant and savage in his accusing of defendants, and   **5**
there were many rivals of his daring: for the princeps's drawing to himself of all
the responsibilities of laws and magistrates had opened up the means for plundering.[12] And no public commodity at all was as venal as the disloyalty of advo-   **2**
cates, to such an extent that Samius, a distinguished Roman equestrian who had
given four hundred thousand sesterces to Suillius and then realized his collusion,[13] fell on his sword at the man's house. Therefore, on the initiative of C.   **3**
Silius, consul designate (whose powerfulness and extermination I shall recall in
time),[14] the fathers rose up and importuned for the Cincian law, by which it
was provided in antiquity that no one should receive money or gift for pleading
a case.[15]

Then, as those for whom that insult was intended started to protest, Silius   **6**
launched a bitter attack on Suillius (with whom he was disaffected), referring to
examples of the orators of old who had regarded fame and successors as the only
prizes of eloquence.[16] What in other circumstances was the finest and principal
of the liberal arts was being defiled, he said, by its sordid administration. Not even
loyalty remained intact when the magnitude of profits was the end in sight. If   **2**
transactions were conducted with no view to anyone's wage, there would be
fewer of them. As it was, however, antagonisms, accusations, hatreds, and injustices were being fostered simply in order that the rottenness of the forum would
bring money to advocates in the same way as the virulence of disease brought
rewards for doctors. They should remember C. Asinius, Messala, and the more recent Arruntius and Aeserninus:[17] they had been raised to the heights without
corrupting their life and fluency.

With the consul designate saying such things, and others agreeing, a motion   **3**
for liability under the law of extortion was in the process of being prepared when
Suillius and Cossutianus[18] and the rest, who saw that it was no trial (its subjects

12. The point is that "any one might be accused when all rested on the caprice of one
man" (Furneaux).

13. The most natural explanation of the story would seem to be that Samius had retained
Suillius to defend him but discovered him subsequently to be in collusion with his op-
ponent(s); but this sits awkwardly with the fact that Suillius, as is clear from the start of
the chapter, was an accuser. An alternative scenario is that Samius had bribed Suillius not
to proceed with a prosecution against him but had been doublecrossed.

14. See 11.12.2–3 and 11.27–35 respectively below.

15. The Lex Cincia of 204 B.C. had already been revived by Augustus in 17 B.C.

16. I.e., orators in the past had not sought monetary reward but wished only for fame
and for followers ("successors"), i.e., future generations of orators who would be inspired
by, and would attempt to rival, them.

17. The first named is the multitalented C. Asinius Pollio (1.12.4n.), whose grandson was
the last named, M. Claudius Marcellus Aeserninus, praetor in A.D. 19 (3.11.2). Messala is the
famous Augustan orator Messala Corvinus (3.34.2, 13.34.1). For L. Arruntius see 1.8.3n.

18. This is the notorious accuser Cossutianus Capito, who will play a prominent role in

but punishment that was being decided, surrounded Caesar
their previous activities. And, on his nod, they began their ac-
Who was the man of such haughtiness that he could presume to
hope for ~~ ~~ nal fame? It was practical to prepare substantial support, lest anyone
for want of an advocate should be exposed to the powerful.[19] Yet eloquence did
not simply happen without cost: family concerns were neglected if one concentrated on someone else's business. Many sustained their existence by soldiering,
some by working the fields; no one followed any pursuit unless he had first fore-

2 seen its fruits. It had been easy for Asinius and Messala, laden with prizes from
the wars between Antonius and Augustus, or for those heirs of rich families, the
Aesernini and Arruntii, to don magnanimity. But they themselves had their own
examples ready: the great wages for which P. Clodius or C. Curio had been ac-

3 customed to discourse.[20] They themselves were modest senators who, with the
state tranquil, sought no emoluments except those of peace. But he should consider the plebs who sparkled in the toga:[21] with the rewards of their studies re-

4 moved, the studies too would perish. —The princeps, deeming these words (if
less becoming) not without point, decided on amounts up to ten thousand sesterces as the limit on the money to be accepted, transgressions of which would
be liable to a charge of extortion.

★

8   At about the same time Mithridates, whose command over the Armenians and
chaining by order of C. Caesar I recalled,[22] on Claudius' advice returned to his
kingdom, relying on the resources of Pharasmanes. The latter, king of the Iberians and Mithridates' brother, announced that the Parthians were disaffected, that
their supreme commander was in doubt, and that lesser matters were being handled carelessly.

---

the remaining narrative, especially as the opponent of Thrasea Paetus (e.g., 16.21.3, 28.1,
33.2). Since he is not given his full name here, T. must have introduced him in a section
of the *Annals* now lost.

19. Whether this is the correct meaning of this highly obscure sentence is quite uncertain.

20. Suillius and his fellow accusers are referring to P. Clodius Pulcher, tribune in 58 B.C.
and an enemy of Cicero (3.27.3n.), and C. Scribonius Curio, tribune in 50 B.C. and friend
of Clodius, who were turbulent political figures of the late republic. See *OCD* 350–1 and
1370.

21. The toga symbolized not only peace as opposed to war (1.12.3 and n.) but also the
pursuits associated with peace, such as oratory. The speakers are reminding Claudius ("he")
that some advocates come from lower down the social scale.

22. For Mithridates I and Armenia see 6.32.3; his subsequent summons to Rome and
imprisonment by Caligula must have been narrated in the portion of the *Annals* which
is now lost.

For Gotarzes among numerous savageries had hastened the execution of Arta-   2
banus and his spouse and son: hence dread on the part of everyone else, and they
summoned Vardanes.[23] He, ready as he was for great acts of daring, in a two-day   3
period advanced three thousand stades[24] and dislodged the unsuspecting and terrified Gotarzes; nor did he hesitate to seize the nearest prefectures,[25] with only
the Seleucians refusing his despotism. Since they had been defectors from his father too, it was anger rather than current circumstances which inflamed him
against them, and he involved himself in the blockading of their city, substantial
as it was and secured by the defensive obstacle of a stream,[26] by a wall, and by
supplies. Meanwhile Gotarzes, augmented by the resources of the Dahae and   4
Hyrcani, renewed the war; and Vardanes, compelled to abandon Seleucia, confronted him on the Bactrian plains with his camp.

It was at that moment, with the forces of the East torn and uncertain in which   9
direction they would lean,[27] that Mithridates was given the chance of occupying
Armenia, with the might of the Roman soldiery to extirpate the steep strongholds, while the Iberian army at the same time scoured the plains. The Armenians did not resist after the rout of the prefect Demonax, who had dared battle.
Some brief hesitation was occasioned by the king of Lesser Armenia, Cotys, cer-   2
tain of the chiefs having turned his way; but then he was restrained by a letter
from Caesar, and everything flowed in the direction of Mithridates, now more
frightening than was advantageous for his new kingdom.

As for the Parthian commanders, however, they suddenly established a treaty   3
just when they were preparing to fight, since they had learned of a plot by their
compatriots which Gotarzes disclosed to his brother. Having convened hesitantly
at first, they then clasped each other's right hand and in front of the altars of the
gods struck a bargain to avenge the treachery of their antagonists and to make
mutual concessions. Vardanes seemed the more able to keep hold of the kingdom;   4
Gotarzes, to avoid any appearance of rivalry, withdrew deep into Hyrcania.

Seleucia surrendered to the returning Vardanes in the seventh year after its defection—not without dishonor for the Parthians, whom one community had
outwitted for so long. Thereupon he visited the most substantial prefectures and   10
was craving+ to recover Armenia, had he not been checked by Vibius Marsus,

23. Gotarzes and Vardanes seem both to have ruled Parthia during the period A.D. 38–51
(see *OCD* 177 s.v. Arsacids), but the precise sequence of events appears most unclear. The
present sentence, which initiates a flashback covering several years (see 11.9.4 "in the seventh year"), has been corrupted in the transmission, and one way of explaining the corruption (though not that adopted here) is to assume a lacuna; such a lacuna might have
contained some further elucidatory material. It is also possible that T. mentioned Parthian
affairs in the narrative which is now lost.

24. Roughly 350 miles, impossible to cover in two days.

25. See 6.42.4n.

26. The River Tigris.

27. Or perhaps "and it was uncertain in which direction they were leaning."

legate of Syria, threatening war.[28] And meanwhile Gotarzes, regretting his concession of the kingdom, and after a call from the nobility (whose servitude in
2   peace is harder), assembled his forces. He was opposed at the Erindes stream, in
the crossing of which, after a considerable struggle, victory went to Vardanes, who
in favorable battles then subdued the intervening nations as far as the River Sindes, which divides the Dahae and Arii. There a limit was placed on his success:
3   for the Parthians, though victorious, spurned a distant campaign. So, having set
up monuments in which he testified to his dominion and that none of the previous Arsacidae had won taxes from those peoples, he returned mighty in glory
and all the more defiant and intolerable to his subjects—who, through a previously arranged trick, killed him while unawares and intent on hunting, still in his
early manhood yet in brilliancy to be ranked with a mere few of the older[+] kings,
if only he had sought the love of his compatriots to the same degree as he found
dread among his enemies.
4   On the execution of Vardanes the affairs of the Parthians were disrupted amid
the uncertainty of who would be received into the kingship. Many leaned toward Gotarzes, some toward Meherdates, the progeny of Phraates, who had been
given to us in hostageship. Afterward it was Gotarzes who prevailed, and, having
gained control of the palace, by his savagery and luxuriousness he drove the
Parthians to send secret pleas to the Roman princeps in which they begged that
Meherdates be admitted to his ancestral pinnacle.

* * *

11 With the same men as consuls,[29] the Secular Games were witnessed in the eight-
hundredth year after Rome's founding, the sixty-fourth from when Augustus
produced them.[30] (I am passing over the calculations of each princeps, sufficiently described as they are in the books in which I compiled the affairs of the
Commander Domitian.[31] For he too produced Secular Games, and I was present at them with particular attentiveness—endowed as I was with the quindec-

---

28. For Vibius Marsus see 2.74.1n.

29. Viz. Claudius and L. Vitellius.

30. The Secular Games, consisting principally of sacrifices and theatrical performances,
celebrated the end of one era or *saeculum* (which in republican times was fixed at 100
years) and the beginning of the next. The most famous such games were those of Augustus in 17 B.C., at which Horace's "Secular Hymn" (*Carmen Saeculare*) was sung. These
games occurred well over a century after the previous celebration (146 B.C.), while
Claudius' games were based on a different cycle altogether (hence T.'s reference to "the
calculations of each princeps" below). For Augustus' games see Sherk 11 = Braund 769,
for Claudius' see Braund 711A = WM 31 (a); also *OCD* 1378.

31. T.'s *Histories,* the later books of which, containing his narrative of Domitian's reign,
are lost. With his Secular Games of A.D. 88 Domitian returned to the Augustan cycle (but
six years early).

imviral priesthood and praetor at the time, which I do not record from boasting but because the college of quindecimvirs has been concerned with them from antiquity, and it was those⁺ magistrates in particular who carried out the duties of the ceremonies.) As Claudius was sitting at the circus games—and while the boy nobles on horseback were embarking on the entertainment of "Troy," among them Britannicus, the Commander's offspring, and L. Domitius, by adoption later admitted into command and the nomenclature of "Nero"—the fact that the goodwill of the plebs was keener toward Domitius was received like a prophecy.[32] And it was publicized that serpents had been present at his infancy in the manner of guards—a fantasy which was assimilated to foreign wonders, for he personally, no detractor of himself, was accustomed to describe how only one snake had been seen in his bedroom. However that may be, the inclination of the people was a survival from their memory of Germanicus, whose only remaining male scion he was; and their pity for his mother, Agrippina, was augmented owing to the savagery of Messalina, who, always ferocious and at the time particularly volatile, was inhibited from setting up charges and accusers only by a new love which bordered on madness.

She had become so inflamed for C. Silius, the finest of the Roman youth, that she evicted Junia Silana, a noble lady,[33] from her marriage to him and took control of a now available adulterer. Nor was Silius unaware of the outrage or the danger; but—with extermination certain if he declined; with some hope of deception; and with the rewards great at the same time—he found consolation in shutting out the future and enjoying the present. She for her part—not stealthily but with a sizable escort—frequented his home, clung to him when he emerged, and lavished wealth and honors upon him; finally, as if the transference of fortune were already complete, slaves, freedmen, and the trappings of the princeps were to be seen at the adulterer's house.

But Claudius, ignorant of his own marriage and exercising his censorial responsibilities, in stern edicts berated the people's recklessness at the theater, because they had hurled abuse at the consular Publius Pomponius (he produced

2

3

12

2

3

13

32. "Troy" was a well-known spectacular at which young men on horseback commemorated the Romans' association with Troy partly by military tattoos and partly by mock battles. Its most famous occurrence was during Augustus' reign; in A.D. 47 it evidently formed part of the circus games (which Augustus had made an integral part of the Secular Games in 17 B.C.). Participating in the "Troy" of 47 were Britannicus, the son born to Claudius and Messalina on 12 February 41, and L. Domitius Ahenobarbus, the son born to Cn. Domitius Ahenobarbus (4.75n.) and the younger Agrippina on 15 December 37. After Claudius married L. Domitius' mother in 49 (12.7.3–8.1), the boy was adopted by the emperor in 50 (12.25) and took Nero as one of his names (12.26.1): from then on he was marked out as Claudius' successor.

33. Junia Silana (on whom there is more at 13.19.2–22.2) was probably the daughter of M. Junius Silanus (3.24.3n.) and sister of Junia Claudilla, a wife of Caligula. For her death see 14.12.4.

2   songs for the stage) and at illustrious ladies.[34] And he carried a law checking the
     savagery of creditors, to prevent their giving money at interest to the sons of fam-
     ilies against their parents' death.[35] He brought into the City sources of water di-
     verted from the Simbruine hills.[36] And he added and publicized new forms of
     letters, having discovered that not even the Greek letter-system had been begun

14   and polished off all at once.[37] —The Egyptians were the first to depict the mind's
     thoughts, by means of animal figures (those most ancient monuments to human
     memory can still be seen, impressed on rock), and they maintain that they them-
     selves were the inventors of letters; and that later the Phoenicians, because they
     were paramount at sea, brought them to Greece and acquired glory for discov-

2   ering what they had only inherited. (For there is a story that Cadmus, sailing with
     the Phoenicians' fleet while the Greek peoples were still at a raw stage, was the
     author of the system. Some, however, recall that the forms of sixteen letters had
     been discovered by Cecrops, the Athenian, or by Linus, the Theban, and, in
     Trojan times, by Palamedes, the Argive, and then the rest by others, principally

3   Simonides.) But in Italy it was the Etruscans who learned from Corinthian
     Demaratus, the Aborigines from the Arcadian, Evander; and indeed the forms of
     Latin letters are those of the oldest of the Greeks, but in our case too they were
     few at first and subsequently added to. It was on this example that Claudius at-
     tached the three letters which, in use during his command but afterward con-
     signed to oblivion, are observed even now on the bronze fixed in forums and
     temples for advertising senate's decisions to the plebs.[+] —

15   Next he placed before the senate a motion concerning the college of divin-
     ers, lest the most olden discipline in Italy should become obsolete through iner-
     tia: they had often been summoned during times adverse for the state, he said,
     and on their advice ceremonies had been revived and handled more correctly
     for the future; and the chiefs of Etruria, of their own accord or at the instigation
     of the Roman fathers, had retained the lore and disseminated it to families,
     something which now happened more sluggishly, given the public listlessness
     surrounding good practices and because foreign superstitions were gaining in ef-

2   fectiveness. Everything was of course delightful at present, yet for this kindness
     of the gods they should render thanks by ensuring that the rites and rituals which
     had been cultivated in times of doubt were not consigned to oblivion during

3   those of prosperity. —As a result a senate's decision was passed that the pontiffs
     should see what aspects of the diviners should be retained and confirmed.

34. For P. Pomponius Secundus, suffect consul in 44, see 5.8.1n.

35. I.e., money which had to be repaid at interest on the father's death.

36. See Braund 812 = Sherk 59 (dating the completion of the work to 52/53).

37. The three letters which Claudius invented were: ⅃ (for the consonantal *u*, to distinguish it from the vocalic *u*, Ⱶ (for the sound between *u* and *i*), and Ɔ (to represent *ps* or
bs). Examples of the first two may still be found in some inscriptions (e.g., that translated
at Braund 218 = WM 35).

★

In the same year the nation of the Cherusci sought a king from Rome, their **16** nobles having been lost in internal wars and only one of their kingly stock remaining, who was being held in the City, by name Italicus. His paternal lineage derived from Flavus, brother of Arminius, his mother from Actumerus, a princeps of the Chatti;[38] the man himself had handsome good looks and was trained in arms and horses according to ancestral custom as well as ours. So Caesar, having enhanced him with money and added some attendants, urged him to undertake his national honor with good heart, saying that he was the first man born at Rome to go, not as hostage but as citizen, to a foreign command.

At first his arrival was welcome to the Germans, and, because of the fact that **2** he was not stained by any of their disaffections but acted with equal enthusiasm toward all, he was celebrated and courted, sometimes practicing affability and moderation, which are resented by none, more often wine-bibbing and lusts, which with barbarians are popular. And already his brilliance was reaching not just among his neighbors but still farther afield when those who had flourished from factions, suspecting his powerfulness, withdrew to the different bordering peoples and testified that the old freedom of Germany was being removed and Roman might was rising up. Was it really the case that there was no one born in **3** the same lands who could fill the position of princeps, if it were not for the fact that an offspring of Flavus the scout was being exalted above everyone? It was pointless to mention Arminius as pretext:[39] if it were *his* son who had grown up on enemy soil and come into the kingdom, he might well be feared, tainted as he would be by upbringing, servitude, culture, and everything foreign. But, if Italicus had his father's mind, no one else had conducted hostilities more ferociously against fatherland and the gods of the hearth than his parent.

By such words as these they gathered considerable forces, and no less was the **17** following of Italicus: he reminded them that he had not burst in upon an unwilling people but had been summoned because he surpassed the rest in nobility; they should test his courage, to see whether he presented himself as worthy of his uncle Arminius and grandfather Actumerus; he did not blush that his fa- **2** ther had never abandoned the loyalty toward the Romans which he had taken up with the Germans' blessing: falsely was the designation "freedom" being used as a screen by those who, lowborn personally and ruinous in public matters, had no hope except through their disaffections. —The crowd bayed its eager approval **3** of him, and, after a great battle between the barbarians, the king was victorious. Then, slipping into haughtiness on account of his good fortune, he was banished; and, restored in turn by the resources of the Langobardi, he remained an affliction on Cheruscan affairs through prosperity and adversity alike.

38. See 2.9.1 and 2.10.1.
39. I.e., it was pointless to defend Italicus on the grounds that Arminius was his uncle.

18   During the same period the Chauci, with no dissension at home and eager on the death of Sanquinius,[40] raided Lower Germany while Corbulo was on the march,[41] their leader being Gannascus, a Canninefate by nationality, who, after earning auxiliary pay for a long time but later a deserter, was now plundering from light vessels and laying waste the coast of the Gauls in particular, not un-

2   aware that they were rich and unwarlike. But Corbulo, having entered the province with great care and soon with the glory of which that campaign was the inception, assembled triremes by way of the channel of the Rhine and the rest of the ships (depending on the adaptability of each) by way of the estuaries and conduits; and, having sunk the enemies' boats, and with Gannascus evicted, when the immediate situation had been adequately settled he brought the legions —shirkers of work and toil, and delighting in pillage—back to their old customs,

3   whereby no one would leave the column, nor enter battle unless ordered. Pickets, watches, daily and nightly responsibilities were carried out under arms; and they maintain that two soldiers—one because he was not properly girded when digging a rampart, and another because he was girded with only a dagger—were punished by death. These excesses, perhaps falsely exaggerated,[+] nevertheless derived their origin from the leader's strictness; and you would know that he was an obsessive, implacable to serious felonies, when such harshness against even trivialities was believed of him.

19   Terror of him affected soldiers and enemies in different ways: our courage was increased, the barbarians' defiance broken. The nation of the Frisians, ferocious or scarcely loyal after the rebellion which began with the disaster to L. Apronius,[42] gave hostages and settled in territory prescribed by Corbulo; he also im-

2   posed a senate, magistrates, and laws. And, lest they should cast aside his orders, he fortified a garrison, dispatching men to entice the Greater Chauci to surrender and at the same time to attack Gannascus by guileful means. Nor was the

3   ambush abortive or, against a deserter and violator of loyalty, improper; but at his slaughter the minds of the Chauci were stirred, and it was Corbulo who was providing the seeds of rebellion, which had a fertile reception in some quarters but in others one of baleful report. Why was he provoking the enemy? Any reverses would fall on the state; but, if he performed successfully, a man of his distinction would constitute an alarm to peace and would weigh too heavily on a cowardly princeps. —Therefore Claudius prohibited any new violence against the Germanies, to such an extent that he ordered the garrisons to be pulled back to this side of the Rhine.

---

40. See 6.4.3; both his appointment to Germany and his death there must have been mentioned in the part of the *Annals* now lost.

41. In the extant *Annals* this is the first reference to Cn. Domitius Corbulo, suffect consul in 39 and a famous general. He was half-brother of the notorious Suillius (11.1.1n.), their mother being Vistilia (5.8.1n.). For Corbulo's father see 3.31.3.

42. See 4.72–3 (A.D. 28).

Corbulo was already constructing a camp on enemy soil when this letter was **20** delivered. At the unexpected development, though many sensations swept over him (dread at the Commander, contempt from the barbarians, mockery from the allies), he made no utterance other than "Happy once were Roman leaders!" and gave the signal for retreat. Nevertheless, so that his soldiery might be divested of **2** their inactivity, he ran a conduit of twenty-three miles in length between the Mosa and Rhine, by means of which the uncertainties of the Ocean could be avoided. Nevertheless Caesar indulged him the insignia of a triumph, although he had denied him a war.

And, not long after, the same honor was acquired by Curtius Rufus, who on **3** Mattiac territory had opened up a shaft in his search for veins of silver; its returns were slender and not long-lasting, but the legions experienced loss as well as toil, digging out watercourses and constructing below ground what would have been hard in the open. Worn down by these tasks, and because their like was being endured across numerous provinces, the soldiery secretly composed a letter in the name of the armies, begging the Commander that, when he was about to entrust someone with an army, he should assign him the triumphal insignia in advance. (Concerning the origin of Curtius Rufus, of whom some have transmitted that **21** he was the offspring of a gladiator, I am not inclined to promulgate falsehoods and it is shaming to follow through with an account of the reality. But, after he had grown up, as the follower of a quaestor to whose lot Africa had fallen, he was spending time by himself in the porticoes—deserted at midday—of the town of Hadrumetum, when he was confronted by a womanly apparition beyond human dimensions and heard a voice saying "You are the one, Rufus, who will come to this province as proconsul." His hopes raised by such an omen, he departed for **2** the City, where through the lavishness of friends as well as his own keen talent he attained the quaestorship and soon, despite there being noble candidates, the praetorship on the vote of the princeps, since Tiberius had veiled the disgraceful circumstances of his birth with these words: "Curtius Rufus seems to me to be born of himself." In a long old age thereafter, and grim sycophancy toward his **3** superiors, arrogant to inferiors and difficult among his equals, he held consular command, the insignia of a triumph and finally Africa; and on his decease there he fulfilled the fateful prophecy.)[43]

★

Meanwhile at Rome, for reasons neither obvious nor recognized later, Cn. Non- **22** ius, a Roman equestrian, was discovered girded with a sword in a throng of the

43. The same ghost story is told in a famous letter by T.'s friend the younger Pliny (7.27.2–3), who adds to the prophecy the vital element (which T. has omitted) that Curtius would die in Africa. The visionary, who became suffect consul in 43, is usually identified with the Curtius who wrote a history of Alexander the Great in ten books (much of which still survives).

princeps's well-wishers. After he had begun to be rent by torture, concerning himself ★★★ he gave up no accomplices, whether concealing any being uncertain.[44]

2   With the same men as consuls, P. Dolabella proposed that a spectacle of gladiators should be celebrated every year at the expense of those who acquired the

3   quaestorship.[45] In ancestral times this had been the reward of excellence, and it was lawful for all citizens who trusted their good qualities to seek magistracies; not even a differentiation of age prevented them from embarking on consulship

4   or dictatorships in early youth. As for quaestors, they were instituted even while the kings were still commanding, as is shown by the resurrection of the curiate law by L. Brutus.[46] The power of selecting them remained with the consuls until the people began to bestow this office too. The first to be created were Valerius Potitus and Aemilius Mamercus, in the sixty-third year after the banish-

5   ment of the Tarquins, so that they might accompany the military chest;[47] then, with their business swelling, two were added to take care at Rome. Later the number was doubled, with Italy now being liable for dues, and revenues accruing

6   from the provinces. After, by a law of Sulla,[48] twenty were created to supplement the senate, to which he had transferred the courts; and, although the equestrians recovered the courts, the quaestorship nevertheless continued to be granted at no cost in accordance with the candidates' status or by the complaisance of those assigning it, until on Dolabella's motion it was (so to speak) put on sale.

★ ★ ★

23   With A. Vitellius and L. Vipstanus as consuls,[49] there was discussion about supplementing the senate and it was chiefs of the Gaul which is called Comata who, having previously achieved treaties and Roman citizenship, were seeking the prerogative of acquiring honors in the City: there was therefore considerable and

44. I.e., it was uncertain whether he had had any accomplices or not. Midway through this sentence there is a lacuna in the manuscript; the sense presumably is "he volunteered nothing and."

45. For P. Dolabella see 3.47.3n.

46. In 509 B.C., when according to tradition Brutus was made one of the two first consuls after his expulsion of Tarquinius Superbus (1.1.1, 3.27.1). A curiate law, at least in the later republic, was one which validated the appointment of magistrates (*OCD* 853 s.v. lex curiata).

47. 446 B.C.

48. 81 B.C.

49. A. Vitellius, son of the previous year's consul (L. Vitellius: 6.28.1n.) and elder brother of one of the current year's suffects (also L. Vitellius), is the future emperor; mentioned again only at 14.49.1. The other consul is L. Vipstanus Poplicola Messalla.

varied rumor on the subject. And in the princeps's presence the matter was dis-   2
puted by those of a different persuasion, asserting that Italy was not so sick that
it could not supply a senate for its own City: once upon a time natives had sufficed for kindred peoples,[50] they said, and no one rued the state of old: indeed
men still recalled the examples which, under old-time conventions, the Roman
character had produced in respect of excellence and glory. Was it not enough that   3
the Veneti and Insubres had burst into the curia, without a throng of aliens being brought in, as if the community had been captured?+ What further honor
would there be for the residual nobility, or for any poor senator who came from
Latium? Everything would be filled by those rich men whose grandfathers and   4
great-grandfathers had been leaders of enemy nations, slaughtering our armies
by the violence of their swords and blockading Divine Julius at Alesia.[51] These
were recent events; but what if there sprang up the memory of those who had
perished when the Capitol and Roman citadel were laid low by the hands of the
same men?+[52] By all means let them enjoy the designation of "citizenship"; but
they should not cheapen the insignia of the fathers or the adornments of the
magistrates

Unmoved by such words as these, the princeps both spoke against them on   **24**
the spot and then embarked as follows after calling the senate:[53] "My ancestors,
of whom the most ancient, Clausus of Sabine origin, was assumed into Roman
citizenship as well as into the families of the patricians, encourage the use of similar counsels in political life, namely the transferring hither of whatever proves to
be exceptional elsewhere. For I am not unaware that the Julii were summoned   2
into the senate from Alba, the Coruncani from Camerium, the Porcii from Tusculum, and (not to explore the past any further+) others from Etruria, Lucania,
and the whole of Italy, and finally that the country itself was advanced to the Alps
so that not only single individuals but lands and peoples might unite in our name.
Then there was unalloyed domestic calm, and in the face of things foreign we   3
flourished alike when the Transpadanes were received into citizenship and when,
under the cover of legions colonized across the globe, the addition of the most
effective provincials rescued our exhausted empire. Surely no one rues the fact
that the Balbi crossed over from Spain, and men no less distinguished from Nar-

50. I.e., in the distant past neighboring peoples such as Latins or Sabines had been content that only natives of the City of Rome were members of the senate.

51. In 52 B.C. (described by Caesar himself in his *Gallic War* 7.68–84).

52. The reference is to the famous events of 390 B.C., when the Senonian Gauls penetrated to the Capitol at Rome. (The text here is extremely corrupt, and what I have
printed is only an expedient.)

53. A substantial portion of Claudius' original speech has been preserved on a bronze
inscription discovered in the sixteenth century at Lyon. Translations of all the extant remains may be found at Braund 570 = WM 34 or in B. Levick, *The Government of the Roman Empire: A Sourcebook* (London ²2000) 178–80; a translation of the second half only is
at Sherk 55.

bonese Gaul? Their posterity survives and does not yield to us in love for this
4   fatherland. What else brought extermination to the Lacedaemonians and Athenians, although they were a force at arms, except the fact that they excluded the
vanquished as being aliens? *Our* founder Romulus, however, was so effective in
his wisdom that he regarded many peoples as enemies and then as citizens on the
same day! Immigrants have reigned over us; bestowing magistracies on the sons
of freedmen is not, as many misconceive it, a recent thing but was done habitu-
5   ally by the people earlier. "But we fought with the Senones." Evidently the Vulsci
and Aequi never drew up their battle lines against us![54] "We were captured by
the Gauls." But we both gave hostages to the Etruscans and went under the Sam-
6   nites' yoke;[55] and, if you were to review every war, it still remains the case that
none was concluded in a shorter space of time than against the Gauls.[56] Thereafter there has been a constant and trusting peace. Now, merged as they are with
us by conventions, attainments, and relationships, let them bring in their gold and
7   wealth rather than keep them to themselves. Everything, conscript fathers, which
is now believed most olden was new: plebeian magistrates came after patrician,
Latin after plebeian, those of the other peoples of Italy after the Latin. This too will
grow old, and what today we defend by examples will be among the examples."
25   The speech of the princeps was followed by a fathers' decision, and the Aedui
were the first to acquire the prerogative of being senators in the City. That was a
concession to their ancient treaty and because, alone of the Gauls, they enjoy the
name of brotherhood with the Roman people.
2   During those same days all the senators of longest standing or those who had
had brilliant parents were enrolled by Caesar among the number of the patricians, given the fewness of the families now remaining which had been called
"Greater" by Romulus and "Lesser" by L. Brutus, and given too the extinction
even of those which had been substituted by the dictator Caesar under the Cassian law and by the princeps Augustus under the Saenian law.[57] And these welcome responsibilities toward the state were embarked on with considerable joy
3   from the censor; but, tense about how he might banish notorious reprobates from
the senate, he adopted a gentle and recently discovered method rather than one
in accordance with old-time strictness, advising each to consider his own position and to seek the right of discarding his rank: permission in that respect would
be easy, he said; and he would post up simultaneously those removed from the

54. References to the famous stories of Cn. Marcius Coriolanus (*OCD* 922) and L.
Quinctius Cincinnatus (*OCD* 1288) in the fifth century B.C.

55. The former refers to a particular version of Lars Porsenna's story in the early sixth
century B.C., already alluded to by T. at *Histories* 3.72.1 (see *OCD* 1227); the latter is the
famous debacle of the Caudine Forks in 321 B.C. (*OCD* 305).

56. 59–50 B.C.

57. The origin of the patriciate, like the mysterious designations of "Greater" and
"Lesser," is uncertain; Caesar's and Octavian's attempts at rebuilding numbers were 45/44
B.C. (Lex Cassia) and 30 B.C. (Lex Saenia). See *OCD* 1123.

senate and those excusing themselves, so that the judgment of the censors and the propriety of those withdrawing voluntarily might, when merged, soften the ignominy.

For these reasons Vipstanus as consul moved that Claudius should be called 4 "Father of the Senate": the nomenclature of "Father of the Fatherland" was, he said, indiscriminate; new services to the state should not be honored by conventional designations. But the princeps personally checked the consul for being excessively indulgent; he also performed the ritual purification, in which 5 5,984,072 citizens were registered. And that was the end of his ignorance toward his own household: not long after, he was driven to recognize and punish the outrages of his wife—thereby ensuring that he would burn for an incestuous wedding later on.[58]

Messalina, having become sated with the simplicity of her adultery, was already 26 drifting to hitherto unrecognized lusts when Silius himself, whether by some fatal derangement or deeming that the remedy for looming danger was danger itself, urged an abrupt end to dissembling. They had not reached this point merely 2 to wait upon the princeps's old age, he said; it was only the guiltless to whom planning was harmless: those whose outrages were clear should seek support from daring. Accomplices with similar dreads were available. He himself was celibate, childless, and prepared for a wedding and for adopting Britannicus; Messalina's power would remain the same, but in addition she would be carefree if they forestalled Claudius, who was as unsuspecting of ambush as he was quick to anger.

His utterance was received grudgingly, not through any love for her husband 3 but lest Silius, on reaching the top, would spurn his adulterer and would soon assess at its true price a crime which had been approved only amid perils. Yet she desired the name of "matrimony" by reason of that magnitude of notoriety which is the ultimate pleasure for the prodigal; and, waiting merely until Claudius set off for Ostia to sacrifice, she celebrated all the solemnities of a wedding. As I 27 am not unaware, it will seem fantastic that any mortals felt such unconcern in a community aware of everything and silent on nothing, still less that a consul designate, on a predicted day and in the presence of signatories, came together with a princeps's wife as if for the purpose of begetting children; that she for her part listened to the words of the officials and[+] sacrificed before the gods; that they reclined at table among party guests; and that there were kisses, embraces, and, finally, a night spent in spousal license. Yet none of this has been compiled to promote a marvel, but I am transmitting what was heard and written by my elders.

Therefore the princeps's household shuddered; and in particular those with 28 whom power lay—and upon whom, if things should change, alarm would descend—no longer muttered in secret exchanges but openly: when it was an actor who trampled over[+] the princeps's bedroom,[59] they said, humiliation had certainly been inflicted but actual extirpation had been only a remote possibility;

58. A forward reference to Claudius' marriage to his niece Agrippina (12.3.1–8.1).
59. The actor in question is Mnester (see 11.36.2 below), one of Messalina's lovers.

but, as things were now, a young noble with dignified good looks, with strength of mind, and with an approaching consulship, was girding himself for a greater prospect: for there was no concealing what remained after such a marriage.

2   Without doubt dread crept over them as they reflected that Claudius was a dullard and shackled to his wife and that many deaths had been perpetrated on Messalina's order; conversely, the very complaisance of the Commander afforded confidence that, if they prevailed owing to the frightfulness of the charge, she could be suppressed, convicted before being tried: the issue turned on whether her defense would be heard and how they might close his ears if she actually confessed.

29   At first Callistus, of whom I have already told in connection with the execution of C. Caesar,[60] and the engineer of the Appian murder, Narcissus,[61] and Pallas, whose influence was then glowing at its brightest, discussed whether they should deflect Messalina from her love for Silius by secret threats, dissembling

2   everything else. But later, dreading that they themselves might be dragged to ruin, they desisted—Pallas through cowardice, Callistus with his experience both of the previous court too and that one's power is more safely kept by careful than by drastic counsel; but Narcissus persisted, his only change being that in no conversation at all would he forewarn her of charge and accuser.

3   Attentive for any opportunity, during Caesar's long delay at Ostia Narcissus used lavishness and promises, as well as the prospect of increased power on the overthrowing of the wife, to compel the denouncement to be undertaken by the

30   two concubines with whose bodies the man was most familiar. Thereupon Calpurnia (that was the concubine's name), groveling at Caesar's knees when they had been granted some privacy, cried out that Messalina had wedded Silius; at the same time she asked Cleopatra (who was standing by, waiting for this very thing) whether she had discovered the same; and, when the latter nodded, she demanded that Narcissus be summoned. He, seeking pardon for his past dissem-

2   bling of Titii, Vettii, and Plautii,[62] said that he would not cast imputations of adultery now either: he[63] should not reclaim his house, slaves, and the other trappings of his fortune; rather let the other enjoy them, but return his wife and rescind the wedding tablets. "Do you know of your divorce?" he said; "her marriage to Silius was seen by the people, senate, and soldiery; and, unless you act quickly, her

31   husband holds the City!" At that point Claudius called the most significant of his friends and first made inquiry of the prefect of the food supply, Turranius, and afterward of Lusius Geta, who was installed over the praetorians. On their ac-

---

60. In the portion of the *Annals* now lost.

61. Narcissus, like Pallas, was one of Claudius' most notorious freedmen, and both appear frequently from now on. Narcissus' "Appian murder" was that of Appius Junius Silanus (4.68.1n.) in 42.

62. The plurals are rhetorical; each name refers to an alleged former lover of Messalina: Titius Proculus (11.35.3), Vettius Valens (11.31.3, 35.3), and Plautius Lateranus (11.36.4).

63. Claudius (but the text of the remainder of the sentence is by no means certain).

knowledgment, the others enveloped him with rival cries: he should go to the army, he should consolidate the praetorian cohorts, he should consider security before revenge. It is generally agreed that Claudius was deluged by such panic that he asked repeatedly whether he himself was in control of the empire and whether Silius was a private citizen.

As for Messalina, never more dissolute in her luxuriousness, with autumn at   2
its height she was celebrating a burlesque of the vintage throughout the house: press-beams were being lowered, vats were flowing, and females girded with pelts were leaping about like sacrificing or raving Bacchants. The woman herself, with flowing hair and waving a wand, and by her side Silius, wreathed with ivy, were wearing buskins and tossing their heads, while a provocative chorus voiced cries all around. It is maintained that Vettius Valens had recklessly struggled up a very   3
tall tree and, when asked what he was looking at, replied "A frightful storm from Ostia," whether such a spectacle had in fact begun or whether an utterance which had slipped out by chance turned into a prophecy.

Meanwhile it was no rumor but messengers who arrived from all sides to bring   **32**
the news that everything was known to Claudius and he was on his way, ready for vengeance. So Messalina and Silius parted, she to the Lucullian Gardens, he, dissembling his dread, to his responsibilities in the forum. As the rest were slipping off in different directions, centurions appeared and clapped chains on whomsoever they discovered in public or in some hiding-place; but Messalina, though ad-   2
versity was depriving her of reason, was not sluggish in determining to meet and be seen by her husband, where she had often found support, and she sent word that Britannicus and Octavia should proceed to their father's embrace. And she begged Vibidia, the most long-standing of the Vestal Virgins, to approach the ears of the high priest and seek clemency. Meanwhile, having covered the length of   3
the City on foot with only three to accompany her (such was her sudden isolation), she started along the Ostian Way in a vehicle by which the clearings from gardens are carried off[+]—to sympathy from no one, because the grotesque nature of her outrages was having too much effect.

Nonetheless there was trepidation on Caesar's part: he[+] did not have sufficient   **33**
trust in Geta, the praetorian prefect, whose attitude toward honor and crookedness alike was one of equal levity. Narcissus therefore, having enlisted the services of men whose dread was the same as his own, affirmed that there was no hope of Caesar's preservation unless he transferred jurisdiction of the soldiers to one of the freedmen for that single day, and he offered himself as the one to undertake it. And, lest Claudius on his journey to the City should have his mind changed to regret by L. Vitellius and Largus Caecina,[64] Narcissus demanded a seat in the same conveyance and was taken along. (There was a frequent report thereafter that in be-   **34**
tween the contrary utterances of the princeps—since sometimes he censured the outrages of his wife, at others he reverted to the memory of his espousal and the infancy of his children—Vitellius' only exclamation was "Oh, the deed! Oh, the

64. C. Caecina Largus had been consul with Claudius in 42.

crime!" Narcissus kept hounding him to clear up its ambiguity[65] and to provide them with access to its meaning; but he still failed to prevail upon him, except to the extent that the man's replies were weighed and likely to come down on whichever side one tipped the scales; and Largus Caecina followed his example.)

2   And already Messalina was in sight and shouting repeatedly that Claudius should listen to the mother of Octavia and Britannicus, when her accuser cried out in protest, referring to Silius and the wedding; at the same time he handed

3   over notes informing on her lusts, to distract Caesar's gaze. And not long after, as the latter was entering the City, their mutual children were in the process of being brought to him, but Narcissus ordered their removal. In the case of Vibidia, however, he was unable to deflect her from importuning, with considerable indignation, that his spouse should not be given up to extermination undefended. So Narcissus replied that the princeps would listen to her and there would be an opportunity of wiping out the charge: meanwhile the Virgin should go and perform her rituals.

35   During all this there was an amazing silence from Claudius; Vitellius was close to incomprehension: there was universal obedience to the freedman. He ordered the adulterer's house to be opened up and the Commander escorted there. And first, in the forecourt, he pointed out a likeness of Silius' father, abolished by a decision of the senate,[66] secondly all the heirlooms of the Nerones and Drusi

2   which had constituted the cost of dishonor. And he took him, now blazing and erupting into threats, to the camp, where there had been arranged a meeting of the soldiers, in whose presence, after a prefatory warning from Narcissus, he spoke only a few words (shame prevented him from manifesting his albeit justified indignation). Thereupon there was one continuous shout from the cohorts, importuning for the names of the accused and their punishment; and, when Silius was moved up to the platform, he attempted no defense, no delay, begging

3   only that his death be speeded up. The same steadfastness was shown by illustrious Roman equestrians too,[67] such was their desire⁺ for a quick execution. Titius Proculus, who had been given by Silius to Messalina as a guard and was offering information, and Vettius Valens, who had confessed, and Pompeius Urbicus and Saufeius Trogus from among her accomplices—all these he ordered to be handed over for reprisals. Decrius Calpurnianus too, prefect of the watchmen, Sulpicius Rufus, procurator of a school,[68] and Juncus Vergilianus, a senator, had the same punishment inflicted on them.

65. Vitellius' exclamation might refer equally to Messalina's wedding or to Narcissus' own campaign against her.

66. Presumably in A.D. 24 in the aftermath of the father's trial and suicide (4.18.1–20.1).

67. Since "steadfastness" does not characterize at least the first of the four men named in the next sentence, it seems unlikely that they are the "illustrious Roman equestrians" mentioned here; perhaps we should assume a lacuna in which the illustrious equestrians were named.

68. Of gladiators. The "watchmen" (above) combined the duties of police and fire brigade.

Only Mnester occasioned some hesitation, his clothing rent, and shouting re-   **36**
peatedly that Claudius should look at the marks of his beatings and remember
the words with which he had made him liable to Messalina's orders:[69] the guilt
of others, he said, was caused by lavishness or by the magnitude of their hopes,
his own by necessity; no one would have had to perish sooner, were Silius in
charge of affairs. Moved by these words, and leaning toward pity, Caesar was com-   2
pelled by his freedmen not to pay heed to an actor when so many illustrious men
had been killed: whether his serious malpractices had been spontaneous or under compulsion made no difference. Not even the defense of Traulus Montanus,   3
a Roman equestrian, was accepted: youthfully modest but distinguished physically, he had been summoned by Messalina of her own accord and within a
single night thrust aside, her recklessness being the same in respect of desire and
disdain. In the cases of Suillius Caesoninus and Plautius Lateranus, death was re-   4
mitted, for the latter because of his uncle's exceptional service;[70] Caesoninus was
protected by his vices, on the grounds that in that foulest of throngs his had been
the passive role of a woman.[71]

Meanwhile Messalina in the Lucullian Gardens was prolonging her life and   **37**
composing a plea with some degree of hope and occasionally of anger (such was
the haughtiness with which she acted in those extreme circumstances); and, had
not Narcissus hastened her slaughter, ruin would have rebounded on her accuser.
For, when Claudius had returned home and been soothed by a timely dinner,   2
on growing warm with wine he ordered someone to go and tell "the pitiable
woman" (this was the expression they maintain he used) to be present on the
next day to make her case. When Narcissus heard this, and anger started to wane
and love return, the approaching night and the man's memory of his wife's bedroom became grounds for fear if there was any hesitation: so he burst out and
told the centurions and the tribune who was present to proceed with the slaughter: such was the Commander's order. Euodus, one of the freedmen, was
provided as guard and agent; and, hurriedly going ahead into the gardens, he dis-   3
covered her stretched on the ground, her mother, Lepida, sitting alongside—who,
without affection for her daughter when she flourished, had been won over to
pity by her final crisis and was urging her not to wait for her assailant: her life
had passed, she said, and there was nothing to be sought except glory in her death.
But in a mind so corrupted by lusts there was no trace of honor: her tearful com-   4
plaints were being drawn out pointlessly when the gates were driven in by the

69. "Claudius ... told Mnester to do whatever he was ordered to do by Messalina" (Dio
60.22.5).

70. Plautius Lateranus later returns to the senate in 55 (13.11.2) and is prominent in the
Pisonian plot against Nero in 65 (15.49.3, 60.1). His uncle was A. Plautius, who led the
invasion of Britain in 43 and stayed on as first governor until 47, when he was awarded
an ovation (13.32.1).

71. Suillius Caesoninus was one of the sons of Suillius Rufus (11.1.1n.) to whom abusive reference was made at 11.2.1.

assault of the arrivals and there stood in front of her the tribune in silence, the
38 freedman berating her with much slavish abuse. That was her first moment of insight into her true situation: she took the sword, and, while tremblingly moving it to her throat and chest in vain, she was transfixed by a blow from the tribune.

2   Her corpse was conceded to her mother, and Claudius was told while dining that Messalina had perished, without its being specified whether by her own or another's hand; and he for his part did not ask: he called for a cup and celebrated

3   the routines of the party. Not even during the following days did he give signs of hatred, joy, anger, sadness, or, in fine, of any human emotion—not when he saw her delighted accusers, not when he saw her children sorrowing. And his oblivion was helped by the senate in voting that her name and likenesses be re-

4   moved from public and private places. Narcissus was decreed quaestorian insignia—the merest triviality for one so disdainful, since he acted above Pallas and Callistus. ★★★ honorable things indeed, but from which the basest would arise, amid the general grimness.[72]

---

72. The last extant "sentence" of Book 11 is corrupt and seems incomplete: hence the hypothesis of a lacuna at the start, in which it would have been made clear what "things" T. is referring to.

Book 12

On the slaughter of Messalina the princeps's household was wrenched apart, **1** competition having arisen among the freedmen as to who would choose a wife for Claudius, intolerant as he was of celibate life and submissive to spouses' commands. No less was the self-aggrandizement with which the ladies burned: each brought into contention her nobility, good looks, and wealth and paraded herself as worthy of so great a marriage; but the greatest dispute was between Lol- **2** lia Paulina, granddaughter of the consular M. Lollius,[1] and Julia Agrippina, the offspring of Germanicus. The latter was being groomed by her supporter, Pallas, the former by hers, Callistus; but Aelia Paetina, from the family of the Tuberones, was favored by Narcissus. Claudius himself, sometimes tending in one direction and sometimes in another (depending on which of the recommendations he had heard), called the quarrelers to a council and ordered them to tender their opinion and adduce reasons.

Narcissus mentioned their old marriage,[2] their mutual daughter (Antonia was **2** Paetina's), and that there would be no strange novelty at his hearth if a familiar spouse returned, one who was not at all likely to look with stepmotherly hatred on Britannicus and Octavia, pledges of affection closest to her own. But for Cal- **2** listus she was rejected by her long-standing divorce, and, if she were taken on again, she would be haughty for that very reason: it would be a long way better, he said, to introduce Lollia, who, since she had borne no children, would be exempt from rivalry and would take the place of a parent for her stepchildren. As **3** for Pallas, he praised especially in Agrippina the fact that with her she brought Germanicus' grandson, altogether worthy of a Commander's fortune:[3] the princeps should espouse a noble stock such as the posterity of the Julian and Claudian families, lest a lady of proved fertility, her youth unimpaired, should take the brilliancy of the Caesars to another household.

It was these points which prevailed, aided by Agrippina's allurements: by go- **3** ing to him very frequently under the guise of their relationship, she lured her uncle with the result that she was preferred to the others and, though not yet his wife, already enjoyed wifely power. For, when she was certain of her own **2** marriage, she laid the foundations of something greater and engineered the wedding of Domitius, whom she had borne to Cn. Ahenobarbus, and Octavia, Caesar's daughter—which could not be accomplished without crime, because Caesar had betrothed Octavia to L. Silanus and by means of triumphal insignia and the magnificence of a gladiatorial show had brought the young man, brilliant as he was in other respects too, to the enthusiastic attention of the pub-

---

1. M. Lollius (1.10.4n., 3.48.2n.) had been consul in 21 B.C.

2. Aelia Paetina had been Claudius' second wife, whom he had divorced roughly a decade earlier.

3. The grandson is L. Domitius, the future emperor Nero (11.11.2).

lic.[4] Yet nothing seemed too steep, given the mentality of a princeps who showed neither approval nor hatred unless each had been implanted and ordered.

4   Therefore Vitellius, cloaking his slavish deceptions under the name of censor, and with a weather eye for impending dominations,[5] wrapped himself in Agrippina's plans in order to procure influence with her, and he brought charges against Silanus, whose admittedly handsome and provocative sister, Junia Calvina, had

2   not long before been Vitellius' daughter-in-law.[6] Hence the starting-point of the accusation: he ascribed the siblings' love—which was not incestuous but indiscreet—to something infamous; and Caesar lent his ear, being all the readier, given

3   his affection for his daughter, to entertain suspicions toward a son-in-law. As for Silanus, unaware of the ambush and by chance praetor in that year, he was suddenly removed from the senatorial order by an edict of Vitellius, despite the senate's having been revised previously and the ritual purification performed.[7] At the same time Claudius broke off his connection with him, and Silanus was driven to forswear his magistracy;[8] the remaining day of his praetorship was conferred on Eprius Marcellus.[9]

★ ★ ★

5   With C. Pompeius and Q. Veranius as consuls,[10] the marriage pact between Claudius and Agrippina was already being reinforced by report and illicit love; but they did not yet dare to celebrate the solemnities of a wedding, there being no precedent for a brother's daughter being escorted to the house of her uncle: in fact it was incestuous; and, if that point were spurned, there was the dread that

2   it would erupt into a public calamity. Their uncertainty was not abandoned un-

4. L. Junius Silanus was son of M. Junius Silanus (the consul of 19: 2.59.1), brother of the consuls of 46 (M. Silanus) and 53 (D. Silanus Torquatus: 12.58.1), and a great-great-grandson of Augustus.

5. "Dominations" is primarily a reference to the reign of L. *Domi*tius, otherwise known as Nero (see further below, 12.8.2). "Censor" is explained by the fact that L. Vitellius was Claudius' colleague in that office (see App. A).

6. She had been married to L. Vitellius' homonymous younger son (11.23.1n.), whom T. nowhere mentions.

7. See 11.23.3–5.

8. To "forswear" in the sense of renouncing or resigning on oath, the oath being that he had observed the laws during the tenure of his magistracy (see the joke at 13.14.1).

9. A notorious accuser (16.22.6, 28.1, 29.1) and suffect consul in 62 and 74; see also 13.33.3.

10. Q. Veranius was son of the homonym featured in the Tiberian books (2.56.4n.) and later governor of Britain in 57 (14.29.1). He was the dedicatee of a work on generalship by the Greek writer Onasander. C. Pompeius is not otherwise known.

til Vitellius undertook to accomplish the matter by means of his own special methods, and he ascertained of Caesar whether he would yield to the orders of the people, to the authority of the senate. When the latter replied that he was only one of the citizens and no match for a consensus, Vitellius ordered him to wait within the Palatium.

Vitellius entered the curia and, claiming that the highest matters of state were   3 at issue, demanded leave to speak before others and began: the very heavy labors involved in the princeps' governing the globe needed some support so that he might be exempt from domestic care when paying heed to the common good. What more honorable solace was there for the censorial mind than to enlist a spouse, a partner in prosperity and doubt, to whom he might entrust his intimate thoughts and his small children, unaccustomed as he was to luxuriousness or pleasures but a man who from early youth had observed the laws?

After he had delivered this preliminary speech to win goodwill, and the fathers'   6 indulgence followed, he made a second beginning: since everyone was urging that the princeps should marry, it was necessary to select a lady who was distinguished in nobility, in childbearing, and in sanctity: it would not take a long examination to find out that, in the brilliancy of her lineage, Agrippina excelled; she had given proof of her fertility; and she had the corresponding honorable attainments. What was exceptional, however, was that, by the foresight of the gods,   2 a widow would be joined to a princeps who had experienced only his own marriages.[11] The senators had heard from their parents—had themselves seen—that spouses were snatched at the whims of the Caesars; but that was remote from the current restraint. Let them establish a paradigm whereby the Commander might receive a wife from the state.[+] It might be said that espousals for the daughters   3 of brothers were a novelty in our case. Yet they were solemnized by other nations and not prohibited by any law; and those of second cousins and cousins,[+] for long ignored, had appeared with the accretion of time. Custom accommodated itself as was advantageous, and this too would be among the things that were soon in general use.

There was no lack of men to erupt from the curia competing to testify that,   7 if Caesar hesitated, they would act by force; an indiscriminate crowd gathered, and shouted repeatedly that the prayer of the Roman people was the same. As   2 for Claudius, he waited no further: in encounters in the forum he presented himself to the well-wishers and, entering the senate, demanded a decree whereby formal weddings between uncles and daughters of brothers should be established, even for the future. (Yet there was discovered but one desirer of such a marriage, Alledius Severus, a Roman equestrian whose motive was maintained by many to have been to gain influence with Agrippina.) It was as a result of this that the   3

11. I.e., he had not been an adulterer (see the following sentence, where "the whims of the Caesars" refers to Augustus (1.10.5, 5.1.2) and Caligula). Agrippina's previous husbands, Cn. Domitius Ahenobarbus (4.75) and C. Passienus Crispus (6.20.1), were now dead: hence her description here as "a widow."

community was overturned, and there was universal obedience to a female who did not, like Messalina, sport with Roman affairs through recklessness: it was a tightly controlled and (so to speak) manlike servitude. Openly there was severity, and more often haughtiness; there was no domestic immorality unless it availed domination. An inordinate desire for gold had as its screen that a bulwark was being prepared for the kingdom.

8   On the day of the wedding Silanus encompassed his own death, whether he had prolonged his hope of life right up to that point or having selected the day to increase resentment. His sister, Calvina, was banished from Italy. Claudius added that rituals had to be offered in accordance with the laws of King Tullus, and expiations by the pontiffs at the grove of Diana—to universal derision that punishments and propitiations for incest were being sought at that precise time.

2   Yet Agrippina, lest she should become known only for evil acts, successfully requested remission of exile on behalf of Annaeus Seneca, and a praetorship too, deeming it would be publicly welcome owing to the brilliancy of his studies; also so that Domitius' boyhood might develop under such a master and they might likewise use his counsel for their hope of domination, because it was believed[12] that Seneca would be loyal to Agrippina owing to the memory of her good deed and ferocious toward Claudius owing to indignation at pain of his wrong.[13]

9   It was next decided to hesitate no further, but by means of mighty promises they induced Mammius Pollio, consul designate, to produce a motion whereby Claudius was begged to betroth Octavia to Domitius, something which was not inappropriate to the age of each and likely to clear the way for still greater things.

2   Pollio proposed in words no different from those of Vitellius recently; and Octavia was betrothed, and Domitius—now son-in-law by troth, in addition to his previous relationship[14]—became the equal of Britannicus through the efforts of his mother and the skill of those who, for having accused Messalina, feared vengeance from her son.

10   During the same period legates of the Parthians, sent (as I have recorded)[15] to ask for Meherdates, entered the senate and began their instructions in this way: they did not come in ignorance of the treaty nor defecting from the family of the Arsacidae but were resorting to the son of Vonones,⁺ grandson of Phraates, against Gotarzes' domination, intolerable as it was to nobility and plebs alike. Already brothers, kin, and those more distantly placed had been swallowed up by

12. By Agrippina and her supporters.

13. In the extant *Annals* this is T.'s first mention of Seneca, the famous and fabulously wealthy author and philosopher who will play a prominent part in the later narrative. In 41 he had been exiled for alleged adultery with Julia Livilla, daughter of Germanicus. Something of Seneca's attitude to Claudius may be gleaned from his satirical *Apocolocyntosis*.

14. Viz. that of stepson and great-nephew (his mother being both Claudius' current wife and daughter of Germanicus, Claudius' brother).

15. See 11.10.4.

his slaughters; now pregnant spouses and small children were being added while, lethargic at home and in war ill-starred, he covered his cowardice by savagery. Their friendship with us was long-standing and had been inaugurated officially, 2 and help should be given to allies who rivaled our resources but yielded to us out of respect. The very purpose of giving their kings' children as hostages was that, if they wearied of their local command, there should be recourse to prin-ceps and fathers, an habituation to whose customs would mean that a better king was adopted.

When they had spoken words such as these, Caesar began a speech on the ex- **11** altedness of Rome and on Parthian compliance, and he made himself the equal to Divine Augustus, recollecting the king sought from the latter but thereby ne-glecting the memory of Tiberius, although he had sent out kings too.[16] He added 2 as precepts (Meherdates was present) that he should think, not in terms of dom-ination over slaves, but of being a guide for citizens, and he should embrace clemency and justice, their unfamiliarity among barbarians making them all the more welcome. Then, turning to the legates, he extolled with praise the City's 3 foster-child, whose modestness up to then had been clear for all to see; never-theless the temperaments of kings had to be borne, and frequent changes were not useful: Roman interests, through a satiety of glory, had advanced to the point where calm was wanted for foreign nations too.

*

Afterward C. Cassius, who was in charge of Syria,[17] was entrusted with escort-ing the young man to the bank of the Euphrates. (At that time it was in his **12** expertise at law that Cassius towered above the rest: for military skills were un-familiar owing to the period of calm, and peace keeps the industrious and the shirkers at the same level. And yet, insofar as was permitted without warfare, he revived the old-time conventions, exercised his legions, and acted with concern and foresight as if an enemy were closing in, deeming this to be worthy of his ancestors and of the Cassian family, celebrated as it was across those nations too.)[18] Having summoned those on whose proposal the king had been sought, he 2 pitched camp at Zeugma (the stream being particularly passable from there); but, after the illustrious Parthians and the king of the Arabs, Acbarus, had arrived, he warned Meherdates that the keen impulses of barbarians either wane with delay or change to disloyalty: thus he should press on with his undertaking. But this 3 warning was spurned owing to foul play from Acbarus, by whom the ignorant

16. The king sent by Augustus was Vonones I (see 2.1.2 and n.); for Tiberius' involve-ment see 6.31–2.

17. C. Cassius Longinus was brother of L. Cassius Longinus (6.15.1) and suffect consul in 30. See further 13.41.4, 13.48, 14.43–4, and elsewhere.

18. C. Cassius Longinus, the assassin of Julius Caesar, had conducted a heroic salvage op-eration in Syria after the notorious defeat of Crassus at Carrhae in 53 B.C.

young man, deeming that the highest fortune consisted in luxuriousness, was
detained for many days at the town of Edessa. And despite a call from Carenes[19]
and his demonstration that things were ready if they arrived quickly,
Meherdates made not directly for Mesopotamia but by a detour for Armenia,
inhospitable at that precise time because winter was commencing. Subse-

13 quently, exhausted by snows and mountains, on their approach to the plains
they joined forces with Carenes; and, having crossed the Tigris stream, they
made their way through the Adiabeni, whose king, Izates, had openly donned
an alliance with Meherdates but in a secret and greater loyalty was inclining to-

2 ward Gotarzes. Yet in their traverse they captured the city of Ninos, the most
olden settlement of Assyria, and a stronghold distinguished by the report that
in the final battle between Darius and Alexander the dominion of the Persians
had collapsed there.

3   Meanwhile Gotarzes, at a mountain whose name is Sanbulos, was offering
vows to the gods of the place—and with particular scrupulousness to Hercules,
who at a regular time warns the priests during their slumber that beside the temple they should station horses caparisoned for hunting. When the horses have
been given quivers laden with weapons, they go roving through the denes, finally returning at night with much panting, their quivers empty. The god once
again in a nighttime appearance indicates where he has wandered through the

14 woods, and wild animals are discovered strewn everywhere. As for Gotarzes, having not yet sufficiently augmented his army, he used the River Corma as a defensive fortification and, though he was challenged to battle in abusive messages,
he wove delays, kept changing his position and, by the dispatch of bribers to strip
away their loyalty, started buying off the enemy. Of these, Izates the Adiabene and
then Acbarus with his army of Arabs withdrew, such being their national fickle-
ness and because it has been recognized by experience that barbarians prefer to

2 seek kings from Rome than to keep them. Meherdates, denuded of effective auxiliaries, and suspecting betrayal from the rest, decided (it was the only thing left)
to commit the matter to chance and to experiment with battle. And Gotarzes
did not decline the fight, defiant as he was with the enemy numbers diminished;
and they converged with great slaughter and uncertain outcome, until Carenes,
carried too far after crushing his opponents, was surrounded by a fresh cluster

3 from the rear. With all hope then lost, Meherdates, following up promises from
Parraces, a client of his father, fell victim to the man's guile and was handed over
to the victor. The latter for his part, berating him as neither kin nor of the race
of Arsaces but an alien and a Roman, ordered him to remain alive with his ears

4 lopped off—an exhibition of his own clemency, and for us a disgrace. (Subsequently Gotarzes died of disease and Vonones, at that time presiding the Medes,
was summoned to the kingdom. He experienced neither prosperity nor adver-

19. Not previously mentioned in the extant narrative but evidently in charge of
Mesopotamia.

sity by which he might be recalled: he completed a brief and inglorious command, and the affairs of the Parthians passed to his son Vologaeses.)[20]

As for Bosporan Mithridates, who was roving about after the loss of his do-   **15**
minion,[21] he learned that Didius, the Roman leader,[22] and the hard core of his
army had departed and that remaining in the new kingdom were Cotys, a raw
young man, and a few cohorts with Julius Aquila, a Roman equestrian; spurning
them both, he roused the nations and enticed deserters; and finally, having gathered an army, he evicted the king of the Dandaridae and took control of his empire. When Aquila and Cotys heard this and considered him to be on the very   2
point of invading Bosporus, they too, distrusting their own forces (because
Zorsines, king of the Siraci, had resumed hostilities), sought foreign kindness by
sending legates to Eunones, who presided over the race of the Aorsi. And it was
no steep task to form an alliance with those who could exhibit Roman power
against the rebel Mithridates. Therefore they fixed that Eunones would direct his
efforts to the cavalry battles, the Romans would undertake blockades of cities.

After that they advanced in a combined column, whose front and rear were pro-   **16**
tected by the Aorsi, its middle by the cohorts and by the Bosporani under our arms.
In this way the enemy was beaten and Soza reached, a town of Dandarica deserted
by Mithridates, which, owing to the ambivalent feelings of the locals, it seemed
proper to hold by leaving a garrison there. Next they proceeded to the Siraci and,   2
crossing the Panda stream, surrounded the city of Uspe, elevated in position and
fortified by walls and ditches, except that the walls, being not of rock but of wicker
hurdles with earth in between, were ineffective against an irruption: the extension
of turrets[23] to a greater height created, with their torches and spears, disruption
among those blockaded; and, had night not broken off the battle, the storming
would have been started and accomplished within the same day. On the next,   **17**
legates were sent begging pardon for all free persons and making an offer of ten
thousand slaves. This the victors spurned, because butchering the surrendered
would be savage, while encircling so large a multitude with a guard would be steep:
rather let them fall by the code of war. And the soldiers who had clambered up on
ladders were given the signal for slaughter.

20. This is Vologeses I, king of Parthia A.D. 51/52–79/80, who will feature prominently
in T.'s later narrative, esp. 15.1–17 and 24–31. See *OCD* 1611.

21. In A.D. 41 Claudius had granted the vacant kingdom of Bosporus to Mithridates
VIII (to be distinguished from the other homonyms mentioned by T.), who within a few
years was removed by Didius Gallus and replaced by a brother, Cotys. This series of events
(see *OCD* 254 and 466–7 s.vv. Bosporus (2) and Didius Gallus) was no doubt narrated in
the portion of the *Annals* which is now lost.

22. A. Didius Gallus, suffect consul in 39, was governor of Moesia from 44 and of Britain
52–7 (12.40.1, 14.29.1).

23. Used in assaults on cities and the like.

2   The extirpation of the Uspenses struck dread into the rest, who deemed nothing safe now that armies, fortifications, impassable or towering positions, and
streams and cities alike were being breached. Therefore, after Zorsines had
weighed up for a long time whether to give thought to Mithridates' extreme situation or to his own ancestral kingdom, national advantage prevailed and, giving hostages, he prostrated himself before a likeness of Caesar—a great glory for
the Roman army, which, unbloodied and victorious, was agreed to be only a

3   three-day journey from the Tanais stream. But on the return its fortune was different, because some of the ships (they were retiring by sea) were carried to the
shores of the Tauri and surrounded by barbarians, with the prefect of a cohort
and numerous auxiliaries killed.

18   Meanwhile Mithridates, with no support in arms, debated whose pity he
might try: his brother Cotys, his betrayer formerly and then his enemy, was an
object of dread; and not one of the Romans present was of the degree of authority to attach much weight to his promises. He turned to Eunones, who lacked
the ferocity of personal hatred and had the influence of a friendship recently

2   joined with us. Therefore, adapting his apparel and appearance as much as possible to his current situation, he entered the palace and groveled at the man's knees,
saying "I, Mithridates, sought by the Romans on land and sea for so many years,
am present of my own accord. Deal as you wish with the progeny of great Achae-

19   menes, the one thing which my enemies have not taken from me." Eunones,
moved by the man's brilliancy, his change of circumstance, and his not unbecoming prayer, raised up the suppliant and praised him for choosing the nation of the
Aorsi and his own right hand for seeking pardon. At the same time he sent legates

2   with a letter to Caesar in this manner: between the Commanders of the Roman
people and the kings of great nations there was first a friendship based on similarity of fortune, but between himself and Claudius there was also a sharing of

3   victory. Wars ended exceptionally well when things were settled by forgiveness:
so, for example, nothing had been seized from the conquered Zorsines; but on
behalf of Mithridates, who deserved sterner treatment, he was begging neither
power nor kingship but that the man should not be subjected to a triumph or
pay the penalty with his life.

20   But Claudius, though mild to foreign nobilities, was nevertheless in doubt
whether it would be better to accept the captive under a pact for his safety or to
reclaim him by arms. In the latter respect he was being driven by indignation at
his wrongs and by a lust for vengeance; but it was said on the other side that a
war would be undertaken along a trackless route, across a harborless sea; in addition to this there were defiant kings, roving peoples, soil devoid of crops, the
weariness of delay, the risks of rushing, the limited praise for the victors, and the
degree of infamy if they were beaten. Why not seize what was offered and preserve the exile, since, the longer a destitute's life, the greater the reprisal?

2   Moved by these words, he wrote to Eunones that Mithridates had indeed deserved the ultimate exemplary treatment, and he himself did not lack the power
to follow it through; but our ancestors had decided that one should show as much

kindness toward suppliants as persistence against an enemy: it was over unbroken
peoples and kingdoms that triumphs were sought. After this, having been handed   **21**
over and conveyed to Rome by Junius Cilo, the procurator of Pontus, Mithridates was said to have spoken before Caesar more defiantly than his fortune warranted, and his voice carried to the public outside in these terms: "I have not
been sent back to you but have come back; if you do not believe me, send me
away and search." His appearance too remained unafraid when, next to the rostra and surrounded by guards, he was presented for the people to behold. To Cilo
were decreed consular insignia, praetorian to Aquila.

★

With the same men as consuls, Agrippina, frightening in her hatred and hostile   **22**
toward Lollia because she had been her competitor over marrying the princeps,
engineered charges and an accuser who would hurl imputations against her about
the Chaldaeans,[24] about magicians, and that the representation of Apollo Clar-
ius had been questioned about the Commander's wedding. Thereupon Claudius,   2
without hearing the defendant, made numerous prefatory remarks before the
senate about her brilliancy—that she was born of L. Volusius' sister, her great uncle was Cotta Messalinus, and she had once been wedded to Memmius Regulus
(he deliberately kept silent about her wedding to C. Caesar)[25] —and then added
that her plans were ruinous to the state and her means for crime should be removed: accordingly, her property confiscated, she should withdraw from Italy.
Thus only five million sesterces from her inordinate wealth were left to the exile. Calpurnia too, an illustrious lady, was overthrown because the princeps had   3
praised her good looks—not in lust but in a chance conversation: hence Agrippina's anger stopped short of the ultimate; but against Lollia was sent a tribune
to drive her to death.[26] Also condemned, under the law of extortion, was Cadius
Rufus, on the accusation of the Bithynians.

To Narbonese Gaul, on account of its exceptional respect for the fathers, per-   **23**
mission was given that senators of the province should be allowed the prerogative, which obtained in Sicily, of visiting their own estates without seeking the
princeps's view of the matter. The Ituraeans and the Judaeans, on the demise of
their kings Sohaemus and Agrippa, were added to the province of Syria. It was
agreed that the augury of Salus, neglected for twenty-five years, should be revived and then continued.[27] And the perimeter of the City was augmented by   2
Caesar—an old-time convention whereby those who extended the empire are

24. See 2.27.2n. for Chaldaeans.

25. Lollia's mother, Volusia, was sister of L. Volusius Saturninus (suffect consul in A.D. 3);
Cotta Messalinus was consul in 20 (2.32.1n., 3.2.3). Her first marriage was to P. Memmius
Regulus, suffect consul in 31 (5.11.1); her brief marriage to Caligula was her second.

26. I.e., to force her to commit suicide.

27. This was an augural inquiry to discover whether the magistrates might properly pray

permitted to enlarge the boundaries of the City also;[28] and yet no Roman leader had put it into practice, despite the great nations subjugated, except L. Sulla and

24 Divine Augustus. (Varying publicity has been given to the self-aggrandizement or glory of the kings in that regard, but I deem it not inappropriate to recognize the beginning of its foundation and what perimeter was laid down by Romulus. So, from the Forum Boarium—where we see the bronze representation of a bull, because that is the species of animal which is harnessed to a plow—it[29] started as a furrow for marking out the town, taking in the great altar of Hercules. From there, at regular distances, stones were interspersed across the base of the Palatine Hill to Consus' altar; next, to the old curiae;[30] then to the shrine of

2 the Lares. The Roman forum and Capitol were believed to have been additions to the City not by Romulus but by Titus Tatius. Later the perimeter was augmented in step with our good fortune; and the boundaries which Claudius laid down at that time are easy to recognize and are written down in the public records.)[31]

★   ★   ★

25 With C. Antistius and M. Suillius as consuls,[32] adoption was being hurried up for Domitius on the instigation of Pallas, who, bound to Agrippina as the arranger of her wedding and soon entangled with her in illicit sex, was goading Claudius to heed the interests of the state and to place a protective cordon of maturity around the boyhood of Britannicus:[33] similarly in the house of Divine Augustus, although he had been supported by his grandsons, his stepsons had thrived;

---

for the safety of the people (*OCD* 214 s.v. augurium salutis). Agrippa (above) is M. Julius Agrippa I, who is thought to have died in 44.

28. See *OCD* 1213–14 s.v. pomerium. Claudius had celebrated a victory over Britain in 43 (see, e.g., Braund 210 (b) = WM 29, an inscription from several years later).

29. Viz. the perimeter (but the precise articulation of this whole passage is highly uncertain).

30. Assembly halls.

31. It is not certain what is meant by the expression "public records" (*publicis actis*), which is also used by T.'s friend, the younger Pliny (*Letters* 5.13.8, 7.33.3, the latter addressed to T. himself). It may be an alternative way of referring to the daily gazette (3.3.2n.).

32. C. Antistius Vetus, who had already been suffect consul in 46, was son of the consul of 23 (4.1.1n.); M. Suillius Nerullinus was son of P. Suillius Rufus (11.1.1n.) and brother of Suillius Caesoninus (11.36.4n.).

33. It is not clear whether this strange expression is a metaphor from military defense (as translated) or from dressing in clothes or armor (like "equip" just below). The meaning is that Britannicus is so young that he needs to be protected from public affairs by Claudius' relying on someone older such as Domitius (*robore* suggests maturity as well as stout protection).

Tiberius, besides his own stock, had enlisted Germanicus: the princeps too should equip himself with the young man likely to take on a share of his cares. Won over   2 by these words, Claudius gave Domitius—the elder by three years—precedence over his son, delivering before the senate a speech along the same lines as those which he had been given by his freedman. (Experts noted that no previous adoption could be discovered among the patrician Claudii and that they had lasted continuously from Attus Clausus.)

Gratitude was expressed to the princeps, with a more studied sycophancy   **26** toward Domitius, and a law was approved whereby he crossed to the Claudian family and its name of "Nero." Agrippina too was augmented with the nomenclature "Augusta."[34] With this accomplished, there was no one so devoid of pity   2 that he was not affected by sorrow at Britannicus' fortune. Gradually forsaken even by his slaves and their services, he turned his stepmother's quite unseasonable dutifulness into mockery, understanding its falsity: he was not slow by nature, they maintain—whether it was true or whether, having been acclaimed for his perils, he retained his reputation without proof.

★

But Agrippina, to display her influence to the allied nations too, successfully re-   **27** quested that at the town of the Ubii, in which she had been born, a colony of veterans should be settled, to which the name assigned was derived from her own designation.[35] (And by chance it had happened that that was the race which, on crossing the Rhine, was received by her grandfather Agrippa into our trust.)[36]

At the same time in Upper Germany there was trepidation at the arrival of   2 the Chatti in their pursuit of banditry. Thereupon P. Pomponius, the legate,[37] sent the auxiliary Vangiones and Nemetae, with the addition of a cavalry wing, warning them to forestall the pillagers or else, should they disperse, to pour around them unexpectedly. The leader's plan was followed by the soldiers' industry, and   3 they were divided into two columns. Those who had made for the left-hand route beset the recently returned enemy just as he had put his plunder to luxurious use and was heavy with sleep (their delight increased because after forty years they had delivered from servitude some of those from the Varian disaster[38]). But those who had gone by the right-hand and nearer shortcuts inflicted a   **28** greater disaster on the enemy, who had risked confronting them in line; and, laden with plunder and fame, they returned to Mount Taunus, where Pomponius was waiting with his legions to see if the Chatti, in a desire for vengeance, would provide the chance of a fight. But they for their part, in dread lest they be   2

34. See 2.14.1n. for the etymological play.
35. Colonia Agrippinensis.
36. The Ubii had asked to be settled across the Rhine in 38 B.C. (Dio 48.49.3).
37. P. Pomponius Secundus (5.8.1n.).
38. In A.D. 9 (1.3.6n.).

surrounded on the one side by the Roman and on the other by the Cherusci (with whom they are perpetually disaffected), sent legates and hostages to the City; and Pomponius was decreed triumphal honor—only a modest part of his fame with posterity, among whom he excels for the glory of his poems.[39]

29   During the same period Vannius, who had been installed over the Suebi by Drusus Caesar, was expelled from his kingdom:[40] brilliant as he was and acceptable to his compatriots in the first stage of his command, later, with its lengthy continuance, he changed to haughtiness and was beset by the hatred of his neighbors as well as by domestic disaffection. The instigators were Vibilius, king of the

2   Hermunduri, and Vangio and Sido, both born to Vannius' sister. Claudius, though often begged, did not interpose arms between the rival barbarians, promising Vannius a safe refuge if he were expelled; and he wrote to Palpellius Hister, who presided Pannonia, to deploy both a legion and, from the province itself, selected auxiliaries along the bank[41] as a support for the conquered and a deterrent to the

3   conquerors, lest, carried away by success, they should disrupt our peace too. For it was an uncountable force—Lugii and other races—which was on the march, given the famed riches of the kingdom which Vannius for thirty years had augmented through plundering and revenues. The king himself had his own unit of infantry, and cavalry from the Sarmatian Iazyges—no match for the enemy multitude, and for that reason he had decided to defense himself by strongholds and

30   to protract the war. But the Iazyges, impatient of blockade and roving across the nearest plains, brought on the necessity of a fight because that was where the Lugii and Hermunduri had closed in. So Vannius left his strongholds and was routed in battle—being praised, despite this reverse, because he both undertook

2   to fight in person and received wounds on the obverse of his body. He nevertheless made his escape to the fleet waiting on the Danube; soon his clients followed and, being given land, were located in Pannonia. Vangio and Sido shared his kingdom between themselves, their loyalty toward us being exceptional, while from their subjects they earned—whether it was due to their own nature or to that of servitude itself—considerable affection during their acquiring of domination but, after its acquisition, a still greater hatred.

31   In Britain P. Ostorius, the propraetor, was welcomed by disruption, the enemy pouring all the more violently into the allies' territory because they deemed that a new leader, with an unfamiliar army and the winter starting, would not go

2   against them.[42] He for his part, aware that it is first outcomes by which dread or confidence is generated, swept his fast cohorts along and, slaughtering the resistance, pursued those who had scattered, and—to prevent them from regrouping

39. See 5.8.1–2, 11.13.1.

40. For Vannius see 2.63.6.

41. Of the Danube (see 12.30.2 below). Sex. Palpellius Hister had been suffect consul in 43.

42. P. Ostorius Scapula, who had been suffect consul in the early 40s, became governor of Britain in 47 (whereas at 12.25.1 T. embarked on his narrative of 50: see 12.40.5).

and a ferocious and faithless peace from allowing no rest at all to either leader or soldiery—prepared to deprive suspects of their arms and to contain everything on this side of the Trisantona and Sabrina currents. This the Iceni were the first **3** to reject (an effective people and not ground down by battles, because they had willingly acceded to an alliance with us); and on their initiative the surrounding nations chose for the fight a place enclosed by a rustic rampart and with a narrow neck, so as not to be passable for cavalry. Such were the defenses which the **4** Roman leader, although he was leading only allied forces without the hard core of the legions, set himself to breach, and, disposing the cohorts, he equipped even the squadrons for the responsibilities of infantrymen. Then at a given signal they broke through the rampart and disrupted an enemy encumbered by their own barriers. The latter for their part, conscious of their rebellion and with their escape routes blocked off, did many brilliant deeds; and in the battle the legate's son, M. Ostorius, earned the honor of saving a citizen.[43]

The disaster to the Iceni calmed those who were hesitating between war and **32** peace, and the army was led against the Decangi. Land was devastated, plunder taken everywhere (the enemy not risking the battle line and, if they tried to pick off the column from concealed positions, having their guile punished), and they had arrived not far from the sea which looks toward the island of Hibernia when disaffection springing up among the Brigantes brought the leader back, fixed as he was in his design not to engineer new achievements without consolidating the earlier.

The Brigantes for their part—after the killing of a few of them who had begun to take up arms, and with pardon given to the rest—quietened down again; **2** but neither fright nor clemency could change the race of the Silures, who engaged in war and required to be suppressed by a legions' camp. So that this might come about more readily, the colony of Camulodunum with a substantial unit of veterans was settled in captured territory as a garrison against rebellion and to imbue the allies with a sense of duty toward the law. An expedition was then **33** made against the Silures, who, besides their natural defiance, relied on the strength of Caratacus, who had been elevated by many equivocal and many successful encounters, so that he towered over the other commanders of the Britons. But on that occasion, with the advantage of a tricky locality but disadvantaged by his force of soldiers, by a stratagem he transferred the war to the territory of the Ordovicae; and, with the addition of those who dreaded peace with us, he resorted to the ultimate hazard, adopting a place for battle so that entry, exit, everything would be unfavorable to us and for the better to his own men, with steep mountains all around,[+] and, wherever a gentle access was possible, he strewed rocks in front in the manner of a rampart. And in front too there flowed a stream with an unsure ford, and companies of armed men had taken up position along the defenses. In addition to this, the nations' leaders went around, encouraging and reinforcing their spirit by diminishing their dread, kindling their hope, and by the **34**

43. For this honor see 3.21.3n. M. Ostorius became suffect consul in 59.

other incitements of war. Moreover Caratacus, flying hither and thither, testified that this was the day, this the battle which would be the start either of the recovery of their freedom or of eternal slavery; and he called out the names of their ancestors who had beaten back the dictator Caesar and through whose courage they themselves, free from the axes and taxation,[44] kept undefiled the bodies of their spouses and children. As he said such things as these, the crowd bayed its approval; each man bound himself by his national sanction: to neither weapons nor wounds would they yield.

35   Their eagerness stunned the Roman leader; at the same time he was terrified by the stream barrier, the additional rampart, the looming ridges, the fact that there was nothing which was not frightening and replete with defenders. But his soldiery demanded battle, shouted repeatedly that everything was assailable with courage; and the prefects and tribunes, by saying similar things, intensified the ar-

2   dor of the army. Then Ostorius, after reconnoitering what was impenetrable and what passable, led his ferocious men onward and forded the stream without difficulty. After their arrival at the embankment, however, more wounds and considerable slaughter occurred on our side as long as the contest was with missiles; but, after the crude constructions of unshaped rocks had been split by the shell which had been formed,[45] and the battle lines at close quarters became matched,

3   the barbarians withdrew to the mountain ridges. But there too the lancers and heavy-armed soldiery burst in, the former dashing forward with their weapons, the latter in serried step, while on the other side there was disruption in the ranks of the Britons, among whom there were no breastplates or helmets to cover them: if they tried to resist the auxiliaries, they were mown down by the swords and javelins of the legionaries, and, if they turned toward the latter, by the claymores and spears of the auxiliaries.

It was a brilliant victory, and Caratacus' wife and daughter were captured and

36   his brothers received in surrender. The man himself had sought sanctuary with Cartimandua, queen of the Brigantes, but (adversity is generally unsafe) he was chained and handed over to the conquerors—in the ninth year after war in Britain began. It was for this reason that his fame carried beyond the island,+ spread through the neighboring provinces, and was celebrated even across Italy, and people craved to see who it was who for so many years had spurned our might.

2   Not even at Rome was the name of Caratacus unknown; and Caesar, in extolling his own prestige, added glory to the victim. The people were summoned as if to a distinctive spectacle; the praetorian cohorts stood under arms on the plain

3   which lies in front of their camp. And then, in a procession of his royal clients, the man's roundels and torques and everything that he had acquired in foreign

44. For axes see 1.59.4n.

45. The term "shell" is used either of a wooden screen to protect those engaged in siege operations or of a tightly packed group of soldiers holding their shields above themselves to form a shell-like covering. The latter is presumably meant here, but the matter is not certain.

wars were carried past, followed by his brothers and spouse and daughter, and finally the man himself on display. The prayers of the others ill became them by reason of their dread; but not Caratacus, who sought pity with neither abject look nor language but, when he stopped at the tribunal, spoke in this manner:

"If the degree of my nobility and fortune had been matched by moderation in success, I would have come to this City as friend rather than as captive, nor would you[46] have disdained to receive with a treaty of peace one sprung from brilliant ancestors and commanding a great many nations. But my present lot, disfiguring as it is for me, is magnificent for you. I had horses, men, arms, and wealth: what wonder if I was unwilling to lose them? If you wish to command everyone, does it really follow that everyone should accept your slavery? If I were now being handed over as one who had surrendered immediately, neither my fortune nor your glory would have achieved brilliance. It is also true that in my case any reprisal will be followed by oblivion. On the other hand, if you preserve me safe and sound, I shall be an eternal example of your clemency."

In response Caesar granted pardon to both him, his spouse and his brothers; and on release from their chains they for their part venerated Agrippina too, conspicuous not far away on another dais, using the same praise and gratitude as they had for the princeps. (It was of course a novelty, quite unfamiliar to the customs of the ancients, for a female to preside over Roman standards; but she was presenting herself as partner in the command once won by her ancestors.)[47]

Summoned afterward, the fathers said many magnificent things about the capture of Caratacus and that it was no less brilliant than when Syphax was displayed to the Roman people by P. Scipio, Perseus by L. Paullus,[48] and any other chained king by anyone else. To Ostorius were voted the insignia of a triumph, his affairs having been successful to that point—though soon equivocal, either because, with the removal of Caratacus, the soldiering on our side was less attentive, as if the war were over, or else the enemy, in their pity for so great a king, blazed more fiercely for vengeance. They poured around the prefect of the camp and the legionary cohorts which had been left to construct garrisons among the Silures; and, had not help come quickly from the nearest strongholds in response to messengers, they would have been laid low by the blockading forces.[49] As it was, the prefect and eight centurions and the readiest men in the maniples fell, and, not long after, they crushed those of our men seeking pasturage and the squadrons

37

2

3

4

38

2

3

---

46. All the second-person references in this speech, with the exception of those in the fourth sentence, are singular and addressed to Claudius.

47. Agrippina was great-granddaughter of Augustus and granddaughter of Agrippa, the architect of many of Augustus' victories: for a brief period after 13 B.C. the two men "had equal formal authority as rulers of the Roman world" (*CAH*² 10.97).

48. The dates were 201 and 167 B.C. respectively.

49. The "blockading forces" are the Britons and "they" (differently from the previous sentence and the next) are the Romans; but both the text and the precise meaning of this sentence are uncertain.

39 sent in support. That was the moment when Ostorius placed the unencumbered cohorts in the way; but, all the same, he would not have halted the flight if the legions had not taken over the battle. With their hard core, the fight leveled and then went the better for us; but the enemy fled off with only slender losses, because the day was declining.

2   There were frequent battles after this, more often in the manner of banditry: through denes, through marshes; dependent on the lot or courage of each man; rashly or with foresight; for anger, for plunder; by order and sometimes even without the leaders' knowledge. A principal factor was the persistence of the Silures, who were inflamed by the publicity given to the Roman commander's utterance that, just as once the Sugambri had been extirpated or transported to

3   the Galliae,[50] so the Silures' name had to be extinguished completely. They cut off two auxiliary cohorts which, on account of the greed of the prefects, were pillaging too incautiously; and, by being lavish with spoils and captives, they were drawing the other nations too into defecting when Ostorius, exhausted by weariness from his cares, departed from life—to the delight of the enemy, in that a

40 leader not to be spurned had been carried off, if not in battle, at least by war. But Caesar, hearing of the legate's death, substituted A. Didius so that the province should not be without a governor.[51] Though traveling there quickly, the latter nevertheless did not find affairs in a healthy state, an adverse fight having been suffered in the meantime by the legion of which Manlius Valens was in charge.[52] And the report of that event was exaggerated on the enemy side in order to terrify the arriving leader, while he for his part exaggerated the hearsay so that greater praise would be granted him for their pacification or, if they held out, a juster exoneration.

It was the Silures who had inflicted these losses too, and they were scouring

2   far and wide until beaten back by an onrush from Didius; but after the capture of Caratacus the principal in knowledge of military affairs was Venutius (from the community of the Brigantes, as I recalled above),[53] loyal for a long time and defended by Roman arms all the while his marriage to queen Cartimandua held; but, on the occurrence of their divorce and of immediate warfare, he had as-

3   sumed hostilities even against us too. Yet at first the struggle was only among themselves, and Cartimandua with her astute calculations cut off Venutius' brother and kinsmen. Inflamed by this, and goaded by the ignominious thought of submitting to her female command, the enemy—effective young men chosen for their armed fighting—invaded her kingdom. This had been foreseen by us, and the cohorts dispatched to help her made it a fierce battle, whose conclu-

4   sion was more welcome than its equivocal beginning. No different in outcome was the fighting of the legion of which Caesius Nasica was in charge: for Did-

---

50. I.e., resettled in the Gallic provinces (in 8 B.C.).

51. For A. Didius Gallus see above, 12.15.1n.

52. Manlius Valens would become consul in 96 at the age of ninety.

53. In the lost portion of the *Annals*.

ius, weighed down by old age and with an abundance of honors, considered it sufficient to act through assistants and merely to hold back the enemy.

(Though these were the achievements of two propraetors, Ostorius and Didi-   5
us, over several years, I linked them together lest their division might not render them as effective as their recollection deserves; but it is to the chronological order that I return.)

★ ★ ★

With Ti. Claudius (for the fifth time) and Servius Cornelius Orfitus as consuls,   **41**
the time was ripe for Nero's toga of manhood to be speeded up for him, so that he should seem adapted to undertake political life. Caesar also conceded gladly to the sycophancies of the senate that in the twentieth year of his age Nero should embark on the consulship and in the meantime, as designate, should hold pro consular command outside the City and be called Princeps of the Youth. Added under his name was a donative for the soldiery, a gratuity for the plebs.[54] At the   2
circus entertainments which were produced to gain the public's enthusiasm, Britannicus rode past in the praetexta, Nero in triumphal clothing: the people had only to look at the latter with his commander's decoration, the former with his boyish garb, and to make the appropriate assumptions about the fortune of each. At the same time those centurions and tribunes who pitied Britannicus' lot were removed for fabricated reasons, some in a show of honor. As for the freedmen, any of incorruptible loyalty were banished too, on an opportunity such as the following. When meeting each other, Nero hailed Britannicus by name, the lat-   3
ter him as "Domitius." Agrippina, with many a complaint, denounced this to her husband as being the start of disaffection: the adoption was being spurned, she said, and what the fathers had voted and the people had ordered was being repudiated within the household; and, unless the prevarication of those teaching such hostility were stopped, it would erupt for the public ruin. Moved by these (as it were) charges, Claudius inflicted exile or death on each of his son's best tutors and installed as his guards those provided by his stepmother.

Nevertheless Agrippina did not yet dare her supreme feat of engineering un-   **42**
less the praetorian cohorts were released from the care of Lusius Geta and Rufrius Crispinus, men whom she believed to be mindful of Messalina and bound to her children.[55] Since Claudius' wife was therefore asserting that the cohorts were being split by the ambitions of the two and that, if they were directed by one man, discipline would be tighter, direction of the cohorts was transferred to Burrus Afranius, a man of exceptional military reputation but aware at whose prompt-

54. The donative (*OCD* 494) was the soldiers' equivalent of the gratuity, for which see 3.29.3n. The two reappear together at 14.11.1; see also 12.69.2.
55. For Crispinus see 11.1.3n.

2   ing he was being placed in charge.[56] Agrippina elevated still higher her own ex-
     altedness too: she entered the Capitol by carriage, a custom whose concession in
     ancient times to priests and sacred objects increased veneration of the lady, whose
     example of being begotten by a commander and of having been sister, spouse,
3   and mother of one who was in charge of affairs is unique to this day.[57] Mean-
     while her principal champion, Vitellius, his influence at its most effective and
     himself at the extremity of life, was seized (so uncertain are the affairs of the pow-
     erful) as the result of an accusation on the denouncement of Junius Lupus, a sen-
     ator. The latter hurled at him imputations of treason and of desire for command;
     and Caesar would have lent his ear, had not Agrippina—by threats rather than
     pleas—changed his mind, with the result that he merely forbade water and fire
     to the accuser. Such had been the limits of Vitellius' wish.

43   Numerous prodigies happened in that year. The Capitol was occupied by omi-
     nous birds; houses were felled by frequent earthquakes and, as dread became more
     widespread, the weak were crushed by the crowd in its trepidation. A scarcity of
     crops too and the famine arising from it were interpreted as prodigies; nor were
     the complaints concealed only: with disruptive cries people encircled Claudius
     as he was dispensing justice and drove him to an extreme part of the forum, press-
     ing upon him violently until, with a cluster of soldiers, he burst through the hos-
2   tile throng. It was agreed that fifteen days' nourishment—no more—remained
     for the City; and only by the gods' great kindness and the mildness of the win-
     ter was the extreme situation rescued. (Yet, as Hercules is my witness, at one time
     Italy transported supplies to distant provinces for the legions! Nor is barrenness
     the trouble even now: rather, we work the land of Africa and Egypt, and it is to
     the risks of ships that the livelihood of the Roman people has been entrusted.)

                                              *

44   In the same year an outbreak of war between the Armenians and Iberians was
2   the cause of the severest tremors for the Parthians and Romans too. The race of
     the Parthians was commanded by Vologaeses, who, on his mother's side the son
     of a Greek concubine, had acquired the kingdom by the concession of his broth-
     ers;[58] the Iberians were held by Pharasmanes in a long-standing tenure, the Ar-
3   menians by his brother Mithridates with our support.[59] Pharasmanes had a son
     by the name of Radamistus, of a becoming tallness, distinctive physical strength,
     well taught in native practices, and with a brilliant reputation among his neigh-

56. Burrus (for whom see Sherk 57 = Braund 461 = WM 37) will become particularly
influential in the reign of Nero.

57. Agrippina's father, Germanicus, had been given the title "commander" in A.D. 15
(1.58.5); she was also the sister of Caligula, the wife of Claudius, and the mother of Nero.

58. Viz. Tiridates and Pacorus (see 12.50.1, 15.2.1).

59. For Vologaeses I see 12.14.4n. above; for Pharasmanes I and Mithridates I see 6.32.3
and n.

bors. His remarks that the modest kingdom of Iberia was being kept from him by his father's old age were too defiant and frequent to conceal his desire. There- 4 fore Pharasmanes—in dread of a young man who was ready for power and equipped with the affection of his compatriots, while his own years were now declining—tried to attract him to a prospect elsewhere and brought Armenia to his attention, recalling that on the expulsion of the Parthians it had been given to Mithridates by himself, but force must be deferred: guile was more potent for overwhelming the man unawares. So Radamistus, pretending disaffection toward 5 his father, and as if no match for his stepmother's hatred, proceeded to his uncle, where, treated by him with great affability like one of his own children, he enticed the chiefs of the Armenians to revolution, with Mithridates still ignorant and decorating him besides.

Assuming an appearance of reconciliation, he returned to his father and said **45** that what could be achieved by treachery was ready; the rest must be followed through by arms. Meanwhile Pharasmanes fabricated reasons for war: while battling against the king of the Albani and summoning the Romans to help, he had, he said, been opposed by his brother, and he would embark on avenging that wrong by means of the man's own extirpation. At the same time he handed over large forces to his son. The latter drove Mithridates, terrified by the sudden ir- 2 ruption and stripped of his plains, into the stronghold of Gorneae, protected by its position and a garrison of soldiers, in charge of whom were Caelius Pollio the prefect and the centurion Casperius. Nothing is so unfamiliar to barbarians as 3 the machinery and strategy of sieges; but to us that part of soldiering is particularly familiar. So Radamistus, after attempting the defenses in vain or with losses, began a blockade; and, when force was abandoned, he began to buy off the greedy 4 prefect—despite Casperius' imploring that neither an allied king nor Armenia, as a gift of the Roman people, should be subverted by a criminal use of money. Finally, because Pollio was pleading enemy numbers, and Radamistus his father's orders, the centurion agreed a truce and left, so that, if he failed to deter Pharasmanes from his war, he could inform Ummidius Quadratus, the governor of Syria, in what state Armenia was.[60]

On the centurion's departure the prefect, as though released from his guard, **46** urged Mithridates to sanction a treaty, referring to the link between brothers, Pharasmanes' priority in age, and the other categories of connection—that he had his brother's daughter in marriage and that he himself was Radamistus' father-in-law. Though at that moment the Iberians were more effective, he said, they were not refusing peace; the Armenians' disloyalty was well-known;[61] and there was no other support than a stronghold devoid of supplies: his preference should be, not to test a doubtful hope[+] by means of arms, but conditions without shedding blood. While Mithridates was hesitating in response, suspecting the 2

60. C. Ummidius Quadratus, who had been suffect consul around 40, was legate of Syria from now until his death (14.26.2).
61. The "disloyalty" is that of the Armenian chiefs (12.44.5 above).

prefect's intentions (because he had polluted a royal concubine and was held to be venal for every lust), Casperius in the meantime reached Pharasmanes and de-
3   manded that the Iberians should withdraw from the blockade. The latter for his part, though his responses were openly indecisive and quite often rather emollient, warned Radamistus by secret messages to accelerate the siege by whatever means. The price of outrage was increased and Pollio by concealed bribery drove the soldiers to importune for peace and to threaten that they would abandon the garrison. Under this constraint Mithridates accepted a day and a place for a treaty and departed from the stronghold.

47   At first Radamistus, effusive in his embraces of him, pretended compliance and called him "father-in-law" and "parent." He added an oath that neither by sword nor by poison would he inflict violence on him. At the same time he drew him into a nearby grove, insisting that the preparations for a sacrifice had been provided there so that the peace might be confirmed with the gods as witnesses.
2   There is a custom among the kings, whenever they meet for an alliance, to entwine their right hands, fasten their thumbs together, and bind them tightly with a knot; then, when the blood has welled up in the extremity of the digits, they coax out the gore with a light blow and lick it in turn. Such a treaty is held to
3   be mystical, in that it has been consecrated by their mutual gore. But on that occasion the man who would attach the fastenings, simulating a fall, went for Mithridates' knees and knocked him down; simultaneously, as more people converged, chains were thrown on him, and in shackles (which are a disgrace for bar-
4   barians) he was dragged away. Soon the public, because of the harsh command under which it had been held, was aiming abuse and blows at him; and on the other side there were those who pitied so great a change of fortune. Following him with their small children was his spouse, filling everywhere with lamentation; they were hidden in separate, covered vehicles until Pharasmanes' orders
5   could be ascertained. The latter's desire for the kingdom was more potent than his brother and daughter, and he was mentally prepared for crime; he nevertheless spared himself the sight of having them killed in his presence. And Radamistus, as if mindful of his oath, produced neither sword nor poison for his sister and uncle but executed them by hurling them to the ground and smothering them with a heavy pile of clothes. Mithridates' sons too, because they had wept at the slaughter of their parents, were butchered.

48   But Quadratus, learning that Mithridates had been betrayed and that his kingdom was being held by his killers, called a council, informed them of the happenings, and debated whether he should avenge them. To a few the public honor was
2   a concern, but the majority spoke for safety: every foreign crime, they said, should be regarded as welcome; in fact the seeds of hatred should actually be sown, just as Roman principes had often made a present of that same Armenia, in apparent lavishness, to disturb the barbarians' minds. Let Radamistus keep control of his ill-gotten gains, provided he was resented and reproached, since that was more to ad-
3   vantage than if he had acquired them with glory. The vote went in favor of this proposal; but, lest they should seem to be endorsing the deed and Caesar might

have different orders, messengers were sent to Pharasmanes that he should with-draw from Armenian territory and remove his son.

The procurator of Cappadocia was Julius Paelignus, despicable for his shirker's   **49**
mentality and for his derided physique alike, but a particular intimate of Claudius
when the latter, as a private citizen, used once to delight his indolent inactivity
by associating with buffoons. The man Paelignus assembled auxiliaries from the
provincials as though to recover Armenia, but, as he plundered the allies rather
than the enemy, he lacked any protection when his own men departed and the
barbarians began raiding, and he went to Radamistus. Won over by his gifts, he
even urged him to assume the royal insignia, and he was present at their assumption as initiator and satellite. When this had been publicized by shameful report,   2
it was to prevent everyone else from being judged by Paelignus' behavior that the
legate Helvidius Priscus was sent with a legion to give heed to the disruption as
suited the moment.[62] Having therefore quickly crossed Mount Taurus, he had
settled things down more by moderation than by force when he was ordered to
return to Syria, lest the start of a war against the Parthians should present itself.

For Vologaeses, deeming that the chance had been offered of invading Arme-   **50**
nia, a possession of his ancestors which a foreign king was holding as the result
of an outrage, assembled forces and prepared to escort his brother Tiridates to the
kingdom so that no part of his family should be without a command. On the
entry of the Parthians, the Iberians were repelled without a formal battle, and the
Armenian cities of Artaxata and Tigranocerta accepted the yoke. But then a   2
frightful winter and ill-provided supplies and the decrepitude arising from both
compelled Vologaeses to abandon his present enterprise. Available once again,
Armenia was invaded by Radamistus, more callous than before against (in his
view) defectors and men likely to rebel at the right moment; and the latter for
their part, though accustomed to servitude, brought their passivity to an abrupt
end and surrounded the palace with arms.

Radamistus had no other recourse than the rapidity of his horses, by which   **51**
he carried off both himself and his spouse. His pregnant wife at first somehow   2
endured the flight owing to her dread of the enemy and her affection for her
husband; but after, when the continuous hurrying made her womb quiver and
her vital organs vibrate, she begged to be delivered from the insults of captivity
by an honorable death. He first embraced, enheartened, and encouraged her, at   3
one moment enthralled by her courage, at another sick with fear that, if left, she
might be possessed by another. Finally, given the violence of his love, and not being raw to action, he unsheathed his scimitar, conveyed the casualty to the bank
of the Araxes, and consigned her to the river, so that even her corpse would be
carried off. He himself made his headlong way through to the Iberians, his ancestral kingdom. Meanwhile Zenobia (that was the woman's name), breathing   4

---

62. This Helvidius Priscus is likely to be identical with the tribune of the plebs mentioned at 13.28.3 and with the famous son-in-law of Thrasea Paetus (16.28.1, 16.29.2,
16.33.2, 16.35.1).

and evidently alive, was noticed in a quiet backwater by some shepherds; and, re-flecting that from her dignified good looks she was not of low birth, they bound her wound, applied rustic medicaments, and, on learning her name and circum-stance, took her to the city of Artaxata. From there, owing to public concern, she was escorted to Tiridates and, welcomed affably, was treated in royal style.

★ ★ ★

A.D. 52

52   With Faustus Sulla and Salvius Otho as consuls,[63] Furius Scribonianus was driven into exile on the grounds that he had been investigating the end of the princeps through the Chaldaeans;[64] woven into the charge was his mother, Vibia, for be-

2   ing allegedly intolerant of her previous plight (she had been relegated).[65] Scri-bonianus' father, Camillus,[66] had mobilized arms across Dalmatia, a factor which Caesar regarded as contributing to his own clemency, because he was saving hos-tile stock for a second time. Nevertheless the exile had no long life thereafter: whether it was by an accidental death or through poison that his life was extin-

3   guished was given publicity depending on what each person believed. Concern-ing the banishment of the astrologers from Italy, there was a senate's decision, frightening and ineffectual.

Afterward, those who on account of straitened family circumstances withdrew from the senatorial order of their own accord were praised in a speech from the princeps; and those who added shamelessness to their poverty by remaining

53   there were removed. It was during this that he placed before the fathers a motion concerning the punishment of females who were espoused to slaves; and it was decided that one who had plunged so far without the master's knowledge

2   should be held in slavery, but, if he had consented, as being a freedwoman. To Pallas, whom Caesar had declared to be the deviser of the motion, the praetorian insignia and fifteen million sesterces were proposed by the consul designate, Barea Soranus.[67] Scipio Cornelius added that gratitude should be expressed publicly because an offspring of Arcadia's kings was subordinating his very old nobility to the public good and was allowing himself to be regarded as one of the

---

63. Faustus Cornelius Sulla Felix, son of the suffect consul of 31, married Antonia (daugh-ter of Claudius: 13.23.1) and was stepbrother of Messalina and nephew of the consul of 33 (6.15.1). He was banished by Nero in 58 (13.47) and murdered in 62 (14.57). L. Salvius Otho Titianus was elder brother of the later emperor Otho (13.12.1n.).

64. See 2.27.2n. for the Chaldaeans.

65. For relegation see App. A.

66. For Camillus Scribonianus see 6.1.1n.

67. For Q. Marcius Barea Soranus, who as suffect consul succeeded Otho, see further 16.21.1, 16.23, 16.30–3.

princeps's servants.[68] Claudius asserted that Pallas was content with the honor only   3
and would stay within the limits of his previous poverty. And fixed in official
bronze was a senate's decision whereby a freedman possessing three hundred million sesterces was heaped with praises for his old-fashioned frugality.[69]

*

But his brother, with the nomenclature Felix, did not act with similar modera-   **54**
tion. Installed now for a long time over Judaea, he deemed that such powerful
backing would guarantee him impunity for all his misdeeds. To be sure, the Jews
had presented an appearance of upheaval, a mutiny having arisen after *** on
the news of his slaughter they had not observed it,[70] there remained the dread that
some future princeps might issue the same commands. And in the meantime   2
Felix by his untimely remedies was fomenting felonies,[71] his rival in baseness being Ventidius Cumanus, by whom part of the province was held—matters being
divided in such a way that the latter was to be obeyed by the nation of the
Galilaeans, Felix by the Samaritans, mutually disaffected as these peoples had been
for a long time and now, in contempt of their rulers, with their hatreds less constrained. Thus there were reciprocal seizures; they sent in groups of bandits; they   3
arranged ambushes and sometimes met in battle; and they took their spoils and
plunder to the procurators. These two for their part were at first delighted; but
when, with the ruinous situation swelling, they intervened with armed soldiers,
it was the soldiers who were slaughtered; and war would have blazed in the
province had not Quadratus, the governor of Syria, come to the rescue. With re-   4
gard to the Jews who had erupted into executing soldiers, there was never much

68. It is uncertain whether this Scipio is the man first mentioned at 3.74.2 (n.) or his son,
the consul of 56 (13.25.1).

69. Light is shed on this last episode by two letters of T.'s friend, the younger Pliny. In
the first (7.29) he says that on the road to Tibur he discovered an inscription referring to
the decree of praetorian insignia and fifteen million sesterces to Pallas, who was "content
with the honor" only (the same words as in T.). In the second (8.6) he says that subsequently he looked up the text of the original decree, from which he proceeds to quote
liberally: the quotations reveal a date (23 January) and instructions for the decree's publication on bronze. Pliny's uncle, the elder Pliny, additionally implies that the decree was
"ordered" by Agrippina (*Natural History* 35.201). Cornelius Scipio's reference (above) to
"Arcadia's kings" rests on the fanciful supposition that Pallas was a descendant of the legendary Pallas who lived in Arcadia and was the ancestor of King Evander, Aeneas' helper
in the *Aeneid* (8.51–4).

70. A lacuna has deprived us of the start of this sentence and the end of the previous one.
From T.'s *Histories* (5.9.2) editors usually supply the sense as follows: ". . . after <they had
been ordered by C. Caesar to place his likeness in the temple; and, although> on the news
of his slaughter."

71. In other words, the measures which Felix was taking against the Jewish population
were only making things worse.

doubt that they would pay the penalty with their lives; but Cumanus and Felix occasioned some hesitation, since Claudius on hearing the causes of the rebellion had granted[72] the prerogative of deciding even about the procurators too. But Quadratus displayed Felix among the judges, where his reception on the tribunal would deter the enthusiasm of his accusers;[73] and it was Cumanus who was condemned for the felonious outrages of the two of them, and calm returned to the province.

55   And, not long after, the nations of rustic Cilicians whose nomenclature is Cietae, and who had often been in upheaval at other times too, under the leadership of Troxoborus now chose their rough mountains for a camp and, descending from there to the shores and cities, dared violence against farmers and
2 townsfolk and particularly merchants and shipowners. The Anemuriensian community was blockaded, and the cavalry sent as help from Syria with the prefect Curtius Severus was disrupted because the harsh locality around about, suited for fighting with infantry, did not permit a cavalry battle. Subsequently the king of that coast, Antiochus, brought disunity to the barbarians' forces by blandishments toward the plebs and foul play against the leader, and then, killing Troxoborus and a few chiefs, quietened the rest by clemency.

★

56 At about the same time, after the mountain between the Fucine Lake and the stream of the Liris had been pierced through,[74] it was so that the magnificence of the work could be viewed by greater numbers that on the lake itself a naval battle was arrayed, just as Augustus, having positioned a pool near the Tiber, had
2 produced one formerly, but with light vessels and a smaller force.[75] Claudius armed triremes and quadriremes and nineteen thousand men, enclosing the periphery with rafts to prevent random escapes, and yet embracing enough space for the violence of oarage, the helmsmen's skills, the thrusts of ships, and battle routines. On the rafts maniples and squadrons of the praetorian cohorts stood by, stationed behind defenses from which catapults and ballistas could be drawn back
3 and aimed; the rest of the lake was held by marines on decked ships. The banks, hills, and mountain heights were filled, like a theater, by an uncountable crowd

---

72. To Quadratus.

73. The procedure seems extraordinary, but in a celebrated murder trial in Kenya the defendant "was not provided with a dock, but sat on the same bench as the assessors" (*The Times* (London), 18 Sept. 1999). See also 13.23.2 below.

74. This project, originally contemplated by Julius Caesar, had occupied thirty-thousand men for eleven years. The excavation was over 3.5 miles (5651m.) in length, partly under Monte Salviano (787 ft. = 240m.). In its final form (see 12.57.1 below) the channel was 8 ft. (2.44m.) wide and over 9 ft. (2.84m.) in depth.

75. In 2 B.C.: see his *Res Gestae* 23, where the extent of his excavations for the "pool" are given.

from the nearest municipalities, and some from the City itself, in their desire to view or out of duty toward the princeps. He himself in a distinctive military cape—and, not far away, Agrippina in a golden chlamys[76]—presided. The battle, though between convicts, was fought in the spirit of brave men, and after a considerable amount of wounding they were exempted from slaying.

But on completion of the spectacle the waterway was opened: the carelessness   **57**
of the work was evident, since it had not been sunk sufficiently to the lowest or even the middle levels of the lake. For that reason, after an interval of time, the cavities were dug out to a greater depth, and, for assembling a crowd yet again, a spectacle of gladiators was produced on bridges superimposed for an infantry fight. Moreover a dinner party too was placed near the outlet of the lake, affect-   2
ing everyone with great alarm because the volume and force of the surging water was sweeping away its immediate surroundings, while the remoter parts shook or were terrified by the crashing sound. At the same time Agrippina took advantage of the princeps's trepidation to accuse Narcissus, the agent for the work, of cupidity and embezzlement; nor did he stay silent for his part, criticizing her womanly unruliness and excessive hopes.

                                       ★   ★   ★

With D. Junius and Q. Haterius as consuls,[77] the sixteen-year-old Nero received   **58**
Octavia, Caesar's daughter, in marriage. And, having taken up the cause of the Ilians so that he could sparkle in honorable pursuits and the glory of eloquence, he went fluently through the Romans' descent from Troy, Aeneas as originator of the Julian stock, and other antiquities not far removed from fantasy, achieving the Ilians' release from all public responsibility.[78] Likewise with him as   2
spokesman the Bononian colony, which had been consumed by fire, was aided by the lavishing of ten million sesterces; to the Rhodians was restored their free-
dom, which had often been taken away or confirmed, depending on whether they had earned it in foreign wars or had offended by mutiny at home; and the Apamaeans, who had been shaken by an earthquake, had their tax remitted for five years.

76. A Greek cloak or cape which, frequently used in military contexts, is often equated with the Roman military cape.

77. D. Junius Silanus Torquatus was a brother of the unfortunate L. Silanus (12.3.2n.); for his enforced suicide in 64 see 15.35. Q. Haterius Antoninus was son of D. Haterius Agrippa (1.77.3n.).

78. I.e., the responsibility of paying taxes. Since public speaking was an essential part of an emperor's job (see esp. 13.3.1–3 below), the young Nero acquired useful practice when he represented the various communities listed in this chapter. See also next n.

59   But Claudius was being driven to produce the utmost savagery by the practices of that same Agrippina,[79] who, gaping for the gardens of Statilius Taurus, a
man illustrious for his wealth, toppled him on the accusation of Tarquitius
Priscus.[80] He, having been Taurus' legate during his rule in Africa with proconsular command, on their return hurled at him a few imputations of extortion but
2   especially some of superstitious magic. The other did not suffer too long his false
accuser and undeserved tatters,[81] putting a violent end to his life before the sentence of the senate. Tarquitius was nevertheless driven from the curia, a victory
which the fathers, owing to their hatred of the denouncer, won in the face of
Agrippina's canvassing.

60   In the same year there was heard quite often from the princeps a statement
that matters judged by his procurators should have the same force as if he had
made the pronouncement himself. And, in case he should be thought to have
made an accidental slip, measures were taken by a senate's decision too, more fully
2   and more expansively than before. (Divine Augustus had ordered legal proceedings to be held in front of the equestrians who presided over Egypt, and their
decrees to be regarded just as if Roman magistrates had pronounced; later, across
other provinces and in the City, numerous matters which once had been inves-
3   tigated by praetors were surrendered.) Claudius handed over the entire judicial
prerogative for which there had been such frequent struggles by mutiny or
arms—for example, when by the Sempronian rogations the equestrian order was
placed in possession of the courts or, conversely, when the Servilian laws restored
the courts to the senate, and when Marius and Sulla once warred principally
4   about this very issue.[82] But in those times the different interests were those of
the orders, whose various victories had a collective validity. It was C. Oppius and
Cornelius Balbus who first were able, through the dominance of Caesar, to handle conditions for peace and adjudication on war; but any subsequent reference
to Matii and Vedii and the other influential names of Roman equestrians would
be pointless, given that Claudius brought his own freedmen, whom he had placed
in charge of his personal estate, up to the same level as both himself and the laws.[83]

79. The words "that same" seem to imply that it was Agrippina who had pushed the
young Nero into delivering the speeches mentioned in the previous chapter.

80. T. Statilius Taurus, son of the homonymous consul of A.D. 11 and nephew of the consul of A.D. 16 (2.1.1n.), had been consul in 44. For the later condemnation of Tarquitius
Priscus see 14.46.1.

81. For tatters see 2.29.1n.

82. The first reference is to Gaius Sempronius Gracchus' Lex Sempronia iudiciaria of 122
B.C., the second to Q. Servilius Caepio's Lex Servilia iudiciaria of 106 B.C. (T. uses plural for singular in each case). In 81 B.C., after intervening vicissitudes which T. omits, Sulla
transferred the courts to the senate (see 11.22.6), although his conflict with Marius had
been several years earlier (88–86 B.C.).

83. Oppius and Balbus were well-known friends of Julius Caesar, although their relevance here, as well as what T. says about them, is obscure. C. Matius and P. Vedius Pollio

Next he put forward a motion about granting immunity to the Coans, recall- **61**
ing many things concerning their antiquity: the Argives or Coeus, the parent of
Latona, had been the most olden tenders of the island, he said; later, with the arrival of Aesculapius, the skill of doctoring had been introduced and had been especially celebrated among that man's posterity—and he referred to the names of
individuals and the periods at which each had thrived: indeed he even said that 2
Xenophon, of whose lore he himself took advantage,[84] was sprung from the same
family and that, in response to his pleas, it should be conceded that the Coans,
free of all taxation for posterity, should tend their island as a sacred place which
ministered only to its god. There can be no doubt that he could have submitted
as evidence their many services to the Roman people and their allied victories;
but Claudius did not use any extraneous aids to veil the concession which, with
his customary complaisance, he had granted to an individual.

But when the Byzantians, on being given the opportunity to speak, begged **62**
before the senate to be excused the magnitude of their burdens, they traced
everything back. Beginning from the treaty which they had struck with us at the
time when we warred against the Macedonian king on whom, as being of low
birth, the designation "Pseudophilippus" was imposed, they recalled their subsequent sending of forces against Antiochus, Perseus, and Aristonicus; their aid for
Antonius in the pirate war;[85] what they had offered Sulla and Lucullus and Pompeius; and then their recent services to the Caesars, since they occupied the kind
of locality which was convenient for leaders and armies traversing by land and
sea as well as for the conveying of supplies. For it was at the narrowest point of **63**
separation between Europe and Asia that Byzantium was sited at the extremity
of Europe by Greeks, who, on consulting Pythian Apollo as to where they should
found a city, received an oracle that they should seek an abode "opposite the land
of the blind." By that conundrum the Chalcedonii were indicated, because, as 2
earlier arrivals who had previewed the advantages of the locality, they had chosen somewhere inferior.[86] For Byzantium has a productive soil and a prolific sea,
because an inordinate volume of fish, bursting out of the Pontus and terrified by
glancing rocks beneath the waves, neglects the curve of the alternative shore and
is carried to its harbors. Hence at first the people were profitable and wealthy; 3

(for whom see 1.10.5n.) were powerful figures of the late republic and early empire (T.
again uses plural for singular).

84. Xenophon was Claudius' personal physician (see also 12.67.2) and honored by his
native island in inscriptions: see Sherk 49B = Braund 467 = WM 36.

85. The Macedonian pretender was Andriscus, 148 B.C. (*OCD* 88): for Antiochus see
2.63.3n., and for Perseus and Aristonicus see 4.55.1n. The pirate war involved M. Antonius Creticus, father of Mark Antony, who was given a special command in 74 B.C. to deal
with piracy.

86. Chalcedon was founded on the eastern shore of the Bosporus, Byzantium on the
western: the same story is told by Herodotus (4.144), though there the words are put into
the mouth of Megabazus.

after, with the pressing magnitude of their burdens, they begged for an end or else a limit—supported earnestly by the princeps, who put forward the fact that they had been exhausted recently by the Thracian and Bosporan wars[87] and that they should be aided. So their taxes were remitted for five years.

★　★　★

A.D. 54

64　With M. Asinius and M'. Acilius as consuls,[88] it was recognized by frequent prodigies that a change of affairs for the worse was being portended. Soldiers' standards and tents blazed with heavenly fire; on the pinnacle of the Capitol a swarm of bees took up occupation; there were two-formed human births;[89] and a sow's issue on which there were hawk's talons. Numbered among the phenomena was the diminished number of all the magistrates, a quaestor, aedile, tribune,

2　praetor, and consul having deceased within a few months. But it was Agrippina who was in a particular panic, dreading an utterance of Claudius (which he had tossed out drunkenly) to the effect that he was fated to bear the outrages of his spouses and then to punish them; and she decided to accelerate her actions, first destroying Domitia Lepida for womanly reasons, because Lepida—an offspring of the younger Antonia, with Augustus as her great-uncle, first cousin once removed of Agrippina, and sister of the latter's husband, Gnaeus[90]—believed her brilliancy

3　equal to Agrippina's own. (Nor was there much difference in good looks, age, and wealth; and, as each was immoral, infamous, and violent, they were rivals no less in vices than in the advantages which they had received from fortune. But the fiercest struggle was whether aunt or mother should be more effective with Nero: Lepida was trying to bind his young mind with blandishments and lavishments, while Agrippina on the other hand was callous and menacing, able to give

65　command to her son but not to endure his commanding.) Yet the imputations which were actually cast were that Lepida had targeted the princeps's spouse with curses and that, with too little restraint over her columns of slaves across Campania, she was disrupting the peace of Italy. On these scores death was the ver-

87. For the Bosporan wars see 12.15–21 above; whether the Thracian wars are those described at 4.46–51 is unclear.

88. The first abbreviation stands for "Marcus," the second for "Manius." Asinius Marcellus was a great-grandson of Asinius Pollio (14.40.2, cf. 1.12.4n.). Acilius Aviola is perhaps son of the man mentioned at 3.41.1 (n.); he became proconsul of Asia.

89. Either two-headed babies (as 15.47.1) or hermaphrodites.

90. Domitia Lepida was in fact the daughter of Antonia the elder, Augustus' niece: T. likewise confuses the elder and the younger Antonia at 4.44.2, his obituary notice for L. Domitius Ahenobarbus (consul in 16 B.C.), husband of the elder and father of Domitia Lepida. For the wedding of Domitia Lepida's brother Gnaeus to the younger Agrippina in A.D. 28 see 4.75.

dict—to much opposition from Narcissus, who, suspecting Agrippina more and more, was said to have produced among his intimates the statement that his own ruin was certain whether Britannicus or Nero were in control of affairs; but Caesar had deserved so well of him that he would expend his life for his benefit. Messalina and Silius, he said, had been condemned: similar reasons for a second 2 accusation existed if Nero were to command; with Britannicus as successor, the princeps would owe him nothing.[91] But it was by the intrigues of the latter's stepmother that the whole household was being wrenched apart, a greater outrage than if he himself had kept silent about the immorality of the previous spouse—though not even immorality was now lacking, with Pallas as her adulterer, lest anyone be in any uncertainty that she held esteem, shame, her body, everything, cheaper than the kingdom. —Insisting thus or in some similar man- 3 ner, he embraced Britannicus, prayed that his strength would mature as speedily as possible, and stretched out his hands sometimes to the gods, sometimes to the youth himself: let him grow up, let him drive off his father's enemies, let him even avenge his mother's killers.

Amid such a storm of concerns Narcissus was seized by adverse health and 66 proceeded to Sinuessa to restore his vigor by the softness of the climate and salubriousness of the waters. It was then that Agrippina—long determined on her crime, quick with the opportunity offered, and not short of servants—debated about the type of poison so that her act would not be betrayed by anything sudden or precipitate; on the other hand, if she selected a slow-wasting one, Claudius on nearing his end might recognize the deception and return to loving his son. She favored something choice, which would disturb his mind and defer his death. She selected an artist in such matters, by designation Locusta, recently convicted 2 of poisoning and long considered one of the instruments of the kingdom. Through the woman's talent a toxin was prepared, whose server was one of the eunuchs, Halotus, accustomed as he was to bringing in food and sampling it by tasting.

Everything soon became so well-known that writers of those times transmit- 67 ted that the poison had been poured into a delectable dish of mushrooms and that the power of the medicament had not been recognized at once, whether through Claudius' insensibility or his wine-bibbing;[+] at the same time an opening of his bowels seemed to have come to his rescue. Agrippina was therefore 2

91. I understand *in se fore* after *nullum principi meritum*. The sentence as a whole is desperately obscure and has been much emended. If the text has been correctly transmitted, one might extract from it the following sense: if Nero were to succeed Claudius, Narcissus would have the same grounds for accusing Agrippina as he had previously in the case of Messalina and Silius, viz. a desire to control the empire, <and hence would need to be silenced by death>; conversely, if Britannicus were to succeed Claudius, the new princeps would owe Narcissus nothing <but would wish to kill him as being responsible for the death of his mother>. Since Agrippina's machinations make the succession of her stepson unlikely, however, the following sentence begins with a contrast ("But").

terrified, and, since she feared the ultimate, she spurned the resentment of immediacy[92] and called upon the complicity (for which she had already provided) of Xenophon, the doctor. He is believed to have inserted into the man's throat, as though to aid his efforts at vomiting, a feather smeared with a quick-seizing poison, not unaware that the most critical crimes are begun with peril but performed with profit.

68   In the meantime the senate was being summoned and the consuls and priests were enunciating vows for the princeps's preservation, since, though already lifeless, he was being covered with clothing and dressings—while matters for con

2 firming Nero's command were being settled. First of all Agrippina, as if overcome by pain and searching for comfort, held Britannicus in an embrace, called his face the true likeness of his father's, and by various means delayed his emerging from

3 the bedroom. She detained Antonia and Octavia too, his sisters; she had closed off all the approaches with guards; and she frequently made it public that the princeps's health was getting better—all so that the soldiery should act in good hope and that the propitious moment of the Chaldaeans' warnings might ar

69 rive.[93] Then, in the middle of the day, on the third before the Ides of October,[94] with the doors of the Palatium suddenly flung open, in the company of Burrus, Nero emerged toward the cohort which, in military fashion, was present as lookout. There, at the prefect's warning, he was welcomed by festive voices and placed in a litter. (They say that some hesitated, looking around and asking repeatedly where Britannicus was; but soon, with no one to authorize differently, they fol

2 lowed what was being offered.) Carried to the camp, and after some preliminary words suited to the moment (and the promise of a donative on the example of his father's lavishness), Nero was hailed as "Commander."

   The verdict of the soldiers was followed by the fathers' decisions, and there

3 was no hesitation in the provinces.[95] Heavenly honors were decreed to Claudius and the Solemnities of his funeral were celebrated in the manner of Divine Augustus', with Agrippina rivaling the magnificence of her great-grandmother Livia. Yet his will was still not read out, lest the preference of stepson to son should, by resentment at its injustice, disturb the disposition of the public.

92. I.e., in the crisis she preferred quick action and was prepared to risk the resentment which an obvious murder might provoke.

93. See 14.9.3 below.

94. 13 October.

95. See Sherk 61 = Braund 235.

BOOK 13

The first death in the new principate was that of Junius Silanus, proconsul of **1**
Asia,[1] contrived without Nero's knowledge through Agrippina's guile, not because any violence of temperament had spurred his extermination (he was sluggish and had been disdained by other dominations, so much so that C. Caesar
was accustomed to call him "the golden sheep"), but Agrippina, having engineered the execution of his brother L. Silanus,[2] dreaded an avenger, given the
frequent reports from the public that in preference to Nero, who had scarcely yet
left boyhood and had acquired his command through crime, there should be
someone of settled years, guiltless, noble, and (something for which there was regard at that time) belonging to the posterity of the Caesars: for Silanus too was
a great-great-grandson of Divine Augustus.[3] This was the reason for his execu-   **2**
tion. Its agents were P. Celerius,[+4] a Roman equestrian, and Helius, a freedman,
both installed over the princeps's estate in Asia. Poison was given by them to the
proconsul during a banquet—too openly to deceive.

With no less speed Narcissus, Claudius' freedman, about whose wrangles with   **3**
Agrippina I have recorded,[5] was driven to death by the harshness of his custody
and by the ultimate necessity—against the will of the princeps, with whose still
hidden vices he was in marvelous accord through his greed and prodigality. And   **2**
the general trend was toward slaughter, had not Afranius Burrus and Annaeus
Seneca stepped in. These mentors of the Commander's youth were mutually har-
monious (a rarity in an alliance of power) and equally forceful by different means,
Burrus in military concerns and the severity of his behavior, Seneca in his precepts for eloquence and an honorable affability, each helping the other so that
they might more easily retain their hold on the slipperiness of the princeps's age
by permitting him pleasures if he spurned virtue.

They both had the same struggle against the defiance of Agrippina, who, blaz-   **2**
ing with all the desires of her evil domination, had Pallas on her side, at whose
instigation Claudius had destroyed himself with his incestuous wedding and the
ruinous adoption. But it was not Nero's instinct, either, to be inferior to slaves,
and Pallas, who with his grim arrogance had exceeded the limits of a freedman, had provoked his antipathy. Nevertheless all honors were palpably heaped   **3**
on her and, when the tribune sought the password in the manner of the mili-

---

1. M. Junius Silanus, consul in 46, was son of the consul of 19 (2.59.1n.).

2. See 12.8.1.

3. Silanus' grandmother, the younger Julia, was the sister of Nero's grandmother, the
elder Agrippina. See Stemma (b).

4. The transmitted reading of the name, commonly changed to *Celer* (after Lipsius)
on the basis of 13.33.1 below, has recently been confirmed on the basis of epigraphic
evidence.

5. See 12.57.2 and 12.65.1.

tary,[6] Nero issued that of "Best Mother." Decreed to her also by the senate were two lictors and a Claudial flamonium,[7] and at the same time to Claudius a censorial funeral and, subsequently, consecration.[8]

3   On the day of the funeral the princeps embarked on a eulogy of the man and was himself as earnest as everyone else while he enumerated the antiquity of Claudius' lineage and the consulships and triumphs of his ancestors; even the recollection of his liberal arts, and that nothing grim had befallen the state at the hands of foreigners during his rule, was listened to with favorable attention. But, after he turned to the man's foresight and wisdom, no one restrained their laughter, although the speech, composed as it was by Seneca, presented considerable refinement, given that the latter's was an attractive talent and one well adapted

2   to contemporary ears. (The elders—whose inactivity consists in comparing past and present—noted that, of those who had been in charge of affairs, Nero was the first to have needed someone else's fluency. For the dictator Caesar was the rival of the highest orators; and Augustus enjoyed a free and flowing eloquence such as became a princeps. Tiberius had skill too in a technique whereby he weighed his words, on such occasions being either effective in his sentiments or purposely ambiguous. Even C. Caesar's disturbed mind did not ruin his power of speech; nor in Claudius' case, whenever he held forth on prepared material,

3   would you have wanted for elegance. But, as for Nero, even in his boyhood years he diverted his lively mind to other things: engraving, painting, practicing songs or his control of horses; and sometimes in the composing of poems he showed that he had elements of learning.)

4   When the imitations of sadness had been performed, he entered the curia and, after a preamble about the authority of the fathers and the consensus of the soldiers, he recalled his exemplars and counsels for undertaking command in an exceptional way. Nor had his youth, he said, been steeped in civil war or domestic disaffection; he brought to his task no hatreds, no wrongs and no desire for

2   vengeance. Then he gave an outline prescription of the future shape of the principate, rejecting in particular those aspects at which resentment had recently blazed: he would not, he said, be the judge of every business, so that, with accusers and defendants shut together in the same house, the powerfulness of a few might spread; nothing at *his* hearth would be venal or open to canvassing: house and state were separate. The senate should hold on to its ancient responsibilities, while Italy and the provinces should attend at the tribunals of the consuls: they[9] would provide access to the fathers, while he himself would pay heed to the armies entrusted to him.

   6. For this practice see 1.7.5.

   7. See App. A.

   8. I.e., deification. For "censorial funeral" see 4.15.2n.

   9. I.e., the consuls, who, sitting in their official seats (on the "tribunals," above), would first receive delegations from Italy or the provinces (e.g., 2.35.2, 3.60–3) before passing them on to the senate at large. In the next sentence Nero refers to the so-called "impe-

Confirmation was not lacking, and many things were settled by the senate's **5** adjudication: that no one should be bought by wage or gifts to plead a case, and that gladiatorial productions should not be required of quaestors designate.[10] In fact it was in the face of opposition from Agrippina (on the ground that Claudius' enactments were being overthrown) that the latter was carried by the fathers, who kept being called to the Palatium precisely so that she might attend,[11] separated by a screen at the doorway added at the rear, which would block their vision but not bar her hearing. And furthermore, when legates of the Armenians **2** were pleading their case before Nero, she was preparing to mount the Commander's dais and to preside next to him, had not Seneca, with everyone else transfixed in panic, warned him to go to meet his advancing mother. Thus disgrace was headed off by a display of devotion.

At the end of the year it was announced in disturbing rumors that there had **6** been a further eruption by the Parthians and that Armenia was being ransacked on their expulsion of Radamistus, who, having often taken control of the kingdom and then been a fugitive, had now too deserted the war.[12] Therefore, in a **2** City greedy for gossip, men inquired in what way a princeps scarcely past seventeen years old could withstand or repel such an onslaught, what support there would be in one who was ruled by a female, whether battles too and sieges of cities and the other aspects of war could be administered by teachers.[13] Others **3** in response said that things had turned out better than if Claudius, ineffectual from old age and from shirking, were being called to the toils of military service, destined to obey servile orders as he was. But Burrus and Seneca were known for their considerable experience of affairs; and how much strength did the Commander lack, when Cn. Pompeius in the eighteenth year of his age and Caesar Octavianus in his nineteenth had sustained civil wars?[14] And at the highest level **4** more was waged by auspices[15] and counsel than by weapons and brawn. He would give clear evidence of whether he was using honorable friends or otherwise if, after putting aside all considerations of resentment, he were to choose an exceptional leader rather than, as the result of canvassing, one who was moneyed and supported by favor.

While words such as these were being aired publicly, Nero ordered that the **7**

---

rial" provinces, which, with their "armies entrusted to him," lay exclusively under his control.

10. Claudian measures are endorsed and reversed by these two decisions: see 11.5.3–7.4 and 11.22.2–6 respectively.

11. For meetings of the senate in the Palatium see 2.37.2n. and 2.83.3n.

12. This continues the narrative from 12.44–7 and 12.50–1 above.

13. Viz. Burrus and Seneca (the sneer is countered below).

14. The references are respectively to 84 B.C. (when Pompey was in fact twenty-three) and 44 B.C.

15. I.e., overall authority (see App. A).

young men recruited in the neighboring provinces should move up to supplement the legions of the East and that the legions themselves should be stationed nearer Armenia; and the two veteran kings, Agrippa and Antiochus,[16] should expedite forces with which they could actually enter the Parthians' territory; and at the same time bridges should be connected across the stream of the Euphrates. And, along with royal insignia, he entrusted Lesser Armenia to Aristobulus and the district of Sophene to Sohaemus.

2   And there arose, just in time, a rival to Vologaeses in his son Vardanes; and the Parthians departed from Armenia, but only as though they were deferring war.

8   Yet in the senate everything received exaggerated celebration in the suggestions of those who proposed supplications and, on the days of the supplications, the triumphal garment for the princeps, and that he should enter the City to an ovation, and a likeness of him of equal size to Mars the Avenger's and in the same temple—all to general delight (quite apart from their customary sycophancy), because he had put Domitius Corbulo in charge of holding on to Armenia, and a place seemed to have been cleared for virtues.[17]

*

2   The forces of the East were divided in such a way that part of the auxiliaries along with two legions remained at the disposal of the province of Syria and its legate Quadratus Ummidius,[18] while an equal number of citizens and allies would be Corbulo's, with the addition of the cohorts and wings which were wintering in Cappadocia. The allied kings were ordered to obey either of them, depending on what would be conducive to the war; but their enthusiasm for Corbulo

3   was the readier. He, to keep pace with+ his reputation (which is a highly effective factor in new undertakings), completed his journey quickly and at Aegeae, a community in Cilicia, found himself confronted by Quadratus, who had advanced there lest Corbulo, if he entered Syria to receive his forces, should attract everyone's attention—mighty in physique as he was, a man of magnificent words and, in addition to his experience and wisdom, impressive even in the irrelevancies of display.

9   As things were, each man had been warning King Vologaeses by messenger that he should prefer peace to war and, having given hostages, should continue his predecessors' customary respect for the Roman people. And Vologaeses, to prepare for war from a position of advantage (or to remove, in the name of "hostages," those suspected of rivalry), handed over the noblest of the family of

2   the Arsacidae. They were received by the centurion Insteius, who had been sent by Ummidius and had approached the king by chance about an earlier mat-

---

16. The former is M. Julius Agrippa II of Judaea, the latter is Antiochus IV of Commagene (12.55.2, 13.37.3, 14.26.2): see *OCD* 779 and 109 respectively.

17. For Corbulo see 11.18.1n.

18. For him see 12.45.4n.

ter.[19] After this became known to Corbulo, he ordered Arrius Varus, prefect of a cohort, to go and recover the hostages. Hence wrangling arose between prefect and centurion, and, lest it should become a protracted spectacle for the foreigners, adjudication of the matter was passed to the hostages and to the legate who led them. And they for their part, on account of his recent glory and because of some tendency even among the enemy, preferred Corbulo. Hence disaffection 3 between the leaders, Ummidius complaining that he had been robbed of what had been realized through his own plans, Corbulo testifying in response that the king had not been converted to offering hostages until his own selection as leader for the war changed the man's hopes to dread. Nero, to reconcile the disputants, ordered publication as follows: on account of successful achievements by Quadratus and Corbulo, laurel was being added to the Commander's fasces. (Events extending into other consulships I have here linked together.)

★

In the same year Caesar sought from the senate a likeness in honor of Cn. Domi-   **10** tius, his father, and consular insignia for Asconius Labeo, who had been his guardian; and he forbade statues to himself of solid silver or gold despite their being offered to him. And, although the fathers had voted that the start of the year should begin in the month of December, in which Nero had been born, he retained the old reverence for the Kalends of January[20] to initiate the year. Nor 2 was Carrinas Celer, a senator, entered among defendants on the accusation of a slave, or Julius Densus, a Roman equestrian, whose goodwill toward Britannicus was given as the charge.

★ ★ ★

With Claudius Nero and L. Antistius as consuls,[21] when the magistrates were   **11** swearing obedience to the principes' enactments, he prevented his colleague Antistius from swearing obedience to his own enactments—to great praise from the fathers, so that his young mind, lifted by glory for even slight matters, might continue to greater ones. And there followed leniency toward Plautius Lateranus, 2 whom, removed from his rank for adultery with Messalina,[22] he restored to the senate, pledging clemency in frequent speeches which Seneca, to testify to the honorableness of his precepts (or for vaunting his talent), publicized in the voice of the princeps.

19. The text is uncertain here.

20. I.e., 1 January.

21. L. Antistius Vetus was son of the consul of 23 (4.1.1n.) and brother of the consul of 50 (12.25.1n.).

22. See 11.30.2 and 11.36.4.

12   Be that as it may, the powerfulness of his mother was gradually broken, as Nero
had slipped into love with a freedwoman whose designation was Acte, and at the
same time had enlisted as accomplices M. Otho and Claudius Senecio, handsome
young men, of whom Otho was born of a consular family, Senecio of a father

2   who was a freedman of Caesar.[23] With his mother's ignorance succeeded by her
vain protests, he[24] had crept his way in thoroughly by the techniques of luxuriousness and ambiguous secrecy, unopposed by even the older friends of the princeps, given that the young woman—without injury to anyone else—was fulfilling
the princeps's desires, since by some fate (or because the illicit always prevails)
he recoiled from his wife Octavia, noble as she was and of demonstrated probity,
and it was dreaded that he might erupt into unlawful sex with illustrious ladies

13   if he were kept from his lust. But Agrippina muttered in womanly fashion about
her "freedwoman rival" and her "daughter-in-law the maid" and other things in
the same style. Nor did she wait for her son's remorse or satiety and, the more
foul her remonstrances, the more fiercely she fired his love until, driven to dis-
traction by its power, he cast off all compliance toward his mother and entrusted
himself to Seneca, one of whose friends, Annaeus Serenus, had screened the juvenile's first desires by pretending love for the same freedwoman and had provided the use of his own name, so that it was he who openly lavished the gifts

2   which the princeps stealthily presented to the young woman. Then Agrippina,
changing her practice, approached her young son with blandishments and offered her own bedroom and lap as an alternative for the concealment of what his
young age and high fortune demanded. Furthermore she acknowledged an "unseasonable severity" and handed over amounts of her own wealth (which was not
far off the Commander's own), being now as unreasonably submissive as she had

3   recently been excessive in restraining her son. But the change did not deceive
Nero; and the closest of his friends dreaded, and begged him to beware, the traps
of a woman who had always been frightening but was now deceitful too.

4   By chance during those days Caesar, inspecting the apparel with which the
spouses and parents of principes had gleamed,[25] selected a garment and jewels
and sent the gift to his mother—without any thought of frugality, since he was
taking the initiative in delivering prime and desirable items. But Agrippina declared that, so far from her costume being enhanced, she was being kept from
everything else, and her son was dividing up possessions which he derived en-

14   tirely from herself. There was no lack of individuals to interpret this for the worse
when they related it; and Nero, hostile to those on whom her womanly haugh-

---

23.   It is not clear which (or whether any particular) emperor is meant by "Caesar." M.
Salvius Otho, son of L. Salvius Otho (suffect consul in 33), is the future emperor; his elder
brother had been consul in 52 (12.52.1n.).

24.   Others take the subject to be either "she" (Acte) or, making the verb plural (Lipsius), "they" (Otho and Senecio).

25.   This seems to suggest that the imperial residence maintained a kind of "gallery" devoted to the clothing worn by great ladies in the past.

tiness depended, removed Pallas from his concern for the matters over which he had been placed by Claudius,[26] where he seemed to operate jurisdiction over the kingdom. And it was maintained that, as Pallas was departing with a great multitude of escorts, Nero said not inappropriately that Pallas was on his way to forswear.[27] (In fact Pallas had struck a bargain that he should not be questioned for any action in the past and that his accounts with the state should be held as balanced.)

After this, Agrippina rushed headlong to terror and threats, nor did she exempt   2
the ears of the princeps from her testimony that Britannicus was now mature, the true and worthy stock for undertaking his father's command, which an adopted scion was exercising through the injustices of his mother. She had no objection,   3
she said, if all the ills of the unhappy house were revealed, her own wedding especially, and her own deed of poisoning; the one providential act of the gods and herself was that her stepson survived. She would go with him to the camp:[28] let them listen to Germanicus' daughter on the one hand and to the crippled Burrus and the exile Seneca on the other, claiming—naturally with maimed hand and professorial tongue—control of the human race! At the same time she brandished her fists, heaped up abuse, and invoked the consecrated Claudius, the shades of the Silani in the underworld,[29] and all her unavailing deeds.

Disturbed by this, and by the fact that on an approaching day Britannicus   **15**
would complete the fourteenth year of his life,[30] Nero began to turn over within himself both his mother's violence and the other's nature, recently known from a demonstration which, though admittedly slight, had nevertheless earned him widespread goodwill. On the festival days for Saturn, amid the general disport-   2
ing of his contemporaries, during the sport of drawing lots for "king" that particular lot had fallen to Nero.[31] For everyone else there were various tasks which would not bring on any blushes; but, when he ordered Britannicus to rise, proceed into the middle, and begin a song (thereby hoping for ridicule of a boy ignorant of even sober, to say nothing of drunken, gatherings), the other embarked steadfastly on a poem in which it was indicated that he had been turned out of his paternal abode and the supremacy. Hence there arose a pity all the more evident because night and its recklessness had removed dissembling. Nero, realiz-   3
ing the resentment, redoubled his hatred; and, under pressure from Agrippina's

26. He had been placed in charge of the imperial accounts (*rationes*), to which T. refers at the end of the paragraph.

27. For the joke in "forswear" see 12.4.3n.

28. Of the Praetorian Guard.

29. See 12.8.1 and 13.1.1–3.

30. In other words, he would be taking the "toga of manhood" (see 3.29.1, 4.4.1, 12.41.1).

31. A game in which orders could be given to the other participants by whoever became "king" on the appropriate throw of the dice. The festival in question was the Saturnalia (17–23 December).

threats, and because there were no grounds for a charge and he did not dare openly to order the slaughter of his brother, he engineered things secretly and ordered poison to be prepared (his agent being Pollio Julius, tribune of a praetorian cohort, in whose care was held a woman convicted of poisoning, Locusta by name, with a considerable criminal reputation).[32] There had been earlier provision that those closest to Britannicus should hold neither law nor loyalty as being of any weight.

4   At first Britannicus received the poison from his actual tutors, but, on the opening of his bowels, he passed what had been insufficiently effective or else

5   had contained a dilution to prevent its savage force from being immediate. But Nero, impatient at the slowness of the crime, threatened the tribune and ordered reprisals for the poisoner on the grounds that, while they were having regard for rumor and preparing their defenses, they were delaying his security. When they then promised as precipitate an execution as one pressed home by the sword, next to Caesar's bedroom a toxin was concocted which, from poisonings beforehand, was known to be quick-seizing.

16   It was a custom that principes' children, sitting with the other nobles of the same age, should eat in the sight of their relatives at their own, more sparing, table. With Britannicus dining there, and because a chosen servant sampled his food and drink by tasting, the following trick was devised to avoid abandoning

2   the routine or betraying the crime by the death of them both. Britannicus was handed a drink, still harmless, very hot, and sipped at the tasting; then, after it was spurned for being scalding, the poison was added in cold water, and it so pervaded his whole frame that his voice and breathing suffered a simultaneous

3   seizure. A shudder came from those sitting around, the misguided scattered; but those of a deeper understanding remained transfixed and gazing at Nero. He for his part, reclining and apparently unwitting, said that this was usual, owing to the epileptic illness with which Britannicus had been afflicted since early boyhood,

4   and that his vision and feeling would return gradually. But, in Agrippina's case, such panic, such mental shock flashed out, despite her attempt to suppress them in her look, that it was agreed that she had been as unaware as Octavia, Britannicus' sister. She had begun to understand that her last source of aid had been seized away and that there was now a precedent for parricide.[33] Octavia too, though raw in years, had learned to hide pain, affection and every emotion. So, after a brief silence, the delightful party resumed.

17   The same night saw Britannicus' pyre juxtaposed with his execution, since there had been earlier provision for his funeral trappings, which were modest. He was nevertheless buried on the Plain of Mars—to such disruptive squalls that the public believed the anger of the gods was being portended against a deed which even many men would forgive when they considered the antiquity of

2   brothers' disaffections and the indivisibility of kingship. (Many writers of those

32. See 12.66.2.

33. Parricide here, as often, denotes the killing of any close relative.

times transmit that, on frequent days before the extermination, Nero had sported with Britannicus' boyhood,[34] so that now his death could be seen as neither premature nor savage, even though—amid the sacred rituals of the table, with no time given even for an embrace of his sisters, and before the eyes of his antagonist—it was hastened against the last of the Claudian bloodline, polluted before the poison by illicit sex.) The speed of the exequies Nero defended in an edict,   3
referring to the fact that it was an established custom of their ancestors to withdraw bitter[35] fatalities from the eye and not to prolong them by eulogies and procession. As things were, he said, his own remaining hopes were placed in the state after the loss of his brother's aid, while the fathers and people must foster all the more a princeps who alone survived from a family born to supreme elevation.[36]

Thereupon he enhanced with lavishness the most influential of his friends.   **18**
There was no lack of critics for men of self-proclaimed austerity who at such a moment had divided houses and villas like plunder. Others believed that compulsion had been applied by the princeps, conscious of his crime and hoping for forgiveness if he obligated the most forceful individuals by lavishments. Yet his   2
mother's anger was softened by no munificence, but she embraced Octavia, held secret meetings frequently with friends (snatching, over and above her inborn greed, money from everywhere as if for support), received tribunes and centurions affably, and held in honor the names and virtues of nobles (who survived even then), as if she were seeking a leader and a faction. That was known to Nero,   3
and he ordered the withdrawal of the military lookouts (which were then being kept for her as the Commander's mother, as they had once been hers as the spouse) and of the Germans (who had been added as guards for the same honorific purpose[+]). And, to prevent her being mobbed by a throng of well-wishers, he made his house separate and transferred his mother to that which had been Antonia's, surrounding himself, whenever he paid a personal visit there, with a crowd of centurions and withdrawing after only a brief kiss.

Nothing in mortal affairs is so unstable and fleeting as the fame of a power   **19**
that relies on a strength not its own. Immediately Agrippina's threshold was deserted: no one consoled her, no one approached her, except a few ladies, whether from love or hate being uncertain. One of these was Junia Silana (whose removal   2
from her marriage to C. Silius by Messalina I recorded above),[37] distinguished by her lineage, good looks, and recklessness, and for a long time very dear to Agrippina; but later there were covert affronts on both sides, because Agrippina had deterred Sextius Africanus, a young noble,[38] from marriage to Silana, insist-

34. The reference is to sexual abuse, as becomes clear at the end of the sentence.

35. Here "bitter" has the sense of "unripe" and hence "untimely."

36. The family is that of the Claudii. Nero had been adopted by Claudius (12.25.1–2), whose brother, Germanicus, was also Nero's grandfather. Britannicus, on the other hand, was Claudius' biological son: hence "the last of the Claudian bloodline" just above.

37. See 11.12.2.

38. T. Sextius Africanus became suffect consul in 59.

ing that she was immoral and declining in years—not so that she might reserve Africanus for herself but lest a husband of Silana's should acquire control of her
3   wealth and childlessness. Now that the prospect of vengeance was offered, Silana procured Iturius and Calvisius, two of her own clients, as accusers, hers being not the old and now hackneyed denouncement that Agrippina was grieving for the death of Britannicus or publicizing the wrongs to Octavia but that she had had designs on exalting Rubellius Plautus—who by his maternal origins was Nero's equal in his remove from Divine Augustus[39]—for revolutionary purposes and, by his espousal of her and by his subsequent command, on assailing the state once
4   more. All this Iturius and Calvisius disclosed to Atimetus, a freedman of Domitia, Nero's aunt;[40] he, delighted with the offering (between Agrippina and Domitia a ferocious rivalry was practiced), drove the actor Paris, himself a freedman of Domitia, to go in haste and frighteningly to denounce the charge.
20   The night had far advanced and was being dragged out by Nero's wine-bibbing when Paris entered, accustomed as he was on other occasions to redouble the princeps's luxuriousness at such an hour, but now composing himself for sorrowfulness; and, having explained the stages of his information, he so terrified his listener that he designed not only to kill his mother and Plautus but also to remove Burrus from the prefecture, on the grounds that he had been advanced by
2   Agrippina's favor and was rendering her a return. (Fabius Rusticus is author of the statement that a note was written to Caecina Tuscus, entrusting the care of the praetorian cohorts to him, but that Burrus retained his rank by help from Seneca; yet Plinius and Cluvius record no doubt about the prefect's loyalty.[41] To be sure, Fabius inclines toward praise of Seneca, by whose friendship he flourished; for myself, with my intention of following an authorial consensus, I shall transmit under their own names any diverging accounts[+] they have handed on.)
3   Nero, trembling and greedy for his mother's killing, could not be put off, until Burrus promised she would be executed if she were confirmed in her deed: anyone, above all a parent, should be granted a defense, he said; nor were there any accusers present: he was being presented with the voice of only one individual from an antagonistic household; he should reflect on the darkness, on the

39. Rubellius Plautus was the son of C. Rubellius Blandus (3.23.2n.) and Julia (6.27.1n.), granddaughter of Tiberius, and was thus great-great-grandson of Augustus, Tiberius' adoptive father. Nero stood in the same relationship to Augustus by direct descent on his mother's side. See Stemma (b); *CAH*[2] 10.990–1.

40. Domitia was sister of Nero's father, Cn. Domitius Ahenobarbus (4.75), and of Domitia Lepida (11.37.3), and had once been married to Passienus Crispus (6.20.1), who divorced her to marry Agrippina: hence the "ferocious rivalry" below.

41. Fabius Rusticus, whom T. elsewhere describes as "the most eloquent of recent authors" (*Agricola* 10.3), is referred to again at 14.2.2 and 15.61.3, but the scope of his history is unknown. The elder Pliny, in addition to his history of the German wars (1.69.2n.), wrote a thirty-one–book history of the later Julio-Claudian period to which T. again refers at 15.53.3. Cluvius Rufus, mentioned again at 14.2.1, was consul (date uncertain) as well as historian, but the exact scope of his work is unknown.

night spent awake in partying, and on the general likelihood of imprudence and ignorance.

With the princeps's dread thus soothed, and the rise of day, a journey was made **21** to Agrippina so that she might know the charges and demolish them or suffer the punishment. It was Burrus who carried out the instructions, with Seneca in attendance; also present were some of the freedmen as witnesses of the conversation. Then from Burrus, after he had explained the charges and their authors, there came a menacing action; and Agrippina, true to her defiance, said: "I do not **2** wonder that Silana, never having given birth, has no knowledge of mothers' emotions: parents do not change their children in the same way as an immoral woman her adulterers. Nor, if Iturius and Calvisius after consuming all their fortunes are repaying a crone with the final service of undertaking an accusation, is that a reason why either I should be subjected to the infamy of parricide or Caesar to complicity therein.[42] As for Domitia, I would thank her for her antagonism if **3** she were competing with me in goodwill toward my Nero; but, as things are, she is using her fornicator Atimetus and her actor Paris to compose stories as if for the stage. (She was developing⁺ aquaria[43] on her Baiae estate when *my* counsels were preparing him for his adoption and his proconsular prerogative and his designation to the consulship and the other aspects of acquiring command.) Alter- **4** natively, let someone appear who can prove that the cohorts in the City have been tampered with, the provinces' loyalty undermined, and, in sum, slaves or freedmen bribed for crime.

"Could *I* have lived on with *Britannicus* in control of affairs? And, if Plautus or **5** any other potential judge of mine should secure the state, there will doubtless be a lack of accusers to impute to me, not the occasional incautious word caused by the impetuosity of affection, but the kind of charges from which I cannot be absolved except by my son!"[44]

Although those present were moved and sought spontaneously to calm her **6** spirits, she demanded a dialogue with her son, where she said nothing on behalf of her innocence (as if in diffidence) nor on her good deeds (as if in remonstrance), but secured vengeance against her denouncers and rewards for her friends. The prefecture of the food supply was entrusted to Faenius Rufus, care **22** of the games which were being prepared by Caesar to Arruntius Stella, and Egypt

42. Parricide is again used, as at 13.16.4 above, of the killing of any close relative, here both of Agrippina's alleged plan to kill Nero, her son, and of Nero's inevitable execution of her if the allegation proved to be true.

43. Lit. "fishponds," but I have preferred a word which plays with "acquiring" at the end of the sentence since T. does the same ("*piscinas . . . apiscendo*").

44. The statement is ironic, implying its opposite. If anyone other than Nero were to become emperor, there would be many people ready and willing to accuse Agrippina of murdering Claudius; and, since Claudius' murder ensured Nero's succession, she is more likely to receive sympathy from her son than from anyone else. It is therefore in her own interests that Nero be preserved.

to Ti. Balbillus. Syria was marked out for P. Anteius; but,[+] having later been out-
2   witted by various means, he was finally detained in the City. As for Silana, she
was driven into exile; Calvisius and Iturius too were relegated. On Atimetus
reprisal was exacted, Paris being too effective an influence on the princeps's lusts
to have punishment inflicted on him. Plautus for the present was passed over in
silence.

23   Subsequently Pallas and Burrus were denounced for having agreed that Cornelius Sulla should be summoned to the command for the brilliancy of his lineage
and his relationship to Claudius, whose son-in-law he was through his wedding
to Antonia.[45] The author of the accusation turned out to be a certain Paetus,
notorious for conducting resales at the treasury[46] and now caught out in an
2   empty falsehood. Pallas' innocence was not as welcome as his haughtiness was
wearisome: when the freedmen of his, whom he was said to have had as accomplices, had been named, he replied that at home he had never indicated anything
except by nod or hand, or, if further clarification were required, he used writing
to avoid vocal communication. Burrus, though a defendant, gave his verdict
among the judges;[47] and exile was imposed on the accuser, and the registers which
he had been using to retrieve the forgotten entries at the treasury were burned.

24   At the end of the year the cohort accustomed to take up position at the games
as a picket was withdrawn so that there should be a greater show of liberty and
in order that the soldiery, if not implicated in theatrical license, might behave less
corruptly and the plebs give proof whether, with the removal of its guards, it
would maintain its restraint. The princeps performed a ritual purification of the
City in accordance with a response of the diviners, because the shrines of Jupiter
and Minerva had been struck from the sky.[48]

★   ★   ★

A.D. 56

25   With Q. Volusius and P. Scipio as consuls,[49] there was inactivity abroad but at
home a foul recklessness, with Nero wandering through the streets of the City
and its love-lairs and distractions in servile apparel, accoutred to dissemble his

---

45. For other references to Faustus Cornelius Sulla, consul in 52, see 12.52.1 (n.),
13.47.1–3, and 14.57.1–4.

46. Paetus was evidently profiting from people who owed a debt to the treasury, but the
precise nature of his private enterprise is unclear.

47. See 12.54.4n.

48. By lightning.

49. Q. Volusius Saturninus was son of L. Volusius Saturninus, suffect consul in A.D. 3
(12.22.2, 13.30.2). P. Cornelius Scipio was son of P. Cornelius Lentulus Scipio (3.74.2n.),
suffect consul in 24.

identity and accompanied by men who would seize things displayed for sale and inflict wounds on passers-by—such being the ignorance of his adversaries that he too received blows and presented the bruises on his face. Later—when it had [2] become known that it was Caesar who was on the prowl, and injuries against distinguished men and women were increasing and some people, now that license was permitted, went unpunished under cover of Nero's name, as they carried on the same behavior with their own personal groups—nighttime was passed as if in a state of captivity; and Julius Montanus, a man of senatorial rank but who had not yet undertaken office, encountered the princeps by chance in the shadows and, because he had fiercely repulsed the other's attempted violence and then on recognizing him had pleaded for pardon, was driven to die—exactly as though he had remonstrated.[50] Nero, now+ in more dread, in the future [3] surrounded himself with soldiers and numerous gladiators, who would allow limited and (as it were) individual brawls to begin; but, if the reaction from the victims was too effective, they went in with their weapons. As for the license at the [4] games and the actors' supporters, he transformed them too almost into pitched battles by offering impunity and prizes and by being a spectator (concealed but usually visible) himself, until, given the conflict among the people and the terror of more serious commotion, no other remedy was devised than that actors should be banished from Italy and the soldiery take up position in the theater once more.

During the same period there was discussion in the senate concerning the in- **26** iquities of freedmen, and it was importuned that in ill-deserving cases patrons should be given the right of revoking their freedom. There was no lack of those to vote in favor, but the consuls, though not daring to instigate a motion without the princeps's knowledge, nevertheless wrote down the consensus of the senate. He for his part hesitated[51] whether to initiate a resolution, seeing that he was [2] in the company of only a few men of different opinions, with some of them muttering that disrespect, reinforced by freedom, had erupted to such a degree that freedmen acted on an equal footing with their patrons, scoffed at+ their opinions, and actually brandished their fists to issue beatings [...] or deprecating their own punishment. What else was allowed to an injured patron except to relegate his freedman beyond the hundredth milestone to the shore of Campania?[52] All [3] other lawsuits were indiscriminate, offering parity to both parties; some weapon should be granted to a patron which could not be spurned. It was no burden for

50. I.e., instead of having pleaded for pardon. Alternatively the meaning may be "on the grounds that he had remonstrated."

51. The transmitted text of this sentence not only lacks a word for "hesitated" but is hopelessly corrupt throughout. I have admitted a minimal level of emendation (e.g., *insultarent*, "scoffed at," for *consultarent*), left a gap where the text seems beyond recall, and translated what is assumed to be the general sense. The scene is thought to be Nero's council ("the company of only a few men"), at which his advisers debate the issue of freedmen.

52. The question is ironic: relegation a hundred miles from Rome, which was evidently

the manumitted[53] to retain their freedom by the same compliance by which they had acquired it. But those clearly caught out in crime would deservedly be dragged back to slavery, so that dread might constrain those whom kindness had not changed.

27   In response it was said that, although the guilt of a few ought to be ruinous for themselves, there should be no detriment to the rights of the whole class. They were a widely spread body: from them, for the most part, came the tribes, the decuriae, the servants of magistrates and priests, and also the cohorts conscripted in the City.[54] In the case of most of the equestrians and very many senators, their origins were derived from nowhere else: if freedmen were given

2   separate treatment, the scarcity of the freeborn would become evident. Not without reason had their ancestors, when dividing off the orders of rank,[55] made freedom common to all. Furthermore, two categories of manumission had been established, to leave room for regret or for some new kindness.[56] Those whom their patron had not freed by formal emancipation were being constrained as if by the chains of slavery. Each man should examine the merits of a case and concede only slowly something which, once given, was not to be taken away.

3   It was the latter opinion which prevailed, and Caesar wrote to the senate that they should weigh the cases of freedmen individually whenever they were accused by their patrons; but there should be no general detriment. And not long after, his aunt was robbed of her freedman Paris as if in accordance with the civil law—not without infamy for the princeps, at whose order the judgment of his freeborn status had been achieved.[57]

28   There remained nonetheless a certain image of the republic. Between the praetor Vibullius and Antistius, tribune of the plebs, there arose a quarrel because the tribune had ordered the release of some of the actors' unrestrained supporters, who had been marched into chains by the praetor. The fathers gave their en-

---

the maximum permitted to patrons, meant that offending freedmen were (so to speak) "compelled" to withdraw to Campania, whose coastline was proverbially attractive.

53. I.e., the freed, emancipated.

54. The term "decuriae" here refers to groups of public officials (or others following the same occupation) organized in societies or clubs. The "cohorts" are those of the watchmen (for whom see 11.35.3 and n.).

55. For the orders see App. A; it is relevant to the present argument that the term "order" in certain senses could be applied also to freedmen (see, e.g., *CAH*[2] 10.877).

56. The two categories of manumission were "formal," to which reference is made in the next sentence, and "informal," which is under discussion: recipients of the latter could be refused the former, if the owner came to regret his earlier decision, or rewarded by it, if the owner wished to offer some further kindness.

57. Paris was a freedman of Domitia, Nero's aunt (see 13.19.4 above). The story was that he had first bought his freedom but then sought to reclaim the sum on the grounds that he was freeborn; the court, not wishing to offend Nero, agreed with him.

dorsement, criticizing the license shown by Antistius.[58] At the same time trib- 2
unes were prevented from preempting the prerogatives of praetors and consuls
or summoning from Italy those with whom legal proceedings could be instituted.[59] L. Piso, the consul designate,[60] added that they should not, by virtue of
their power, take measures within their own houses and that no fine announced
by them should be recorded in the public registers by the quaestors of the treasury until after four months. In the intervening period it should be lawful to make
a counterannouncement, and the consuls should decide on the matter. The power
of the aediles too was restricted more narrowly, and it was decided how much of
a pledge should be seized, and how much of a penalty invoked, by the curule and
plebeian respectively.[61] And Helvidius Priscus, tribune of the plebs, conducted a 3
personal dispute against Obultronius Sabinus, quaestor of the treasury, on the
grounds that he was enlarging unmercifully his prerogative of the spear[62] against
the destitute. Then the princeps transferred the care of the public registers[63] from
quaestors to prefects.

(The arrangements in that respect have been variously handled and often **29**
changed. Augustus permitted the senate to choose prefects; then, after suspicions
of canvassing for votes, those who were to be in charge were drawn by lot from
the category of praetors. And that did not survive for long, because the lot strayed
to persons too little suited. Next Claudius installed quaestors again and, lest they 2
should pay too sluggish attention through dread of causing offense, promised
them extraordinary honors;[64] but those undertaking it as their first magistracy
lacked the strength of years. So Nero chose former praetors who were proved by
experience.)

With the same men as consuls, Vipsanius Laenas was condemned for his greedy **30**
handling of the province of Syria. Acquitted of extortion was Cestius Proculus,
accused by the Cretans. Clodius Quirinalis anticipated by poison his condemna-

---

58. For the later fortunes of Antistius Sosianus, praetor in 62, see 14.48–9, 16.14, and
16.21.2.

59. No one seems to know exactly what is meant by the latter part of this sentence, but
it appears that tribunes were henceforth prevented from summoning to Rome cases
which could be dealt with locally elsewhere in Italy.

60. L. Calpurnius Piso (13.31.1, 15.18.3) was son of L. (formerly Cn.) Calpurnius Piso
(3.17.4, 4.62.1) and grandson of the disgraced Cn. Piso (1.13.2n.).

61. The "pledge" liable for seizure is a reference to property, upon which the aedile
could order a distraint if, for example, a senator failed to meet an official obligation. For
the two types of aedile see App. A s.v. curule.

62. See 3.31.5n. For Helvidius Priscus see 12.49.2n.

63. Another way of referring to the treasury, which is the subject of the following di-
gression and to which the words "in that respect" in the following sentence refer.

64. They passed directly to the praetorship without the intervening stages of tribune or
aedile.

tion on the grounds that as prefect of the rowers who were held at Ravenna he had blighted Italy, as if it were the lowest of nations, by his luxury and savagery.

2   Caninius Rebilus, one of the leaders in terms of his skill at law and the size of his fortune, escaped the rackings of an ill old age by emitting his blood from his veins, though he was not believed capable of the steadfastness needed for choosing death, owing to the womanly disreputableness of his lusts. As for L. Volusius, he passed away with an exceptional reputation, a man who had a life span of ninety-three years, outstanding wealth procured+ by good practice, and the uninterrupted friendship of a great many Commanders.[65]

★ ★ ★

31   With Nero (for the second time) and L. Piso as consuls, there were few events worth recalling—unless anyone finds it pleasant to fill volumes with praising the foundations and beams with which Caesar had set up a massive amphitheater on the Plain of Mars, despite the finding that what accords with the worthiness of the Roman people is that illustrious matters should be entrusted to annals but

2   things such as these to the daily record of the City.[66] Be that as it may, the colonies of Capua and Nuceria were consolidated by the addition of veterans, and as a gratuity to the plebs four hundred sesterces a man were given,[67] and forty million were paid into the treasury to maintain the people's credit. Also the tax of four percent on the sale of menials was remitted—a show rather than a reality, because, since the seller was ordered to pay it, it devolved upon buyers as an additional part of the price.

3   And Caesar issued an edict that no magistrate or procurator should produce, in the province which he held, a spectacle of gladiators or of wild beasts or any other form of games. (Previously they had been blighting their subjects as much by such lavishness as by seizing their money, in that they courted popularity to defend the

32   felonies which they had committed through lust.)[68] There was also passed, for the purposes of retribution and security alike, a senate's decision that, if anyone was killed by his slaves, those manumitted in his will who had stayed under the same roof should also suffer reprisals along with the slaves.

2   Restored to his rank was the consular, Lurius Varus, formerly struck down on charges of greed; and Pomponia Graecina, a distinguished lady and wedded to

---

65. For him see 12.22.2n. and 13.25.1n.

66. For the gazette see also 3.3.2 (and n.), 16.22.3.

67.   For the gratuity see 3.29.3n.

68. T. seems to mean that public spectacles, which were popular, were financed by the very money which governors greedily extorted from the provincials (hence "lust"). It was a vicious circle, which Nero attempted to break.

the Plautius whose ovation over the Britons I recorded,[69] became a defendant indicted for a foreign superstition and was entrusted to the judgment of her husband. In accordance with the old-time custom, it was in front of their relations that he investigated the question of his spouse's jeopardy and reputation and pronounced her guiltless.[70] (This Pomponia had a long life of unbroken sadness. **3** After the killing of Julia, Drusus' daughter, by Messalina's guile,[71] for forty years she went about with no garb except that of grief,[72] no spirit except that of sorrow; and this behavior, which passed with impunity during the command of Claudius, later turned to her glory.)

The same year saw further defendants, among whose cases was that of P. **33** Celerius,+ accused by Asia; because Caesar could not acquit, he dragged it out until the man met his death from old age: for Celerius,+ after killing—as I have recalled[73]—the proconsul Silanus, used the magnitude of the crime to cover up his other outrages. The Cilicians had denounced Cossutianus Capito, a blemished **2** and foul individual who deemed he had the same daring prerogative in his province as he had exercised in the City; but, belabored by the persistence of their accusation, he finally abandoned his defense and was condemned under the law of extortion. On behalf of Eprius Marcellus,[74] from whom the Lycians sought **3** restitution, canvassing was so successful that some of his accusers were penalized by exile on the grounds that they had endangered a guiltless man.

★   ★   ★

With Nero as consul for the third time, there embarked simultaneously on the **34** consulship Valerius Messalla, whose great-grandfather, the orator Corvinus, was remembered by a few men (now old) as having been colleague to Divine Augustus, the great-great-grandfather of Nero, in the same magistracy.[75] But the noble family had its honor augmented by the gift of five hundred thousand sesterces each year, with which Messalla could sustain a blameless poverty. For

69. Evidently in the lost portion of Book 11.

70. For such investigations by husbands and family members see 2.50.3 and 2.85.3. The "foreign superstition" of which Pomponia was accused has sometimes been thought to have been Christianity.

71. In A.D. 43, so presumably also in the lost portion of Book 11.

72. See 2.29.1n. for the clothing of grief.

73. At 13.1.2 above, where the confirmation of the transmitted name *Celerius* (see n.) requires emending the name to that same form here.

74. For him see 12.4.3n.

75. In 31 B.C. The present consul, M. Valerius Messalla Corvinus, was son of the consul of 20 (3.2.3n.).

Aurelius Cotta and Haterius Antoninus too the princeps established an annual sum, although it was through luxuriousness that they had dissipated their ancestral wealth.

★

2   At the beginning of that year the war between Parthians and Romans concerning the holding of Armenia, which had been postponed in its initial (and still mild) stages,[76] was taken up fiercely, because Vologaeses for his part would not allow his brother Tiridates to be deprived of the kingdom he had given him or to hold it as the gift of a foreign power, while Corbulo deemed it worthy of the greatness of the Roman people to recover what had once been acquired by Lucullus and Pompeius.[77] In addition, the Armenians with ambiguous loyalty invited the armies of each side, though in the situation of their country and the similarity of their habits they were closer to the Parthians, and, having merged with them through intermarriage and being ignorant of freedom, they inclined rather in their direction, toward servitude.

35   But Corbulo had greater trouble with his soldiers' shirking than against the enemy's disloyalty: for the legions transplanted from Syria,[78] sluggish from a lengthy peace, were enduring only with the greatest difficulty the responsibilities of Romans. It was generally agreed that there were in his army veterans who had gone on neither pickets nor watches, who viewed rampart and ditch as novelties and marvels, without helmets and breastplates as they were, sleek profiteers, their en-

2   tire service spent in towns. Therefore, dismissing those whose old age or health was against them, he sought reinforcement; and levies were held across Galatia and Cappadocia, and a legion was added from Germany, together with cavalry

3   auxiliaries and infantry cohorts.[79] The whole army was kept under pelt[80] despite the winter's being so savage that the ground, with its covering of ice, provided no place for tents unless it was dug out. Many men's limbs were scorched by the force of the cold, and some expired while on lookout; and one soldier was noted carrying a bundle of wood whose hands were so deeply frozen that they stuck to his burden and dropped off from the stumps of his arms. But Corbulo him-

4   self, in light clothing and head uncovered, was in regular attendance in the column and amid their toils, offering praise to the energetic, comfort to the unhealthy, and an example to all. Later, because in the harshness of the climate and service many were refusing and deserting, a remedy was found in severity: it was not the case that pardon attended a first or second offense, as in other armies, but

76. See 13.7.2–9.3 above.

77. In the Third Mithridatic War (74/73–63 B.C.).

78. Legion III Gallica and Legion VI Ferrata (cf. 13.8.2, 13.38.4).

79. Apparently an error: the legion (VI Scythica) was from Moesia, not Germany, and it went to Syria to compensate for the troops which had left there.

80. I.e., in tents made from hide.

anyone who left the standards paid the penalty at once with his life. And that that was wholesome in practice and an improvement on sympathy was apparent, since fewer deserted that camp than those in which reprieve was common.

Meanwhile Corbulo kept the legions within the camp until spring matured, **36** and, deploying the auxiliary cohorts in suitable positions, prescribed that they should not be the first to dare battle. Care of the garrisons he entrusted to Pac- cius Orfitus, who had discharged the honor of first rank.[81] Although the latter 2 had written that the barbarians were incautious and that the chance of a success- ful operation was being offered, he was ordered to hold himself within the for- tifications and wait for larger forces. But, breaking the command after a few squadrons had arrived from the nearest strongholds and in their inexperience were demanding battle, he engaged with the enemy and was routed. His loss ter- rified those who ought to have brought support, and each returned to his own camp in trembling flight. Corbulo took this heavily and ordered the chastened 3 Paccius and his prefects and soldiers to pitch tent outside the rampart; and in that insulting detention they were kept, and not released except by the pleas of the entire army.

As for Tiridates, aided by help from his brother Vologaeses besides his personal **37** clients, he no longer struck at Armenia stealthily but openly in war, and he rav- aged those whom he deemed loyal to us; and, if forces were led against him, he outwitted them and, flying here and there, caused more terror by rumor than by fighting. Therefore Corbulo, frustrated by his long search for battle and com- 2 pelled by the enemy's example to peddle the war, divided his forces so that the legates and prefects should attack different places simultaneously. At the same 3 time he advised King Antiochus to make for the prefectures nearest to him.[82] For Pharasmanes, having killed his son Radamistus as a traitor,[83] was exercising more readily his old hatred against the Armenians in order to testify to his loy- alty to us. And that was the first time the Moschi were enticed over, and a nation allied before all others to the Romans raided the trackless areas of Armenia.

Thus Tiridates' plans were being reversed, and he sent advocates to demand, 4 in his own and the Parthians' name, why, having recently given hostages and re- vived a friendship which was supposed to clear the way for new benefits too, he was being expelled from his old possession of Armenia. It was precisely because they preferred to deal in reason rather than violence that Vologaeses himself had not yet made a move, he said; but, if war was persevered with, the Arsacidae would not lack the courage and fortune which so often now had been proved by a Ro- man disaster. In response Corbulo, having discovered to his own satisfaction that 5 Vologaeses was being held up by the defection of Hyrcania, urged Tiridates to

81. He was evidently a "first-ranker" (see App. B), but his description as "of the first rank" at 15.12.2 below seems to imply that he was demoted as a result of the present episode. (In the next sentence "written" means that he had sent a report to Corbulo.)

82. For "prefectures" see 6.42.4n. The reference is to Antiochus IV (12.55.2, 13.7.1).

83. For these two see 6.32–5, 12.44–51, and 13.6.1.

approach Caesar with a plea. It was possible, he said, that a stable kingdom and bloodless future would befall him if, abandoning a distant and tardy prospect, he pursued an immediate and more likely possibility.

38   It was then agreed—because despite the exchanges of messengers no progress was being made toward the goal of peace—that a time and place be determined for a dialogue between the men themselves. Tiridates said that he would have with him a thousand cavalry as escort; he would not lay down the number and type of soldiers that might attend Corbulo, provided that, having placed aside

2   their breastplates and helmets, they came with the face of peace. To any mortal, let alone a veteran and provident leader, the barbarian strategy would have been patent. It was precisely to prepare a trick that a restricted number was being defined on the one side and a larger offered on the other: for, if uncovered bodies were exposed to cavalry trained in the use of arrows, a multitude would be of no

3   advantage. Corbulo nevertheless dissembled his understanding, replying that it would be more correct to discuss issues of public interest with whole armies present. And he chose a place where half the area was hills, rising gently to accommodate ranks of infantry, while the other half stretched into level ground, for the deployment of cavalry squadrons.

4   On the appointed day it was Corbulo who first positioned the allied cohorts and the auxiliaries of the kings along the edges, and in the middle the Sixth Legion, with which he had merged three thousand of the Third (whom he had summoned during the night from a different camp), but with a single eagle, as if just one and the same legion were being looked at. It was only when the day was already declining that Tiridates presented himself, at a distance from which he could be seen rather than heard. Thus, without meeting, the Roman leader or-

39   dered his soldiery to withdraw, each to his own camp. The king, whether suspecting a trap (because there was simultaneous movement in several directions) or to cut off the supplies of ours which were arriving by the Pontic sea and the town of Trapezus, hastily retired.

Yet he was unable to do violence to the supplies, because they were led through mountains occupied by our garrisons; and Corbulo for his part, lest the war should drag on aimlessly and to compel the Armenians onto the defensive, prepared to extirpate their strongholds. The most substantial in the prefecture, Volandum by nomenclature, he adopted for himself; the lesser were entrusted to

2   Cornelius Flaccus, a legate, and Insteius Capito, camp prefect. Then, having reconnoitered the fortifications and made suitable provision for their storming, he urged the soldiers that the roving enemy, who was prepared for neither peace nor battle but who acknowledged by flight his disloyalty and shirking, should be

3   divested of his abodes; to glory and spoils they should pay equal heed. Then, dividing his army into four, he led forward one group (clustered together into a shell)[84] to undermine the rampart, another he ordered to move ladders up to the walls, a considerable number to shoot torches and spears from launchers. To the

---

84. See 12.35.2n.

throwers and slingers was assigned a position from which they could launch pellets at a distance, so that no section could bring support to those in difficulty, the dread being equal everywhere.

So great thereupon was the ardor of the army's competitiveness that by the 4 third part of the day the walls were denuded of defenders, the barriers of the gates overturned, the fortifications captured on the ascent, and all the adults butchered—without the loss of a single soldier, and just a few wounded. The mass of noncombatants was put up for sale under wreath;[85] the remaining plunder went to the victors. Equally good fortune was enjoyed by the legate and prefect, 5 and, with three strongholds stormed on one day, the rest in terror (and some at the wish of their inhabitants) entered into surrender.

Hence arose the confidence to attack the capital of the race, Artaxata. The le- 6 gions were nevertheless not led by the nearest route, for, if they crossed the Araxes stream (which laps the walls) by the bridge, they brought themselves within striking range; they traversed at a distance by means of a rather wide ford. But Tiri- **40** dates was ashamed that his impotence would become obvious if he yielded to the blockade, and he dreaded that he would entangle himself and his cavalry forces on impassable ground if he tried to prevent it: so he decided finally to show his battle line and, if given the day, to start a battle or, by the pretence of flight, to prepare the ground for some trick. Therefore he suddenly poured around the Roman column, but not without the awareness of our leader, who had arranged his army for marching and fighting alike. (The Third Legion was proceeding on 2 the right flank, the Sixth on the left, with the pick of the Tenth in the middle. The baggage was sheltered within the ranks, and the rear was guarded by a thousand cavalry, whom Corbulo had ordered to resist being hounded at close quarters but not to pursue any retreat. On the edges went the infantry archers and the remaining unit of cavalry, being more extended on the left edge across the foothills so that the enemy, if he entered, would be received simultaneously at the front and by an arc.) Tiridates made dashes from separate directions, not as 3 far as the range of weapons, but threatening at one moment and with a display of trepidation at another, to see if he could loosen the ranks and pursue them separately. But, when no break occurred through any rash reaction, and the rest had only been confirmed in their compliance by the example of a cavalry officer who had advanced too boldly and been transfixed by arrows, he withdrew as darkness was already approaching.

As for Corbulo, having laid out his camp on the spot, he debated whether to **41** march to Artaxata by night with his legions unencumbered and to surround it by blockade, deeming that Tiridates had retired there. But then, after scouts had brought news that the king's journey was a lengthy one and it was uncertain whether he was making for the Medes or the Albani, he waited for the dawn,

85. Wreaths were worn by slaves at auction. The proceeds of the sale of captives went to the state: hence "the remaining plunder" (below) must refer to their possessions, valuables, etc.

and the light armor was sent ahead to encircle the walls in the meantime and to
2   begin the siege at a distance. But the townsfolk, opening the gates of their own
accord, surrendered themselves and their possessions to the Romans—which was
their salvation. Artaxata was set on fire, destroyed, and leveled to the ground, because it could not be held without a substantial garrison owing to the size of its
walls, nor did we have the forces to divide between strengthening the garrison
and conducting the war, whereas, if it were left untouched and unguarded, there
3   was no advantage or glory in the fact of its capture. (There was the addition of
a marvel, as if offered by a divinity: everything outside was in bright sunshine as
far as the buildings;[+] but suddenly the area enclosed by the walls was so completely covered by dark cloud and streaked[+] by lightning that, as though the gods
were conducting an assault, it was believed that it was being handed over for extermination.)

*

4   On this account Nero was hailed as "commander," and by a senate's decision supplications were held; and there was a decree of statues and arches and successive
consulships for the princeps, and also that among the festival days there should
be included those on which the victory had been accomplished, on which it had
been announced, and on which there had been a motion concerning it—and
other items of the same kind, so outstripping any limit that C. Cassius, having
agreed in the case of the other honors, said that, if gratitude were to be expressed
to the gods in proportion with the kindness of fortune, not even the whole year
would suffice for the supplications and it was therefore necessary for sacred and
business days to be shared out, so that they might worship things divine without
obstructing things human.

42   Next a defendant who had been buffeted by various circumstances and had
earned the hatred of many was condemned—though not without resentment
against Seneca. The man was Publius Suillius,[86] terrifying and venal during the
command of Claudius and not as downcast by the change in the times as his
antagonists desired, preferring himself to be seen as a guilty party rather than as
suppliant. (It was for the sake of suppressing him in particular that the senate's
decision was believed to have been reinstated, as well as the penalty of the Cin-
2   cian law against those who pleaded cases at a price.)[87] Suillius would not refrain
from complaint and remonstrance, being free-spoken in his extreme old age—
quite apart from his natural defiance—and berating Seneca for hostility to the
3   friends of Claudius, under whom he had borne a highly justified exile:[88] at the
same time, he said, Seneca was accustomed to aimless studies and the inexperi-

86. See 11.1.1n.

87. The "senate's decision" is that of A.D. 47 (see 11.5–7, including a reference to the
Cincian law); its reinstatement is that of 13.5.1 above.

88. For Seneca's exile see 12.8.2n. From here to the end of the chapter Suillius in indi-

ence of youths, and was green with envy at those who employed a lively and in-corruptible eloquence to protect citizens. While he himself had been Germanicus' quaestor, Seneca was an adulterer in his household;[89] or was it to be reckoned a more serious matter to acquire a prize for honest effort at the wish of a litigant than to corrupt the bedrooms of principes' ladies? By what wisdom, by which   4
precepts of the philosophers had he procured three hundred million sesterces within a four-year period of royal friendship? At Rome the wills of the childless were being caught (as it were) in his net, Italy and the provinces were being drained by his inordinate usury; but in his own case his money was limited and won by toil: he himself would endure charge, danger, indeed anything, rather than subject his old and modestly[+] gained status to such sudden prosperity.

Now there was no lack of people to denounce this in the same words—or   **43**
changed for the worse—to Seneca; and accusers were discovered, and they de-nounced that the allies had been ransacked when Suillius ruled the province of Asia, and that there had been embezzlement of public money. Subsequently, be-cause they had successfully requested a yearlong investigation, it seemed quicker to begin with the charges relating to the City, for which there were witnesses available. The latter's imputations—that by an acrimonious accusation Q. Pom-   2
ponius had been forced to the necessity of civil war; that Julia, Drusus' daughter, and Sabina Poppaea had been driven to death; that Valerius Asiaticus, Lusius Sat-urninus, and Cornelius Lupus had been ensnared;[90] finally that whole columns of Roman equestrians had been convicted, and all of Claudius' savagery—were hurled against Suillius. His defense was that none of these matters had been un-   3
dertaken voluntarily but that he had only been obeying the princeps—until Cae-sar curbed the speech by referring to his own discovery in his father's records that the latter had compelled no accusation of anyone. Suillius' next pretext was   4
orders from Messalina, and his defense began to totter: why had no one else been chosen as the mouthpiece of that immoral savage? The agents of atrocities must be punished when, having acquired rewards for their crimes, they ascribed the crimes themselves to others. So, deprived of half his property (half was conceded   5
to his son and granddaughter, and also exempt was what they had received in their mother's, or grandmother's, will), he was banished to the Balearic Islands, broken in spirit neither during the crisis itself nor after his conviction; and he was said to have endured his seclusion there by means of a well-supplied and soft lifestyle. When his son Nerullinus was attacked by accusers relying on resentment of his father and charges of extortion, the princeps intervened to the effect that vengeance had been amply fulfilled.

---

rect speech systematically contrasts Seneca's alleged failings with his own alleged virtues.

89. Julia Livilla, with whom Seneca had allegedly conducted his adulterous liaison, was Germanicus' daughter.

90. The story about Pomponius (6.18.1) must have been in a part of the *Annals* now lost; the death of Julia is alluded to at 13.32.3; for the deaths of Poppaea and Valerius Asi-aticus see 11.1–3.

44   During the same period Octavius Sagitta, a tribune of the plebs, deranged with love for Pontia, a wedded woman, by means of mighty gifts bribed her into adultery and, next, to leave her husband—his own promise of marriage being met with her agreement to the wedding. But, when the woman was free, she wove delays, alleged that her father's wish was against it, and, on discovering the

2   prospect of a richer spouse, cast aside her promises. Octavius reacted by alternating between complaints and threats, invoking his lost reputation and drained money, and finally committing his life, which was "the only thing left," to her adjudication. And, after he had begun to be spurned, he demanded as consolation

3   a single night, soothed by which he might control himself in future. The night was decided upon, and Pontia entrusted custody of the bedroom to a maidservant accomplice; he for his part, with a single freedman, carried in a sword, concealed in his clothing. Then, as is customary in love and anger, there were wrangles, pleas, remonstrance, and reconciliation; and a period of darkness was reserved for lust. As if that had inflamed him, he stabbed her through, devoid of dread as she was, with the sword; he frightened off the maidservant, who came run-

4   ning up, with a wound; and burst forth from the bedroom. On the next day the slaughter was revealed, the assailant not in doubt (he was proved to have lodged with her). But the freedman announced that the deed was his: he had avenged the wrong to his patron. And he had influenced some people by the greatness of his example, until the maidservant, recovered from her wound, dis-

5   closed the truth. Arraigned before the consuls by the father of the woman he had killed, after leaving his tribunate he was convicted by a vote of the fathers and the law concerning assassins.

45   No less distinctive in that year was the immorality which marked the beginning of massive calamities for the state. There was in the community Sabina Poppaea, begotten with T. Ollius as her father, but she had adopted the name of her maternal grandfather, Poppaeus Sabinus,[91] of illustrious memory, a consular who outshone the other in triumphal luster (Ollius was overthrown by Sejanus'

2   friendship without having yet discharged any honors). This woman had everything else except honorableness. Her mother,[92] outstripping in beauty the ladies of her age, had given her both glory and good looks alike; her wealth sufficed for

3   the brilliancy of her lineage. Her conversation was affable, and her talent not inappropriate. She paraded modestness and practiced recklessness, rarely emerging in public, and then only with part of her face screened by a veil, lest she satisfy people's gaze or because it became her. She never spared her reputation, making no distinction between husbands and adulterers; susceptible to neither her own nor another's emotion, she would transfer her lust wherever advantage showed.

4   While she was living in marriage to Rufrius Crispinus, a Roman equestrian to whom she had borne a son, Otho enticed her by his youth and luxuriousness

---

91. Consul in A.D. 9 and awarded the triumphal insignia in 26: see 1.80.1, 4.46–51, 5.10.2–3, and 6.39.3.

92. The Poppaea of 11.1–4.

and because he was regarded as the most ardent in Nero's friendship.[93] And there
was no delay before adultery was followed by marriage. Otho would praise his   **46**
wife's good looks and elegance in the princeps's presence, whether being incautious through love or so that he might inflame him and, if they both possessed
the same lady, that that bond might add to his powerfulness. Often, rising from
a dinner party of Caesar's, he was heard saying that he was the one going to her,+
to him had been granted nobility and beauty— things which were the wish of
everyone and the joy of the fortunate. With spurs such as these, no long hesita-   2
tion was interposed. With an approach accepted, Poppaea first achieved influence
by means of skillful blandishments, pretending that she was unequal to her desire and captured by Nero's good looks; but soon, with the princeps's love now
fierce, she changed to haughtiness, insisting, if she were detained beyond a night
or two, that she was a wedded woman and could not give up her married state,
bound as she was to Otho by the kind of life which no one could equal: he was
a man of magnificent spirit and refinement, she said, in him she saw things deserving of the highest fortune; whereas Nero, bound by custom to a maidservant
concubine,+ had derived nothing from his servile cohabitation except sordid
abasement. Otho was toppled from his accustomed intimacy, then from all en-   3
counter and companionship, and finally, to prevent his living as a rival in the City,
he was placed over the province of Lusitania, where up to the time of the civil
war he lived, not in accordance with his previous infamy, but wholesomely and
righteously—a man provocative in inactivity and more restrained in power.

   To that extent Nero found screens for his outrages and crimes; but he was par-   **47**
ticularly suspicious of Cornelius Sulla,[94] interpreting his temperamental insensibility for its opposite and construing him as an astute pretender. His dread was
intensified by Graptus—one of Caesar's freedmen, who because of his experience and old age had become well versed in the household of the principes ever
since Tiberius—through the following lie. The Mulvian Bridge at that time was   2
celebrated for its nocturnal allurements; and Nero went there frequently, so that
his recklessness might find greater release outside the City. Graptus' story—that
an ambush had been arranged for Nero's return by the Flaminian Way and had
been avoided only by fate, since he had retired to the Sallustian Gardens by a different route, and that the instigator of the trap had been Sulla—was all lies,
based on the chance fact that certain individuals, owing to the youthful licen-
tiousness which was then generally prevalent, had produced a groundless dread
in some of the princeps's servants on their way home. Not one of Sulla's slaves   3
or clients had been recognized, and in particular his despicable nature, incapable
of any daring, was inconsistent with the charge; nevertheless, just as if it had been
proved, he was ordered to leave his native land and be confined within the walls
of the Massilians.

   93. Otho is the future emperor (13.12.1n.); for Rufrius Crispinus see 11.1.3 (n.), 11.4.3,
and 12.42.1.
   94. See 13.23.1n.

48   With the same men as consuls, legations from the Puteolani were heard, which the rank[95] and plebs had sent separately to the senate, the former berating the violence of the multitude, the latter the greed of the magistrates and first citizens. Lest the mutiny, which had gone as far as rocks and threats of arson, should incite executions and arms, C. Cassius was chosen to apply a remedy.[96] Because they would not endure his severity, concern for the matter was transferred at his own request to the Scribonii brothers, who were given a praetorian cohort, in terror of which, and after reprisals against a few individuals, harmony returned to the townsfolk.

49   I would not record a quite commonplace senate's decision by which it was permitted to the community of the Syracusans to exceed the defined number for gladiatorial productions, had not Paetus Thrasea spoken against it and pre-

2   sented his disparagers with material for criticizing his opinion.[97] Why, if he believed that the state needed senatorial freedom, was he pursuing such trivialities? Should not his persuasion or dissuasion be concerned rather with war or peace, with revenues and laws, and with whatever else formed the basis of things Roman? It was allowed to the fathers, whenever it was their turn for the prerogative of giving their opinion, to express whatever they wished and to require a

3   motion in respect of it: was this the only topic worthy of an amendment, namely, that spectacles at Syracuse should not be produced more lavishly? Was everything else across all parts of the empire as exceptionally good as if, not Nero, but Thrasea were holding the reins? On the other hand, if dissembling the highest matters led to their being overlooked, how much more should one refrain from the irrelevant!

4   Thrasea's response, when his friends demanded an explanation, was to reply that it was not ignorance of present circumstances which made him seek to rectify decisions of that kind, but he was in fact honoring the fathers by making it clear that concern for important matters would not be dissembled by those who turned their attention even to the most trivial.

50   In the same year, after frequent importuning by the people, who were blaming the unrestraint of collectors,[98] Nero considered whether to order all revenues

2   to be abandoned and to give that as his finest gift to the race of mortals. But his impulse, after much preliminary praise for his magnanimity, was checked by the senators, warning of the empire's dissolution if the incomes by which the state was sustained were reduced: if the tolls were removed, they said, the consequence

3   would be a demand for the abolition of taxes. Many of the revenue companies had been set up by consuls and tribunes of the plebs at a time when the Roman

95. The technical term for a local town-senate.

96. For him see 12.11.3n.

97. In the extant *Annals* this is T.'s first reference to Thrasea Paetus, suffect consul in 56 and an increasingly heroic figure in the later narrative, which breaks off in the course of his suicide (16.35.1–2).

98. I.e., tax collectors (see *OCD* 1275–6 s.v. publicani).

people's freedom was still keen; the remainder had been provided subsequently so that the profit account and the necessary disbursements would balance each other. Yet plainly the collectors' desires should be moderated, lest what had been endured without complaint for so many years should develop into resentment because of new embitterments.

Therefore the princeps issued an edict that the laws of each collecting body, **51** concealed up to that time, should be advertised; abandoned claims should not be resumed beyond a year; at Rome the praetor, and in the provinces whoever was propraetor or proconsul, should dispense justice out of turn in the case of collectors; the immunity of soldiers should be preserved, except for those engaged in selling; and other perfectly fair measures, which, though observed for a short while, were then frustrated. (Nevertheless there still survives the abolition of the **2** "fortieth" and "fiftieth" and the other names which the collectors had invented for their unlawful impositions.)[99] The cost of transporting grain in overseas provinces was modified, and it was laid down that ships were not to be entered in the assessments of businessmen and they should not pay tax on them.

Defendants from the province of Africa who had held proconsular command **52** there, Sulpicius Camerinus and Pompeius Silvanus, were acquitted by Caesar — Camerinus in the face of a few private individuals who were hurling against him charges of savagery rather than of stealing money. Silvanus had been beset by a **2** large army of accusers and they were demanding time for the summoning of witnesses; but their victim was requiring that he defend himself on the spot, and he prevailed on account of his moneyed childlessness and an old age which he prolonged beyond the life of those by whose canvassing he had escaped.[100]

*

Up to that time affairs in Germany had been quiet owing to the ingenuity of its **53** leaders, who, now that the insignia of a triumph had become commonplace, hoped for greater luster if they maintained unbroken peace. Paulinus Pompeius **2** and L. Vetus were in charge of the army at that period.[101] But, to prevent their soldiery from being kept sluggish, the former finished off the embankment begun sixty-three years before by Drusus for curbing the Rhine; Vetus was preparing to connect the Moselle and Arar by making a conduit between the two, so that provisions transported by sea[102] and then along the Rhone and Arar might travel by means of the conduit and thereafter along the stream of the Moselle into the Rhine and thence to the Ocean, and that, with the difficulties removed

99. Evidently taxes at the rates of 2 ½ and 2 percent.

100. His bribery had consisted in promising legacies in his will. Silvanus had been suffect consul in 45, Camerinus (above) in the following year.

101. A. Pompeius Paullinus (again at 15.18.3) had been suffect consul in (probably) 54; L. Antistius Vetus is the consul of 55 (13.11.1n.).

102. The Mediterranean.

from the route, the shores of the West and North might be navigable between
3   each other. But the task was resented by Aelius Gracilis, legate of Belgica, in the
form of deterring Vetus from bringing his legions into someone else's province
and from striving after the affections of the Galliae—his insistence that it would
constitute an alarm for the Commander being one by which honorable ventures
are generally prevented.[103]

54   However, given the unbroken inactivity of the armies, a rumor started that the
legates' prerogative of leading against the enemy had been snatched away from
them; and for that reason the Frisians moved their young men to the bank[104] by
means of the denes and marshes, and those of noncombatant age across the lakes,
and they settled on the vacant land reserved for the soldiers' use, the instigators
being Verritus and Malorix, who were rulers of that nation (insofar as Germans
2   are ruled at all). Already they had planted their homes, had introduced seed into
the plow land, and were working the ground as if it were ancestral, when Dubius Avitus,[105] receiving the province from Paulinus, and threatening the Frisians
with Roman might unless they withdrew to their old locations or made a successful request for their new abode from Caesar, drove Verritus and Malorix to
3   undertake the presentation of the plea. They set off for Rome, and, while they
waited for Nero (intent on other concerns), in the course of the sights normally
shown to barbarians they entered Pompey's theater to observe the size of the
population. While they idled away their time there (in their ignorance they took
no delight in the entertainment), they inquired about the assembly in the audi-
torium, the distinctions between the ranks, which the equestrians were, where
the senate—and they noticed some people in foreign dress in the senators' seats.
When, on asking who they were, they were told that that was an honor given to
legates of those peoples who excelled in courage and in Roman friendship, they
exclaimed that no mortals were ahead of Germans in arms or loyalty, and they
4   went down and sat among the fathers—an action received affably by its observers
as typical of a primitive impulse and in fine rivalry. Nero presented them both
with Roman citizenship—and ordered the Frisians to depart from the territory.
When this was spurned, the sudden sending in of auxiliary cavalry enforced its
necessity, with the capture or slaughter of those whose opposition had been too
persistent.

55   The same territory was occupied by the Ampsivarii, a more effective race owing not only to their own resources but to the pity of the adjacent peoples, because, driven out by the Chauci and lacking an abode, they were begging for a
safe place of exile. And they had the assistance of a man brilliant among those
races and loyal to us too, by name Boiocalus, who reported that he had been

103. Gracilis is implying that Vetus has ulterior motives in proposing to operate in Gaul,
a traditional trouble spot (3.40–7, 11.1.2).

104. Of the Rhine.

105. Suffect consul in 56.

bound in chains by order of Arminius in the Cheruscan rebellion,[106] had later performed military service under the leadership of Tiberius and Germanicus, and to his fifty years' compliance was added also the fact that he was subjecting his own race to our jurisdiction. How small, he said, was the stretch of plain, to which   2
the soldiers' livestock and herds might occasionally be transferred! *Naturally* they should reserve refuges for flocks even though humans were starving, provided only that they did not prefer desolate wastes to friendly peoples![107] That had once been the plow land of the Chamavi, then of the Tubantes, and afterward of the Usipi. Land had been given to the race of mortals as the sky to the gods; and that which was vacant was common property. Then, looking up to the sun and call-   3
ing on the other planets, he inquired (as if in their presence) whether they wanted to gaze on ground that was empty; rather let them deluge it with the sea in the face of "the seizers of land"!

Avitus was unmoved+ by this speech: they should tolerate the commands of   **56**
their betters, he said; what the gods whom they were imploring had decided was that any verdict should remain with the Romans as to what was granted and what taken away, and the latter should tolerate no other judges than themselves. This was his public response to the Ampsivarii; but to Boiocalus himself it was that he would grant him territory in memory of his friendship. But this the man spurned as the bribe for betrayal, adding "We may lack a land in which to live, but not in which to die." And so, with hostility on each side, they parted.

The Ampsivarii called the Bructeri, Tencteri, and even more distant nations   2
too as allies for the war; but Avitus, having written to Curtilius Mancia, legate of the upper army, that he should cross the Rhine and make a show of arms in the rear, led his legions in person into the territory of the Tencteri, threatening them with extirpation unless they dissociated themselves from the allied cause. As they   3
therefore desisted, the Bructeri were terrorized by a like dread; and, as the rest too were protecting themselves against a danger not their own, the now isolated race of the Ampsivarii withdrew back to the Usipi and Tubantes. Driven off from their land in turn, they made for the Chatti and Cherusci, and in the course of their long wandering were transformed from needy guests into enemies on alien ground, where all their young men were slaughtered and those of noncombatant age were shared out as plunder.

In the same season there was a dispute between the Hermunduri and Chatti   **57**
in the form of a great battle, as they tried to annex by force a river which was fertile in generating salt and bordered on them both—having had implanted in them, besides a lust to conduct everything by means of arms, a religious belief

106. A reference to the Varian disaster of A.D. 9.

107. This sentence seems only to make sense if the preceding sentence is ironic, implying its opposite: namely, that the territory in question is very large and will accommodate both livestock and the Ampsivarii, provided that the Romans do not actually give preference to animals at the expense of humans.

that that locality in particular is close to heaven and that the prayers of mortals are nowhere listened to more closely by the gods. Hence it was by the beneficence of the divinities, they thought, that in that stream and those woods salt was produced in the way that it was⁺ (not, as among other races, by waves drying out in a deposit of the sea but by water poured over a pile of burning trees—a consolidation from the mutually contrary elements of fire and water). The war was successful for the Hermunduri, more ruinous for the Chatti, because the victors consecrated the opposing line to Mars and Mercury, a vow by which they consign horses, men, and everything vanquished for slaying.

3   Whereas the enemies' threats recoiled only upon themselves, the community of the Ubii, an ally of ours, was afflicted by an unforeseen calamity. Fires, issuing from the earth, seized villas, plow land, and villages far and wide and were carried into the actual walls of the recently founded colony.[108] Nor could they be extinguished—not if rain fell, not if they were drenched by river water or any other moisture—until some countryfolk, in their need for a remedy and in anger at the disaster, hurled rocks from a distance and then, as the flames came to a halt, approached more closely, repelling them with blows from rods and other forms of beating, as if they were wild animals. Finally they hurled on coverings torn from their bodies, those more sordid and soiled by use being proportionately the more likely to overwhelm the fires.

*

58   In the same year the fact that the Ruminal tree in the Comitium, which eight hundred thirty years before had protected Remus and Romulus in their infancy,[109] had shriveled, its twigs dead and its trunk drying out, was held as a prodigy, until it revived with new growth.

108. See 12.27.1 (A.D. 50).

109. The "Ruminal fig" (*ficus Ruminalis*) was an ancient tree which stood in the area near the foot of the Capitoline Hill and was said to be the tree under which Romulus and Remus were suckled by the famous wolf.

Book 14

A.D. 59

With Gaius Vipstanus and C. Fonteius as consuls,[1] Nero deferred no further the **1** long contemplated crime, his daring strengthened by his protracted experience of command and himself being daily more inflamed with love for Poppaea, who, despairing of marriage for herself and of his divorce from Octavia as long as Agrippina was preserved, censured the princeps with regular reproaches and sometimes by way of a witticism called him "the ward," susceptible to the orders of another and lacking not only command but even freedom. Why was her wed- **2** ding being deferred? Evidently her looks were displeasing, and her triumphal grandfathers; or was it her fertility[2] and true heart? No, the fear was that, at least as a wife, she might disclose the wrongs done to the fathers and the wrath of the people against the haughtiness and greed of his mother. But, if Agrippina could bear no daughter-in-law who was not hostile to her son, she herself should be restored to her espousal to Otho: she would go anywhere on earth where she could only hear the insults to the Commander rather than witness them and be enmeshed in his perils. —No one attempted to prevent such penetrating words **3** as these, accompanied as they were by the artful tears of an adulteress, since all desired his mother's power broken and none believed that her son's hatred would harden into slaughter.

Cluvius[3] transmits that Agrippina was so carried away by the fervor of retain- **2** ing her powerfulness that in the middle of the day, at a time when Nero was warm with wine and with banqueting, she quite often offered herself to him in his drunken state, smartly made up and prepared for incest; and that, as those clos- est to them were already noting their reckless kisses and the blandishments which heralded outrage, Seneca sought from a female some defense against these wom- anly allurements and sent in the freedwoman Acte, who, tense though she was at the danger to herself and at Nero's infamy alike, was to tell him that their incest had been publicized by his mother's boasting and that the soldiers would not tol- erate the command of a perverted princeps. (Fabius Rusticus[4] recalls that the de- **2** sire was not Agrippina's but Nero's and that it was thwarted by a stratagem of the same freedwoman; but the other authors too have relayed the same as Cluvius, and tradition inclines in their direction—whether Agrippina in fact conceived such monstrousness in her mind or whether the contemplation of a novel lust seemed more credible in one who in her girlhood years had committed illicit sex with Lepidus in the hope of despotism, having groveled even before the whims of Pallas with a similar desire and been trained for every outrage by her

1. C. Vipstanus Apronianus was son of the consul of 48 (11.23.1); C. Fonteius Capito was perhaps son or grandson of the consul of A.D. 12 (4.36.3).
2. She already had a son by Rufrius Crispinus (13.45.4).
3. See 13.20.2n.
4. See 13.20.2n.

3 wedding to her uncle.)[5] Therefore Nero avoided private encounters with her and, on her withdrawal to her gardens or to her Tusculan or Antian estates, praised her pursuit of inactivity; finally, deeming her overburdensome wherever she was, he decided to kill her, debating only whether by poison or the sword or some other violence.

2   The favorite at first was poison; but, if it were administered during a banquet of the princeps, it could not be referred to chance, such having already been the means of Britannicus' extermination; and it seemed a steep task to manipulate the servants of a woman alerted against subterfuge by her own experience in crime; and in fact she had personally fortified her body by taking prophylactic remedies. As for slaughter by the sword, no one could devise how it might be concealed; and he dreaded that his orders might be spurned by anyone chosen for so great a deed.

3   An ingenious offer came from the freedman Anicetus, prefect of the fleet at Misenum, a tutor of Nero's boyhood and resented by Agrippina with a hatred that was mutual. He explained that a ship could be assembled, part of which might be detached by artifice while out at sea, ejecting the unsuspecting woman. Nothing, he said, was so capable of chance occurrences as the sea; and, if she were cut off by shipwreck, who would be so unfair as to assign to crime something for which the winds and billows were to blame? The princeps could add a tem-
4 ple for the deceased, and altars and all the other manifestations of devotion. Such artfulness found favor, helped as it was by the moment too, since he was cele-brating the festival days of the Quinquatrus at Baiae.[6] There he lured his mother, insisting that the rages of parents should be borne and tempers calmed—all so that he might produce a rumor of reconciliation which Agrippina might accept, the credulity of females being responsive to joyful news.

2   On her subsequent arrival he met her on the shore (she was coming from An-tium), welcomed her with his hand and an embrace and led her to Bauli. (That is the name of a villa which is lapped by the sea as it curves between the promon-
3 tory of Misenum and the Baian lake.) There stood among other ships one more ornate, as if that too were a tribute to his mother's honor (she had been accus-tomed to travel in a trireme with marines as oarsmen). And then she had been invited to a banquet, so that nighttime might be pressed into concealing the deed.
4 There was general assent that a betrayer had presented himself and that Agrip-pina, after hearing of the subterfuge but ambivalent about believing it, had trav-eled to Baiae[+] by the conveyance of a chair. But there blandishments removed her dread, after her affable reception and being placed above her host:[7] for, when

5. M. Aemilius Lepidus, son of the consul of A.D. 6 (1.13.2n.) and great-grandson of Augustus, was married to Drusilla (sister of Agrippina and Caligula) and was executed in 39 as an accomplice in the conspiracy of Lentulus Gaetulicus, in which Agrippina was also involved. The "uncle" is Claudius, whom she married in 49 (12.3–8).

6. A festival of Minerva (see 14.12.1 below) on 19–23 March.

7. The place of honor (3.14.1n.).

he had dragged out the party for a long time by numerous conversations, at one moment in youthful intimacy and at another frowning as if communicating something serious, Nero escorted her on her departure, fastening particularly closely upon her eyes and breast—either to complete his pretense or else the final gaze on his doomed mother checked even his bestial heart.

That the night was illuminated by stars and peaceful with a calm sea was ensured by the gods, as if to prove criminality. The ship had not made much progress (with Agrippina accompanied by two from the number of her establishment, of whom Crepereius Gallus was standing not far from the tiller, while Acerronia, leaning over the feet of her reclining mistress, was recalling in joy the remorse of the son and his mother's recovery of favor), when at a given signal the shelter over the area collapsed from its heavy load of lead, and Crepereius was crushed and immediately rendered lifeless. Agrippina and Acerronia were sheltered by the bed's towering sides, which by chance were too substantial to yield to the weight. Nor did the detachment of the vessel follow, given the general disturbance and because even the accomplices were impeded by the numbers of the ignorant. It seemed therefore to the rowers that they should lean to one side and so sink the ship; but there was no ready agreement among themselves as regards the emergency, and others straining in the opposite direction provided the opportunity for a gentler plunge into the sea. Yet Acerronia—misguidedly (she kept shouting that she was Agrippina and that the princeps's mother must be rescued)—was dispatched with pikes and oars and whatever naval weapons chance offered. Agrippina, silent and therefore less recognized (she nevertheless received one wound to the shoulder), swam and then encountered some skiffs; conveyed thus to the Lucrine Lake, she was carried to her own villa.

Reflecting there that she had been deliberately summoned by a treacherous letter and had been the principal recipient of honor, and how it was next to the shore, not driven by winds or dashed on rocks, that her ship had collapsed from its uppermost part like a terrestrial device; observing too the execution of Acerronia, and at the same time looking at her own wound, she realized that her only remedy against subterfuge was to seem not to understand it.[+] She sent her freedman Agermus to announce to her son that by the gods' kindness and his good fortune she had escaped a serious disaster. She begged, she said, that, no matter how scared by the danger to his mother, he should defer any concern to visit her: what *she* needed at present was rest. Meanwhile, pretending unconcern, she applied medication to her wound and dressings to her body and[+] ordered Acerronia's will to be sought and her property sealed (that alone not in pretense).

As for Nero, waiting for news of the completed deed, he was told that she had escaped, injured by only a light blow, her brush with the crisis extending only to her being in no doubt as to its instigator. Thereupon, choking with panic, he claimed that she would soon—soon!—be here, hurrying for vengeance. If she armed the slaves or inflamed the soldiery, or if she made her way through to the senate and people with allegations of shipwreck and wounding and murdered friends, what would be his defense against her, unless Burrus and Seneca came

up with something? To try them out,[+] he had immediately summoned them (it
3   being doubtful whether they were ignorant even before this). There was thus a
long silence from each, lest their dissuasion be unavailing—or else they believed
that things had reached such depths that, unless Agrippina were forestalled, Nero
must perish. Afterward Seneca was the readier to the extent that he looked at
Burrus and inquired whether her slaughter should be commanded of the sol-
4   diery; the other replied that the praetorians, bound to the whole house of the
Caesars and mindful of Germanicus, would not venture anything frightful against
5   his progeny: let Anicetus complete what he had promised. And he for his part
had no hesitation but actually demanded the climax of the crime. In response to
these words, Nero professed that that was the day on which command was being
given to him, and the author of so great a gift was a freedman: Anicetus should
6   go rapidly, he said, and take with him those readiest for his orders. He himself,
on hearing that Agermus had arrived as a messenger on a mission from Agrippina, set the stage for an accusation of his own and, while the man was conveying her instructions, threw down a sword at his feet and then ordered him to be
thrown into chains as if apprehended in the act—all so that he could fabricate a
story to the effect that the extermination of the princeps had been set in motion
by his mother and, in shame at the apprehension of the crime, she had chosen
death of her own accord.

8   Meanwhile Agrippina's danger had become public, the assumption being that
it had happened by accident, and each person on hearing of it ran down to the
shore. Some climbed on the piled breakwaters, some on the closest boats; others
waded into the sea as far as their bodies allowed; still others stretched out their
hands. The whole beach was filled with the complaints, vows, and shouting of
those asking their different questions or answering in uncertain terms. A mighty
multitude with lights streamed down, and, when it became known that she had
been preserved, they prepared themselves to offer congratulations—until they
scattered at the sight of an armed and menacing column.
2   Anicetus surrounded her villa with pickets and, breaking down the entrance,
seized any slaves he encountered until he came to the doors of the bedroom,
where a few still stood fast, the rest having been terrified away in terror of the
3   onrushers. In the bedroom there was only a modest light and one of the maids,
while Agrippina was more and more tense that no one, not even Agermus, arrived from her son. Welcome circumstances would wear a different face, she
thought; as it was, there was isolation and sudden noises and the symptoms of a
4   final affliction. When next the maid departed, she said "Are you too deserting
me?", then looked around to see Anicetus, accompanied by the trierarch Her-
culeius and Obaritus, a marine centurion. If he had come to visit, she said, he
might report that she had recovered; but, if to perpetrate a crime, she would not
5   believe it of her son: there had been no command for parricide.[8] But the assailants surrounded her bed, and initially the trierarch struck her head with his

8. For parricide see 13.16.4n.

cudgel; and, as the centurion was already drawing his sword for death, she proffered her womb, crying out "Stab my belly!"; and with many wounds she was dispatched.

On these matters the tradition is in agreement; but, as to whether Nero gazed **9** at his lifeless mother and praised the look of her body, there are those who have transmitted it and there are those who deny it. She was cremated the same night, on a party couch[9] and with cheap obsequies. (Nor, while Nero was in charge of affairs, was the earth piled up or encased;[10] later, through the concern of her domestics, she received an insignificant tomb alongside the road to Misenum and the villa of the dictator Caesar, which enjoys an elevated prospect of the bays beneath.) With the pyre lit, a freedman of hers with the nomenclature Mnester **2** pierced himself with a sword, whether through affection for his patron or dread of extermination being uncertain.

This was the end which Agrippina many years before had believed would be **3** hers and had belittled: when she was consulting the Chaldaeans about Nero, they replied that he would achieve command and would slaughter his mother; and she for her part said, "Let him slaughter, provided he achieves command."[11]

But, on Caesar's part, it was only when the crime was at last accomplished that **10** its magnitude was understood. For the remainder of the night, sometimes transfixed in silence, but more often rising in panic and devoid of reason, he awaited the dawn as if it would bring his extermination. It was the sycophancy of the **2** centurions and tribunes which first, at Burrus' instigation, fortified him to hope, as they grasped his hand and congratulated him on his escape from the unforeseen crisis of his mother's deed. Then his friends approached the temples, and, the example being set, the nearest municipalities in Campania testified to their delight with victims[12] and legations—the man himself being sorrowful with the opposite pretense[13] and as if bitter at his own preservation and bewailing his parent's death. Yet, because the faces of localities do not change as do the counte- **3** nances of men, and he was confronted by the oppressive sight of that sea and its shores (and there were those who believed that the sound of a trumpet was heard in the hills rising around, and breast-beating at his mother's tomb), he withdrew to Naples and sent a letter to the senate, of which the essence was that the assailant Agermus, from Agrippina's most intimate freedmen, had been discovered with a sword and that she had paid the penalty in conscience at the crime which she had arranged.[14] He added charges drawn from the more distant past: that she **11**

9. I.e., a couch on which one would recline at parties or banquets.

10. Sc. by a stone monument or similar.

11. See 2.27.2n. for the Chaldaeans, and possibly 6.22.4 for this prophecy (but no reference to Chaldaeans).

12. Sacrificial animals.

13. I.e., the celebrations of his friends and of the Campanian townships were as insincere as Nero's sorrow.

14. The precise text of this last clause is uncertain.

had hoped for partnership in command; for the praetorian cohorts to swear allegiance to a female; and for the same dishonor on the part of senate and people; and, after she had been thwarted,[15] in her hostility to the soldiery, fathers, and plebs, she had deprecated the donative and gratuity[16] and contrived dangers for illustrious men. By what effort of his own had it been achieved that she did not

2   burst into the curia, nor issue replies to foreign peoples![17] In a glancing assault on the Claudian period too he transferred all the outrages of that despotism to his mother, referring to the fact that her life had been extinguished by public good fortune. For he narrated the shipwreck also; but who could be found so dull as to believe that it had been a chance occurrence? Or that a shipwrecked woman had sent a single man with a weapon to break through the cohorts and

3   fleets of the Commander? Therefore it was no longer Nero, whose monstrousness outstripped the complaints of all, but Seneca who was the subject of adverse rumor, because in such a speech he had inscribed a confession.

12   Nevertheless, with remarkable rivalry on the part of the leaders, there were decrees of supplications at all the cushioned couches[18] and that the Quinquatrus, during which the subterfuge had been disclosed, should be celebrated by annual games; that a golden representation of Minerva should be set up in the curia and an image of the princeps alongside; and that Agrippina's birthday should be included among the disqualified days.[19] Thrasea Paetus, accustomed as he had been to pass over previous sycophancies in silence or with only brief assent, on that occasion made an exit from the senate, thereby providing grounds for danger to himself but not presenting the others with their entry to freedom.

2   Portents too intervened, frequent and unavailing: a woman gave birth to a snake, and another in intercourse with her husband was rendered lifeless by a thunderbolt; again, the sun was suddenly darkened and the fourteen districts of the City were struck from the sky.[20] All of which happened without any concern of the gods, to such an extent that for many years afterward Nero contin-

3   ued his command and his crimes. Yet, to aggravate the resentment toward his mother and to testify to his own increased mildness with her removed, he restored to their ancestral abodes Junia and Calpurnia, illustrious ladies,[21] and Valerius Capito and Licinius Gabolus, former praetors who had been banished by

4   Agrippina.[22] He even permitted the ashes of Lollia Paulina to be brought back

15. The text of this clause too is uncertain.

16. For these see 12.41.1n.

17. For these two "achievements" see 13.5.1–2.

18. Ritual couches, on which images of gods, etc., might be placed: see *OCD* 837 s.v. lectisternium.

19. No public business could be transacted on "disqualified days" (*dies nefasti*), in this case 6 November.

20. By lightning. For the fourteen districts of Rome see 15.40.2n.

21. For Junia Calvina see 12.4.1–2 and 12.8.1; for Calpurnia see 12.22.3.

22. Nothing is known of them.

and a sepulchre set up;[23] and those whom he himself had recently relegated, Iturius and Calvisius, he released from their penalty.[24] As for Silana, she had succumbed to fate after returning to Tarentum from distant exile, at a time when Agrippina, through whose antagonism she had fallen,[25] was already tottering or had mellowed.[+]

And yet he tarried[26] in the towns of Campania, tense as to the precise man-   **13** ner in which he should go into the City, and whether he would discover compliance from the senate or enthusiasm from the plebs. Conversely all the basest people, of whom no other court has been more fertile, said that Agrippina's name was resented and the people's goodwill fired by her death: he should go without trembling and should experience in person their veneration of him. At the same time they demanded to precede him, and found everything readier than their re-   2 assurances: the tribes along the route, the senate in festive adornment, columns of spouses and children arranged by sex and age, and, set up where he would process, tiers of observation-platforms, in the way that triumphs are viewed. Hence it was as a haughty victor over public servitude that he approached the Capitol, repaid his debt of gratitude, and released himself into all the lusts which, though ill curbed, had nevertheless been retarded by such respect as he had had for his mother.

It was an old desire of his to stand in the races of a four-horse team, and a no   **14** less foul enthusiasm to sing to the lyre as if at the games. He would recall that competing with chariot and horses was a royal pursuit and practiced by ancient leaders, and that too one celebrated in the praises of bards and offered as an honor to the gods; moreover singing was sacred to Apollo, he said, and it was in such garb[27] that that principal and prescient divinity stood not only in Greek cities but throughout Roman temples. And it was only when he could no longer be   2 checked that Seneca and Burrus decided that, to prevent his winning on both counts, they should concede one. An area was enclosed in the Vatican valley in which he could drive his horses without its becoming an indiscriminate spectacle; but soon the Roman people were actually invited, and they extolled him with their praises, seeing how the public is desirous of pleasures and delighted if a princeps inclines in the same direction. Yet the publicizing of his shame did not   3 bring satiety, as they had deemed it would, but incentive; and, deeming that his dishonor would be mitigated if he defiled others, he brought onto the stage the descendants of noble families whose need had made them venal. They have since succumbed to their fate, and I think it should be granted to their ancestors that I do not transmit their names. Also, the outrage is that of him who gave money

23. For her see 12.22.1–3.

24. See 13.22.2.

25. See 13.19.2–22.2.

26. The text of the start of this sentence and the end of the previous one is uncertain: I have translated *uel mitigata. ac tamen cunctari* (Wellesley).

27. Viz. that of singer/lyre-player.

in return for felonies rather than to prevent the felonies from being committed.[28]

4   Notable Roman equestrians too were driven by mighty gifts to promise their services to the arena, except that wages from one who can order carry with them the force of compulsion.

15   However, so that he should not yet be dishonored in the public theater, he instituted games with the designation "Juvenalian," for which people everywhere entered their names. Neither nobility nor age nor the holding of offices served as a hindrance to anyone's practicing the art of a Greek or Latin actor, right down

2   to gestures and rhythms which were quite unmanly. Indeed illustrious ladies too gave grotesque performances; and, in the copse which Augustus placed around the naval pool,[29] there were constructed trysting-places and taverns; and spurs to luxuriousness were placed on sale, and coins distributed, which the good were

3   to spend from compulsion, the profligate from self-glorification.[30] Hence outrages and infamy swelled, and nothing made a greater contribution of lust to the long-standing corruption of behavior than did that cesspit. It is only with difficulty that decency is upheld even by honorable attainments; still less among the competing vices was purity or restraint or any element of upright behavior pre-

4   served. Last of all the man himself took the stage, testing his lyre with much concern and rehearsing with the assistance of his voice-trainers. There had arrived too a cohort of soldiers, and centurions and tribunes, and a sorrowing Burrus—

5   with his praises. That was the first time that Roman equestrians were enrolled with the nomenclature of "Augustiani,"[31] conspicuous for their youthful stamina, some temperamentally provocative, others in the hope of power. And for days and nights they resounded with applause, calling the princeps's good looks and voice by divine designations: as if because of some excellence of theirs, they lived brilliant and honored lives.

16   However, so that his skills as Commander should not be known only at the games, he adopted an enthusiasm for poetry too, gathering together those who had a certain as yet unrecognized facility for composing. The young men[32] sat down with him and strung together verses they had brought or had invented on the spot, while supplementing the man's own words in whatever meter they were produced—something which is exposed by the actual character of the poems, flowing as they do with neither impulse nor inspiration nor a uniform move-

28. This sentence was deleted by Fuchs.

29. See 12.56.1n. for Augustus' construction of the pool.

30. The point seems to be that purchase of the "spurs to luxuriousness" was encouraged by Nero in the form of his distributing coins to the would-be purchasers: men with conscience would feel obliged to spend them through fear of what would happen if they refused; the unscrupulous would take advantage of the free gift to promote their own careers.

31. Nero's personal claque. It came to comprise several thousand individuals who were notable for their hairstyles and dress and who adopted special forms of rhythmical applause (Suetonius, *Nero* 20.3).

32. "Young men" is a guess at T.'s meaning; the text is highly uncertain.

ment.+ After a banquet he would also share his time with the exponents of wis-   2
dom,[33] being one who+ enjoyed the disagreement of those arguing opposite positions; nor were there lacking those who, amid the royal delectations, desired to
be noticed for their grim expression and look.

At about the same time from a trivial dispute there sprang up between the   **17**
Nucerian and Pompeian colonists a frightful slaughter at a gladiatorial spectacle
which Livineius Regulus, whose removal from the senate I have recorded,[34] was
producing. Assailing each other with the recklessness of townsfolk, they resorted
to abuse, then rocks and finally the sword, the more effective being the plebs of
the Pompeians, among whom the spectacle was being produced. As a result many
of the Nucerians were transferred to the City, their bodies maimed by wounds,
and very many had the deaths of children and parents to lament. Judgment on   2
the affair was passed from princeps to senate, from senate to consuls; and, the affair being referred back to the fathers, the Pompeians were officially prevented
from holding gatherings of that type for ten years, and the leagues which they
had instituted illegally were dissolved;[35] Livineius and the others who had stirred
up the riot were penalized by exile.

Removed from the senate also was Pedius Blaesus, on the Cyrenaeans' accu-   **18**
sation that he had violated the treasury of Aesculapius and tampered with a military levy by favoritism at a price. The Cyrenaeans likewise made a defendant of   2
Acilius Strabo, who had had experience of praetorian power and been sent by
Claudius as arbitrator of the estates which, once the ancestral holdings of King
Apion and left to the Roman people along with his kingdom,[36] all the neighboring proprietors had invaded, and they were now relying on the longevity of
their licensed illegality as if on legitimacy and fairness. So, when the judgment   3
on the estates went against them, resentment sprang up against the judge; and the
senate's response was that it was unaware of Claudius' instructions and the princeps should be consulted. Nero, approving Strabo's verdict, wrote that he was
nevertheless helping the allies and was conceding what they had asserted as their
right.

There followed the deaths of the illustrious men Domitius Afer and M. Servil-   **19**
ius, who had thrived in the highest offices and by considerable eloquence, the
former in pleading cases, Servilius for a long time in the forum but later celebrated for transmitting Roman affairs and for the elegance of a life which he
made more brilliant in that the equality of his talent was matched by the dissimilarity of his behavior.[37]

33. Here "wisdom" means "philosophy" (6.6.2n.), as often from now on (14.56.3,
14.59.1, 15.62.2, 15.71.4): hence its "exponents" are "philosophers."

34. In a passage no longer extant.

35. Whether the "leagues" were fan clubs, supporting the gladiators, or cadet corps, actually performing gladiatorial exercises, seems unclear.

36. In 96 B.C. (*OCD* 422 s.v. Cyrene).

37. I.e., behavior dissimilar to that of Domitius Afer (suffect consul in 39), who had been

★   ★   ★

A.D. 60

20   With Nero (for the fourth time) and Cornelius Cossus as consuls,[38] the quinquennial games were instituted at Rome after the fashion of a Greek competition—to variable report, as is the case with almost all new things.

2   There were those who maintained that even Cn. Pompeius had been censured
by his elders because he established a lasting abode for the theater: previously,
they said, games had customarily been produced with improvised tiers and a stage
set up temporarily, or, if you traced back to more olden days, the people had
watched standing, lest, if they sat down at the theater, they should spend one

3   whole day after another in shirking. Of course the ancient character of the spectacles should be preserved whenever praetors produced them,[+] with no com-

4   pulsion on any one of the citizens to compete; but ancestral morality, having
fallen gradually into disuse, was now being overthrown fundamentally by imported debauchery, with the result that whatever anywhere could be corrupted
or could corrupt was on view in the City, and the youth was degenerating on
account of foreign pursuits, indulging in gymnasia and inactivity and shameful
love at the instigation of a princeps and senate who not only granted license to
vice but applied force, so that leading Romans, under the pretext of speeches and
poems, were being polluted on the stage. What remained, except that they should
also bare their bodies and take up boxing gloves and perform fights of that type

5   instead of soldiering and weapons? Would justice be improved and the decuriae
of equestrians fulfill better their exceptional responsibility of judging[39] if they
listened expertly to the fractured sounds of sweet voices? Even nighttime had
contributed to the disgrace, so that no period should be left for decency but in
an indiscriminate throng all the most depraved might dare by dark what they desired by day.

21   But with the majority the license itself found favor, and yet they screened it
with honorable names: even their ancestors, they said, had not recoiled from the
delectations which (given the conditions obtaining in those times) were provided
by spectacles, and for that reason actors had been imported from the Etruscans
and competitions of horses from Thurii; once Achaea and Asia had become possessions, more care had been devoted to the production of games, and yet at Rome
no one born in an honorable station had degenerated to theatrical skills, despite
its now being two hundred years from the triumph of L. Mummius, who was the

---

an accuser under Tiberius (see 4.52.1, 4.52.4, 4.66.1). M. Servilius Nonianus (consul in
35: 6.31.1), whose life was thus "more brilliant" than Afer's, became a historian, though
the period of "Roman affairs" which he "transmitted" to posterity is unknown.

38. Cossus was son of the consul of 25 (4.34.1n.).

39. Here "decuriae" means boards or panels which each consisted of one thousand
equestrians and from which jurors were selected: see *OCD* 552 s.v. equites.

first to present that kind of spectacle in the City.[40] But heed had also been paid   2
to frugality, in that the theater was located in a permanent abode rather than that
it should arise and be leveled[+] at inordinate cost each year. Magistrates would not
drain their personal resources in the same way, or the people have reason to importune the magistrates for Greek competitions, since the state discharged the
cost. The victories of orators and bards would provide an incentive for talent; and   3
no judge would find it heavy to lend his ears to honorable pursuits and to permitted pleasures. It was to delight rather than to debauchery that a few nights of
the whole quinquennium were given, during which there was such illumination
from lights that nothing illicit could be concealed.

At any rate the spectacle passed without any significant disreputableness; and   4
the enthusiasms of the plebs did not flare up even moderately, because pantomimes, though restored to the stage, were prevented from the sacred competitions.[41] No one carried off the First for eloquence, but it was announced that
the victor was Caesar. (Greek attire, in which during those days many people had
paraded, at that point became obsolete.)

It was during this that a comet gleamed out, on which the opinion of the pub-   22
lic is that it portends a change for kingdoms.[+] Therefore, as if Nero were already
deposed, they began to ask who should be selected; and frequently on the lips of
all was Rubellius Plautus, whose nobility came from the Julian family through his
mother.[42] (The man himself cultivated the preferences of his ancestors,[43] being of
serious deportment, his household chaste and private, and, the more he concealed
himself through dread, the more reputation he acquired.) The rumor was rein-   2
forced by an interpretation—which sprang up from an equally groundless base—
of a flash of lightning. A meal of Nero's (who was reclining near the Simbruine
pools in a villa whose name is Sublaqueum) had been struck and his table shattered, and it had happened in the territory of the Tiburtines, whence derived the
paternal origins of Plautus:[44] the people therefore believed that he was the one
marked out by the will of the gods; and his cause was fostered by the many whose
greedy—and usually deluded—ambition is to be first in cultivating the novel and
the equivocal. Nero therefore, agitated by this, sent a letter to Plautus: he should   3
pay heed to the City's tranquillity and remove himself from those who were
spreading prevarications; he had ancestral estates across Asia in which he might
enjoy a secure and undisturbed youth. So that is where, with his spouse Antistia
and a few of his establishment, he withdrew.

40. Achaea and Asia came under Roman control in 146 and 133 B.C. respectively; L.
Mummius celebrated a triumph over Achaea in 145 B.C.

41. Pantomime actors had been expelled in A.D. 56 (13.25.4); "sacred competitions" was
a standard description of the famous Greek games, which were religious occasions: the
Actian games are similarly described at 15.23.2.

42. See 13.19.3n.

43. Evidently a reference to Stoicism (see 14.59.1 below).

44. See 6.27.1.

4   During the same days Nero's excessive desire for luxuriousness brought him infamy and danger, because he had gone to swim in the source of water diverted by Q. Marcius[+] into the City: by bathing his body he seemed to have polluted the sacred draught and the sanctity of the place, and his subsequent ambiguous health confirmed the anger of the gods.

*

23   As for Corbulo, deeming that after the destruction of Artaxata[45] he should capitalize on this fresh terror to occupy Tigranocerta (by the extirpation of which he might intensify the enemies' dread or, if he spared it, acquire a reputation for clemency), he proceeded in that direction—with no ferocity on the part of his army, lest the prospect of pardon be removed, and yet with no relaxation of concern, aware that they were a people prone to change, being as untrustworthy
2   when faced by opportunities as they were sluggish when by danger. As for the barbarians, depending on their individual disposition some offered prayers, others deserted their villages and deviated into trackless areas, and there were those who hid themselves in caverns, and their dearest things with them. Therefore the Roman leader used different techniques, sympathy toward the suppliants, speed against the fugitives, and, ruthless to those who had settled in hiding-places, he filled up the mouths and outlets of the caves with loppings and brushwood and burned them out by fire.
3   He in his turn, while bypassing their territory, was raided by the Mardi, who are trained in banditry and protected against an invader by mountains; Corbulo, sending in the Iberians, devastated them and avenged the enemy's daring with
24   only foreign blood.[46] But, though without losses from the battle, he and his army were becoming exhausted from want and toil, being driven to ward off hunger by the flesh of livestock.[47] In addition, the scarcity of water, the blazing summer season, and the long journeys were mitigated only by the perseverance of the
2   leader, enduring the same and more as the troop soldiery. Subsequently they came to a cultivated locality and reaped the crops, and, of the two strongholds into which the Armenians had fled, one was taken by assault; those who had repelled
3   the first force were subdued by blockade.[48] Crossing from there to the district of the Tauronites, he avoided an unexpected danger. Not far from his tent, a not ignoble barbarian was discovered with a weapon, who under torture revealed the stages of the ambush, himself as its instigator, and his allies; and those who

45. For which see 13.41.1–3; the narrative of those events is continued here.

46. I.e., the Romans suffered no losses themselves, as T. explains in the next sentence.

47. Compare Caesar, *Gallic War* 7.17.3 "The army was afflicted by the utmost difficulty in its grain supply . . . so much so that for several days the soldiers had no grain and bore up against extreme hunger only by driving in herds from the more distant villages."

48. The last sentence refers to the inhabitants of the second of the two strongholds.

had been arranging the trap under a show of friendship were condemned and punished.

It was not long afterward that legates sent from[49] Tigranocerta brought word   4
that its battlements were lying open, the locals attentive for his orders; at the same time they handed over a golden crown as a gift of hospitality. He accepted it with grace, and nothing was removed from the city, so that its inhabitants, being unscathed, might more readily sustain their compliance. But the garrison of   **25**
Legerda, which its defiant youth had closed, was stormed—yet not without a struggle: they had dared a battle before the walls, and, when driven within the fortifications, yielded at last only to an embankment[50] and to the arms of those who rushed in.

These operations burgeoned more easily because the Parthians were detained   2
by the Hyrcanian war.[51] The Hyrcani had sent to the Roman princeps to beg for an alliance, pointing out, as a pledge of their friendship, that they were hold-ing up Vologaeses. On their return, lest after crossing the Euphrates they should find themselves surrounded by the enemies' guardposts, Corbulo gave them a convoy and escorted them to the shores of the Red Sea,[52] whence, avoiding the territory of the Parthians, they retired to their native abode. Moreover, as Tiri-   **26**
dates for his part was entering the margins of Armenia by way of the Medes, Corbulo sent ahead the legate Verulanus with auxiliaries and he himself accom-panied the speeding legions, by these means forcing the man to depart to a dis-tance and to abandon any hope of war. As for those whom he knew to be [...],[53] he pillaged them using slaughter and fire and was in the process of asserting the right to possession of Armenia when Tigranes arrived, having been selected by Nero to undertake its command, a member of the nobility of the Cappadocians and grandson of King Archelaus, but, because for a long time he had been a hostage in the City, reduced to a servile passivity.[54] There was no consensus about   2
his acceptance, given the lasting goodwill in some quarters toward the Arsacidae; but the majority, hating greatly the haughtiness of the Parthians, preferred a king given by the Romans. Additional support came in the form of a garrison: a thou-sand legionaries, three cohorts of allies, and two wings of cavalry. And, so that he could protect his new kingdom more easily, the parts of Armenia which bor-dered on each were ordered to obey Pharasmanes, Polemon, Aristobulus, and

49. Or perhaps "to."

50. Constructed for the purposes of a siege.

51. See 13.37.5.

52. In Latin "Red Sea" can mean either our Red Sea or the Persian Gulf (see 2.61.2n.), but scholars think that here the Caspian Sea must be meant: if so, it is not clear whether the mistake is T.'s or a scribe's (Lipsius proposed to emend *rubri* to *sui,* "their own sea").

53. The received text makes no sense and no satisfactory emendation has been pro-posed; scholars assume the meaning to be "hostile to ourselves."

54. For Tigranes V see *OCD* 1525. For Archelaus see 2.42.2–4.

Antiochus respectively.[55] Corbulo withdrew into Syria, vacant on the death of its legate Ummidius and now granted to him.

★

27 In the same year one of the illustrious cities of Asia, Laodicea, which had collapsed from an earth tremor, recovered by means of its own resources without any remedy from us. In Italy the old town of Puteoli acquired the prerogative

2 and nomenclature of a colony from Nero.[56] Veterans were enrolled at Tarentum and Antium but still failed to help the depletion of the localities, the majority slipping off to the provinces in which they had completed their service; and, unaccustomed to undertaking espousals and to rearing children, they left homes or-

3 phaned and without descendants. (It was not the case, as formerly, that whole legions were settled along with their tribunes and centurions and individual soldiers of the same unit, so that they would produce a "commonwealth" based on accord and affection; but, unknown to one another, from different maniples, without a guide, without mutual feelings, they were suddenly collected together as if from some other category of mortals, a numerical total rather than a colony.)

28 Because the election of praetors (usually held under the jurisdiction of the senate) had flared up from keener canvassing, the princeps brought it under control by placing in charge of legions the three who were seeking office above the numerical total.[57] And he increased the honor of the fathers by deciding that those who appealed to the senate against civil judges should risk the same money as those who petitioned the Commander (previously that had been an unre-

2 stricted procedure and exempt from penalty). At the end of the year Vibius Secundus, a Roman equestrian, was condemned for extortion on the accusation of the Mauri and driven from Italy, avoiding the infliction of a heavier penalty by relying on the wealth of Vibius Crispus, his brother.[58]

★   ★   ★

A.D. 61

29 With Caesennius Paetus and with Petronius Turpilianus as consuls, a heavy disaster was suffered in Britain, where the legate A. Didius, as I have recalled,[59] had merely held on to the gains, and his successor Veranius, having pillaged the Sil-

55. For Pharasmanes I see 6.32.3n.; Polemon II is son of the Pontic king Polemon mentioned at 2.56.2; for Aristobulus and Antiochus see 13.7.1.

56. Its new title was "Colonia Claudia Augusta Neronensis."

57. There were twelve vacancies (1.14.4) and fifteen candidates.

58. Crispus was suffect consul in 61 (probably), 74, and 83, and a famous orator and accuser.

59. See 12.40.4.

ures in only modest sallies, was prevented by death from developing the war further—a man with a great reputation for severity while he lived, but convicted of self-aggrandizement by the last words of his will: with considerable syco-phancy toward Nero, he added that he would have made the province subject to him if he had lived for the next two years.[60]

It was now Paulinus Suetonius who had hold over the Britons,[61] a competi-tor of Corbulo in his knowledge of soldiering and in popular rumor (which lets no one lack a rival), and desiring to match the prestige of the recovery of Arme-nia by taming the foe. Therefore he prepared to attack the island of Mona, for-midable owing to its inhabitants and a retreat for fugitives; and he manufactured ships with flat hulls for the perilous shallows. Thus did the infantry cross, the cav-alry by following in the shoals or by swimming beside their horses through the deeper water. **2** **3**

There stood along the shore a diverse line, dense with arms and men, and with females running in between: in funereal clothing and with tumbling hair, they were flourishing firebrands after the manner of Furies; and Druids around about, pouring forth ominous prayers with their hands raised to the sky, stunned the soldiery by the strangeness of their appearance, so that, as if their limbs were stuck fast, their bodies presented a stationary target for wounds. Then, after exhorta-tions from their leader and goading themselves not to panic at a womanly and fanatical column, they advanced the standards, laid low those in their way, and engulfed them in their own fire. After this a garrison was imposed on the con-quered and their groves were extirpated, consecrated as they were to savage su-perstition: they held it right to grill captive gore on their altars and to consult their gods with the entrails of men. **30** **2** **3**

It was while Suetonius was conducting these operations that the sudden de-fection of the province was announced. The king of the Iceni, Prasutagus, con-spicuous for his long-standing wealthiness, had written down Caesar as his heir along with his two daughters, deeming that by such compliance both his king-dom and his household would stay clear of injury. The opposite turned out to be the case, so much so that his kingdom was devastated by centurions, his house-hold by slaves—as though both were captured property. At the very start his wife Boudicca had beatings inflicted on her and their daughters were violated by rape; all the principals of the Iceni, as if they[62] had received the entire district as a gift, were stripped of their ancestral property, and the king's relatives were held like menials. At this insult, and in dread of worse (since they had succumbed to the status of a province), they seized arms and stirred into rebellion the Trinovantes **31** **2**

60. Veranius (12.5.1n.), whose career is recorded on his tomb (Braund 404 (c) = WM 30), had succeeded Didius in 57 but died within a year (*Agricola* 14.2).

61. He had been suffect consul in (probably) 43 and his son would be one of the reg-ular consuls in 66 (16.14.1).

62. I.e., the Romans (the change of subject is awkward and the text has been ques-tioned).

and any others who, not yet broken by servitude, had struck an agreement in secret conspiracies to regain their freedom, their fiercest hatred being for the vet-

3   erans. (Having been recently settled in the colony of Camulodunum, they had been driving people from their homes, evicting them from their estates, calling them captives and slaves—the veterans' unruliness being abetted by the soldiers

4   because of their like lifestyle and their hope of identical license. In addition, the temple set up to Divine Claudius appeared as a citadel of everlasting despotism, and its chosen priests were pouring away entire fortunes in a show of religion.) And it did not seem a steep task to extirpate a colony encircled by no fortifications—something for which our leaders had made too little provision, inasmuch as more heed was paid to attractiveness than to practicality.

32   Meanwhile, for no obvious reason, the representation of Victory at Camulodunum collapsed and turned upside down, as if succumbing to an enemy. And females, disturbed to frenzy, prophesied that extermination was at hand, and that foreign cries had been heard in their[63] curia, the theater had resounded with howling, and there had been seen in the estuary of the Thames an image of the colony overturned. Again, Ocean had a gory appearance, and likenesses of human bodies had been left by the ebbing tide. As the Britons were drawn toward

2   hope, so were the veterans toward dread;[64] but, because Suetonius was some distance away, they sought help from the procurator, Catus Decianus. He for his part sent no more than two hundred men without their regular arms; and inside[65] there was only a modest unit of soldiers.

Relying on the protection of the temple, and impeded by accomplices in the rebellion who secretly disrupted their plans, they neither ran an outer ditch or rampart nor was it the case that the old men and females were moved, with the youth alone resisting; incautious as if in the mid of peace, they were surrounded

3   by a multitude of barbarians. Everything else was ransacked or burned in the assault; the temple, into which the soldiery had clustered, was blockaded for two days and stormed. The victorious Britons, encountering Petilius Cerialis,[66] the legate of the Ninth Legion who was coming to the rescue, routed the legion and killed its infantry element; Cerialis with the cavalry escaped to the camp and defended himself in its fortifications. Trembling at the disaster and at the hatred of the province which his greed had driven to war, the procurator Catus crossed to Gaul.

33   But Suetonius, with marvelous steadfastness, made his way through the midst of the enemy to Londinium, a place not distinguished by the nomenclature of a colony but particularly celebrated for the quantity of its businessmen and commerce. Once there, he was uncertain whether he should select it as a site for war;

63. I.e., the inhabitants', a reference to the Roman settlers at Camulodunum.

64. Scholars have variously questioned the passage of which this sentence is part. I have translated the transmitted text, punctuated thus: . . . *effigies relictae. ut Britanni ad spem, ita ueterani ad metum trahebantur; sed* . . .

65. I.e., inside Camulodunum.

66. Suffect consul in 70 (probably) and 74, and governor of Britain between those dates.

looking around at the depletion of the soldiery, however, and after the sufficiently strong lesson that Petilius' rashness had been checked,[67] he determined on saving the totality to the detriment of an individual town. The weeping and tears of those begging his help did not sway him from giving the signal for departure and from accepting as part of his column only those who would accompany him; any kept back by their noncombatant sex or the exhaustion of age or the charm of the locality were overwhelmed by the enemy.

There was the same disaster for the municipality of Verulamium, because the barbarians, neglecting the strongholds and garrisons of the military, and as delighted by plunder as they were sluggish for toil, sought out the areas most fruitful for a despoiler and unprotected by defenders. It has been agreed that about seventy thousand citizens and allies fell in the places which I have recalled. There was neither capturing nor selling or any other feature of the trade of war, but they speeded up their slaughtering, gibbets, fire, and crosses—as though destined to pay in reprisals, but in the meantime preempting revenge.

Suetonius already had the Fourteenth Legion, with the banner-men of the Twentieth and auxiliaries from nearby, roughly ten thousand armed men, when he prepared to abandon delay and come to an engagement in the line. And he selected a place with narrow jaws and enclosed by a wood at the rear, knowing well enough that there were no enemy elements except in front and that the flat ground was open, without the dread of an ambush. So the legion stood by in crowded ranks, the light armor all around, the cavalry clustered on the edges. But the forces of the Britons were prancing about by company and squadron, a larger number than on any other occasion, and in such defiant spirit that they even brought their spouses with them as testifiers to their victory and placed them in wagons which they had placed beyond the outermost perimeter of the plain. As Boudicca, carrying her daughters before her in a chariot, approached each tribe, she testified that it was of course customary for the Britons to take the field under female leadership; yet now she was not, as one sprung from great ancestors, avenging her kingdom and wealth but, as one of the people, her lost freedom, her body battered by beatings, and the abused chastity of her daughters. The desires of the Romans had advanced to the point where they left no bodies, not even old age or virginity, unpolluted; yet the gods were assisting their justified vengeance: the legion which had dared battle had fallen; the rest were concealing themselves in camp or looking around for flight: they would not bear even the noise and shouting of so many thousands, still less their assault and brawn. If they weighed up within themselves their resources in armed men and their reasons for war, they must conquer in that line or fall. That was the design of a woman; the men could survive—and be slaves!

Nor was Suetonius for his part silent in such a great crisis. Although he had confidence in their courage, he nevertheless blended exhortations and pleas that

----

67. Others translate "and seeing that Petilius' rashness had been dealt a sufficiently strong lesson."

they should spurn the sounds and empty threats of the barbarians: more females than young men were observable there; unwarlike and unarmed, they would yield immediately when they recognized, after so many routs already, the steel

2 and courage of their conquerors. Even in the case of many legions there were only a few men whose bearing on battles was decisive; and it would be an extra yield on their glory that a modest unit acquired the fame of an entire army. Concentrated together, their javelins discharged, they must merely continue the devastation and slaughter afterward with shield-bosses and swords, forgetful of plunder: with victory gained, everything would yield to them.

3 Such was the ardor which followed the leader's words, such the expeditiousness which the veteran soldiery—with its considerable experience of battles—had shown for the launching of its javelins, that Suetonius, sure of the outcome,

37 gave the signal for the fight. At first the legion was motionless in its stance, keeping the narrowness of the place as a fortification; but, after they had used up their weapons with sure aim against the closer approach of the enemy, they burst out as in a wedge. The auxiliaries' attack was the same; and the cavalry, extending their spears, broke through every effective obstacle. The rest presented their backs despite the difficulty of escape (because the surrounding vehicles had cordoned off the ways out). And the soldiery did not refrain from the execution even of women; and baggage-animals too, transfixed by weapons, had enlarged the heaps

2 of bodies. Brilliant was the praise acquired that day, and the equal of ancient victories. There are those who transmit that a little less than eighty thousand Britons fell, with roughly four hundred soldiers[68] killed and not many more wounded.

3 Boudicca ended her life by poison. And Poenius Postumus, prefect of the camp of the Second Legion, learning of the successful affairs of the Fourteenths and Twentieths and because he had cheated his own legion of equal glory and had refused his leader's orders contrary to the conventions of military service, pierced himself with a sword.

38 The whole army was then assembled and held under pelt[69] with a view to completing the remainder of the war. And Caesar increased the forces by sending from Germany two thousand legionaries, eight cohorts of auxiliaries, and a thousand cavalry, on whose arrival the Nines were supplemented with legionary

2 soldiery. The cohorts and wings were located in new winter quarters, and every doubtful or adverse element among the tribes was devastated with fire and sword. But nothing so much as hunger afflicted the enemy, who were indifferent to sowing crops, with every age-group being turned over to the war, while they marked

3 out our supplies for themselves. And, defiant peoples that they were, they inclined more slowly to peace because Julius Classicianus, sent as successor to Catus and in discord with Suetonius, was hampering the general good with his private feud and had spread word that a new legate was to be awaited who, without the anger of an enemy or victorious haughtiness, would pay merciful heed to those who

68. I.e., on the Roman side.
69. See 13.35.3n.

surrendered.[70] At the same time his instructions for the City were that they should expect no end to battles unless someone succeeded Suetonius, whose troubles he attributed to the man's own perversity, his prosperity to fortune.

So, to view the state of Britain, there was sent Polyclitus, one of the freedmen, **39** Nero's great hope being that his authority would make it possible not only that harmony would be engendered between legate and procurator but also that peace would settle the barbarians' rebellious temper. And Polyclitus, whose **2** mighty column had been an oppression on Italy and Gaul, did not fail, after he had crossed the Ocean, to advance in a manner which terrified even our soldiers. But he was a laughingstock to an enemy among whom freedom still blazed even then and the powerfulness of freedmen was not yet known; and they marveled that a leader and an army, the dispatchers of so great a war, should obey slaves. Yet everything was reported to the Commander in milder terms, and Suetonius **3** was retained to conduct affairs; but, because afterward he had lost a few ships on the shore and the oarsmen in them, he was ordered, on grounds of the war's continuance, to hand over his army to Petronius Turpilianus, who by now had left the consulship.[71] He, neither spurring on the enemy nor harassed himself, imposed the honorable name of peace upon sluggish inactivity.

✦

In the same year at Rome distinctive crimes were committed through daring— **40** a senator's in one case, in the other a slave's.

Domitius Balbus was a praetorian, vulnerable to intrigue owing both to his lengthy old age and to his childlessness and money. His relative, Valerius Fabianus, **2** who was marked out for a political career, substituted a will, his accessories being Vinicius Rufinus and Terentius Lentinus, Roman equestrians. They had allied Antonius Primus and Asinius Marcellus. (Antonius was a man of ready daring;[72] Marcellus was regarded as brilliant on account of his great-grandfather Asinius Pollio and as not to be spurned for his behavior, except that he believed poverty the principal of afflictions.)[73] So Fabianus, in the presence of⁺ those whom I have **3** recalled and others less illustrious, sealed the tablets.[74] This was proved before the fathers, and Fabianus and Antonius along with Rufinus and Terentius were con-

70. An inscription honoring Classicianus after his death (Braund 473 = WM 38) reveals that his wife was the daughter of the Julius Indus mentioned by T. at 3.42.3.

71. The text, articulation, and logic of the whole of this sentence are uncertain.

72. He features prominently in T.'s *Histories* (note the brief sketch of his personality at *Histories* 2.86.2) since he was a major player in the civil war of 68–69: as a supporter of Vespasian (the eventual winner) in the latter year, he led the invasion of Italy and captured Rome but later fell from Vespasian's favor owing to the machinations of Licinius Mucianus.

73. Asinius Marcellus had been consul in 54 (12.64.1n.).

74. I.e., the writing tablets which comprised the will.

demned under the Cornelian law;[75] as for Marcellus, the memory of his ancestors and the pleas of Caesar excused him from punishment rather than from infamy.

41   The same day struck down Pompeius Aelianus too, a young quaestorian, on the grounds of his knowledge of Fabianus' outrages; and Italy and Spain, where he had been born, were forbidden to him. Valerius Ponticus had similar ignominy inflicted on him because, to prevent the defendants' being accused before the prefect of the City, he had denounced them to the praetor, intending to outwit retribution by a legal pretext in the meantime and by colluding later on. It was added to the senate's decision that whoever bought or sold such services should be liable for punishment exactly as one convicted of calumny by a public court.[76]

42   Not long after, the prefect of the City, Pedanius Secundus, was killed by a slave of his—either on the denial of his freedom, for which he had struck a price, or being inflamed with love for a pathic and intolerant of his master's being a rival.

2   Whatever the case, since according to an old custom it was required that the entire establishment which had lodged under the protection of the same roof should be led off for reprisal,[77] matters reached the point of mutiny in the throng of the plebs which was for protecting so many blameless individuals; and in the senate itself there was support from those spurning excessive severity, despite the majority's proposing that nothing be changed. Of these, C. Cassius at his turn for an opinion spoke in this way:[78]

43   "Times out of number, conscript fathers, I have been present in this assembly when new senate's decrees were being demanded contrary to the institutions and laws of our ancestors; nor did I oppose, not because I had any doubt that with reference to every item of business better and truer provision had been made in the past, and that what was being transformed was being changed for the worse, but lest it should seem that, owing to an excessive passion for ancient fashion, I

2   was promoting a pursuit of my own.[79] At the same time I judged that, whatever authority it is that I have, it should not be destroyed by constant contradicting, so that it might remain unimpaired if ever the state needed counsel. And that has happened today, a consular man[80] having been killed in his own house in a slavish ambush which no one blocked or betrayed, although nothing had yet shaken the senate's decision which threatened the whole establishment with reprisal.

3   "As Hercules is my witness, decree impunity! But who will be rescued by his

75. A Sullan law of 81 B.C. which dealt with wills.

76. The senate's decision in question became known as the Senatus Consultum Turpillianum (after one of the consuls: see 14.29.1) and it penalized accusers who withdrew from criminal proceedings without a good reason.

77. The "old custom" had already been made more severe by a senate's decision of 57 (see 13.32.1).

78. For Cassius' fame as a jurist see 12.12.1.

79. By "a pursuit of my own" Cassius means the law, lawyers being notoriously addicted to precedent.

80. Pedanius Secundus had been suffect consul in 43.

rank, when it profited not the prefect of the City?[81] Who will be guarded by the number of his slaves, when four hundred did not protect Pedanius Secundus? To whom will assistance be rendered by his establishment, which not even in an atmosphere of dread noticed the dangers to us? Or, as some do not blush to fab-   4
ricate, is it the case that the killer avenged his own injustices because he had reached agreement over his father's finances or a menial of his grandfather's was being removed from him?[82] In fact, let our verdict be that the master appears to have been justly slain!

"Is it really your pleasure to rake up arguments on an issue which was delib-   **44**
erated by wiser men? But, even if we now had the decision to make for the first time, do you believe that a slave so formed the resolution of killing his master that he let drop no threatening utterance, made no announcement through rash-ness? Doubtless he concealed his plan, prepared his weapon among the ignorant! Even so, surely it was impossible to go past the lookouts, open the doors of the bedroom, carry in a light, and accomplish the slaughter—all without anyone's knowledge? Many indications precede a crime. If slaves betray them, we are able   2
to live as individuals amid greater numbers, safe amid their tenseness, and finally, if perish we must, not unavenged amid the guilty.

"Our ancestors were suspicious of the instincts of slaves even when they were   3
born in the same estates or houses and immediately conceived an affection for their masters. But, now that we have in our establishments whole nations whose rites are different and rituals foreign (or nonexistent), you will not suppress a cesspit like that except by dread. "But some guiltless ones will perish." Yes, and when every tenth man of a stricken army is struck by cudgel,[83] the energetic too are drawn by lot. Each great example has some element of unfairness, which, as against individuals, is balanced by public expediency."

Although no one member dared to go against the opinion of Cassius, there   **45**
were responses from the dissonant voices of those pitying the number or age or sex and the indubitable innocence of the majority; nevertheless the section which was for decreeing reprisal prevailed. But compliance proved impossible, given the multitude which clustered around and menaced with rocks and torches. There-   2
upon Caesar berated the people in an edict and lined with military detachments the entire route along which the condemned were to be led to punishment. Cin-

---

81. The precise text of this and of many of the subsequent sentences is not certain.

82. Cassius' sarcastic allusion to the motives offered at 14.42.1 (above) is based on the fact that slaves had no legal rights whatsoever: in law it was impossible for the father to have possessed money or the grandfather to have had slaves. (It may be that the Latin *aui-tum mancipium* means "an ancestral menial" more generally rather than "a menial of his grandfather's," but the point still stands.) But the sarcasm makes no allowance for the re-ality, which was that slaves might be allowed to administer assets and that these assets might be extensive (see *OCD* 1130 s.v. peculium). A slave would have felt especially aggrieved if he were deprived of something to which he considered himself morally entitled.

83. A reference to the practice of decimation (see 3.21.1).

gonius Varro had proposed that the freedmen too who had lived under the same roof should be deported from Italy; but that was prohibited by the princeps, lest an ancient custom which pity had not mitigated should be intensified through savagery.

46   Condemned with the same men as consuls was Tarquitius Priscus for extortion on the interrogation of the Bithynians, to the great joy of the fathers because they remembered that he had accused Statilius Taurus, his own proconsul.[84] Censuses were carried out across the Galliae by Q. Volusius and Sextius Africanus and Trebellius Maximus, Volusius and Africanus being mutual rivals owing to their nobility; inasmuch as each of them disdained Trebellius, they elevated him above themselves.[85]

47   In that same year there met his death Memmius Regulus, whose authority, steadfastness, and reputation made him (insofar as is allowed by the Commander's overshadowing eminence) brilliant—so much so that Nero, in ill health and with sycophants around who said that the end of the empire was close if his suffering should prove fateful, replied that the state had a reinforcement; and to their subsequent question "Wherein particularly?" he had added "In Memmius Regulus." Regulus nevertheless survived after this, protected by his quietude and because he was a man of a new brilliancy of lineage and of unresented wealth.[86]

2   A gymnasium was dedicated by Nero in that year and oil presented to equestrians and senate (a Greek convenience).[87]

★ ★ ★

48   With P. Marius and L. Afinius as consuls, Antistius, a praetor whose licentious behavior during his tribunate I have recalled,[88] scribbled slanderous poems against the princeps and publicized them at a populous party while he was dining at the house of Ostorius Scapula.[89] Thereupon Cossutianus Capito, who had recently

---

84. See 12.59.1.

85. Volusius had been consul in 56 (13.25.1); Africanus (13.19.2) suffect consul in 59; and Trebellius (perhaps identical with the man mentioned at 6.41.1) suffect consul in 55. T.'s meaning seems to be that Volusius and Africanus were so preoccupied with their personal rivalry that Trebellius rose above them. He was governor of Britain 63–69, a role which T. elsewhere treats with contempt (*Agricola* 16.3–4).

86. Regulus had been suffect consul in 31; his son was consul in 63 (15.23.1).

87. In Greece oil was provided free of charge to those exercising in the gymnasia; Nero's presentation is a strong hint that upper-class Romans should start to adopt Greek practice.

88. See 13.28.1.

89. Already mentioned at 12.31.4 as being son of the P. Ostorius Scapula who was governor of Britain A.D. 47–52.

recovered his senatorial rank through the pleas of his father-in-law Tigellinus,[90] denounced him for treason. (That was the first time the law was revived; and it 2 was believed that the aim was not so much Antistius' extermination as glory for the Commander, so that the latter by his tribunician intercession might release from death a man condemned by the senate.) When Ostorius by way of testimony said that he had heard nothing, those who testified to the contrary were believed; and Junius Marullus as consul designate proposed that the defendant's praetorship be removed from him and that he should be executed according to ancestral custom.[91] As everyone else was agreeing to this, Paetus Thrasea, with 3 much honor toward Caesar and berating Antistius very fiercely, said that what a guilty defendant deserved to suffer should *not* be decided by a senate under an exceptional princeps and bound by no constraint. The executioner and his noose 4 had long since fallen out of use, he said, and there were punishments laid down by the laws whereby reprisals were decreed without either savagery from the judges or infamy for the times. Rather, on an island, with his property confiscated, the longer he dragged out his culpable life, the more pitiful would he be personally, and a very great example of official clemency.

The free-speaking of Thrasea exploded the servitude of others, and, after the **49** consul had permitted a division, they went to vote in favor of his proposal—with a few exceptions, among whom the readiest with his sycophancy was A. Vitellius,[92] harassing all the best individuals with his wrangling and reticent when they responded (as panicky temperaments are accustomed). But the consuls, not daring to endorse the decree of the senate, wrote to Caesar about the general consensus. He for his part, hesitating between shame and anger, finally wrote back that, un- 2 provoked by any wrong, Antistius had spoken the gravest insults against the princeps. Retribution for them had been demanded by the fathers, he said, and it would have been right to decide the punishment in accordance with the magnitude of the felony; but, since he would have blocked any severity on the part of those framing the decree, he was not now forbidding restraint. They should decide as they wished; they had been given license even to acquit.

With remarks such as these read out, and his affront clear, neither did the con- 3 suls change the motion on that account nor did Thrasea withdraw his proposal or the others abandon what they had approved—some of them to avoid the appearance of having exposed the princeps to resentment,[93] the majority safe in numbers, Thrasea because of his usual firmness of spirit and lest his glory should fall out of sight.

90. Cossutianus (11.6.3n.) had been deprived of his rank in 57 (see 13.33.2). This is T.'s first reference to Nero's notorious henchman Ofonius Tigellinus, prefect of the praetorians (14.51.2), who will play a malign part in the narrative from now on.

91. See 2.32.3n.

92. Consul in 48 (11.23.1n.) and later emperor in 69.

93. They did not want people to think that they had changed their minds owing to the princeps's vindictiveness.

50   Fabricius Veiento was belabored by the not dissimilar charge that he had composed many slanders against fathers and priests in the books to which he had
given the name of "Codicils."[94] His accuser Tullius Geminus added that sales
had been conducted by him of the princeps's gifts and of the rights to acquire

2   office.[95] That was Nero's reason for undertaking the judgment, and he drove the
convicted Veiento from Italy and ordered his books to be burned—collectors'
items and much read so long as there was peril in their procurement; subsequently the license to hold them ensured their oblivion.

51   But, as the public maladies grew worse from day to day, relief was diminishing: Burrus departed from life, whether through ill health or poison being
uncertain. Ill health was inferred from the fact that, when he stopped breathing,
his gullet had been gradually distending inward, and his passageway was blocked;
but the majority asserted that on Nero's order, as if some remedy were being applied, his palate had been smeared with a noxious medicament and that Burrus,
realizing the crime and averting his gaze when the princeps came to visit him,

2   had given no other reply to his persistent queries than "*I* am well." He remained
a great loss to the community owing to its recollection of his excellence and to
the sluggish innocence of one of his successors and the blazing outrages of the
other. For Caesar had placed two men over the praetorian cohorts: Faenius Rufus, in response to the goodwill of the public (because he had been handling the
food supply without profit to himself),[96] and Ofonius Tigellinus, of whose in-

3   veterate immorality and infamy he had been a follower. And they for their part
fared in accordance with their known behavior—Tigellinus more influential on
the princeps's mind and enlisted for his most intimate lusts, Rufus with a favorable reputation among people and soldiers, which meant that from Nero he experienced the opposite.

52   The death of Burrus broke Seneca's powerfulness, because good practice
lacked its previous strength with the removal of one of its two (so to speak) lead-

2   ers, and Nero was all for inclining toward baser men. These rose up against Seneca
with various charges, to the effect that he was still increasing his mighty wealth,
which had exceeded all private limits, and that he was turning the affections of
the citizens toward himself; and in the attractiveness of his gardens and the mag-

3   nificence of his villas it was as if he were surpassing the princeps. They cast against
him too the charge that he was arrogating praise for eloquence to himself exclusively and was scribbling poems more frequently, now that Nero's love of them
had emerged (he was, they said, being openly prejudiced against the princeps's

94. The books were written in the form of a make-believe will, wills being posthumous
documents and a favorite vehicle for delivering personal attacks. Fabricius Veiento was a
notorious accuser in the reign of Domitian, under whom he held his third consulship in
(probably) 83.

95. Veiento was being accused of accepting bribes in return for using his influence with
the emperor to secure either imperial favors for third parties or their nomination for office.

96. Faenius Rufus had been appointed to the food supply in 55 (see 13.22.1).

delectations, depreciating his power in controlling horses and making sport of his voice whenever he sang): what pass would need to be reached before there   4 was nothing brilliant in the state which was not believed to be of Seneca's devising? Surely Nero's boyhood had passed and he now had the strength of a young man: he should cast off his master, equipped as he was with sufficiently plentiful teachers in his own ancestors.

But Seneca, not unaware of his accusers (betrayed as they were by those who   **53** had some concern for honorableness), and as Caesar increasingly spurned familiarity with him, begged time for a conversation, and, on receiving it, began thus: "It is the fourteenth year, Caesar, since I became associated with your prospects,   2 the eighth that you have held command: in that interval of time you have heaped such honors and wealth upon me that my happiness lacks nothing except its moderation. I shall resort to great exemplars, and not of my situation but of yours.   3 Your great-great-grandfather Augustus permitted a Mytilenean seclusion to Marcus Agrippa and (so to speak) a foreign furlough within the City itself to C. Maecenas:[97] the one an ally in war, the other buffeted by numerous toils at Rome, they had of course received plentiful rewards, but in return for mighty deserts. In my case, what else could I contribute to your munificence than my   4 studies, nurtured as they were (if I may so express it) in the shade, and which have emerged with brilliancy only because I am seen to have attended to the rudiments of your youth—a great prize for such a thing? Yet you have surrounded   5 me with immeasurable favor, with money uncountable, so much so that often within myself I turn over these thoughts: 'Am I really counted among the leaders of the community, born as I was in an equestrian and provincial station? Has my newness sparkled amid the nobles and those flaunting a long line of adornments?[98] Where is that spirit, content with modestness? Does it construct such gardens as mine and walk through these suburban areas and abound in such large stretches of land and such wide investment?' I am confronted with only one defense, that I was obliged not to defy your gifts.

"But each of us has reached his full measure—you, as much as a princeps   **54** could grant to a friend, and I, as much as a friend receive from a princeps. Every surplus increases resentment, which of course (like all mortal things) occupies a level far beneath your greatness but hangs over me and requires me to be rescued. Just as, if exhausted by campaign or travel, I might beg the ministration of   2 a stick, so, as an old man at this point in his journey through life and unequal to even the slightest of cares, I seek support, since I cannot sustain my wealth further. Order my estate to be administered by your procurators and accepted as

97. In 23 B.C. Agrippa was sent on a mission to the eastern provinces and based himself at Mytilene. According to one tradition he had fallen out of favor with Augustus, although he was given further commands on his recall two years later. As for Maecenas, there is evidence that he was less influential with Augustus from about the same period and withdrew increasingly from affairs (see 3.30.4).

98. I.e., distinguished ancestors.

3 part of your fortune. Not that I shall drag myself down into poverty, but, having
handed over the things which dazzle me by their flash, I shall reclaim for my
mind the time which is set aside for the care of my gardens and villas. In front of
you lie your strength and, as seen over so many years, the control which comes
with eminence;[99] we older friends can demand our due rest. This too will re-
dound to your glory—to have conveyed to the heights those who could tolerate modest levels too."

55   To this Nero replied approximately thus: "The fact that I can confront immediately your prepared speech I hold to be your first gift to me, since you taught
2 me to express not only foreseen but also improvised words. My great-great-
grandfather Augustus allowed Agrippa and Maecenas to take up furloughs after
their toils but was himself at an age when his authority could protect whatever
he granted and whatever its nature; and yet he stripped neither of them of the
3 rewards he had given them. They had deserved them, in war and danger: for it
was in such areas that Augustus' youth was spent. Not that I would have lacked
your weapons and brawn in a life of arms; but, as the immediate situation demanded, you fostered my boyhood and then my youth with reasoning, counsel,
4 and precepts. And of course *your* gifts to me will be everlasting as long as my life
continues; what you have from me—gardens and investments and villas—is susceptible to hazard. And, although it seems a lot, more has been held by numerous
5 men who are in no way equal to your artistic skills. It is too shaming to refer
to the freedmen who are conspicuously richer: hence I blush also at the fact that
56 you, the principal in my affection, do not yet surpass all in fortune. On the other
hand, not only are you at an effective age which is adequate to affairs and to the
fruits of affairs, but I am embarking on the first stretches of command—unless
perchance you consider either yourself inferior to Vitellius, three times consul,
or me to Claudius, and my lavishness toward you is unable to match the fulfil-
ment which lifelong frugality brought to Volusius.[100] If in any respect there is a
decline in the slippery slope of my adolescence, why not reclaim it and provide
more emphatic control for the youthful strength which you graced with your
2 support? It will be neither your moderation, should you return the money, nor
your rest, should you abandon your princeps, but my greed and the dread of
my cruelty which will be on the lips of all; and, however much your self-denial

---

99. There is considerable uncertainty about the meaning of this sentence and especially
of its latter part, where the text is also uncertain.

100. The point of this very difficult sentence seems to be as follows: Nero has plenty of
time ahead of him in which to make up any deficiencies in Seneca's fortune, while Seneca
is still not too old to repay such generosity with service to the state—unless, of course,
Seneca considers himself less capable of serving Nero than was L. Vitellius (thrice consul
and the most successful politician of his age) of serving Claudius, and unless he imagines
Nero to be less generous than Claudius had been. For Volusius and his wealth see 13.30.2.
Other scholars transpose the clause "unless perchance . . . to Volusius" so that it follows on
from the end of either of the two previous sentences (". . . artistic skills" or ". . . in fortune").

may be praised, it will certainly not be appropriate for a wise man to accept glory from the same circumstance as procures infamy for his friend."

To these words he added an embrace and kisses, being constituted by nature 3 and trained by habit to screen his hatred by treacherous blandishments. Seneca (such being the end of all conversations with one's master) expressed his gratitude; but he reversed the routines of his previous powerfulness: he stopped the throngs of well-wishers, avoided companions and was rarely in the City, as if detained at home by adverse health or the study of wisdom.

With Seneca struck down, circumstances were ready for the diminishing of **57** Rufus Faenius, in his case the charge being friendship with Agrippina.[101] And Tigellinus—more effective each day and deeming that his evil practices, which alone made him a force, would be more welcome if he bound the princeps in an alliance of crime—probed the latter's dread; and, on discovering that Plautus and Sulla were particularly feared (Plautus recently removed to Asia, Sulla to Narbonese Gaul),[102] he recalled their nobility and the proximity of the armies of the East to the former and of Germany's to the latter. He himself was not, like Burrus, holding incompatible hopes in view,[103] he said, but only Nero's preservation, 2 in respect of which every possible precaution against urban intrigue was being taken by his care on the spot; but in what way could distant movements be suppressed? The Galliae had pricked up their ears at the dictatorial name, and no less were the peoples of Asia hanging on the brilliancy of such a grandfather as Drusus.[104] Sulla, he said, was destitute, whence came his prime daring, and a sim- 3 ulator of sluggishness until he could discover an opportunity for his rashness; Plautus with his great wealth was not even fabricating a desire for inactivity but flaunted his imitations of the old Romans, adopting too the arrogance of the Stoics' sect, which made men disruptive and hungry for action.

There was no further delay: on the sixth day afterward, by assailants on assign- 4 ment to Massilia, Sulla was killed while reclining for dinner, before rumor could cause him dread. His head was brought back, and Nero mocked it to the effect that with its premature greyness it was grotesque. But the procurement of Plau- **58** tus' execution was not concealed to the same degree, because his safety was the concern of more people and the distance of the journey by land and sea, as well as the interval of time, had mobilized the news. The general fabrication was that 2

101. After a statement such as this, it is odd that Faenius Rufus is not mentioned again until 15.50.3 (A.D. 65); perhaps one should suppose a lacuna, in which T. made some reference to the postponement of Rufus' case (as he did at 4.19.1 apropos of Titius Sabinus). For Rufus' recent appointment as praetorian prefect see 14.51.2 above.

102. For Plautus see 14.22.1–3 above; for Sulla see 13.47.1–3.

103. Burrus had been appointed prefect of the Praetorian Guard through the influence of Agrippina (12.42.1) and so could be said to have had divided loyalties.

104. Sulla had the same name as, and was a direct descendant of, the famous Sulla who had been dictator in 82/81 B.C.; Plautus' maternal grandfather was Drusus, son of the emperor Tiberius.

he had gone to Corbulo, then presiding over great armies and, if brilliant and guiltless men were to be killed, a prime target for danger; moreover, it was said, Asia too had taken up arms in goodwill toward the young man, and the soldiers sent on their errand of crime—neither substantial in number nor ready in spirit—had transferred to the prospective revolution after they had proved un-

3   able to carry out their orders. This empty talk, in the habit of news, was exaggerated by the inactivity of the credulous; but in reality a freedman of Plautus, given the speed of the winds, forestalled the centurion[105] and brought instructions from

4   his father-in-law, L. Antistius:[106] he should shun a sluggish death;[107] nor was there any refuge in inactivity,+ and, with the sympathy for his great name,[108] he would discover allies in good and daring men; no support should be spurned in the meantime: if he repelled the sixty soldiers (such was the number arriving), then, during the time it took for a message to be sent back to Nero and another unit to make its way through, there could be many developments which might evolve into war. In short, either safety could be found by such a plan as this or his inevitable suffering would be no worse for his being daring rather than a shirker.

59   But his words did not move Plautus, whether because he could foresee no assistance, unarmed and exiled as he was, or through an aversion to an equivocal prospect, or through love of his spouse and children, to whom he deemed the princeps would be more amenable if not disturbed by any worry. There are those who say that another message arrived from his father-in-law, to the effect that nothing frightening was looming and that his teachers of wisdom, Coeranus and Musonius (of Greek and Tuscan lineage respectively), had urged steadfastness in

2   waiting for death in preference to an uncertain and trembling life.[109] At all events, he was discovered in the middle of the day, naked for physical training; in this state the centurion butchered him in the presence of Pelago, a eunuch whom Nero had placed in charge of the centurion and his maniple like a royal servant

3   over satellites. The murdered man's head was brought back, and at the sight of it (I shall record the princeps's very words) Nero said "Why ★★★?"[110] And, dropping his dread, he prepared to hasten his wedding to Poppaea, which had been deferred on account of terrors of that kind, and also to dislodge his spouse, Oc-

---

105. Who had been sent to kill Plautus.

106. The consul of 55 (13.11.1).

107. I.e., suicide.

108. See what is said about Plautus at 14.22.1 above.

109. Coeranus is scarcely otherwise known, but C. Musonius Rufus was a famous Stoic philosopher (see further 15.71.4), born at Vulsinii in Etruria. For "wisdom" see 14.16.2n.; "steadfastness" (*constantia*) was a Stoic virtue—one of Seneca's essays was entitled "On the Steadfastness of the Wise Man" (*De constantia sapientis*).

110. Given the extreme rarity with which T. claims to reproduce a person's actual words, it is singularly unfortunate that here a lacuna deprives us of what Nero said. According to Dio (62.14.1), he made a remark about the size of Plautus' nose (see 14.57.4 above, on Sulla).

tavia, who despite her modest behavior was oppressive to him because of her father's name and the people's affection. Yet to the senate he sent a letter confessing nothing about the slaughter of Sulla and Plautus: each, however, had a disruptive temperament, he said, and he was upholding the preservation of the state with great care. Under this title supplications were decreed, and also that Sulla and Plautus be removed from the senate—the mockeries now being more oppressive than the maladies.[111]   4

So, on the acceptance of the fathers' decision, and after he saw that all of his own crimes were being accepted as exceptional deeds, he evicted Octavia, insisting she was sterile; thereupon he was espoused to Poppaea. The long-standing concubine, who controlled Nero first as her adulterer and then as her husband, drove one of Octavia's servants to cast against her the charge of a servile love affair; and the defendant marked out was someone by the nomenclature Eucaerus,[112] Alexandrian by birth and expert at performing on the flute. Investigations of her maids were started with that in view, and, though some fell victim to the violence of their tortures with the result that they nodded their assent to falsehoods, the majority persevered in defending the purity of their mistress—one of them replying to Tigellinus' hounding that Octavia's womanly parts were more chaste than his mouth. She was removed nevertheless, at first in a show of civil divorce, and she received Burrus' house and Plautus' estates (inauspicious gifts); later she was banished to Campania, with the addition of a military guard. Hence frequent and unconcealed complaints from the public, whose prudence is less and, given the meanness of their fortune, dangers fewer.   60   2   3   4   5

In response *** though Nero, in remorse at his outrage, recalled Octavia as his spouse.[113] Thereupon the people delightedly climbed the Capitol and at last venerated the gods. They felled likenesses of Poppaea, carried Octavia's images on their shoulders, strewed them with flowers, and set them up in the forum and temples. Matters even reached praise for the princeps,+ and they were already filling the Palatium too with their numbers and their shouting when clusters of soldiers were sent out, who disrupted and scattered them by beatings and by brandishing steel. Everything which they had overthrown in their mutiny was changed, and Poppaea's honor was restored.   61

She for her part—always frightening in her hatred but now too from her dread that either the violence of the public might pose a fiercer threat or Nero be changed by the people's inclination—groveled at his knees, saying that her affairs were not being driven to the point where she was competing for her marriage,   2

111. For a similar remark at the end of a paragraph see 16.11.3.

112. The name means "opportune" or "timely."

113. Since this sentence is defective, it is impossible to be sure whether T. wrote "although," as transmitted by the manuscript, or "as though," as scholars have suggested. It nevertheless seems highly unlikely that Octavia was in fact recalled, especially as there is no reference to her being sent back again to Campania, which is where she is below (14.61.3).

although it meant more to her than life, but that her life itself had been taken to the brink by Octavia's clients and slaves, who, bestowing on themselves the role

3 of the plebs,[114] dared in peacetime things which scarcely happened in war. Those arms, she said, had been taken up against the princeps; the only lack was a leader, who, once things were mobilized, would be discovered easily: all she had to do was abandon Campania and proceed to the City in person, that absent woman

4 at whose nod such ferment was roused! Besides, what had been her own felony? What her offense to anyone? Or was it because she was about to present the hearth of the Caesars with true progeny? Did the Roman people really prefer the offspring of an Egyptian flute-player[115] to be introduced into the heights of the Commander's court? In short, if it was of material advantage, he should be willing rather than compelled to summon the woman who had mastery over him—or else let him pay heed to his security! The first disorders had subsided through justified vengeance and moderate remedies; but, if people despaired that Octavia would ever be Nero's wife, they would soon give the woman a husband!

62 The variation in her talk, adapted as it was to the dread and anger of her listener, terrified as well as inflamed him. But suspicion in the case of a slave[116] was too ineffectual and had been outwitted by the interrogation of the maids. It was therefore decided that a confession be sought from someone against whom a

2 charge of revolution might also be fabricated; and Anicetus, perpetrator of the maternal execution, seemed a suitable candidate, the prefect (as I have recalled)[117] of the fleet at Misenum and recipient of only slight favor after his criminal commission and then of a weightier hatred subsequently, because those who administer evil deeds are perceived as constantly remonstrating. Once summoned,

3 therefore, he was reminded by Caesar of his previous service: he alone had come to the rescue of the princeps's preservation in the face of a mother's intrigue; the chance of no less a favor was at hand, if he could remove a ferocious spouse. There was no need of brawn or weapon: he should merely confess adultery with Octavia. —Nero promised rewards, concealed for the moment but large, and an at-

4 tractive retirement; or, if he refused, he brandished the prospect of execution. The other, with an innate derangement and an ease derived from his previous outrages, fabricated even more than had been ordered, and made the confession in front of friends whom the princeps had assembled as if for a council. Then he was banished to Sardinia, where he endured no destitute exile and met a nat-

63 ural death. But Nero recalled in an edict that Octavia had bribed the prefect in the hope of allying his fleet and (quite forgetting his accusation of sterility a while before) that she had expelled a fetus in consciousness of her lusts, and

114. "Plebs" here represents riot and sedition (as Poppaea proceeds to imply), although slaves did not of course constitute any part of the plebs.

115. The flute-player is Eucaerus (14.60.2).

116. Viz. Eucaerus (14.60.2).

117. See 14.3.3.

that he himself had discovered all this; and he shut away Octavia on the island of Pandateria.

No other exiled woman afflicted the eyes of onlookers with greater pity. Some   2
still remembered Agrippina's banishment by Tiberius, and confronting them was the more recent memory of Julia's by Claudius.[118] Yet those two had had the strength of years: they had seen some happy times and could alleviate their present savagery by the recollection of better fortune once. But for this woman her   3
wedding day might as well have been a funeral in the first place, escorted as she had been to a house in which she was to have only grief, her father snatched away by poison and her brother immediately after;[119] then there was the maid, more influential than her mistress,[120] and Poppaea, wedded only for the ruin of a wife; and finally the charge, heavier to bear than any extermination. And the girl, in   **64**
the twentieth year of her age, amid centurions and soldiers, already released from life by the presentiment of evil, could nevertheless not yet rest in death. Subsequently, after an interval of a few days, she was ordered to die, although she testified that she was now a widow and no more than a sister,[121] and she invoked the Germanici, whom they had in common,[122] and finally the name of Agrippina, during whose lifetime she had sustained a marriage admittedly unhappy but exempt from extermination. She was restrained with bonds, and the veins in all   2
her limbs were severed; and because her blood, staunched by panic, trickled too slowly, she was executed by means of the steam from an extra-hot bath.[123] And there was the addition of a more frightful savagery, in that her head, amputated and carried into the City, was seen by Poppaea.

Gifts were decreed to the temples for this; and for how long shall I be recall-   3
ing them?+ Whoever becomes acquainted with the misfortunes of those times, either through my authorship or that of others, may hold the presumption that, whenever the princeps ordered exile and slaughter, on every occasion gratitude was expressed to the gods, and that what were once the distinctions of success were now those of public disaster. And yet we shall not be silent if any senate's decision was novel in its sycophancy or unsurpassable in its passivity.

118. Agrippina's banishment in 29 will have been told in the lost part of Book 5; Julia Livilla, daughter of Germanicus, had been banished in 41 for her alleged adultery with Seneca (see 13.42.3).

119. Respectively Claudius (12.67–8) and Britannicus (13.16.2–17.1).

120. I.e., Acte (see 13.12.1–2).

121. To Nero, who had been adopted by Claudius, Octavia's natural father.

122. Octavia's grandfather was the elder Drusus, who had been given the name Germanicus on his death; one of his sons, the "famous" Germanicus (viz. Claudius' brother), was Nero's grandfather.

123.   She is said to have died on the same day as Nero, who is thought to have died on 9 June six years later. There survives under the name of the younger Seneca a play entitled *Octavia*, which deals with the young woman's last days.

65   In the same year he was believed to have killed by poison the most powerful
       of his freedmen: Doryphorus as having opposed his wedding to Poppaea, Pallas
       on the grounds that he was tying up inordinate money by the length of his old
2   age. Romanus in secret charges had censured Seneca for being an ally of C. Piso,
       but he was struck down more efficiently on the same indictment by Seneca him-
       self. Hence fear on Piso's part, and there arose against Nero a storm of intrigue,
       great and ill-starred.[124]

124. T.'s closing statements seem to imply that the so-called Pisonian Conspiracy started
in A.D. 62 but are regarded by many scholars with the greatest skepticism, since T.'s own
narrative of the conspiracy is not given until 15.48–74 (A.D. 65).

BOOK 15

Meanwhile the king of the Parthians, Vologaeses—learning of Corbulo's affairs **1** and that the alien-born Tigranes had been installed as king in Armenia, and in addition wanting to embark on avenging the eminence of the Arsacidae, which had been spurned with the banishment of his brother Tiridates—was being drawn contrariwise to different concerns by the greatness of Rome and by his respect for the unbroken treaty, being a hesitator by instinct and tangled up in the defection of the Hyrcani, an effective people, and in the many wars resulting therefrom.[1]

While in two minds, he was goaded by word of a new and additional insult: **2** having left Armenia, Tigranes had devastated the bordering nation of the Adiabeni too extensively and lengthily for mere banditry, and the chiefs of the peoples were enduring it only with difficulty: had they descended to such a point of contemptibility that they were being raided not even under Roman leadership but because of the temerity of a hostage held for so many years among menials?[2] Their pain was inflamed by Monobazus (with whom control of the Adiabeni **3** rested), urgently asking what support he should seek or from where: already, he said, there had been a concession over Armenia; neighboring areas were being drawn in; and, unless the Parthians defended them, their servitude to the Romans would be lighter if they surrendered than if they were captured. Tiridates **4** too, a refugee from his kingdom, was all the weightier for his silence or in his modest complaints. It was not by shirking, he said, that great empires were maintained: the competition of men and arms was a necessity; at the highest level of fortune, power was identical with fairness, and, whereas to retain one's own property was the characteristic of a private household, to compete for that of foreigners was a kingly virtue.

Vologaeses, convinced by this, therefore called a council and set Tiridates next **2** to himself and began thus: "Although this man, born of the same father as myself, had conceded the supreme name to me by reason of age, I escorted him to the possession of Armenia,[3] which is regarded as the third rank in powerfulness (Pacorus had previously taken the Medes); and I seemed, contrary to the old hatreds and competitions of brothers, to have achieved a proper settlement for our family's household gods. But the Romans are preventing it, and the peace, which **2** they have never challenged with advantage to themselves, they are now again severing, to their own extermination. I shall not embark on denial: I should have **3** preferred to retain by fairness rather than by bloodshed, by reason rather than by

---

1. For the Parthians' Hyrcanian war, Corbulo's expulsion of Tiridates, and Nero's installation of Tigranes, see 14.25.2–26.2, of which the present narrative is the continuation. The treaty is the accommodation which Augustus reached with the Parthians in 20 B.C.

2. For Tigranes' sojourn in Rome see 14.26.1.

3. See 12.50.1.

arms, the acquisitions of our ancestors. If I have failed through hesitation, I shall rectify it through courage. At least *your* strength and glory remain intact, with the addition of a reputation for modestness which is not to be spurned by the high-

4 est of mortals and is valued by the gods."[4] So saying, he wreathed Tiridates' head with a diadem; he handed to Monaeses, a noble man, the ready unit of cavalry which by custom follows the king, adding some auxiliaries of the Adiabeni, and he entrusted him with the eviction of Tigranes from Armenia; while he himself, putting aside his disaffection with the Hyrcani, summoned up his internal forces and the storm of war, menacing the Roman provinces.

3   When Corbulo heard of this from reliable messengers, he dispatched two le- gions with Verulanus Severus and Vettius Bolanus as support for Tigranes, with the secret instruction that they should conduct everything calmly rather than hastily.[5] He preferred to have the war at his disposal rather than to wage it, and he had also written to Caesar of the need for Armenia to be defended by a leader

2 of its own, saying that Syria, should Vologaeses swoop, was in a keener crisis. And meanwhile he situated the remaining legions along the bank of the Euphrates, armed an irregular unit of provincials, cut off enemy approaches with garrisons, and, because the region is lacking in water, strongholds were installed at springs, and some watercourses he buried by piling up sand.

4   While such were the preparations being made by Corbulo for the protection of Syria, Monaeses, despite having driven his driving column rapidly to forestall any report of himself, failed even so to come upon Tigranes in a state of igno-

2 rance or incautiousness. He had occupied Tigranocerta, an effective city owing to the abundance of its defenders and the bulk of its battlements. In addition, the Nicephorius stream, of a width not to be spurned, streamed around part of the walls, and a mighty ditch had been run where the current inspired no confidence. And inside there were soldiers, and previously provided supplies, at the trans- portation of which a few men had advanced too greedily; their sudden surround- ing by the enemy had inflamed the others with anger rather than with dread.

3 But the Parthian has no hand-to-hand daring for the execution of blockades: with his occasional arrows he cannot terrify those shut inside and he becomes frustrated. When the Adiabeni began to move up ladders and machines, they were easily dislodged and then, as our men burst out, slaughtered.

5   Nevertheless Corbulo, despite his success, deemed some moderation of his for- tune to be necessary and dispatched men to Vologaeses to protest that violence had been inflicted on the province: those being invested were an allied and friendly king and Roman cohorts; it would be better for the blockade to be aban-

2 doned, or he himself too would station a camp on enemy territory. Casperius, the centurion selected for the legation, approached the king at the town of Nis-

---

4. Vologaeses has been speaking to a council, so "*your*" in this last sentence is plural and refers to his listeners.

5. Verulanus, mentioned earlier at 14.26.1, would be suffect consul in (?) 66; M. Vet- tius Bolanus would also be suffect consul in (?) 66 and governor of Britain 69–71.

ibis (thirty-seven miles distant from Tigranocerta) and defiantly issued the instructions. It was deeply entrenched in Vologaeses from of old that he should   3
avoid Roman arms; nor were present circumstances running favorably: the blockade was unavailing, Tigranes was protected by brawn and resources, those who
had undertaken the storming were put to flight, legions were dispatched to Armenia, and others along the frontier of Syria were prepared for a spontaneous irruption—and how weak his own cavalry were for want of pasturage! (With the
appearance of a swarm of locusts, there was an absence of any grass or leaf.) So,   4
his dread concealed, in a more conciliatory gesture he replied that he would dispatch legates to the Roman Commander concerning his request for Armenia
and the consolidation of peace. He ordered Monaeses to abandon Tigranocerta,
while he himself withdrew in retreat.

The majority extolled this as a magnificent accomplishment that was due to   6
the king's alarm and the threats of Corbulo; but others interpreted that a secret
bargain had been struck whereby, on the abandonment of the war by both sides
and Vologaeses' departure, Tigranes too would leave Armenia. For why had the   2
Roman army been removed from Tigranocerta? Why during peacetime had they
deserted what they had defended in war? Was it really better to have wintered at
the extremity of Cappadocia, in hastily erected shacks, than in the seat of a kingdom recently retained? Of course! The fighting had been deferred so that Vologaeses might compete with someone other than Corbulo and that Corbulo
might not endanger further the glory won over so many years! For, as I have   3
recorded, he had demanded that Armenia be protected by a leader of its own,
and it had been heard that Caesennius Paetus was arriving.[6]

And now he had appeared, the forces being divided in such a way that the
Fourth and Twelfth Legions, with the addition of the Fifth (which had recently
been summoned from the Moesians), as well as the Pontic and Galatians' and
Cappadocians' auxiliaries, should obey Paetus, while the Third, Sixth, and Tenth
Legions and the earlier soldiery of Syria should remain with Corbulo;[7] everything else they would combine or assign according to the needs of the moment.
But Corbulo was intolerant of a rival, and Paetus, who would have had sufficient   4
glory if he had been regarded as second to him, despised his achievements, insisting that there had been no slaughter or plunder and that the "stormings of
cities" which he frequently cited were nominal only: he would impose on the
vanquished taxes and laws and, instead of a mere shadow of a king, the jurisdiction of Rome.

About the same time Vologaeses' legates, whose dispatch to the princeps I have   7
recalled,[8] returned in failure, and war was adopted openly by the Parthians. And

6. See 15.3.1 above for Corbulo's demand. L. Caesennius Paetus had been consul in
61 (14.29.1).

7. For inscriptions relating to Legions III and VI see Sherk 65A and B (= Braund 245
= WM 43).

8. At 15.5.4 above.

Paetus did not decline it, but with two legions (of which the Fourth was directed by Funisulanus Vettonianus at that time, the Twelfth by Calavius Sabinus[9]) en-
2   tered Armenia—to a grim omen. In the crossing of the Euphrates, which they were going across by bridge, the horse which was carrying the consular insignia became agitated for no obvious reason and escaped to the rear; and a victim,[10] standing by the winter quarters as they were being fortified, burst through the half-completed works in flight and ejected itself from the rampart; and the soldiers' javelins caught fire—a more distinctive prodigy because in combat the
8   Parthian enemy uses missiles as weapons. But Paetus, spurning the omens, and with his winter quarters not yet sufficiently consolidated and no provision of grain, swept his army across Mount Taurus to recover (so he maintained) Tigra-
2   nocerta and to ravage the areas which Corbulo had abandoned untouched. Some strongholds were captured, and some glory and plunder acquired—except that he handled neither his glory with moderation nor his plunder with care, over-running on distant marches places which could not be held, and with the supplies that he had captured being contaminated; and, with winter now encroaching, he withdrew his army and composed a letter to Caesar as if on the basis of the war's completion—magnificent words, empty of substance.

9   Meanwhile Corbulo installed himself on the bank of the Euphrates (which he had never neglected) with more frequent garrisons; and, to prevent the enemy squadrons from creating some obstacle to the superimposition of a bridge (already they were flying over the surrounding plains in a great display), across the stream he strung ships of outstanding size, connected by timbers and heightened with turrets; and with catapults and ballistas he thrust aside the barbarians, against whom the trajectory of rocks and spears was farther than could be matched by
2   their countering discharge of arrows. Then the bridge was joined up, and the hills opposite were occupied by allied cohorts and afterward by the legions' camp—with such speed and evident strength that the Parthians, abandoning their preparations for the invasion of Syria, turned all their hopes on Armenia, where Paetus, unaware of what loomed, was holding the Fifth Legion far away in Pontus and had weakened the rest by indiscriminate grants of leave to the soldiers, until it was heard that Vologaeses was arriving with a considerable and ferocious column.

10   The Twelfth Legion was summoned, and the tactic which Paetus had hoped would report the increase in his army served only to betray its depletion. Yet he would still have been able to hold the camp with it and to outwit the Parthian by dragging out the war, had he been steadfast in his own decisions or in those of others; but, just when he had been fortified by military men against some pressing contingency, contrarily, to prevent the appearance of needing another's opin-
2   ion, he would convert to a different and more detrimental plan. So now, leaving his winter camp, crying that he had been given neither ditch nor rampart but

9. Funisulanus would be consul in 78; Calavius is otherwise unknown.
10. A sacrificial animal.

bodies and arms to fight the enemy, he led his legions as if for combat in battle;
then, after losing a centurion and the few soldiers whom he had sent ahead to
observe the enemy's forces, he retired in trepidation. And, because Vologaeses' 3
hounding had been none too fierce, with an empty and contrary confidence he
installed three thousand selected infantry on the neighboring ridge of the Taurus to prevent the king's passage. He also situated Pannonian wing-men, the hard
core of his cavalry, on part of the plain. His spouse and son were concealed in a
stronghold whose name is Arsamosata, and he gave them a cohort as garrison—
thereby dispersing soldiery which, if kept in one place, would more readily have
withstood the roving enemy. It is maintained that he was compelled only with 4
difficulty to admit to Corbulo that they were hounding him; nor was there any
hurry on Corbulo's part, so that, as the dangers swelled, the praise for his support
might also be magnified. The latter nevertheless ordered a thousand from each
of the three legions, eight hundred wing-men and a similar number from the cohorts to be expedited for the journey.

But, although Vologaeses had heard that the routes were blockaded by Paetus **11**
with infantry in one place and cavalry in another, without changing his plan but
by threats and by force respectively he terrified the wing-men and crushed the
legionaries—only one centurion, Tarquitius Crescens, daring to defend the tower
in which he was keeping garrison, making frequent eruptions and slaughtering
any barbarians who moved in too close, until he was surrounded by the discharging of fire-brands. Any uninjured infantrymen made for distant and trackless ar- 2
eas, the wounded again for the camp, emphasizing in their dread the courage of
the king and the savagery and number of his peoples—all to the easy credulity
of those who shared the same panic. Not even their leader grappled with the re- 3
verses but had abandoned all the responsibilities of soldiering, dispatching again
to Corbulo a plea that he should hurry in coming and protect the standards and
eagles of the unlucky army, and what was left of its name; meanwhile he and his
men would retain their loyalty while life lasted.

Corbulo for his part was unafraid and, leaving some of his forces in Syria to **12**
hold the fortifications installed on the Euphrates, he made for the Commagene
region by the nearest route which was not lacking in supplies, then for Cappadocia, and thence for the Armenians. Accompanying the army, apart from the things
generally common in war, was a considerable number of camels laden with grain
so that he might repel hunger as well as the enemy. The first of the stricken whom 2
he encountered was Paccius (the centurion of the first rank),[11] then quite a few
of the soldiers, whom, when they offered different reasons for their flight, he
warned to return to their standards and to try out the clemency of Paetus: he
himself, he said, was ruthless except to victors. At the same time he went among 3
his own legions, encouraging, reminding them of the past and pointing out new
glories: it was not the villages or towns of the Armenians, he said, but a Roman
camp and the two legions within it which were the aim and prize of their toil;

11. See 13.36.1 and n.

if the principal crown for rescuing a citizen[12] was to be bestowed on individual maniple regulars by the Commander's hand, what a fine and great honor it would be when the total of those who had brought salvation was observed to equal that

4 of those who had received it! Collectively eager after words such as these (and some were inflamed by personal spurs in the form of perils to their brothers or relatives), they persisted day and night with their hurried journey.

13   It was therefore all the more intensively that Vologaeses pressed those blockaded, at one moment assaulting the legions' rampart, at another the stronghold where those of noncombatant age were being defended, approaching more closely than is the Parthians' custom to see if by such temerity he could entice

2 the enemy to battle. But they could scarcely be drawn out of their billets and did nothing but protect the fortifications, some at the order of their leader, others through personal cowardice or waiting for Corbulo and, if violence threatened, with premonitions of the disastrous precedents of Caudium and Numantia—and the violence of Samnites or Spaniards was hardly the same as that of the Roman empire's rivals![+13] Though valiant and praised, antiquity too, they said, had paid heed to its salvation whenever fortune delivered an adverse verdict.

3   Though the leader was overwhelmed by such despair in his army, the first letter which he composed to Vologaeses was nevertheless in no way supplicatory but in the manner of a complaint that it was on behalf of the Armenians, who had always been under Roman jurisdiction or subject to a king chosen by the Commander, that he was conducting hostilities: peace was equally useful to both of them; he should not look only at the present: he had come against a mere two Roman legions with all the forces of his kingdom, but the Romans had the rest of the globe with which to aid the war.

14   In reply Vologaeses wrote back nothing of relevance but that he must wait for his brothers, Pacorus and Tiridates: that was the place and time which had been marked out for their consideration of what to decide about Armenia; it was the gods who had added—something worthy of the Arsacidae!—that simultaneously

2 they should reach a settlement about the Roman legions. After this, messengers were dispatched by Paetus and a dialogue was sought with the king, who ordered Vasaces, his prefect of cavalry, to go. Thereupon Paetus for his part recalled the Luculli, the Pompeii, and everything the Caesars had done for the maintaining or bestowing of Armenia; Vasaces, that only the phantom of retaining or lavish-

3 ing rested with us: the reality of that power lay with the Parthians. And, after much dispute on both sides, the Adiabene Monobazus was called in for the following day to witness what terms they had struck; and it was agreed that the legions should be freed from the blockade and all the soldiery withdraw from the Armenians' territory and the strongholds and supplies be handed to the Parthi-

12. The civic crown (3.21.3 and n.).

13. After the disaster of the Caudine Forks in 321 B.C. the Roman army was forced to pass under the Samnite yoke (11.24.5); in 137 B.C. the Romans suffered a disgraceful defeat at Numantia in Spain. The Roman empire's "rivals" are the Parthians (see 12.10.2).

ans, on the conclusion of which Vologaeses should have the opportunity of dispatching legates to Nero.

In the meantime Paetus installed a bridge over the River Arsanias (it flowed **15** past the camp) in a show of expediting a route there for himself, although in fact the Parthians had ordered it as evidence of their victory. (It was they who used it; our men went in an opposite direction.) Rumor added both that the legions **2** had been sent beneath the yoke and other ill-starred episodes drawn from history, the like of which the Armenians appropriated by performing them themselves: they entered the fortifications before the Roman column could withdraw and stood around the streets, recognizing and reclaiming their previously captured menials or cattle; clothing too was seized, and arms secured, the soldiery acquiescing in panic lest any pretext for battle should arise. Vologaeses, with the **3** arms and bodies of the slaughtered piled up to testify to our disaster, refrained from viewing the fleeing legions: he was seeking a reputation for moderation, now that his haughtiness had had its fill. Sitting on an elephant, he charged across the River Arsanias, as did the king's entourage on a team of straining horses, because a rumor had circulated that the bridge would yield under their weight owing to the guile of its manufacturers; but those who dared to go onto it ascertained its sturdiness and reliability.

All the same, it was agreed that those blockaded had had so plentiful a grain **16** supply that they set fire to their storehouses; conversely Corbulo has transmitted[14] that the Parthians, lacking in supplies and with their pasturage cropped right down, were about to abandon the siege and that he himself had been no more than three days' journey distant. He adds that with an oath from Paetus measures **2** were taken in front of the standards, in the presence of those whom the king had sent as witnesses, that no Roman would enter Armenia until the return of Nero's letter, saying whether he assented to the peace. Even on the assumption that he **3** composed all this to magnify the man's infamy, there is considered to be no obscurity about the rest: that in a single day Paetus had covered a distance of forty miles,[15] abandoning the injured on all sides, and that the trepidation of the fugitives was no less grotesque than if they had turned their backs in the line of battle.

Corbulo with his own forces, encountering them on the bank of the Eu- **4** phrates, did not present such a display of insignia and arms as to reproach the others for their dissimilarity; his mournful maniples, commiserating with the lot of their fellow soldiers, did not restrain even their tears: scarcely were greetings exchanged through weeping. All competition in courage and all ambition for glory—the feelings of fortunate men—had passed away; pity alone prevailed, and more largely among the lesser ranks. There followed a brief conversation of the **17** leaders between themselves, the one complaining that his toils had been unavailing: the war could have been finished by the flight of the Parthians. The other

14. In his memoirs, by which T.'s narrative is believed to have been greatly influenced.

15. Double the normal daily rate of twenty miles and one of the fastest recorded marches in Roman history.

313

replied that the circumstances of each of them were unaffected: they should turn the eagles around and jointly invade an Armenia weakened by Vologaeses' depar-

2   ture. But "he did not have such instructions from the Commander" was Corbulo's reply; it was because he had been moved by the legions' peril that he had left his province; since the attempts of the Parthians remained in uncertainty, he would make for Syria again; but even so he must pray for the best of fortune, namely that his infantry, worn out by the stages of their journey, might overtake an eager cavalry which, given the favorability of the plains, could outrun them.[16]

3   Afterward Paetus wintered here and there in Cappadocia; but Vologaeses sent messengers to Corbulo that he should tear down his strongholds across the Euphrates and make the stream, as before, the border between them. Corbulo for his part demanded that Armenia too should be emptied of its various garrisons. Finally the king yielded; and the places which Corbulo had fortified beyond the Euphrates were destroyed, and the Armenians were left without an arbiter.

★

18   At Rome the trophies and arches which were being set up on account of the Parthians in the middle of the Capitoline Hill had been decreed by the senate with the war still undecided and were not now abandoned—a consideration for

2   appearances which meant the spurning of conscience. Moreover, to dissemble his concern at foreign affairs, Nero threw the plebs' grain, which was rotten with age, into the Tiber in order to bolster unconcern for the food supply. No addition was made to its price, although roughly two hundred ships had been demolished in the actual harbor by the violence of a storm, and a hundred others

3   sailing up the Tiber by a chance fire. Then he placed three consulars—L. Piso, Ducenius Geminus, and Pompeius Paulinus[17]—in charge of the public revenues, with an assault on earlier principes whose weight of expenditure had outstripped the due returns. He himself, he said, was lavishing an annual amount of sixty million sesterces on the state.

19   There had grown up at that time a crooked custom whereby at the approach of an election or a ballot for provinces numerous childless men took on sons by fabricated adoptions and, having been allotted praetorships and provinces alongside genuine fathers, immediately dismissed from their charge those whom they

2   had adopted—all to considerable resentment.[18] An appeal was made to the sen-

---

16. Corbulo cannot be hoping that his infantry might literally "overtake" the Parthian cavalry (which he evidently imagines as being likely to invade Syria); presumably he means that, if he gets a head start, the rate of his infantry's progress might result in their reaching Syria before the Parthians.

17. L. Piso (13.28.2n.) had been consul in 57 (13.31.1), A. Ducenius Geminus suffect consul in 61 or 62, and Pompeius Paullinus (13.53.2) suffect in (probably) 54.

18. The Lex Papia Poppaea of A.D. 9 privileged the fathers of children at the expense of the childless (see 2.51.1, 3.25.1, 3.28.3).

ate by men who enumerated the rights[+] of nature and the toils of rearing, as opposed to the deceit and artificiality of the brief adoptions: the childless enjoyed
adequate rewards in that, with considerable unconcern and no burdens, they had
influence, honors, indeed everything, ready and waiting; but, as for themselves, the
long-awaited promises of the legislation were being turned into a mockery when
someone—a parent without the anxiety, childless without the grief—could equal
in an instant the long-standing prayers of fathers. As a result there was passed a   3
senate's decision that simulated adoption should be of no help in any area of public responsibility and no advantage even for claiming inheritances.

Next, Claudius Timarchus, a Cretan, appeared as a defendant on the general   **20**
charges customary for those paramount provincials whose elevation to excessive
wealth results in injury to lesser people; but one utterance of his had gone so far
as to insult the senate, namely his insistence that it lay within his own power
whether gratitude should be expressed to the proconsuls who held Crete.[19] Pae-   2
tus Thrasea turned the occasion to public benefit and, after he had proposed that
the defendant be expelled from the province of Crete, added this: "It has been   3
proved by experience, conscript fathers, that exceptional laws and honorable
precedents are generated among good men by the felonies of others. Thus the
Cincian rogation was born from the license of advocates, the Julian laws from the
bribery of candidates, the Calpurnian resolutions from the greed of magistrates:[20]
fault is prior in time to punishment, amendment later than malpractice. Therefore   4
against the new haughtiness of provincials let us adopt a policy worthy of Roman
reliability and steadfastness, whereby, without any detriment to the protection of
our allies, we depart from the opinion that what each man is held to be like rests
somewhere other than in the judgment of his fellow citizens.[21] At one time, of   **21**
course, not only a praetor or consul but even private members were sent to visit
provinces and to report their views on the compliance of each; and nations trembled upon the evaluation of individuals. But now we court foreigners and are sycophantic toward them; and, just as gratitude is decreed at the nod of one of them,
so—and more readily—is an accusation. Let it be decreed! And let provincials keep   2
the prerogative[+] of exhibiting their powerfulness in such a way! But, if their praise
is false and extracted only by pleas, let it be curbed in the same way as wicked-
ness and cruelty. Often there is more malpractice in obliging than in offending;   3
in fact, certain virtues are a source of hatred: a determined severity, a spirit invin-

19. Scholars infer (largely from the present episode) that there was a custom whereby,
when a provincial governor's term of office was concluded, a delegation of provincials
would travel to Rome to deliver a formal speech of thanks (*gratiarum actio*) in the senate.

20. For the Cincian law of 204 B.C., forbidding payments to advocates, see 11.5.3 (and
13.42.1); the Julian laws are those of 18 and 8 B.C. against electoral bribery; in 149 B.C.
L. Calpurnius Piso Frugi as tribune established the first standing court to deal with cases
of extortion by Roman officials in the provinces (mentioned again at 15.21.4 below).

21. I.e., Romans must accept that they should be judged only by their fellow citizens
in Rome.

4   cible against influence. Hence it is the debuts of our magistrates which are usually better, and there is decline at the end, when, in the manner of candidates, we are looking for votes. If all this were stopped, the provinces will be ruled more uniformly and consistently. Just as greed has been foiled by dread of the extortion trial, so canvassing will be curbed if thanksgivings are forbidden.'

22   Considerable agreement greeted the proposal, but a senate's decision could nevertheless not be completed, since the consuls denied that there had been a motion on the subject. Later, at the princeps's instigation, they sanctioned that no one at a council of allies should move that gratitude must be expressed to propraetors or proconsuls in front of the senate, and that no one should perform such a legation.

2   With the same men as consuls the gymnasium[22] burned down after being struck by lightning, and the likeness of Nero within it melted to shapeless bronze. And in an earthquake a crowded town in Campania, Pompeii, was largely demolished. And there was the decease of the Vestal Virgin, Laelia, in whose place Cornelia, of the family of the Cossi, was appointed.

★ ★ ★

A.D. 63

23   With Memmius Regulus and with Verginius Rufus as consuls,[23] Nero welcomed with more than mortal joy the daughter born to him by Poppaea,[24] and he called her Augusta, the same nomenclature being given also to Poppaea. The place for the childbirth was the colony of Antium, where he himself had been brought

2   forth. Already the senate had commended Poppaea's womb to the gods and had publicly undertaken vows, which were multiplied and discharged. And supplications were added, and a temple of Fertility and a contest on the model of the Actian religious festival were decreed, and also that golden likenesses of the Fortunes[25] should be sited on the throne of Capitoline Jupiter; and circus games, as for the Julian family at Bovillae, should be produced for the Claudian and Domitian at Antium.

3   It was all fleeting, the infant being deceased within four months. And once again there arose the sycophancies of those proposing the honor of her being a goddess, and a cushioned couch, a shrine, and a priest.[26] As for the man himself,

22. Presumably the same gymnasium as had been dedicated in A.D. 61 (see 14.47.2).

23. C. Memmius Regulus was son of P. Memmius Regulus (consul in 31: 5.11.1–2), who had died in the previous year (14.47.1). L. Verginius Rufus held his third consulship in 97, the year of his death; his funeral oration was delivered by Tacitus as suffect consul (Introduction, p. x).

24. On 21 January.

25. Two local goddesses regarded as sisters, the "Antian Fortunes."

26. For the couch see 14.12.1n.

he behaved as immoderately in sorrow as he had in happiness. (It was noted that,   4
with the whole senate pouring to Antium after the recent delivery, Thrasea was
prevented, accepting with spirit unmoved the insult which prophesied his looming slaughter. It is maintained that this was followed by an utterance from Caesar, in which he boasted to Seneca that he had been reconciled with Thrasea, and
that Seneca had congratulated Caesar. Hence the glory of these exceptional
men—and their dangers—continued to swell.)[27]

Meanwhile, at the beginning of spring, the legates of the Parthians[28] brought in-   **24**
structions from King Vologaeses and a letter along the same lines: he was now abandoning his previous and frequent boasts about retaining Armenia, he said, because
the gods, those arbiters of peoples however powerful, had handed its possession to
the Parthians, and not without Roman ignominy; recently Tigranes had been be-   2
set; afterward, when he could have crushed Paetus and his legions, he had released
them safe and sound: there had been sufficient proof of his strength; evidence had
been given also of his leniency; and Tiridates would not have declined to come to
the City to receive his diadem if he were not detained by the impediment of his
priesthood;[29] but he would go to the standards and to the likenesses of the princeps, where in the presence of the legions he could inaugurate his reign.

Such being Vologaeses' letter, it was because Paetus was writing differently, as   **25**
though matters were still undecided, that the centurion who had arrived with
the legates was asked in what state Armenia was, and he replied that the Romans
had all withdrawn. Then, appreciating the derision of barbarians who sought   2
what they had seized, Nero consulted among the chiefs of the community
whether a precarious war or dishonorable peace was their pleasure. There was no
hesitation about war; and Corbulo, knowledgeable of his soldiers and of the enemy for so many years, was placed in charge of conducting affairs lest through
someone else's ignorance there should be further mistakes, because Paetus had
been a source of disgust. —So they were sent back in failure, but with gifts to   3
encourage the hope that similar advocacy from Tiridates would not be in vain if
he brought his pleas in person.

The administration of Syria was entrusted to C. Cestius, the military forces to
Corbulo; and the Fifteenth Legion, in the process of being led by Marius Celsus
from Pannonia, was added.[30] The tetrarchs and kings and prefects and procurators and those praetors who controlled the bordering provinces were written to
that they should comply with Corbulo's orders, his power having been more or

27. Seneca's congratulations implied that Thrasea's friendship was worth more to Nero
than Nero's to him, an implication which gave glory both to Seneca (for his free speaking) and to Thrasea (by acknowledging his influence).

28. The dispatch of these legates to Nero was mentioned at 15.14.3 above.

29. According to the elder Pliny (*Natural History* 30.16), Tiridates was a Magian and
scrupled to cross the sea.

30. C. Cestius Gallus had been suffect consul in 42; Marius Celsus would be suffect consul in 69.

less increased to the very considerable limit which the Roman people had given
4   Cn. Pompeius for his conduct of the pirate war.[31] Though Paetus on his return
had been dreading greater severity, Caesar was content merely to assail him with
a witticism in more or less these terms: he was pardoning him at once, lest one
so prone to panic should fall ill from a lengthier anxiety.

★

26   As for Corbulo, having transferred the Fourth and Twelfth Legions (which, after
the loss of their bravest men and with the rest terrified, seemed scarcely fit for
battle) to Syria, he led from there to Armenia the Sixth and Third Legions, sol-
2   diery that was fresh and trained by frequent and successful toils. He added the
Fifth Legion, whose time in Pontus had been free from disaster, as well as the Fif-
teenths (recently moved up) and detachments of picked men from Illyricum and
Egypt and their wings and cohorts, and the kings' auxiliaries that had been concentrated into a body at Melitene, where he was preparing to cross the Euphrates.
3   Then, after performing the ritual purification of the army, he called it to a meeting and began speaking in magnificent fashion about the Commander's auspices
and his own achievements, diverting responsibility for the reverses onto the ignorance of Paetus, and all with that considerable authority which served as the
military man's fluency.
27   Soon he proceeded along the route once penetrated by L. Lucullus,[32] opening up the places which time had obstructed. And on the arrival of Tiridates' and
Vologaeses' legates concerning peace, he did not spurn them but attached to them
centurions with instructions that were in no way ruthless: it had not come to the
2   point where there was need of a final contest; the Romans had had numerous
successes, but some things had gone the Parthians' way as a lesson against haughtiness. Accordingly, not only was it advantageous to Tiridates to receive as a gift
a kingdom untouched by devastation but Vologaeses would pay better heed to
the Parthian people by a Roman alliance than by mutual losses. He[33] knew the
extent of internal disaffection and how untamed and defiant were the nations he
ruled; by contrast his own Commander enjoyed an undisturbed peace every-
3   where and this was his only war. —At the same time he backed up his advice
with terror and drove the Armenian magnates, who had been the first to defect
from us, from their abodes, extirpated their strongholds, and filled the lowlands
and highlands, the powerful and the powerless, with equal dread.
28   Even the barbarians did not regard Corbulo's name as hostile or with an enemy hatred, and for that reason they believed his counsel trustworthy. Therefore

---

31. In 67 B.C. Pompey the Great was given unprecedented powers to deal with the continuing pirate menace (see also 12.62 above).

32. On his advance to Tigranocerta in 69 B.C.

33. It is not clear whether Corbulo is referring to himself or to Vologaeses; at the end
of this sentence "he ruled" of course refers to the latter.

Vologaeses did not react frighteningly to the main issue and actually sought a truce
for certain prefectures;[34] Tiridates demanded a place and day for a dialogue. The   2
time was soon; the place—that in which the legions had recently been blockaded
with Paetus—was chosen by the barbarians for its memory of a happier affair there
and yet was not avoided by Corbulo, in order that the dissimilarity of their two
fortunes should increase his glory. Nor was he made tense by the infamy of Paetus, as was revealed above all by the fact that he commanded the man's son, a tribune, to lead some maniples and to cover over the relics of the disastrous battle.

On the agreed day Tiberius Alexander, an illustrious Roman equestrian who   3
had been provided as administrator for the war, and Vinicianus Annius, Corbulo's
son-in-law who was not yet of senatorial age but placed over the Fifth Legion
in the capacity of legate, came to Tiridates' camp as an honor to the man and so
that he should not dread a trap with such a form of surety.[35] Next, twenty cavalry were enlisted by both sides; and, seeing Corbulo, the king was the first to
spring down from his horse; and Corbulo did not hesitate either, but each man
on foot clasped the other's right hand. Thereupon the Roman praised the young   **29**
man for abandoning headstrong policies and for the adoption of those safe and
salutary; the other for his part, after a long preamble on the nobility of his lineage, added the rest of his words with restraint: he would go to Rome and bring
a novel prestige to Caesar—a suppliant Arsacid at a time of no reverses for the
Parthians! It was then decided that Tiridates should place his royal decoration before the likeness of Caesar and not take it up again except from the hand of Nero.
And the dialogue ended with a kiss.

Later, after a few days' intermission, in a great scene on both sides, the cavalry   2
on the one hand was arranged by squadron and with native insignia, the columns
of legions on the other stood with glittering eagles and standards, and representations of gods in the manner of a temple; in the center a tribunal held a curule
seat, and the seat a likeness of Nero. Approaching it, Tiridates, after slaughtering   3
the customary victims,[36] removed the diadem from his head and placed it beneath the image—making on everyone's mind a considerable impression, magnified by the slaughter or blockading of Roman armies which was still imprinted
on their eyes. But now the circumstances were reversed! Tiridates would be going to be exhibited to the nations! How little short of a captive! Corbulo added   **30**
to his glory the affability of a banquet; and, with the king asking for explanations
whenever he noticed some novelty (such as that the beginnings of the watches
were announced by a centurion, the party was dismissed by a bugle, and the altar constructed in front of the augural tent[37] was lit by a torch placed under-

34. See 6.42.4n. for prefectures.

35. Tiberius Julius Alexander, nephew of the Jewish writer and philosopher Philo, had
been governor of Judaea in the 40s and would become prefect of Egypt. Annius Vinicianus
was son of L. Annius Vinicianus and came from a family of conspirators (6.9.4n., 15.56.4).

36. Sacrificial animals.

37. See 2.13.1n.

neath), Corbulo exaggerated everything, arousing in him an admiration for old-
time convention.

2   On the next day Tiridates begged for an interval in which, as he was about to
embark on such a great journey, he might first visit his brothers and mother;
meanwhile he handed over his daughter, as a hostage, and a supplicatory letter

31   for Nero. On departing he found Pacorus with the Medes but Vologaeses at Ecbatana in a state of concern for his brother: he had even requested of Corbulo
by personal messengers that Tiridates should not present[+] any semblance of servitude or hand over his sword or be prevented from embracing the holders of
provinces or be kept standing at their doors, and that at Rome he should enjoy
as much honor as the consuls. Evidently, habituated as he was to foreign haughtiness, he had no understanding of us, by whom the reality of empire is rated but
the trumpery disregarded.

★

32   In the same year Caesar transferred the nations of the maritime Alps to the prerogative of Latium.[38] He moved the places for the Roman equestrians so that
they were in front of the plebs' seating at the circus (up to that date they had entered indiscriminately, because the Roscian law sanctioned nothing except for
the Fourteen Rows).[39] As for the spectacles of gladiators, that year saw them with
a magnificence matching their predecessors; but several of the illustrious ladies
and senators were defiled by appearing in the arena.

★   ★   ★

A.D. 64

33   With C. Laecanius and M. Licinius as consuls,[40] Nero was being driven by a desire which grew fiercer each day to appear on the public stage. (Hitherto he had
sung only in his house or gardens at the Juvenalian Games,[41] which he had begun to spurn as insufficiently celebrated and as too confined for so great a voice.)

2   Not daring to make his debut at Rome, however, he selected Naples as being a
Greek city: that would be the starting-point for his crossing to Achaea, where,
after acquiring the distinguished crowns which had been sacred from antiquity,

3   he could by a greater reputation elicit the enthusiasm of his citizens. Therefore

38. The "prerogative of Latium" or "Latin right" was a form of Roman citizenship much
prized by provincials (*OCD* 790–1 s.v. *ius Latii*); the "maritime Alps" was the area north
of Nice which was constituted as a province by Augustus in 14 B.C. (*OCD* 68).

39. The Roscian law of 67 B.C. (see 2.83.4n.) applied only to the theater; here the
equestrians' privilege is extended to the circus also.

40. M. Licinius Crassus Frugi was son of the consul of 27 (4.62.1).

41. See 14.15.1.

there gathered a crowd of townsfolk, and those whom report of the affair had stirred from the nearby colonies and municipalities, and those who followed Caesar out of respect or for various purposes, and even maniples of soldiers; and they filled the Neapolitans' theater.

There an event took place that was regarded by many as grim but by the man **34** himself as providential instead and blessed by the divinities. After the attendant populace had gone out, the empty theater, without harm to anyone, collapsed. Therefore in specially composed songs he celebrated his gratitude to the gods and the good fortune of the recent downfall; and, intending to make for the crossing-places of the Adriatic Sea, in the meantime he settled at Beneventum, where Vatinius was producing his celebrated gladiatorial show. (Vatinius was among the **2** foulest phenomena of his court, the child of a shoe-making shop, with a twisted physique and buffoonlike wit: enlisted initially as a butt for insults, by issuing charges against all the best people he later became so effective that in influence, money, and a capacity to harm he towered even over evil men.)

While appearing at the man's show, Nero even amid his pleasures allowed him- **35** self no respite from his crimes. During those very same days Torquatus Silanus was driven to die because, besides the brilliancy of his Junian family, he had Divine Augustus as his great-great-grandfather.[42] Accusers were ordered to cast **2** against him the imputation that he was prodigal with lavishments and had no hope other than in revolution: indeed, they said, he had unknowns+ whom he called "For Letters" and "For Petitions" and "For Accounts," titles which were the concern of the supremacy—and rehearsals for it.[43] The most intimate of his **3** freedmen were then bound and swept off; and, when condemnation loomed, Torquatus sundered the veins in his arms. And there followed Nero's customary speech that, however culpable and rightly distrustful of his defense, he would nevertheless have lived if only he had waited for the clemency of his judge.

Not long after, abandoning Achaea for the present (his reasons were uncer- **36** tain), Nero revisited the City, churning over the provinces of the East, particularly Egypt, in his private visualizings. Then, testifying by edict that his would be no long absence and that everything in the state would be as undisturbed as it was prosperous, he approached the Capitol about his departure. There he venerated **2** the gods, but, after he had entered the temple of Vesta too, suddenly trembling in all his limbs (whether terrified by the divinity or, through the recollection of

---

42. D. Junius Silanus Torquatus (consul in 53: 12.58.1) was son of M. Junius Silanus Torquatus (consul in 19), who had married Aemilia Lepida, a great-granddaughter of Augustus.

43. At the time of which T. is speaking, emperors were assisted by powerful freedmen, three of whom had the official titles listed here (respectively *ab epistulis, a libellis,* and *a rationibus*). Narcissus had held the post "For Letters," Pallas that of "For Accounts." Thus the allegation, though T.'s Latin defies simple interpretation, is that Torquatus is mimicking the imperial staff, as if ready to take over as princeps himself. See further 16.8.1 below on Torquatus' nephew.

his deeds, being never empty of fear), he relinquished his undertaking, insisting
that all his concerns were trivial when compared to his love for his fatherland:

3   he had seen the sorrowful looks of the citizens, he could hear the secret complaints that he would be embarking on so great a journey when they could not
endure even his limited excursions, accustomed as they were to being rekindled
by the sight of their princeps to counteract the effects of chance events. Therefore, just as in private relationships one's closest connections were the most effective, so it was the Roman people who exerted on him the greatest influence,
and he must obey if they kept him back.

4   Words such as these were welcome to the plebs, with its desire for pleasure and
dreading a straitened grain supply (which is its primary concern) if he were absent. The senate and leaders were uncertain whether he should be regarded as
more frightening when at a distance or before them. (Subsequently—such is the
nature of great fear—they came to believe that that which had happened was

37 worse.) As for the man himself, to acquire credibility that nothing anywhere was
as delightful for him, he set up parties in public places and treated the whole City
as his own house; and especially celebrated for its luxuriousness and reputation
was the banquet prepared by Tigellinus, which I shall record as an example, to
avoid the obligation of narrating too often the same prodigality.

2   It was in Agrippa's pool, then, that he manufactured a pontoon,[44] on which a
party was mounted and moved along by towing from other ships. The ships were
picked out in gold and ivory, and their pathic rowers arranged by age and expertise at lust. He had sought birds and wild beasts from far-flung lands, and sea

3   animals all the way from Ocean. On the dykes of the pool stood love-lairs filled
with illustrious ladies, and, opposite, whores could be seen with naked bodies.
Already the gestures and movements were obscene; and, after darkness had started
to come on, every adjacent copse and the surrounding housing resounded with

4   singing and shone with lights. As for the man himself, defiled by acts both permitted and proscribed, he had omitted no outrage in his pursuit of increasingly
corrupt behavior—except that after a few days he took one of that herd of
perverts (his name was Pythagoras) in the fashion of a solemn espousal to be his
husband: there was placed on the Commander a bridal veil, the officials were admitted,[+] there was a dowry, marriage-bed, and wedding torches. Everything, in
short, was observed which even in the case of a female is covered by night.

38   There followed a disaster—whether by chance or by the princeps's cunning
being uncertain (authors have transmitted each alternative), but one more serious and frightening than any which have befallen this City through violent fires.

2   Its beginning arose in that part of the circus which adjoins the Palatine and
Caelian Hills, where, among shops in which there was the kind of merchandise
by which flames are fed, the fire had no sooner started than gathered strength
and, fanned by the wind, took hold along the length of the circus. There were

44. Agrippa's pool is thought to be associated with Agrippa's Baths, close to the
Pantheon.

no houses enclosed by fortifications or temples girded by walls, nor did any other
form of hindrance lie in its path. In its attack the conflagration—ranging across   3
the level at first, then surging to the heights and contrariwise ravaging the de-
pressions—outstripped all remedies in the speed of its malignancy and with the
City being susceptible owing to its confined streets winding this way and that
and its irregular blocks, as was the nature of old Rome. In addition, the lamen-   4
tations of the panic-stricken—of women, those worn out by age or in their raw
youth—and individuals who paid heed to themselves or to others, as they
dragged the infirm or waited for them, impeded everything, some by dilatori-
ness, others hurrying.[45] And often, while they looked back to the rear, they were   5
surrounded on the flanks or in front, or, if they emerged in some nearby area,
with the fire having taken hold there too they discovered that even places which
they had believed distant from it were in the same predicament. Finally, in two   6
minds as to what they should avoid and what they should make for, they filled
the roads or scattered over the fields. Some perished after the loss of all their fortune and even that of their daily livelihood, others from affection for the relatives whom they had been unable to rescue; yet in both cases escape had been
open. Nor did anyone dare to fight back the fire, given the frequency of threats   7
from the numbers who prevented quenching it, and because others openly threw
torches and shouted that they had authorization—whether to conduct their
looting more licentiously or by order.

At the time Nero was at Antium, not returning to the City until the fire neared   **39**
the house of his by which he had linked the Palatium with Maecenas' Gardens;
yet it still could not be stopped from consuming the Palatium and house and
everything around about. But, as a relief for the evicted and fugitive people, he   2
opened up the Plain of Mars and the monuments of Agrippa,[46] in fact even his
own gardens, and he set up improvised buildings to receive the destitute multitude; and comestibles were sailed up from Ostia and nearby municipalities, and
the price of grain was reduced to three sesterces. All of which, though popular,   3
proved unavailing, because a rumor had spread that at the very time of the City's
blaze he had actually mounted his domestic stage and sung of the extirpation of
Troy, assimilating present calamities to olden disasters.

Finally on the sixth day, at the foot of the Esquiline, an end was put to the con-   **40**
flagration by the widespread demolition of buildings, so that its relentless violence should encounter an expanse and (as it were) unoccupied sky. But dread
had not yet been laid aside, or hope returned to the plebs:[+] once again the fire
raged, more in the open places of the City; and for that reason the wreckage of
persons was less, but the shrines of the gods and the porticoes designated as attractions toppled more extensively. And more infamy attached to that particular   2
conflagration because it had erupted from the Aemilian estates of Tigellinus, and

45. The text of this sentence is not certain.

46. Presumably the various buildings northeast of the Pantheon complex (above,
15.37.2n.), between it and the Plain of Agrippa.

Nero seemed to be seeking the glory of founding a new City and calling it after his own nomenclature.[47]

41 Rome is divided into fourteen districts,[48] of which only four remained untouched and three were leveled to the ground; in the other seven there survived a few traces of housing, mauled and charred. Of the houses and tenements and temples that were lost, it would not be easy to arrive at the total; but the most olden religious buildings—that which had been consecrated to Luna by Servius Tullius, and the great altar and fane to Praesens Hercules by Arcadian Evander, and the temple of Stator Jupiter vowed by Romulus, and Numa's Regia, and the shrine of Vesta with the Penates of the Roman People—were all burned down; next, there was the wealth acquired in so many victories, and glories of Greek art; then ancient and unspoiled monuments of genius—although older men, despite being surrounded by the great beauty of the resurgent City, remember many things which could not

2 be restored.[49] (There were those who noted that the start of this conflagration arose on the fourteenth day before the Kalends of Sextilis, on which the Senones too ignited the captured City; others have gone to such trouble as to total the same number of years, months, and days between each of these conflagrations.)[50]

42 As for Nero, he capitalized on the ruins of his fatherland and constructed a house in which it was not so much jewels and gold that would be a marvel (they were long since familiar as the commonplaces of luxuriousness) as fields and pools and, in the fashion of wildernesses, woods here and open spaces and vistas there— all under the expert engineers Severus and Celer, whose daring genius it was to attempt through technology even what nature had denied, and to sport with the

2 princeps's resources. (They had promised to sink a navigable conduit from Lake Avernus right to the Tiber mouth along the barren shore or through mountain obstacles: that is to say, where no other wet area for generating water is encountered except the Pomptine marshes; the rest is precipitous or parched and, if it could be pierced, the work would be unendurable and the reasons inadequate. Nevertheless Nero, desirous of the incredible as he was, struggled to dig out the ridges closest to Avernus; and there still remain the traces of his thwarted hope.)

43 As for the parts of the City which survived his house, they were not (as after the Gallic conflagrations) built up without demarcation or at random but with the rows of blocks measured out and wide spaces for roads and the height of buildings curtailed and areas left open and porticoes added (which would pro-

47. "Neropolis," according to Suetonius (*Nero* 55).

48. This division was introduced by Augustus when he reorganized the administration of the City in 7 B.C. The districts were known by their numbers, which began in the southeast corner of Rome and went roughly counterclockwise. See *OCD* 1297 s.v. *regio*.

49. The text of the end of this sentence is uncertain. The "monuments of genius" are works of literature, presumably housed in the Palatine Library.

50. The day was 19 July, the year of the Senonian Gauls' capturing of Rome (11.24.5) was 390 B.C. Counting inclusively from that year to A.D. 64, there are 454 years, which may be divided into 418 years + 418 months + 418 days.

tect the front of tenements). These porticoes Nero guaranteed to construct with   2
his own money, and he would hand over the cleared areas to their owners. He
added rewards in proportion to each person's rank and family resources, and he
defined the time within which, on completion of houses or tenements, they were
to be acquired. For the reception of rubble he marked out the Ostian marshes,   3
and the ships which had sailed grain up the Tiber were to hurry back laden with
rubble; buildings themselves, to a specified extent, should be without beams and
consolidated by Gabine or Alban rock, because such stone was impervious to fire;
next, there should be guards so that the water supply, which had been intercepted   4
by private individuals taking liberties, would flow more lavishly and in more
places for the public benefit; and aids for curbing fires should be kept to the fore
by each person; and each building should be enclosed, not by shared partitions,
but by its own walls. All of this, welcomed for its practicality, brought luster too   5
to the new City; but there were those who believed that its old design had been
more conducive to health, because the narrowness of the streets and the height
of the housing were not so easily pierced by the boiling sun; whereas now the
open expanses, unprotected by any shade, scorched under the more severe heat.

    Such were the provisions made by human plans; next, expiations for the gods   **44**
were sought and the books of the Sibyl were appealed to, as a result of which
supplication was made to Vulcan, Ceres, and Proserpina, and Juno was propiti-
ated by matrons,[51] first on the Capitol and then at the nearest stretch of sea, from
which water was drawn to besprinkle the temple and the representation of the
goddess; and sittings[52] and vigils were celebrated by ladies who had husbands.
But despite the human help, despite the princeps's lavishments and the appease-   2
ments of the gods, there was no getting away from the infamous belief that the
conflagration had been ordered. Therefore, to dispel the rumor, Nero supplied
defendants and inflicted the choicest punishments on those, resented for their
outrages, whom the public called Chrestiani.[53] (The source of the name was   3
Christus, on whom, during the command of Tiberius, reprisal had been inflicted
by the procurator Pontius Pilatus; and, though the baleful superstition had been
stifled for the moment, there was now another outbreak, not only across Judaea,
the origin of the malignancy, but also across the City, where everything frightful
or shameful, of whatever provenance, converges and is celebrated.)

---

51. I.e., married women.

52. These were ritual banquets offered to goddesses, who were provided with chairs
upon which to sit (see *OCD* 1382 s.v. *sellisternium*).

53. "Chrestiani" is the form of the name which appears first in manuscript M but which
the scribe has then changed to "Christiani," no doubt influenced by what T. says in the
next sentence. Yet the coexistence of "Chrestiani" and "Christus" is not impossible: T.
would be drawing a muted contrast between the common (i.e., pagan) name for the sect,
evidently attributed to the Christians through a confusion with the Greek word *chrēstos*
("good," "honorable"), and the true origin of the name. For a succinct discussion of the
nomenclature see *The Oxford Dictionary of the Christian Church* (Oxford 1997) 333.

4   The first to be seized were those who confessed,[54] then, on their information,
a mighty number was convicted, not so much on the charge of the conflagration as for their hatred of the human race. And, as they perished, mockeries were
added, so that, covered in the hides of wild beasts, they expired from mutilation
by dogs or, fixed to crosses and made flammable,[+] on the dwindling of daylight
5   they were burned for use as nocturnal illumination. Nero had offered his gardens for the spectacle and he produced circus games, mingling with the plebs in
the dress of a charioteer or standing in his racer.[55] Hence there arose—albeit for
culprits who deserved the ultimate exemplary treatment—a feeling of pity, as
though it were not in the public interest, but for one man's savagery, that they
were being eliminated.

45   Meanwhile, for contributions of money, Italy was being laid waste and the
provinces ransacked, as well as allied peoples and those communities which are
called free.[56] To that plunder even the gods subscribed, their temples in the City
despoiled, and their gold carried off—gold which during triumphs and vows
every generation of the Roman people had consecrated in prosperity and dread
2   respectively. Indeed across Asia and Achaea it was not only gifts to but representations of divinities which were looted, after the dispatch of Acratus and Secundus
Carrinas to those provinces. The one was a freedman, ready for whatever outrage;
the other, drilled in Greek learning to the tip of his tongue, had not imbued[+]
3   his mind with good qualities. (It was maintained that Seneca, to avert from himself any resentment at the sacrilege, had pleaded for retirement to the distant
countryside and, when that was not granted, fabricated ill health and, as if with
a muscular disease, did not emerge from his bedroom. Some have transmitted
that poison was prepared for him by his own freedman—whose name was
Cleonicus—at Nero's order and that it was avoided by Seneca either through the
freedman's betrayal or his own alarm, inasmuch as he supported life by a simple
livelihood of wild fruit and, if prompted by thirst, springwater.)

46   About the same time gladiators at the town of Praeneste, attempting a breakout, were restrained by the garrison of soldiery which was there as a guard, although rumors of Spartacus[57] and old calamities were already being circulated
2   by the people, desiring and panicking at revolution as they do. And, not long after, a naval disaster was sustained—not in war (at no other time was peace so
undisturbed), but Nero had ordered the fleet to return to Campania by a specific
day, no allowance being made for the hazards of the sea. Therefore the helmsmen, though the open main was raging, moved off from Formiae; and in a se-

54. The statement is rather odd: we might have expected T. rather to say that seizure
preceded confession. R. J. Getty proposed to read *qui<dam>* ("the first few who were
seized confessed").

55. For which see 14.14.1.

56. These were communities which enjoyed local autonomy, at least in theory.

57. See 3.73.2n.

vere African,[58] while they struggled to round the promontory of Misenum, they were dashed against the Cumaean shores and lost several of the triremes and smaller craft everywhere.

At the end of the year publicity was given to prodigies announcing looming **47** calamities: the discharge of lightning at no other time more frequent, and a comet, something always expiated by Nero with illustrious blood; two-headed fetuses of humans and other animals, respectively discarded in public and discovered during the sacrifices at which it is the custom to immolate pregnant victims. And in Pla- **2** centine territory next to a road a calf was born whose "head was on its leg"; and there followed the diviners' interpretation that in preparation there was another head of human affairs, but it would not be effective or concealed, because it had been suppressed in the womb and delivered by the wayside.

★ ★ ★

There next embarked on the consulship Silius Nerva[59] and Atticus Vestinus, af- **48** ter the start and simultaneous augmentation of a conspiracy for which senators, equestrians, soldiery, and even females had competed to sign up, through both hatred of Nero and goodwill toward C. Piso. Born of Calpurnian lineage and in- **2** corporating through his father's nobility many distinguished families, he enjoyed a brilliant reputation among the public for his virtue—or displays which resem- bled virtues.[60] He employed his fluency for the protection of citizens, and lav- **3** ishness toward his friends; and with strangers too he was affable in conversation and encounter. He also had the chance advantages of a lofty physique and a hand- some appearance. But gravity of behavior and frugality in pleasures were alien to him: he indulged in levity, magnificence, and sometimes luxuriousness, and that earned him the approval of the numerous persons who, given the sweetness of the vices surrounding them, do not wish the supreme command to be either re- strictive or oversevere.

Embarking on the conspiracy came not from any desire of his own, and yet I **49** could not easily recall[61] who was initially the author or at whose instigation came the summons which so many took up. That the readiest proved to be Subrius **2** Flavus, the tribune of a praetorian cohort, and Sulpicius Asper, a centurion, was learned from the steadfastness of their deaths; and Lucanus Annaeus and Plautius **3**

58. An "African" is a wind from the southwest.

59. A. Licinius Nerva Silianus was grandson of the homonymous consul of A.D. 7, who was himself son of P. Silius Nerva (consul in 20 B.C.).

60. C. Calpurnius Piso, suffect consul at an unknown date, is assumed to be the subject of the poem known as the *Laus Pisonis* or "Praise of Piso."

61. Sc. for my readers.

Lateranus each contributed vital hatred.[62] (Lucanus had his own reasons inflaming him, since Nero, in a vain attempt at assimilation,[63] was trying to suppress the fame of his poems and had prevented him from showing them off. As for Lateranus, the consul designate, it was no injustice but love for the state which made him an ally.)

4   Flavius Scaevinus and Afranius Quintianus, each of senatorial rank, belied their own reputations by undertaking principal parts in so great a deed: for Scaevinus' mind was dissolute from luxuriousness, and his life correspondingly languid from somnolence; Quintianus was infamous for physical softness[64] and, defamed by Nero in an abusive poem, was proceeding to avenge the insult.

50   Therefore, among themselves or among friends, they bandied the princeps's crimes and the fact that the end of his command was near and that someone must be chosen to relieve the general exhaustion; and meanwhile they herded together a troop consisting of Claudius Senecio, Cervarius Proculus, Vulcacius Araricus, Julius Augurinus, Munatius Gratus, Antonius Natalis, and Marcius Festus, Roman

2   equestrians. (Of these, Senecio, one of Nero's principal circle of intimates,[65] still maintained even then a show of friendship with him and for that reason contended with danger more often; Natalis was a partner in Piso's every secret; the

3   rest were seeking hope through revolution.) Military hands, in addition to Subrius and Sulpicius (about whom I have recorded), were brought in: Gavius Silvanus[66] and Statius Proximus, tribunes of the praetorian cohorts, and Maximus Scaurus and Venetus Paulus, centurions. But the hard core seemed above all to be comprised of Faenius Rufus, the prefect,[67] who was praised for his reputable life, although it was Tigellinus who, owing to his savagery and immorality, had priority in the princeps's mind, wearying the other man with repeated charges and having often reduced him to dread with the allegation that he had been Agrippina's adulterer and was intent on avenging her loss.

4   So, when the conspirators were convinced by his own frequent conversations that the prefect of the praetorian too had joined their company, they began, more readily now, to agitate about the time and place for the slaughter. (And Subrius Flavus was said to have conceived an impulse to attack Nero as he sang on the stage or when, his house burning,[68] he roamed here and there unguarded

---

62. M. Annaeus Lucanus is Lucan, son of Seneca's younger brother Annaeus Mela (16.17.3–4) and author of the epic poem on the civil war between Pompey and Caesar. For Plautius Lateranus see 11.30.2, 11.36.4n.

63. I.e., Nero boastfully but fruitlessly tried to rival Lucan.

64. See 11.2.1n.

65. See 13.12.1.

66. His career is recorded on an inscription (Sherk 49A = Braund 517).

67. See 14.51.2–3, where it is noted that he shared command with Tigellinus (who is about to be mentioned).

68. The word "burning" (*ardente*) has been suspected, partly because it seems to refer so obviously to the events of the previous year; but none of the suggested emendations car-

through the night. In the latter case it was the opportunity of his solitude, in the former the actual throng—the finest of witnesses to such an exploit—that had spurred his spirit, except that he was restrained by the desire for impunity, always a barrier to great attempts.) Meanwhile, as they hesitated and prolonged their **51** hope and dread, one Epicharis—her means of information uncertain (and previously she had had no concern for matters of honor)—repeatedly inflamed and impugned the conspirators and eventually, tired of their slowness and finding herself in Campania, strove to undermine the officers of the Misenan marines and to involve them in complicity, beginning as follows.

There was a marshal in the fleet there, Volusius Proculus, who had been among   2 the assistants in slaying Nero's mother but was not (as he deemed it) promoted in proportion to the magnitude of the crime. Long known to the woman (or else their friendship had recently arisen), he disclosed to her his services for Nero and how unavailing they had proved, and he added complaints and his designs on revenge if the chance should arise, thereby offering her the hope that he could be swayed and win over others. The assistance of the fleet would not be trivial, she reflected, and there would be frequent opportunities because Nero took considerable delight in seafaring at Puteoli and Misenum. Epicharis therefore went   3 further and started on all the princeps's crimes: the senate, she continued, had nothing left, but the means had been provided whereby he might be punished for having overturned the state: Proculus had only to gird himself, marshal[69] his energies, and lead the fiercest of the soldiers to side with them, and he could expect a worthy reward. On the names of the conspirators, however, she kept silent. Hence Proculus' information was unavailing, although he had denounced to   4 Nero what he had heard: for, though Epicharis was summoned and confronted with the informant, she easily refuted him without witnesses on whom he might rely. But she was kept in custody, on Nero's suspicion that the matter was not false, even if it could not be proved true.

The conspirators nevertheless, moved by the dread of betrayal, decided to has- **52** ten the slaughter at Baiae in Piso's villa, the attractiveness of which had captivated Caesar, who often went and participated in baths and banquets, neglecting lookouts and the pressures of his station. But Piso refused, his pretext being the resentment if table rituals and the gods of hospitality were bloodied by the slaughter of a princeps of any kind: it would be better if it were in the City, in that resented house constructed from the spoils of the citizens, or in public, that they accomplished what they had undertaken on behalf of the state. This for gen-   2 eral consumption, but with the hidden fear that L. Silanus, with his exceptional nobility and raised to every brilliancy by the training of C. Cassius, in whose house he had been brought up, might march into a command which would be

---

ries conviction. If T. is in fact referring to the present year, this passage will not be a parenthesis and the brackets around it should be removed.

69. T.'s choice of verb (*nauare*) seems designed to play on the man's position as "marshal" (*nauarchus*) at the start of the paragraph.

readily offered to him by people whom the conspiracy had not touched and who
3 would pity Nero as though he had been criminally killed.[70] Several believed that
Piso had avoided the sharp intelligence of the consul Vestinus too, in case he
should rise for freedom or, by choosing someone else as Commander, make the
state a matter of his own gift. For he was no party to the conspiracy, although it
was on that charge that Nero satisfied his long-standing hatred for a guiltless man.

53   At last they decided to follow through their designs on the day of the circus
games which is celebrated for Ceres,[71] because Caesar, rare to emerge and shut
in his house or gardens, went often to the entertainments of the circus and there
2 was readier access to him because of his delight in the spectacle. They had
arranged the stages of the ambush: as if begging support for his patrimony, Lateranus, entreating and falling at the princeps's knees, would knock him over all
unsuspecting and pin him down (being of a strong mind and mighty in
physique); then, as he lay trapped, the tribunes and centurions and the others, depending on their degree of daringness, would run up and butcher him—with
the leading role being demanded for himself by Scaevinus, who had removed a
dagger from a temple of Salus in Etruria or, as others have transmitted, of Fortune in a Frentane town[+72] and was carrying it about as if consecrated for some
3 great task. Meanwhile Piso would be waiting at the shrine of Ceres, from where
the prefect Faenius and the others would summon him and carry him to the
camp in the company of Antonia, Claudius Caesar's daughter, to elicit the good-
4 will of the public. (This is what C. Plinius recalls;[73] as for myself, it was not my
intention to conceal it, whatever the form of its transmission, although it seemed
incongruous either that Antonia had lent her name to and risked danger for an
empty prospect or that Piso, known for his love of his wife, had pledged himself
to another marriage—unless of course the desire for despotism flares stronger
than every feeling.)

54   It is amazing how among people of different lineage, rank, age, and sex, rich
and poor, everything was contained in silence until betrayal began from the house
of Scaevinus. On the day before the ambush, after a long conversation with Antonius Natalis he returned home and sealed his will; producing the dagger (about
which I recorded above) from its sheath, and berating its bluntness from age,
he ordered it to be sharpened on a rock and gleaming to a point; and that he
2 entrusted to the concern of Milichus, a freedman. At the same time a more afflu-
ent party than usual was embarked upon, and the dearest of his slaves were pre-

70. L. Junius Silanus Torquatus was son of M. Silanus (consul in 46), nephew of D. Silanus
(15.35.1n., 16.8.1), and a direct descendant of Augustus through the princeps's daughter,
Julia. Cassius is the famous jurist (12.11.3–12.1) and, by his marriage to Junia Lepida
(16.8.2), L. Silanus' uncle. See Stemma (b).

71. The festival of Ceres was held on 12–19 April, and there were circus games on the
first and last of those days.

72. The term "Frentane" has been suspected.

73. For the elder Pliny see 13.20.2n.

sented with their freedom and others with money; and, as for Scaevinus himself, he was depressed and demonstrably deep in thought, however much he pretended delight during random conversations. Finally he began to sort out ligatures for wounds and things by which bleeding is stopped, and he warned Milichus to do the same,[+] the man being either aware of the conspiracy and hitherto reliable or else ignorant and only then seizing on suspicions for the first time (as several have transmitted). About the sequel there is agreement.[74] Whenever his slavish mind reflected on the prizes of perfidy, and at the same time the thought of inordinate money and power confronted him, obligation and his patron's very life and the memory of his gift of freedom all receded. And in fact from his wife too he had enlisted advice, womanly and baser, for she in addition was brandishing a prospect of dread; also, she said, many freedmen and slaves had stood by who had seen the same things: no advantage would accrue from one man's silence, but the prizes would fall to the one man who with his information achieved priority. So, at the start of daylight, Milichus proceeded to the Servilian Gardens;[75] and, when he was turned away from the entrance, he insisted that he brought important and frightening news. Led by the doorkeepers to Nero's freedman Epaphroditus, and then by him to Nero, he informed him of the pressing danger, the seriousness of the conspirators, and the other things which he had heard or inferred. He also showed the weapon intended for the other's execution, and ordered the culprit to be summoned.

Seized by soldiers, Scaevinus began his defense by responding that the blade which was the subject of the accusation had for a long time been revered with ancestral scruple and kept in his bedroom and seized secretly by the deceitful freedman; the tablets of his will he had sealed often enough and without any careful attention to the days in question; money and freedom had been given to slaves as gifts previously too, but more lavishly on that occasion for the simple reason that, with his patrimony already slender and creditors hounding him, he distrusted his will; certainly he had always been liberal in setting up banquets, his life being an attractive one and scarcely approved of by hard judges;[+] there had been no dressings for wounds by any order of his, but his accuser, who had clearly hurled his other imputations in vain, was appending a charge in which he could make himself both informant and testifier. Scaevinus added steadfastness to his words: he in turn censured the man for being a detestable criminal—with such unconcern in delivery and demeanor that the information was collapsing, except that Milichus' wife reminded him that Antonius Natalis had had a long and private dialogue with Scaevinus and that both were intimates of C. Piso.

Therefore Natalis was summoned, and they were asked separately about the nature and subject of their conversation. Suspicions then arose, because their replies had not corresponded; and they were clapped in chains. They could not

74. On the assumption that T. wrote something like *de sequentibus constat,* but the text is most uncertain.

75. The location of this imperial property is uncertain.

2   bear the sight and threats of torture; but Natalis was the first, being more knowledgeable of the whole conspiracy and at the same time more unskilled in excul-
pation.[+] He confessed first about Piso, then added Annaeus Seneca (either because
he was an intermediary between him and Piso or else in order to obtain influence with Nero, who, hostile to Seneca, had been searching for every means to
3   overwhelm him). Then, learning of Natalis' information, Scaevinus too—with
equal feebleness, or believing everything now to be disclosed and that there was
4   no profit in silence—gave up the others. Of these, Lucanus and Quintianus and
Senecio long maintained their disclaimers; after, bribed by the promise of impunity, and to excuse their tardiness, Lucanus provided the name of his own
mother, Acilia, Quintianus that of Glitius Gallus, and Senecio that of Annius Pollio, their principal friends.[76]

57   Meanwhile Nero, recalling that on Volusius Proculus' information Epicharis
was being detained, and deeming her womanly body unequal to pain, ordered
her to be mauled by torture. But in her case neither beatings nor fires nor the
torturers' anger (all the fiercer, lest they be spurned by a female) prevailed over
2   her denials of the imputations. Thus was the first day of inquisition passed.[+] On
the next, when she was being dragged back to the same rackings by the conveyance of a chair (she was unable to stand on her dislocated limbs), she attached
to the canopy of the chair, in the manner of a noose, the banded fastening which
she had torn from her bosom, and, inserting her neck and straining with the
weight of her body, she expelled her now faint breath—a woman and freedwoman defending, by her more brilliant example in such an extremity, others
whom she scarcely knew, when the freeborn—men and Roman equestrians and
senators, all untouched by torture—were each betraying the dearest of those to
whom they were bound.

58   For Lucanus too and Senecio and Quintianus were not neglecting to give up
their accomplices on all sides, to the ever increasing panic of Nero, although he
2   had surrounded himself with redoubled lookouts. Moreover the City too, its walls
taken over by maniples and even the sea and stream[77] under occupation, he put
into custody, as it were; and there flew through the forums and houses, through
the countryside too and nearby municipalities, infantry and cavalry, interspersed
3   with Germans, whom the princeps trusted as being foreign.[78] As a result, constant columns of chained men were dragged along and left lying at the entrance
to the gardens;[79] and, whenever they went in to plead their case, it was not only
services[+] for the conspirators but a chance conversation or unplanned encounters—if they had coincided at a party or spectacle—that were interpreted as
criminal, since, in addition to the savage inquiries of Nero and Tigellinus, Faenius Rufus too was pressing violently, having not yet been named by the inform-

---

76. For Pollio see 6.9.3n.
77. I.e., the Tiber.
78. For the tombstone of one of these Germans see Sherk 76.
79. See 15.55.1n.

ants and, to achieve credibility for his ignorance, behaving frighteningly toward his partners. (Likewise, when Subrius Flavus was standing near and nodding his   4 head to ask whether he should draw his sword and accomplish the slaughter during the actual investigation, Rufus threw back his own head and inhibited the impulsiveness of one whose hand was already carrying to his hilt.)

There were those who, after the betrayal of the conspiracy and while Milichus   **59** was being heard and Scaevinus hesitating, urged Piso to proceed to the camp[80] or mount the rostra and test the enthusiasm of soldiers and people: if his accomplices flocked to his attempt, they said, the uninvolved too would follow; and great would be the report of what they had set in motion, something particularly effective in revolutionary plans. No provision against such things had been   2 made by Nero: even brave men were terrified by unplanned developments; still less would that stage-performer, accompanied for sure by Tigellinus and his concubines, stir up arms against them. Many things were brought about by experiment, though to sluggards they seemed a steep task; it was pointless to hope for   3 silence and loyalty in the hearts and frames of so many accomplices: to the rack or reward all things were susceptible. Men would come to shackle him too and finally to inflict upon him an undignified execution; how much more laudably would he perish while embracing the state and while summoning help for freedom! Rather let the soldiery be absent and the plebs abandon him, provided that he personally, should his life be cut short, justified his death to his ancestors and to posterity!

Unmoved by these words and circulating briefly in public, Piso afterward   4 sought seclusion at home, fortifying himself against the final moments, until there arrived a unit of soldiers whom Nero had chosen as being recruits or new to the service (his veteran soldiery was feared as though[+] imbued with goodwill).[81] He   5 died by rupturing the veins in his arms. His will, with its foul sycophancies toward Nero, was a concession to his love for his wife, whom, lowborn and recommended only by her physical good looks, he had snatched from her marriage to a friend. (The woman's name was Satria Galla, that of her earlier husband Domitius Silus: the latter by his passivity, the former by her immorality, disseminated the infamy of Piso.)[82]

As the next execution Nero added that of Plautius Lateranus, the consul des-   **60** ignate—and so quickly that he permitted him neither to embrace his children nor the usual brief discretion over his death:[83] swept off to the place reserved for slavish punishments, he was butchered at the hands of Statius, the tribune, maintaining a steadfast silence and failing to taunt the tribune with his own complicity.[84]

80. Of the Praetorian Guard.
81. I.e., goodwill toward the conspirators.
82. The point of this remark is unknown.
83. I.e., the choice to commit suicide (as at 11.3.1 and 16.33.2).
84. For Statius' participation in the conspiracy see 15.50.3 above.

2   There followed the slaughter of Annaeus Seneca (a highly welcome prospect for the princeps, not because he had discovered him in the act of conspiracy but so that he could make progress with the sword, since poison had not suc-

3   ceeded).[85] Natalis—and he alone—produced the statement, limited as it was, that he had been sent to visit the ailing Seneca and to issue the complaint of why he had barred Piso from access to him: it would be better if they gave practical expression to their friendship by meeting sociably. And Seneca had replied that conversational exchanges and frequent dialogues were of advantage to neither party, whereas his own life depended upon Piso's preservation.

4   Gavius Silvanus, the tribune of a praetorian cohort, was ordered to convey all this to Seneca and to inquire whether he acknowledged the words of Natalis and his own reply. By chance or deliberately, Seneca had returned from Campania that day and had halted at the fourth milestone in the suburban countryside. It was there, on the approach of evening, that the tribune came and encircled the villa with clusters of soldiers; then, while the man himself was dining with his wife Pompeia Paulina and two friends, he issued the Commander's instructions.

61   Seneca replied that Natalis had been sent to him and had complained in Piso's name that he was being kept from visiting him; his excuses had been the current state of his health and his love of quiet; he had had no reason for giving the life of a private individual precedence over his own preservation, nor did he have a ready temperament for sycophancy—and that was known to none better than Nero, who had more often experienced free speaking from Seneca than servitude.

2   When this was relayed by the tribune in the presence of Poppaea and Tigellinus (who constituted the princeps's most intimate counselors when he was savage), Nero asked whether Seneca was intending a voluntary death. Thereupon the tribune confirmed that there had been no signs of panic; nothing gloomy had been detected in his language or look. So he was ordered to go back with

3   the indictment of death. Fabius Rusticus transmits that his return was not along the route he had come but that he deviated to Faenius, the prefect, and, after explaining Caesar's orders, asked whether he should comply; and was advised by the other that he should follow them through—the shirking of them all being

4   fated.[86] For Silvanus too was one of the conspirators and was augmenting the crimes to whose avenging he had consented. He nevertheless spared his voice and gaze, and sent in one of the centurions to announce to Seneca the final necessity.

62   The latter, unafraid, demanded the tablets of his will and testament; and, on the centurion's refusal, he turned to his friends and testified that, since he was prevented from rendering thanks for their services, he was leaving them the image of his life, which was the only thing—but still the finest thing—he had; if they were mindful of it, men so steadfast in friendship would carry with them

85. See 15.45.3.

86. Faenius by this last remark means that, in the light of the conspiracy's discovery, there was no point in any conspirator's displaying bravery by going against Nero's person or his orders. For Fabius Rusticus (above) see 13.20.2n.

the reputation for good qualities.[87] At the same time, partly by conversation and   2
partly in the more intense role of a reprimander, he recalled them from their tears
to fortitude, asking repeatedly where were the precepts of their wisdom? Where,
after contemplating it for so many years, was that reasoning in the face of looming adversity? For who had not known of the savagery of Nero? Nothing else
remained, after the killing of his mother and brother, except that he should add
the execution of his tutor and preceptor.

When Seneca had spoken such words as these as if for general consumption,   **63**
he embraced his wife and, softening for a moment in the face of her manifest
alarm,+ asked and begged that she should moderate her pain and not accept it
for ever, but, by reflecting upon a life lived in virtue, she should use this honorable consolation to make tolerable the loss of her husband. In reply she asserted
that she too had designs on death, and demanded the assailant's hand. Thereupon   2
Seneca, not opposed to her glory, and at the same time tenderly reluctant to abandon his only beloved to injury, said: "I had pointed out the palliatives of life to
you, but you prefer the prestige of death. I shall not begrudge you your example. In such a brave outcome as this, let equal steadfastness be within reach of us
both—but the greater brilliancy in that ending of yours." After that they sliced
their arms with the same blow of the sword.

Seneca, because his elderly body had shrunk owing to his spare livelihood[88]   3
and it was providing only a slow escape for his blood, ruptured also the veins in
his legs and the backs of his knees; and, exhausted by the savage rackings, he per-
suaded his wife to retire to another bedroom lest, by reason of his own pain, he
should break her spirit and he himself, by seeing her torments, should slip into
irresolution. And, since even at the very last moment his eloquence was in plentiful supply, he called his scribes and transmitted a very considerable amount
which, issued to the public in his version, I forbear to convert.[89] But Nero, with   **64**
no personal hatred for Paulina, and lest resentment at his cruelty should swell,
ordered her death to be stopped. To exhortations from the soldiers, the slaves and
freedmen bound up her arms and staunched the bleeding, but whether she was
unconscious remains uncertain. (For—such is the readiness of the public for baser   2
alternatives—there was no lack of those who believed that, as long as she feared
Nero's implacability, she had sought the fame of a death allied to her husband's;
but then, with the offer of a gentler prospect, she had been overcome by the blandishments of life—to which, in fact, she added a few further years, laudably
mindful of her husband, and with her complexion and limbs paling into such
wanness as was a constant advertisement that much of her vital spirit had been

87. The text here is most uncertain.

88. For which see 15.45.3.

89. How else could Seneca's final utterances have been issued to the public except "in
his version" (lit. "in his words," *eius uerbis*)? As transmitted, T.'s statement, though much
quoted, is extremely odd; Hartman proposed *meis* for *eius* ("which, issued to the public, I
forbear to convert in my own version/words").

3   discharged.) Seneca meanwhile, as the protracted slowness of his death endured,
     begged Statius Annaeus, long esteemed for the loyalty of his friendship and for
     his skill at medicine, to produce the poison, previously prepared, "by which those
     condemned by the Athenians' public court had their lives extinguished."[90] But,
     when it was brought, he swallowed it in vain, being already cold in his joints, and
4   his body blocked against the power of the poison. Finally he entered the hot-
     water pool, splashing the nearest of his slaves and adding the utterance that the
     liquid was his libation to Jupiter the Liberator. Thereafter, having been carried
     into the bath, where he was asphyxiated by the steam, he was cremated without
     any of the solemnity of a funeral. Such had been the prescription in his codicils,
     since, even when at the peak of his prosperity and power, he had been paying
     heed to his final moments.

65   There was a report that Subrius Flavus along with the centurions, concealing
     their intention and yet not without Seneca's knowledge, had designed that, after
     Nero had been slaughtered by Piso's efforts, Piso too should be killed and com-
     mand handed to Seneca, as if he had been chosen for the supreme elevation by
     guiltless men on account of the brilliancy of his virtues. Moreover, Flavus' words
     too were publicized: that, in terms of disgrace, it made no difference if a lyre-
     player were removed and a tragedy-player succeeded him (since, just as Nero sang
66   to the lyre, so did Piso in tragic costume). But the military conspiracy too went
     unnoticed no longer, with the informants burning to betray Faenius Rufus,
     whom as simultaneously accomplice and inquisitor they could not endure.
     Therefore, in the midst of the man's hounding and menacing, Scaevinus smiled
     back at him with the remark that no one knew more than *he* did; and he urged
2   him that of his own accord he should do such a fine princeps a good turn. No
     utterance came from Faenius in response, no silence, but, gulping his words and
     in incriminating panic, as everyone else (and especially Cervarius Proculus, a Ro-
     man equestrian) concentrated on convicting him, on the Commander's order he
     was seized and bound by Cassius, a soldier who, on account of his distinctive
     physical strength, was standing by.

67   Subsequently, on information from the same men, the tribune Subrius Flavus
     was overthrown. At first he brought the dissimilarity of his behavior to his de-
     fense: as an armed man he would never have allied himself to unarmed effemi-
2   nates for so great a deed! Then, after he was pressed, he embraced the glory of
     confessing and, asked by Nero what reasons had led him to forget his oath, he
     said: "I hated you, and yet none of your soldiers was more loyal to you as long as
     you deserved affection. I began to hate you only after you turned out to be the
     parricide[91] of your mother and wife, a charioteer and an actor and an arsonist."
3   (I have recorded his actual words, because they were not, as were Seneca's, pub-

90. The reference is to Socrates' famous death by hemlock (399 B.C.); in T. the verb "extinguished" (*exstinguerentur*) is in the subjunctive, indicating that Seneca's own words are
imagined as being quoted.

91. See 13.16.4n. for parricide.

licized, and it was no less fitting for the military man's feelings to become known, unadorned and yet effective as they were.) It was agreed that nothing in that conspiracy weighed more heavily on the ears of Nero, who, though ready for the commission of crimes, was unaccustomed to hear of what he was committing. Flavus' punishment was entrusted to Veianius Niger, a tribune. In a neighboring   4 field he ordered a pit to be dug out, which Flavus criticized as shallow and narrow, saying to the soldiers standing around, "Not even this is in line with your training!"; and, warned to extend his neck bravely, he remarked "I hope you will strike equally bravely!" The other, greatly trembling, scarcely amputated the head with two blows, but boasted of his savagery to Nero, saying that he had killed the man with a "blow-and-a-half."

The next example of steadfastness was provided by the centurion Sulpicius   **68** Asper, who, when Nero asked why he had conspired in his slaughter, replied briefly that for so many outrages there could have been no other relief; he then received the punishment ordered. Nor did the other centurions demean themselves when suffering their reprisals; but not Faenius Rufus, whose spirit was unequal to it: he transferred his wailings even to his will.

Nero was waiting for the consul Vestinus too to be drawn into a charge, deem-   2 ing him violent and hostile; but none of the conspirators had shared their plans with Vestinus, some because of olden feuds with him, the majority because they believed him headstrong and incompatible. (Nero's hatred for Vestinus had be-   3 gun from a close fellowship, inasmuch as the one despised the princeps's shirking, of which he had profound knowledge, and the other dreaded his friend's defiance, having often been made sport of in rough witticisms, which, whenever they draw much on truth, leave a sharp memory of themselves. In addition there had been the unanticipated circumstance that Vestinus had joined Statilia Messalina to himself in marriage, not unaware that Caesar too was among her adulterers.)[92] Since he therefore could not, in the absence of both charge and accuser,   **69** assume the role of judge, he resorted to his despot's power and sent in the tribune Gerellanus with a cohort of soldiers, ordering them to forestall the consul's attempts, to occupy his so-called citadel, and to overwhelm his picked youth (Vestinus had a house looming over the forum and handsome slaves all of a similar age).

Vestinus had fulfilled all his consul's responsibilities for that day and was cele-   2 brating a party, dreading nothing (or dissembling his dread), when the soldiers entered and said that he was being summoned by the tribune. Without delay he rose, and everything was speeded up simultaneously: he shut himself in his bedroom, the doctor was at hand, his veins were cut, he was carried (still vigorous) into the bath and immersed in hot water, uttering no sound of self-pity. Those   3 who had reclined with him[93] were surrounded by guards and not released until

92. Statilia Messalina, great-great-granddaughter of the famous T. Statilius Taurus (3.72.1n.), became Nero's third wife after the death of Poppaea (16.6.1).

93. At the dinner table.

the night was advanced—after Nero, visualizing and vilifying the panic of those waiting for death after dinner, had remarked that they had suffered sufficient reprisal for their consular banquet.

70   Thereupon he commanded the slaughter of Annaeus Lucanus. As his blood poured forth, and he realized that his feet and hands were chilling and that the pulse was gradually withdrawing from his extremities, yet his breast was still warm and in control of his mind,[94] he recalled a poetic composition of his in which he had transmitted that a wounded soldier had met a form of death of the same

2   sort; he repeated the actual verses, and they were his final utterance. After this there perished Senecio and Quintianus and Scaevinus, belying the former softness of their lives, and soon the rest of the conspirators, without any memorable deed or word.

71   Meanwhile, however, the City was filling with funerals, the Capitol with victims:[95] one man after another, on the killing of son or brother or relative or friend, expressed gratitude to the gods, decorated the house with laurel, fell at the knees of Nero himself, and wearied his right hand with kisses. And he for his part, believing that to be joy, recompensed Antonius Natalis and Cervarius Proculus for their quick information by granting them impunity. Milichus, enriched with rewards, adopted for himself the name "Savior" (in the Greek designation thereof); of the tribunes, Gavius Silvanus, though acquitted, fell by his

2   own hand; Statius Proximus spoiled by the vainness of his departing the pardon which he had received from the Commander.[96] Next, Pompeius,[97] Cornelius Martialis, Flavius Nepos, and Statius Domitius were stripped of the tribunate on the grounds, not indeed that they hated the princeps, but that they were thought

3   to do so. Exile was given to Novius Priscus for his friendship with Seneca and to Glitius Gallus and Annius Pollio as having been discredited rather than convicted: Priscus was accompanied by his spouse Artoria Flacilla, Gallus by Egnatia Maximilla, her great wealth at first untouched but later taken away from her,

4   each of which circumstance increased her glory. Also banished was Rufrius Crispinus, the conspiracy providing the opportunity, but in fact he was resented by Nero because he had once been married to Poppaea. As for Verginius Flavus and Musonius Rufus, it was the brilliancy of their names which drove them out: Verginius fostered the studies of young men by his eloquence, Musonius by the precepts of wisdom.[98] To Cluvidienus Quietus, Julius Agrippa, Blitius Catulinus, Petronius Priscus, and Julius Altinus, as if to make up the numbers of the se-

5   quence, islands in the Aegean Sea were allowed; but Caedicia, wife of Scaevinus, and Caesennius Maximus were merely debarred from Italy, discovering only from

94. The breast (*pectus*) could be regarded as the seat of intellectual faculties.

95. I.e., sacrificial animals.

96. Nothing is known of the story of Proximus' death to which T. is referring.

97. It is thought that a scribe may have omitted a praenomen before, or a cognomen after, Pompeius' name.

98. For Musonius see 14.59.1 and n.

their punishment that they had been on trial. Acilia, mother of Annaeus Lucanus, without acquittal and without reprisal, was conveniently forgotten.

After accomplishing all this, Nero held a meeting of the soldiers and distrib-   **72** uted to the maniple regulars two thousand sesterces a man, adding without cost the grain which previously they had had at market rate. Then, as if to expound achievements in war, he called the senate and bestowed triumphal honors on Petronius Turpilianus, a consular,[99] Cocceius Nerva, praetor designate,[100] and Tigellinus, prefect of the praetorian, so extolling Tigellinus and Nerva that, in addition to their triumphal images in the forum, he placed likenesses of them at the Palatium too. Consular insignia for Nymphidius were decreed. (About   **2** Nymphidius,[101] because this is his first appearance, I shall give some brief background: for he too will have a part in the disasters of Rome. Sprung from a freedwoman mother who had made her handsome body publicly available among the slaves and freedmen of principes, he maintained that he was the offspring of C. Caesar, because by some chance he was lofty in build and of brutal demeanor, or else C. Caesar, desirous also of whores, had sported with the man's mother too. ★★★)[102]

As for Nero, after summoning the senate and delivering his speech amid the   **73** fathers, he added an edict for the people and all the information which had been collected in book form[103] and the confessions of the condemned. For he was being mauled in a persistent rumor among the public to the effect that he had extinguished the brilliant and the guiltless merely through resentment or dread. But   **2** that there had been a conspiracy which began and developed and was overthrown was not doubted at the time by those whose concern was with knowing the truth, and is admitted by those who after Nero's demise returned to the City.

But in the senate, as each of those whose sorrow was greatest all plunged into   **3** sycophancy, Junius Gallio, panicked by the death of his brother Seneca and supplicating for his own preservation, was berated by Salienus Clemens, who kept calling him an enemy and a parricide, until he was deterred by a consensus of the fathers: he should not seem to be misusing public calamities for the opportunity of a private hatred, nor should he reinstate fresh savagery where, thanks to the princeps's forbearance, things were now settled or forgotten.[104] Next, gifts   **74**

99. Consul in 61 (14.29.1) and then governor of Britain (14.39.3).

100. The future emperor.

101. The words "were decreed. About Nymphidius" are insertions: it is assumed that a scribe's eye jumped from the first mention of the man's name to the second. Nymphidius Sabinus, not mentioned again in the extant *Annals,* was a powerful and ambitious figure who played a significant role in the events of A.D. 68. See *OCD* 1055.

102. Scholars assume a lacuna here, in which more of Nymphidius' background was described. C. Caesar is the emperor, Gaius Caligula.

103. T. seems to be referring to the written records of the interrogation sessions, as at 6.47.3.

104. Seneca's elder brother, adopted by the Junius Gallio mentioned at 6.3.1, had been

and gratitude were decreed to the gods, and a particular honor for Sol,[105] who had an old shrine at the circus where the deed had been intended and who "by his divinity had uncovered the secret of the conspiracy"; and the Cerial circus games should be celebrated with more horse-races, and the month of April should receive the nomenclature of "Nero"; a temple to Salus should be set up

2   at the precise point where+ Scaevinus had produced his blade.[106] Nero himself consecrated the dagger on the Capitol and inscribed it to Jupiter the Vindicator (something unnoticed at the time, but after the armed rising of Julius Vindex it

3   was interpreted as an augury and presage of future vengeance).[107] I discover in the records of the senate[108] that Cerialis Anicius, the consul designate, gave it as his proposal that a temple to Divine Nero should be founded as soon as possible with public money. Admittedly he intended his decree to have as its grounds that the princeps had surpassed mortal exaltedness and deserved the veneration of men; *** of certain people it should turn into an ill-omened sign+ of his own departing.[109] The honor of gods is not given to a princeps until his life among men has ceased.

---

suffect consul in 55 and proconsul of Achaea (see *Acts* 18.12–17); Clemens is otherwise unknown.

105. I.e., the sun.

106. Perhaps a reference to Scaevinus' house (see 15.54.1), now liable to total or partial destruction; but the text of the sentence is problematic.

107. Vindex was to lead an armed uprising against Nero in Gaul in the spring of 68: see *OCD* 787.

108. This is the only place in the extant *Annals* where T. certainly refers to his own consultation of the *acta senatus* (for which see 5.4.1), characteristically using a synonym (*commentarii*) to describe them.

109. The lacuna at the start of this sentence is assumed to have contained something like "but the man himself [viz. Nero] prevented it, lest in the interpretation." The ending of the sentence is also corrupt: "an ill-omened sign" is just a guess at T.'s meaning.

Book 16

Sport was next made of Nero by Fortune owing to his own foolishness and the **1** promises of Caesellius Bassus, who, Punic by origin and of disturbed mind, construed a vision in his nighttime slumber as the prospect of a certainty. Traveling to Rome, and purchasing access to the princeps, he explained that there had been discovered on his land a cavity at an inordinate depth which contained a substantial amount of gold,[1] not in the form of money but in a raw and ancient mass: there was a layer of really heavy bars, with piles standing nearby in another area. **2** He said that they had been concealed for so great an age in order to augment present blessings, but that, as his own interpretation showed, it had been Phoenician Dido who, as a fugitive from Tyre, had hidden the wealth when founding Carthage, lest her new people should become reckless with too much money or else the kings of the Numidians, already hostile for other reasons, should be inflamed to war by a desire for the gold. So Nero—without examining sufficiently **2** the trustworthiness either of the author or of the business itself, and without sending inspectors to ascertain whether the news was true—augmented the rumor further and sent men to fetch the plunder with which he seemed to have been presented. Triremes were provided, and rowers[+] were selected to improve their speed.

Nothing else during those days was discussed by the people (with credulity) or by the perspicacious (with reporting of a different kind). And by chance the **2** quinquennial games were being celebrated for the second five-year period:[2] by bards and orators it was enlisted as a principal subject in their praise of the princeps: not only was there production of the usual crops and of gold contaminated by other metals, they said, but the earth was burgeoning with a new fecundity and the gods were granting a windfall of wealth—and all the other servilities which, with the utmost fluency and no less sycophancy, they fabricated, confident in the complaisance of their believer.[3] Meanwhile his luxury was swelling **3** on the strength of an idle prospect, and old wealth was being consumed on the apparent offer of some which he could squander over many years. In fact his lavishness was already drawing upon this source too; and the expectation of riches was among the reasons for public poverty.

For Bassus dug up his land and the broad fields around about, all the time asserting that this or that was the place of the promised cavity, and followed not **2** only by soldiers but by a veritable populace of rustics enlisted for carrying out the task; but, at last rid of his derangement, and saying in astonishment that his dreams had not been false before and that that was the first time he had been deluded, he escaped shame and dread only by a voluntary death. (Some have trans-

---

1. "Dream guided treasure hunter to Roman coins" (headline in *The Times* (London), 11 December 1998).

2. See 14.20–1 above; also Braund 254 = WM 39 for a commemorative coin.

3. Viz. Nero.

mitted that he was bound and later released, having been deprived of his property as replacement for the royal treasure.)

4   Meanwhile, with the five-yearly contest now near, the senate, to avert disgrace, offered the Commander the victory in singing and added the crown for fluency,
2 by which a disfiguring performance might be screened.[4] But Nero, insisting that there was no need of canvassing or the power of the senate, that he would be equal to his rivals and would win from the scrupulousness of the judges his
3 deserved praise, at first recited a poem on the stage. Then, with the public importuning that he should communicate to them the complete range of his enthusiasms (these were the words they spoke), he entered the theater, complying with all the laws of the lyre:[5] not to sit down when tired, not to wipe off sweat except with the garment which he wore as clothing, and that no emissions from
4 mouth or nostrils be visible. Finally, bending his knee and venerating the crowd with his hand, he awaited the verdicts of the judges in fabricated panic.

For its part the plebs of the City, accustomed as it was to encourage the gestures of actors too, resounded with regular rhythms and organized applause.[6] You would have believed them delighted—and perhaps they were delighted, in their
5 indifference to public outrage. But those from remote municipalities and an Italy still austere and retentive of ancient custom, and those who had arrived on official legations or some private errand, unused to recklessness in their distant provinces, neither tolerated the sight of it all nor were competent for the dishonorable task, since with their untrained hands they grew weary, they disrupted the experts, and often they were beaten by soldiers, who stood between the blocks[7] in case a single moment of time should pass in inadequate shouting or sluggish
2 silence. It was agreed that several of the equestrians, while they struggled out through the narrow accesses and the oncoming crowds, had been crushed, and others, while they spent day and night on the benches, had been seized by fatal illness. For a weightier dread lurked if they missed the spectacle, since many people openly (and more in secret) were on hand to examine the names and
3 faces, the eagerness and sourness, of the assembly. As a result, on those of more slender means reprisals were imposed immediately; in the case of the illustrious, hatred was dissembled for the present but later repaid. They maintained that Vespasian, berated by the freedman Phoebus for closing his eyes in sleep and protected only with difficulty by the pleas of better parties, had later escaped looming ruin because of his greater destiny.[8]

4. The sense seems unclear: perhaps the idea was that the crown would distract the audience's attention from Nero's performance.

5. In other words, his first appearance was as a poet, his second as a lyre-player. Suetonius implies that he had left the theater after his recitation (*Vitellius* 4).

6. For this kind of thing see N. Horsfall, *The Culture of the Roman Plebs* (London 2003) 31–42.

7. Of seats. Or perhaps T. means "stood in block formation."

8. Vespasian was to become emperor in A.D. 69.

After the end of the games Poppaea met her death owing to the chance rage **6**
of her husband, by whom she was struck, when pregnant, with a blow from his
heel. (I am not inclined to believe it was poison, although certain writers so transmit, in hatred rather than from conviction: for he was desirous of children and
submissive to the love of his wife.) Her body was not destroyed by fire, as is the **2**
Roman custom, but, in the practice of foreign kings, was packed with perfumes,
preserved, and carried into the tomb of the Julii.[9] Nevertheless, public exequies
were conducted, and at the rostra Nero himself praised her good looks, the fact
that she had been parent of a divine infant, and her other gifts of fortune—in
place of virtues. The death of Poppaea—openly sad but welcome to those recall- **7**
ing her immorality and savagery—was rounded off by a new and additional
instance of Nero's resentment when he kept C. Cassius from his duty at the exequies. This was the first indication of trouble; and it was not deferred for long,
but Silanus[10] was added, theirs being no crime except that Cassius was preeminent for his olden wealth and the gravity of his behavior, Silanus for the brilliancy of his lineage and youthful modesty. So, dispatching a speech to the senate, **2**
Nero said that each should be removed from the state, and against Cassius he
hurled the imputation that among the images of his ancestors he had worshiped
also a likeness of C. Cassius, thus inscribed: "To the Leader of the Party."[11] The
seeds of civil war and defection from the house of the Caesars had been his aim,
he said; and, lest he should rely merely on the memory of a hated name for his
disaffection, he had enlisted L. Silanus, a young man of noble lineage, precipitate
in spirit, whom he could display for the purposes of revolution.[12] Then he be- **8**
rated Silanus himself for the same things as his uncle Torquatus, to the effect that
he was already disposing the concerns of command and was placing freedmen in
charge of accounts and petitions and letters[13]—accusations as empty as they were
false: Silanus was too strained from dread and, after the extermination of his uncle, terrified into being on his guard. Next, under the designation of "inform- **2**
ants," men were introduced to fabricate against Lepida—Cassius' wife, Silanus'
aunt—charges of incest with her brother's son and ominous rites and rituals.[14]
Dragged in as accomplices were Volcacius Tullinus and Marcellus Cornelius, sen- **3**
ators, and Calpurnius Fabatus, a Roman equestrian,[15] all of whom thwarted their

9. The Mausoleum of Augustus.

10. This is the L. Silanus Torquatus of 15.52.2. Cassius is the famous jurist (12.11.3–12.1).

11. Likenesses of C. Cassius, one of the principal assassins of Julius Caesar, may have been
banned (see 3.76.2), although Cremutius Cordus defended his praise of the man by saying that Cassius was known from his likenesses (4.35.2).

12. Since Silanus was descended from Augustus (15.52.2n.), Nero's accusation is that he
would make a suitable figurehead for Cassius' alleged plot.

13. See 15.35.2 and n.

14. Junia Lepida was also the sister of Junia Calvina (12.4.1–2, 12.8.1, 14.12.3).

15. Grandfather of Calpurnia, wife of the younger Pliny, who addresses some of his letters to him.

impending condemnation by an appeal to the princeps and then later, when Nero was distracted by the magnitude of the crimes by which he was surrounded, escaped him by virtue of their relative insignificance.

9   Then, by decision of the senate, exile was decreed for Cassius and Silanus; about Lepida Caesar should determine. Cassius was deported to the island of Sardinia, where the outcome of his old age was awaited; Silanus, as though he were being conveyed to Naxus, was removed to Ostia and afterward shut up in the

2 municipality in Apulia whose name is Barium. It was there, while enduring wisely his quite unjustified fate, that he was seized by the centurion sent for his slaughter; and, as the latter urged him to rupture his veins, he said that, though in his mind he had designed to die, he would not relieve his assailant of the glory of his commission. But the centurion, observing that, though unarmed, he was exceptionally capable and closer to anger than to fear, ordered him to be overpowered by the soldiers. Yet Silanus did not neglect to struggle and to aim blows (insofar as he had the capability with his bare hands), until he fell, as if in battle, under frontal wounds from the centurion.

10   No less ready for undergoing execution were L. Vetus and his mother-in-law Sextia and his daughter Pollitta,[16] who were resented by the princeps as if they were a living remonstrance against the killing of Rubellius Plautus, son-in-law

2 of Lucius Vetus;[17] but the occasion for the uncovering of his[18] savagery was provided when the freedman Fortunatus, after diverting his patron's property, transformed himself into an accuser and summoned help from Claudius Demianus, whom, imprisoned for his outrages by Vetus when proconsul of Asia, Nero released as reward for his accusation. When this became known to the defendant, and that he and his freedman were matched on equal terms, he withdrew to his Formian estate.

3   It was there that soldiers surrounded him with a secret guard. His daughter was present, who, besides the impending danger, was in a frightening state from the prolonged pain she had suffered since seeing the assailants of Plautus, her husband; and, having nursed his gory neck, she had kept his blood-stained clothing, a widow vanquished[+] by constant grief, her only nourishment that which would

4 ward off death. Then, at the urging of her father, she proceeded to Naples; and, because she was prevented from access to Nero, she put his departures under blockade:[19] sometimes with womanly shrieking, at others with a ferocity of voice in which she departed from her sex, she repeatedly shouted that he should listen to a guiltless man and not surrender to a freedman the onetime colleague of his

16. L. Antistius Vetus was the consul of 55 (13.11.1n.) and the adviser of Rubellius Plautus (14.58.3–4); his daughter, here named Pollitta, is the Antistia of 14.22.3.

17. See 14.57–9.

18. I.e., Nero's.

19. For the elaborate and formalized departures of a great man from his residence, etc., see 3.33.4n.; Antistia Pollitta is here imagined as lying in wait for Nero and laying siege to him on such occasions.

own consulship[20]—until the princeps showed himself unmoved by pleas and indignation alike.

Therefore she announced to her father that she was casting hope aside and **11** submitting to necessity;[21] at the same time news was brought that a senatorial investigation was being prepared, and a callous verdict. Nor were there lacking those who advised him to denominate Caesar as his majority heir and in this way to give thought to his grandchildren concerning the remainder.[22] This he spurned, lest he should defile with an ultimate act of servitude a life lived next to freedom, and he lavished upon his slaves what money there was to hand; and he ordered each to remove for himself whatever could be carried off, only three pallets being retained for their final moments.

Then, in the same bedroom, with the same blade, they cut their veins and— **2** each dressed for decency in a single drape—were carried quickly to the baths, the father gazing at his daughter, the grandmother at her grandchild, and she at both, all praying in rivalry for a speedy outcome to their faltering lives so that they might leave their relatives surviving and moribund. And Fortune kept them in order, the elders being extinguished first, then she whose age was still young.[23] They were accused after their burial, and it was decreed that they be punished **3** according to ancestral custom;[24] and Nero intervened to permit death without a witness:[25] such were the mockeries added after the accomplishment of their slaughter.

Publius Gallus, a Roman equestrian, was barred from water and fire because he **12** had been an intimate of Faenius Rufus and no stranger to Vetus. To the freedman— and accuser—there was given, as the reward for his trouble, a place in the theater among the tribunician couriers.[26] And the months which followed April/ **2** Neroneus[27]—May and June—were changed to the designations of "Claudius" and "Germanicus," the testimony of Cornelius Orfitus, who had made the proposal, being that the precise reason for passing over the month of June was that now two Torquati had been killed for their crimes, making the name "June" unpropitious.[28]

A year foul with so many misdeeds was distinguished by the gods too with **13** storms and illnesses. Campania was devastated by a whirlwind which scattered

20. Vetus' colleague in the consulship of 55 had been Nero (13.11.1).

21. Others translate "that he should cast hope aside and submit to necessity."

22. For other examples of similar precautions see 14.31.1 and 16.17.5.

23. The text here is uncertain.

24. See 2.32.3n.

25. "Death without a witness" means suicide and is a variant on the expressions at 11.3.1, 15.60.1, and 16.33.2.

26. Couriers were employed by Roman magistrates for official errands.

27. For the change of name from "April" to "Neroneus" see 15.74.1.

28. Junius was the family name of both L. Silanus Torquatus (16.7–9 above) and his uncle, D. Silanus Torquatus (15.35 above). Orfitus had been consul in 51 (12.41.1).

farms, plantations, and crops everywhere and brought its violence to the vicinity of the City, in which every class of mortals was being ravaged by the force of an epidemic, though without any climatic disorder that was obvious to the eye.

2   Yet houses were filling with lifeless bodies, streets with funerals; neither sex nor age was exempt from danger; slaves and freeborn plebs alike were being speedily extinguished amid the lamentations of spouses and children, who, as they sat by and wailed, were often cremated on the same pyre. (The demise of equestrians and senators, though indiscriminate, was less bewailed, as if by their share in the mortalities they were forestalling the savagery of the princeps.)

3   In the same year levies were held across Narbonese Gaul and Africa and Asia to supplement the legions of Illyricum, where those exhausted for reasons of age or health were being discharged from their oath. For a Lugdunensian disaster[29] the princeps's consolation was four million sesterces to restore the city's losses. (It was the same sum of money which the Lugdunensians had previously offered for the misfortunes of the City.)

★ ★ ★

14   With C. Suetonius[30] and Luccius Telesinus as consuls, Antistius Sosianus—who, as I have said,[31] had been penalized by exile for scribbling abusive poems against Nero—heard of the honor given to informers and of the princeps's propensity to slaughter. Temperamentally restless and not sluggish at opportunities, he used the similarity of his own fortune to that of Pammenes to win over the latter, who was an exile in the same place and, being well-known for the Chaldaeans' skill,[32] was connected in friendship with numerous men. Deeming it was not without purpose that messengers came to Pammenes frequently for consultations, he learned at the same time that an annual sum of money was being supplied to him by P. Anteius;[33] and he was not unaware that Anteius was resented by Nero on account of his affection for Agrippina and that his wealth was a principal means of enticing that covetousness which was the reason for the extermination of

2   many. So, intercepting a letter from Anteius and stealing also a document in which his natal day and (according to Pammenes' secrets) future were concealed, and at the same time discovering what had been compiled about the birth and life of Ostorius Scapula,[34] he wrote to the princeps that he would bring important news

29. The great fire at Lugdunum about which Seneca writes (*Letters* 91) is thought to be identical with the "disaster" mentioned here, though there are problems over the dating.

30. For his father see 14.29.2n.

31. See 14.48.4–49.3.

32. For which see 2.27.2n.

33. For him see 13.22.1.

34. For him see 14.48.1n.

which was conducive to his preservation, if only his request for a brief remission in his exile were successful. Anteius and Ostorius were looming over affairs, he said, and were investigating their own and Caesar's fates.

Therefore Liburnians[35] were dispatched and Sosianus arrived quickly. On the 3 communication of his information, Anteius and Ostorius were considered as being among the condemned rather than among the defendants—so much so that no one would have signed Anteius' will,[36] had not Tigellinus presented himself to authorize it, first warning Anteius that his final tablets should not be delayed. His response was to swallow poison, but, detesting its slowness, he quickened his death by slicing his veins. As for Ostorius, at that point in time he was on a dis- 15 tant estate near the border with the Ligurians:[37] it was to there that a centurion was dispatched to hasten his slaughter. The reason for hurrying arose from the fact that Ostorius, with his considerable military reputation and having won the civic crown in Britain,[38] had, by his mighty physical strength and knowledge of arms, created in Nero a dread that he might assail him—panicking as he always was and, after the recent discovery of the conspiracy, all the more terrified. So 2 the centurion, when he had closed the escape routes from the villa, revealed the Commander's orders to Ostorius. The latter turned upon himself the courage which he had often displayed against the enemy; and, because his veins (although ruptured) poured out too little blood, relying on the grip of a slave to the limited extent that he held out a dagger steady, he drew the other's right hand nearer and met it with his throat.

Even if it were foreign wars, and deaths met on behalf of the state, that I were 16 commemorating with such similarity of circumstance, not only would I have been afflicted by satiety myself but I would be expecting aversion from others who feel repugnance at the departures of citizens which, however honorable, are nevertheless grim and constant; but, as it is, servile passivity and so much blood wasted at home weary the spirit and numb it with sorrowfulness. And yet, from 2 those to whom such matters will become known, I would be inclined to demand no other justification than that I do not reject those perishing so sluggishly.[39] This was the anger of the divinities against Roman affairs, and one cannot, as in the case of disasters to armies or the capture of cities, pass over it after but a single reference. Let this concession be granted to the posterity of illustrious men: just as it is by their exequies that they are excepted from indiscriminate burial,

35. A type of fast ship.

36. Sc. as witnesses.

37. Liguria was an administrative district in northwest Italy.

38. See 12.31.4 and n.

39. Both text and meaning of this difficult sentence are disputed. T. appears to be saying that he expects his future readers ("those to whom such matters will become known") to defend his practice, and, as seems to be made clear in the two following sentences, the one defense he desires is the simple fact that he has described each "departure" (i.e., death).

so in the transmission of their final moments may they receive and retain their individual memorial.

17   For within a few days Annaeus Mela, Cerialis Anicius, Rufrius Crispinus, and Petronius all fell in a single sequence, Mela and Crispinus being Roman eques-

2   trians with senatorial rank.[40] The latter, once prefect of the praetorian and presented with consular insignia, but recently banished to Sardinia on the charge of

3   conspiracy,[41] killed himself on receiving news of the order for his death. Mela, born from the same parents as Gallio and Seneca, had abstained from seeking office, having the inverted ambition that as a Roman equestrian he might match consulars in powerfulness. At the same time he believed that a shorter way of acquiring money was through procuratorships for administering the princeps's

4   business. He had also begotten Annaeus Lucanus, a significant aid to his brilliancy. While he was keenly requisitioning the latter's family resources after his killing,[42] he provoked an accuser in Fabius Romanus, one of Lucanus' intimate friends. That knowledge of the conspiracy had been shared between father and son was fabricated on the basis of a forged letter from Lucanus, which Nero, after inspect-

5   ing it, ordered to be taken to the man, for whose wealth he was gaping. But Mela severed his veins (which was then the readiest route to death), having written a codicil in which he disbursed a significant sum of money to Tigellinus and his son-in-law, Cossutianus Capito,[43] so that the remainder might survive unchanged.

6   To the codicil it was added (as if he had written in this way to complain about the unfairness of his extermination) that, while he himself was dying without there being any reasons for the reprisal, Rufrius Crispinus and Anicius Cerialis were enjoying life, though hostile to the princeps. These were believed to have been inventions—in Crispinus' case because he had been killed, in Cerialis' so that he should be killed.[44] And in fact the latter did violence to himself not long after, attracting less pity than the others because people remembered that a conspiracy had been betrayed by him to C. Caesar.[45]

40. I.e., they had the necessary property qualification and were entitled to wear the broad-striped toga. Annaeus Mela was the younger brother of Seneca and the father of the poet Lucan (see below); for Anicius Cerialis see 15.74.3n.; for Rufrius Crispinus see 13.45.4n.; for Petronius see 16.18.1n. below.

41. See 11.4.3 for his insignia (described there as praetorian, not consular) and 15.71.4 for his banishment.

42. For Lucan's suicide see 15.70.1. Mela has been recovering dues owed to Lucan by his debtors, one of whom may have been Fabius Romanus.

43. The relationship between Tigellinus and Capito was previously mentioned at 14.48.1.

44. In other words, the belief was that the additions to Mela's will had been forged on behalf of Nero to provide retrospective justification for the death of Crispinus and a pretext for the death of Cerialis.

45. Almost nothing is known of the conspiracy or its betrayal to Caligula apart from the date of A.D. 40.

In C. Petronius' case some brief background must be given.[46] On his part, the **18** day was spent in sleep, the night on duties and the delectations of life; and, just as others are projected to fame by their industriousness, so had he been by shirking, and he was considered, not a glutton and profligate (as are very many of those who drain their own resources), but a man of educated luxuriousness. And, the greater the laxity of his words and deeds, parading as they did a certain indifference to self, the more gladly were they interpreted as a specimen of his straightforwardness. Nevertheless, as proconsul of Bithynia and later as consul, he showed himself vig- **2** orous and equal to business. Then, recoiling into vice, or by imitations of vice, he was enlisted by Nero among a few of his establishment as the arbiter of elegance, inasmuch as he thought that nothing was attractive or had the soft feeling of afflu- ence except what Petronius had approved for him.

Hence the resentment of Tigellinus, as if against a rival and a superior expert **3** in pleasures. He therefore made an appeal to the princeps's cruelty, to which all other lusts submitted, imputing to Petronius a friendship with Scaevinus, after bribing a slave to give information and having removed his opportunity for de- fense and swept the greater part of his establishment into chains. By chance dur- **19** ing those days Caesar had made for Campania, and Petronius, having proceeded as far as Cumae, was detained there. He bore no further delay in his fear or hope, yet neither did he expel his life precipitately, but, having slit his veins and bound **2** them up at whim, he opened them again and addressed his friends, though not in grave terms or such as would bring him the glory of steadfastness. And he lis- tened to them speaking, not about the immortality of the soul and the tenets of the wise,[47] but light poems and easy verses. Of his slaves, he treated some to his lavishness, others to beatings. He embarked on a banquet, indulged in sleep, so that his death, though forced, might resemble the natural. Not even in his codi- **3** cils (like many of those perishing) was he sycophantic to Nero or Tigellinus or any other of the powerful, but he listed the princeps's outrages (under the names of the pathics and females) and the novelty of each sexual crime, and dispatched the signed contents to Nero. He also broke his ring, lest later it should prove use- ful for the manufacturing of danger.[48]

In the midst of Nero's debating about the way in which his nights' ingenuities **20** were becoming known, the name of Silia occurred to him—noted for her mar- riage to a senator, adopted by himself for every lust, and particularly familiar with Petronius. She was driven into exile on the grounds that she had not kept silent

46. Whether T.'s consular Petronius is identical with a P. Petronius Niger who was suf- fect consul in 62, or with any of the other Petronii attested at this period, is disputed. T.'s Petronius is generally believed to be the author of the novel entitled *Satyrica*. See E. Court- ney, *A Companion to Petronius* (Oxford 2001) 5–11; *OCD* 1149–50 s.vv. Petronius and Petronius Arbiter.

47. I.e., philosophers.

48. Presumably Lucan's signet ring had been used to establish the "authenticity" of the letter forged in his name (16.17.4 above).

2 about what she had seen and suffered, his hatred here being personal. But in the case of Minucius Thermus, a former praetor, he yielded him up to the feuding of Tigellinus, because a freedman of Thermus had denounced certain charges about Tigellinus. For these the man himself paid with the rackings of torture, his patron with an undeserved execution.

21 After the butchery of so many distinguished men, Nero finally desired to extirpate virtue itself by killing Thrasea Paetus and Barea Soranus, being long hostile to each and with additional reasons against Thrasea because he left the senate when there was a motion concerning Agrippina, as I have recalled,[49] and because at the Juvenalian Games he had provided insufficiently conspicuous service. The latter was the offense which penetrated deeper, because it was the same Thrasea who at Patavium, his place of origin, had sung in tragic costume at the

2 metropolitan+ games instituted by the Trojan Antenor. Also, on the day on which the praetor Antistius was condemned to death for abusive compositions against Nero, he proposed and secured milder measures;[50] and, deliberately absent when divine honors were being decreed for Poppaea, he had not attended her funeral.

3 All of this Capito Cossutianus would not allow to be forgotten, since, quite apart from his headlong tendency to outrage, he was prejudiced against Thrasea because it was through his influence, in helping the Cilicians' legates when they

22 had been questioning Capito for extortion,[51] that he had lost his case. Moreover he hurled other imputations too against him: that at the beginning of the year Thrasea would avoid the solemn oath; he was not present at the enunciation of vows, although endowed with a quindecimviral priesthood;[52] he had never sacrificed for the health of the princeps or for his heavenly voice; regular and tireless at one time, a man who showed himself a supporter or opponent of even commonplace fathers' decisions,[53] for three years he had not entered the curia, and very recently, when they were competing with one another to convene quickly for the curbing of Silanus and Vetus,[54] he had preferred to give his time to the pri-

2 vate business of his clients. That was already secession and factionalism, and, if many proved equally bold, it was war! "Just as once it was C. Caesar and M. Cato,"[55] he said, "so now it is you, Nero, and Thrasea that the community speaks of in its greed for examples of disaffection. And he has followers, or rather satellites, who follow, not yet the truculence of his opinions, but his demeanor and look—stiff and grim

3 as these people are, in order to remonstrate against your 'recklessness.' He is the only man by whom your preservation is not entreated,+ your arts not honored.

49. See 14.12.1.
50. See 14.48.4–49.3.
51. See 13.33.2.
52. For the oath see 1.72.1n.; for the vows see, e.g., 4.17.1.
53. A reference to the episode at 13.49 (A.D. 58).
54. See 16.7–11 above.
55. A reference to the opposition between Julius Caesar and the younger Cato in the late republic.

He snubs the princeps's successes; is he not sated even with your grief and pain? It is one and the same attitude which is characterized by a failure to believe that Poppaea is divine and by a failure to swear obedience to the enactments of Divine Augustus and Divine Julius. He spurns religion, ignores the law. The journal of the Roman people[56] is read with extra care throughout the provinces, throughout the armies, to find out what Thrasea has not done. Either let us transfer to those doctrines of his, if they are so superior, or let the desirers of revolution be deprived of their leader and instigator. That sect of his produced the Tuberones and Favonii, names unwelcome even to the state of old.[57] To overturn the empire, they make a parade of freedom; but, if they overthrow it, they will attack freedom itself. In vain did you remove Cassius,[58] if you are to allow the rivals of the Bruti to swell and thrive! In short, write nothing yourself about Thrasea; leave the senate to be the arbitrator between us." Cossutianus' temper, so ready with anger, was encouraged by Nero, and he drafted in also Marcellus Eprius, with his fierce eloquence.[59]

4

5

6

As for Barea Soranus, already Ostorius Sabinus, a Roman equestrian, had demanded him as a defendant for himself after his proconsulship of Asia,[60] when by his justice and industriousness he increased the affronts felt by the princeps, and because he had expended care in opening the port of the Ephesians and had neglected to take revenge on the influential Pergamene community when it prevented Acratus, Caesar's freedman, from carrying off statues and pictures.[61] But the actual charges given were friendship with Plautus and the ambition of winning over his province to hopes of revolution.

23

The time chosen for the condemnation was that at which Tiridates was arriving to receive the kingdom of Armenia,[62] so that an internal crime might be eclipsed by foreign-directed rumors—or so that he might exhibit his Commander's greatness by the slaughter of distinguished men, as if by a kingly deed. As the whole community therefore poured out to welcome the princeps and to see the king, Thrasea, who was debarred from the reception, was not cast down but composed a note for Nero, asking for the allegations and asserting that he would clear himself if he had knowledge of the charges and a chance of wiping them out. Nero took the note quickly, in the hope that a terrified Thrasea had writ-

2

24

2

56. See 3.3.2n.

57. Q. Aelius Tubero was an opponent of the Gracchi in the late second century B.C. M. Favonius was an admirer of the younger Cato but an opponent of almost everyone else. Both were Stoics and had reputations for being awkward.

58. See 16.7.1–9.1 above.

59. For him see 12.4.3n.

60. Soranus had been suffect consul in 52 (12.53.2); the precise date of his proconsulship of Asia is unknown.

61. See 15.45.2.

62. A reference back to the narrative at 15.29–31; for a coin which perhaps commemorates the occasion see Braund 247 = WM 44.

ten something which would emphasize the brilliancy of the princeps and dishonor his own reputation. But, when he did not find it, [+] instead he became afraid of the looks and spiritedness and free-speaking of a guiltless man, and he ordered the fathers to be called.

25   Then Thrasea debated among his intimates whether he should attempt a defense or spurn it. Different advice was forthcoming. Those who favored his entering the curia said that they were unconcerned about his steadfastness: in their

2   opinion he would say nothing except what would augment his glory. It was the sluggish and the panic-stricken who surrounded their final moments with secrecy; let the people gaze on a true man facing death, let the senate hear utterances which were truly more than human, as if from some divinity: it was possible that even Nero would be impressed by a veritable marvel; but, if he persisted in his cruelty, at least among posterity the memory of an honorable departure would be differentiated from the shirking of those perishing in silence.

26   On the other hand, those who thought he should wait at home said the same things about Thrasea himself but that mockery and insults were looming: he

2   should withdraw his ears from disparagement and abuse. It was not only Cossutianus and Eprius who were ready for crime, they said; there were plenty of others who in their monstrousness would perhaps dare blows with their hands: even the good would follow in dread. Let him rather deprive the senate, which he had always adorned, of the infamy of so great an outrage, and let him leave it uncertain what the fathers, had they seen Thrasea as a defendant, would have decreed.

3   That Nero would be afflicted by shame at his outrages was an idle hope by which to be exercised; it was much more to be feared that he would direct his savagery against Thrasea's spouse, daughter, and other ties. Accordingly, undefiled and unpolluted, in the glory of those whose footsteps and study had guided his life, let him seek his end.

4   Present at the council was Rusticus Arulenus, a fiery young man, and in his desire for praise he offered to intervene in the senate's decision (he was a trib-

5   une of the plebs).[63] But Thrasea curbed his spirit: he should not take any empty initiative, of no advantage to the defendant and ruinous to the intervener. His own time was over, he said, and there was no deserting a system of life which had been constant for so many years; but Rusticus was merely at the inception of his magistracies, and what lay in front of him was still intact: he should weigh carefully beforehand the route on which, at such a time, he embarked for undertaking a political career.

         As for Thrasea himself, he left to his own contemplation the question whether

27   it was proper to come to the senate. But at next light two armed praetorian cohorts took up position in the temple of Genetrix Venus. Access to the senate was blockaded by a cluster of men in togas, but with swords unconcealed, and wedges

---

63. See App. A for tribunician intervention. L. Junius Arulenus Rusticus, another Stoic, would be praetor in 69; he was executed under Domitian for having written a biography of Thrasea (*Agricola* 2.1).

of soldiers dispersed through the forums and basilicas. It was under their gaze and threats that the senators entered the curia, and they listened to the princeps's speech through the agency of his quaestor.[64] Addressing no one by name, he 2 criticized the fathers on the grounds that they were abandoning their official responsibilities, and it was by their example that Roman equestrians were being converted to sluggishness. What wonder that none came from distant provinces, when many who had acquired the consulship and priesthoods preferred to be enslaved to the attractions of their gardens?

This was like a weapon, and the accusers seized it. While Cossutianus made a **28** start, Marcellus with greater force cried out that the highest matters of state were at issue: the truculence of inferiors was curtailing the mildness of the Commander. Up to the present day, he said, the fathers had been too soft in allowing themselves to be outwitted with impunity by the defecting Thrasea, by his son-in-law Helvidius Priscus, of the same mad persuasion,[65] as well as by Paconius Agrippinus, heir to his father's hatred for principes,[66] and by Curtius Montanus, scribbling his execrable poems. What he missed was a consular at the senate, a priest 2 at the vows, a citizen at the oath—unless, contrary to the established practices and ceremonies of their ancestors, Thrasea had openly put on the traitor and the enemy. In short, let him act the senator and, accustomed as he was to protecting the disparagers of the principes, let him come and propose what he wished corrected or changed: it would be easier for them to tolerate his censuring of single items than it was now to tolerate the silence of his universal condemnation. Was it peace across the globe or victories without loss to the armies that dis- 3 pleased him? A man sorrowful at the public good, who regarded forums, theaters, and temples as a wilderness, and who threatened his own exile, should not have his twisted ambition fulfilled. But to him their decisions did not seem real, nor did the magistrates or the Roman City. Let him sever his life from the community, his gaze on which, like his former affection for it, he had now cast aside.

Brutal and threatening as Marcellus was, there was fire in his language, look, **29** and eyes throughout speeches such as this, during which there was none of that normal and (given the frequency of the dangers) now customary sorrowfulness in the senate, but a new and deeper panic affected them as they observed the hands of the soldiers on their weapons. At the same time a vision of the venera- 2 ble Thrasea himself confronted them; and there were those who pitied Helvidius too, about to be punished for a blameless relationship. What was the allegation against Agrippinus, except the grim fate of his father (since he too, equally

64. I.e., Nero's speech was read out for him by his personal quaestor, an office which T. himself would later hold (see Introduction, p. x).

65. Another prominent Stoic, who would become praetor in 70 (see also 12.49.2 and 13.28.3). His wife (Thrasea's daughter) was Fannia, who appears memorably in Pliny's letters (3.11.3, 3.16, 7.19, 9.13.3–5): see also 16.34.2 below.

66. Agrippinus was also a well-known Stoic; his father was M. Paconius (3.67.1), who is thought to have died in the aftermath of the fall of Sejanus (see 16.29.2 below).

innocent, had fallen by Tiberius' savagery)? And as for Montanus, a young man of probity rather than of defamatory poetry, he was being banished as an outcast because he had proclaimed his talent.

30   Meanwhile Ostorius Sabinus, the accuser of Soranus, entered and started off on his friendship with Rubellius Plautus and the fact that Soranus had conducted a proconsulship of Asia accommodated rather to his own brilliance than in the
2   interests of the common welfare, by fostering sedition in the communities. These were old charges; a recent one, which connected his daughter to her father's plight, was that she had lavished money on magicians. (That had of course come about owing to the devotion of Servilia—that was the girl's name—who, from affection for her parent as well as the misguidedness of youth, had nevertheless made no other consultation than that concerning the preservation of her family and whether Nero was amenable and whether the senate's investigation would
3   result in no frightening development.) So she was summoned to the senate, and, facing each other before the consuls' tribunal, there stood a parent of great age and, opposite, a daughter in the nineteenth year of her life, widowed and desolate by the recent driving of her husband Annius Pollio into exile,[67] and not even looking at her father, whose dangers she seemed to have aggravated.

31   Then, as her accuser asked whether she had offered her trousseau for sale, or the necklace torn from her throat, to accumulate money for the performance of magic rituals, she first prostrated herself on the ground in a long and tearful silence and then, clasping the altar-fittings and altar, she said: "No impious gods, no curses did I invoke with inauspicious prayers, nor anything other than that
2   you, Caesar, and you, fathers, should continue to preserve this best of fathers. My jewels and clothes, the insignia of my rank, I gave exactly as I would my life and blood, if they had demanded them. It is for *them*—men of whom I had no previous knowledge—to see to it what name they used,[+] what skills they practice; *no* mention of the princeps was made by me, except among the divinities. In any case, my most pitiable father knows nothing, and, if there has been a crime, I alone am the culprit."

32   Soranus took up her words as she was still speaking, and announced that she had not departed with him to his province, that she could not have been known to Plautus because of her age, and that she had not been connected with the crimes of her husband. Guilty only of excessive devotion, she should be dissociated from his case; and he for his part should undergo whatever was his lot. At the same time he dashed toward the embrace of his onrushing daughter, but lictors interposed themselves, standing in the way of each.
2   Next it was the witnesses' turn; and, great as was the pity which the savagery of the accusation had stirred, it was equaled by the anger which P. Egnatius as wit-
3   ness provoked.[68] A client of Soranus, and now bought to overwhelm his friend, he had been parading the authority of the Stoic sect, disciplined to display an im-

67. See 15.71.3.
68. In 70 P. Egnatius Celer was sentenced to exile for the part he plays here.

age of honesty in demeanor and voice but in reality faithless and guileful at heart, concealing his greed and lust. But, after these qualities had been exposed by money, he exemplified the fact that the guard one takes against those enveloped in intrigue or stained by iniquity needs to be matched by that against those treacherous in their show of good features and traitorous in friendship. Yet the same day **33** brought also the honorable example of Cassius Asclepiodotus, principal among the Bithynians for the magnitude of his wealth, who, with the same compliance as he had honored Soranus when he flourished, did not abandon him when he was tottering, and was stripped of all his fortune and driven into exile—such being the evenhandedness of the gods toward good and evil.+

Thrasea, Soranus, and Servilia were allowed discretion over their deaths;[69] Helvidius and Paconius were banished from Italy; Montanus was yielded up to his father, with the provision that he should not stay in politics. To the accusers Eprius and Cossutianus were granted five million sesterces each, to Ostorius twelve hundred thousand and quaestorian insignia. Then to Thrasea, who was in his garden, **34** the consul's quaestor was dispatched as day was already turning to evening.

He had collected a substantial throng of illustrious men and ladies, giving his particular attention to Demetrius, a teacher of the Cynic doctrine, with whom (as was possible to infer from the attentiveness on his face and from overhearing the more distinct parts of their talk) he was inquiring about the nature of the soul and the separation of spirit and body— until Domitius Caecilianus arrived, one of his closest friends, who reported to him what the senate had voted. Thrasea therefore urged those present, weeping and protesting as they were, to **2** make off quickly and not to share their own dangers with the lot of a condemned man. As regards Arria, who was for attempting to follow her husband's final moments and the example of her mother Arria,[70] he warned her to hold on to life and not to deprive their mutual daughter of her one and only support. Then he **35** proceeded to the portico, where the quaestor discovered him in a state approaching delight, because he had learned that Helvidius, his own son-in-law, was only being debarred from Italy.

Receiving then the senate's decision, he led Helvidius and Demetrius to the bedroom; and, extending the veins in each arm and sprinkling upon the ground the gore which he poured out, he called the quaestor to approach and said: "We are making a libation to Jupiter the Liberator. Look, young man! May the gods avert the omen, of course, but you have been born into times when it is expedient to strengthen the spirit with steadfast examples." After, as the slowness of **2** his departure was bringing on severe rackings, turning to Demetrius ★★★[71]

69. I.e., allowed to commit suicide (15.60.1 and n.).

70. The celebrated suicide of the elder Arria is commemorated by, among others, the younger Pliny in a famous letter (3.16).

71. At this poignant and dramatic moment, with Thrasea turning (presumably his eyes, since *obuersis* is plural) to Demetrius, our text of the *Annals* breaks off.

APPENDIX A

POLITICAL AND MILITARY TERMS

The following list contains definitions and explanations of various terms encountered in this translation of the *Annals*. Some terms which are at least as topographical as they are political (e.g., the rostra) will be found in Appendix C; for some military terms (e.g., "banner-men" or "first-rankers") see Appendix B. Further information on the terms listed below may usually be found in *OCD*, which also provides bibliographical references. Bold type in a definition indicates that a term is explained elsewhere in this list.

aediles   These **magistrates** were senior to **quaestors** but junior to **praetors** and had various responsibilities chiefly relating to the City of Rome. See also **curule.**

augurs   They constituted one of the four major priestly **colleges;** augurs practiced and were experts on divination.

auspices   A form of divination carried out by **magistrates,** e.g., before military enterprises (as at 2.14.1). Wars could be said to be waged "under the auspices of" a **commander** (who under the empire was usually the emperor himself, whether or not he was conducting the campaign in person: 2.41.1): hence the term comes to have a secondary meaning of "leadership" or "authority" or "command" (e.g., 13.6.4, 15.26.3).

censors   Senior Roman **magistrates** who were elected as a pair and were responsible for revising the official list of Roman citizens and the membership of the **senate.** Under the republic they were normally elected every five years for an eighteen-month term; under the empire the office lapsed, its functions being discharged by the emperors. Claudius, as one of his antiquarian revivals, held the office in A.D. 47–48 with Lucius Vitellius (see 11.13.1, 11.25.2–5).

college   The Latin term *collegium* is used (a) for boards or associations of priests, of which the four most important were the **augurs,** the **pontiffs,** the **quindecimvirs,** and the septemvirs (3.64.3 and n.); (b) for partnerships in a **magistracy.** I have used "college" for the former (6.12.2, 11.11.1, 11.15.1; cf. 1.73.2) but "collegiality" for the latter (3.16.4, 3.31.1).

command   (*imperium*) The power to command an army or execute the law. It was held by senior **magistrates,** by the emperor, and by others who received it as a special grant (e.g., 2.43.1 and n., 12.37.4 and n., 12.41.2). It was symbolized by the **fasces** and **lictors.** *Imperium,* from which our "empire" derives, was also used in a concrete geographical sense of the lands commanded by a people such as the Romans or Parthians (the "Roman empire"): see 2.56.1. See also next entry.

commander   (*imperator*) *Imperator* was originally a generic term for a Roman general, and after a victory a general was hailed as "*imperator*" by his troops. In the 30s B.C. Octavian (the future Augustus) adopted *Imperator* as a first name (*praenomen*), and from the time of Vespasian the term was in standard use as a title to denote the emperor (a word which derives from it). T. reflects the usage of his own day by regularly (but largely anachronistically) referring to the Julio-Claudian emperors as *imperator* (a usage which I distinguish by printing "Commander" with a capital letter).

356

Only a holder of **command** (*imperium*) could be hailed as "commander," and this had consequences under the empire. When the **legate** of an imperial province won a victory, as the emperor's delegate he was not entitled to be hailed as "commander": that privilege belonged to the emperor himself, and the title came to be monopolized by the emperor (e.g., 1.9.2) and by members of his family who had received grants of command (1.58.5, 12.42.2). It was in keeping with this trend that a **proconsul** (who had *imperium* in his own right) was last hailed as "commander" in A.D. 22 (3.74.4).

consul In the republic the consuls were the two highest **magistrates** in the state: they held office in pairs and for a year at a time. Consuls continued to be elected under the empire: those who took up office on 1 January were the "regular consuls" (*c. ordinarii*), and it was their names which were used to date each year; but they were generally replaced by "suffect consuls" (*c. suffecti*) later in the year.

consular The term used for an ex-consul.

curia The senate house in the Roman Forum (see Appendix C).

curule An adjective used to describe (a) the official chair or seat in which certain **magistrates** were entitled to sit, (b) those magistrates themselves (by an extension of meaning). **Consuls** and **praetors** (cf. 1.75.1) were automatically curule magistrates; **aediles** were divided into "curule" (cf. 1.3.1) and "plebeian" (13.28.2). Sometimes a curule seat was awarded by virtue of one's holding a priesthood (2.83.1).

dictator In the earlier republic a dictator was a **magistrate** appointed for a limited term to deal with some specific emergency or task. After their victories in civil war both Sulla and Julius Caesar were appointed dictator. Sulla soon resigned his dictatorship, but Caesar's appointment as dictator for life in 44 B.C. prompted his assassination, after which the office was abolished. T. often refers to Julius Caesar as "(the) dictator Caesar."

diviners (*haruspices*) Religious experts from Etruria. They formed a **college** of their own, and they were called upon to explain and interpret various phenomena. See esp. 11.15.

equestrian(s) (*eques*, pl. *equites*) Members of the "equestrian **order**": those citizens who were not senators but whose capital wealth amounted to not less than 400,000 sesterces (see 2.33.3n.). They constituted a numerous upper class, many of whom were active as equestrian military officers (see App. B) or in the imperial administration (see **prefect** and **procurator**). Some equestrians chose to make their fortunes, and hoped to acquire power and influence, by deliberately not embarking on a senatorial career.

fasces This plural noun (pron. "faskays") denotes a bundle of rods tied together and carried by a **lictor** before a **magistrate**, symbolizing the latter's **command** (the higher its grade, the greater the number of bundles and lictors). Outside Rome the bundle would also include an axe (see 1.59.4, 12.34). From 19 B.C. Augustus was entitled to the fasces for life.

fiscus This term denotes the private funds of the emperor. The funds were administered alongside the **treasury**, from which the fiscus was technically distinct (see esp. 6.2.1)

flamen (pron. "flahmen") The technical name for a certain type of priest who belonged to the **college** of the **pontiffs** and was responsible for the cult of a particular god. The three principal flamines (pron. "flahminays") were entitled Dialis, Martialis, and Quirinalis (see esp. 3.58) and were devoted respectively to Jupiter, Mars, and Quirinus. Flamines were also assigned to the cult of an emperor after his death (1.10.6; see 13.2.3).

flaminica The term for a **flamen**'s wife (4.16.3).

flamonium The term for the priesthood of a **flamen** (4.16.2, 13.2.3).

357

honor(s) (*honor, honores*) This term may be used of any distinction but often has the narrower and technical sense of "office" or "**magistracy**" (such as the consulship). *Cursus honorum* (lit. "path of honors") is the phrase used conventionally to denote a political career, starting at the lowest stage and ending up with one of the top posts.

intervention (*intercessio*) **Tribunes** of the plebs traditionally had the right to veto (*intercedere*) the proposals or procedures of a **magistrate** (see, e.g., 16.26.4). Emperors could exercise such a veto by virtue of their tribunician power (1.13.4, 14.48.2).

legate A term used in several different ways. (a) A delegate or envoy (e.g., 3.60.2 and very frequently). (b) A "legionary legate" (*legatus legionis*) was the officer in charge of a legion (e.g., 2.20.1 and also very frequently). Such a man was usually an ex-praetor. (c) The governor of an "imperial" **province**, his full title being *legatus Augusti pro praetore*. Such a man would be either an ex-praetor or an ex-consul. See, e.g., 2.80.2 and again very frequently. (d) An assistant to a provincial governor (3.67.1).

lictors Attendants who accompanied **magistrates** and carried the **fasces** which symbolized the latter's **command**. As a special mark of honor an imperial lady might be granted the right to be accompanied by lictors (13.2.3; cf. 1.14.2).

magistracy, magistrate The former is the technical term for an elective senatorial office, the latter for its holder: the principal magistrates were (in ascending order of seniority) **quaestor, tribune, aedile, praetor, consul** (see 12.64.1).

noble, nobility Terms used of those who could boast a **consul** among their ancestors.

order(s) In the earlier republic the two "orders" were the **patricians** and the **plebs** (see 3.27.1). In the later republic, and during the empire, the term is used collectively to denote senators and **equestrians** (the "senatorial and equestrian orders"): see esp. 12.60.3–4.

ovation See **triumph**.

patrician(s) The patriciate was an exclusive subgroup of the Roman aristocracy. In the early republic the patricians had enjoyed a near monopoly of political power, but after the fourth century B.C. the distinction between patricians and **plebs** was of little practical importance. For most of the republic patrician status could only be inherited by birth. Since the number of patricians dwindled, however, new members of the patriciate were created by Julius Caesar, as later by Augustus and (see 11.25.2) Claudius. See esp. 11.24–5; for the patricians' special form of marriage see 4.16.1.

people, the (Roman) (*populus (Romanus)*) The expressions "the people" or (more fully) "the Roman people" denote the entire citizen body (i.e., excluding women and children). These expressions thus have a different connotation from "**plebs.**" In the well-known coupling "the senate and people" (e.g., 4.12.1) the distinction is between those members of the people who hold or have held office and those who do not or have not. Occasionally, however, "people" is used as a synonym for "plebs" (3.27.1); and, like plebs, "people" is also used by T. of foreign nations (e.g., 6.42.1, 6.42.3).

plebs In the earlier republic the plebs was that large body of citizens which was not of patrician status: **patricians** and plebs were the two "**orders,**" the latter seeking to extend its rights and privileges at the expense of the former. By the later republic, however, the term "plebs" denoted the lower social classes (i.e., those who were neither senators nor equestrians), and it is in this sense that the term is used most frequently by T., who also uses it analogously of foreign nations (e.g., 1.55.2). I have retained the term in the translation to distinguish it from "the **people.**"

pontiffs These were priests who formed one of the four major **colleges** and included the **flamines** within their number. The chief priest was the *pontifex maximus* or "high pontiff," who under the empire was always the emperor himself (see 3.58.3, 11.32.2).

praetexta The name given to the toga with a purple border which was worn by boys before their formal assumption of the "toga of manhood" (1.3.2, 12.41.2) and by certain officeholders (cf. 2.14.1).

praetor The penultimate **magistracy** of a political career before the climax of the consulship. Among other responsibilities (e.g., 14.20.3), praetors presided over the criminal courts (as 1.75.1). One of T.'s idiosyncratic archaisms is to use "praetor" of provincial governors (e.g., 1.74.1, 2.77.1, 4.43.3, 12.60.2).

praetorian A term used in two principal senses. (a) An ex-praetor. Such a man might be a legionary **legate** or governor of certain **provinces**. The Latin term is *praetorius*. (b) "Praetorian" may also be used either as a noun = "the Praetorian Guard" (e.g., 15.72.1), for which the Latin is *praetorium*, or as an adjective to describe the Guard itself or anything connected with it (e.g., 1.8.2, 6.3.1), for which the Latin is either *praetorianus* or *praetorius.*

prefect(ure) A "prefect" is one who is "placed in charge," and the term is used of those overseeing the food supply (1.7.2, 11.31.1), the **treasury** (5.8.1, 13.28.3–29.1), the watchmen (11.35.3), the fleet (14.3.3, 14.62.2), units of allied soldiers (e.g., 13.9.2), military camps (e.g., 1.20.1). The prefects of the food supply and of the Praetorian Guard followed the consuls in swearing allegiance to Tiberius (1.7.2), indicating their importance; other significant prefectures were those of the City of Rome (6.10.3–11.3, 14.42.1) and of the province of Egypt. The prefect of the City, like that of the **treasury**, was a senator; the others were equestrians. T. also uses the same terminology to denote the various districts of the kingdoms of Armenia and Parthia and the men in charge of them (e.g., 11.9.1, 11.10.1).

princeps, pl. **principes** (pron. "prinkeps" and "prinkipays") The basic meaning of this word is "foremost," "chief," or "leader": during the republic there was a "leader of the senate" (*p. senatus*), and the unqualified term *principes* was also used of the most influential senators (the "leading men"). Augustus used the term to refer to himself, after which it became one of the standard designations of the emperor: I have retained it in the translation, partly in order to preserve the link with "principate," one of the equally standard terms denoting imperial rule. The term recurs in the expression "Princeps of the Youth," an honorific title given in the first place to Augustus' grandsons (1.3.2) and subsequently to young members of the imperial family who seemed destined for the succession (thus Nero at 12.41.1). As is also the case with "the **people**" and "**plebs**," T. uses "princeps" with reference to foreign nations too (e.g., 2.7.2).

proconsul The name for the governor of a public (i.e., nonimperial) **province**. In most cases the governor would be an ex-praetor, but certain provinces (e.g., Africa and Asia) received ex-consuls.

procurator This term, which denotes one who has "care" or "concern" (*cura*) for a matter, was used for certain **equestrians** employed in the service of the emperor or other members of the imperial family. (a) Most procurators had financial responsibilities. Each province had an imperial procurator: in the public provinces, the procurator looked after the emperor's estates; in the imperial provinces he was also responsible for the collection of taxes and payment of troops (like Julius Classicianus in Britain: 14.38–9). (b) Certain minor imperial provinces had equestrian governors, who were known at first as **prefects**

but from the time of Claudius as procurators (e.g., Pontius Pilate in Judaea: 15.44.3). Claudius evidently assigned certain judicial functions too to procurators, but T.'s report is unclear (12.60).

propraetor An alternative title for a "**legate** of Augustus," whose full name was *legatus Augusti pro praetore*. See esp. 13.51.1 and 15.22.1, where these men are distinguished from **proconsuls.**

province (*prouincia*) Originally *prouincia* denoted the sphere of duty of a **magistrate,** but the term came to be used mainly of the overseas territories under permanent Roman administration. Under the empire the provinces were divided between the Roman **people** (the "public" provinces) and the emperor (the "imperial" provinces): see the table in *CAH²* 10.369–70. The public provinces were governed by **proconsuls,** chosen by lot from former **praetors** and **consuls.** The governors of the imperial provinces were the emperor's appointees and held **command** only by delegation from him. Most imperial provinces were governed by senatorial **legates,** but some were governed by **equestrians** (minor provinces under their **procurators,** and Egypt under its **prefect**). The public provinces were nonmilitary (except for Africa, which still retained a legion, commanded by the proconsul until A.D. 39, when it was placed under a legate).

quaestor The lowest of the regular Roman **magistracies.** From the time of the late republic, the office of quaestor brought with it membership of the **senate.** Some of the history and functions of quaestors are described at 11.22.2–6. Under the empire two of the twenty quaestors every year would each be called *quaestor Caesaris* or *Augusti* ("quaestor of Caesar" or "of Augustus"), an appointment given by the emperor himself to young men of particular promise: it seems likely that T. himself was such a quaestor (see Introduction, page x). An ex-quaestor is a "quaestorian" (14.41.1).

quindecimvir "One of the Fifteen," the Fifteen (*quindecimuiri*) being one of the four major priestly **colleges** (its full complement was in fact sixteen members). These priests were associated particularly with the Sibylline Books (6.12.1–3) and, as T. tells us with reference to himself, the production of the Secular Games (11.11.1).

relegation A less severe form of banishment or exile, often to an island, and involving confiscation of property.

rogation A proposal (lit. "request") placed before an assembly of the Roman people for approval as a law.

senate Formally the advisory council of the **consuls,** the senate under the republic had been in effect the governing body of Rome. Under the empire it retained wide-ranging functions, acquired a judicial role, and from A.D. 14 chose the **magistrates;** but the political reality was that it operated in the shadow of the emperor's superior power. The senate comprised current and past magistrates, and membership was automatic on attaining the quaestorship. Members of the senate are "senators," although T. very frequently refers to them by the archaizing term "fathers" (*patres*); when addressed in speeches, members might be termed "conscript (lit. 'enlisted') fathers." It is thought that the total membership in the Julio-Claudian period was approximately six hundred; we know from epigraphic evidence that, when the senate's decision on Cn. Calpurnius Piso was passed in A.D. 20 (see 3.12–18), three hundred one senators were in attendance.

senate's decision My translation of the standard *senatus consultum,* used for a resolution passed by the senate. In a typical variation, however, T. twice transposes the words to produce "decision of the senate" (11.35.1, 16.9.1); and quite often he varies it again by substituting "decree" (*decretum*) for "decision" (e.g., 2.85.1).

treasury   (*aerarium*) The principal treasury of Rome was the "Treasury of Saturn" (*aer. Saturni*), in whose temple on the Capitol it was situated. It was here that state documents such as **senate's decisions** were deposited (3.51.2). For the history of the various types of official placed in charge of the treasury see 13.28.3–29.2. Augustus also founded a "military treasury" on the Capitol to fund the pensions of demobilized soldiers (1.78.2; cf. 5.8.1). See also **fiscus.**

tribunes, tribunician power   (a) Military tribunes (*tribuni militum*) were **equestrian** officers in the Roman army: see Appendix B. (b) Tribunes of the plebs (*tribuni plebis*) originated in the early republic as officers who would champion the interests of the **plebs.** Their person was sacrosanct and they possessed a range of powers including the right to initiate and (see **intervention**) to veto legislation. The office continued under the empire as one of the earlier steps on a political career (see esp. the case of Arulenus Rusticus at 16.26.4–5). (c) In 23 B.C. Augustus resigned the consulship and, though not himself a tribune of the plebs, was given tribunician power (*tribunicia potestas*) for life, by which he came to date the years of his principate (thus "TRIB. POT. XXXVII" in A.D. 14, the year of his death: see 1.9.2). The power became one of the foundations of imperial rule and was also bestowed on members of the imperial family to mark them out as successors. See esp. 3.56.

triumph   The ritual procession of a victorious returning **commander** into the City of Rome. Triumphs were occasions for magnificent display: the commander rode in a chariot, followed by his troops, prisoners, and spoils, and the procession culminated on the Capitol, where the commander dedicated the laurels from his **fasces** to Jupiter. Under the republic triumphs were common, but under the empire the division of the **provinces,** which gave the emperor a near monopoly of the armies, effectively ended senators' opportunities of winning a triumph: the last triumph celebrated by a commander outside the imperial family was in 19 B.C. Thereafter triumphs were held only by emperors or by members of their family who had received independent grants of **command** (*imperium*), e.g., Germanicus (1.55.1, 2.41.2). Generals who won victories as the emperor's legate had to be content with the "triumphal insignia" (e.g., 4.46.1), which entitled them to wear the triumphal laurel wreath at the games. An ovation was a lesser form of triumph, in which the commander wore myrtle rather than laurel.

triumvir   (lit. "one of three") Most commonly used (as at 1.2.1 and 5.1.1) to refer to a member of the triumvirate (3.28.2), which was established between Mark Antony, M. Aemilius Lepidus, and Octavian (the future Augustus) in 43 B.C. and lasted for ten years. The nominal purpose of the arrangement was "to stabilize the state" (*rei publicae constituendae*), but its effect was to divide the Roman world geographically between the triumvirs. The term is also used (as at 5.9.2) of the so-called "capital triumvirs" (*tresuiri capitales*), a board of three junior officers who supervised executions.

APPENDIX B

THE FIRST-CENTURY A.D. ROMAN ARMY AND THE *ANNALS*

The Roman army is a complicated and controversial subject, and during the Julio-Claudian period it was in the process of developing many of the organizational elements and features which are described below. The army was divided into (a) legionary soldiers and (b) auxiliaries. Each may be discussed in turn, as by T. himself (4.5.1–4).

Legionary soldiers came increasingly from the provinces, rather than from Rome or Italy, and they held Roman citizenship. In Book 1 they are made to complain that their service is too long, that they are kept "under the banner" as reservists after discharge, and that they are poorly paid (1.17); but the concessions which they later think they have won through mutiny, including a fixed period of sixteen years' service, are revoked by Tiberius, who makes twenty years the norm (1.78.2).

Each legion comprised roughly between five thousand and six thousand men, divided into ten cohorts. Each cohort in turn was constituted of six centuries (1.21.2), each of these consisting of approximately eighty men (except that the first of a legion's ten cohorts came to have more men than the other nine). Two centuries together formed a maniple (*manipulus*): though the maniple had long since been abandoned as a tactical unit, T. continues to refer frequently to maniples, individual members of which were "maniple-regulars" (*manipulares*).

A legion was normally commanded by a legionary legate (*legatus legionis*), who was a senator of—usually but not (see 2.36.1) always—praetorian rank and was subordinate to the governor of the province in which the legion was based; in provinces where only one legion was based, the governor himself normally commanded the legion. Subordinate to the legionary commander were the officers of equestrian rank: the camp prefect (*praefectus castrorum*) and the six military tribunes (*tribuni militum*). The former was an experienced soldier who had risen up through the centurionate, like Aufidienus Rufus in Pannonia (1.20) or Poenius Postumus in Britain (14.37.3). The six military tribunes were usually young men: the senior tribune (*tribunus laticlauius* or "broad-striped tribune") was a prospective senator in his early twenties, who would then go on to enter the senate as quaestor; the other five (*tribuni angusticlauii* or "narrow-striped tribunes") regarded their post as part of an equestrian career.

Next in the line of command came the centurions (each of the sixty centuries was under a centurion): most of these men had risen through the ranks and were highly experienced. The centurion who commanded the first century of the first cohort was the senior centurion of the legion or "centurion of the first rank" (15.12.2 *primi pili centurio*); "first-rankers" (*primipilares*: 2.11.1, 4.72.1) is the term for former holders of this position. The common soldiers were *gregarii milites* or "troop-soldiers" (*grex* = "a herd").

Under Augustus there were twenty-eight legions, but three of them (XVII–*XIX) were lost in Germany in the Varian disaster of A.D. 9 (1.3.6 and elsewhere). Thereafter the establishment remained at twenty-five legions until two more were raised by Gaius Caligula or Claudius in A.D. 39–42. The legions and their stations in the period covered by the *Annals* are as follows (asterisks indicate those mentioned by T.):

*I	Germanica	Lower Germany
*II	Augusta	Upper Germany; Britain from A.D. 43
III	Augusta	Africa
III	Cyrenaica	Egypt
*III	Gallica	Syria
IV	Macedonica	Spain; on the Rhine from A.D. 43
*IV	Scythica	Moesia; Syria from A.D. 56/57
*V	Alaudae	Lower Germany
*V	Macedonica	Moesia
*VI	Ferrata	Syria
VI	Victrix	Spain
VII	Claudia	Dalmatia; Moesia from perhaps A.D. 56/57
*VIII	Augusta	Pannonia; Moesia from c. A.D. 45
*IX	Hispana	Pannonia (Africa A.D. 20–24); Britain from 43
*X	Fretensis	Syria
X	Gemina	Spain (Pannonia A.D. 63–68)
XI	Claudia	Dalmatia
*XII	Fulminata	Syria
*XIII	Gemina	Upper Germany; Pannonia from c. A.D. 45
*XIV	Gemina	Upper Germany (Britain A.D. 43–67)
*XV	Apollinaris	Pannonia
XV	Primigenia	Upper, later Lower Germany (formed A.D. 39–42)
*XVI	Gallica	Upper, later Lower Germany
*XX	Valeria Victrix	Lower Germany; Britain from A.D. 43
*XXI	Rapax	Lower Germany
XXII	Deiotariana	Egypt
XXII	Primigenia	Upper Germany (formed A.D. 39–42)

Each legion would have its own "eagle" (*aquila,* e.g., 1.60.3 "the Nineteenth Legion's eagle"); smaller units would have their own banner (*uexillum*); a more general term is the "standard" (*signum*). A special detachment of troops was also called a *uexillum* (e.g., 4.73.1, 15.26.2): its members were *uexillarii* or "banner-men" (e.g., 1.38.1, 14.34.1), not to be confused with the veteran reservists kept "under the banner" (above).

Though each legion would normally come to have one hundred twenty legionary cavalry attached to it, the principal cavalry forces were supplied by the auxiliaries. T.'s frequent references to "wings" (*alae*), and his few references to "wing-men" (*alares, alarii*), denote auxiliary cavalry units approximately five-hundred–strong (though sometimes they were double that number), smaller groups of which (c. thirty men) are called "squadrons" (*turmae*). The auxiliaries also supplied substantial infantry forces known as "(the) cohorts" (*cohortes*), but sometimes called "allied cohorts" (e.g., 1.49.4 *sociae cohortes*) or simply "the allies" (*socii,* e.g., 1.56.1). At times these forces would fight the main infantry action in a battle, with the legionary troops holding back and entering the fray only if the auxiliaries found themselves too hard pressed.

Auxiliary troops were recruited from various of the Roman provinces and were not Roman citizens, though they could expect to receive citizenship (sanctioned by the *diploma*) at the end of their service. T. puts the total auxiliary strength in A.D. 23 as equivalent to that of the legions, but adds that precision is impossible because auxiliaries moved around and varied in numbers from time to time (4.5.4).

The Praetorian Guard, initially comprising nine cohorts (4.5.3) but later increased to twelve, was stationed in Rome but would sometimes go on campaign (e.g., 2.16.3, 2.20.3). Also stationed at Rome were the three urban cohorts (4.5.3), each under the command of a tribune (6.9.3) and together under the overall command of the Prefect of the City.

Finally it is worth noting that T. reserves the word "soldiers" (*milites*)—or his favored alternative, the collective "soldiery" (*miles*)—almost exclusively for troops on the Roman side; the enemy's forces are never (or virtually never) described as "soldiers."

For further information see Y. Le Bohec, *The Imperial Roman Army* (London 2000).

APPENDIX C

THE CITY OF ROME

The following list, like the skeletal map on page 398, is intended merely to explain the relative topography of the various places in the City of Rome which Tacitus mentions. (Sometimes I have referred to the more detailed maps in P. Zanker, *The Power of Images in the Age of Augustus* (Ann Arbor, MI 1988), A. Wallace-Hadrill, *Augustan Rome* (London 1993), or A. Claridge, *Rome: An Oxford Archaeological Guide* (Oxford 1998).) For further information consult *OCD* or especially L. Richardson, Jr., *A New Topographical Dictionary of Ancient Rome* (Baltimore/London 1992).

altar   See **Consus' altar** and **temple** (Hercules).

Basilica of Paulus   On the northern side of the Roman Forum; named after L. Aemilius Paulus (cos. 50 B.C.).

Capitol, Capitoline (Hill)   Capitol is both an alternative term for the whole of the Capitoline Hill (full form at 15.18.1), the smallest of Rome's seven hills, and the specific name for the southern of its twin summits and/or the buildings thereon, one of which was the temple of Capitoline Jupiter. The more northerly summit was called Arx or "Citadel" (11.23.4).

Circus   This term, when used alone, invariably refers to the Circus Maximus (full form at 2.49.1) between the Aventine, Palatine, and Caelian Hills (6.45.1, 15.38.2).

Comitium   An area (originally for popular assemblies) adjacent to the Curia in the Roman Forum (see Zanker 80).

Consus' altar   A subterranean altar in the Circus Maximus which was uncovered only on the god's festival days.

Curia   The senate house of Rome, on the northern side of the Roman Forum and separated from the Basilica of Paulus by the street known as Argiletum. See also maps in Zanker 80, Wallace-Hadrill 52.

forum   The word *forum* means a public square or marketplace in the center of a town. In the context of Rome it is often used, by a form of metonymy, to refer to the law courts (e.g., 11.6.2); but, when used literally and without further qualification in a Roman context, the word (in the singular) refers to the Roman Forum (full form at 12.24.2), which lay to the east of the Capitol on an axis roughly WNW/ESE. The Forum of Augustus (4.15.2) lay directly to the north of the Roman Forum and almost at right angle to it (see Wallace-Hadrill 52). The Forum Boarium (12.24.1: the name suggests cattle) was the area bounded by the Capitoline, Palatine, and Aventine Hills, while the Forum Holitorium (2.49.1: the name suggests vegetables) lay to the northwest of it, between the Capitol and the River Tiber.

Gardens   The various estates or parklands in Rome were known by the names of their original owners:

Caesar's (the dictator Julius Caesar): on the right bank of the Tiber, southwest of the City proper.

Lucullian (L. Licinius Lucullus, cos. 74 B.C.): one of the most famous estates, lying in the north of Rome to the west of the Salarian Way.

Maecenas': on the Esquiline Hill in the eastern area of the City.

Sallustian (C. Sallustius Crispus, the historian Sallust): the most celebrated estate in Rome, extending over a very wide area in the north of the City to the east of the Salarian Way.

Servilian (possibly named after M. Servilius Nonianus, cos. A.D. 35: see 14.19): often assumed to be in the southwestern area of the City.

Taurus' (T. Statilius Taurus, cos. A.D. 44): on the Esquiline Hill.

Gemonian Steps, Gemonians   A flight of steps leading from the jail up toward the summit of the Capitol and used to display the bodies of those executed as criminals (5.9.2, 6.25.3).

jail   At the foot of the Capitoline Hill between the temple of Concord and the Curia. Its underground part was called the Tullianum.

Marcellus' theater.   See **theaters.**

Mausoleum of Augustus   At the northern end of the Plain of Mars, between the Flaminian Way and the River Tiber (see 3.9.2). See also Zanker 140, Wallace-Hadrill 59.

Mulvian Bridge   Outside the city proper, the bridge carried the Flaminian Way across the Tiber to the north.

Nero's houses   Nero's first palace was the so-called "Domus Transitoria" (Suetonius, *Nero* 31.1), which connected, as its name suggests, the imperial complex on the Palatine with Maecenas' Gardens on the Esquiline (15.39.1). When this was burned down in the fire of A.D. 64, Nero built the famous "Golden House" or "Domus Aurea," which was similar in orientation but even more extensive. See Claridge 268–9, with Fig. 129.

Palatine (Hill), Palatium   Palatium is both an alternative term for Palatine Hill (full form at 12.24.1, 15.38.2), one of the seven hills of Rome, and the name for the emperors' residential complex on the hill. The temple of Apollo was part of this complex and, though never named by T., was a regular meeting place of the senate (see 2.37.2 and note).

Plain of Mars   This is T.'s name for what other authors call the Campus Martius or Martial Plain. Originally an open area in the northwest of the City and suitable for athletic training and the like, it was gradually built up, especially by Agrippa (15.37.2, 39.2): its edifices included Pompey's theater and (see 13.31.1) Nero's amphitheater, but one of its most spectacular was the Mausoleum of Augustus (1.8.5, 3.4.1, 13.17.1). The Plain was also the traditional meeting place of the "centuriate" assembly, responsible for the election of consuls and praetors (1.15.1). See Zanker 140, Wallace-Hadrill 59.

prison   See **jail.**

regia   The "office" (as it were) of the high pontiff (*pontifex maximus*); situated at the eastern end of the Roman Forum.

the Rock   (2.32.3, 4.29.2) See **Tarpeian Rock.**

rostra   In imperial times the rostra (a plural word meaning "beaks") were at the northwestern end of the Roman Forum and constituted a raised area or platform from which various types of formal public speaking could take place. The term derives from the "beaks" of enemy ships with which the platform and its various predecessors were traditionally adorned.

shrine   See **temple.**

Tarpeian Rock   A precipitous area of the Capitoline Hill from which criminals were thrown as a form of execution. It overlooked the Roman Forum.

temple   The temples or shrines mentioned by T. are those of:

Augustus: exact location uncertain but thought to lie behind the Basilica Julia. The temple was said to have been used by Gaius Caligula to help support his bridge or walkway between the Palatine and Capitoline Hills.

Capitoline Jupiter: the famous temple to Jupiter Best and Greatest (*Optimus Maximus*) on the Capitol was shared with Minerva (see 13.24.2).

Flora: near the Circus Maximus and the temple of Liber, Libera, and Ceres, with which it is often associated (as by T. at 2.49.1, no doubt to distinguish it from another temple of Flora on the Quirinal).

Fors Fortuna: on the right bank of the Tiber in Caesar's Gardens.

Hercules: there were numerous temples of Hercules. That mentioned by T. (15.41.1) is associated with the "great altar" of Hercules, which was in the Forum Boarium (12.24.1). Thus the temple is presumably that of Hercules Victor, which was in the Forum Boarium.

Hope: in the Forum Holitorium.

Janus: specified by T. (2.49.1) as being in the Forum Holitorium in order to distinguish it from the more famous shrine of Janus Geminus (or Quirinus) in the Roman Forum.

Jupiter Stator: evidently in the area of the Palatine and described by T. as "vowed by Romulus" (15.41.1) to distinguish it from a homonymous temple in the Circus Flaminius.

Liber, Libera, and Ceres (often abbreviated simply to Ceres, as at 15.53.3): on the lower slope of the Aventine, near the northwest end of the Circus Maximus.

Luna: on the Aventine near the Circus.

Mars the Avenger: in the Forum of Augustus.

Saturn: on the slope of the Capitol.

Sol: an ancient temple at the southwest corner of the Circus.

Venus Genetrix: in the Julian Forum.

Vesta: at the southeast end of the Roman Forum, at the foot of the Palatine.

theaters   Marcellus' theater was on the southern edge of the Plain of Mars, opposite the bridge connecting with Tiber Island; Pompey's theater, the first permanent theater in Rome (14.20.2), was also in the Plain of Mars but farther to the northwest.

Tuscan Street   Ran from the Roman Forum (between the temple of Castor and the Basilica Julia) in the direction of the Forum Boarium.

Vatican valley   Approximately the site of the piazza and basilica of St. Peter.

Appendix D
Peoples and Places (Excluding Rome)

In general I have used ancient rather than modern forms of names but have not been absolutely consistent: thus "Vahalis" instead of Waal and "Mosa" instead of Meuse or Maas occur alongside "Rhine" at 2.6.4. Further information on some of the following entries may be found in *OCD;* a standard work of reference is the *Barrington Atlas of the Greek and Roman World* (Princeton 2000). In the following list, modern-day equivalents are *italicized;* all distances are approximate. For the legions stationed in the various provinces, see Appendix B.

Achaea　Roman province (from 27 B.C.), comprising all of the Peloponnese and part of northern Greece. Modern *Achaía* covers a much smaller area in the north of the Peloponnese.

Actium　Promontory located on the west coast of Greece on the entrance to the bay Amvrakikós Kólpos; the modern settlement is *Áktio.* Site of famous victory by Octavian (Augustus) over Antony and Cleopatra in 31 B.C.

Adiabene　Region which was situated west of the River Tigris in modern Iraq.

Adrana　The River *Eder,* western Germany.

Adriatic Sea　Arm of the Mediterranean Sea which lies between the Italian and Balkan peninsulas.

Aedui　A Celtic people who lived in the area of Burgundy (Bourgogne), France. Their capital was Augustodunum (*Autun*).

Aegeae　(a) 2.47.3: ancient town inland from Çandarlı Körfezi, western Turkey, northeast of the modern town of Aliağa.

(b) 13.8.3: ancient town near the modern settlement of Yumurtalık, on the Gulf of Iskenderun (İskenderun Körfezi) in southern Turkey.

Aegean Sea　Arm of the Mediterranean Sea which lies between Greece and Turkey.

Aegium　Town on the north coast of the Peloponnese; now *Aígio.*

Aequi　Old Italian tribe living east of Rome.

Africa　Comprised Africa Proconsularis (including Numidia) and Cyrenaica, roughly Tunisia and northern Libya.

Alba (Longa)　Ancient settlement southeast of Rome which was located near Castel Gandolfo.

Albani　A people living west of the Caspian Sea in modern Georgia.

Albis　The *Elbe* river, which rises in the Czech Republic and flows north through Germany to the North Sea.

Alesia　Ancient settlement near Alise-Sainte-Reine, northwest of Dijon, France.

Alexandria　Modern-day *Alexandria* (*Al Iskandarīyah*), in Egypt, on the Mediterranean coast.

Aliso　A stronghold near the Lippe river, western Germany.

Alps   Not only the mountain range to the north of Italy (11.24.2) but also the name of a Roman province (see 15.32 and n.).

Amanus   A mountain range in southern Turkey, now known as *Nur Dağları;* an arm of the Taurus Mountains.

Amisia   The *Ems* river in northwestern Germany.

Amorgus   One of the Cyclades Islands, Greece, in the Aegean Sea; *Amorgós.*

Ampsivarii   Germanic tribe living east of the Frisii (northwestern Netherlands), between the Ems and Weser rivers.

Amynclan Sea   Off Formiae on the west coast of Italy.

Ancona   Seaport on the east coast of Italy on the Adriatic Sea; *Ancona.*

Andecavi   Tribe living in the area of Anjou, northwest France, around Angers.

Anemurium   Ancient town whose site is located close to the modern town of Anamur, on the Mediterranean coast of Turkey.

Angrivarii   Germanic tribe living around the River Weser, Germany.

Anthemusias   Town in ancient Mesopotamia.

Antioch   Modern-day *Antakya,* a city in southern Turkey. In Roman times, Antioch was the capital of the province of Syria.

Antium   A city of ancient Latium; now *Anzio.* Situated on the west coast of Italy, south of Rome.

Aorsi   Sarmatian tribe living east of the Sea of Azov in what is now Russia.

Apamea   Ancient city on the River Meander (Büyükmenderes Nehri). The modern town of Dinar, in western Turkey, is built on part of its site.

Aphrodisias   Ancient city whose site lies near the modern settlement of Geyre, southwest of Denizli, southwestern Turkey.

Apollonis   City in western Turkey.

Appian Way   The road between Rome and Brundisium.

Apulia   A region in southeast Italy (*Puglia*).

Arabia   The vast peninsula between the Red Sea and the Persian Gulf. Its inhabitants were the Arabs.

Arar   The River *Saône* in the east of France.

Araxes   The River *Aras,* which rises in Turkey south of Erzurum and flows east, forming parts of the boundary between Turkey and Armenia, between Iran and Armenia and between Iran and Azerbaijan. It flows into the River Kura in Azerbaijan.

Arcadia   A mountainous region of the Peloponnese, Greece. The modern administrative department *Arkadía* is roughly coextensive with the ancient region.

Arduenna   *Ardennes,* a forested region in Belgium and France. In ancient geography, the forest covered the area from the Rhine at Koblenz (Germany) to the River Sambre (west Belgium/northeast France).

Arii   Inhabitants of ancient Aria, a region corresponding roughly to northwest Afghanistan and eastern Iran.

Armenia   A country divided by the Romans in the late 60s B.C. into Armenia Maior (Greater Armenia) and Armenia Minor (Lesser Armenia). Lesser Armenia (11.9.2, 13.7.1) was located in what is now northeastern Turkey, west of the River Euphrates. Greater Armenia was east of the Euphrates.

Arnus   The River *Arno,* in Tuscany, Italy.

Arsamosata   A stronghold of ancient Armenia, near the River Arsanias.

Arsanias   *Murat Nehri,* a river in northeastern Turkey.

Artaxata   The modern city of *Artashat,* about 15 miles south of Yerevan, Armenia.

Artemita   A Parthian town. It was located near Ba'qūbah, a town about 35 miles northeast of Baghdad, Iraq.

Asia   Roman province comprising a large area of modern western Turkey.

Assyria   An ancient country in what is now northern Iraq.

Athens   *Athens (Athína),* capital of modern Greece.

Attica   The district (*Attikí*) around Athens.

Augustodonum   *Autun* in east central France, about 45 miles southwest of Dijon.

Auzea   *Sour El Ghozlane* in northern Algeria, 55 miles southeast of Algiers.

Avernus, Lake   *Lago d'Averno,* a small crater lake near Cumae in southern Italy.

Bactria   Ancient country occupying a vast area that lay between the Amu Darya river (historically the Oxus) to the north and the Hindu Kush to the south. Its capital was Bactra, the modern city of Balkh in northern Afghanistan.

Baiae   Ancient seaside resort on the west coast of Italy; the modern *Baia.*

Balearic Islands   Island group in the Mediterranean Sea, near the east coast of Spain to which they now belong.

Barium   *Bari,* a port in southeastern Italy on the Adriatic Sea.

Bastarnae   Germanic tribe living in an area north of the Black Sea around the lower Danube.

Batavi   A Germanic people living in an area between the Rhine and Waal rivers (the area known today as Betuwe, in the Netherlands).

Belgae   A people living to the north of the Seine and Marne rivers, in the province of Gallia Belgica.

Beneventum   *Benevento,* a town in southern Italy on the River Calore; about 34 miles northeast of Naples.

Bithynia   Ancient region which bordered the Black Sea and Sea of Marmara, in what is now northern Turkey. Later incorporated into the Roman province of Bithynia and Pontus (63 B.C.).

Bononia   *Bologna,* northern Italy.

Bosporus   (a) 12.15.1: a kingdom on the Kerch Strait which connects the Black Sea with the Sea of Azov. (b) 12.63.6: narrow strait connecting the Black Sea with the Sea of Marmara.

Bovillae   Ancient town which was about 10 miles southeast of Rome, on the Appian Way.

Brigantes   Extensive tribe in north Britain, whose capital was possibly Isurium (now the delightful village of Aldborough in North Yorkshire).

Britain   (Britons) Roman province.

Bructeri   Germanic people living around the River Lippe, in northwest Germany.

Brundisium   *Brindisi,* port in southern Italy on the Adriatic Sea.

Byzantium   Ancient city, known later as Constantinople, now *Istanbul,* Turkey.

Cadra   Unidentified hill in Asia Minor.

Caesian Wood   Somewhere in Germany, perhaps south of the River Lippe.

Calabria   In Roman times, the "heel" of Italy was called Calabria; modern Calabria is a region in the "toe."

Cales   Near the modern settlement of *Calvi Risorta,* about 25 miles north of Naples.

Camerium   Ancient settlement in Latium.

Campania   A region in southern Italy noted in antiquity for its beauty and fertility. It was a favorite resort of distinguished Romans and contained the ancient cities of Capua, Cumae, Baiae, Herculaneum, Neapolis, Nola, Pompeii, and Puteoli.

Camulodunum   *Colchester,* a town in Essex, southeast England.

Canninefates   A Germanic tribe living in a coastal area of Holland, north of the Rhine delta.

Canopus   In ancient geography, a city of Egypt situated about 10 miles east of Alexandria, near what was then the westernmost mouth of the Nile (the Canopic Mouth), long since silted up. The approximate site of ancient Canopus is the modern village of Abū Qīr.

Cappadocia   Ancient region in what is now east central Turkey. The name was applied at various times to territories of varying size. Rome annexed the region in A.D. 17.

Capri   *Capri* (ancient Capreae), island in the Gulf of Naples, near the town of Sorrento, southern Italy.

Capua   Ancient city about 15 miles north of Naples. The modern village of *Santa Maria di Capua Vetere* is on its site.

Carmania   Ancient region extending north from the Persian Gulf, in the area around the modern city of Kermān, southeast Iran.

Carthage   Ancient city and state of North Africa. The city was located 5 miles northeast of modern Tunis (*Tunisia*); it later became the capital of the Roman province Africa Proconsularis.

Caspian route   Probably the *Dariel Pass* (*Darialis Kheoba*) in northern Georgia, a narrow gorge in the Caucasus Mountains, on the Georgian Military Highway along the Terek river.

Celenderis   Ancient settlement whose ruins are near the village of Aydıncık, on the Mediterranean coast of Turkey, east of Anamur.

Cenchreus   A river near Ephesus (Efes), Turkey.

Cercina   The *Ile Chergui,* largest of the *Iles de Kerkenah,* a group of islands off the east coast of Tunisia, to which they now belong.

Chalcedonii   The inhabitants of Chalcedon, now *Kadıköy.* The modern settlement is a suburb of the city of Istanbul, Turkey. It is on the east side of the entrance to the Bosporus.

Chamavi   Germanic people living east of the Batavi in the area of the River Ijssel, Netherlands.

Chatti   Powerful Germanic people from the area around the upper Weser and Diemel rivers, Germany.

Chauci   Germanic people who lived in the area along the North Sea coast between the Elbe and Ems rivers.

Cherusci   Germanic people from the region of the middle River Weser, Germany.

Cibyra   Ancient town whose site is near the modern town of Gölhisar, southwest of Burdur, in southwestern Turkey.

Cietae   Mountain tribe in ancient Cilicia (southern Turkey).

Cilicia   The eastern part of southern Asia Minor between the Mediterranean Sea and the Taurus Mountains, in what is now southern Turkey. Became a Roman province in the first century B.C.

Cinithii   A people of north Africa.

Cirtenses   Inhabitants of Cirta, the main town of ancient Numidia; the modern city of *Constantine* in northeast Algeria.

Clanis   The River *Chiana* in Tuscany, Italy.

Coelaletae   A Thracian tribe in southern Bulgaria.

Colchi   Inhabitants of Colchis, an ancient country east of the Black Sea and south of the Caucasus mountains, corresponding to the western part of modern Georgia.

Colonia Agrippinensis   *Cologne* (*Köln*), city in Germany on the banks of the Rhine.

Colophon   Ancient city whose site is near the modern village of Değirmendere in western Turkey, about 19 miles south of İzmir.

Commagene   A kingdom lying between the River Euphrates and the Taurus Mountains.

Corcyra   *Corfu* (*Kérkyra*), an island of Greece, in the Ionian Sea.

Corinth   *Corinth* (*Kórinthos*) in the Peloponnese, Greece. The ruins of ancient Corinth are 3 miles southwest of the modern town.

Corma   Unidentified tributary of the River Tigris.

Cos   *Kos,* an island of Greece in the Aegean Sea.

Cosa   The modern settlement of *Ansedoni* in Tuscany, Italy, on the Mediterranean coast near the town of Orbetello.

Crete   *Crete* (*Kríti*), Greek island in the Mediterranean Sea.

Ctesiphon   Ancient city whose ruins (*Ṭāq Kisrá*) lie about 20 miles southeast of Baghdad, Iraq.

Cumae   Coastal town of ancient Campania, Italy, whose site (*Cuma*) is on the coast west of Naples.

Cusus   Possibly either the River Váh, west Slovakia, or the River Hron, central Slovakia.

Cyclades Islands   *Cyclades* (*Kykládes*), Greek island group in the Aegean Sea.

Cyme   Ancient city whose site is on the west coast of Turkey, about 25 miles northwest of İzmir.

Cyprus   Island in the Mediterranean Sea.

Cyrene   Ancient city in north Africa, at the modern-day settlement of *Shaḥḥāt,* on the coast of Libya.

Cyrrus   Town of ancient Syria. It was located about 60 miles northeast of Antakya (Antioch).

Cythnus *Kýthnos,* an island of the Cyclades group, Greece.

Cyziceni Inhabitants of Cyzicus, an ancient city south of the Sea of Marmara in what is now western Turkey. Its remains are approximately 4 miles from the modern settlement of Bandırma.

Dahae Scythian tribe southeast of the Caspian Sea in modern Turkmenistan.

Dalmatia Roman province on the eastern seaboard of the Adriatic Sea.

Dandarica Area to the north of the Black Sea, home to the Dandaridae, a Scythian tribe.

Danube River flowing through many countries of Central Europe.

Davara Unidentified hill in Cappadocia.

Decangi Tribe in north Wales.

Delos Smallest island of the Cyclades, Greece, in the Aegean Sea. Traditionally regarded as the center of the Cyclades.

Delphi Site of famous ancient sanctuary at *Delfoí,* a town in Greece near the northern shore of the Gulf of Corinth.

Denthaliatis A district of Messenia at the head of the middle prong of the Peloponnese.

Dii Tribe in southern Bulgaria.

Donusa *Donoúsa,* an island east of Náxos, in the Cyclades, Greece.

Ecbatana The modern city of *Hamadān,* western Iran, 175 miles southwest of Tehran.

Edessa Şanlıurfa, a city in southeastern Turkey, about 25 miles from the border with Syria.

Egypt After the death of Cleopatra (30 B.C.), Octavian (Augustus) annexed Egypt to Rome.

Elephantine *Jazırat Aswān,* an island, southern Egypt, in the River Nile opposite Aswān.

Elymaei Inhabitants of the ancient kingdom of Elam, a country east of the River Tigris, north of the head of the Persian Gulf, in what is now southwest Iran.

Ephesus *Efes.* Site of the ancient city is near the coast of the Aegean Sea in western Turkey, south of İzmir and near the modern settlement of Selçuk.

Epidaphne Garden suburb of Antioch (more strictly just Daphne).

Erindes Unidentified river in northern Iran.

Erycus *Monte San Giuliano,* a mountain in northwest Sicily, about 4 miles northeast of Trapani. The modern town of Erice sits on top of the mountain.

Erythrae The site of this ancient city lies partly covered by the modern settlement of İldır, about 45 miles due west of İzmir, Turkey.

Ethiopia Ancient Ethiopia was an ill-defined territory south of Egypt.

Etruria Ancient region of Italy northwest of Rome, covering an area now in Tuscany and part of Umbria. Inhabitants were the Etruscans.

Euboea *Évvoia.* A Greek island, lying in the Aegean Sea alongside the east coast of central mainland Greece.

Euphrates *River Euphrates: Al Furāt* (Arabic); *Fırat Nehri* (Turkish). The river is formed from two headstreams in east central Turkey; it then flows through Turkey and Syria to

Iraq where it joins the River Tigris near Basra, forming the Shatt al Arab waterway which flows into the Persian Gulf.

Fidenae   Ancient town about 5 miles north of Rome, situated on the Tiber.

Flaminian Way   The road which ran from Rome to Ariminum (*Rimini*).

Flevum   Stronghold on the coast of the Netherlands whose name perhaps survives as Vlieland.

Florentini   Inhabitants of ancient Florentia, modern *Florence* (*Firenze*).

Formiae   Modern *Formia,* a town on the coast about 50 miles northwest of Naples, Italy; near Gaeta.

Forum Julium   *Fréjus,* southeast France, about 30 miles southwest of Nice. T. also calls it "the Forojulian town" (4.5.1).

Frentani   Samnite tribe who lived on the east coast of central Italy.

Frisii   A people from the northwestern Netherlands (modern *Friesland*).

Fucine Lake   Former lake in central Italy, east of Avezzano (drained 1854–75).

Fundi   *Fondi,* a town in south central Italy, about 20 miles northwest of Gaeta.

Gabii   Town of ancient Latium, 12 miles east of Rome on the road to Praeneste (*Palestrina*).

Galatia   Ancient region covering an area now in west central Turkey. A Roman province from 25 B.C.

Galileans   Inhabitants of Galilee.

Galliae   ("The Gauls") Four provinces, each called Gallia ("Gaul"), were established by Augustus: Aquitania, Belgica (13.53.3), Lugdunensis, and Narbonensis ("Narbonese Gaul": 2.63.5, 12.23.1, 14.57.1, 16.13.3). Earlier there had been only one established Gallic province (equivalent to Narbonese Gaul); beyond that was Gallia Comata or "Hairy Gaul" (a reference to the conventional hirsuteness of barbarians: 11.23.1). To avoid confusion in the cases of plural forms, I have retained "Galliae" for the region and used "Gauls" for the inhabitants.

Garamantes   North African tribe in the area of modern Fezzan, southwest Libya.

Germany, the Germanies   The Roman militarized zone of Germany comprised two divisions: "Lower Germany" (1.31.2–3, 3.41.2, 4.73.1) on the northern Rhine, whose capital was Cologne, and "Upper Germany" (1.31.2, 6.30.2, 12.27.2, 13.56.2) on the southern Rhine, whose capital was Mainz.

Getae   Thracian tribe on the lower Danube.

Gorneae   Stronghold whose ruins are at *Garni,* southeast of Yerevan, Armenia.

Gotones   A people living to the east of the lower Vistula (Wisła) in what is now Poland. Usually regarded as being the same tribe as that which was later known as the Goths.

Gyarus   *Gyáros,* an island of the Cyclades, in the Aegean Sea.

Hadrumetum   The modern port of *Sousse* on the east coast of Tunisia.

Haemus   Ancient name for the *Balkan Mountains,* a range of mountains extending from Yugoslavia across central Bulgaria to the Black Sea.

Halicarnassus   Coastal city in southwest Turkey, now *Bodrum*.

Halus   Unidentified Parthian town, presumably near Artemita.

Heliopolis   Ancient city whose ruins lie about 5 miles northeast of Cairo, Egypt.

Heniochi   A Caucasian people.

Hercynia   The forested uplands adjacent to the Rhine in Germany, between Düsseldorf and Mainz, and extending eastward to the Carpathians.

Hermunduri   Extensive Germanic tribe living in the area from Regensburg on the Danube north into Thuringia (Thüringen).

Hibernia   The island of Ireland.

Hierocaesaria   Ancient town located northeast of İzmir in western Turkey.

Homonadenses   A people on the western border of Cilicia.

Hypaepa   Ancient town located inland from İzmir in western Turkey.

Hyrcania   An ancient region which bordered the Caspian Sea, corresponding to modern-day northeast Iran.

Iazyges   Nomadic Sarmatian tribe occupying the plain between the Danube and Tisza rivers.

Iberia   An ancient region roughly equivalent to southern and eastern Georgia.

Iceni   British tribe around modern Norfolk and Suffolk.

Idisiovisa   Unidentified place in Germany (Old High German for "Nymphs' Meadow").

Ilium   Alternative ancient name for Troy, used especially of the later settlement. *Truva,* the site of Troy, is situated near the coast in northwest Turkey, south of Çanakkale.

Illyricum   General name for the vast hinterland to the east of the Adriatic. The Roman province of Illyricum was later (from A.D. 9) divided into the two provinces of Dalmatia and Pannonia.

Insubres   A Gallic tribe living north of the Po, around modern Milan.

Interamna   *Terni* in Umbria, Italy.

Ionian Sea   Section of the Mediterranean Sea between the southeastern coast of Italy and western Greece.

Ituraei   An Arab people living in the region northwest of Damascus.

Jews   Inhabitants of Judaea (their Latin name is Iudaei).

Judaea   Roman province from A.D. 6.

Lacedaemonians   Alternative name for Spartans.

Langobardi   Germanic tribe on lower River Elbe.

Lanuvium   *Lanuvio,* about 15 miles south of Rome, in the Alban Hills.

Laodicea   (a) 4.55.2, 14.27.1: Laodicea-on-Lycus lay east of the Lycus' confluence with the Meander (Büyükmenderes Nehri). Its site lies just north of the modern town of Denizli, in southwest Turkey.

   (b) 2.79.2: Laodicea-on-Sea, seaport opposite the northern tip of Cyprus. Now *Latakia* (*Al Lādhiqīyah*) in Syria.

Latium   The area around and to the south of Rome, approximately modern-day *Lazio.*

Legerda   Stronghold northwest of Tigranocerta, near the source of the Tigris river, Turkey.

Lepcitani   Inhabitants of Leptis, the name of two ancient coastal cities of north Africa, Leptis Magna and Leptis Minor. The site of Leptis Magna (Labdah) is near the modern town of Al Khums on the coast of Libya; Leptis Minor (Lamta) is southeast of Sousse, Tunisia. It is unclear to which Tacitus refers (3.74.2).

Lesbos   *Lésvos,* an island of Greece, in the Aegean Sea, just off the northwest coast of Turkey.

Leucophrys   The name of an ancient village near Magnesia-on-Meander.

Libya   Libya was the old Greek name for north Africa outside of Egypt. Under the Romans the region was divided into Marmarica and Cyrenaica.

Liguria   The ancient region of the Ligurians, an area of northwest Italy and southeastern France. The area covered was east of Marseille along toward the River Po. The name survives with a more limited extent as an area centered on Genoa, Italy.

Limnae   Town in southwest Peloponnese, Greece.

Liris   The *Liri* river, in south central Italy. It rises in the Apennines and flows to the Gulf of Gaeta (Golfo di Gaeta).

Londinium   Roman settlement on the River Thames (*London*).

Lucania   Roughly equal to modern *Basilicata,* a mountainous region of southern Italy.

Lucrine Lake   Coastal lagoon between Puteoli and Baiae.

Lugdunum   *Lyon,* a city in east central France at the confluence of the Rhône and Saône rivers.

Lugii   A people of eastern Germany living between the Gotones to the northeast and the Hermunduri to the southwest.

Lupia   The River *Lippe* in northwest Germany.

Lusitania   Roman province which included all of modern central Portugal and much of western Spain.

Lycia   Ancient mountainous region occupying an area now in southwest Turkey. Combined with Pamphylia in A.D. 43 to form a new Roman province.

Lydia   Ancient country occupying an area now in western Turkey. Its capital was at Sardis. Under the Romans, it was part of the province of Asia.

Macedonia   A Roman province lying between the Adriatic and the Aegean seas, north of the province of Achaea.

Magnesia   (a) Magnesia-on-Meander (3.62.1, 4.55.2): ancient city on the River Meander (Büyükmenderes Nehri), whose site is located in western Turkey, about 8 miles north of the modern settlement of Söke. (b) Magnesia-by-Sipylus (2.47.3): *Manisa,* located about 20 miles northeast of İzmir in western Turkey.

Marcomanni   Germanic tribe living between the upper reaches of the Elbe and Danube rivers.

Mardi   A people located both south of the Caspian Sea and near the Persian Gulf.

Marsi   A Germanic people, living south of the Lippe river.

Marus   The *March/Morava* river in Central Europe.

Massilia   *Marseille,* Mediterranean seaport city, southeast France.

Mattiaci   Evidently a subdivision of the Chatti (whose capital was called Mattium) and living in the area of modern Wiesbaden, Germany.

Mattium   Unidentified capital of the Chatti, perhaps on the River Eder.

Mauri   People inhabiting the ancient region of north Africa roughly equivalent to Morocco.

Medes   A people living south of the Caspian Sea.

Melitene   The name of a district located in what is now east central Turkey. The name was also given to a town close to the Euphrates whose site is about 8 miles northeast of the modern settlement of Malayta.

Mesopotamia   The "country between the rivers" (the meaning of the name: 6.37.3) Tigris and Euphrates.

Messenia   A division of ancient Greece in the southwest Peloponnese. Its capital was Messene, site of the modern village of Mavrommáti near the modern town of Messíni, Greece.

Miletus   Ancient city situated near the mouth of the Meander (Büyükmenderes Nehri) in what is now southwest Turkey. In ancient times it stood on a promontory; now the site is inland, near the modern village of Balat, about 18 miles southwest of Söke.

Misenum   Ancient town situated on a promontory known today as *Miseno,* northwest of the Bay of Naples.

Moesia   Roman province extending along the lower Danube from the River Drina to the Black Sea.

Mona   *Anglesey,* an island off northwest Wales.

Mosa   The *Meuse/Maas* river, which rises in France and flows through Belgium and the Netherlands to the North Sea.

Moschi   A people of south Georgia.

Mosella   The River *Moselle,* which rises in northeast France and flows through Germany and into the Rhine at Koblenz.

Mosteni   Inhabitants of the ancient town of Mostene which was situated in western Turkey, southeast of Magnesia-by-Sipylus (Manisa).

Musulamii   A tribe of north Africa.

Myrina   Ancient town whose ruins lie near Aliağa, on Çandarlı Körfezi, a bay in western Turkey.

Mytilene   *Mytilíni,* port on the southeastern shore of the island of Lésvos, Greece, in the Aegean Sea.

Nabataei   An Arab people whose kingdom was centered on Petra, present-day Jordan.

Naples   *Naples (Napoli),* seaport city in southern Italy.

Nar   The river *Nera* in central Italy. It flows out of the Apennines southwest into the Tiber.

Narnia   *Narni,* a town in Umbria, Italy, on a hill above the River Nera, near Terni.

Nauportus   Present-day *Vrhnika,* about 15 miles southeast of Ljubljana, Slovenia.

Naxus   Náxos, the largest island of the Cyclades, Greece, in the Aegean Sea.

Nemetes   Germanic tribe from around the area of the modern settlement of Speyer, Germany.

Nicephorium   A town on the River Euphrates; present-day *Ar Raqqah* in Syria.

Nicopolis   City founded by Augustus to commemorate his famous victory at Actium in 31 B.C. Situated at the entrance to the bay Amvrakikós Kólpos opposite Áktio (Actium) on the west coast of Greece; modern *Nikópoli*.

Nile   Major river of Africa. In ancient times the delta had seven branches; now it has two principal mouths.

Ninos   Another name for the city of Nineveh. Its ruins (*Nīnawâ*) are situated on the east bank of the Tigris opposite what is now Mosul (Al Mawşil) in northern Iraq.

Nisibis   Now *Nusaybin* in southeastern Turkey, on the border with Syria, about 35 miles southeast of Mardin.

Nola   *Nola* near Naples, southern Italy.

Noricum   A Roman province in the eastern Alps. It corresponded roughly to modern Austria south of the Danube and west of Vienna, a small area of southern Germany and a small area of northeast Slovenia. It was bordered on the west by the province of Raetia, and on the east by the province of Pannonia.

Nuceria   *Nocera Inferiore*, a town in southern Italy, about 10 miles northwest of Salerno.

Numantia   Ancient city in what is now north central Spain, near the River Duero, on Garray Hill, 3 miles north of Soria.

Numidians   Inhabitants of Numidia, a region of north Africa roughly corresponding to eastern Algeria and northern Tunisia. It was later included in the Roman province of Africa Proconsularis.

Ocean   The name given to the great river which in ancient thought was believed to encircle the earth. The North Sea was regarded as part of it.

Odrusae   A Thracian tribe who lived on the River Maritsa in southern Bulgaria.

Ordovices   A tribe living in central and north Wales.

Ostia   The port of ancient Rome, at the mouth of the Tiber in central Italy. The port lay just to the north of the modern Lido di Ostia.

Pagyda   Unidentified river in north Africa.

Panda   Unidentified river north of the Black Sea.

Pandateria   *Ventotene*, an island west of the Bay of Naples.

Pannonia   Roman province, north of the province of Dalmatia and to the east of the province of Noricum, lying south and west of the Danube in the valleys of the Sava and Drava rivers. It included parts of modern Austria, Hungary, Slovenia, Croatia, and Yugoslavia.

Paphos   *Paphos,* coastal town in southwest Cyprus.

Parthia   Kingdom of southwest Asia which at its height constituted the vast territory stretching from the Euphrates to the Indus.

Patavium   *Padua (Padova),* north Italy, approximately 20 miles west of Venice.

Peloponnese *Peloponnese (Pelopónnisos)*. Peninsula forming the south of the mainland of Greece. Under the Romans it was part of the province of Achaea.

Pergamum Modern-day *Bergama*, western Turkey, about 50 miles north of İzmir.

Perinthus *Marmaraereğlisi*, a port on the north shore of the Sea of Marmara, about 50 miles west of Istanbul, Turkey.

Persia The ancient Persian empire of the sixth to fourth centuries B.C. extended from the River Indus to the Mediterranean and from the Caucasus Mountains to the Indian Ocean. Its heartland lay northeast of the Persian Gulf.

Perusia *Perugia*, central Italy, east of Lake Trasimeno.

Pharsalus Town where Caesar famously defeated Pompey in 48 B.C. Modern *Fársala*, in Thessaly, central Greece.

Philadelphini Inhabitants of ancient Philadelphia, the modern settlement of *Alaşehir* in western Turkey, about 75 miles east of İzmir.

Philippi Modern *Fílippoi* in northern Greece, about 10 miles north of Kavála. It was here that Octavian and Mark Antony defeated Brutus and Cassius in 42 B.C.

Philippopolis *Plovdiv*, a city of south central Bulgaria on the River Maritsa north of the Rhodope Mountains.

Phoenicia The region on the east Mediterranean coast between modern Syria and southern Lebanon.

Picenum Ancient district in east central Italy on the Adriatic coast.

Piraeus The modern *Peiraiás*, the port of Athens, Greece.

Placentia *Piacenza*, a city in north central Italy on the River Po.

Planasia *Pianosa*, a small island of Italy in the Mediterranean Sea, southwest of the island of Elba.

Poeni Alternative name for Carthaginians.

Pomptine Marshes *Agro Pontino (Pontine Marshes)*, an area southeast of Rome.

Pontus (a) The Black Sea (2.54.1, 12.63.2, 13.39.1). (b) Kingdom and subsequently a Roman province along the southern shore of the Black Sea (2.56.2, 12.21, 15.6.3, 15.26.2).

Praeneste *Palestrina*, a town in central Italy, about 20 miles east of Rome.

Propontis *Sea of Marmara*, between the Aegean Sea and the Black Sea.

Puteoli *Pozzuoli*, a town in southern Italy on the coast west of Naples.

Pyramus *Ceyhan Nehri*, a river in southern Turkey which flows from the Anti-Taurus Mountains to the Gulf of Iskenderun.

Quadi Germanic tribe of the upper River Danube, east of the Marcomanni and northwest of Budapest.

Raetia Roman province bounded on the east by the province of Noricum and on the west by Germany and Gaul. It included most of Tirol and Vorarlberg in Austria, part of southern Germany, and part of Switzerland.

Ravenna *Ravenna*, a city in northern Italy on the Adriatic, about 60 miles northeast of Florence.

Reatini   Inhabitants of Reate, the modern *Rieti,* central Italy, about 45 miles north of Rome.

Red Sea   (See 2.61.2n.)

Regini   Inhabitants of Regium, the modern *Reggio di Calabria,* a port on the east coast of the Strait of Messina, Italy.

Rhine   Major river of Western Europe. It flows from the Alps to the North Sea and passes through or borders on Switzerland, Liechtenstein, Austria, Germany, France, and the Netherlands.

Rhodanus   The *Rhône,* a river in Switzerland and southeast France.

Rhodes   *Rhodes (Ródos),* largest island in the Dodecanese, Greece, in the Aegean Sea.

Sabines   Ancient Italian people living northeast of Rome.

Sabrina   The River *Severn* in Wales and western England.

Salamis   An ancient city of Cyprus, whose site lies near Famagusta.

Samaritans   People of Samaria, the area between Galilee and Judaea.

Samnites   Samnium was an ancient district in the area of the Apennines.

Samos   *Sámos,* Greek island of the Aegean Sea, off the western coast of Turkey.

Samothrace   *Samothrace (Samothráki),* a Greek island in the northeast Aegean Sea.

Sanbulos   Perhaps Sunbula Kūh, a mountain range in northwestern Iran.

Santoni   Tribe in western Gaul.

Sardinia   Island of Italy in the Mediterranean Sea.

Sardis   Capital of the ancient kingdom of Lydia, absorbed by the Romans into the province of Asia. The small village of Sartmustafa in western Turkey (about 50 miles east of İzmir) occupies part of its site.

Sarmatians   A general name for nomadic tribes beyond the Vistula (Wisła) who moved gradually westward in about 250 B.C.–A.D. 50. They included principally the Iazyges and the Roxolani.

Scythia   Ancient region of undefined boundaries inhabited by the nomadic Scythians. The area covered parts of modern Kazakhstan, Russia, and Ukraine. The heart of the region was to the north of the Black Sea and to the east of the Aral Sea.

Segesta   Ancient city of western Sicily, whose location was near the modern settlement of Calatafini.

Seleucia   (a) Seleucia Pieria (2.69.2) was the port of Antioch. Its ruins lie just north of the modern seaside resort of Samandağı, southwest of Antakya, Turkey. (b) Seleucia-on-Tigris (6.42.3, 6.44.2, 11.8.3–4) was a royal city on the River Tigris. Its site is in Iraq, about 20 miles southeast of Baghdad, opposite the ruins of Ctesiphon.

Semnones   Germanic tribe living between the middle Elbe and Oder rivers.

Senones   Gallic tribe of the Seine valley, some of whom had migrated to Umbria. Their chief city was Agendicum, now *Sens,* about 60 miles southeast of Paris.

Sequani   Tribe of eastern Gaul between the Saône and Rhône rivers.

Seriphos   *Sérifos,* island of the Cyclades, Greece, in the Aegean Sea.

Sicily   Island of Italy in the Mediterranean Sea.

Silures   Tribe in southern Wales.

Simbruvium   District in the Sabine hills around the Aniene river (known in classical times as the Anio).

Sindes   Unidentified river, perhaps in northern Iran.

Sinuessa   Coastal town about 30 miles northwest of Naples; the modern *Mondragone* is on its site.

Siraci   A people living north and east of the Black Sea.

Smyrna   *İzmir,* western Turkey.

Sophene   District in ancient Armenia, east of the River Euphrates, occupying an area in what is now eastern Turkey.

Soza   Unidentified town north of the Black Sea.

Spain, the Spains   There were three Roman provinces in the Iberian peninsula: Baetica (orig. Farther Spain: 4.13.2, 4.37.1) in the south, Hispania Tarraconensis (1.78.1, orig. Nearer Spain: 4.45.1) in the north and east, and Lusitania (13.46) in the west.

Sparta   The once powerful city in the southern Peloponnese, now *Spárti,* Greece.

Spelunca   *Sperlonga,* port in Italy on the Gulf of Gaeta.

Stratonicea   The ruins of this ancient city lie near Eskihisar, northwest of Muğla in southwest Turkey.

Sublaqueum   *Subiaco,* a town in central Italy, east of Rome.

Suebi   A catch-all term for various Germanic tribes including the Hermunduri, Marcomanni, Quadi, and (especially) the Semnones.

Sugambri   Germanic tribe on the east of the lower Rhine, north of the Ubii.

Surrentum   *Sorrento* in southern Italy.

Syene   *Aswān* in southern Egypt, on the east side of the upper Nile.

Syria   Roman province east of Cilicia, whose capital was Antioch.

Tanais   The *Don* river, southwest Russia. It rises southeast of Tula and flows to the Sea of Azov.

Tarentum   *Taranto* in southeast Italy.

Tarracina   *Terracina* in south central Italy, on the Gulf of Gaeta.

Tarraco   A town on the northeastern coast of Spain (*Tarragona*), referred to by T. as "the Tarraconensian colony" (1.78.1).

Taunus   *Taunus,* mountain range in western Germany.

Tauronites   A people perhaps belonging to a district in the Taurus range.

Tauri   Inhabitants of the southwestern Crimea, Ukraine.

Taurus   *Taurus Mountains* (*Toros Dağları*), mountain range in southern Turkey.

Teleboae   Inhabitants of a group of islands known in ancient times as Teleboides or Taphiae, the modern Kálamos, Meganísi, etc., off the northwest coast of Greece.

Temnus   Ancient town whose site is about 14 miles north of İzmir, western Turkey.

Tencteri   Germanic tribe of the lower Rhine, to the east of Cologne.

Tenos   *Tínos,* an island of the Cyclades, Greece, in the Aegean Sea.

Termestini   A people whose capital was ancient Termes near the source of the River Duero in northern Spain.

Teutoburgian dene Now thought to be in the area of modern Kalkriese, 10 miles north of Osnabrück.

Thala Ancient town in north Africa, perhaps (but not certainly) *Thala,* in western Tunisia.

Thames A principal river of England, flowing through London.

Thebes Ancient city of Egypt. Luxor (Al Uqşur), Al Karnak, and Al Qurnah now occupy parts of its site.

Thermae *Thermaïkós Kólpos,* arm of the Aegean Sea in northeast Greece.

Thessalians Inhabitants of Thessaly, an ancient region of Greece which corresponds roughly with the current administrative division of *Thessalía.* It includes the east central part of the Greek mainland.

Thrace A region of southeast Europe, of varying extent at different times. Ancient Thrace corresponded generally to central and southern Bulgaria, European Turkey, and northeastern Greece. A Roman province from A.D. 46.

Thubuscum Unidentified African town.

Thurii Ancient city on the Gulf of Taranto, Italy, which was situated near the modern town of Sibari.

Tiber *Tiber (Tevere),* the river of Rome.

Tibur *Tivoli* near Rome, Italy.

Ticinum *Pavia,* a settlement on the River Ticino, south of Milan, northern Italy.

Tigranocerta *Silvan,* about 20 miles north of Batman in eastern Turkey.

Tigris *River Tigris: Nahr Dijlah* (Arabic), *Dicle Nehri* (Turkish). It rises south of Elaziğ, Turkey, flows through Iraq, and unites with the River Euphrates in southeast Iraq to form the Shatt al Arab which then flows into the Persian Gulf.

Tmolus A town near Boz Dağlar, a mountain range in western Turkey, east of İzmir.

Toronaean Gulf *Kólpos Kassándras,* an inlet of the north Aegean Sea between the Sithonía and Kassándra peninsulas of Chalkidikí, northeast Greece.

Tralles Ancient town on the River Meander (Büyükmenderes Nehri). Now *Aydın,* approximately 55 miles southeast of İzmir.

Trapezus *Trabzon (Trebizond),* city on the Black Sea, in northeast Turkey.

Treveri A tribe whose capital was Trier, a city in western Germany near the border with Luxembourg.

Trimerus One of the *Tremiti Islands,* a group of five small islands in the Adriatic Sea off the southeastern coast of Italy.

Trinovantes British tribe based in modern Suffolk and Essex, England.

Trisantona The River *Trent* in central England.

Troy *Truva,* the site of Troy, is situated near the coast in northwest Turkey, south of Çanakkale.

Tubantes Germanic people who, over the course of time, moved from the modern Netherlands to south of the River Ruhr in Germany.

Turoni Tribe in the area of the modern Touraine, whose chief city was Tours, northwest France.

Tusculum Town of ancient Latium, located about 15 miles southeast of Rome. Its ruins lie near the town of Frascati.

Tyre *Tyre (Soûr),* Mediterranean coastal town, southern Lebanon.

Ubii   Germanic tribe originally from east of the Rhine but in 38 B.C. transferred to the west bank (12.27.1). Their capital ("The Town of the Ubii") in due course became Cologne.

Umbria   In Roman times, a region in Italy situated east of Etruria. Modern Umbria is a region of Italy surrounded by the regions of Tuscany, Marche, and Lazio.

Usipi, Usipetes   Germanic tribe of the lower Rhine.

Uspe   Unidentified town north of the Black Sea.

Vahalis   The River *Waal* in the Netherlands.

Vangiones   Germanic tribe in the area of modern Worms, south of Mainz, Germany.

Velinus, Lake   *Lago di Piediluco,* a small lake south of Terni, central Italy.

Veneti   A Gallic tribe north of the River Po, Italy.

Verulamium   St. Albans, southeast England.

Vesuvius   *Vesuvio,* a volcano on the east side of the Bay of Naples, Italy.

Vetera   An Augustan military base near Xanten in western Germany.

Vienne   A principal town (modern *Vienne*) of Narbonese Gaul.

Vindelici   Tribe inhabiting the region east and northeast of Lake Constance; modern Augsburg is on the site of Augusta Vindelicorum, a Tiberian foundation in their territory.

Visurgis   The River *Weser,* northwest Germany.

Volandum   A fortress of ancient Armenia. Possibly equates to modern-day İğdir, southeast Turkey.

Volsci   Ancient people of central Italy.

Vulsinii   A town of ancient Etruria. Now *Bolsena,* a town in central Italy, about 60 miles northwest of Rome.

Zeugma   Ancient town also known as Balkis, on the west side of the River Euphrates, near the modern town of Birecik in southeastern Turkey. Strategically situated on a curve of the Euphrates, it was noted as an important crossing point.

Appendix E
Textual Variants

Experience shows that those who read the *Annals* in Latin are likely to use a wide variety of different editions. The old Oxford text of C. D. Fisher (Oxford 1906) remains surprisingly popular, but also in use are the various Teubner (Leipzig) editions of E. Koestermann (mine is the 1965 version). More recently, Teubner editions of the whole work were produced by H. Heubner (Stuttgart 1983) and of Books 1–6 by S. Borzsák (Stuttgart/Leipzig 1992) and of Books 11–16 by K. Wellesley (Leipzig 1986). This variety is such that, in practice, it is impossible to provide a systematic comparison with the text which I have chosen to translate: here I have therefore merely listed the places, signaled in the translation by a superscript +, which seem likely to cause surprise or which differ from what may loosely be called the vulgate text. Unattributed emendations are either my own or a composite of those of others.

Book 1

8.3 uisos (*Lenchantin*)

27.2 digredientem [eum Caesare] (*Fuchs*)

31.1 trac<ta>turis

35.2 nec (*Courtney*)

42.3 non[dum] (*Shackleton Bailey*)

44.5 <co>egit (*Hiller*)

61.2 primo (*Kohler*)

65.7 amissis (*Goodyear*) . . . geritur (*M*)

69.3 <studia> (*Doederlein/C. Heraeus*)

Book 2

16.1 Idisiouisa (*Hartman*)

23.2 [aut uelis] impelli

24.1 uasto [et] profundo (*Haase*)

43.4 ei (*Goodyear*)

67.1 ingre<sso re>gi

69.1 <in>tentabantur (*Wurm*)

78.2 alto (*Lipsius*)

88.1 scriptores [senatoresque]

BOOK 3

7.1 ultioni set (*after Heinsius*)

12.2 non ut princeps (*Lipsius*)

13.2 post quae (*Baiter*)

19.2 ulciscendo

22.2 reticeri (*Acidalius*)

26.3 ac primo (*Sirker*)

31.1 triennio (*Nipperdey*)

35.3 haud <difficulter> uictus est

38.2 fratris <filio> (*Muretus*)

38.3 incusantes

46.2 conuincite

47.2 omisisse urbem (*Freinsheim*)

49.1 legerat (*M*)

52.1 <non> inturbidus

53.4 quis [lapidum causa]

67.4 missis (*Faernus*)

68.2 alia (*M*)

70.3 egregia (*Martin*) in publicum

BOOK 4

12.2 ferax (*Hartman*)

26.2 et culpae conscia (*Lipsius*)

33.2 rerum <salute> (*Bringmann*)

49.3 simulque (*Lipsius*)

51.2 paratae (*Watt*)

52.3 arreptamque

59.2 genu utroque

59.3 uindicis (*Shackleton Bailey*)

67.3 amoenitatibus

69.3 <cautissime> agens (*Martin*)

Appendix E

BOOK 5

4.1 Germanici fatum

4.2 faustisque (*Muretus*)

BOOK 6

5.7.1 absistere (*Draeger/Pfitzner*)

5.10.3 Actiaco

6.9.2 uincla

10.1 qu<ae qui>a

21.1 ta<nto> (*Ruperti*)

22.1 sectas (*Wurm*)

29.2 arguebatur (*Ernesti*)

30.1 accusatores <ipsi> si

35.1 conserta acies ut

BOOK 11

1.1 excolebat (*late MS, Watt*)

10.1 auebat (*Lipsius*)

10.3 se<nior>um

11.1 <ii> magistratus (*Shaw-Smith*)

14.3 publicandis plebi senatus consultis (*Grotius*)

18.3 aucta (*late MS*)

23.3 coetus ... uelut capt<a sit c>iuitas (*Haase*)

23.4 arce ... stratis perissent?

24.2 uetera <ultra>

27 [subisse] (*late MSS, Urlichs*)

28.1 histrio ... insultauerit (*Bipontine ed.*)

32.3 egeruntur (*Heinsius*)

33 fidebat (*late MSS*)

35.3 <ea> cupido ... fuit (*Walter*)

BOOK 12

6.2 <a re publica> acciperet (*Orelli*)

6.3 sobrinarum <et consobrinarum> (*Nipperdey*)

10.1 ad (*Rhenanus*) . . . accedere (*M*)

33 circum montibus arduis

36.1 insulam (*Heinsius*)

46.1 dubi<am spem ten>tare

67.1 Claudii an (*Rhenanus*)

BOOK 13

1.2 P. Celerius (*M*)

8.3 ut famae <instaret> (*Haase*)

18.3 Germanos per eundem honorem (*Andresen*)

20.2 quae (*late MSS*)

21.3 excolebat (*Watt*)

22.1 <s>et (*Heinsius*)

25.3 Nero iam metuentior (*Halm*)

26.2 insultarent (*Ruperti*)

30.2 artibus <paratae> (*after Syme*)

33.1 Celerium . . . Celerius (*Eck*)

41.3 tectis tenus (*Lipsius*)

distinctum (*Watt*)

42.4 ac modeste partam

46.1 se <esse> qui ire<t>

46.2 paelici ancillae adsuetudine [Actes] (*Wellesley*)

56.1 nec commotus (*Lipsius*)

57.1 it<a sal>em prouenire (*Wellesley*)

BOOK 14

4.4 Baias (*Puteolanus*)

6.1 esse <sensit> (*Anquetil*) si non intelleg<i uid>erentur

6.3 adhibet <et> testamentum

7.2 quos experiens

12.4–13.1 uel mitigata. ac tamen cunctari (*Wellesley*)

16.1 nec <ten>ore uno (*Acidalius*)

16.2 ut qui (*Ritter*)

20.3 praetores ederent (*Lipsius*)

21.2 sterneretur (*Willis*)

22.1 regnis (*Bentley*)

22.4 aquae <a Q.> Marcio (*Jackson*)

40.3 <adhibitis> iis (*Fuchs*)

58.4 <nec in> otio suffugium et (*after Wurm*)

61.1 [repetitum uenerantium] (*Acidalius/Ritter*)

64.3 decreta; quae <quem> ad finem memorabimus?

Book 15

13.2 Numantinaeque <cladis: neque> eandem uim Samnitibus [Italico populo] aut <His>panis <quae> Romani imperii aemulis (*mostly Ritter*)

19.1–2 magna cum inuidia. senatum adeunt qui ius (*Wellesley, after Ernesti/Ritter*)

21.2 prouincialibus <ius> (*W.A. Schmidt*)

31 praeferret

35.2 quin ignobiles (*after Ritter*)

37.4 admissi

40.1 necdum positus (*Jacob*) metus aut redierat plebi spes (*Madvig*)

44.4 aut crucibus adfixi ac flammandi, [atque] ubi (*after Weyman/Linck*)

45.2 imbuerat (*Lipsius*)

53.2 Frentano in oppido (*M*)

54.3 sanguis <dis>pertiebat <at>que eadem (*after Oelschlaeger*)

55.3 uita amoena et ... probata (*Hartman*)

56.2 purgandi imperitior

57.1 consumptus (*Prammer*)

58.3 <non meri>ta tantum

59.4 tamquam (*Rhenanus*)

63.1 formidinem (*late MSS*)

74.1 [ex] quo

74.3 ad omen dol<end>um

BOOK 16

1.2 demonstrat (*M*)

2.1 remigium (*Boxhorn*)

10.3 uicta

21.1 ludis asticis (*Lipsius*)

22.3 sine <precatione> (*Courtney*)

24.2 <in>uenit (*Hartman*)

31.2 <usi> sint

33.1 erga bona malaque [documenta] (*Martin*)

APPENDIX F
ROMAN EMPERORS FROM AUGUSTUS TO HADRIAN

Augustus	31 B.C.–A.D. 14
Tiberius	A.D. 14–37
Caligula	37–41
Claudius	41–54
Nero	54–68
Galba	68–69
Otho	69
Vitellius	69
Vespasian	69–79
Titus	79–81
Domitian	81–96
Nerva	96–98
Trajan	98–117
Hadrian	117–138

Appendix G

The Imperial Family

The following stemmata illustrate the major family connections of (a) Augustus and Tiberius, (b) Gaius (Caligula), Claudius, and Nero.

Note:

1. Dates are A.D. unless otherwise indicated; "cos." = "consul" and "pr." = "praetor"; + refers to death date.

2. Descendants are not always arranged in their order of birth.

3. Parenthetic numbers directly before or after a name refer to marriages.

4. The names of emperors are CAPITALIZED.

5. Names appearing in both stemmata are *italicized*.

6. In (a), the names of Nero and his parents are listed twice; in (b), the name of Claudius is listed twice.

7. The stemmata, though complex, are by no means complete.

? = (1) L. Marcius Philippus (2) = (2) Atia (1) = (2) C. Octavius (pr. 61 B.C.)

L. Marcius Philippus = Atia

Paullus Fabius Maximus = Marcia
(cos. 11 B.C.)

Sex. Appuleius = (1) Fabia (2) = M. Plautius Silvanus
(cos. 14)   Numantina   (pr. 24)

Ti. Claudius Nero = (1) Livia (2) = (3) AUGUSTUS (2) = Scribonia
(pr. 42 B.C.)   (+29)   (+14)

? = Q. Haterius
(cos. 5 B.C.,
+ A.D. 26)

M. Vipsanius Agrippa
(cos. 37, 28, 27 B.C.)

C. Asinius Pollio
(cos. 40 B.C.)

? = C. Asinius Gallus = (2) Vipsania (1) = (1) TIBERIUS (2) = (3) Julia (2)
(cos. 8 B.C., +33)   (d. of Agrippa)   (+37)   the Elder

M. Claudius = Asinia
Marcellus Aeserninus
(cos. 22 B.C.)

C. Asinius Pollio
(cos. 23)

M. Asinius Agrippa
(cos. 25)

M. Claudius
Marcellus Aeserninus
(pr. 19)

Germanicus = Agrippina the Elder
(cos. 12, 18, +19)   (+33)

M. Aemilius Lepidus
(cos. 6)

Drusus Caesar = Aemilia
(+33)   Lepida

M. Aemilius = (2) Drusilla (1) = L. Cassius
Lepidus   (Longinus
(+41)   cos. 30)

C. Junius Silanus
(cos. 10)

D. Jun. Silanus   M. Jun. Silanus   Junia Torquata
(cos. 15)   (Vestal)

C. Appius Junius Silanus
(cos. 28)

Agrippa Postumus
(+14)

L. Caesar
(+2)

C. Caesar
(cos. 1, +4)

Julia the
Younger (+28)

Julia = M. Vinicius
Livilla   (cos. 30, 45)

Cn. Domitius = Agrippina (1)
Ahenobarbus   the Younger
(cos. 32)

GAIUS
(CALIGULA)
(+41)

NERO
(+68)

C. Claudius Marcellus = (1) Octavia (2) = (4) M. Antonius
(cos. 50 B.C.)   (cos. 44, 34 B.C.)

L. Domitius Ahenobarbus
(cos. 54 B.C.)

Cn. Domitius Ahenobarbus
(cos. 32 B.C.)

Antonia
the Younger

Nero Claudius Drusus
(cos 9 B.C.)

L. Domitius = Antonia
Ahenobarbus   the Elder
(cos. 16 B.C.)

Cn. Domitius = (1) Agrippina the
Ahenobarbus   Younger
(cos. 32)

NERO
(+68)

CLAUDIUS
(+54)

Drusus Caesar = Livi(l)la

C. Rubellius = (2) Julia (1) = Nero Caesar
Blandus   (+31)
(cos. 18)

Germanicus   Tib. Gemellus   Drusus Caesar
(+23)   (+37/38)   (cos. 15, 21, +23)

Marcella = Iullus Antonius
the Elder   (cos. 10 B.C.)

L. Antonius
(+25)

Marcella = (1) M. Valerius Messalla Appianus
the Younger   (cos. 12 B.C.)

P. Quintilius = Claudia Pulchra
Varus
(cos. 13 B.C.)

Quintilius Varus

M. Valerius
Messalla Barbatus

= (1) Domitia Lepida (3) = C. Appius Junius Silanus

Valeria Messalina

M. Marcellus
(+23 B.C.)

(b) GAIUS, CLAUDIUS, and NERO

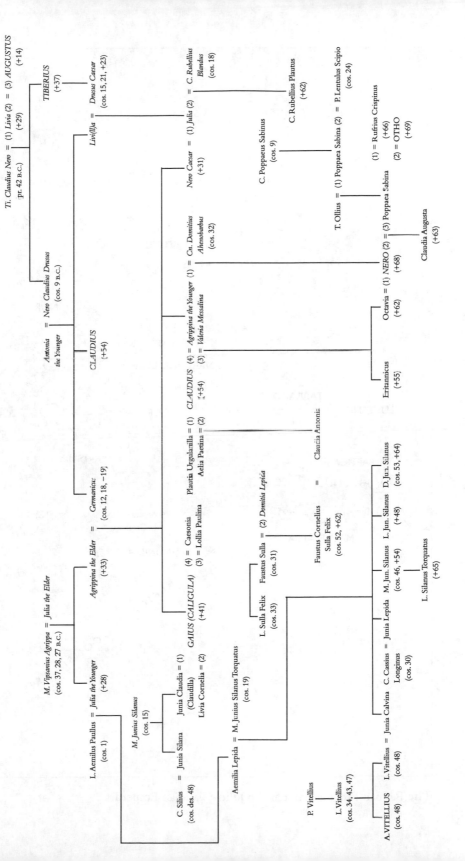

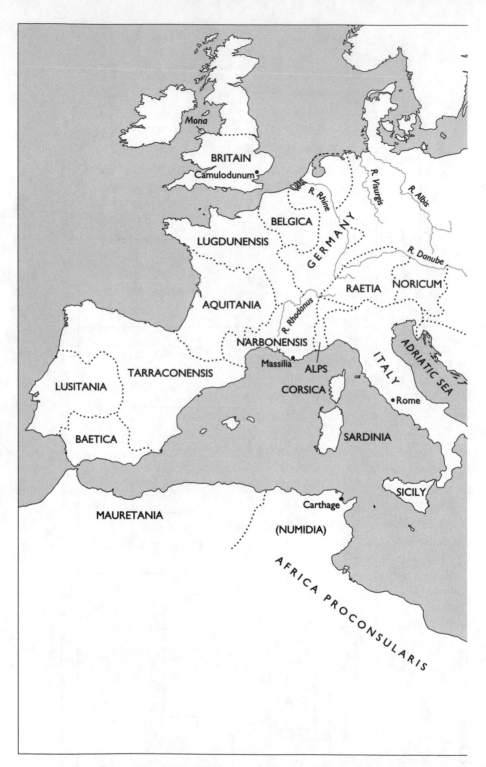

The Roman Provinces under the Julio-Claudian Emperors

CASPIAN
SEA

PANNONIA

R. Danube

DALMATIA

MOESIA

BLACK SEA

THRACE

Byzantium

Armenia

MACEDONIA

IONIAN
SEA

ACHAEA

AEGEAN
SEA

ASIA

GALATIA

CAPPADOCIA

Parthia

R. Tigris

Mesopotamia

R. Euphrates

Antioch

SYRIA

LYCIA

CRETE

CYPRUS

M E D I T E R R A N E A N   S E A

JUDAEA

Alexandria

CYRENAICA

EGYPT

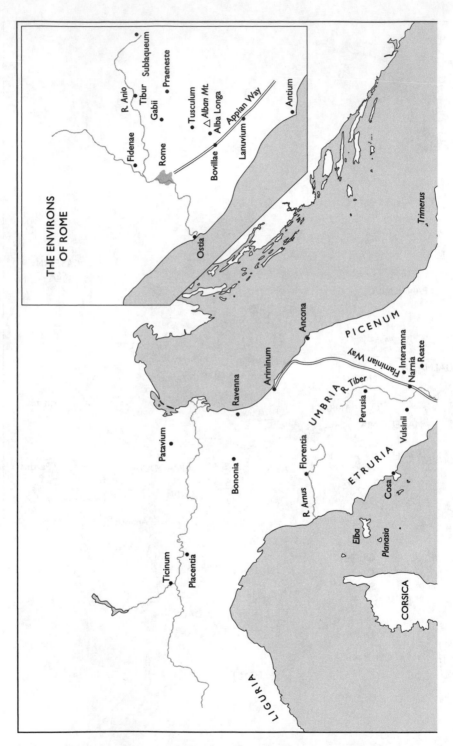

THE ENVIRONS
OF ROME

Sublaqueum
R. Anio
Tibur
Praeneste
Gabii
Tusculum
Alban Mt.
Alba Longa
Appian Way
Antium
Fidenae
Rome
Bovillae
Lanuvium
Ostia

Trimerus

Ancona

PICENUM

Ariminum

Flaminian Way
Interamna
Narnia
Reate

Ravenna

UMBRIA
R. Tiber

Perusia

Patavium

Bononia

Florentia

ETRURIA
Vulsinii

R. Arnus

Cosa

Elba

Planasia

Ticinum
Placentia

CORSICA

LIGURIA

Italy, the Environs of Rome, and the Bay of Naples

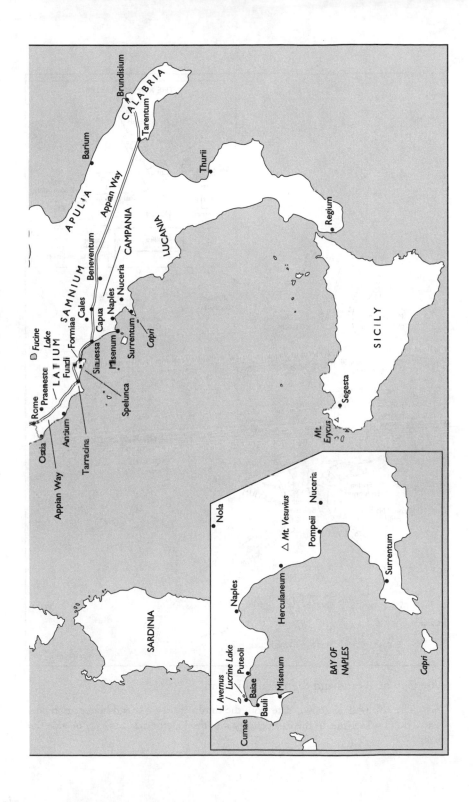

Main map labels:

Brundisium
CALABRIA
Barium
Tarentum
APULIA
Appian Way
Thurii
Beneventum
CAMPANIA
SAMNIUM
Regium
LUCANIA
Cales
Capua
Nuceria
Naples
Fucine
Lake
LATIUM
Formiae
Sinuessa
Capri
Surrentum
Misenum
Rome
Praeneste
Fundi
Speluncа
SICILY
Antium
Tarracina
Ostia
Appian Way
Mt.
Erycus
Segesta

Inset map (BAY OF NAPLES):

SARDINIA
Nola
△ Mt. Vesuvius
Nuceria
Naples
Pompeii
Herculaneum
Surrentum
L. Avernus
Lucrine Lake
Puteoli
Baiae
Misenum
Bauli
Cumae
BAY OF NAPLES
Capri

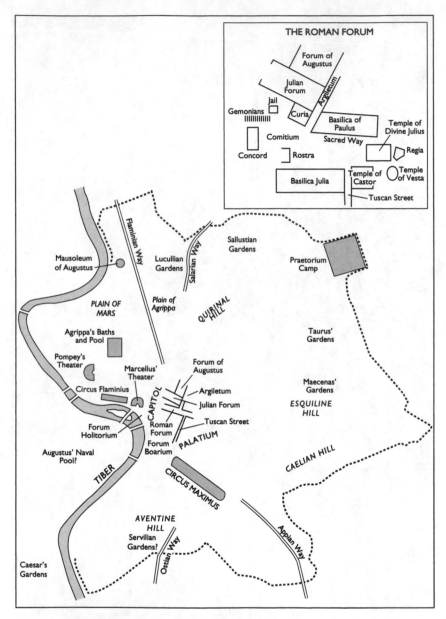

The City of Rome and the Roman Forum

Note: The city walls as shown date from the third century A.D and hence are represented by a broken line. In the first century A.D. the Praetorian Camp lay outside the walls.

INDEX

Note: "cos." = consul, "suff." = suffect consul, "pr." = praetor. The names of emperors are capitalized. All dates are A.D. unless indicated otherwise. Question marks indicate places where identity, date, magisterial office, and the like are uncertain.

Index